# Geospatial Analysis

## A Comprehensive Guide to Principles, Techniques and Software Tools
### - Third Edition -

Michael J de Smith

Michael F Goodchild

Paul A Longley

# Copyright and licensing information

## Disclaimer

This publication is designed to offer accurate and authoritative information in regard to the subject matter. It is provided on the understanding that it is not supplied as a form of professional or advisory service. References to software products, datasets or publications are purely made for information purposes and the inclusion or exclusion of any such item does not imply recommendation or otherwise of the product or material in question.

## Licensing and ordering

For ordering (printed and special PDF versions), licensing and contact details please refer to the Guide's website: www.spatialanalysisonline.com

Published by Matador (an imprint of Troubador Publishing Ltd) on behalf of The Winchelsea Press
Printed in Great Britain by the MPG Books Group, Bodmin and King's Lynn

Postal address: Matador, 9 De Montfort Mews, Leicester, LE1 7FW, UK. Tel: +44 (0)116 255 9311

Matador email address: books@troubador.co.uk; Web: www.troubador.co.uk

Chinese edition: Publishing House of Electronics Industry, Beijing, PRC, www.phei.com.cn

### British Library Cataloguing in Publishing Data

ISBN 13: 9781848761582          (soft cover version)

ISBN 13: 9781848761575          (hard cover version)


Production of this edition has been generously supported by a Fellowship award to Dr de Smith from the UK HEFCE SPLINT initiative:

# 3D visualization of modeled road-related noise levels

# in an urbanized area

*Visualization using CadnaA software, courtesy of Accon GmbH & DataKustik GmbH.*
*See Section 3.3 for more details*

# Optimized service center location and allocated demand

## Tripolis, in Arcadia, Greece

*Coverage or p-center location optimization problem. See Section 7.4.2 for more details. Map produced using S-Distance software, courtesy of S A Sirigos, Greece*

# Contents, figures and tables

# List of Figures

# List of Tables

# Foreword to the Third Edition

**Changes from the 2ⁿᵈ edition:**

This 3ʳᵈ edition includes the following principal changes from earlier editions: the print version is now provided in full color; embedded links (applicable to the PDF and Web versions) are highlighted in the body of the printed text in dark blue type; there has been extensive revision and updating of Chapters 3 and 8; removal of tables of software products — these are now all referenced via the accompanying website page which is regularly updated: www.spatialanalysisonline.com/software.html; addition of new sections, including geospatial modeling, Knox and Mantel tests, cartogram production, and space syntax; extended discussion of geovisualization techniques in many sections; expansion and revision of the sections covering distance transforms (DTs) and join count statistics (JCS); inclusion of many new diagrams and examples (e.g. fire, pollution, wind and noise modeling) and re-implementation of many existing diagrams; addition of links to downloadable PDF files of the out-of-print CATMOG publication series — although rather 'historic' those referenced include useful discussions of many of the topics mentioned in this Guide; provision of Google mapping links for many placenames cited; and updates to many sections to reflect recent technological advances, particularly in software tools. These include the addition of information on analytical tools not previously covered such as PySal, PASSaGE, SAM, and R Spatial (see further the selected summary "R-Project spatial statistics software packages" at the end of this Guide).

*Geospatial Analysis: A Comprehensive Guide to Principles, Techniques and Software Tools* originated as a document to accompany the spatial analysis module of the MSc in Geographic Information Science at University College London delivered by the principal author, Dr Mike de Smith. As is often the case, from its conception through to completion of the first draft it developed a life of its own, growing into a substantial Guide designed for use by a wide audience. Once several of the chapters had been written — notably those covering the building blocks of spatial analysis and on surface analysis — the project was discussed with Professors Longley and Goodchild. They kindly agreed to contribute to the contents of the Guide itself. As such, this Guide may be seen as a companion to the pioneering book on *Geographic Information Systems and Science* by Longley, Goodchild, Maguire and Rhind, particularly the chapters of that work which deal with spatial analysis and modeling. Their participation has also facilitated links with broader "spatial literacy" and spatial analysis programmes. Notable amongst these are the *GIS&T Body of Knowledge* materials provided by the Association of American Geographers at www.aag.org/bok/ together with the spatial educational programmes provided at www.spatial-literacy.org, www.spatial.ucsb.edu, www.ncgia.ucsb.edu and www.csiss.org.

The three formats in which this Guide has been published: Printed, Web and E-book (PDF) versions have proved to be extremely popular, encouraging us to seek to improve and extend the material and associated resources further. Many academics and industry professionals have provided helpful comments on previous editions, and universities in several parts of the world have now developed courses which make use of the Guide and the accompanying resources. Workshops based on these materials have been run in Ireland, the USA, East Africa, Italy and Japan, and a Chinese version of the Guide has been published by the Publishing House of Electronics Industry, Beijing, PRC, www.phei.com.cn in 2009.

A unique, ongoing, feature of this Guide is its independent evaluation of software, in particular the set of readily available tools and packages for conducting various forms of geospatial analysis. To our knowledge, there is no similarly extensive resource that is available in printed or electronic form. We remain convinced that there is a need for guidance on where to find and how to apply selected tools. Inevitably, some topics have been omitted, primarily where there is little or no readily available commercial or open source software to support particular analytical operations. Other topics, whilst included, have been covered relatively briefly and/or with limited examples, reflecting the inevitable constraints of time and the authors' limited access to some of the available software resources.

Every effort has been made to ensure the information provided is up-to-date, accurate, compact, comprehensive and representative — we do not claim it to be exhaustive. However, with fast-moving changes in the software industry and in the development of new techniques it would be impractical and uneconomic to publish the material in a conventional manner. Accordingly the Guide has been prepared without intermediary typesetting. This has enabled the time between producing the text and delivery in electronic (web, e-book) and printed formats to be greatly reduced, thereby ensuring that the work is as current as possible. It also enables the work to be updated on a regular basis, with embedded hyperlinks to external resources and suppliers (highlighted and activated in the Web and PDF versions), thus making the Guide a more dynamic and extensive resource than would otherwise be possible. This approach does come with some minor disadvantages. These include: the need to provide rather more subsections to chapters and keywording of terms than would normally be the case in order to support topic selection within the web-based version; and the need for careful use of symbology and embedded graphic symbols at various points within the text to ensure that the web-based output correctly displays Greek letters and other symbols across a range of web browsers.

As with the previous editions, comments and suggestions regarding the scope, detailed content and associated materials (e.g. case studies) are welcome and amendments will be made available via the Guide web site, www.spatialanalysisonline.com. We would like to thank all those users of the web site, electronic version of the Guide and of the printed book, for their comments and suggestions which have assisted us in producing this third edition.

Mike de Smith, Edinburgh ♦ Mike Goodchild, Santa Barbara ♦ Paul Longley, London

June 2009 (3$^{rd}$ Edition)

# Acknowledgements

The authors would like to express their particular thanks to the following individuals and organizations: Accon GmbH, Greifenberg, Germany for permission to use the noise mapping images on the inside cover of this Guide and in Figure 3-4; Prof D Martin for permission to use Figure 4-19 and Figure 4-20; Prof D Dorling and colleagues for permission to use Figure 4-50 and Figure 4-52; Dr K McGarigal for permission to use the Fragstats summary in Section 5.3.4; Dr H Kristinsson, Faculty of Engineering, University of Iceland for permission to use Figure 4-69; Dr S Rana, formerly of the Center for Transport Studies, University College London for permission to use Figure 6-24; Prof B Jiang, Department of Technology and Built Environment of University of Gävle, Sweden for permission to use the Axwoman software and sample data in Section 6.3.3.2; Dr G Dubois, European Commission (EC), Joint Research Center Directorate (DG JRC) for comments on parts of Chapter 6 and permission to use material from the original AI-Geostats website; Geovariances (France) for provision of an evaluation copy of their Isatis geostatistical software; F O'Sullivan for use of Figure 6-41; Profs A Okabe, K Okunuki and S Shiode (Center for Spatial Information Science, Tokyo University, Japan) for use of their SANET software and sample data; and S A Sirigos, University of Thesally, Greece for permission to use his Tripolis dataset in the Figure at the front of this Guide, the provision of his S-Distance software, and comments on part of Chapter 7. Sections 8.1 and 8.2 of Chapter 8 are substantially derived from material researched and written by Christian Castle and Andrew Crooks (and updated for the latest edition by Andrew) with the financial support of the Economic and Social Research Council (ESRC), Camden Primary Care Trust (PCT), and the Greater London Authority (GLA) Economics Unit. The front cover has been designed by Dr Alex Singleton.

A number of the maps displayed in this Guide, notably those in Chapter 6, have been created using GB Ordnance Survey data provided via the EDINA Digimap/JISC service. These datasets and other GB OS data illustrated is © Crown Copyright. Every effort has been made to acknowledge and establish copyright of materials used in this publication. Anyone with a query regarding any such item should contact the authors via the Guide's website, www.spatialanalysisonline.com

# 1 Introduction and terminology

## 1.1 Motivation and Media

Our objective in producing this Guide is to be comprehensive in terms of concepts and techniques (but not necessarily exhaustive), representative and independent in terms of software tools, and above all practical in terms of application and implementation. However, we believe that it is no longer appropriate to think of a standard, discipline-specific textbook as capable of satisfying every kind of new user need. Accordingly, an innovative feature of our approach here is the range of formats and channels through which we disseminate the material.

### 1.1.1 Guide overview

In this Guide we address the full spectrum of spatial analysis and associated modeling techniques that are provided within currently available and widely used geographic information systems (GIS) and associated software. Collectively such techniques and tools are often now described as *geospatial analysis*, although we use the more common form, *spatial analysis*, in most of our discussions.

The term 'GIS' is widely attributed to Roger Tomlinson and colleagues, who used it in 1963 to describe their activities in building a digital natural resource inventory system for Canada (Tomlinson 1967, 1970). The history of the field has been charted in an edited volume by Foresman (1998) containing contributions by many of its early protagonists. A timeline of many of the formative influences upon the field up to the year 2000 is available via: www.casa.ucl.ac.uk/gistimeline/; a printed summary is provided by Longley *et al.* (2005, and Chapter 1 of the forthcoming 3$^{rd}$ edition), and useful background information may be found at the GIS History Project web site based at the NCGIA (Buffalo): http://www.ncgia.buffalo.edu/gishist/. Each of these sources makes the unassailable point

that the success of GIS as an area of activity has fundamentally been driven by the success of its applications in solving real world problems. Many applications are illustrated in Longley *et al.* (Chapter 2 of the forthcoming 3$^{rd}$ edition, "A gallery of applications"). In a similar vein the web site for this Guide provides companion material focusing on applications. Amongst these are a series of sector-specific case studies drawing on recent work in and around London (UK), together with a number of international case studies.

In order to cover such a wide range of topics, this Guide has been divided into a number of main sections or chapters. These are then further subdivided, in part to identify distinct topics as closely as possible, facilitating the creation of a web site from the text of the Guide. Hyperlinks embedded within the document enable users of the web and PDF versions of this document to navigate around the Guide and to external sources of information, data, software, maps, and reading materials.

Chapter 2 provides an introduction to spatial thinking, recently described by some as "spatial literacy", and addresses the central issues and problems associated with spatial data that need to be considered in any analytical exercise. In practice, real-world applications are likely to be governed by the organizational *practices* and *procedures* that prevail with respect to particular *places*. Not only are there wide differences in the volume and remit of data that the public sector collects about population characteristics in different parts of the world, but there are differences in the ways in which data are collected, assembled and disseminated (e.g. general purpose censuses versus statistical modeling of social surveys, property registers and tax payments). There are also differences in the ways in which different data holdings can legally be merged and the purposes for which data may be used — particularly with regard to health and law enforcement data. Finally, there are geographical differences in the cost of geographically referenced data. Some organizations, such as the US Geological Survey, are bound by statute to limit charges for data to sundry costs such as media used for delivering data while others, such as most national mapping organizations in Europe, are required to exact much heavier charges in order to recoup much or all of the cost of data creation. Analysts may already be aware of these contextual considerations through local knowledge, and other considerations may become apparent through browsing metadata catalogues. GIS applications must by definition be sensitive to context, since they represent unique locations on the Earth's surface.

This initial discussion is followed in Chapter 3 by an examination of the methodological background to GIS analysis. Initially we examine a number of formal methodologies and then apply ideas drawn from these to the specific case of spatial analysis. A process known by its initials, PPDAC (Problem, Plan, Data, Analysis, Conclusions) is described as a methodological framework that may be applied to a very wide range of spatial analysis problems and projects. We conclude Chapter 3 with a discussion on model-building, with particular reference to the various types of model that can be constructed to address geospatial problems.

Subsequent Chapters present the various analytical methods supported within widely available software tools. The majority of the methods described in Chapter 4 and many of those in Chapter 6 are implemented as standard facilities in modern commercial GIS packages such as ArcGIS, MapInfo, Manifold, TNTMips and Geomedia. Many are also provided in more specialized GIS products such as Idrisi, GRASS, Terraseer and ENVI. In addition we discuss a number of more specialized tools, designed to address the needs of specific sectors or technical problems that are otherwise not well-supported within the core GIS packages at present. Chapter 5, which focuses on statistical methods, and Chapters 7 and 8 which address Network and Location Analysis, and Geocomputation, are much less commonly supported in GIS packages, but may provide loose- or close-coupling with such systems, depending upon the application area. In all instances we provide detailed examples and commentary on software tools that are readily available.

As noted above, throughout this Guide examples are drawn from and refer to specific products — these have been selected purely as examples and are not intended as recommendations. Extensive use has also been made of tabulated information, providing abbreviated summaries of techniques and formulas for reasons of both compactness and coverage. These tables are designed to provide a quick reference to the various topics covered and are, therefore, not intended as a substitute for fuller details on the various items covered. We provide limited discussion of novel 2D and 3D mapping facilities, and the support for digital globe formats (e.g. KML and KMZ), which is increasingly being embedded into general-purpose and specialized data analysis toolsets. These developments confirm the trend towards integration of geospatial data and presentation layers into mainstream software systems and services, both terrestrial and planetary (see, for example, the KML images of Mars DEMs at the end of this Guide).

Just as all datasets and software packages contain errors, known and unknown, so too do all books and websites, and the authors of this Guide expect that there will be errors despite our best efforts to remove these! Some may be genuine errors or misprints, whilst others may reflect our use of specific versions of software packages and their documentation. Inevitably with respect to the latter, new versions of the packages that we have used to illustrate this Guide will have appeared even before publication, so specific examples, illustrations and comments on scope or restrictions may have been superseded. In all cases the user should review the documentation provided with the software version they plan to use, check release notes for changes and known bugs, and look at any relevant online services (e.g. user/developer forums and blogs on the web) for additional materials and insights.

The interactive web version of this Guide may be accessed via the associated Internet site: www.spatialanalysisonline.com. The contents and sample sections of the PDF version may also be accessed from this site. In both cases the information is regularly updated. The Internet is now well established as society's principal mode of information exchange, and most aspiring GIS users are accustomed to searching for material that can easily be customized to specific needs. Our objective for such users is to provide an independent, reliable and authoritative first port of call for conceptual, technical, software and applications material that addresses the panoply of new user requirements.

Readers wishing to obtain a more in-depth understanding of the background to many of the topics covered in this Guide should review the Suggested Reading topic (Section 1.2.2). Those seeking examples of software tools that might be used for geospatial analysis should refer to Section 1.1.2.

### 1.1.2 Spatial analysis, GIS and software tools

Given the vast range of spatial analysis techniques that have been developed over the past half century many topics can only be covered to a limited depth, whilst others have been omitted because they are not implemented in current mainstream GIS products. This is a rapidly changing field and increasingly GIS packages are including analytical tools as standard built-in facilities or as optional *toolsets*, *add-ins* or *analysts*. In many instances such facilities are provided by the original software suppliers (commercial vendors or collaborative non-commercial development teams) whilst in other cases facilities have been developed and are provided by third parties. Many products offer software development kits (SDKs), programming languages and language support, scripting facilities and/or special interfaces for developing one's own analytical tools or variants.

In addition, a wide variety of web-based or web-deployed tools have become available, enabling datasets to be analyzed and mapped, including dynamic interaction and drill-down capabilities, without the need for local GIS software installation. These tools include the widespread use of Java applets, Flash-based

mapping, AJAX and Web 2.0 applications, and interactive Virtual Globe explorers, some of which are described in this Guide. They provide an illustration of the direction that many toolset and service providers are taking.

Throughout this Guide there are numerous examples of the use of software tools that facilitate geospatial analysis. In addition, some subsections of the Guide and the software section of the accompanying website, provide summary information about such tools and links to their suppliers. Commercial software products rarely provide access to source code or full details of the algorithms employed. Typically they provide references to books and articles on which procedures are based, coupled with online help and "white papers" describing their parameters and applications. This means that results produced using one package on a given dataset can rarely be exactly matched to those produced using any other package or through hand-crafted coding. There are many reasons for these inconsistencies including: differences in the software architectures of the various packages and the algorithms used to implement individual methods; errors in the source materials or their interpretation; coding errors; inconsistencies arising out of the ways in which different GIS packages model, store and manipulate information; and differing treatments of special cases (e.g. missing values, boundaries, adjacency, obstacles, distance computations etc.).

Non-commercial packages sometimes provide source code and test data for some or all of the analytical functions provided, although it is important to understand that "non-commercial" often does not mean that users can download the full source code. Source code greatly aids understanding, reproducibility and further development. Such software will often also provide details of known bugs and restrictions associated with functions — although this information may also be provided with commercial products it is generally less transparent. In this respect non-commercial software may meet the requirements of scientific rigor more fully than many commercial offerings, but is often provided with limited documentation, training tools, cross-platform testing and/or technical support, and thus is generally more demanding on the users and system administrators. In many instances open source and similar not-for-profit GIS software may also be less generic, focusing on a particular form of spatial representation (e.g. a grid or raster spatial model). Like some commercial software, it may also be designed with particular application areas in mind, such as addressing problems in hydrology or epidemiology.

The process of selecting software tools encourages us to ask: (i) "what is meant by geospatial analysis techniques?" and (ii) "what should we consider to be GIS software?" To some extent the answer to the second question is the simpler, if we are prepared to be guided by self-selection. For our purposes we focus principally on products that claim to provide geographic information systems capabilities, supporting at least 2D mapping (display and output) of raster (grid based) and/or vector (point/line/polygon based) data, with a minimum of basic map manipulation facilities. We concentrate our review on a number of the products most widely used or with the most readily accessible analytical facilities. This leads us beyond the realm of pure GIS. For example: we use examples drawn from packages that do not directly provide mapping facilities (e.g. Crimestat) but which provide input and/or output in widely used GIS map-able formats; products that include some mapping facilities but whose primary purpose is spatial or spatio-temporal data exploration and analysis (e.g. GS+, STIS, GeoDa, PySal); and products that are general- or special-purpose analytical engines incorporating mapping capabilities (e.g. MATLab with the Mapping Toolbox, WinBUGS with GeoBUGS) — for more details on these and other example software tools, please see the website page:

www.spatialanalysisonline.com/software.html

The more difficult of the two questions above is the first — what should be considered as "geospatial analysis"? In conceptual terms, the phrase identifies the subset of techniques that are applicable when, as a minimum, data can be referenced on a two-dimensional frame and relate to terrestrial activities. The results of geospatial analysis will change if the location or extent of the frame changes, or if objects are repositioned within it: if they do not, then "everywhere is nowhere", location is unimportant, and it is simpler and more appropriate to use conventional, *aspatial*, techniques.

Many GIS products apply the term (geo)spatial analysis in a very narrow context. In the case of vector-based GIS this typically means operations such as: map overlay (combining two or more maps or map layers according to predefined rules); simple buffering (identifying regions of a map within a specified distance of one or more features, such as towns, roads or rivers); and similar basic operations. This reflects (and is reflected in) the use of the term *spatial analysis* within the Open Geospatial Consortium (OGC) "simple feature specifications" (see further Table 4-2). For raster-based GIS, widely used in the environmental sciences and remote sensing, this typically means a range of actions applied to the grid cells of one or more maps (or images) often involving filtering and/or algebraic operations (*map algebra*). These techniques involve processing one or more raster layers according to simple rules resulting in a new map layer, for example replacing each cell value with some combination of its neighbors' values, or computing the sum or difference of specific attribute values for each grid cell in two matching raster datasets. Descriptive statistics, such as cell counts, means, variances, maxima, minima, cumulative values, frequencies and a number of other measures and distance computations are also often included in this generic term "spatial analysis".

However, at this point only the most basic of facilities have been included, albeit those that may be the most frequently used by the greatest number of GIS professionals. To this initial set must be added a large variety of statistical techniques (descriptive, exploratory, explanatory and predictive) that have been designed specifically for spatial and spatio-temporal data. Today such techniques are of great importance in social and political sciences, despite the fact that their origins may often be traced back to problems in the environmental and life sciences, in particular ecology, geology and epidemiology. It is also to be noted that spatial statistics is largely an observational science (like astronomy) rather than an experimental science (like agronomy or pharmaceutical research). This aspect of geospatial science has important implications for analysis, particularly the application of a range of statistical methods to spatial problems.

Limiting the definition of geospatial analysis to 2D mapping operations and spatial statistics remains too restrictive for our purposes. There are other very important areas to be considered. These include: surface analysis —in particular analyzing the properties of physical surfaces, such as gradient, aspect and visibility, and analyzing surface-like data "fields"; network analysis — examining the properties of natural and man-made networks in order to understand the behavior of flows within and around such networks; and locational analysis. GIS-based network analysis may be used to address a wide range of practical problems such as route selection and facility location, and problems involving flows such as those found in hydrology. In many instances location problems relate to networks and as such are often best addressed with tools designed for this purpose, but in others existing networks may have little or no relevance or may be impractical to incorporate within the modeling process. Problems that are not specifically network constrained, such as new road or pipeline routing, regional warehouse location, mobile phone mast positioning, pedestrian movement or the selection of rural community health care sites, may be effectively analyzed (at least initially) without reference to existing physical networks. Locational analysis "in the plane" is also applicable where suitable network datasets are not available, or are too large or expensive to be utilized, or where the location algorithm is very complex or involves the

examination or simulation of a very large number of alternative configurations.

A further important aspect of geospatial analysis is visualization ( or *geovisualization*) — the use, creation and manipulation of images, maps, diagrams, charts, 3D static and dynamic views, high resolution satellite imagery and digital globes, and their associated tabular datasets (see further, Slocum *et al.*, 2008, Dodge *et al.*, 2008, Longley *et al.* (Chapter 13 in the forthcoming 3$^{rd}$ edition) and the work of the GeoVista project team). For further insights into how some of these developments may be applied, see Andrew Hudson-Smith (2008) "Digital Geography: Geographic visualization for urban environments" and Martin Dodge and Rob Kitchin's earlier "Atlas of Cyberspace" which is now available as a free downloadable document.

GIS packages and web-based services increasingly incorporate a range of such tools, providing static or rotating views, draping images over 2.5D surface representations, providing animations and fly-throughs, dynamic linking and brushing and spatio-temporal visualizations. This latter class of tools has been, until recently, the least developed, reflecting in part the limited range of suitable compatible datasets and the limited set of analytical methods available, although this picture is changing rapidly. One recent example is the availability of image time series from NASA's Earth Observation Satellites, yielding vast quantities of data on a daily basis (e.g. Aqua mission, commenced 2002; Terra mission, commenced 1999).

Geovisualization is the subject of ongoing research by the International Cartographic Association (ICA), Commission on Geovisualization, who have organized a series of workshops and publications addressing developments in geovisualization, notably with a cartographic focus.

As datasets, software tools and processing capabilities develop, 3D geometric and photo-realistic visualization are becoming a *sine qua non* of modern geospatial systems and services — see Andy Hudson-Smith's "Digital Urban" blog for a regularly updated commentary on this field. We expect to see an explosion of tools and services and datasets in this area over the coming years — many examples are included as illustrations in this Guide. Other examples readers may wish to explore include: the static and dynamic visualizations at 3DNature and similar sites; the 2D and 3D Atlas of Switzerland; Urban 3D modeling programmes such as LandExplorer and CityGML; and the integration of GIS technologies and data with digital globe software, e.g. data from Digital Globe and GeoEye, and Earth-based frameworks such as Google Earth, Microsoft Virtual Earth, NASA Worldwind and Edushi (Chinese). There are also automated translators between GIS packages such as ArcGIS and digital Earth models (see for example Arc2Earth).

These novel visualization tools and facilities augment the core tools utilized in spatial analysis throughout many parts of the analytical process: exploration of data; identification of patterns and relationships; construction of models; dynamic interaction with models; and communication of results — see, for example, the recent work of the city of Portland, Oregon, who have used 3D visualization to communicate the results of zoning, crime analysis and other key local variables to the public. Another example is the 3D visualizations provided as part of the web-accessible London Air Quality network (see example at the front of this Guide). These are designed to enable:

- users to visualize air pollution in the areas that they work, live or walk

- transport planners to identify the most polluted parts of London.

- urban planners to see how building density affects pollution concentrations in the City and other high density areas, and

- students to understand pollution sources and dispersion characteristics

Physical 3D models and hybrid physical-digital models are also being developed and applied to practical analysis problems. For example: 3D physical models constructed from plaster, wood, paper and plastics have been used for many years in architectural and engineering planning projects; hybrid sandtables are being used to help firefighters in California visualize the progress of wildfires (see Figure 1-1A); very large sculptured solid terrain models (e.g. see STM) are being used for educational purposes, to assist land use modeling programmes, and to facilitate participatory 3D modeling in less-developed communities (P3DM); and 3D digital printing technology is being used to rapidly generate 3D landscapes and cityscapes from GIS, CAD and/or VRML files with planning, security, architectural, archaeological and geological applications (see Figure 1-1B and the websites of Z corporation, Landprint and Dimension Printing for more details. To create large landscape models multiple individual prints, which are typically only around 20cm x 20cm x 5cm, are made, in much the same manner as raster file mosaics.

### Figure 1-1 3D Physical GIS models

A. Sand-in-a-box model, Albuquerque, USA

B. 3D GIS printing

GIS software, notably in the commercial sphere, is driven primarily by demand and applicability, as manifest in willingness to pay.

Hence, to an extent, the facilities available often reflect commercial and resourcing realities (including the development of improvements in processing and display hardware, and the ready availability of high quality datasets) rather than the status of development in geospatial science. Indeed, there may be many capabilities available in software packages that are provided simply because it is extremely easy for the designers and programmers to implement them, especially those employing object-oriented programming and data models. For example, a given operation may be provided for polygonal features in response to a well-understood application requirement, which is then easily enabled for other features (e.g. point sets, polylines) despite the fact that there may be no known or likely requirement for the facility.

Despite this cautionary note, for specific well-defined or *core* problems, software developers will frequently utilize the most up-to-date research on algorithms in order to improve the quality (accuracy, optimality) and efficiency (speed, memory usage) of their products. For further information on algorithms and data structures, see the online NIST Dictionary of algorithms and data structures.

Furthermore, the quality, variety and efficiency of spatial analysis facilities provide an important discriminator between commercial offerings in an increasingly competitive and open market for software. However, the ready availability of analysis tools does not imply that one product is necessarily better or more complete than another — it is the selection and application of *appropriate* tools in a manner that is *fit for purpose* that is important. Guidance documents exist in some disciplines that assist users in this process, e.g. Perry *et al.* (2002) dealing with ecological data analysis, and to a significant degree we hope that this Guide will assist users from many disciplines in the selection process.

### 1.1.3   Intended audience and scope

This Guide has been designed to be accessible to a wide range of readers — from undergraduates and postgraduates studying GIS

and spatial analysis, to GIS practitioners and professional analysts. It is intended to be much more than a cookbook of formulas, algorithms and techniques — its aim is to provide an explanation of the key techniques of spatial analysis using examples from widely available software packages. It stops short, however, of attempting a systematic evaluation of competing software products. A substantial range of application examples are provided, but any specific selection inevitably illustrates only a small subset of the huge range of facilities available. Wherever possible, examples have been drawn from non-academic sources, highlighting the growing understanding and acceptance of GIS technology in the commercial and government sectors.

The scope of this Guide incorporates the various spatial analysis topics included within the NCGIA Core Curriculum (Goodchild and Kemp, 1990) and as such may provide a useful accompaniment to GIS Analysis courses based closely or loosely on this programme. More recently the Education Committee of the University Consortium for Geographic Information Science (UCGIS) in conjunction with the Association of American Geographers (AAG) has produced a comprehensive "Body of Knowledge" (BoK) document, which is available from the AAG website (http://www.aag.org/bok/). This Guide covers materials that primarily relate to the BoK sections **CF**: Conceptual Foundations; **AM**: Analytical Methods and **GC**: Geocomputation. In the general introduction to the **AM** knowledge area the authors of the BoK summarize this component as follows:

"This knowledge area encompasses a wide variety of operations whose objective is to derive analytical results from geospatial data. Data analysis seeks to understand both first-order (environmental) effects and second-order (interaction) effects. Approaches that are both data-driven (exploration of geospatial data) and model-driven (testing hypotheses and creating models) are included. Data-driven techniques derive summary descriptions of data, evoke insights about characteristics of data, contribute to the development of research hypotheses, and lead to the derivation of analytical results. The goal of model-driven analysis is to create and test geospatial process models. In general, model-driven analysis is an advanced knowledge area where previous experience with exploratory spatial data analysis would constitute a desired prerequisite." (BoK, p83 of the e-book version).

# 1.2 Software tools and Companion Materials

## 1.2.1 GIS and related software tools

The GIS software and analysis tools that an individual, group or corporate body chooses to use will depend very much on the purposes to which they will be put. There is an enormous difference between the requirements of academic researchers and educators, and those with responsibility for planning and delivery of emergency control systems or large scale physical infrastructure projects. The spectrum of products that may be described as a GIS includes (amongst others):

- highly specialized, sector specific packages: for example civil engineering design and costing systems; satellite image processing systems; and utility infrastructure management systems

- transportation and logistics management systems

- civil and military control room systems

- systems for visualizing the built environment for architectural purposes, for public consultation or as part of simulated environments for interactive gaming

- land registration systems

- census data management systems

- commercial location services and Digital Earth models

The list of software functions and applications is long and in some instances suppliers would not describe their offerings as a GIS. In many cases such systems fulfill specific operational needs, solving a well-defined subset of spatial problems and providing mapped output as an incidental but essential part of their operation. Many of the capabilities may be found in generic GIS products. In other instances a specialized package may utilize a GIS engine for the display and in some cases processing of spatial data (directly, or indirectly through interfacing or file

input/output mechanisms). For this reason, and in order to draw a boundary around the present work, reference to application-specific GIS will be limited.

A number of GIS packages and related toolsets have particularly strong facilities for processing and analyzing binary, grayscale and color images. They may have been designed originally for the processing of remote sensed data from satellite and aerial surveys, but many have developed into much more sophisticated and complete GIS tools, e.g. Clark Lab's Idrisi software; MicroImage's TNTMips product set; the ERDAS suite of products; and ENVI with associated packages such as RiverTools. Alternatively, image handling may have been deliberately included within the original design parameters for a generic GIS package (e.g. Manifold), or simply be toolsets for image processing that may be combined with mapping tools (e.g. the MATLab Image Processing Toolbox). Whatever their origins, a central purpose of such tools has been the capture, manipulation and interpretation of image data, rather than spatial analysis per se, although the latter inevitably follows from the former.

In this Guide we do not provide a separate chapter on image processing, despite its considerable importance in GIS, focusing instead on those areas where image processing tools and concepts are applied for spatial analysis (e.g. surface analysis). We have adopted a similar position with respect to other forms of data capture, such as field and geodetic survey systems and data cleansing software — although these incorporate analytical tools, their primary function remains the recording and georeferencing of datasets, rather than the analysis of such datasets once stored.

For most GIS professionals, spatial analysis and associated modeling is an infrequent activity. Even for those whose job focuses on analysis the range of techniques employed tends to be quite narrow and application focused. GIS consultants, researchers and academics on the other hand are continually exploring and developing analytical techniques. For the first group and for consultants, especially in commercial environments, the imperatives of financial considerations, timeliness and corporate policy loom large, directing attention to: delivery of solutions within well-defined time and cost parameters; working within commercial constraints on the cost and availability of software, datasets and staffing; ensuring that solutions are fit for purpose/meet client and end-user expectations and agreed standards; and in some cases, meeting "political" expectations.

For the second group of users it is common to make use of a variety of tools, data and programming facilities developed in the academic sphere. Increasingly these make use of non-commercial wide-ranging spatial analysis software libraries, such as the R-Spatial project (in "R"); PySal (in "Python"); and Splancs (in "S").

### 1.2.1.1  Sample software products

The principal products we have included in this latest edition of the Guide are included on the accompanying website's software page. Many of these products are free whilst others are available (at least in some form) for a small fee for all or selected groups of users. Others are licensed at varying per user prices, from a few hundred to over a thousand US dollars per user. Our tests and examples have largely been carried out using desktop/Windows versions of these software products. Different versions that support Unix-based operating systems and more sophisticated back-end database engines have not been utilized. In the context of this Guide we do not believe these selections affect our discussions in any substantial manner, although such issues may have performance and systems architecture implications that are extremely important for many users. OGC compliant software products are listed on the OGC resources web page: http://www.opengeospatial.org/resource/pro ducts/compliant. To quote from the OGC: "The OGC Compliance Testing Program provides a formal process for testing compliance of products that implement OpenGIS® Standards. Compliance Testing determines that a specific product implementation of a particular OpenGIS® Standard complies with all mandatory elements as specified in the standard and that these elements operate as described in the standard."

### 1.2.1.2  Software performance

Suppliers should be able to provide advice on performance issues (e.g. see the ESRI web site, "Services" area for relevant documents relating to their products) and in some cases such information is provided within product Help files (e.g. see the Performance Tips section within the Manifold GIS help file). Some analytical tasks are very processor- and memory-hungry, particularly as the number of elements involved increases. For example, vector overlay and buffering is relatively fast with a few objects and layers, but slows appreciably as the number of elements involved increases. This increase is generally at least linear with the number of layers and features, but for some problems grows in a highly non-linear (i.e. geometric) manner. Many optimization tasks, such as optimal routing through networks or trip distribution modeling, are known to be extremely hard or impossible to solve optimally and methods to achieve a best solution with a large dataset can take a considerable time to run (see Section 7.1.4 for a fuller discussion of this topic). Similar problems exist with the processing and display of raster files, especially large images or sets of images. Geocomputational methods, some of which are beginning to appear within GIS packages and related toolsets, are almost by definition computationally intensive. This certainly applies to large-scale (Monte Carlo) simulation models, cellular automata and agent-based models and some raster-based optimization techniques, especially where modeling extends into the time domain.

A frequent criticism of GIS software is that it is over-complicated, resource-hungry and requires specialist expertise to understand and use. Such criticisms are often valid and for many problems it may prove simpler, faster and more transparent to utilize specialized tools for the analytical work and draw on the strengths of GIS in data management and mapping to provide input/output and visualization functionality. Example approaches include: (i) using high-level programming facilities within a GIS (e.g. macros, scripts, VBA, Python) – many add-ins are developed in this way; (ii) using wide-ranging programmable spatial analysis software libraries and toolsets that incorporate GIS file reading, writing and display, such as the R-Spatial and PySal projects noted earlier; (iii) using general purpose data processing toolsets (e.g. MATLab, Excel, Python's Matplotlib, Numeric Python (Numpy) and other libraries from Enthought; or (iv) directly utilizing mainstream programming languages (e.g. Java, C++). The advantage of these approaches is control and transparency, the disadvantages are that software development is never trivial, is often subject to frustrating and unforeseen delays and errors, and generally requires ongoing maintenance. In some instances analytical applications may be well-suited to parallel or grid-enabled processing – as for example is the case with GWR (see Harris *et al.*, 2006).

At present there are no standardized tests for the quality, speed and accuracy of GIS procedures. It remains the buyer's and user's responsibility and duty to evaluate the software they wish to use for the specific task at hand, and by systematic controlled tests or by other means establish that the product and facility within that product they choose to use is truly fit for purpose — *caveat emptor*! Details of how to obtain these products are provided on the software page of the website that accompanies this book. The list maintained on Wikipedia is also a useful source of information and links, although is far from being complete or independent. A number of trade magazines and websites (such as Geoplace and Geocommunity) provide ad hoc reviews of GIS software offerings, especially new releases, although coverage of analytical functionality may be limited.

## 1.2.2 Suggested reading

There are numerous excellent modern books on GIS and spatial analysis, although few address software facilities and developments. Hypertext links are provided here, and throughout the text where they are cited, to the more recent publications and web resources listed.

As a background to this Guide any readers unfamiliar with GIS are encouraged to first tackle "Geographic Information Systems and Science" (GISSc) by Longley *et al.* (2005) – this work is soon to be updated in a 3rd edition. GISSc seeks to provide a comprehensive and highly accessible introduction to the subject as a whole. The GB Ordnance Survey's "GIS Files" document, downloadable from their website also provides an excellent brief introduction to GIS and its application.

Some of the basic mathematics and statistics of relevance to GIS analysis is covered in Dale (2005) and Allan (2004). For detailed information on datums and map projections, see Iliffe and Lott (2008). A useful online resource for those involved in data analysis, particularly with a statistical content, is the e-Handbook of Statistical Methods produced by the US National Institute on Standards and Technology, NIST). The more informally produced set of articles on statistical topics provided under the Wikipedia umbrella are also an extremely useful resource. These works, and the mathematics reference site, Mathworld, are referred to (with hypertext links) at various points throughout this document. For more specific sources on geostatistics and associated software packages, the European Commission's AI-GEOSTATS website (www.ai-geostats.org) is highly recommended, as is the web site of the Center for Computational Geostatistics (CCG) at the University of Alberta. For those who find mathematics and statistics something of a mystery, de Smith (2006) and Bluman (2003) provide useful starting points. For guidance on how to avoid the many pitfalls of statistical data analysis readers are recommended the material in the classic work by Huff (1993) "How to lie with statistics", and the 2008 book by Blastland and Dilnot "The tiger that isn't".

A relatively new development has been the increasing availability of out-of-print published books, articles and guides as free downloads in PDF format. These include: the series of 59 short guides published under the CATMOG umbrella (Concepts and Methods in Modern Geography), published between 1975 and 1995, most of which are now available at the QMRG website (a full list of all the guides is provided at the end of this book); the AutoCarto archives (1972-1997); the Atlas of Cyberspace by Dodge and Kitchin; and Fractal Cities, by Batty and Longley.

Undergraduates and MSc programme students will find Burrough and McDonnell (1998) provides excellent coverage of many aspects of geospatial analysis, especially from an environmental sciences perspective. Valuable guidance on the relationship between spatial process and spatial modeling may be found in Cliff and Ord (1981) and Bailey and Gatrell (1995). The latter provides an excellent introduction to the application of statistical methods to spatial data analysis. O'Sullivan and Unwin (2003) is a more broad-ranging book covering the topic the authors describe as "Geographic Information Analysis". This work is best suited to advanced undergraduates and first year postgraduate students. In many respects a deeper and more challenging work is Haining's (2003) "Spatial Data Analysis — Theory and Practice". This book is strongly recommended as a companion to the present Guide for postgraduate researchers and professional analysts involved in using GIS in conjunction with statistical analysis.

However, these authors do not address the broader spectrum of geospatial analysis and associated modeling as we have defined it. For example, problems relating to networks and location are often not covered and the literature relating to this area is scattered across many disciplines, being founded upon the mathematics of graph theory, with applications ranging from electronic circuit design to computer networking and from transport planning to the design of complex molecular structures. Useful books addressing this field include Miller and Shaw (2001) "Geographic Information Systems for Transportation" (especially Chapters 3, 5 and 6), and Rodrigue et al. (2006) "The geography of transport systems" (see further: http://people.hofstra.edu/geotrans/).

As companion reading on these topics for the present Guide we suggest the two volumes from the Handbooks in Operations Research and Management Science series by Ball et al. (1995): "Network Models", and "Network Routing". These rather expensive volumes provide collections of reviews covering many classes of network problems, from the core optimization problems of shortest paths and arc routing (e.g. street cleaning), to the complex problems of dynamic routing in variable networks, and a great deal more besides. This is challenging material and many readers may prefer to seek out more approachable material, available in a number of other books and articles, e.g. Ahuja et al. (1993), Mark Daskin's excellent book "Network and Discrete Location" (1995) and the earlier seminal works by Haggett and Chorley (1969), and Scott (1971), together with the widely available online materials accessible via the Internet. Final recommendations here are Stephen Wise's excellent GIS Basics (2002) and Worboys and Duckham (2004) which address GIS from a computing perspective. Both these volumes covers many topics, including the central issues of data modeling and data structures, key algorithms, system architectures and interfaces.

Many recent books described as covering (geo)spatial analysis are essentially edited collections of papers or brief articles. As such most do not seek to provide comprehensive coverage of the field, but tend to cover information on recent developments, often with a specific application focus (e.g. health, transport, archaeology). The latter is particularly common where these works are selections from sector- or discipline-specific conference proceedings, whilst in other cases they are carefully chosen or specially written papers. Classic amongst these is Berry and Marble (1968) "Spatial Analysis: A reader in statistical geography". More recent examples include "GIS, Spatial Analysis and Modeling" edited by Maguire, Batty and Goodchild (2005), and the excellent (but costly) compendium work "The SAGE handbook of Spatial Analysis" edited by Fotheringham and Rogerson (2008).

A second category of companion materials to the present work is the extensive product-specific documentation available from software suppliers. Some of the online help files and product manuals are excellent, as are associated example data files, tutorials, worked examples and white papers (see for example, ESRI's GIS site: http://www.gis.com/ which provides a wide-ranging guide to GIS. In many instances we utilize these to illustrate the capabilities of specific pieces of software and to enable readers to replicate our results using readily available materials. In addition some suppliers, notably ESRI, have a substantial publishing operation, including more general (i.e. not product specific) books of relevance to the present work. Amongst their publications we strongly recommend the "ESRI Guide to GIS Analysis Volume 1: Geographic patterns and relationships" (1999) by Andy Mitchell, which is full of valuable tips and examples. This is a basic introduction to GIS Analysis, which he defines in this context as "a process for looking at geographic patterns and relationships between features". Mitchell's Volume 2 (July 2005) covers more advanced techniques of data analysis, notably some of the more accessible and widely supported methods of spatial statistics, and is equally highly recommended. A number of the topics covered in his Volume 2 also appear in this Guide. Those considering using Open Source software should investigate the recent books by Neteler and Mitasova (2008), Tyler Mitchell (2005) and Sherman (2008).

In parallel with the increasing range and sophistication of spatial analysis facilities to be found within GIS packages, there has been a major change in spatial analytical techniques. In large measure this has come about as a result of technological developments and the related availability of software tools and detailed publicly available datasets. One aspect of this has been noted already — the move towards network-based location modeling where in the past this would have been unfeasible. More general shifts can be seen in the move towards local rather than simply global analysis, for example in the field of exploratory data analysis; in the increasing use of advanced forms of visualization as an aid to analysis and communication; and in the development of a wide range of computationally intensive and simulation methods that address problems through micro-scale processes (geocomputational methods). These trends are addressed at many points throughout this Guide.

# 1.3 Terminology and Abbreviations

GIS, like all disciplines, utilizes a wide range of terms and abbreviations, many of which have well-understood and recognized meanings. For a large number of commonly used terms online dictionaries have been developed, for example: those created by the Association for Geographic Information (AGI); the Open Geospatial Consortium (OGC); and by various software suppliers. The latter includes many terms and definitions that are particular to specific products, but remain a valuable resource. The University of California maintains an online dictionary of abbreviations and acronyms used in GIS, cartography and remote sensing. Web site details for each of these are provided at the end of this Guide.

## 1.3.1 Definitions

Geospatial analysis utilizes many of these terms, but many others are drawn from disciplines such as mathematics and statistics. The result that the same terms may mean entirely different things depending on their context and in many cases, on the software provider utilizing them. In most instances terms used in this Guide are defined on the first occasion they are used, but a number warrant defining at this stage. Table 1-1 provides a selection of such terms, utilizing definitions from widely recognized sources where available and appropriate.

*Table 1-1 Selected terminology*

| Term | Definition |
|------|------------|
| Adjacency | The sharing of a common side or boundary by two or more polygons (AGI). Note that adjacency may also apply to features that lie either side of a common boundary where these features are not necessarily polygons |
| Arc | Commonly used to refer to a straight line segment connecting two nodes or vertices of a polyline or polygon. Arcs may include segments or circles, spline functions or other forms of smooth curve. In connection with graphs and networks, arcs may be directed or undirected, and may have other attributes (e.g. cost, capacity etc.) |
| Artifact | A result (observation or set of observations) that appears to show something unusual (e.g. a spike in the surface of a 3D plot) but which is of no significance. Artifacts may be generated by the way in which data have been collected, defined or re-computed (e.g. resolution changing), or as a result of a computational operation (e.g. rounding error or substantive software error). Linear artifacts are sometimes referred to as "ghost lines" |
| Aspect | The direction in which slope is maximized for a selected point on a surface (see also, Gradient and Slope) |
| Attribute | A data item associated with an individual object (record) in a spatial database. Attributes may be explicit, in which case they are typically stored as one or more fields in tables linked to a set of objects, or they may be implicit (sometimes referred to as *intrinsic*), being either stored but hidden or computed as and when required (e.g. polyline length, polygon centroid). Raster/grid datasets typically have a single explicit attribute (a value) associated with each cell, rather than an attribute table containing as many records as there are cells in the grid |
| Azimuth | The horizontal direction of a vector, measured clockwise in degrees of rotation from the positive Y-axis, for example, degrees on a compass (AGI) |
| Azimuthal Projection | A type of map projection constructed as if a plane were to be placed at a tangent to the Earth's surface and the area to be mapped were projected onto the plane. |

| Term | Definition |
|------|-----------|
| | All points on this projection keep their true compass bearing (AGI) |
| (Spatial) Autocorrelation | The degree of relationship that exists between two or more (spatial) variables, such that when one changes, the other(s) also change. This change can either be in the same direction, which is a positive autocorrelation, or in the opposite direction, which is a negative autocorrelation (AGI). The term autocorrelation is usually applied to ordered datasets, such as those relating to time series or spatial data ordered by distance band. The existence of such a relationship suggests but does not definitely establish causality |
| Cartogram | A cartogram is a form of map in which some variable such as Population Size or Gross National Product typically is substituted for land area. The geometry or space of the map is distorted in order to convey the information of this alternate variable. Cartograms use a variety of approaches to map distortion, including the use of continuous and discrete regions. The term cartogram (or *linear cartogram*) is also used on occasion to refer to maps that distort distance for particular display purposes, such as the London Underground map |
| Choropleth | A thematic map [i.e. a map showing a theme, such as soil types or rainfall levels] portraying properties of a surface using area symbols such as shading [or color]. Area symbols on a choropleth map usually represent categorized classes of the mapped phenomenon (AGI) |
| Conflation | A term used to describe the process of combining (merging) information from two data sources into a single source, reconciling disparities where possible (e.g. by rubber-sheeting — see below). The term is distinct from *concatenation* which refers to combinations of data sources (e.g. by overlaying one upon another) but retaining access to their distinct components |
| Contiguity | The topological identification of adjacent polygons by recording the left and right polygons of each arc. Contiguity is not concerned with the exact locations of polygons, only their relative positions. Contiguity data can be stored in a table, matrix or simply as [i.e. in] a list, that can be cross-referenced to the relevant co-ordinate data if required (AGI). |
| Curve | A one-dimensional geometric object stored as a sequence of points, with the subtype of curve specifying the form of interpolation between points. A curve is simple if it does not pass through the same point twice (OGC). A LineString (or polyline — see below) is a subtype of a curve |
| Datum | Strictly speaking, the singular of *data*. In GIS the word datum usually relates to a reference level (surface) applying on a nationally or internationally defined basis from which elevation is to be calculated. In the context of terrestrial geodesy datum is usually defined by a model of the Earth or section of the Earth, such as WGS84 (see below). The term is also used for horizontal referencing of measurements; see Iliffe and Lott (2008) for full details |
| DEM | Digital elevation model (a DEM is a particular kind of DTM, see below) |
| DTM | Digital terrain model |
| EDM | Electronic distance measurement |
| EDA, ESDA | Exploratory data analysis/Exploratory spatial data analysis |
| Ellipsoid/Spheroid | An ellipse rotated about its minor axis determines a spheroid (sphere-like object), |

| Term | Definition |
|------|------------|
| | also known as an ellipsoid of revolution (see also, WGS84) |
| Feature | Frequently used within GIS referring to point, line (including polyline and mathematical functions defining arcs), polygon and sometimes text (annotation) objects (see also, vector) |
| Geoid | An imaginary shape for the Earth defined by mean sea level and its imagined continuation under the continents at the same level of gravitational potential (AGI) |
| Geodemographics | The analysis of people by where they live, in particular by type of neighborhood. Such localized classifications have been shown to be powerful discriminators of consumer behavior and related social and behavioral patterns |
| Geospatial | Referring to location relative to the Earth's surface. "Geospatial" is more precise in many GI contexts than "geographic," because geospatial information is often used in ways that do not involve a graphic representation, or map, of the information. OGC |
| Geostatistics | Statistical methods developed for and applied to geographic data. These statistical methods are required because geographic data do not usually conform to the requirements of standard statistical procedures, due to spatial autocorrelation and other problems associated with spatial data (AGI). The term is widely used to refer to a family of tools used in connection with spatial interpolation (prediction) of (piecewise) continuous datasets and is widely applied in the environmental sciences. Spatial statistics is a term more commonly applied to the analysis of discrete objects (e.g. points, areas) and is particularly associated with the social and health sciences |
| Geovisualization | A family of techniques that provide visualizations of spatial and spatio-temporal datasets, extending from static, 2D maps and cartograms, to representations of 3D using perspective and shading, solid terrain modeling and increasingly extending into dynamic visualization interfaces such as linked windows, digital globes, fly-throughs, animations, virtual reality and immersive systems. Geovisualization is the subject of ongoing research by the International Cartographic Association (ICA), Commission on Geovisualization |
| GIS-T | GIS applied to transportation problems |
| GPS/ DGPS | Global positioning system; Differential global positioning system — DGPS provides improved accuracy over standard GPS by the use of one or more fixed reference stations that provide corrections to GPS data |
| Gradient | Used in spatial analysis with reference to surfaces (scalar fields). Gradient is a vector field comprised of the *aspect* (direction of maximum slope) and *slope* computed in this direction (magnitude of rise over run) at each point of the surface. The magnitude of the gradient (the slope or inclination) is sometimes itself referred to as the gradient (see also, Slope and Aspect) |
| Graph | A collection of vertices and edges (links between vertices) constitutes a graph. The mathematical study of the properties of graphs and paths through graphs is known as graph theory |
| Heuristic | A term derived from the same Greek root as Eureka, heuristic refers to procedures for finding solutions to problems that may be difficult or impossible to solve by direct means. In the context of optimization heuristic algorithms are systematic procedures that seek a good or near optimal solution to a well-defined |

| Term | Definition |
|------|-----------|
| | problem, but not one that is necessarily optimal. They are often based on some form of intelligent trial and error or search procedure |
| *iid* | An abbreviation for "independently and identically distributed". Used in statistical analysis in connection with the distribution of errors or residuals |
| Invariance | In the context of GIS invariance refers to properties of features that remain unchanged under one or more (spatial) transformations |
| Kernel | Literally, the core or central part of an item. Often used in computer science to refer to the central part of an operating system, the term kernel in geospatial analysis refers to methods (e.g. density modeling, local grid analysis) that involve calculations using a well-defined local neighborhood (block of cells, radially symmetric function) |
| Layer | A collection of geographic entities of the same type (e.g. points, lines or polygons). Grouped layers may combine layers of different geometric types |
| Map algebra | A range of actions applied to the grid cells of one or more maps (or images) often involving filtering and/or algebraic operations. These techniques involve processing one or more raster layers according to simple rules resulting in a new map layer, for example replacing each cell value with some combination of its neighbors' values, or computing the sum or difference of specific attribute values for each grid cell in two matching raster datasets |
| Mashup | A recently coined term used to describe websites whose content is composed from multiple (often distinct) data sources, such as a mapping service and property price information, constructed using programmable interfaces to these sources (as opposed to simple compositing or embedding) |
| MBR/ MER | Minimum bounding rectangle/Minimum enclosing (or envelope) rectangle (of a feature set) |
| Planar/non-planar/planar enforced | Literally, lying entirely within a plane surface. A polygon set is said to be planar enforced if every point in the set lies in exactly one polygon, or on the boundary between two or more polygons. See also, planar graph. A graph or network with edges crossing (e.g. bridges/underpasses) is non-planar |
| Planar graph | If a graph can be drawn in the plane (embedded) in such a way as to ensure edges only intersect at points that are vertices then the graph is described as planar |
| Pixel/image | Picture element — a single defined point of an image. Pixels have a "color" attribute whose value will depend on the encoding method used. They are typically either binary (0/1 values), grayscale (effectively a color mapping with values, typically in the integer range [0,255]), or color with values from 0 upwards depending on the number of colors supported. Image files can be regarded as a particular form of raster or grid file |
| Polygon | A closed figure in the plane, typically comprised of an ordered set of connected vertices, $v_1,v_2,...v_{n-1},v_n=v_1$ where the connections (edges) are provided by straight line segments. If the sequence of edges is not self-crossing it is called a simple polygon. A point is inside a simple polygon if traversing the boundary in a clockwise direction the point is always on the right of the observer. If every pair of points inside a polygon can be joined by a straight line that also lies inside the polygon then the polygon is described as being convex (i.e. the interior is a connected point set). The OGC definition of a polygon is "a planar surface defined by 1 exterior boundary and 0 or more interior boundaries. Each interior boundary |

| Term | Definition |
|------|-----------|
| | defines a hole in the polygon" |
| Polyhedral surface | A Polyhedral surface is a contiguous collection of polygons, which share common boundary segments (OGC). See also, Tesseral/Tessellation |
| Polyline | An ordered set of connected vertices, $v_1, v_2, ... v_{n-1}, v_n, v_1$ where the connections (edges) are provided by straight line segments. The vertex $v_1$ is referred to as the start of the polyline and $v_n$ as the end of the polyline. The OGC specification uses the term LineString which it defines as: a curve with linear interpolation between points. Each consecutive pair of points defines a line segment |
| Raster/grid | A data model in which geographic features are represented using discrete cells, generally squares, arranged as a (contiguous) rectangular grid. A single grid is essentially the same as a two-dimensional matrix, but is typically referenced from the lower left corner rather than the norm for matrices, which are referenced from the upper left. Raster files may have one or more values (attributes or bands) associated with each cell position or pixel |
| Resampling | 1. Procedures for (automatically) adjusting one or more raster datasets to ensure that the grid resolutions of all sets match when carrying out combination operations. Resampling is often performed to match the coarsest resolution of a set of input rasters. Increasing resolution rather than decreasing requires an interpolation procedure such as bicubic spline. |
| | 2. The process of reducing image dataset size by representing a group of pixels with a single pixel. Thus, pixel count is lowered, individual pixel size is increased, and overall image geographic extent is retained. Resampled images are "coarse" and have less information than the images from which they are taken. Conversely, this process can also be executed in the reverse (AGI) |
| | 3. In a statistical context the term resampling (or re-sampling) is sometimes used to describe the process of selecting a subset of the original data, such that the samples can reasonably be expected to be independent |
| Rubber sheeting | A procedure to adjust the co-ordinates all of the data points in a dataset to allow a more accurate match between known locations and a few data points within the dataset. Rubber sheeting ... preserves the interconnectivity or topology, between points and objects through stretching, shrinking or re-orienting their interconnecting lines (AGI). Rubber-sheeting techniques are widely used in the production of Cartograms (*op. cit.*) |
| Slope | The amount of *rise* of a surface (change in elevation) divided by the distance over which this rise is computed (the *run*), along a straight line transect in a specified direction. The run is usually defined as the *planar* distance, in which case the slope is the tan() function. Unless the surface is flat the slope at a given point on a surface will (typically) have a maximum value in a particular direction (depending on the surface and the way in which the calculations are carried out). This direction is known as the *aspect*. The *vector* consisting of the slope and aspect is the *gradient* of the surface at that point (see also, Gradient and Aspect) |
| Spatial econometrics | A subset of econometric methods that is concerned with spatial aspects present in cross-sectional and space-time observations. These methods focus in particular on two forms of so-called spatial effects in econometric models, referred to as spatial dependence and spatial heterogeneity (Anselin, 1988, 2006) |
| Spheroid | A flattened (oblate) form of a sphere, or ellipse of revolution. The most widely used model of the Earth is that of a spheroid, although the detailed form is |

| Term | Definition |
|---|---|
| | slightly different from a true spheroid |
| SQL/Structured Query Language | Within GIS software SQL extensions known as spatial queries are frequently implemented. These support queries that are based on spatial relationships rather than simply attribute values |
| Surface | A 2D geometric object. A simple surface consists of a single 'patch' that is associated with one exterior boundary and 0 or more interior boundaries. Simple surfaces in 3D are isomorphic to planar surfaces. Polyhedral surfaces are formed by 'stitching' together simple surfaces along their boundaries (OGC). Surfaces may be regarded as scalar fields, i.e. fields with a single value, e.g. elevation or temperature, at every point |
| Tesseral/Tessellation | A gridded representation of a plane surface into disjoint polygons. These polygons are normally either square (raster), triangular (TIN — see below), or hexagonal. These models can be built into hierarchical structures, and have a range of algorithms available to navigate through them. A (regular or irregular) 2D tessellation involves the subdivision of a 2-dimensional plane into polygonal tiles (polyhedral blocks) that completely cover a plane (AGI). The term lattice is sometimes used to describe the complete division of the plane into regular or irregular disjoint polygons. More generally the subdivision of the plane may be achieved using arcs that are not necessarily straight lines |
| TIN | Triangulated irregular network. A form of the tesseral model based on triangles. The vertices of the triangles form irregularly spaced nodes. Unlike the grid, the TIN allows dense information in complex areas, and sparse information in simpler or more homogeneous areas. The TIN dataset includes topological relationships between points and their neighboring triangles. Each sample point has an $X,Y$ co-ordinate and a surface, or Z-Value. These points are connected by edges to form a set of non-overlapping triangles used to represent the surface. TINs are also called irregular triangular mesh or irregular triangular surface model (AGI) |
| Topology | The relative location of geographic phenomena independent of their exact position. In digital data, topological relationships such as connectivity, adjacency and relative position are usually expressed as relationships between nodes, links and polygons. For example, the topology of a line includes its from- and to-nodes, and its left and right polygons (AGI). In mathematics, a property is said to be *topological* if it survives stretching and distorting of space |
| Transformation 1. Map | Map transformation: A computational process of converting an image or map from one coordinate system to another. Transformation … typically involves rotation and scaling of grid cells, and thus requires resampling of values (AGI) |
| Transformation 2. Affine | Affine transformation: When a map is digitized, the $X$ and $Y$ coordinates are initially held in digitizer measurements. To make these $X,Y$ pairs useful they must be converted to a real world coordinate system. The affine transformation is a combination of linear transformations that converts digitizer coordinates into Cartesian coordinates. The basic property of an affine transformation is that parallel lines remain parallel (AGI, with modifications). The principal affine transformations are contraction, expansion, dilation, reflection, rotation, shear and translation |

| Term | Definition |
|---|---|
| Transformation 3. Data | Data transformation (see also, subsection 6.7.1.10): A mathematical procedure (usually a one-to-one mapping or function) applied to an initial dataset to produce a result dataset. An example might be the transformation of a set of sampled values $\{x_i\}$ using the log() function, to create the set $\{\log(x_i)\}$. Affine and map transformations are examples of mathematical transformations applied to coordinate datasets. Note that operations on transformed data, e.g. checking whether a value is within 10% of a target value, is not equivalent to the same operation on untransformed data, even after back transformation |
| Transformation 4. Back | Back transformation: If a set of sampled values $\{x_i\}$ has been transformed by a one-to-one mapping function $f()$ into the set $\{f(x_i)\}$, and $f()$ has a one-to-one inverse mapping function $f^{-1}()$, then the process of computing $f^{-1}\{f(x_i)\}=\{x_i\}$ is known as back transformation. Example $f()=\ln()$ and $f^{-1}=\exp()$ |
| Vector | 1. Within GIS the term vector refers to data that are comprised of lines or arcs, defined by beginning and end points, which meet at nodes. The locations of these nodes and the topological structure are usually stored explicitly. Features are defined by their boundaries only and curved lines are represented as a series of connecting arcs. Vector storage involves the storage of explicit topology, which raises overheads, however it only stores those points which define a feature and all space outside these features is "non-existent" (AGI)<br><br>2. In mathematics the term refers to a directed line, i.e. a line with a defined origin, direction and orientation. The same term is used to refer to a single column or row of a matrix, in which case it is denoted by a bold letter, usually in lower case |
| Viewshed | Regions of visibility observable from one or more observation points. Typically a viewshed will be defined by the numerical or color coding of a raster image, indicating whether the (target) cell can be seen from (or probably seen from) the (source) observation points. By definition a cell that can be viewed from a specific observation point is inter-visible with that point (each location can see the other). Viewsheds are usually determined for optically defined visibility within a maximum range |
| WGS84 | World Geodetic System, 1984 version. This models the Earth as a spheroid with major axis 6378.137 kms and flattening factor of 1:298.257, i.e. roughly 0.3% flatter at the poles than a perfect sphere. One of a number of such global models |

*Note: Where cited, references are drawn from the Association for Geographic Information (AGI), and the Open Geospatial Consortium (OGC). Square bracketed text denotes insertion by the present authors into these definitions. For OGC definitions see: Open Geospatial Consortium Inc (2006) in References section*

# 1.4 Common Measures and Notation

## 1.4.1 Notation

Throughout this Guide a number of terms and associated formulas are used that are common to many analytical procedures. In this section we provide a brief summary of those that fall into this category. Others, that are more specific to a particular field of analysis, are treated within the section to which they primarily apply. Many of the measures we list will be familiar to readers, since they originate from standard single variable (univariate) statistics. For brevity we provide details of these in tabular form. In order to clarify the expressions used here and elsewhere in the text, we use the notation shown in Table 1-2. *Italics* are used within the text and formulas to denote variables and parameters, as well as selected terms.

*Table 1-2 Notation and symbology*

| | |
|---|---|
| [a,b] | A closed interval of the Real line, for example [0,1] means the set of all values between 0 and 1, including 0 and 1 |
| (a,b) | An open interval of the Real line, for example (0,1) means the set of all values between 0 and 1, NOT including 0 and 1. This should not be confused with the notation for coordinate pairs, (x,y), or its use within bivariate functions such as f(x,y), or in connection with graph edges (see below) — the meaning should be clear from the context |
| (i,j) | In the context of graph theory, which forms the basis for network analysis, this pairwise notation is often used to define an edge connecting the two vertices $i$ and $j$ |
| (x,y) | A (spatial) data pair, usually representing a pair of coordinates in two dimensions. Terrestrial coordinates are typically Cartesian (i.e. in the plane, or *planar*) based on a pre-specified projection of the sphere, or Spherical (latitude, longitude). Spherical coordinates are often quoted in positive or negative degrees from the Equator and the Greenwich meridian, so may have the ranges [-90,+90] for latitude (north-south measurement) and [-180,180] for longitude (east-west measurement) |
| (x,y,z) | A (spatial) data triple, usually representing a pair of coordinates in two dimensions, plus a third coordinate (usually height or depth) or an attribute value, such as soil type or household income |
| $\{x_i\}$ | A *set* of $n$ values $x_1, x_2, x_3, \dots x_n$, typically continuous ratio-scaled variables in the range $(-\infty,\infty)$ or $[0,\infty)$. The values may represent measurements or attributes of distinct objects, or values that represent a collection of objects (for example the population of a census tract) |
| $\{X_i\}$ | An ordered set of $n$ values $X_1, X_2, X_3, \dots X_n$, such that $X_i \leq X_{i+1}$ for all $i$ |
| X,x | The use of bold symbols in expressions indicates matrices (upper case) and vectors (lower case) |
| $\{f_i\}$ | A set of $k$ frequencies ($k<=n$), derived from a dataset $\{x_i\}$. If $\{x_i\}$ contains discrete values, some of which occur multiple times, then $\{f_i\}$ represents the number of occurrences or the *count* of each distinct value. $\{f_i\}$ may also represent the number of occurrences of values that lie in a range or set of ranges, $\{r_i\}$. If a dataset contains $n$ values, then the sum $\Sigma f_i = n$. The set $\{f_i\}$ can also be written $f(x_i)$. If $\{f_i\}$ is regarded as a set of weights (for example attribute values) associated with the $\{x_i\}$, it may be written as the set $\{w_i\}$ or $w(x_i)$ |
| $\{p_i\}$ | A set of $k$ probabilities ($k<=n$), estimated from a dataset or theoretically derived. With a finite set of values $\{x_i\}$, $p_i=f_i/n$. If $\{x_i\}$ represents a set of $k$ classes or ranges then $p_i$ is the probability of finding an occurrence in the $i^{th}$ class or range, i.e. the proportion of events or values occurring in |

| | |
|---|---|
| | that class or range. The sum $\sum p_i = 1$. If a set of frequencies, $\{f_i\}$, have been standardized by dividing each value $f_i$ by their sum, $\sum f_i$, then $\{p_i\}$ is equivalent to $\{f_i\}$ |
| $\sum$ | Summation symbol, e.g. $x_1 + x_2 + x_3 + \ldots + x_n$. If no limits are shown the sum is assumed to apply to all subsequent elements, otherwise upper and/or lower limits for summation are provided |
| $\Pi$ | Product symbol, e.g. $x_1 \cdot x_2 \cdot x_3 \cdot \ldots \cdot x_n$. If no limits are shown the product is assumed to apply to all subsequent elements, otherwise upper and/or lower limits for multiplication are provided |
| $\wedge$ | Used here in conjunction with Greek symbols (directly above) to indicate a value is an estimate of the true population value. Sometimes referred to as "hat" |
| $\sim$ | Is distributed as, for example $y \sim N(0,1)$ means the variable $y$ has a distribution that is Normal with a mean of 0 and standard deviation of 1 |
| ! | Factorial symbol. $z = x!$ means $z = x(x-1)(x-2) \ldots 1$. $x \geq 0$. Usually applied to integer values of $x$. May be defined for fractional values of $x$ using the Gamma function (Table 1-3, Section 1.4.2.8) |
| $\equiv$ | 'Equivalent to' symbol |
| $\approx$ | 'Approximately equal to' symbol |
| $\in$ | 'Belongs to' symbol, e.g. $x \in [0,2]$ means that $x$ belongs to/is drawn from the set of all values in the closed interval [0,2]; $x \in \{0,1\}$ means that $x$ can take the values 0 and 1 |
| $\leq$ | Less than or equal to, represented in the text where necessary by <= (provided in this form to support display by some web browsers) |
| $\geq$ | Greater than or equal to, represented in the text where necessary by >= (provided in this form to support display by some web browsers) |

## 1.4.2 Statistical measures and related formulas

Table 1-3 provides a list of common measures (univariate statistics) applied to datasets, and associated formulas for calculating the measure from a sample dataset in summation form (rather than integral form) where necessary. In some instances these formulas are adjusted to provide estimates of the population values rather than those obtained from the sample of data one is working on.

Many of the measures can be extended to two-dimensional forms in a very straightforward manner, and thus they provide the basis for numerous standard formulas in spatial statistics. For a number of univariate statistics (variance, skewness, kurtosis) we refer to the notion of (estimated) *moments* about the mean. These are computations of the form

$$\sum (x_i - \bar{x})^r, r = 1, 2, 3 \ldots$$

When $r=1$ this summation will be 0, since this is just the difference of all values from the mean. For values of $r>1$ the expression provides measures that are useful for describing the shape (spread, skewness, peakedness) of a distribution, and simple variations on the formula are used to define

the correlation between two or more datasets (the *product moment* correlation). The term *moment* in this context comes from physics, i.e. like 'momentum' and 'moment of inertia', and in a spatial (2D) context provides the basis for the definition of a centroid — the center of mass or center of gravity of an object, such as a polygon (see further, Section 4.2.5).

### Table 1-3 Common formulas and statistical measures

This table of measures has been divided into 9 subsections for ease of use. Each is provided with its own subheading:

- Counts and specific values
- Measures of centrality
- Measures of spread
- Measures of distribution shape
- Measures of complexity and dimensionality
- Common distributions
- Data transforms and back transforms
- Selected functions
- Matrix expressions

### 1.4.2.1 Counts and specific values

| Measure | Definition | Expression(s) |
|---|---|---|
| Count | The number of data values in a set | $Count(\{x_i\})=n$ |
| Top $m$, Bottom $m$ | The set of the largest (smallest) $m$ values from a set. May be generated via an SQL command | $Top_m\{x_i\}=\{X_{n-m+1}, \ldots X_{n-1}, X_n\};$ <br><br> $Bot_m\{x_i\}=\{X_1, X_2, \ldots X_m\};$ |
| Variety | The number of distinct i.e. different data values in a set. Some packages refer to the variety as diversity, which should not be confused with information theoretic and other diversity measures | |
| Majority | The most common i.e. most frequent data values in a set. Similar to mode (see below), but often applied to raster datasets at the neighborhood or zonal level. For general datasets the term should only be applied to cases where a given class is 50%+ | |

| Measure | Definition | Expression(s) |
|---|---|---|
| | of the total | |
| Minority | The least common i.e. least frequently occurring data values in a set. Often applied to raster datasets at the neighborhood or zonal level | |
| Maximum, *Max* | The maximum value of a set of values. May not be unique | $Max\{x_i\}=X_n$ |
| Minimum, *Min* | The minimum value of a set of values. May not be unique | $Min\{x_i\}=X_1$ |
| Sum | The sum of a set of data values | $\displaystyle\sum_{i=1}^{n} x_i$ |

### 1.4.2.2 Measures of centrality

| Measure | Definition | Expression(s) |
|---|---|---|
| Mean (arithmetic) | The arithmetic average of a set of data values (also known as the *sample mean* where the data are a sample from a larger population). Note that if the set $\{f_i\}$ are regarded as weights rather than frequencies the result is known as the *weighted mean*. Other mean values include the geometric and harmonic mean. The population mean is often denoted by the symbol $\mu$. In many instances the sample mean is the best (unbiased) estimate of the population mean and is sometimes denoted by $\mu$ with a ^ symbol above it) or as a variable such as $x$ with a bar above it. | $\displaystyle\bar{x} = \frac{1}{n}\sum_{i=1}^{n} x_i$ $\displaystyle\bar{x} = \sum_{i=1}^{n} f_i x_i \Big/ \sum_{i=1}^{n} f_i$ $\displaystyle\bar{x} = \sum_{i=1}^{n} p_i x_i$ |
| Mean (harmonic) | The harmonic mean, $H$, is the mean of the reciprocals of the data values, which is then adjusted by taking the reciprocal of the result. The harmonic mean is less than or equal to the geometric mean, which is less than or equal to the arithmetic mean | $\displaystyle H = \left(\frac{1}{n}\sum_{i=1}^{n}\frac{1}{x_i}\right)^{-1}$ |
| Mean (geometric) | The geometric mean, $G$, is the mean defined by taking the products of the data values and then adjusting the value by taking the $n^{th}$ root of the result. The geometric mean is greater than or equal to the harmonic mean and is less than or equal to the arithmetic mean | $\displaystyle G = \left(\prod_{i=1}^{n} x_i\right)^{1/n}$ , hence $\displaystyle\log(G) = \frac{1}{n}\sum_{i=1}^{n}\log(x_i)$ |
| Mean (power) | The general (limit) expression for mean values. Values for $p$ give the following means: $p=1$ arithmetic; $p=2$ root mean | $\displaystyle M = \left(\frac{1}{n}\sum_{i=1}^{n} x_i^{\,p}\right)^{1/p}$ |

| Measure | Definition | Expression(s) |
|---|---|---|
| | square; $p$=-1 harmonic. Limit values for $p$ (i.e. as $p$ tends to these values) give the following means: $p$=0 geometric; $p$=-$\infty$ minimum; $p$=$\infty$ maximum | |
| Trim-mean, $TM$, $t$, Olympic mean | The mean value computed with a specified percentage (proportion), $t/2$, of values removed from each tail to eliminate the highest and lowest outliers and extreme values. For small samples a specific number of observations (e.g. 1) rather than a percentage, may be ignored. In general an equal number, $k$, of high and low values should be removed and the number of observations summed should equal $n(1$-$t)$ expressed as an integer. This variant is sometimes described as the Olympic mean, as is used in scoring Olympic gymnastics for example | $TM = \dfrac{1}{n(1-t)} \displaystyle\sum_{i=nt/2}^{n(1-t/2)} X_i \ , \ t\in [0,1]$ |
| Mode | The most common or frequently occurring value in a set. Where a set has one dominant value or range of values it is said to be unimodal; if there are several commonly occurring values or ranges it is described as multi-modal. Note that arithmetic mean-mode$\approx$3 (arithmetic mean-median) for many unimodal distributions | |
| Median, $Med$ | The middle value in an ordered set of data if the set contains an odd number of values, or the average of the two middle values if the set contains an even number of values. For a continuous distribution the median is the 50% point (0.5) obtained from the cumulative distribution of the values or function | $Med\{x_i\}$=$X_{(n+1)/2}$ ; $n$ odd <br><br> $Med\{x_i\}$=$iX_{n/2}$+$X_{n/2+1})/2$; $n$ even |
| Mid-range, $MR$ | The middle value of the Range | $MR\{x_i\}$=Range$/2$ |
| Root mean square ($RMS$) | The root of the mean of squared data values. Squaring removes negative values | $\sqrt{\dfrac{1}{n}\displaystyle\sum_{i=1}^{n} x_i^2}$ |

### 1.4.2.3 Measures of spread

| Measure | Definition | Expression(s) |
|---|---|---|
| Range | The difference between the maximum and minimum values of a set | $Range\{x_i\}$=$X_n$-$X_1$ |
| Lower quartile (25%), $LQ$ | In an ordered set, 25% of data items are less than or equal to the upper bound of this range. For a continuous distribution | $LQ$=$\{X_1, \ldots X_{(n+1)/4}\}$ |

| Measure | Definition | Expression(s) |
|---|---|---|
| | the LQ is the set of values from 0% to 25% (0.25) obtained from the cumulative distribution of the values or function. Treatment of cases where $n$ is even and $n$ is odd, and when $i$ runs from 1 to n or 0 to $n$ vary | |
| Upper quartile (75%), $UQ$ | In an ordered set 75% of data items are less than or equal to the upper bound of this range. For a continuous distribution the UQ is the set of values from 75% (0.75) to 100% obtained from the cumulative distribution of the values or function. Treatment of cases where $n$ is even and $n$ is odd, and when $i$ runs from 1 to n or 0 to $n$ vary | $UQ = \{X_{3(n+1)/4}, ... X_n\}$ |
| Inter-quartile range, $IQR$ | The difference between the lower and upper quartile values, hence covering the middle 50% of the distribution. The inter-quartile range can be obtained by taking the median of the dataset, then finding the median of the upper and lower halves of the set. The IQR is then the difference between these two secondary medians | $IQR = UQ - LQ$ |
| Trim-range, $TR$, $t$ | The range computed with a specified percentage (proportion), $t/2$, of the highest and lowest values removed to eliminate outliers and extreme values. For small samples a specific number of observations (e.g. 1) rather than a percentage, may be ignored. In general an equal number, $k$, of high and low values are removed (if possible) | $TR_t = X_{n(1-t/2)} - X_{nt/2}$, $t \in [0,1]$<br><br>$TR_{50\%} = IQR$ |
| Variance, $Var$, $\sigma^2$, $s^2$, $\mu_2$ | The average squared difference of values in a dataset from their population mean, $\mu$, or from the sample mean (also known as the sample variance where the data are a sample from a larger population). Differences are squared to remove the effect of negative values (the summation would otherwise be 0). The third formula is the frequency form, where frequencies have been standardized, i.e. $\Sigma f_i = 1$. $Var$ is a function of the $2^{nd}$ moment about the mean. The population variance is often denoted by the symbol $\mu_2$ or $\sigma^2$.<br><br>The estimated population variance is often denoted by $s^2$ or by $\sigma^2$ with a ^ symbol above it | $Var = \sigma^2 = \dfrac{1}{n}\sum_{i=1}^{n}(x_i - \mu)^2$<br><br>$Var = \dfrac{1}{n}\sum_{i=1}^{n}(x_i - \bar{x})^2$<br><br>$Var = \sum_{i=1}^{n} f_i(x_i - \bar{x})^2$<br><br>$Var = \dfrac{1}{n}\sum_{i=1}^{n}(x_i - \bar{x})(x_i - \bar{x})$<br><br>$s^2 = \hat{\sigma}^2 = \dfrac{1}{n-1}\sum_{i=1}^{n}(x_i - \bar{x})^2$ |

| Measure | Definition | Expression(s) |
|---------|-----------|---------------|
| Standard deviation, SD, s or RMSD | The square root of the variance, hence it is the Root Mean Squared Deviation (RMSD). The population standard deviation is often denoted by the symbol $\sigma$. SD* shows the estimated population standard deviation (sometimes denoted by $\sigma$ with a ^ symbol above it or by s) | $SD = \sqrt{Var} = \sigma$ $$SD = \sqrt{\frac{1}{n}\sum_{i=1}^{n}(x_i - \bar{x})^2}$$ $$SD^* = \hat{\sigma} = \sqrt{\frac{1}{n-1}\sum_{i=1}^{n}(x_i - \bar{x})^2}$$ |
| Standard error of the mean, SE | The estimated standard deviation of the mean values of $n$ samples from the same population. It is simply the sample standard deviation reduced by a factor equal to the square root of the number of samples, $n>=1$ | $$SE = \frac{SD}{\sqrt{n}}$$ |
| Root mean squared error, RMSE | The standard deviation of samples from a known set of true values, $x_i^*$. If $x_i^*$ are estimated by the mean of sampled values RMSE is equivalent to RMSD | $$RMSE = \sqrt{\frac{1}{n}\sum_{i=1}^{n}\left(x_i - x_i^*\right)^2}$$ |
| Mean deviation/error, MD or ME | The mean deviation of samples from the known set of true values, $x_i^*$ | $$MD = \frac{1}{n}\sum_{i=1}^{n}\left(x_i - x_i^*\right)$$ |
| Mean absolute deviation/error, MAD or MAE | The mean absolute deviation of samples from the known set of true values, $x_i^*$ | $$MAE = \frac{1}{n}\sum_{i=1}^{n}\left|x_i - x_i^*\right|$$ |
| Covariance, Cov | Literally the pattern of common (or co-) variation observed in a collection of two (or more) datasets, or partitions of a single dataset. Note that if the two sets are the same the covariance is the same as the variance | $$Cov(x,y) = \frac{1}{n}\sum_{i=1}^{n}(x_i - \bar{x})(y_i - \bar{y})$$ $Cov(x,x)=Var(x)$ |
| Correlation/ product moment or Pearson's correlation coefficient, r | A measure of the similarity between two (or more) paired datasets. The correlation coefficient is the ratio of the covariance to the product of the standard deviations. If the two datasets are the same or perfectly matched this will give a result=1 | $r=Cov(x,y)/SD_x SD_y$ $$r = \frac{\sum_{i=1}^{n}(x_i - \bar{x})(y_i - \bar{y})}{\sqrt{\sum_{i=1}^{n}(x_i - \bar{x})^2}\sqrt{\sum_{i=1}^{n}(y_i - \bar{y})^2}}$$ |
| Coefficient of variation, CV | The ratio of the standard deviation to the mean, sometime computed as a percentage. If this ratio is close to 1, and the distribution is strongly left skewed, it may suggest the underlying distribution is Exponential. Note, mean values close to 0 may produce unstable results | $CV= SD / \bar{x}$ |

| Measure | Definition | Expression(s) |
|---------|------------|---------------|
| Variance mean ratio, VMR | The ratio of the variance to the mean, sometime computed as a percentage. If this ratio is close to 1, and the distribution is unimodal and relates to count data, it may suggest the underlying distribution is Poisson. Note, mean values close to 0 may produce unstable results | $VMR = Var / \bar{x}$ |

#### 1.4.2.4 Measures of distribution shape

| Measure | Definition | Expression(s) |
|---------|------------|---------------|
| Skewness, $\alpha_3$ | If a frequency distribution is unimodal and symmetric about the mean it has a skewness of 0. Values greater than 0 suggest skewness of a unimodal distribution to the right, whilst values less than 0 indicate skewness to the left. A function of the $3^{rd}$ moment about the mean (denoted by $\alpha_3$ with a ^ symbol above it for the sample skewness) | $$\alpha_3 = \frac{1}{n\sigma^3} \sum_{i=1}^{n} (x_i - \mu)^3$$ $$\alpha_3 = \frac{1}{n\hat{\sigma}^3} \sum_{i=1}^{n} (x_i - \bar{x})^3$$ $$\hat{\alpha}_3 = \frac{n}{(n-1)(n-2)\hat{\sigma}^3} \sum_{i=1}^{n} (x_i - \bar{x})^3$$ |
| Kurtosis, $\alpha_4$ | A measure of the peakedness of a frequency distribution. More pointy distributions tend to have high kurtosis values. A function of the $4^{th}$ moment about the mean. It is customary to subtract 3 from the raw kurtosis value (which is the kurtosis of the Normal distribution) to give a figure relative to the Normal (denoted by $\alpha_4$ with a ^ symbol above it for the sample kurtosis) | $$\alpha_4 = \frac{1}{n\sigma^4} \sum_{i=1}^{n} (x_i - \mu)^4$$ $$\alpha_4 = \frac{1}{n\hat{\sigma}^4} \sum_{i=1}^{n} (x_i - \bar{x})^4$$ $$\hat{\alpha}_4 = \frac{a}{\hat{\sigma}^4} \sum_{i=1}^{n} (x_i - \bar{x})^4 - b \text{ where}$$ $$a = \frac{n(n+1)}{(n-1)(n-2)(n-3)},$$ $$b = \frac{3(n-1)^2}{(n-2)(n-3)}$$ |

#### 1.4.2.5 Measures of complexity and dimensionality

| Measure | Definition | Expression(s) |
|---------|------------|---------------|
| Information statistic (Entropy), $I$ (Shannon's) | A measure of the amount of pattern, disorder or *information*, in a set $\{x_i\}$ where $p_i$ is the proportion of events or values occurring in the $i^{th}$ class or range. Note that if $p_i=0$ then $p_i \log_2(p_i)$ is 0. $I$ takes values in the range $[0, \log_2(k)]$. The lower value | $$I = -\sum_{i=1}^{k} p_i \log_2(p_i)$$ |

| Measure | Definition | Expression(s) |
|---|---|---|
| | means all data falls into 1 category, whilst the upper means all data are evenly spread | |
| Information statistic (Diversity), Div | Shannon's entropy statistic (see above) standardized by the number of classes, $k$, to give a range of values from 0 to 1 | $$Div = \frac{-\sum_{i=1}^{k} p_i \log_2(p_i)}{\log_2(k)}$$ |
| Dimension (topological), $D_T$ | Broadly, the number of (intrinsic) coordinates needed to refer to a single point anywhere on the object. The dimension of a point=0, a rectifiable line=1, a surface=2 and a solid=3. See text for fuller explanation. The value 2.5 (often denoted 2.5D) is used in GIS to denote a planar region over which a single-valued attribute has been defined at each point (e.g. height). In mathematics topological dimension is now equated to a definition similar to cover dimension (see below) | $D_T$=0,1,2,3,... |
| Dimension (capacity, cover or fractal), $D_c$ | Let $N(h)$ represent the number of small elements of edge length $h$ required to cover an object. For a line, length 1, each element has length $1/h$. For a plane surface each element (small square of side length $1/h$) has area $1/h^2$, and for a volume, each element is a cube with volume $1/h^3$. More generally $N(h)=1/h^D$, where D is the topological dimension, so $N(h)= h^{-D}$ and thus $\log(N(h))=-D\log(h)$ and so $D_c=-\log(N(h))/\log(h)$. $D_c$ may be fractional, in which case the term *fractal* is used | $$D_c = -\lim \frac{\ln N(h)}{\ln(h)}, h \to 0^+$$ $D_c$>=0 |

### 1.4.2.6  Common distributions

| Measure | Definition | Expression(s) |
|---|---|---|
| Uniform (continuous) | All values in the range are equally likely. Mean=$a/2$, variance=$a^2/12$. Here we use $f(x)$ to denote the probability distribution associated with continuous valued variables $x$, also described as a *probability density function* | $$f(x) = \frac{1}{a}; x \in [0,a]$$ |
| Binomial (discrete) | The terms of the Binomial give the probability of $x$ successes out of $n$ trials, for example 3 heads in 10 tosses of a coin, where $p$=probability of success and $q=1-p$=probability of failure. Mean, $m=np$, variance=$npq$. Here we use $p(x)$ to denote the probability distribution associated with discrete valued variables $x$ | $$p(x) = \frac{n!}{(n-x)!\,x!} p^x q^{1-x}; x=1,2,...n$$ |

| Measure | Definition | Expression(s) |
|---------|-----------|---------------|
| Poisson (discrete) | An approximation to the Binomial when $p$ is very small and $n$ is large (>100), but the mean $m=np$ is fixed and finite (usually not large). Mean=variance=$m$ | $p(x) = \dfrac{m^x}{x!} e^{-m}$ ; $x=1,2,...n$ |
| Normal (continuous) | The distribution of a measurement, $x$, that is subject to a large number of independent, random, additive errors. The Normal distribution may also be derived as an approximation to the Binomial when $p$ is not small (e.g. $p \approx 1/2$) and $n$ is large. If $\mu$=mean and $\sigma$=standard deviation, we write $N(\mu,\sigma)$ as the Normal distribution with these parameters. The Normal- or z-transform $z=(x-\mu)/\sigma$ changes (normalizes) the distribution so that it has a zero mean and unit variance, N(0,1). The distribution of $n$ mean values of independent random variables drawn from *any* underlying distribution is also Normal (*Central Limit Theorem*) | $f(z) = \dfrac{1}{\sqrt{2\pi}} e^{-z/2}$ ; $z \in [-\infty, \infty]$ |

### 1.4.2.7 Data transforms and back transforms

| Measure | Definition | Expression(s) |
|---------|-----------|---------------|
| Log | If the frequency distribution for a dataset is broadly unimodal and left-skewed, the natural log transform (logarithms base e) will adjust the pattern to make it more symmetric/similar to a Normal distribution. For variates whose values may range from 0 upwards a value of 1 is often added to the transform. Back transform with the exp() function | $z=\ln(x)$ or<br><br>$z=\ln(x+1)$<br><br>*n.b.* $\ln(x)=\log_e(x)=\log_{10}(x) \cdot \log_{10}(e)$<br><br>$x=\exp(z)$ or<br><br>$x=\exp(z)-1$ |
| Square root (Freeman-Tukey) | A transform that may adjust the dataset to make it more similar to a Normal distribution. For variates whose values may range from 0 upwards a value of 1 is often added to the transform. For 0<=x<=1 (e.g. rate data) the combined form of the transform is often used, and is known as the Freeman-Tukey (FT) transform | $z = \sqrt{x}$, or<br><br>$z = \sqrt{x+1}$, or<br><br>$z = \sqrt{x} + \sqrt{x+1}$ (FT)<br><br>$x = z^2$, or $x=z^2-1$ |
| Logit | Often used to transform binary response data, such as survival/non-survival or present/absent, to provide a continuous value in the range ($-\infty,\infty$), where $p$ is the proportion of the sample that is 1 (or 0). The inverse or back-transform is shown as $p$ in terms of $z$. This transform avoids concentration of values at the ends of the | $z = \ln\left(\dfrac{p}{1-p}\right), p \in [0,1]$<br><br>$p = \dfrac{e^z}{1+e^z}$ |

| Measure | Definition | Expression(s) |
|---------|-----------|---------------|
| | range. For samples where proportions $p$ may take the values 0 or 1 a modified form of the transform may be used. This is typically achieved by adding $1/2n$ to the numerator and denominator, where $n$ is the sample size. Often used to correct S-shaped (*logistic*) relationships between response and explanatory variables | |
| Normal, z-transform | This transform normalizes or standardizes the distribution so that it has a zero mean and unit variance. If $\{x_i\}$ is a set of $n$ sample *mean* values from *any* probability distribution with mean $\mu$ and variance $\sigma^2$ then the z-transform shown here as $z_2$ will be distributed N(0,1) for large $n$ (Central Limit Theorem). The divisor in this instance is the standard error. In both instances the standard deviation must be non-zero | $z_1 = \dfrac{(x - \mu)}{\sigma}$ <br><br> $z_2 = \dfrac{(x - \mu)}{\sigma / \sqrt{n}}$ |
| Box-Cox, power transforms | A family of transforms defined for positive data values only, that often can make datasets more Normal; $k$ is a parameter. The inverse or back-transform is also shown as $x$ in terms of $z$ | $z = \dfrac{(x^k - 1)}{k}, k > 0, x > 0$ <br><br> $x = (kz + 1)^{1/k}, k > 0$ |
| Angular transforms (Freeman-Tukey) | A transform for proportions, $p$, designed to spread the set of values near the end of the range. $k$ is typically 0.5. Often used to correct S-shaped relationships between response and explanatory variables. If $p=x/n$ then the Freeman-Tukey (FT) version of this transform is the averaged version shown. This is a variance-stabilizing transform | $z = \sin^{-1}\left(p^k\right),$ <br><br> $p = \sin(z)^{1/k}$ <br><br> $z = \sin^{-1}\left(\sqrt{\dfrac{x}{n+1}}\right) +$ <br><br> $\sin^{-1}\left(\sqrt{\dfrac{x+1}{n+1}}\right)$ (FT) |

### 1.4.2.8  Selected functions

| Measure | Definition | Expression(s) |
|---------|-----------|---------------|
| Bessel function of the first kind | Bessel functions occur as the solution to specific differential equations. They are described with reference to a parameter known as the order, shown as a subscript. For integer orders Bessel functions can be represented as an infinite series. Order 0 and Order 1 expansions are shown here. The graph of a Bessel function is similar to a dampening sine wave. Usage in spatial analysis arises in connection with directional statistics and spline curve fitting. See the Mathworld website entry for more details | $I_0(\kappa) = \displaystyle\sum_{i=0}^{\infty} \dfrac{(-1)^i (\kappa/2)^{2i}}{(i!)^2}$ , and <br><br> $I_1(\kappa) = \dfrac{\kappa}{2} \displaystyle\sum_{i=0}^{\infty} \dfrac{(-1)^i (\kappa/2)^{2i+1}}{i!(i+1)!}$ |

| Measure | Definition | Expression(s) |
|---|---|---|
| Exponential integral function, $E_1(x)$ | A definite integral function. Used in association with spline curve fitting. See the Mathworld website entry for more details | $$E_1(x) = \int_1^\infty \frac{e^{-tx}}{t}\, dt$$ |
| Gamma function, $\Gamma$ | A widely used definite integral function. For integer values of $x$: $\Gamma(x)=(x\text{-}1)!$ and $\Gamma(x/2)=(x/2\text{-}1)!$ so $\Gamma(3/2)=(1/2)!/2=(\sqrt\pi)/2$ See the Mathworld website entry for more details | $$\Gamma(x) = \int_0^\infty x^{1/2} e^{-x}\, dx$$ $$\Gamma(1/2) = \sqrt\pi$$ |

### 1.4.2.9 Matrix expressions

| Measure | Definition | Expression(s) |
|---|---|---|
| Identity | A matrix with diagonal elements 1 and off-diagonal elements 0 | $$I = \begin{bmatrix} 1 & 0 & 0 & 0 \\ 0 & 1 & 0 & 0 \\ .. & .. & .. & .. \\ 0 & 0 & 0 & 1 \end{bmatrix}$$ |
| Determinant | Determinants are only defined for square matrices. Let **A** be an $n$ by $n$ matrix with elements $\{a_{ij}\}$. The matrix $\mathbf{M}_{ij}$ here is a subset of **A** known as the *minor*, formed by eliminating row $i$ and column $j$ from **A**. An $n$ by $n$ matrix, **A**, with Det=0 is described as *singular*, and such a matrix has no inverse. If Det(**A**) is very close to 0 it is described as *ill-conditioned* | $\lvert A \rvert$, Det(**A**) $$\lvert A \rvert = \sum_i^n a_{ij} a^{ij}, \text{ where}$$ $$a^{ij} = (-1)^{i+j} M_{ij}$$ |
| Inverse | The matrix equivalent of division in conventional algebra. For a matrix, **A**, to be invertible its determinant must be non-zero, and ideally not very close to zero. A matrix that has an inverse is by definition non-singular. A symmetric real-valued matrix is *positive definite* if all its eigenvalues are positive, whereas a *positive semi-definite* matrix allows for some eigenvalues to be 0. A matrix, **A**, that is invertible satisfies the relation $\mathbf{AA}^{-1}=\mathbf{I}$ | $\mathbf{A}^{-1}$ |
| Transpose | A matrix operation in which the rows and columns are transposed, i.e. in which elements $a_{ij}$ are swapped with $a_{ji}$ for all $i,j$. The inverse of a transposed matrix is the same as the transpose of the matrix inverse | $\mathbf{A}^T$ or $\mathbf{A'}$ $(\mathbf{A}^T)^{-1}=(\mathbf{A}^{-1})^T$ |
| Symmetric | A matrix in which element $a_{ij}=a_{ji}$ for all $i,j$ | $\mathbf{A}=\mathbf{A}^T$ |

| Measure | Definition | Expression(s) |
|---------|-----------|---------------|
| Trace | The sum of the diagonal elements of a matrix, $a_{ii}$ — the sum of the eigenvalues of a matrix equals its trace | $Tr(\mathbf{A})$ |
| Eigenvalue, Eigenvector | If $\mathbf{A}$ is a real-valued $k$ by $k$ square matrix and $\mathbf{x}$ is a non-zero real-valued vector, then a scalar $\lambda$ that satisfies the equation shown in the adjacent column is known as an eigenvalue of $\mathbf{A}$ and $\mathbf{x}$ is an eigenvector of $\mathbf{A}$. There are $k$ eigenvalues of $\mathbf{A}$, each with a corresponding eigenvector. The matrix $\mathbf{A}$ can be decomposed into three parts, as shown, where $\mathbf{E}$ is a matrix of its eigenvectors and $\mathbf{D}$ is a diagonal matrix of its eigenvalues | $(\mathbf{A}-\lambda\mathbf{I})\mathbf{x}=\mathbf{0}$ <br><br> $\mathbf{A}=\mathbf{EDE}^{-1}$ (diagonalization) |

# 2 Conceptual Frameworks for Spatial Analysis

## 2.1 The geospatial perspective

Geospatial analysis provides a distinct perspective on the world, a unique lens through which to examine events, patterns, and processes that operate on or near the surface of our planet. It makes sense, then, to introduce the main elements of this perspective, the conceptual framework that provides the background to spatial analysis, as a preliminary to the main body of this Guide's material. This chapter provides that introduction. It is divided into four main sections. The first describes the basic components of this view of the world — the classes of things that a spatial analyst recognizes in the world, and the beginnings of a system of organization of geographic knowledge. The second section describes some of the structures that are built with these basic components and the relationships between them that interest geographers and others. The third section introduces the concepts of spatial statistics, including probability, that provide perhaps the most sophisticated elements of the conceptual framework. Finally, the fourth section discusses some of the basic components of the data infrastructure that increasingly provides the essential facilities for spatial analysis.

The domain of geospatial analysis is the surface of the Earth, extending upwards in the analysis of topography and the atmosphere, and downwards in the analysis of groundwater and geology. In scale it extends from the most local, when archaeologists record the locations of pieces of pottery to the nearest centimeter or property boundaries are surveyed to the nearest millimeter, to the global, in the analysis of sea surface temperatures or global warming. In time it extends backwards from the present into the analysis of historical population migrations, the discovery of patterns in archaeological sites, or the detailed mapping of the movement of continents, and into the future in attempts to predict the tracks of hurricanes, the melting of the Greenland ice-cap, or the likely growth of urban areas. Methods of spatial analysis are robust and capable of operating over a range of spatial and temporal scales.

Ultimately, geospatial analysis concerns *what* happens *where*, and makes use of geographic information that links features and phenomena on the Earth's surface to their locations. This sounds very simple and straightforward, and it is not so much the basic information as the structures and arguments that can be built on it that provide the richness of spatial analysis. In principle there is no limit to the complexity of spatial analytic techniques that might find some application in the world, and might be used to tease out interesting insights and support practical actions and decisions. In reality, some techniques are simpler, more useful, or more insightful than others, and the contents of this Guide reflect that reality. This chapter is about the underlying concepts that are employed, whether it be in simple, intuitive techniques or in advanced, complex mathematical or computational ones.

Spatial analysis exists at the interface between the human and the computer, and both play important roles. The concepts that humans use to understand, navigate, and exploit the world around them are mirrored in the concepts of spatial analysis. So the discussion that follows will often appear to be following parallel tracks — the track of human intuition on the one hand, with all its vagueness and informality, and the track of the formal, precise world of spatial analysis on the other. The relationship between these two tracks forms one of the recurring themes of this Guide.

# 2.2 Basic Primitives

## 2.2.1 Place

At the center of all spatial analysis is the concept of *place*. The Earth's surface comprises some 500,000,000 sq km, so there would be room to pack half a billion industrial sites of 1 sq km each (assuming that nothing else required space, and that the two-thirds of the Earth's surface that is covered by water was as acceptable as the one-third that is land); and 500 trillion sites of 1 sq m each (roughly the space occupied by a sleeping human). People identify with places of various sizes and shapes, from the room to the parcel of land, to the neighborhood, the city, the county, the state or province, or the nation-state. Places may overlap, as when a watershed spans the boundary of two counties, and places may be nested hierarchically, as when counties combine to form a state or province.

Places often have names, and people use these to talk about and distinguish between places. Some names are official, having been recognized by national or state agencies charged with bringing order to geographic names. In the U.S., for example, the Board on Geographic Names exists to ensure that all agencies of the federal government use the same name in referring to a place, and to ensure as far as possible that duplicate names are removed from the landscape. A list of officially sanctioned names is termed a *gazetteer*, though that word has come to be used for any list of geographic names.

Places change continually, as people move, climate changes, cities expand, and a myriad of social and physical processes affect virtually every spot on the Earth's surface. For some purposes it is sufficient to treat places as if they were static, especially if the processes that affect them are comparatively slow to operate. It is difficult, for example, to come up with instances of the need to modify maps as continents move and mountains grow or shrink in response to earthquakes and erosion. On the other hand it would be foolish to ignore the rapid changes that occur in the social and economic makeup of cities, or the constant movement that characterizes modern life. Throughout this Guide, it will be important to distinguish between these two cases, and to judge whether time is or is not important.

People associate a vast amount of information with places. Three Mile Island, Sellafield, and Chernobyl are associated with nuclear reactors and accidents, while Tahiti and Waikiki conjure images of (perhaps somewhat faded) tropical paradise. One of the roles of places and their names is to link together what is known in useful ways. So for example the statements "I am going to London next week" and "There's always something going on in London" imply that I will be having an exciting time next week. But while "London" plays a useful role, it is nevertheless vague, since it might refer to the area administered by the Greater London Authority, the area inside the M25 motorway, or something even less precise and determined by the context in which the name is used. Science clearly needs something better, if information is to be linked exactly to places, and if places are to be matched, measured, and subjected to the rigors of spatial analysis.

The basis of rigorous and precise definition of place is a *coordinate system*, a set of measurements that allows place to be specified unambiguously and in a way that is meaningful to everyone. The Meridian Convention of 1884 established the Greenwich Observatory in London as the basis of longitude, replacing a confusing multitude of earlier systems. Today, the World Geodetic System of 1984 and subsequent adjustments provide a highly accurate pair of coordinates for every location on the Earth's surface (and incidentally place the line of zero longitude about 100m east of the Greenwich Observatory). Elevation continues to be problematic, however, since countries and even agencies within countries insist on their own definitions of what marks zero elevation, or exactly how to define "sea level". Many other coordinate systems are in use, but most are easily converted to and from latitude/longitude. Today it is possible to measure location directly, using the Global

Positioning System (GPS) or its Russian counterpart GLONASS (and in future its European counterpart Galileo). Spatial analysis is most often applied in a two-dimensional space. But applications that extend above or below the surface of the Earth must often be handled as three-dimensional. Time sometimes adds a fourth dimension, particularly in studies that examine the dynamic nature of phenomena.

## 2.2.2 Attributes

*Attribute* has become the preferred term for any recorded characteristic or property of a place (see Table 1-1 for a more formal definition). A place's name is an obvious example of an attribute, but a vast array of other options has proven useful for various purposes. Some are measured, including elevation, temperature, or rainfall. Others are the result of classification, including soil type, land-use or land cover type, or rock type. Government agencies provide a host of attributes in the form of statistics, for places ranging in size from countries all the way down to neighborhoods and streets. The

characteristics that people assign rightly or mistakenly to places, such as "expensive", "exciting", "smelly", or "dangerous" are also examples of attributes. Attributes can be more than simple values or terms, and today it is possible to construct information systems that contain entire collections of images as attributes of hotels, or recordings of birdsong as attributes of natural areas. But while these are certainly feasible, they are beyond the bounds of most techniques of spatial analysis.

Within GIS the term *attribute* usually refers to records in a data table associated with individual features in a vector map or cells in a grid (*raster* or image file). Sample vector data attributes are illustrated in Figure 2-1A where details of major wildfires recorded in Alaska are listed. Each row relates to a single polygon feature that identifies the spatial extent of the fire recorded. Most GIS packages do not display a separate attribute table for raster data, since each grid cell contains a single data item, which is the value at that point and can be readily examined. ArcGIS is somewhat unusual in that it provides an attribute table for raster data (see Figure 2-1B).

*Figure 2-1 Attribute tables - spatial datasets*

*A. Alaskan fire dataset - polygon attributes*

| | OBJECTID | HA_BURNED | ACRES_BURN | YEAR_ | BOUNDARY | COUNTRY | SITENAME |
|---|---|---|---|---|---|---|---|
| 1 | 1 | 2571 | 6352 | 2004 | Y | AK | 446 |
| 2 | 2 | 25518 | 63057 | 2004 | Y | AK | 342 |
| 3 | 3 | 281 | 695 | 2004 | Y | AK | 348 |
| 4 | 4 | 8789 | 21719 | 2004 | Y | AK | 578 |
| 5 | 5 | 1968 | 4864 | 2004 | Y | AK | 164 |
| 6 | 6 | 60 | 149 | 2004 | Y | AK | 533 |
| 7 | 7 | 75 | 186 | 2004 | Y | AK | 452 |
| 8 | 8 | 86953 | 214869 | 2004 | Y | AK | 158 |
| 9 | 9 | 135 | 333 | 2004 | Y | AK | 213 |

*B. DEM dataset - raster file attribute table (ArcGIS)*

| ObjectID | Value | Count |
|---|---|---|
| 275 | 449 | 167 |
| 276 | 450 | 212 |
| 277 | 451 | 166 |
| 278 | 452 | 159 |
| 279 | 453 | 144 |

Rows in this raster attribute table provide a count of the number of grid cells (pixels) in the raster that have a given value, e.g. 144 cells have a value of 453 meters. Furthermore, the linking between the attribute table visualization and mapped data enables all cells with elevation=453 to be selected and highlighted on the map.

Many terms have been adopted to describe attributes. From the perspective of spatial analysis the most useful divides attributes into scales or levels of measurement, as follows:

- **Nominal**. An attribute is nominal if it successfully distinguishes between locations, but without any implied ranking or potential for arithmetic. For example, a telephone number can be a useful attribute of a place, but the number itself generally has no numeric meaning. It would make no sense to add or divide telephone numbers, and there is no sense in which the number 9680244 is more or better than the number 8938049. Likewise, assigning arbitrary numerical values to classes of land type, e.g. 1=arable, 2=woodland, 3=marsh, 4=other is simply a convenient form of naming (the values are nominal). SITENAME in Figure 2-1A is an example of a nominal attribute, as is OBJECTID, even though both happen to be numeric

- **Ordinal**. An attribute is ordinal if it implies a ranking, in the sense that Class 1 may be better than Class 2, but as with nominal attributes no arithmetic operations make sense, and there is no implication that Class 3 is worse than Class 2 by the precise amount by which Class 2 is worse than Class 1. An example of an ordinal scale might be preferred locations for residences — an individual may prefer some areas of a city to others, but such differences between areas may be barely noticeable or quite profound. Note that although OBJECTID in Figure 2-1A appears to be an ordinal variable it is not, because the IDs are provided as unique names only, and could equally well be in any order and use any values that provided uniqueness (and

typically, in this example, are required to be integers)

- **Interval**. The remaining three types of attributes are all quantitative, representing various types of measurements. Attributes are interval if differences make sense, as they do for example with measurements of temperature on the Celsius or Fahrenheit scales, or for measurements of elevation above sea level

- **Ratio**. Attributes are ratio if it makes sense to divide one measurement by another. For example, it makes sense to say that one person weighs twice as much as another person, but it makes no sense to say that a temperature of 20 Celsius is twice as warm as a temperature of 10 Celsius, because while weight has an absolute zero Celsius temperature does not (but on an absolute scale of temperature, such as the Kelvin scale, 200 degrees can indeed be said to be twice as warm as 100 degrees). It follows that negative values cannot exist on a ratio scale. HA_BURNED and ACRES_BURN in Figure 2-1A are examples of ratio attributes. Note that only one of these two attribute columns is required, since they are simple multiples of one another

- **Cyclic**. Finally, it is not uncommon to encounter measurements of attributes that represent directions or cyclic phenomena, and to encounter the awkward property that two distinct points on the scale can be equal — for example, 0 and 360 degrees are equal. Directional data are cyclic (Figure 2-2), as are calendar dates. Arithmetic operations are problematic with cyclic data, and special techniques are needed, such as the techniques used to overcome the Y2K problem, when the year after (19)99 was (20)00. For example, it makes no sense to average 1° and 359° to get 180°, since the average of two directions close to north clearly is not south. Mardia and Jupp (1999) provide a comprehensive review of the analysis of directional or cyclic data (see further, Section 4.5.1)

*Figure 2-2 Cyclic attribute data — Wind direction, single location*

| | A | | C | | D | | E | |
|---|---|---|---|---|---|---|---|---|
| Type | Angles | ▼ | ▼ Date | ▼ | Month of year | ▼ | Time | ▼ |
| Name | Direction | | Date | | Month | | Time | |
| 1 | 265.000 | | 15/06/2002 | June | | ▼ | | 12:00 |
| 2 | 248.000 | | 15/06/2002 | June | | ▼ | | 13:00 |
| 3 | 232.000 | | 15/06/2002 | June | | ▼ | | 14:00 |
| 4 | 186.000 | | 15/06/2002 | June | | ▼ | | 15:00 |
| 5 | 222.000 | | 15/06/2002 | June | | ▼ | | 16:00 |
| 6 | 252.000 | | 15/06/2002 | June | | ▼ | | 17:00 |
| 7 | 239.000 | | 15/06/2002 | June | | ▼ | | 18:00 |
| 8 | 250.000 | | 15/06/2002 | June | | ▼ | | 19:00 |
| 9 | 237.000 | | 15/06/2002 | June | | ▼ | | 20:00 |

While this terminology of measurement types is standard, spatial analysts find that another distinction is particularly important. This is the distinction between attributes that are termed *spatially intensive* and *spatially extensive*. Spatially extensive attributes include total population, measures of a place's area or perimeter length, and total income — they are true *only of the place as a whole*.

Spatially intensive attributes include population density, average income, and percent unemployed, and if the place is homogeneous they will be true of any part of the place as well as of the whole. For many purposes it is necessary to keep spatially intensive and spatially extensive attributes apart, because they respond very differently when places are merged or split, and when many types of spatial analysis are conducted.

Since attributes are essentially measured or computed data items associated with a given location or set of locations, they are subject to the same issues as any conventional dataset: sampling error; measurement errors and limitations; mistakes and miscalculations; missing values; temporal and thematic errors and similar issues. Metadata accompanying spatial datasets should assist in assessing the quality of such attribute data, but at least the same level of caution should be applied to spatial attribute data as with any other form of data that one might wish to use or analyze.

### 2.2.3 Objects

The places discussed in Section 2.2.1 vary enormously in size and shape. Weather observations are obtained from stations that may occupy only a few square meters of the Earth's surface (from instruments that occupy only a small fraction of the station's area), whereas statistics published for Russia are based on a land area of more than 17 million sq km. In spatial analysis it is customary to refer to places as *objects*. In studies of roads or rivers the objects of interest are long and thin, and will often be represented as lines of zero width. In studies of climate the objects of interest may be weather stations of minimal extent, and will often be represented as points. On the other hand many studies of social or economic patterns may need to consider the two-dimensional extent of places, which will therefore be represented as areas, and in some studies where elevations or depths are important it may be appropriate to represent places as volumes. To a spatial statistician, these points, lines, areas, or volumes are known as the attributes' *spatial support*.

Each of these four classes of objects has its own techniques of representation in digital systems. The software for capturing and storing spatial data, analyzing and visualizing them, and reporting the results of analysis must recognize and handle each of these classes. But digital systems must ultimately represent everything in a language of just two characters, 0 and 1 or "off" and "on", and special techniques are required to represent complex objects in this way. In practice, points, lines, and areas are most often represented in the following standard forms:

- **Points** as pairs of coordinates, in latitude/longitude or some other standard system

- **Lines** as ordered sequences of points connected by straight lines

- **Areas** as ordered rings of points, also connected by straight lines to form polygons. In some cases areas may contain holes, and may include separate islands, such as in representing the State of Michigan with its separate Upper Peninsula, or the State of Georgia with its offshore islands. This use of polygons to represent areas is so pervasive that many spatial analysts refer to all areas as polygons, whether or not their edges are actually straight

Lines represented in this way are often termed *polylines*, by analogy to polygons (see Table 1-1 for a more formal definition). Three-dimensional volumes are represented in several different ways, and as yet no one method has become widely adopted as a standard. The related term *edge* is used in several ways within GIS. These include: to denote the border of polygonal regions; to identify the individual links connecting nodes or vertices in a network; and as a general term relating to the distinct or indistinct boundary of areas or zones. In many parts of spatial analysis the related term, *edge effect* is applied. This refers to possible bias in the analysis which arises specifically due to proximity of features to one or more edges. For example, in point pattern analysis computation of distances to the nearest neighboring point, or calculation of the density of points per unit area, may both be subject to edge effects.

Figure 2-3 shows a simple example of points, lines, and areas, as represented in a typical map display. The hospital, boat ramp, and swimming area will be stored in the database as points with associated attributes, and symbolized for display. The roads will be stored as polylines, and the road type symbols (U.S. Highway, Interstate Highway) generated from the attributes when each object is displayed. The lake will be stored as two polygons with appropriate attributes. Note how the lake consists of two geometrically disconnected pieces, linked in the database to a single set of attributes — objects in a GIS may consist of multiple parts, as long as each part is of the same type.

*Figure 2-3 An example map showing points, lines, and areas appropriately symbolized*

*see text for explanation*

It can be expensive and time-consuming to create the polygon representations of complex area objects, and so analysts often resort to simpler approaches, such as choosing a single *representative point*. But while this may be satisfactory for some purposes, there are obvious problems with representing the entirety of a large country such as Russia as a single point. For example, the distance from Canada to the U.S. computed between representative points in this way would be very misleading, given that they share a very long common boundary.

### 2.2.4 Maps

Historically, maps have been the primary means to store and communicate spatial data. Objects and their attributes can be readily depicted, and the human eye can quickly discern patterns and anomalies in a well-designed map. Points can be shown as symbols of various kinds, depicting anything from a windmill to a church; lines can be symbolized to distinguish between major roads, minor roads, and rivers; and areas can be symbolized with color, shading, or annotation.

Maps have traditionally existed on paper, as individual sheets or bound into atlases (a term that originated with Mercator, who produced one of the first atlases in the late 16th century). The advent of digital computers has broadened the concept of a map substantially, however. Maps can now take the form of images displayed on the screens of computers or even mobile phones. They can be dynamic, showing the Earth spinning on its axis or tracking the movement of migrating birds. Their designs can now go far beyond what was traditionally possible when maps had to be drawn by hand, incorporating a far greater range of color and texture, and even integrating sound.

## 2.2.5 Multiple properties of places

Dividing objects into points, lines, areas, and volumes is only the crudest of the many ways in which humans classify the things they find surrounding them in their environment. A topographic map may show areas of woodland, rivers, roads, contours, windmills, and several hundred other kinds of objects, each of them classifiable as points, lines, areas, or volumes. Objects may overlap — a river may pass through a wood, a road may cross a river, and all three may lie inside the area shown as "Montara, California".

Spatial analysts think of multiple classes of objects as forming *layers* of information superimposed on each other (see Figure 2-4). A study might be conducted on just one layer, analyzing the patterns formed by the objects in that layer and looking for clues as to the processes that created the pattern. In other cases the patterns of one layer might be analyzed in relation to other layers. For example, the pattern of cases of cancer in an area might be studied to see if it bears any relationship to the pattern of roads or electrical transmission lines in the area, or to the chemistry of drinking water.

Sometimes many different attributes are collected and published for the same sets of places (see Section 2.2.2). Census agencies do this when they compile hundreds of attributes for census tracts, counties, or states. In such cases comparing layers is a simple matter of comparing the different attributes assigned to the same places. But more generally the objects in two layers may not be the same, creating difficulties for analysis. For example, suppose a study is being conducted of people's perception of noise in a neighborhood near an airport. Monitoring devices have been positioned at points around the neighborhood, providing a layer of noise measurements. Residents have been interviewed, providing another layer of perceptual data. The analysis now moves to a comparison of the contents of the two layers, but it is hampered by the fact that the objects in the two layers are in different locations.

*Figure 2-4 Layers and overlay*

*Layers: streams, roads, terrain, & combined*

*Source: Manifold GIS sample dataset, Montara CA*

## 2.2.6  Fields

The idea that the Earth's surface is a space littered with various kinds of objects certainly matches the ways humans tend to think about the world around them. Scenes perceived by the eye are immediately parsed by the brain into "tree", "car", "house", and other discrete objects. But in other cases the world may appear more continuous than discrete. Ground elevation (or ocean depth), for example, is in broad terms a continuously varying property that can be measured anywhere on the Earth's surface, as is atmospheric temperature, or, within an urbanized area, average level of noise or pollution (Figure 2-5).

### Figure 2-5 Noise level raster

*Each pixel of this image indicates the measured or modeled level of traffic-related noise in decibels - reds are the highest levels, gray indicates buildings*

In essence there are two ways of thinking about phenomena on the Earth's surface. In the first, the *discrete-object* view, reality is like an empty table-top littered with discrete, countable objects that can be assigned to different classes. In the second, the *continuous-field* view, reality is a collection of continuous surfaces, each representing the variation of one property, such as elevation, over the Earth's surface (Figure 2-4, layer 3). When it is necessary to differentiate by height, the field becomes three-dimensional rather than two-dimensional, and time may add a fourth dimension. Mathematically, a field is a continuous function mapping every location to the value of some property of interest.

### Figure 2-6 Filled contour view of field data

The distinction between continuous fields and discrete objects is merely conceptual, and there is no test that can be applied to the contents of a database to determine which view is operative. But it is a very important distinction that underlies the choices that analysts make in selecting appropriate techniques. Points, polylines, and polygons arise in both cases, and yet their meanings are very different. For example, points might represent the locations where a continuous field of temperature is measured, or they might represent isolated instances of a disease — in the latter case, which falls within the discrete-object view, there is no implication that anything happens in between the cases, whereas in the former case one would expect temperature to vary smoothly between measurement sites. Polylines might represent the connected pieces of a stream network (as in Figure 2-4, uppermost layer), or they might represent the contours of an elevation surface — in the latter case, the polylines would collectively represent a field, and would consequently not be allowed to cross each other. If filled contours rather than separate contour lines are generated then polygons rather than polylines define the field values (Figure 2-6; source as per Figure 2-4).

## 2.2.7 Networks

Mention has already been made of the lines that often constitute the objects of spatial data. They include streets, roads, railroads, and highways; rivers, canals, and streams; and the more abstract interpersonal networks studied by sociologists. Networks constitute one-dimensional structures embedded in two or three dimensions. Discrete point objects may be distributed on the network, representing such phenomena as landmarks or bridges on road networks, or observation points on rivers. Discrete line objects may also be found, in the form of tunnels, stretches of highway with a constant number of lanes, or river reaches. Continuous fields may also be distributed over the one-dimensional network, defining such variables as travel speed, railroad gradient, traffic density, or stream velocity. Mathematically, a network forms a *graph*, and many techniques developed for graphs have applications to networks. These include various ways of measuring a network's connectivity, or of finding shortest paths between pairs of points on a network. These methods are explored in detail in Chapter 7.

## 2.2.8 Density estimation

One of the more useful concepts in spatial analysis is *density* — the density of humans in a crowded city, or the density of tracks across a stretch of desert, or the density of retail stores in a shopping center. Density provides an effective link between the discrete-object

and continuous-field conceptualizations, since density expresses the number of discrete objects per unit of area, and is itself a continuous field. Mathematically, the density of some kind of object is calculated by counting the number of such objects in an area, and dividing by the size of the area. This is easily done when calculating population density from census data, for example, by dividing the population of each census tract or county by its physical area. But this leads to multiple values of density, depending on the objects selected and the definition of the areas used to make the calculation. Techniques of *density estimation* try to avoid this problem and are discussed in detail in Section 4.3.4. The book by Silverman (1998) provides additional background reading on this issue.

## 2.2.9 Detail, resolution, and scale

The surface of the planet is almost infinitely complex, revealing more and more detail the closer one looks. An apparently simple concept such as a coastline turns out to be problematic in practice — should its representation as a polyline include every indentation, every protruding rock, even every grain of sand? It is clearly impossible to build a representation that includes every detail, and in reality decisions must be made about the amount of detail to include. *Spatial resolution* is the term given to a threshold distance below which the analyst has decided that detail is unnecessary or irrelevant. For example, one might decide to represent a coastline at a spatial resolution of 100m, meaning that all crenulations, indentations, and protuberances that are no wider than 100m are omitted from the representation. In other words, the representation of the phenomenon appears simpler and smoother than it really is.

Cartographers use a somewhat different approach to the omission of detail from maps. A map is said to have a *scale* or *representative fraction*, being the ratio of distances on the map to their corresponding distances in the real world. For example, if a map shows Los Angeles and Santa Barbara as 10cm apart, and in reality they are 100km apart as the crow flies, then the map's scale is 1:1,000,000 (note that in principle, because of projection from a curved to a flat surface, no map's scale can be exactly uniform although this clearly does not apply to globes). This approach to defining level of detail is problematic, however, if the dataset in question is not on paper. Data that are *born digital* do not have a representative fraction, and the representative fraction for data displayed on a computer screen depends on the dimensions of the screen. Project onto a larger screen and the representative fraction will change, irrespective of the value shown on the screen. So it is better to use spatial resolution to describe the level of detail of digital data. As a general rule of thumb the spatial resolution of a paper map is roughly 0.5mm at the scale of the map (500m on a 1:1,000,000 map, or 5m on a 1:10,000 map), a figure that takes into account the widths of lines on maps and the cartographic practice of smoothing what is perceived as excessive detail.

When digital map data is displayed decisions have to made, manually and/or automatically, as to how much detail should be displayed, and how feature data should be *generalized* in order to produce a visually acceptable and meaningful result. This has been the subject of much research, some of which continues to the present day. For a recent book (of collected papers) on this subject, see Mackaness *et al.* (2007). In a white paper produced by ESRI (1996) they summarized the major generalization operators that they planned to implement at that time, as follows:

- **Preselection**: deciding on which features to include and which to exclude (e.g. major roads only, ignore footpaths etc.)
- **Elimination**: removal of features that are too small/short (below some threshold)
- **Simplification**: simplifying (smoothing, straightening) linear or polygon boundaries whilst retaining their basic form (see also, Section 4.2.4)
- **Aggregation**: combining distinct features into a larger composite object (e.g. a cluster of houses into a polygonal 'urbanized area')

- **Collapse**: reduction of feature dimensionality, as for example when a town is represented by a point or a broad river by a line
- **Typification**: reduction of the level of detail by replacing multiple objects by a smaller number of the same objects occupying broadly the same locations
- **Exaggeration**: emphasizing important features that might otherwise be removed
- **Classification and symbolization**: grouping together similar features and using different symbology to represent the new arrangement
- **Conflict resolution (displacement)**: identifying and resolving feature conflicts (e.g. overlaps, labeling), and
- **Refinement**: altering feature geometry and alignment to improve aethetics

### 2.2.10 Topology

In mathematics, a property is said to be *topological* if it survives stretching and distorting of space. Draw a circle on a rubber sheet, and no amount of stretching or distorting of the sheet will make it into a line or a point. Draw two touching circles, and no amount of stretching or distorting will pull them apart or make them overlap. It turns out that many properties of importance to spatial analysis are topological, including:

- **Dimensionality**: the distinction between point, line, area, and volume, which are said to have topological dimensions of 0, 1, 2, and 3 respectively
- **Adjacency**: including the touching of land parcels, counties, and nation-states
- **Connectivity**: including junctions between streets, roads, railroads, and rivers
- **Containment**: when a point lies inside rather than outside an area

Many phenomena are subject to topological constraints: for example, two counties cannot overlap, two contours cannot cross, and the boundary of an area cannot cross itself.

Topology is an important concept therefore in constructing and editing spatial databases. Figure 2-7 illustrates the concept of topology, using the example of two areas that share a common boundary. While stretching of the space can change the shapes of the areas, they will remain in contact however much stretching is applied.

*Figure 2-7 Topological relationships*

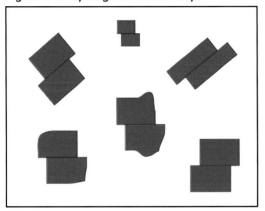

*Topological properties are those that cannot be destroyed by stretching or distorting the space. In this case the adjacency of the two areas is preserved in all the illustrations, no matter how much distortion is applied*

# 2.3 Spatial Relationships

Despite the emphasis placed on it in Section 2.2, and in spatial analysis generally, location is not in itself very interesting. While latitude does generally tend to predict average annual temperature, there are obvious exceptions (Iceland is much warmer in winter than Irkutsk, yet it is further north), and longitude is essentially arbitrary. The power of location comes not from location itself, but from the linkages or relationships that it establishes — from relative positions rather than absolute ones. This section looks at examples of those relationships, as fundamental concepts in spatial analysis. Some have already been mentioned as examples of topological properties, including adjacency, connectivity, and containment. Others are introduced in the subsections that follow, with examples of their significance.

Another way to think about this important point is to examine how the results of spatial analysis are affected by imagined changes in location. The patterns of crime in Los Angeles would be as interesting whether the city was analyzed in its correct location, or if it were arbitrarily relocated to another place on the Earth's surface — patterns are *invariant under displacement*. Similarly the city could be rotated, or analyzed in its mirror image, without substantially affecting the insights that spatial analysis would reveal. Under all of these operations — displacement, rotation, and mirror imaging — the *relative* locations of objects remain the same, and it is these relative locations that provide insight.

## 2.3.1   Co-location

Many useful insights can come from comparing the attributes of co-located places. For example, a cluster of cases of lung cancer in a port city might be explained by knowing that asbestos was widely used in the construction of ships in that city in the Second World War. There is also merit in examining occurrences of co-location in point datasets — in many instances the same coordinates are assigned to multiple points in a sample, which only becomes apparent when the attribute table is examined since mapping will obscure the existence of multiple points at the same location. In Section 2.2.5 a distinction was made between cases where multiple attributes are compared for the same set of objects, and cases where the attributes to be compared are attached to distinct, overlapping objects. In the latter case analysis will require the use of special techniques, such as those discussed in Section 2.3.8. Analysts often use the term *overlay* to refer to the superimposition and analysis of layers of geographic data about the same place. Overlay may require the superimposition of area on area, or line on area, or point on area, or line on line, or point on line, depending on the nature of the objects in the database.

## 2.3.2   Distance, direction and spatial weights matrices

Knowledge of location also allows the analyst to determine the distance and direction between objects. Distance between points is easily calculated using formulas for straight-line distance on the plane or on the curved surface of the Earth, and with a little more effort it is possible to determine the actual distance that would be travelled through the road or street network, and even to predict the time that it would take to make the journey. Distance and direction between lines or areas are often calculated by using representative points, but this can be misleading (as noted in Section 2.2.3). They can also be calculated using the nearest pair of points in the two objects, or as the average distance and direction between all pairs of points (note the difficulties of averaging direction, however, as mentioned in Section 2.2.2).

Many types of spatial analysis require the calculation of a table or matrix expressing the relative proximity of pairs of places, often denoted by **W** (a *spatial weights matrix*). Proximity can be a powerful explanatory factor in accounting for variation in a host of phenomena, including flows of migrants, intensity of social interaction, or the speed of diffusion of an epidemic. Software packages will commonly provide several alternative ways of determining the elements of **W**, including:

- 1 if the places share a common boundary, else 0

- the length of any common boundary between the places, else 0

- a decreasing function of the distance between the places, or between their representative points, or their $k^{th}$ nearest neighbors

In Figure 2-8 we show a section of the map of counties in North Carolina, USA. Two of the 100 counties have been highlighted, counties 1 and 3. An extract from a simple binary spatial weights matrix generated by the GeoDa software package based on 'Queen's move adjacency' (by analogy with the game of chess) is shown below for each of these counties (represented in this instance as a text list for compactness, rather than a sparse binary matrix):

```
1 3
19 18 2
3 5
25 23 18 10 2
```

Here, the first line indicates that county 1 (the most westerly of the two highlighted) has 3 neighbors. Line two shows that their IDs are 19 18 and 2. County 3 is shown as having 5 neighbors, 4 of which share a boundary with it (Rook's move) and one of which (25) appears to share a corner (Bishop's move: Rook's move plus Bishop's move equal Queen's move) but in fact shares a very short boundary. Instead of pure adjacency a set of spatial weights could have been computed based on the Euclidean distance separating the centroids of the various counties. In this case the matching entries for the weights matrix would have the form:

| | | |
|---|---|---|
| 1 | 19 | 0.3290 |
| 1 | 2 | 0.3138 |
| 1 | 18 | 0.2535 |
| 3 | 18 | 0.4985 |
| 3 | 2 | 0.4077 |
| 3 | 23 | 0.1738 |
| 3 | 25 | 0.4475 |

| | | |
|---|---|---|
| 3 | 40 | 0.5202 |

Here the pairwise connections are listed with the distances between the centroids, and entries may include counties that are not adjacent but perhaps lie within some threshold distance (n.b. distances computed by GeoDa in this example are not in meaningful units, i.e. *not* in miles; *arc distance* must be specified to produce distances in miles).

*Figure 2-8 Spatial weights computation*

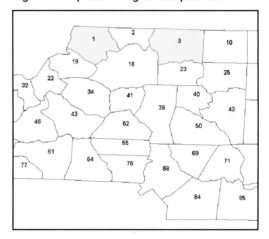

In such analyses it will be **W** that captures the spatial aspects of the problem, and the actual coordinates become irrelevant once the matrix is calculated. Note that under Euclidean measure **W** will be invariant with respect to displacement (translation), rotation, and mirror imaging (reflection). Also note that edge effects may be significant – North Carolina is not an isolated State but has the counties of the State of Virginia to its north. Thus there are counties adjacent to those we have highlighted that have been excluded from our analysis purely because of the way we have selected our study area. Likewise, adjacency models based on immediate neighbors (e.g. rook's move) have a substantial effect on resulting computations, for example on computed correlation coefficients (see further Dubin, 2008, for a fuller discussion of these effects).

### 2.3.3 Multidimensional scaling

Multidimensional scaling (MDS) is the general term given to the problem of reconstructing locations from knowledge of proximities. Tobler and Wineberg (1971) provided an excellent example in which the unknown locations of 33 ancient pre-Hittite settlements in Cappadocia were inferred from knowledge of their interactions with other settlements whose locations were known, based on the assumption that interaction declined systematically with distance (see further, Section 4.4.5). Scaling techniques have been used to create a wide range of specialized maps, including maps on which distances reflect travel times rather than actual distances, or the similarity of the species found in each place, or the perceptions of relative proximities in the minds of local residents (Golledge and Rushton, 1972).

### 2.3.4 Spatial context

Much useful insight can often be gained by comparing the attributes of objects with those of other objects in close proximity. The behavior of a person on a crowded street might be explained in terms of the proximity of other people; the price of a house might be due in part to the existence of expensive homes in the immediate vicinity; and an area might find its homes losing value because of proximity to a polluting industrial plant. Location establishes context, by allowing distances between objects to be determined, and by providing information on their relevant attributes.

### 2.3.5 Neighborhood

People think of themselves as living in neighborhoods, or places that are sufficiently close to be experienced on a day-to-day basis. Very often neighborhood is the basis of spatial context, characterizing the nature of a person's surroundings. Neighborhoods are often conceived as partitioning an urban space, such that every point lies in exactly one neighborhood, but this may conflict with individual perceptions of neighborhood, and by the expectation that neighborhood extends in all directions around every individual's location. Figure 2-9 shows three examples of possible neighborhood definitions.

*Figure 2-9 Three alternative ways of defining neighborhood, using simple GIS functions*

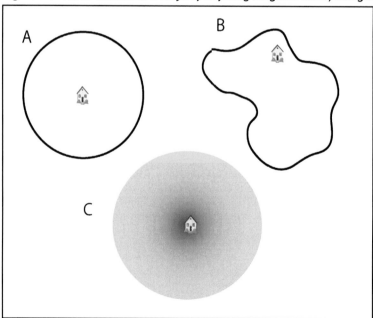

In Figure 2-9A the neighborhood is defined as a circle centered on the house, extending equally in all directions. In Figure 2-9B neighborhood is equated with an existing zone, such as a census tract or precinct, reflecting the common strategy of using existing aggregated data to characterize a household's surroundings. In Figure 2-9C weights are applied to surroundings based on distance, allowing neighborhood to be defined as a *convolution* (see further, Section 2.3.10) with weight decreasing as a simple function of distance.

In many geospatial analysis applications the term neighborhood is used to refer to the set of zones or cells that are immediately adjacent to a selected zone or cell. For example, a raster model is generally defined using a regular grid of square cells. The set of 8 cells that surround each cell (omitting the grid's edge cells) is often referred to as the 'Moore' neighborhood (see further, Section 8.2.2) or 'Queen's move' neighborhood (by analogy with the game of chess). Likewise the subset that consists of just the direct North, South, East and West neighbors is sometime called the 'von Neumann' or 'Rook's move' neighborhood (see further, Section 8.2.2). Note that whilst such neighborhoods apply to regular grids, irregular lattices (e.g. administrative areas) also have neighborhood structures of that may be described in this or a similar manner.

## 2.3.6 Spatial heterogeneity

The Earth's surface displays almost incredible variety, from the landscapes of the Tibetan plateau to the deserts of Australia and the urban complexity of London or Tokyo. Nowhere can be reasonably described as an *average place* and it is difficult to imagine any subset of the Earth's surface being a representative sample of the whole. The results of any analysis over a limited area can be expected to change as that limited area is relocated, and to be different from the results that would be obtained for the surface of the Earth as a whole. These concepts are collectively described as *spatial heterogeneity*, and they tend to affect almost any kind of spatial analysis conducted on

geographic data. Many techniques such as Geographically Weighted Regression (Fotheringham, Brunsdon, and Charlton, 2002, discussed in Section 5.6.3 of this Guide) take spatial heterogeneity as given — as a universally observed property of the Earth's surface — and focus on providing results that are specific to each area, and can be used as evidence in support of local policies. Such techniques are often termed *place-based* or *local*.

## 2.3.7 Spatial dependence

Notwithstanding the comments in Section 2.3.6 about spatial heterogeneity, anyone examining the Earth's surface in detail would be struck by how conditions tend to persist locally, and how it is possible to divide the surface into regions that exhibit substantial internal similarity. For example, the desert regions are characterized by lack of rainfall, the tropical rainforests by abundant rainfall and dense vegetation, and the Polar Regions by extreme cold. Conditions at nearby points are not sampled independently and randomly from global distributions, but instead show remarkable levels of interdependence. Of course there are exceptions, where conditions change very rapidly over short distances, for example between the plains of India and the high Himalayas, or between coastal plains and adjacent ocean.

The general term for this phenomenon is *spatial dependence*. Its pervasiveness was aptly captured by Tobler in what has become known as his First Law of Geography: "All things are related, but nearby things are more related than distant things". The magnitude of the effect can be measured using a number of statistics of *spatial autocorrelation* (Cliff and Ord, 1981, Goodchild CATMOG 47). It also underlies the discipline known as *geostatistics*, which describes spatial variation in terms of a function (known as a *correlogram*) that shows how spatial autocorrelation decreases with increasing distance (for a general overview of geostatistics see Section 6.7.1, and the book by Isaaks and Srivastava, 1989). This correlogram reaches zero, or independence, at a distance known as the *range*. The implications of Tobler's observation are profound. If it were not true, the full range of conditions anywhere on the Earth's surface could in principle be found packed within any small area. There would be no regions of approximately homogeneous conditions to be described by giving attributes to area objects. Topographic surfaces would vary chaotically, with slopes that were everywhere infinite, and the contours of such surfaces would be infinitely dense and contorted. Spatial analysis, and indeed life itself, would be impossible.

## 2.3.8 Spatial sampling

One of the implications of Tobler's First Law and spatial dependence is that it is possible to capture a reasonably accurate description of the Earth's surface with a few well-placed samples. Meteorologists capture weather patterns by sampling at measuring stations, knowing that conditions between these sample locations will vary systematically and smoothly. Geographers describe the contents of entire regions with a few well-chosen statements, provided that the regions have been defined to enclose approximately uniform conditions. Census data are published in spatially aggregated form to protect the confidentiality of individual returns, and Tobler's First Law ensures that the variance within each aggregate unit is not so large as to render the aggregated data meaningless.

Numerous approaches to spatial sampling exist, depending on the nature of the questions being asked. Perhaps the simplest occurs when sample observations are made in order to obtain a best estimate of average conditions within an area. For example, to show that average temperatures across the globe are increasing due to global warming, one would want to ensure that every location on the globe had an equal chance of being sampled (in reality weather stations are distributed far from randomly, often co-located with airports, and more common on land and in heavily populated areas). In other cases it might be more important to characterize various regions, by placing an equal number of sample points in each region, or to characterize each of a number of vegetation or soil types. If the objective is to

characterize the pattern of spatial dependence in an area, then it may be more important to place samples so as to obtain equally reliable estimates of similarity in every range of distances. A discussion of spatial sampling can be found in the book by Longley *et al.* (forthcoming 3rd edition, Section 4.4) and in Section 5.1.2 of this Guide.

## 2.3.9 Spatial interpolation

If spatial sampling is an efficient way of capturing knowledge of spatial variation, then there must be reliable ways of filling in the unknown variation between sample points. Spatial interpolation attempts to do this, by providing a method of estimating the value of a field anywhere from a limited number of sample points. Spatial interpolation is no more and no less than intelligent guesswork, supported by Tobler's First Law. For example, in Figure 2-10 we may wish to estimate the value at location (5,5) utilizing knowledge of the values of nearby locations.

In this example a total of 5 nearby points have been selected and the value at location (5,5) will be estimated as some combination of the known values at other locations, for example as a weighted average of these values. Typically weights are chosen to be larger for nearby values (e.g. point 4, with value 4 and point 5 with value 6) than more distant sites, such as location 2 with value 4. For example, weights could be chosen as a simple inverse function of the distance between the point to be evaluated and the measured locations – the further away a known location is the less its contribution (or weight) will be to the estimated value at (5,5). For the example shown this yields an estimated value of 4.18 at location (5,5), with point 4 contributing 44% to this estimate, whilst point 3 contributes only 8%.

Many methods of spatial interpolation exist, all of them based to some extent on the principle that conditions vary smoothly over the Earth's surface. Methods have even been devised to cope with exceptions to Tobler's First Law, by recognizing the discontinuities that exist in some geographic phenomena, such as faults in geologic structures, or the barriers to human interaction created by international boundaries.

*Figure 2-10 Simple interpolation modeling*

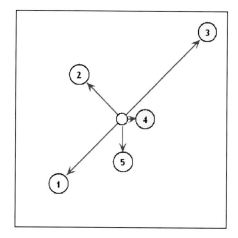

Arguably the most rigorous approach to interpolation is Kriging, a family of techniques based on the theory of geostatistics (Isaaks and Srivastava, 1989). Kriging and a wide range of other interpolation methods are described in Chapter 6 of this Guide.

## 2.3.10 Smoothing and sharpening

The Earth's surface is very dynamic, particularly in those aspects that fall in the social domain. People move, houses are constructed, areas are devastated by war, and severe storms modify coastlines. Patterns of phenomena on the Earth's surface reflect these processes, and each process tends to leave a distinctive footprint. Interpreting those footprints in order to gain insight into process is one of the most important motivations for spatial analysis.

The pervasiveness of Tobler's First Law suggests that processes that leave a smooth pattern on the Earth's surface are generally more prevalent than those that cause sharp discontinuities, but spatial analysts have developed many ideas in both categories.

Many processes involve some form of *convolution*, when the outcome at a point is determined by the conditions in some immediate neighborhood. For example, many social outcomes are responses to neighborhood conditions — individual obesity may result in part from a physical design of the neighborhood that discourages walking, alcoholism may be due in part to the availability of alcohol in the neighborhood, and asthma incidence rates may be raised due to pollution caused by high local density of traffic. Mathematically, a convolution is a weighted average of a point's neighborhood, the weights decreasing with distance from the point, and bears a strong technical relationship to density estimation. As long as the weights are positive, the resulting pattern will be smoother than the inputs. The blurring of an out-of-focus image is a form of convolution.

## 2.3.11 First- and second-order processes

In the analysis of point patterns, a *first-order process* is one that produces a variation in point density in response to some causal variable. For example, the density of cases of malaria echoes the density of particular species of mosquito, which in turn reflects the abundance of warm stagnant water for breeding. Because both mosquitoes and people move around, the pattern of malaria density can be expected to be smoother than the patterns of either mosquito density or stagnant-water abundance.

A *second-order process* results from interactions, when the presence of one point makes others more likely in the immediate vicinity. Patterns of contagious disease reflect second-order processes, when the disease is passed from an initial carrier to family members, co-workers, sexual partners, and others who come into contact with infectious carriers. The result will be a pattern that clusters around carriers (Figure 2-11B and D). Both first- and second-order processes produce clustering and smooth variations in density, but the mechanisms involved and the relationships to other variables are very different.

Competition for space provides a familiar example of a form of second-order process that results in an exception to Tobler's First Law. The presence of a shopping center in an area generally discourages other shopping centers from locating nearby, particularly when the focus is on convenience goods and services. It is unusual, for example, to find two supermarkets next to each other, or two outlets of the same fast-food chain. These are examples of *dispersed* rather than clustered point patterns (Figure 2-11C), in which the presence of one point makes others less rather than more likely in the immediate vicinity.

**Figure 2-11 Four distinct patterns of twelve points in a study area**
*(A) random, (B) clustered, (C) dispersed, (D) clustered*

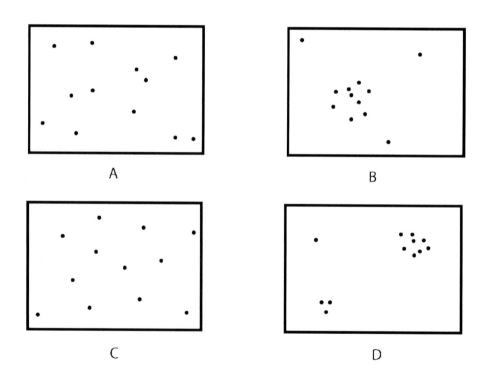

# 2.4 Spatial Statistics

## 2.4.1 Spatial probability

Humans will never have a complete understanding of everything that happens on the Earth's surface, and so it is often convenient to resort to thinking in terms of probabilities. In principle one could completely characterize the physics of a human hand and a coin, but in practice it is much more productive to assign probabilities to the outcomes of a coin toss. In similar fashion spatial analysts may avoid the virtual impossibility of predicting exactly where landslides will occur by assigning them probabilities based on patterns of known causes, such as clay soils, rainfall, and earthquakes. A map of probabilities assigns each location a value between 0 and 1, forming a probability field.

Such a map considers only the probability of a single, isolated event, however. The probability that two points a short distance apart will both be subject to landslide is not simply the product of the two probabilities, as it would be if the two outcomes were independent, a conclusion that can be seen as another manifestation of Tobler's First Law. For example, if the probability of a landslide at Point A is ½ and at Point B a short distance away is also ½, the probability that both will be affected is more than ½x½=¼, and possibly even as much as ½. Technically, the *marginal* probabilities of isolated events may not be as useful as the *joint* probabilities of related events – and joint probabilities are properties of pairs of points and thus impossible to display in map form unless the number of points is very small.

## 2.4.2 Probability density

One of the most useful applications of probability to the Earth's surface concerns uncertainty about location. Suppose the location of a point has been measured using GPS, but inevitably the measurements are subject to uncertainty, in this case amounting to an average error of 5m in both the east-west and north-south directions. Standard

methods exist for analyzing measurement error, based on the assumption, well justified by theory, that errors in a measurement form a bell curve or *Gaussian* distribution. Spatially, one can think of the east-west and north-south bell curves as combining to form a bell. But the surface formed by the bell is not a surface of probability in the sense of Section 2.4.1 – it does not vary between 0 and 1, and it does not give the marginal probability of the presence of the point. Instead, the bell is a surface of *probability density*, and the probability that the point lies within any defined area is equal to the volume of the bell's surface over that area. The volume of the entire bell is exactly 1, reflecting the fact that the point is certain to lie somewhere.

It is easy to confuse probability density with spatial probability, since both are fields. But they have very different purposes and contexts. Probability density is most often encountered in analyses of positional uncertainty, including uncertainty over the locations of points and lines.

## 2.4.3 Uncertainty

Any geographic dataset is only a representation of reality, and it inevitably leaves its user with uncertainty about the nature of the real world that is being represented. This uncertainty may concern positions, as discussed in the Section 2.4.2, but it may also concern attributes, and even topological relationships. Uncertainty in data will propagate into uncertainty about conclusions derived from data. For example, uncertainty in positions will cause uncertainty in distances computed from those positions, in the elements of a **W** matrix, and in the results of analyses based on that matrix.

Uncertainty can be due to the inaccuracy or limitations of measuring instruments, since an instrument that measures a property to limited accuracy leaves its user uncertain about the true value of the property. It can be due to vagueness in definitions, when land is assigned to classes that are not rigorously defined, so that different observers may classify the same land differently. Uncertainty can also be due to missing or inadequate documentation, when the user is left to guess as to the meaning or definitions of certain aspects of the data. Clearly it is important to spatial analysts to know about the uncertainties present in data, and to investigate how those uncertainties impact the results of analysis. A range of techniques have been developed, and there is a rich literature on uncertainty in spatial data and its impacts (see further, Zhang and Goodchild, 2002 and Longley *et al.* (Chapter 6 in the forthcoming 3rd edition).

### 2.4.4 Statistical inference

One of the most important tools of science is statistical inference, the practice of reasoning from the analysis of samples to conclusions about the larger populations from which the samples were drawn. Entire courses are devoted to the topic, and to its detailed techniques — the *t*, *F*, and Chi-Squared tests, linear modeling, and many more. Today it is generally accepted that any result obtained from an experiment, through the analysis of a sample of measurements or responses to a survey, will be subjected to a *significance test* to determine what conclusions can reasonably be drawn about the larger world that is represented by the measurements or responses.

The earliest developments in statistical inference were made in the context of controlled experiments. For example, much was learned about agriculture by sowing test plots with new kinds of seeds, or submitting test plots to specific treatments. In such experiments it is reasonable to assume that every sample was created through a random process, and that the samples collectively represent what might have happened had the sample been much larger — in other words, what might be expected to happen under similar conditions in the universe of all similar experiments, whether conducted by the experimenter or by a farmer. Because there is variation in the experiment, it is important to know whether the variation observed in the sample is sufficiently large to reach conclusions about variation in the universe as a whole. Figure 2-12 illustrates this process of statistical inference. A sample is drawn from the population by a random process. Data are then collected about the sample, and analyzed. Finally, inferences are made about the characteristics of the population, within the bounds of uncertainty inherent in the sampling process.

*Figure 2-12 The process of statistical inference*

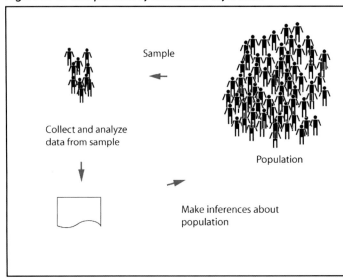

These techniques have become part of the standard apparatus of science, and it is unusual for scientists to question the assumptions that underlie them. But the techniques of spatial analysis are applied in very different circumstances from the controlled experiments of the agricultural scientist or psychologist. Rather than creating a sample by laying out experimental plots or recruiting participants in a survey, the spatial analyst typically has to rely on so-called *natural* experiments, in which the variation among samples is the result of circumstances beyond the analyst's control.

In this context the two fundamental principles of statistical inference raise important questions: (i) were the members of the sample selected randomly and independently from a larger population, or did Tobler's First Law virtually ensure lack of independence, and/or did the basic heterogeneity of the Earth's surface virtually ensure that samples drawn in another location would be different? (ii) what universe is represented by the samples? and (iii) is it possible to reason from the results of the analysis to conclusions about the universe?

All too often the answers to these questions are negative. Spatial analysis is often conducted on all of the available data, so there is no concept of a universe from which the data were drawn, and about which inferences are to be made. It is rarely possible to argue that sample observations were drawn independently, unless they are spaced far apart. Specialized methods have been devised that circumvent these problems to some degree, and they will be discussed at various points in the book. More often, however, the analyst must be content with results that apply only to the sample under analysis, and cannot be generalized to some larger universe.

# 2.5 Spatial Data Infrastructure

This final section introduces some of the basic concepts associated with what has become known as *spatial data infrastructure*, the set of representations created using recognized standards and other arrangements that provide sources of spatial data and tools, in ways that support spatial analysis. Spatial data infrastructures provide some of the raw ingredients to spatial analysis, as well as a framework for the display of results that enable ready interpretation by users.

Until the 1980s it was generally accepted that responsibility for the acquisition and dissemination of spatial data lay with national mapping agencies, which produced topographic maps and other information at public expense. Parts of this system began to degrade and decentralize around 1990, however, for a number of reasons. On the one hand, governments became less and less willing to foot the steadily increasing bill; particularly as new technologies created demands for increasingly high value information products. One the other hand, some of the same developments in computing technology and GPS had made it possible for virtually anyone to become a creator of spatial data at low cost; and the 'creative commons of the Internet allowed the creation of spatial data infrastructures by communities of volunteers. For example, Figure 2-13 shows the results of calculating a school catchment area and an analysis of pupil educational attainment in and around the area, mapped against a backcloth of data from www.openstreetmap.org. Related to this second trend has been the commercial sector lobby for new markets for its products, arguing that subsidized government production of spatial data constituted unfair competition. The movement of the search engines of Google and Microsoft into Internet mapping has resulted in spatial data infrastructures becoming available to any non commercial user at zero cost, on the presumption that the supply of such data can be funded through an advertising driven business model. Today, many countries now have extensive spatial data infrastructures, and responsibility for the acquisition and dissemination of spatial data is now shared between numerous agencies, companies, and individuals.

## 2.5.1 Geoportals

A *geoportal* is a Web site providing a single point of access to spatial data, allowing its users to browse through extensive collections of data and related materials, evaluating their potential fitness for use. Geoportals may include data that are in the public domain or are otherwise available free of charge, and may also support licensing and purchasing of proprietary data. They include the ability to search through catalogues, examining the contents and quality of data.

The www.publicprofiler.org geoportal shown in Figure 2-13 is a UK example of a geoportal that brings together datasets concerned with pupil and student education, along with associated population characteristics and framework data. Geoportals include standard layers of data on topography, roads and streets, rivers and streams, named places, imagery, and political boundaries; and may also provide access to more specialized data. A number of geoportals are listed in the Web links: "Selected national and international data and information sources" Annex to this Guide.

*Figure 2-13 Pupil performance and a school catchment area in the East Riding of Yorkshire, UK*

## 2.5.2 Metadata

Fundamental to the operation of a geoportal are *metadata*, the catalogue entries that allow users to search for datasets and to assess their contents. Metadata may include information on contents, quality, the data production process, details of formats and coordinate systems, and many other topics. For more details see the UK Geospatial Information Gateway: http://www.gigateway.org.uk/ or the US National Spatial Data Infrastructure site: http://www.fgdc.gov/nsdi/nsdi.html

## 2.5.3 Interoperability

Over the past four decades many hundreds of formats have been devised and implemented for spatial data. Some are open, while others are proprietary. The development of an effective spatial data infrastructure has required extensive efforts to achieve *interoperability*, in other words the ability of systems to exchange and use data without major effort. The standards that make this possible have been devised and promulgated by several organizations, including national mapping agencies, international standards bodies, and the Open Geospatial Consortium (OGC): www.opengeospatial.org

## 2.5.4 Conclusion

This chapter has provided a brief overview of some of the more important and fundamental concepts that underpin spatial analysis. Many more will be encountered at various points in this book, and many more can be found in the background readings cited in Section 1.2.2. These concepts and others together frame the theory of (geo)spatial analysis, just as the field of statistics is framed by the concepts of statistical analysis. While much of spatial analysis will appear intuitive, it is important to recognize that it is underpinned by concepts and terms whose meanings are often far from intuitive, and require explicit recognition.

# 3 Methodological Context

## 3.1 Spatial analysis as a process

In many instances the process of spatial analysis follows a number of well-defined (often iterative) stages: problem formulation; planning; data gathering; exploratory analysis; hypothesis formulation; modeling and testing; consultation and review; and ultimately final reporting and/or implementation of the findings. GIS and related software tools that perform analytical functions only address the middle sections of this process, and even then may be relatively "blunt" instruments.

Having first identified and formulated the problem to be addressed (often a significant task in itself), and developed an outline plan, the first task typically involves obtaining the data which are to be the subject of analysis. This immediately raises many questions that have an important bearing on subsequent stages: what assumptions have been invoked in order to represent the "real-world" and what are the implications of this for subsequent analysis? how complete are the data – spatially and temporarily? how accurate are the data (spatially, temporarily and in terms of measured attributes)? are all of the datasets compatible and consistent with one another – what sources are they drawn from and how do they compare in terms of scale, projection, accuracy, modeling, orientation, date of capture and attribute definition? are the data adequate to address the problem at hand? Can the available data be combined and processed with the resources available?

The second stage, once the data have been obtained and accepted as fit for purpose (and/or as the best available), is often exploratory. This may involve: simple mapping of the data, points, lines, regions, grids, surfaces, computation of rates, indices, densities, slopes, directional trends, level sets, classifications etc.; or more complex and dynamic exploration of the data, such as brushing and linking (see further, Section 5.2.1). One or more analytical techniques and tools may be utilized at this and subsequent stages.

The third stage will depend upon the objective of the analysis. In many instances presentation of the results of exploratory analysis in the form of commentary, maps, descriptive statistics and associated documents will complete the process. In others it will involve the development and testing of hypotheses about the patterns observed, and/or modeling of the data in order to undertake some predictive or optimization exercise. Frequently the result of this process is a series of possible outcomes (scenarios) which then need to be summarized and presented for final analysis and decision-making by stakeholders, interest groups, policy makers or entrepreneurs. The process may then iterate until an agreed or stable and robust flow is achieved, from problem specification to data selection, and thence to analysis and outcomes.

This kind of process can be formalized and may be implemented as a standard procedure in operational systems or as part of a planning process. Such procedures may involve relatively lengthy decision cycles (e.g. identifying the next location for a new warehouse as customer demand grows) or highly dynamic environments, for example controlling road traffic lights and routing to reflect the type and density of traffic in real time.

To a substantial degree spatial analysis can be seen as part of a decision support infrastructure, whether such decision-making reflects purely academic interest or commercial, governmental or community interests (see further Batty and Densham, 1996; Miller and Shaw, 2001, Chapter 8). Increasingly, to reflect this trend, GIS vendors have developed tools to facilitate such processes. This has been through the provision of Internet-enabled input, output and processing facilities, and through improved usability, speed, interactivity, spatial decision support systems (SDSS) and visualization techniques. Increasingly these have involved the use of formal decision-support systems, from simple cost-benefit analysis and Multi-Criteria Evaluation (MCE) techniques to the more sophisticated and formalized multi-criteria process such as Saaty's Analytical Hierarchical Process (AHP) and his more recent Analytical Network Process (ANP) models — see Saaty (1980, 1999), commercialized as the Decision Lens and the Superdecisions suites of software.

With these improvements in data and toolsets the range and experience of users has grown and will continue to develop. For this reason it is essential that the underlying principles are well-understood and not misused, accidentally or deliberately, leading to ill-informed or invalid decision-making. All providers and users of such systems have a responsibility to ensure that information generated is communicated in an unambiguous and unbiased manner, and to ensure that limitations and assumptions made are transparent and well-understood. These concerns are of particular importance and relevance to those in the print and broadcast media, especially television, where visualization is so important and timeslots for presentation so brief.

# 3.2 Analytical methodologies

As with all scientific disciplines, spatial analysis has its fair share of terminology, abbreviations, methods and tools. In this subsection we start by examining spatial analysis in the broader context of analytical methodologies, and attempt to highlight the similarities with methods applied in a range of disciplines. We then extend the discussion to consider some of the distinctive aspects of spatial and GIS analysis.

Earlier we suggested that the process of spatial analysis often proceeds in a simple sequence from problem specification to outcome. In reality this is an over-simplification — the analytical process is far more complex and iterative than this summary of steps suggests. So, for example, Mitchell (2005) suggests the sequence for spatial *data* analysis shown in Figure 3-1. Here it appears that there is a natural flow from start to finish, but this is rarely the case. Not only is the process iterative, but at each stage one often looks back to the previous step and re-evaluates the validity of the decisions made. Explicit recognition of this need is incorporated in the approach of Haining (2003, p.359) to "Data-driven statistical modeling", which is otherwise very similar to Mitchell's model.

The need for a more iterative approach is partly a reflection of adopting scientific methods, but also a recognition that most analytical tasks take place within a much broader context. For example, pragmatic decisions often have to be made based on a series of common questions:

- how well defined is the problem I am seeking to address?

- how much time, money and resource can I afford to apply to this problem?

- what research has previously been carried out on problems of this type, and what strengths and weaknesses have these shown?

*Figure 3-1 Analytical process — Mitchell*

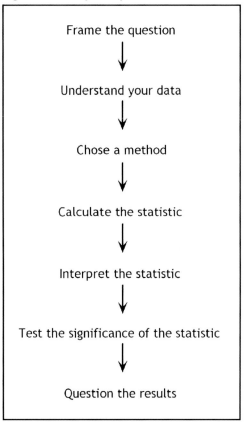

After Mitchell (2005)

- who will be the recipient of the results, and what are their expectations and requirements?

- if I commence by examining the requirements of the outcome closely, what implications does this have on my selection of techniques and data, and what caveats should I apply to the scope and validity of my analyses — e.g. in relation to sample/region size, timespan, attribute set, validation etc.?

- how will I deal with data inadequacies — e.g. missing data, unsuitable data, delays in receiving or obtaining access to key datasets?

- how will I deal with limitations and errors in the software I have chosen to use?

- what are the implications of producing wrong or misleading results?

- are there independent and verifiable means for validating results obtained?

This list is by no means exhaustive but serves to illustrate the kind of questioning that should form part of any analytical exercise, in GIS and many other fields. In the context of GIS, readers are strongly recommended to study the "Framework for theory" section of the paper by Steinitz (1993), which proposes a six step approach to landscape planning, with many resonances in our own methodological discussions, below. Also recommended is the more recent technical report by Stratton (2006) "Guidance on spatial wildfire analysis", which again echoes many of the observations we make in the following subsections.

In supplier-client relationships it is often useful to start with the customer requirements and expectations, including the form of presentation of results (visualizations, data analyses, reports, public participation exercises etc.). From a clear understanding of the problem and expectations, one can then work *back* through the process stages identifying what needs to be included and might be excluded in order to have the best chance of meeting those expectations and requirements within the timescale and resourcing available. Echoes of these ideas are found in the commentary on cartographic modeling provided with the Idrisi GIS package:

*"In developing a cartographic model we find it most useful to begin with the final product and proceed backwards in a step-by-step manner towards the existing data. This process guards against the tendency to let the available data shape the final product."*

An interesting example of the modern analytical process at work is a study of the incidence of childhood cancer in relation to distance from high voltage power lines by Draper *et al.* (2005). The client in this instance was not a single person or organization, but health policy makers and practitioners, together with academic and medical

specialists in the field. With such scrutiny, political sensitivity and implications for the health of many children, great care in defining the problem to be addressed, selecting the data, conducting the analysis and reporting the findings was essential. In this instance some of their initial findings were reported by the press and radio prior to the intended publication date, so the authors took the decision to publish ahead of schedule despite the issues this might raise. The researchers summarized their approach in the form shown in Figure 3-2:

*Figure 3-2 Analytical process — Draper*

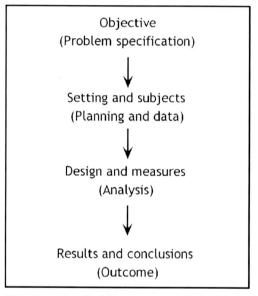

After Draper et al. (2005)

Each step of this process is described clearly, qualifying the information and referring to earlier work where appropriate. In addition the paper clarifies the roles of the various participants in the research, addresses issues relating to competing interests (one of the researchers involved was an employee of the main power grid company), and deals with issues of funding and ethical approval. All of these elements provide transparency and enable "clients" to evaluate the quality and importance of the research. The form of publication (via the British Medical Journal) also facilitated extensive online discussion, with comments on the paper by acknowledged experts from around the world being published electronically, as well as the author's responses to these comments.

An interesting aspect of this research, and a significant number of similar studies, is that it deals with rare events. In general it is far more difficult to be confident about drawing definitive conclusions about such events, but this does not detract from the importance of attempting to carry out research of this kind. What it does highlight is the need to identify and report on the scope of the study, and attempt to identify and highlight any obvious weaknesses in the data or methodology. In the cancer study just cited, for example, the datasets used were details of the location of power grid lines (by type, including any changes that had occurred during the 30+ year study period) together with around 30,000 records stored in the national cancer registry. No active participation from patients or their families was involved, and homes were not visited to measure actual levels of Electro-Magnetic (EM) radiation. These observations raise important but *unstated* questions: how accurate are the grid line datasets and the cancer registry records? is home address *at birth* an appropriate measure (surrogate for exposure to EM radiation)? is vertical as well as horizontal proximity to high voltage lines of importance? is proximity to pylons carrying insulators and junction equipment rather than just the lines an important factor? is voltage variability important? were the controls similarly located relative to the power lines as the cases — if not, could this account for some aspects of the results reported? given that the research findings identified a pattern of increased risk for certain cancers that was *not* a monotonic function of distance, can this result be explained, are the observations purely chance occurrences, or are there some other factors at work?

The latter issue is often described as *confounding*, i.e. identifying a result which is thought to be explained by a factor that has been identified, but is in reality related to one or more other factors that did not form part of the analysis. For example, in this instance one might also consider that: (i) socio-economic status and lifestyle factors may be associated with proximity to overhead power lines, pylons and transformers; (ii) population densities may vary with distance from power lines; (iii) pre-natal exposure may be important; and (iv) the location of nurseries and playgroups may be relevant. Any of these factors may be important to incorporate in the research. In this instance the authors did analyze some of these points but did not include them in their reporting, whilst other points remain for them to consider further and comment on in a future publication. The "distance from power lines" study is an example of modern scientific research in action — indeed, it has provided an important input to the debate on health and safety, leading to national recommendations affecting future residential building programmes.

Mackay and Oldford (2002) have produced an excellent discussion of the context and role of (statistical) analysis within the broader framework of scientific research methods: "Scientific method, statistical method and the speed of light". Their paper studies the work carried out in 1879 by A A Michelson, a 24-year old Naval ensign, and his (largely successful) efforts to obtain an accurate estimate of the speed of light. The paper is both an exercise in understanding the role of statistical analysis within scientific research, and a fascinating perspective on a cornerstone of spatial analysis, that of distance determination. They conclude that statistical analysis is defined in large measure by its methodology, in particular its focus on seeking an understanding of a population from sample data. In a similar way spatial analysis and GIS analysis are defined by the methods they adopt, focusing on the investigation of spatial patterns and relationships as a guide to a broader understanding of spatial patterns and processes. As such spatial analysis is defined by both its material (spatial datasets) and its methods. Within this set of methods are the full range of univariate and multivariate statistical methods, coupled with a wide range of specifically spatial tools, and a broad mix of modeling and optimization techniques.

Mackay and Oldford describe the *statistical method* in terms of a sequence of steps they label *PPDAC*: Problem; Plan; Data; Analysis; and Conclusions. This methodology is very similar to those we have already described, although a little broader in scope. They then expand upon each step and in the paper relate each step to the process adopted by Michelson. This approach emphasizes the place of formal analysis as very much a part of a process, rather than a distinct discipline that can be considered in isolation. Daskin (1995, Ch. 9) makes a very similar case within the context of planning facility locations, and sees this as an iterative process culminating in implementation and ongoing monitoring. Spatial analysis as a whole may be considered to follow very similar lines — however the steps need clarification and some amendment to Mackay and Oldford's formulation.

A summary of a revised PPDAC approach is shown in Figure 3-3. As can be seen from the diagram, although the clockwise sequence (1→5) applies as the principal flow, each stage may and often will feed back to the previous stage. In addition, it may well be beneficial to examine the process in the reverse direction, starting with Problem definition and then examining expectations as to the format and structure of the Conclusions (without pre-judging the outcomes!). This procedure then continues, step-by-step, in an anti-clockwise manner (e→a) determining the implications of these expectations for each stage of the process. A more detailed commentary on the PPDAC stages, particularly as they relate to problems in spatial analysis, is provided in Section 3.3. In addition, an example application of the methodology to noise mapping is provided on the accompanying website in the RESOURCES section.

*Figure 3-3 PPDAC as an iterative process*

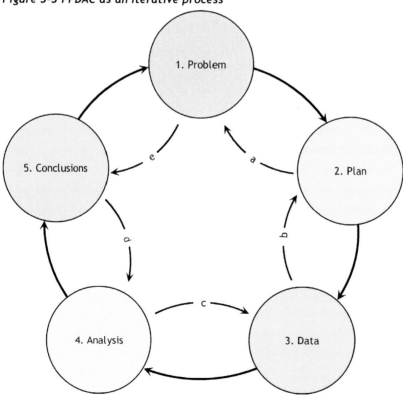

# 3.3 Spatial analysis and the PPDAC model

Mackay and Oldford's perspective, discussed in the preceding section, is a little too narrow for many complex real-world situations. It also tends to focus on problems that have scientific research focus rather than the broader range of practical problems that the GIS analyst is likely to encounter.

The approach we describe in the following subsections is intended to provide a strong framework for undertaking projects that have a significant geospatial component. For example, the framework might be used to guide the process of preparing a response to an initial government-initiated RFI (request for information). It might subsequently used to help guide the development of a full-scale costed proposal in response to an RFP (request for proposals), or to address a subset of a larger project within which the geospatial element is a small element. Alternatively, the PPDAC methodology can be applied to problems in which the collection and analysis of particular datasets is the central task, as may be the case with primary environmental, socio-economic or epidemiological research.

PPDAC is a flexible and dynamic methodology, not a rigid set of procedures or forms, and thus may be applied at several stages of a project. An example 'case study' of the use of the PPDAC approach is provided on the accompanying website under the section entitled RESOURCES. This case study examines the hypothetical response to an RFP covering noise mapping of urban areas (in order to produce maps of the type illustrated in Figure 3-4, showing noise levels in Augsburg, Germany). The example is illustrative only and is not based on actual application of the PPDAC methodology to a specific project that has been implemented. However, it draws on a wide range of materials relating to this topic that have been developed at a national and international level (notably the European IMAGINE programme).

*Figure 3-4 Noise map, Augsburg*

*Source: Accon & DataKustnik GmbH, Germany*

In respect of problems that the GIS user is likely to meet there are a number of reasons for treating spatial problems as 'special'. These include the following:

- Spatial analysis is particularly concerned with problems that have an explicit spatial context, and frequently data at one location is not independent of data at other locations (see Sections 2.3 and 2.4). Indeed such associations (spatial correlations) are the norm, especially for measurements taken at locations that are near to one another. Identifying and analyzing such patterns is often the goal of analysis, at least at the early stages of investigation

- Many problems must be considered in a spatio-temporal context rather than simply a spatial context. Time of day/week/month/year may have great relevance to obtaining an understanding of particular spatial problems, especially those of an environmental nature and problems relating to infrastructure usage and planning

- The theoretical foundations of statistics rely on a set of assumptions and sampling procedures that are often more applicable to experimental datasets than purely observational data. Very few problems addressed by spatial analysis fall into the category of truly experimental research

- Often the purpose of spatial analysis is not merely to identify pattern, but to construct models, if possible by gaining an understanding of process. In some instances this will involve the development of new models, whereas in others it will involve the use and/or development of existing models (see further, Section 3.4 and the discussion on Agent-based modeling in Section 8.2.7)

- Spatial patterns are rarely if ever uniquely determined by a single process, hence spatial analysis is often the start of further investigations into process and model building, and rarely an end in itself. Where explicitly spatial factors, such as distance or contiguity, are identified as important or significant, the question why? must follow: is the problem under consideration directly or indirectly affected by purely spatial factors; or is the spatial element a surrogate for one or more explanatory variables that have not be adequately modeled or are unobtainable?

- Spatial datasets are often provided by third parties, such as national mapping agencies, census units and third party data vendors. Metadata provided with such material may or may not provide adequate information on the quality, accuracy, consistency, completeness and provenance of the information. In many areas of spatial research these elements are pre-determined, although they are often augmented by corporate datasets (e.g. customer databases, crime incident records, medical case details) or field research (e.g. georeferenced collection of soil samples or plant locations, market

research exercises, bathymetric surveys, remote-sensed data etc.)

Each of these factors serves to distinguish spatial analysis from analysis in other disciplines, whilst at the same time recognizing the considerable similarities and overlap of methodologies and techniques.

In subsections 3.3.1 to 3.3.5 we examine each step of the PPDAC model in the context of spatial analysis. In this "revised" version of the PPDAC approach the Plan stage is much broader than in Mackay and Oldford's model. In their approach the Plan stage focuses largely on the data collection procedures to be adopted. In our case it covers all aspects of project planning, including preparation for data acquisition and analysis, and considerations of feasibility within given project constraints.

For many problems that arise in spatial analysis there will be multiple instances of the process described, especially for the data and analysis stages, where several different but related datasets are to be studied in order to address the problem at hand. Finally, in instances where the geospatial analyst is simply presented with the data and asked to carry out appropriate analyses, it is essential that the context is first understood (i.e. Problem, Plan, Data and Conclusions) even if these cannot be influenced or revisited.

### 3.3.1 Problem: Framing the question

Understanding and defining the problem to be studied is often a substantial part of the overall analytical process — clarity at the start is obviously a key factor in determining whether a programme of analysis is a success or a failure. Success here is defined in terms of outcomes rather than methods. And outcomes are typically judged and evaluated by third parties — customers, supervisors, employers — so their active involvement in problem specification and sometimes throughout the entire process is essential. Breaking problems down into key components, and simplifying problems to focus on their essential and most important and relevant components, are often very effective first steps. This not only helps identify many of the issues to be addressed, likely data requirements, tools and procedures, but also can be used within the iterative process of clarifying the customer's requirements and expectations. Problems that involve a large number of key components tend to be more complex and take more time than problems which involve a more limited set. This is fairly obvious – but perhaps less obvious is the need to examine the interactions and dependencies between these key components. The greater the number of such interactions and dependencies the more complex the problem will be to address, and as the numbers increase complexity tends to grow exponentially.

Analysis of existing information, traditionally described as "desk research", is an essential part of this process and far more straightforward now with the advantage of online/Internet-based resources. Obtaining relevant information from the client/sponsor (if any), interested third parties, information gatekeepers and any regulatory authorities, forms a further and fundamental aspect to problem formulation and specification.

Spatial analysts also need to be particularly aware of a number of well-known problems associated with grouped data in general, and spatial data in particular. This applies to both problems in which the analyst contributes to the entire PPDAC process as well as the common situation in which the analyst is presented with the problem or task and maybe the (broad) approach to be taken by another party (for example an academic or business supervisor, a technical committee, or even a client). Issues requiring particular attention in the case of spatial problems include:

- spatial scale factors: over what study region is the work to be carried out, and what are the implications of altering this for some or all datasets? Do the same scale factors apply for all the data of interest?

- statistical scale factors: at what levels of grouping are data to be analyzed and reported?

- spatial arrangement factors: does the specification of the spatial arrangement or re-arrangement of subsections of the study area have an impact on the analysis?

- does the problem formulation require data of types, sizes or quality standards that are available, within the time, budget and resources available? if not, compromises will be necessary

- are conclusions regarding spatially grouped data being sought that imply the grouping (e.g. at the county level, at the farm level) is truly representative of all the components in the group (e.g. individuals living within the county, fields within the farm)? If so, the grouped regions must be entirely or largely homogeneous in order to avoid the so-called *ecological fallacy* – ascribing characteristics to members of a group when only the overall group characteristics are known (special statistical techniques have been devised to address certain problems of this type, for example as discussed in King *et al.*, 2004)

- are conclusions regarding spatial grouped data being sought based on the measured characteristics of sampled individuals? If so, the sample must be entirely or highly representative of the grouping in order to avoid the so-called *atomistic fallacy* – ascribing characteristics to members of a group based on a potentially unrepresentative sample of members

Framing the question is not always a one-time exercise. Once an initial problem specification has been drafted, it may be altered in the light of preliminary investigations, technical or commercial considerations, or unforeseen events (Figure 3-3, feedback loops). As far as possible, however, only essential changes should be made (and documented as such) once problem formulation has been completed and documented, and all interested parties have agreed on problem content. GIS has a particular role to play here, in providing tools (principally mapping related) for storing and visualizing existing data and facilitating discussion of aspects of the problem prior to subsequent stages in the process. This role may continue throughout the various stages of a project, assisting in the interpretation, analysis and presentation of results. Careful consideration should be given to change control management, documentation and reporting, especially in commercial and governmental environments.

Note that in many instances it will be difficult if not impossible to compute the timescale and budget required to address a particular problem without a preliminary study or project. For example, it is quite common for there to be preliminary project involving the preparation of a detailed Requirements Specification (RS) and/or undertaking a smaller-scale or feasibility project, e.g. confined to a small, but representative, area.

### 3.3.2   Plan: Formulating the approach

Having agreed on the problem definition the next stage is to formulate an approach that has the best possible chance of addressing the problem and achieving answers (outcomes) that meet expectations. Although the PLAN phase is next in the sequence, the iterative nature of the PPDAC process emphasizes the need to define and then re-visit each component. Thus whilst an outline project plan would be defined at this stage, one would have to consider each of the subsequent stages (DATA, ANALYSIS, CONCLUSIONS) before firming up on the detail of the plan. With projects that are more experimental in nature, drawing up the main elements of the PLAN takes place at this stage. With projects for which pre-existing datasets and analysis tools are expected to be used, the PLAN stage is much more an integrated part of the whole PPDAC exercise.

The output of the PLAN stage is often formulated as a detailed project plan, with allocation of tasks, resources, timescales, analysis of critical path(s) and activities, and estimated costs of data, equipment, software tools, manpower, services etc. Frequently project plans are produced with the aid of formal tools, which may be paper-based or software assisted. In many instances this will involve determining all the major tasks or task blocks that need to be carried out, identifying the interconnections between these building

blocks (and their sequencing), and then examining how each task block is broken down into sub-elements. This process then translates into an initial programme of work once estimated timings and resources are included, which can then be modified and fine-tuned as an improved understanding of the project is developed. In some instances this will be part of the Planning process itself, where a formal functional specification and/or pilot project forms part of the overall plan.

As with other parts of the PPDAC process, the PLAN stage is not a one-shot static component, but typically includes a process of monitoring and re-evaluation of the plan, such that issues of timeliness, budget, resourcing and quality can be monitored and reported in a well-defined manner.

The approach adopted involves consideration of many issues, including:

- the nature of the problem and project — is it purely investigative, or a formal research exercise; is it essentially descriptive, including identification of structures and relationships, or more concerned with processes, in which clearer understanding of causes and effects may be required, especially if predictive models are to be developed and/or prescriptive measures are anticipated as an output?

- does it require commercial costings and/or cost-benefit analysis?

- are particular decision-support tools and procedures needed?

- what level of public involvement and public awareness is involved, if any?

- what particular operational needs and conditions are associated with the exercise?

- what time is available to conduct the research and are there any critical (final or intermediate) deadlines?

- what funds and other resources are available?

- is the project considered technically feasible, what assessable risk is there of failure and how is this affected by problem complexity?

- what are the client (commercial, governmental, academic) expectations?

- are there specifications, standards, quality parameters and/or procedures that must be used (for example to comply with national guidelines)?

- how does the research relate to other studies on the same or similar problems?

- what data components are needed and how will they be obtained (existing sources, collected datasets)?

- are the data to be studied (units) to be selected from the target population, or will the sample be distinct in some way and applied to the population subsequently (in which case one must consider not just sampling error but so-called study error also)?

When deciding upon the design approach and analytical methods/tools it is essential to identify available datasets, examine their quality, strengths and weaknesses, and carry out exploratory work on subsets or samples in order to clarify the kind of approach that will be both practical and effective. There will always be unknowns at this stage, but the aim should be to minimize these at the earliest opportunity, if necessary by working through the entire process, up to and including drafting the presentation of results based on sample, hypothetical or simulated data.

The application of a single analytical technique or software tool is often to be avoided unless one is extremely confident of the outcome, or it is the analytical technique or approach itself that is the subject of investigation, or that this approach or toolset has already been approved for use in such cases. If analysis is not limited to single approaches, and a series of outputs, visualizations, techniques and tests all suggest a similar outcome then confidence in the findings tends to be greatly increased. If such

techniques suggest different outcomes the analyst is encouraged to explain the differences, by re-examining the design, the data and/or the analytical techniques and tools applied. Ultimately the original problem definition may have to be reviewed.

The impact on research of exceptions — rare events, spatial outliers, extreme values, unusual clusters — is extremely important in geospatial analysis. Exploratory methods, such as mapping and examining cases and producing box-plots (see further, Section 5.2.2.2), help to determine whether these observations are valid and important, or require removal from the study set.

Some analytical techniques are described as being more *robust* than others. By this is meant that they are less susceptible to data extremes or unusual datasets — for example the median or middle value of a dataset is generally regarded as more robust than the mean or average value, because it is unaffected by the specific values of the set. However, the *spatial* mean and median exhibit different properties from those applied to individual tabulated attributes, and other measures of centrality (e.g. the central feature of a set) may be more appropriate in some instances. Likewise, statistical tests that make no assumptions about the underlying distribution of the dataset tend to be more robust than those that assume particular distributional characteristics — for example non-parametric versus parametric tests. However, increasing robustness may result in loss of *power* in the sense that some methods are described as being more powerful than others, i.e. they are less likely to accept hypotheses that are incorrect or reject hypotheses that are correct.

### 3.3.3 Data: Data acquisition

Spatial analysis is somewhat unusual, in that key datasets are often provided by or acquired from third parties rather than being produced as part of the research. Analysis is often of these pre-existing spatial datasets, so understanding their quality and provenance is extremely important. It also means that in many instances this phase of the PPDAC process involves selection of one or more existing datasets from those available. In practice not all such datasets will have the same quality, cost, licensing arrangements, availability, completeness, format, timeliness and detail. Compromises have to be made in most instances, with the over-riding guideline being fitness for purpose. If the datasets available are unsuitable for addressing the problem in a satisfactory manner, even if these are the only data that one has to work with, then the problem should either not be tackled or must be re-specified in such a way as to ensure it is possible to provide an acceptable process of analysis leading to worthwhile outcomes.

A major issue related to data sourcing is the question of the compatibility of different data sets: in formats and encoding; in temporal, geographic and thematic coverage; in quality and completeness. In general datasets from different sources and/or times will not match precisely, so resolution of mismatches can become a major task in the data phase of any project. And as part of this process the issue of how and where to store the data arises, which again warrants early consideration, not merely to ensure consistency and retrievability but also for convenient analysis and reporting.

Almost by definition no dataset is perfect. All may contain errors, missing values, have a finite resolution, include distortions as a result modeling the real world with discrete mathematical forms, incorporate measurement errors and uncertainties, and may exhibit deliberate or designed adjustment of positional and/or attribute data (e.g. for privacy reasons, as part of aggregation procedures). Spatial analysis tools may or may not incorporate facilities for explicitly handling some of the more obvious of these factors. For example, special GIS tools exist for handling issues such as:

- boundary definition and density estimation
- coding schemes that provide for missing data and for masking out invalid regions and/or data items

- modeling procedures that automatically adjust faulty topologies and poorly matched datasets, or datasets of varying resolutions and/or projections
- a wide range of procedures exist to handle difficulties in classification
- data transformation, weighting, smoothing and normalization facilities exist to facilitate comparison and combination of datasets of differing data types and extents
- lack of continuity in field data can be explicitly handled via breaklines and similar methods
- a range of techniques exist for modeling data problems and generating error bounds, confidence envelopes and alternative realizations

In other words, many facilities now exist within GIS and related software packages that support analysis even when the datasets available are less than ideal. It is worth emphasizing that here we are referring to the analytical stage, not the data cleansing stage of operations. For many spatial data this cleansing has been conducted by the data supplier, and thus is outside of the analyst's direct control. Of course for data collected or obtained within a project, or supplied in raw form (e.g. original, untouched hyperspectral imagery) data cleansing becomes one element in the overall analytical process.

For many problems important components of the project involve intangible data, such as perceptions or concerns relating to pollution, risk or noise levels. Quantifying such components in a manner that is accepted by the key participants, and in a form suitable for analysis, is a difficult process. This is an area in which a number of formal methodologies have been established and widely tested (including spatial decision support tools and cost-benefit analysis tools). Such tools are almost always applied separately and then utilized to generate or qualify input to GIS software (e.g. weightings).

An additional issue arises when data are generated as part of a research exercise. This may be as a result of applying a particular procedure to one or more pre-supplied datasets, or as a result of a simulation or randomization exercise. In these latter cases the generated datasets should be subjected to the same critical analysis and inspection as source datasets, and careful consideration should be given to generated and magnified distortions and errors produced by the processing carried out. A brief discussion of such issues is provided in Burrough and McDonnell (1998, Ch.10) whilst Zhang and Goodchild (2002) address these questions in considerable detail. For further discussion of the nature of spatial data and some of the key issues raised when undertaking analyses using such datasets, see Haining (2008).

### 3.3.4   Analysis: Analytical methods and tools

One of the principal purposes of this Guide is to assist readers in selecting appropriate analytical methods, tools and models from those readily available in the GIS and related marketplace. Since analysis takes place well down the chain in what we have described as the analytical methodology, initial selection of methods and tools should have been made well before the analytical stage has been reached. *Simplicity and parsimony* — using the simplest and clearest tools, models and forms of visualization — and *fit to the problem* and objectives are the key criteria that should be applied. Other factors include: the availability of appropriate tools; time and cost constraints; the need to provide validity and robustness checks, which could be via internal and/or external checks on consistency, sensitivity and quality; conformance to relevant standards; the use of multiple techniques; and the use of independent and/or additional datasets or sampling.

There are a very large number of software tools available for performing spatial analysis: both for simple data summarizing and exploratory spatial data analysis (ESDA), which will often form the initial stage of analysis; and to assist the development and/or application of specific techniques or models.

Longley *et al.* (Chapters 14-16 of the forthcoming 3rd edition) consider *spatial analysis* to be characterized by static analysis, searching for readily visible or hidden patterns or anomalies, leading to new ideas and hypotheses. This they contrast with *spatial modeling,* which they regard as typically being: multi-stage or dynamic in nature; often implementing ideas and hypotheses (e.g. standard process flow models) rather than investigating concepts; and in a significant number of applications, involving experimentation with policy options and scenarios. This distinction between spatial analysis and spatial modeling is useful, but should not be regarded as over-restrictive. Frequently model-building and spatial analysis are very closely coupled, with the output of one leading to revisions in the other. This is particularly true of micro-modeling techniques, such as geosimulation, where results often 'emerge' from the modeling exercise and reveal unexpected patterns and behaviors which in turn lead to revised ideas and hypotheses (see for example, Section 8.2.3 on Agent Based Models).

All products describing themselves as geographic information systems have a core set of analytical facilities, including many of those we describe in this Guide. We cannot hope to draw examples from even a representative sample of products, so we have made our own selection, which we hope will provide sufficient coverage to illustrate the range of analytical techniques implemented in readily available toolsets. In addition to mainstream GIS products we have included a number of specialist tools that have specific spatial analysis functionality, and which provide either some GIS functionality and/or GIS file format input and/or output. Throughout this Guide there are many examples of the application of tools and models to geospatial problems. In addition, in Section 3.4, we discuss the application of certain types of modeling, particularly high-level process-flow models, to geospatial problems.

A recurrent theme in spatial analysis is the notion of *pattern*. Frequently the objective of analysis is described as being the identification and description of spatial patterns, leading on to attempts to understand and model the processes that have given rise to the observed patterns. Unfortunately the word 'pattern' has a very wide range of meanings and interpretations. One way of defining whether a particular set of observations constitute a spatial pattern is by attempting to define the opposite, i.e. what arrangements of objects are not considered to constitute a pattern. The generally agreed notion of *not a pattern* is a set of objects or an arrangement that provides no information to the observer. From a practical point of view no information is often the situation when the arrangement is truly random, or is indistinguishable from a random arrangement. An alternative definition might be an even arrangement of objects, with deviations from this uniformity considered as patterns. Thus spatial pattern is a relative concept, where a model of *not a pattern* (e.g. Complete Spatial Randomness or CSR) is a pre-condition (see for example, Figure 2-11).

Observed spatial arrangements are frequently of indirect or *mapped data* rather than direct observations — the process of data capture and storage (e.g. as points and lines or remote sensed images) has already imposed a model upon the source dataset and to an extent pre-determined aspects of the observable arrangements. The method(s) of visualization and the full and/or sampled extent of the dataset may also impose pre-conditions on the interpretation and investigation of spatial patterns.

Identification of spatial pattern is thus closely associated with a number of assumptions or pre-conditions: (i) the definition of what constitutes *not a pattern* for the purposes of the investigation; (ii) the definition of the dataset being studied (events/observations) and the spatial (and temporal) extent or scale of the observations; and (iii) the way in which the observations are made, modeled and recorded.

Observed patterns may *suggest* a causal relationship with one or more principal processes, but they do not provide a secure means of inference about process. For example, consider the case of the distribution of insect larvae. Imagine that an insect lays its eggs at a location in a large region at least 200 meters from the egg sites of other insects of the same species, and then flies away or dies. Other insects of the same species do likewise, at approximately the same time, each laying a random number of eggs, most of which hatch to form larvae that slowly crawl away in random directions from the original site for up to 100 meters. At some point in time shortly thereafter an observer samples a number of sites and records the pattern of all larvae within a given radius, say 10 meters. This pattern for each sampled site is then individually mapped and examined. The observer might find that the mapped patterns appear entirely random or might have a gradient of larvae density across the sampled regions. Zooming out to a 100m radius (i.e. using a larger region for sampling) a different pattern might have been observed, with a distinct center and decreasing numbers of larvae scattered in the sampled region away from this point. However, if observations had been made over 1km squares in a 10kmx10km region it might only have been practical to identify the centers or egg sites. At this scale the pattern may appear regular since we implied that each egg site is not randomly distributed, but is influenced by the location of other sites. However, it could equally well be the case that egg sites are actually random, but only eggs on those sites that are laid on suitable regularly distributed vegetation survive and go on to produce live larvae. Zooming out again to 100kmx100km the observer might find that all egg sites are located in particular sub-regions of the study area, thus appearing strongly clustered, a pattern perhaps related to an attraction factor between insects or uneven large-scale vegetation cover or some other environmental variable. The mapped patterns at any given scale may not be sufficient to enable the analyst to determine whether a given set of observations are random, evenly spread, clustered or exhibit some specific characteristic such as radial spread, nor to infer with any reliability that some particular process is at work (as discussed in Section

2.2.9: Detail, resolution, and scale and Section 5.4, Point Sets and Distance Statistics).

On the other hand it is fairly straightforward to generate particular spatial patterns, in the manner described above, using simple (stochastic) process models (see further, Section 5.4). These patterns are specific realizations of the models used, but there is no guarantee that the same pattern could not have been generated by an entirely different process. A specific mapped dataset *may* be regarded as a specific outcome of a set of (known and unknown) processes, and as such is but one of many possible outcomes or *process realizations*. To this extent, and perhaps to this extent only, such datasets can be thought of as samples (see further, Sections 2.3.8 and 2.4.4).

Thus the ANALYSIS phase can be seen as a multi-part exercise. It commences with the review of data collected and the manipulation of the many inputs to produce consistent and usable data. It then extends into the pure analytical phase, where the data is subjected to study in order to identify patterns of various kinds then help to develop new ideas and hypotheses regarding form and process. And this in turn may lead on to the use of or development of one or more models within a formal build-fit-criticize cycle. Finally the output of the models and analysis is examined, and where necessary the dataset and data gathering is re-visited, working back up the PPDAC model chain, prior to moving on to producing the output from the project and delivering this in the Conclusion stage.

### 3.3.5 Conclusions: Delivering the results

The last stage of the PPDAC process is that of reaching conclusions based upon the analyses conducted, and communicating these to others. Note that implementation of findings (e.g. actually proceeding with building a bypass, designating an area as unfit for habitation, or implementing a vaccination programme) does not form part of this model process, but lies beyond its confines.

*"The purpose of the Conclusion stage is to report the results of the study in the language of the Problem. Concise numerical summaries and presentation graphics [tabulations, maps, geovisualizations] should be used to clarify the discussion. Statistical jargon should be avoided. As well, the Conclusion provides an opportunity to discuss the strengths and weaknesses of the Plan, Data and Analysis especially in regards to possible errors that may have arisen"* Mackay and Oldford (2002)

For many problems treated in spatial analysis this summary is sufficient. For others the conclusions stage will be the start of additional work: re-visiting the problem and iterating the entire process or parts of the process; a new project; implementing proposals; wider consultation, such as public participation GIS (PPGIS, Communityviz), Geoweb applications (such as Digital globes and StreetView) and participatory 3D modeling (P3DM); and/or the development of models that help to understand or explain the observations, guide future data gathering, and predict data values at locations/times not included within the analysis.

# 3.4 Geospatial analysis and model building

Geospatial analysis often involves the design and execution of one or more 'models'. In many instances pre-existing models or simple variants of these are used. Such models may be provided within standard GIS packages, or they may be offered by third parties as add-ons, or they may have been specially developed for specific applications, such as airborne pollution dispersal modeling, flood modeling, wildfire management or traffic forecasting. In other cases models are designed using a number of approaches and tools, and then applied to address the specific problem at hand. The construction of such models follows the well-trodden procedure known as the "build-fit-criticize" cycle. This envisages the designer building a model on paper or computer or using a physical analogue, and then developing the model by evaluating its behavior under various conditions and datasets. By examining the performance of the model (the criticize part of the cycle) in terms of outputs, performance speed, completeness, robustness, efficiency, quality and ultimately, fitness for purpose, the model can be progressively improved and fine-tuned to meet the requirements.

Elsewhere in this Guide are many examples of specific and generic models that have been developed for use in the geospatial field. These range from simple deterministic models of behavior (distance decay models), to so-called 'cartographic modeling' (essentially map algebra and related operations), through to complex micro-simulation modeling frameworks that may be used for a wide range of bottom-up and dynamic modeling problems. Extended discussion of models and modeling in the context of geospatial analysis has been provided by Harvey (1968, Chs. 10-12), Goodchild et al. (1993) and Longley et al. (Chapters 8 and 16 of the forthcoming 3rd edition) and readers are recommended to review these discussions before embarking upon spatial model building. In particular Longley et al. characterize geospatial modeling, as opposed to analysis, as involving: multiple stages (perhaps representing different points in time); implementing ideas and hypotheses; and experimenting with policy options and scenarios.

Unfortunately, as with many other areas of GIS, the term model has acquired a wide range of meanings. In a number of GIS packages, such as ArcGIS and Idrisi, model building refers specifically to the use of graphical tools to design and execute a series of geoprocessing tasks. This provides both a way of designing and communicating the workflow associated with a task, and a means of implementing that workflow in a convenient manner. A very simple ArcGIS example illustrates this (Figure 3-5).

*Figure 3-5 Simple GIS graphical model (ESRI ArcGIS)*

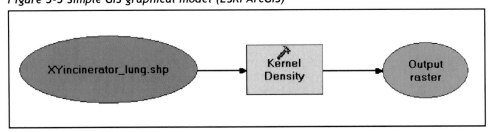

In this example two items have been dragged to the ArcGIS ModelBuilder design window: the first is a point set file (a shapefile of lung cancer cases from Lancashire, UK, which is an X,Y point set); the second is the geoprocessing function, Kernel Density, which generates two linked items in the graphical window, the processing function itself and the output raster. All that remains is to link the input shapefile to the processing function (identifying the input and flow) and then to run the 'model'. Each of the graphical entities can be clicked to specify attributes and parameters, and the model saved for future use. When the model is run an output raster of density data is generated, according to the parameters set in the model.

Clearly this is a trivial example — it is essentially an example of the simple form of general-purpose model structure:

INPUT → PROCESS → OUTPUT

This form of model can readily be developed in a number of ways. For example, in Figure 3-5 we have a single input, single output and single process. Many single geospatial processing operations require more than one input - for example, the *Overlay* and *Intersect* functions (note that the order in which links are established may be important). Likewise, some processing functions will produce multiple outputs.

Even this reflects a very simple model structure. In many real-world workflow situations a whole series of input → process → output steps are involved, with connections between the various outputs and the next stage of inputs. Such models may be structured into a series of sub-models, nested within a broader overall structure, designed to address a broader range of problems or a complex task. The process of analyzing a large task and breaking it down into smaller, more manageable components, is typical of systems analysis and business analysis exercises, which precede the process of systems design and implementation.

A very wide range of models can be constructed using this kind of approach, and optionally exported to a high-level programming language or script, such as Python or VBscript. Once in the explicit form of the preferred scripting language the functionality of the model can be examined closely, the ordering of links double-checked, extra functionality added, test datasets used to validate the model and outputs, and the 'program' retained for repeated use, perhaps with more complex parameterization of inputs.

The type of model described above is relatively simple, in that it flows from input to output in a well-defined manner, using pre-existing processing functionality. This is a static, deterministic model – the result is a specific output which will always be generated in the same manner from a given input. This is ideal for a range well-defined processing tasks, but is still limited in terms of model functionality.

One way to make high-level models of this type become more like traditional concepts of high-level or 'top-down' model-building is to incorporate new, purpose-designed, processing modules within the flow. This could involve entirely new model component design, or the development of components that incorporate pre-existing facilities within the GIS package or from third party toolsets (which may or may not be GIS-package related). Typically such models are designed as block diagrams with flows, rather as with the simple models described earlier, but with a much wider range of operations within and between blocks permitted. In particular, one development of the high-level model framework is to permit iterative behavior, leading to models with a dynamic-like structure. In such models one or more output datasets becomes the input data for the next iteration. A series of iterations are then run, with intermediate outputs providing a time-like profile for the model. Indeed, generating a large number of iterations may produce a series of raster grids which provide a sufficient number of data 'frames' to generate a video of the process as it develops.

Another common development for high-level models is to build-in stochastic behavior for some components, thus enabling a range of outcomes to be generated from a single starting set of data. In such models the results are obtained after repeated runs of the model, generating a range of outcomes and a probability 'envelope' of results. Non-deterministic models of this type are especially appropriate in forecasting or predictive studies.

Figure 3-6 illustrates the kind of model of this type that can be constructed using Idrisi. In this instance a static model was initially designed to predict areas of likely residential expansion within land use classes designated as 'forest'. The initial input is the pattern of residential land use in 1991 (RESIDENTIAL91) together with a pre-existing low density residential suitability raster (LDRESSUIT) which is based on factors such as proximity to roads, terrain etc. Both these input files are grids with matching size (565x452 cells) and resolution. In the model diagram rectangular boxes are grids and processing modules are parallelograms. The details of the model are not especially important here, but one can see that the process flows from top left (inputs) to bottom right) output, and is concluded with an overlay of the original input grid and the model output grid (NEWRESID) to produce a map which highlights the predicted growth.

*Figure 3-6 Dynamic residential growth model (Idrisi)*

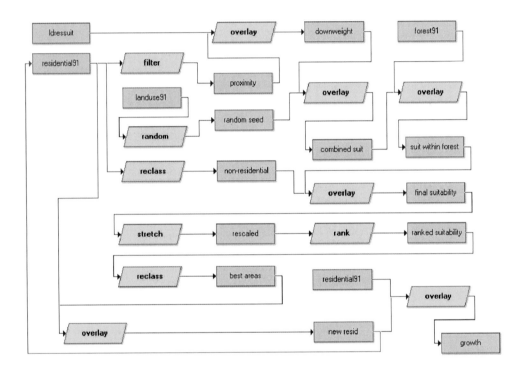

This static model forms part of the tutorial data distributed with the software, so readers can work through this example themselves if they have access to Idrisi. There are two aspects of this particular model we wish to highlight: the first is the process box marked RANDOM which appears early in the process – this takes as input the LANDUSE91 grid and introduces a small random chance that forested land might convert to residential in any part of the study area; the second aspect is the red line at the bottom of the model, which takes the output (NEWRESID) and feeds it back as the input for the next iteration of the model. This feedback loop provides a form of dynamic modeling, and enables the overall model to be run for a number of iterations, with intermediate growth maps and associated data being optionally retained for closer examination. Clearly these kinds of macro-level models can provide a very powerful framework for certain classes of geospatial analysis, especially when addressing complex recurring processing tasks and when examining alternative scenarios in multi-criteria decision making problems.

GIS data and analytical processes often contribute a part of a larger multi-disciplinary modeling process. Consider, for example, the FlamMap wildfire modeling system. Input to this model includes eight GIS raster layers that describe the 'fuels' and topography: elevation, slope, aspect, fuel model, canopy cover, canopy height, crown base height and crown bulk density; these layers are then combined in the model with an Initial Fuel Moistures file, and optional components including the inclusion of a custom Fuel Model, weather, and wind files. Within the model further models are applied in combination: a surface fire model; crown fire initiation model; crown fire

spread model and a dead fuel moisture model. This example serves to illustrate how many components make up many real-world operational models. In this instance GIS provides key inputs, and also is used to map key outputs, which are produced in the form of both raster and vector files for subsequent mapping. These outputs are then utilized in a second stage of spatial analysis, covering issues such as risk and impact assessment (Figure 3-7), fire management planning, and comparing modeled minimum travel time (MTT) and travel paths of a fire front to actual data. The FlamMap input and output data used to create Figure 3-7, with accompanying metadata and output files, is available from ForestERA.

*Figure 3-7 Modeling wildfire risks, Arizona, USA*

## Fire risk assessment - western Mogollon Plateau

*© Forest Ecosystem Restoration Analysis (ForestERA) project, Northern Arizona University (NAU).*

Dynamic modeling may be implemented in many other ways. These range from traditional mathematical models, e.g. using computational fluid dynamics (CFD) to model flow processes; to micro-scale simulation using agent-based modeling (ABM, see further Section 8.1 on Geocomputation and Section 8.2 which addresses Geosimulation); and a variety of real-time dynamical systems. Examples of the latter include systems that support interfaces for receiving geospatial data in real-time (such as satellite and mobile field-based georeferenced data), and systems that provide interactive interfaces that allow users to explore and manipulate the physical and parameter space of the models they are using. In this context new forms of interactive and dynamic visualization are of increasing importance, facilitating and supporting the analysis and decision-making process.

Models that generate relatively narrow solution envelopes, that have been validated with current or past datasets, may provide greater confidence in forecast values than models that have a wide spread of possible outcomes. On the other hand, such models may give a narrow range of results because they are built to mimic existing data (as occurs with many neural network models) or because the range of possible outcomes has been limited by the model design and parameterization. Models that generate consistently good predictions over time, with a wide range of input data, can reasonably be regarded as more robust and less uncertain, and hence to this degree are 'better' than models that have limited predictive success or which have had limited testing with real-world data. It is highly desirable that models that provide predictions (spatial, temporal) include estimates of the uncertainty associated with these predictions, as this helps the end user when making judgments about the results presented, for example in risk assessment situations. For example, the FlamMap output used to create Figure 3-7 includes a matching uncertainty raster, as does the modeling of zinc concentrations in the soil in Figure 6-46B and Figure 6-47B. Ideally, for major areas of long-term concern, models are continually refined and improved in the light of experience, testing and new and improved source of data and infrastructure.

In many types of geospatial model it is normal for the outcomes to vary according to the way in which input parameters are varied and the relative importance, or weight, that is attached to the various model components – these elements can be thought of as the 'parameter space' for a given model. For example, the decision as to where to locate a waste-processing plant will depend on a large number of input variables. Each may have a different weight or set of weights that might be applied: construction costs; air pollution; noise; transport access; proximity to water supplies; proximity to existing and planned residential areas; usage costs; visibility etc. The selection of these weights, typically by specialists in the individual disciplines and/or involving public participation, will influence the range of outcomes that might subsequently be evaluated by the planning team. Although not widely available within GIS packages, such multi-criteria decision making (MCDM) frameworks can and have been formalized (e.g. using AHP, ANP and similar procedures), and are implemented in some GIS packages (such as Idrisi).

It is important to note that such procedures can be extremely heavy users of computer resource, not just processing power but also memory and disk storage, especially where sizeable intermediate raster files are generated and retained. This in turn leads to important questions as to model design and implementation. For example, it may be effective to use a high-level modeling facility to create the basic structure and program for a particular problem, and then to re-implement all or part of this process by modifying the generated code or implementing the model in a different software environment. This might be a high-resource environment such as a network service or Grid computing facility or a high performance special application. An example of a simple alteration to the storage of intermediate grids would be to store the initial grid plus the changes between grids (i.e. incremental differences), since the latter can generally be stored in a far more compact manner.

An illustration of the value of implementing geospatial models in a different software environment is the widespread use of application-specific modeling tools that accept standard GIS files as input and generate GIS data files as optional output (sometimes referred to as 'loose coupling'). Many engineering-based models adopt this approach — examples include: hydrographic modeling (e.g. the Groundwater Modeling System from EMS-i); sound and pollution modeling (e.g. the CadnaA noise mapping facilities from DataKustik); telecommunications planning (e.g. the Cellular Expert software from HNIC-Baltic — actually an example of close-coupling); and wildfire management (see, for example, the FlamMap fire behavior modeling and mapping system discussed earlier). Researchers and analysts in the GIS field should always ensure that they investigate work carried out in other disciplines, especially where there are strong application-specific features of the problem under investigation. In such cases there may well be tools, models, datasets and techniques readily available or suitable for modification that can be of enormous assistance.

# 3.5 The changing context of GIScience

The preceding discussion of the PPDAC methodology has illustrated how the data used for decision-making in a wide range of applications areas often have a spatial component. The general context to the supply and provision of spatially referenced data has changed profoundly over the last 20 years and this has had far-reaching implications for the practice of applications-led science. Specifically:

- Most developed countries now have advanced spatial data infrastructures, comprising 'framework' data. Such data typically record the variable nature of the Earth's surface, landscape characteristics, and a range of artificial structures ranging from roads to mail delivery points. This provides valuable context for decision-making. Even in parts of the world where this is not the case, high resolution remote sensing imagery or the data sources assembled into the 'virtual Earths' of Google and Microsoft can provide an acceptable framework from which environmental, population and infrastructure characteristics can be ascertained

- Advances in data dissemination technologies, such as geoportals, have encouraged governments to disseminate public sector data on social, health, economic, demographic, labor market and business activity to the widest possible audiences (e.g. www.statistics.gov.uk; www.geodata.gov). Many geoportals include metadata ('data about data') on their holdings, which can be used to establish the provenance of a dataset for a given application. The advent of geoportals is having a catalytic role in stimulating public participation in GIS (PPGIS, Communityviz, MapTube), and for example amongst genealogists when historic census data are put online. Of more central importance to professional users, geoportals empower very many more users to assemble datasets across domains and create added value information products for specific uses

- Advances in data capture and collection are leading to conventional data sources being supplemented, and in some cases partially replaced, with additional measures of physical, social and environmental information. Developments in the supply and assembly of volunteered geographic information are creating new spatial data infrastructures such as OpenStreetMap (www.openstreetmap.org), that help to contextualize spatial data and enhance geovisualization. Additional framework data sources are being provided by the likes of Microsoft and Google, underpinned by an advertising led business model. This is creating challenges for those national mapping agencies that are required to recover most of their costs through user charges and copyright enforcement. One scenario is that the monolithic structure of parts of the data industry may become obsolete. In the socio-economic realm, Longley and Harris (1999) have written about the ways in which routine customer transactions in retailing, for example, are captured and may be used to supplement census-based measures of store catchment characteristics. Although the provenance of such data sources is less certain than that of conventional censuses and other government surveys, there is nonetheless some movement towards adoption of rolling surveys and other sample-based methods to replace conventional censuses

- There is now a greater focus upon metadata. As suggested above, the proliferation of data sources from formal and informal sources is leading to greater concern with the quality and provenance of data, and the situations in which such data are fit for purpose. This is particularly important post the innovation of the Internet, since data collectors, custodians and users are often now much more dispersed in space and time, and Internet GIS enables much greater apparent ease in conflating and concatenating remotely located data

- Allied to the previous two points, there is a wider realization that the potential of data collected by public sector agencies at the local level or at fine levels of granularity, remains under-exploited. There exist very good prospects for public sector organizations to 'pool' data pertaining to their local operations, to the good of the populations that they serve. Innovations such as Google Earth are making it easy for organizations with no previous experience of GIS to add spatial context to their own data

- The practice of science itself is changing. Goodchild and Longley (1999) have written of the increasingly interdisciplinary setting to the creation of GIS applications, of the creation and maintenance of updates of GIS databases in real time, and of the assembly and disbanding of task-centered GIS teams — most obviously in emergency scenarios, but increasingly across the entire domain of GIS activity

Each of these developments potentially contributes to the development of GIS applications that are much more data rich than hitherto. Yet such applications may be misguided if the analyst is unaware of the scientific basis to data collection, the assumptions implicitly invoked in conflation and concatenation of different datasets, or general issues of data quality. Additionally, the creation of GIS applications and the dissemination of results may be subject to a range of ethical considerations, and issues of accountability and data ownership. The remaining sections of this Guide give the flavor of these issues, and illustrate the ways in which GIS based representations are sensitive to the properties of software and the data that are used. In an ideal world, all data and software would be freely available, but in practice such a world would be unlikely to prioritize investments for future applications development. In the case of software, public domain sources are by no means all open source, but it is possible to form a view as to the quality of a software product by examining the nature of the results that it yields compared against those obtained using similar software offerings and known results with test datasets. Gauging the provenance of data sources is often an altogether trickier proposition, however. In seeking to validate one dataset with reference to a second, as in the comparison of two digitized street network products or the classification of two remotely sensed data resources, analysis of mismatches is more likely to suggest uncertainties than pinpoint precisely measurable inaccuracies. Discrepancies are only ultimately reconcilable through time-consuming field measurement, although models of error propagation and understanding of data lineage or classification method may optimize use of scarce validation resources.

While it is possible to validate some of the data used in representations of built or natural environments, validation of social measurements is an altogether more problematic task (Kempf-Leonard, 2005). Repeated measurement designs are usually prohibitively expensive, and some of the attitudes and behaviors that are under investigation may in any case be transient or ephemeral in nature. In general terms it is helpful to distinguish between *direct* versus *indirect* indicators of human populations. A direct indicator bears a clear and identifiable correspondence with a focus of interest: net (earned plus unearned) income, along with measures of wealth accumulated in assets provides a direct indicator of affluence. Direct indicators may be time-consuming or difficult to measure in practice (how affluent are you?), as well as being invasive of personal privacy. Thus many data sources rely upon indirect indicators, which are easier to assemble in practice, but which bear a less direct correspondence with the phenomenon of interest — housing tenure, car ownership and possession of selected consumer durables might be used in a composite indicator of affluence, for example.

Many of these issues are crystallized in the current focus upon 'spatial literacy', which has been defined by the National Research Council (NRC), part of the US National Academy of

Sciences, as comprising the following integrated components:

- understanding spatial relationships
- developing knowledge about how geographic space is represented; and
- the ability to reason and make key decisions about spatial concepts

In this Guide we seek to demonstrate how the *practice* of GIS is fundamentally about finding out about the real (geographic) world. To quote the NRC (2006):

*Spatial thinking is a cognitive skill that can be used in everyday life, the workplace, and science to structure problems, find answers, and express solutions using the properties of space*

# 4 Building Blocks of Spatial Analysis

## 4.1 Spatial Data Models and Methods

Spatial datasets make it possible to build operational models of the real world based upon the field and object conceptions discussed in Section 2.2.6 and the use of coordinate geometry to represent the object classes described in Section 2.2.3. These include: discrete sets of point locations; ordered sets of points (open sets forming composite lines or *polylines*, and closed, non-crossing sets, forming *simple polygons*); and a variety of representations of continuously varying phenomena, sometimes described as surfaces or fields. The latter are frequently represented as a continuous grid of square cells, each containing a value indicating the (estimated) average height or strength of the field in that cell. In most of the literature and within software packages the points/ lines/ areas model is described as vector data, whilst the grid model is described as raster (or image) data.

Longley *et al.* (2005, and in the forthcoming 3$^{rd}$ edition) provide a summary of spatial data models used in GIS and example applications (Table 4-1). The distinctions are not as clear-cut as they may appear, however. For example, vector data may be converted (or transformed) into a raster representation, and vice versa. Transformation in most cases will result in a loss of information (e.g. resolution, topological structure) and thus such transformations may not be reversible. For example, suppose we have a raster map containing a number of distinct zones (groups of adjacent cells) representing soil type. To convert this map to vector form you will need to specify the target vector form you wish to end up with (polygon in this example) and then apply a conversion operation that will locate the boundaries of the zones and replace these with a complex jagged set of polygons following the outline of the grid form. These

polygons may then be automatically or selectively smoothed to provide a simplified and more acceptable vector representation of the data. Reversing this process, by taking the smoothed vector map and generating a raster output, will generally result in a slightly different output file from the one we started with, for various reasons including: the degree of boundary detection and simplification undertaken during vectorization; the precise nature of the boundary detection and conversion algorithms applied both when vectorising and rasterizing; and the way in which special cases are handled, e.g. edges of the map, "open zones", isolated cells or cells with missing values.

*Table 4-1 Geographic data models*

| Data model | Example application |
|---|---|
| Computer-aided design (CAD) | Automated engineering design and drafting |
| Graphical (non-topological) | Simple mapping |
| Image | Image processing and simple grid analysis |
| Raster/grid | Spatial analysis and modeling, especially in environmental and natural resource applications |
| Vector/Geo-relational topological | Many operations on vector geometric features in cartography, socio-economic and resource analysis, and modeling |
| Network | Network analysis in transportation, hydrology and utilities |
| Triangulated irregular network (TIN) | Surface/terrain visualization |
| Object | Many operations on all types of entities (raster/vector/TIN etc.) in all types of application |

Similar issues arise when vector or raster datasets are manipulated and/or combined in various ways (e.g. filtering, resampling). In the following sections we describe a large variety of such operations that are provided in many of the leading software packages. We concentrate on those operations which directly or indirectly form part of analysis and/or modeling procedures, rather than those relating to data collection, referencing and management. These processes include the various "methods" that form part of the OGC simple "feature specifications" (Table 4-2) and test protocols, including the procedures for determining convex hulls, buffering, distances, set-like

operators (e.g. spatial intersection, union etc.) and similar spatial operations. In each case it is important to be aware that data manipulation will almost always alter the data in both expected and unexpected ways, in many instances resulting in some loss of information. For this reason it is usual for new map layers and associated tables, and/or output files, to be created or augmented rather than source datasets modified. In many cases these procedures are closely related to the discipline known as Computational Geometry.

*Table 4-2 OGC OpenGIS Simple Features Specification — Principal Methods*

| Method | Description |
|---|---|
| **Spatial relations** | |
| Equals | spatially equal to: $a=b$ |
| Disjoint | spatially disjoint: equivalent to $a \cap b = \varnothing$ |
| Intersects | spatially intersects: $[a \cap b]$ is equivalent to [not $a$ disjoint($b$)] |
| Touches | spatially touches: equivalent to $[a \cap b = \varnothing$ and $I(a) \cap I(b) = \varnothing]$; does not apply if $a$ and $b$ are points |
| Crosses | spatially crosses: equivalent to $[\dim(I(a) \cap I(b)) < \max\{\dim(I(a)), \dim(I(b))\}$ and $a \cap b \neq a$ and $a \cap b \neq b]$ |
| Within | spatially within: within($b$) is equivalent to $[a \cap b = a$ and $I(a) \cap I(b) \neq \varnothing]$ |
| Contains | spatially contains: [$a$ contains($b$)] is equivalent to [$b$ within($a$)] |
| Overlaps | spatially overlaps: equivalent to $[\dim(I(a) \cap I(b)) = \dim(I(a)) = \dim(I(b))$ and $a \cap b \neq a$ and $a \cap b \neq b]$ |
| Relate | spatially relates, tested by checking for intersections between the interior, boundary and exterior of the two components |
| **Spatial analysis** | |
| Distance | the shortest distance between any two points in the two geometries as calculated in the spatial reference system of this geometry |
| Buffer | all points whose distance from this geometry is less than or equal to a specified distance value |
| Convex Hull | the convex hull of this geometry (see further, Section 4.2.13.1) |
| Intersection | the point set intersection of the current geometry with another selected geometry |
| Union | the point set union of the current geometry with another selected geometry |
| Difference | the point set difference of the current geometry with another selected geometry |
| Symmetric difference | the point set symmetric difference of the current geometry with another selected geometry (logical XOR) |

**Note:** $a$ and $b$ are two geometries (one or more geometric objects or features — points, line objects, polygons, surfaces including their boundaries); $I(x)$ is the interior of $x$; $\dim(x)$ is the dimension of $x$, or maximum dimension if $x$ is the result of a relational operation

# 4.2 Geometric and Related Operations

Individual vector features (e.g. polygons) and groups of grid cells exhibit a range of distinctive spatial attributes — for example the *length* of a polyline or polygon boundary and the *area* of a polygon or grid patch. In this section we examine a number of basic geometric attributes that apply to such features. These basic attributes may be included in the attribute table record associated with each feature, or may be treated as an *intrinsic* attribute that may be computed on demand and optionally added as a field in the associated table. If it is necessary to perform operations on these attributes, for example sorting areas by size, or calculating the ratio of areas to perimeters, it is helpful and often more efficient to add the data as an explicit field if it is not already available.

## 4.2.1 Length and area for vector data

Since the majority of GIS mapping involves the use of datasets that are provided in projected, plane coordinates, distances and associated operations such as area calculations are carried out using Euclidean geometry. Polygon areas (and the areas of sections of polygons) are calculated using integration by the trapezoidal or Simpson's rule, taking advantage of the fact that progressing clockwise around all the polygon vertices generates the desired result.

For example, in Figure 4-1 the area between the x-axis and the two vertical lines at $x_1$ and $x_2$ is simply the width between the two lines, i.e. $(x_2-x_1)$ times the average height of the two verticals, i.e. $(y_1+y_2)/2$, giving a rectangle like the first one shown to the right of the polygon. Thus this rectangle has area:

$$A_1 = \frac{1}{2}(x_2 - x_1)(y_1 + y_2)$$

The area between the x-axis and the two verticals at $x_2$ and $x_3$ is shown by the second narrow rectangle, and if we then subtract the shorter and wider rectangle, which represents the area outside of the polygon between the two vertical lines of interest, we obtain the area of the part of the overall polygon we are interested in (A,B,C,D). More generally, if we take the $(n-1)$ distinct coordinates of the polygon vertices to be the set $\{x_i,y_i\}$ with $(x_n,y_n)=(x_1,y_1)$ then the total area of the polygon is given by:

$$A = \frac{1}{2}\sum_{i=1}^{n-1}(x_{i+1} - x_i)(y_i + y_{i+1})$$

*Figure 4-1 Area calculation using Simpson's rule*

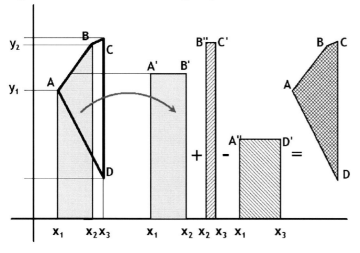

Traversing a polygon in a clockwise direction generates a sequence of positive and negative rectangular sections (negative when $x_i$ is less than $x_{i+1}$) whose total sums to a positive value, the area of the polygon. Multiplying out the brackets the formula can also be written as

$$A = \frac{1}{2}\sum_{i=1}^{n-1}(x_{i+1}y_i - x_iy_{i+1})$$

This is an expression we use again in Section 4.2.5.1, in connection with the determination of polygon centroids. If the order is reversed the total is the same but has a negative sign. This feature can be used to remove unwanted polygons contained within the main polygon (e.g. areas of water or built-up zones within a district when calculating available land area for farming or the area to be included and excluded in density or similar areal computations). The procedure fails if the polygon is self-crossing (which should not occur in well-structure GIS files) or if some of the y-coordinates are negative — in this latter case either positive-only coordinate systems should be used or a fixed value added (temporarily) to all y-coordinate values to ensure they all remain positive during the calculation process.

Lengths and areas are normally computed using Cartesian (x,y) coordinates, which is satisfactory for most purposes where small regions (under 100 kms x 100 kms) are involved. For larger areas, such as entire countries or continents, and where data are stored and manipulated in latitude/longitude form, lengths (distances) and areas should be computed using spherical or similar measures (e.g. ellipsoidal, geoidal). If one uses Cartesian calculations over large regions the results will be incorrect — for example, using the standard ArcGIS measure tool to show the distance between Cairo and Capetown on a map of Africa will give a value substantially different from the "true", great circle distance (depending on the projection applied in ArcGIS v9.3 and above the great circle distance can be obtained if the SHIFT key is held down whilst using the measure tool). Computation of polygon areas using spherical or ellipsoidal

models is complex, requiring careful numerical integration. Functions such as AREAINT in the Mapping Toolbox of MATLab provide such facilities, and the source code for the module can be inspected and amended if required. It should also be noted that in most cases only two coordinates are utilized, whereas on surfaces with variable heights three dimensional distances, areas and volumetric analysis may be more appropriate (see further, Section 4.2.3).

In some cases GIS software products will select the appropriate calculation method based on the dataset, whilst in others (e.g. MapInfo) the option to specify Cartesian or Spherical computation may be provided where relevant. If we identify two mapped locations as having Cartesian coordinates $(x_i,y_i)$ and $(x_j,y_j)$ then the distance between them, $d_{ij}$, is simply the familiar:

$$d_{ij} = \sqrt{(x_i - x_j)^2 + (y_i - y_j)^2}$$

The length of a polyline or perimeter length of a polygon is then computed as the sum of the individual segments comprising the feature. Distances calculated using this formula, or the 3D equivalent, we shall denote $d_E$, or Euclidean distance.

A straight line, $l$, in the x-y plane can be expressed as an equation: $ax+by+c=0$, where $a$, $b$ and $c$ are constants. Using this formulation the Euclidean distance of a point $p(x_p,y_p)$ from this line is given by:

$$d_{(p,l)} = \frac{|ax_p + by_p + c|}{\sqrt{(a^2 + b^2)}}$$

Within GIS the distance from a point to a line segment or set of line segments (e.g. a polyline) is frequently needed. This requires computation of one of three possible distances for each (point, line segment) pair: (i) if a line can be extended from the sample point that is orthogonal to the line segment, then the distance can be computed using the general formula $d_{p,l}$ provided above; (ii) and (iii) if case (i) does not apply, the sample point must lie in a position that means the closest point of the line segment is one of its two end points. The minimum of these two is taken in this instance. The process is then repeated for each part of the polyline and the minimum of all the lengths computed selected.

In spherical coordinates the (great circle) distance equation often quoted is the so-called Cosine formula:

$$d_{ij} = R\cos^{-1}\left[\sin\varphi_i \sin\varphi_j + \cos\varphi_i \cos\varphi_j \cos(\lambda_i - \lambda_j)\right]$$

where: $R$ is the radius of the Earth (e.g. the average radius of the WGS84 ellipsoid); $(\varphi, \lambda)$ pairs are the latitude and longitude values for the points under consideration; and $-180 \le \lambda \le 180$, $-90 \le \varphi \le 90$ (in degrees, although such calculations normally are computed using radians; n.b. 180 degrees=Pi radians and one radian=57.30 degrees). This formula is sensitive to computational errors in some instances (very small angular differences). A safer equation to use is the Haversine formula:

$$d_{ij} = 2R\sin^{-1}\left(\sqrt{\sin^2(A) + \sin^2(B)\cos\varphi_i \cos\varphi_j}\right)$$

where: $A = \dfrac{\varphi_i - \varphi_j}{2}, B = \dfrac{\lambda_i - \lambda_j}{2}$

Most GIS packages do not specify how they carry out such operations, although in many cases basic computations are made using the Euclidean metric and reported in decimal degrees. Distances calculated using the Haversine formula we shall denote $d_S$, or Spherical distance.

## 4.2.2 Length and area for raster datasets

Length and area computations may also be meaningful for grid datasets, and in this case the base calculations are very simple, reflecting the grid cell size or resolution (summing the number of cells and multiplying by the edge length or edge length squared, as appropriate). The difficulty in this case is in the definition of what comprises a line or "polygon". A set of contiguous cells (a clump or patch) with a common attribute value or classification (e.g. deciduous woodland) has an area determined by the number of cells in the clump and the grid resolution. The perimeter length of the clump is a little less obvious. Taking the perimeter as the length of the external boundary of each cell in the clump appears to be the simplest definition, although this will be much longer than a vectorised (smoothed) equivalent measure (typically around 50% longer). Furthermore, depending on the software used, differences in definition of what a clump is (for example, whether a clump can include holes, open edges that are not part of the perimeter, cells whose attributes do not match those of the remaining cells) will result in variations in both area and perimeter calculation.

Many environmental science datasets (e.g. soil type, land-use, vegetation cover) show a near continuous spread of attribute values across cells, with few if any distinct sharp breaks. In this case boundaries are less definitive, determined more by common consent or other procedures (see further, Section 4.2.9) than by clear demarcation of cell values. The determination of areas and perimeters of zones in such cases is less clear, although some progress has been made using the concept of *membership functions* (MFs). A further issue with gridded data is that the gridding model (or imaging process) results in distortions or constraints on the way in which data are processed. The distortions are primarily of three kinds — Orientation, Metrics and Resolution:

**Orientation** — with a single rectangular grid the allocation of source data values to cells and the calculations of lengths and areas will alter if the grid is first rotated; with two or more grids common orientation and resolution are essential if data are to be combined in any way. This may mean that source data (e.g. remote sensed images) will have been manipulated prior to provision of the gridded data to ensure matching is possible, with each source item receiving separate treatment to achieve this end, and/or that data will require resampling during processing. Of course, with multi-band data relating to a single image the orientation and resolution will always match.

**Metrics** — in order to compute distances for gridded data it is common to add up the number of cells comprising a line or boundary and multiplying this number by the cell edge length, $E$. This is essentially a "rook's move" calculation, zig-zagging across the grid, although it may be adjusted by allowing diagonal or "bishop's moves" also (see Figure 4-2). Diagonal lengths are then taken as $E\sqrt{2}$.

*Figure 4-2 3x3 grid neighborhood*

This 3x3 neighborhood model is used in many areas of geospatial analysis, including distance computations, image processing, cellular automata methods (where the complete 8-cell set that surrounds the central cell is known as the Moore neighborhood (see further, Section 8.2.2), surface analysis, and spatial autocorrelation analysis amongst others.

These methods only provide correct values for the distance between cells in 4 or 8 directions, with global distances to all other directions (for example, those highlighted in gray in Figure 4-3) being in error by up to 41% for the 4-point rook's move model and 7.6% for the 8-point queen's move model. Each of the squares shown in gray below are 2.24 units from the central cell but would be calculated as either 3 units away (rook's move) or 2.41 units (queen's move). The position of these gray squares is sometimes described as Knight's move, again by reference to the movement of chess pieces.

*Figure 4-3 5x5 grid neighborhood*

Similar issues arise in computations of cost distance, path alignment and the calculation of surface gradient, aspect and related measures (e.g. material flows). This is not always a question of what is correct or incorrect in some absolute sense, since this will be determined by the application and adequacy or appropriateness of the approach adopted, but it is a significant issue to be aware of.

**Resolution** — the cell size (and shape) of a grid or image file and the range of attribute values assigned to cells has an important role to play in spatial measures and analysis. Amongst the more obvious is the fact that finer resolution images/grids provide more detailed representation of points, lines and areas, as well as a finer breakdown of associated attribute data. But there are many additional factors to be considered, including the increase in data and processing overhead with finer resolutions. Another factor is the implication that an attribute value assigned to a cell applies throughout the cell, so larger cells imply a greater degree of averaging, including the possibility of missing important variations within the cell. At one extreme, assuming cells are assigned a single attribute value, a grid consisting of a single huge cell will show no variation in attribute values at all, whilst variation between cells will tend to increase as cell sizes are reduced and the number of cells increases. At the other extreme, with cell sizes that are extremely small (and thus very large in number) every cell may be different and contain a unique value or a single observation (presence/ absence). Likewise, with attributes showing binary presence/ absence all cells will show either presence or absence, whilst with continuous variables (e.g. terrain height, soil moisture levels) entries may be continuous (e.g. any real positive number) or categorized (e.g. coded as 0-255 in an 8-bit attribute coding). Cell entries may also be counts of events, in which cases the earlier comments on cell size have a direct bearing — with one large cell all $N$ observations will fall in the single grid cell, whilst with smaller cell sizes there will be a range of values $0 \leq n \leq N$ until with very small cell sizes the only values for $n$

will be 0 and 1 unless events are precisely co-located.

### 4.2.3 Surface area

#### 4.2.3.1 Projected surfaces

Most GIS packages report planar area, not surface area. Some packages, such as ArcGIS (3D Analyst) and Surfer provide the option to compute surface area. Computation of surface areas will result in a value that is greater than or equal to the equivalent planar projection of the surface. The ratio between the two values provides a crude index of surface roughness.

If a surface is represented in TIN form, the surface area is simply the sum of the areas of the triangular elements that make up the TIN. Let $T_j=\{x_{ij},y_{ij},z_{ij}\}$ $i=1,2,3$ be the coordinates of the corner points of the $j^{th}$ TIN element. Then the surface area of the planar triangular (or *planimetric* area) determined when z=constant, can be calculated from a series of simple cross-products:

$$A_j = \frac{1}{2}\begin{pmatrix} + x_{2j}y_{1j} + x_{3j}y_{2j} + x_{1j}y_{3j} \\ - x_{1j}y_{2j} - x_{2j}y_{3j} - x_{3j}y_{1j} \end{pmatrix}$$

Note that this expression is the same as the polygon area formula we provided earlier, but for a (n-1)=3-vertex polygon:

$$A = \frac{1}{2}\sum_{i=1}^{3}(x_{i+1}y_i - x_iy_{i+1})$$

where i+1=4 is defined as the first point, i=1. The term inside the brackets is the entire area of a parallelogram, and half this gives us our triangle area. This expression can also be written in a convenient matrix determinant form (ignoring the j's for now) as:

$$A = -\frac{1}{2}\begin{vmatrix} x_1 & y_1 & 1 \\ x_2 & y_2 & 1 \\ x_3 & y_3 & 1 \end{vmatrix}$$

If the slope of $T_j$, $\theta_j$, is already known or easily computed, the area of $T_j$ can be directly estimated as $A_j/cos(\theta_j)$ (Figure 4-4). Alternatively the three dimensional equivalent of the matrix expression above can be written in a similar form, as:

$$A = \frac{1}{2}\sqrt{\begin{vmatrix} x_1 & y_1 & 1 \\ x_2 & y_2 & 1 \\ x_3 & y_3 & 1 \end{vmatrix}^2 + \begin{vmatrix} y_1 & z_1 & 1 \\ y_2 & z_2 & 1 \\ y_3 & z_3 & 1 \end{vmatrix}^2 + \begin{vmatrix} z_1 & x_1 & 1 \\ z_2 & x_2 & 1 \\ z_3 & x_3 & 1 \end{vmatrix}^2}$$

If z=0 for all *i*, the second and third terms in this expression disappear and we are left with the result for the plane. Suppose that we have a plane right angled triangle with sides 1,1 and √2, defined by the 3D coordinates: (0,0,0), (1,0,0) and (1,1,0). This plane triangle has area of one half of a square of side length 1, so its area is 0.5 units, as can be confirmed using the first formula above. If we now set one corner, say the point (1,1,0) to have a z-value (height) of 1, its coordinate becomes (1,1,1) and the area increases to 0.7071 units, i.e. by around 40%.

*Figure 4-4 Planimetric and surface area of a 3D triangle*

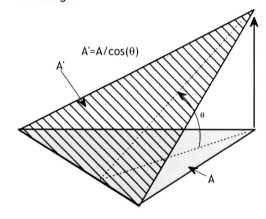

If the surface representation is not in TIN form, but represented as a grid or DEM, surface area can again be computed by TIN-like computations. In this case the 8-position immediate neighborhood of each cell can be remapped as a set of 8 triangles connecting the center-points of each cell to the target cell. Connecting all cell centers in this way creates a form of TIN and surface computation proceeds as described above – this is the procedure used in ArcGIS (3D Analyst). A more sophisticated method involves a similar form of computation but calculated on a cell-by-cell weighted basis. In this procedure the surface area for each cell is taken as a weighted sum of eight small triangular areas. The area of triangles centered on the target cell are computed and 25% of each such area is assigned to the central cell (shaded gray in Figure 4-5B).

### Figure 4-5 DEM surface area

A. 3x3 DEM element

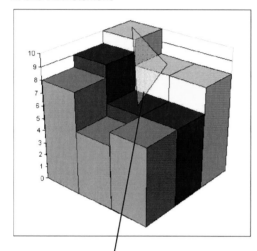

B. Plan view of triangular components

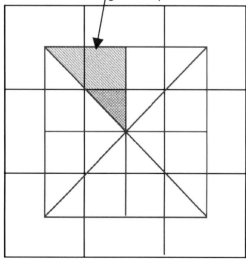

Research has suggested that the resulting total surface area for the cell is close to that produced by TIN models for grids of 250+ cells. We can examine this model more closely by taking a specific example. Let us assume that the 3x3 DEM surface segment in Figure 4-5 has cells which are 1 meter square and elevation values given in meters as shown below:

```
10  8  8
 9  6  6
 8  5  6
```

The nine individual cells can be referenced in various ways – below use a simple numerical referencing around the central or target cell:

```
1  2  3
8  0  4
7  6  5
```

The planar area of each cell is simply 1x1, so 1 square meter. To compute the estimated *surface* area we need to calculate the area of each of the 8 sloping triangles and allocate 25% of this area to the central cell. To do this we use the determinant expression shown earlier. For the triangle shown in Figure 4-5A (the triangle connecting cells 1-2-0) this gives an area of 3/2, so 25% of this gives 3/8 units as opposed to the 1/8 units that to a flat triangle such as 0-4-5. Continuing this computation for all 8 triangles gives the overall estimated surface area using this algorithm as 2.5 sq.m. The process is then repeated for every pixel, adjusting for edge effects where necessary as with many other operations of this type (e.g. by adding a temporary row or column to each edge that duplicates the existing values).

This example is unrealistic of course since In most DEM datasets the horizontal and vertical scales are not the same. For example, if the individual cell sizes in the example above are 10 meters x 10 meters and the vertical measurements are in meters, the procedure yields a surface area approximately 3% greater than the planar area. Grid surface areas can also be computed using the slope adjustment method described above assuming that a slope grid has been first been computed, or using grid data with linear interpolation to facilitate simpler 3D quadrilateral computations.

Surface areas are computed relative to a reference plane, usually $z=z_{min}$ or $z=0$. In some instances it may be necessary to specify the value to be associated with the reference plane, and whether the absolute values, positive values and/or negative values are to be computed. Surfer, for example, supports all three options which it describes as positive planar and surface area, negative planar and surface area and total planar and surface area.

For example, consider the surface illustrated in Figure 4-6. This shows a surface model of a GB Ordnance Survey DEM for tile TQ81NE, which we shall use as a test surface in various sections of this Guide. This is a 5000mx5000m area provided as a 10mx10m grid of elevations, with an elevation range from around 10m-70m. Using a reference plane of $z=30$m the surface area above this reference plane is roughly 1.3sq kms and below 30m is roughly 2.1sq kms (3.4sq kms in total compared to 2.5sq kms for the planar area). For details of volume computations, which also use reference surfaces, see Section 6.2.6.

*Figure 4-6 Surface model of DEM*

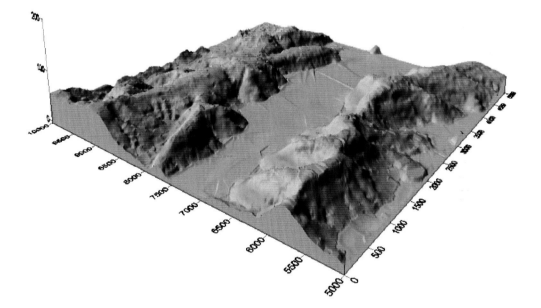

#### 4.2.3.2 Terrestrial (unprojected) surface area

For large regions (e.g. "rectangular" regions with sides greater than several hundred kilometers) surface areas will be noticeably affected by the curvature of the Earth. Such computations apply at large State and continental levels, or where the areas of ocean, ice or cloud cover are required over large regions. Computation of areas using spherical trigonometry or numerical integration is preferable in such cases.

The area of a spherical rectangular region defined by fixed latitude and longitude *coordinates* is greater than the area bounded by *lines* of constant latitude — the latter are not great circles, although the lines of longitude are. This effect increases rapidly nearer the poles and is weakest close to the equator. The MATLab Mapping Toolbox (MMT) function AREAQUAD provides a convenient way of computing the area of a latitude-longitude "quadrangle", although it can be computed without too much difficulty using spherical trigonometry. The area north of a line of latitude, $\varphi$, is the key factor in the calculation (the surface area of an entire sphere is $4\pi R^2$). The former area is:

$$A = 2\pi(1-\sin\varphi)R^2$$

where $R$ is the radius of the spherical Earth, e.g. 6378.137 kms. The area of the quadrangle is then simply the difference between the areas, $A_1$ and $A_2$, north of each of the two lines of latitude, $\varphi_1$ and $\varphi_2$, adjusted by the proportion of the Earth included in the difference in longitude values, $\lambda_1$ and $\lambda_2$:

$$A = \frac{\pi}{180}|A_1 - A_2||\lambda_1 - \lambda_2|R^2$$

A (simple) polygon with $n$ vertices on the surface of the Earth has sides that are great circles and area:

$$A = \left(\sum_i \theta_i - (n-2)\pi\right)R^2$$

where again $R$ is the radius of the Earth and the $\theta_i$ are the internal angles of the polygon in radians measured at each polygon vertex. The simplest spherical polygon is a triangle ($n$=3 so $n$-2=1) and on a sphere the sum of its internal angles must be greater than 180° ($\pi$), so the formula equates to 0 when the triangle is vanishingly small. A spherical triangle with internal angles that are all 180° is the largest possible, and is itself a great circle. In this case the formula yields $A$=2$\pi R^2$, as expected.

All polygon arcs must be represented by great circles and internal angles are to be measured with respect to these curved arcs. The term in brackets is sometimes known as the *spherical excess* and denoted with the letter $E$, thus $A$=$ER^2$. Note that every simple polygon on a sphere divides it into two sections, one smaller than the other unless all vertices lie on a great circle. If only the latitude and longitude values are known, the internal angles must be computed by calculating the true great circle bearing (or *azimuth*) from each vertex to the next — this can be achieved using spherical

trigonometry or, for example, the MMT function AZIMUTH, which supports explicit geoid values. Azimuth values are reported from due north, so computations of internal angles need to adjust for this factor. Alternatively the MMT function AREAINT may be used, ideally with high point density (i.e. introducing additional vertices along the polygon arcs). This latter function computes the enclosed area numerically. The open source GIS, GRASS, provides a number of similar functions, including the source code modules area_poly1, which computes polygon areas on an ellipsoid where connecting lines are grid lines rather than great circles, and area_poly2 which computes planimetric polygon area.

### 4.2.4 Line Smoothing and point-weeding

Polylines and polygons that have a large number of segments may be considered over-complex or poor representations of the original features, or unsuitable for display and printing at all map scales (a problem of *map generalization*). A range of procedures exist to achieve simplification of lines in such cases, including those illustrated in Figure 4-7.

A. Point weeding is a procedure largely due to Douglas and Peuker (1973) — for a fuller discussion, see Whyatt and Wade (1988) and Visvalingam and Whyatt (1991). For an interactive tool for line simplification of SHP files using a variety of algorithms see the web-based MapShaper software. In the example shown in Figure 4-7a the original black line connecting all the vertices 1 to 10 is progressively simplified to form the green line shown. The procedure commences by connecting point 1 (the anchor) to point 10 (the floating point) with a temporary line (the initial segment). This enables point 8 to be identified as the vertex that deviates from this initial segment by the greatest distance (and more than a user-defined tolerance level, shown here by the bar symbol on the left of the upper diagram). Euclidean distance squared is sufficient for this algorithm and is significantly faster to compute. Point 10 is then directly connected to point 8 and point 9 is dropped. A new temporary line is drawn between point 8 (the new floating point) and 1 and the process is repeated. This time points 5, 6 and 7 are dropped. Finally point 3 is dropped and the final line contains only 4 segments and 5 nodes (1, 2, 4, 8 and 10).

This process can be iterated by moving the initial anchor point to the previous floating point and repeating the process for further simplification. Some implementations of this algorithm, including those of the original authors, fail to handle exceptions where the furthest point from the initial segment is one end of a line that itself lies close to the initial segment. Ebisch (2002) addresses this error and provides corrected code for the procedure. The procedure is very sensitive to the tolerance value selected, with larger values resulting in elimination of more intermediate points.

*Figure 4-7 Smoothing techniques*

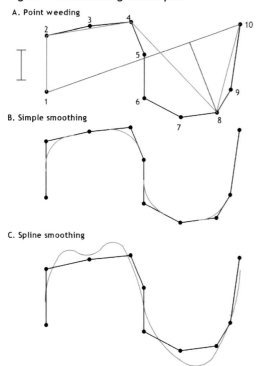

A. Point weeding

B. Simple smoothing

C. Spline smoothing

A number of GIS products provide a range of simplification methods. The default in ArcGIS is point-weeding (POINT_REMOVE) but an alternative BEND_SIMPLIFY which removes extraneous bends is also available.

**B. Simple smoothing** utilizes a family of procedures in which the set of points is replaced by a smooth line consisting of a set of curves and straight line segments, closely following but not necessarily passing through the nodes of the original polyline. This may be achieved in many ways with Figure 4-7b showing one example.

**C. Spline smoothing** typically involves replacing the original polyline with a curve that passes through the nodes of the polyline but does not necessarily align with it anywhere else, or approximates the point set rather like a regression fit (Figure 4-7c). A range of spline functions and modes of operation are available (including in some cases Bézier curves and their extension, B-splines), many of which involve using a series of smoothly connected cubic curves. In some cases additional temporary nodes or "knots" are introduced (e.g. half way between each existing vertex) to force the spline function to remain close to the original polyline form.

Each method and implementation (including the selection of parameters and constraints for each variant) will have different results within and across different GIS packages and the process will not generally be reversible. Furthermore, different GIS packages tend to offer only one or two smoothing procedures, so obtaining consistent results across implementations is almost impossible. Note that once a polyline or polygon has been subject to smoothing its length will be altered, becoming shorter in many cases, and enclosed areas will also be altered though generally by a lesser amount in percentage terms. The orientation of the line segments also changes dramatically, but not the relative positions of the two end nodes, so the end-node to end-node orientation is retained. Determination of the length and area of amended features may require numerical integration utilizing fine division of the smoothed objects rather than the simple procedures we have described in Section 4.2. Further discussion of smoothing, including additional approaches, is provided in

Chapter 6. These methods have been described by McMaster and Shea (1992) as forms of *feature generalization* (see also, Section 2.2.9). Other forms of generalization include: *amalgamation* (replacing a large number of separate area features or cells by a smaller number, e.g. a single feature); *merging* (replacing several line features with a single line feature); and *collapse* (replacing an area object by a point, cells or a combination of points and lines, or replacing dual lines by a single centerline. For a fuller discussion of generalization issues see the ESRI (1996) white paper, available via the ESRI web site.

## 4.2.5 Centroids and centers

The terms center and centroid have a variety of different meanings and formulas, depending on the writer and/or software package in which they are implemented. There are also specific measures used for polygons, point sets and lines so we treat each separately below. Centers or centroids are provided in many GIS packages for multiple polygons and/or lines, and in such cases the combined location is typically computed in the same manner as for point sets, using the centers or centroids of the individual objects as the input points. In almost all cases the metric utilized is $d_E$ or $d_S$, although other metrics may be more appropriate for some problems. Centroids are often defined as the nominal center of gravity for an object or collection of objects, but many other measures of centrality are commonly employed within GIS and related packages. In these latter instances the term center (qualified where necessary by how this center has been determined) is more appropriate than centroid, the latter being a term that should be reserved for the center of gravity.

### 4.2.5.1 Polygon centroids and centers

Polygon centers have many important functions in GIS: they are sometimes used as "handle points", by which an object may be selected, moved or rotated; they may be the default position for labeling; and for analytical purposes they are often used to "represent" the polygon, for example in distance calculations (zone to zone) and when assigning

zone attribute values to a point location (e.g. income per capita, disease incidence, soil composition). The effect of such assignment is to assume that the variable of interest is well approximated by assigning values to a single point, which essentially involves loss of information. This is satisfactory for some problems, especially where the polygons are small, homogeneous and relatively compact (e.g. unit ZIP-code or postcode areas, residential land parcels), but in other cases warrants closer examination.

With a number of raster-based GIS packages the process of vector file importing may utilize polygon centers as an alternative to the polygons themselves, applying interpolation to the values at these centroids in order to create a continuously varying grid rather than the common procedure of creating a gridded version of discretely classified polygonal areas (see further Chapter 6). Similar procedures may be applied in vector-based systems as part of their vector-to-raster conversion algorithms.

If $(x_i, y_i)$ are the coordinate pairs of a point set or defining a single polygon, we have for the Mean Center, M1:

$$M1 = \left( \sum_i \frac{x_i}{n}, \sum_i \frac{y_i}{n} \right) = (\bar{x}, \bar{y})$$

The Mean Center is not the same as the center of gravity for a polygon (although it is for an unweighted point set, see subsection 4.2.5.2). A weighted version of this expression is sometimes used:

Mean Center (weighted), M1*:

$$M1^* = \left( \frac{\sum_i w_i x_i}{\sum_i w_i}, \frac{\sum_i w_i y_i}{\sum_i w_i} \right)$$

The RMS variation of the point set $\{x_i, y_i\}$ about the mean center is known as the *standard distance*. It is computed using the expressions:

$$SDis = \sqrt{\sum_i \frac{(x_i - \overline{x})^2}{n} + \sum_i \frac{(y_i - \overline{y})^2}{n}},$$

or weighted:

$$SDis^* = \sqrt{\frac{\sum_i w_i (x_i - \overline{x})^2}{\sum_i w_i} + \frac{\sum_i w_i (y_i - \overline{y})^2}{\sum_i w_i}}$$

As noted above, the term *centroid* for a polygon is widely used to refer to its assumed center of gravity. By this is meant the point about which the polygon would balance if it was made of a uniform thin sheet of material with a constant density, such as a sheet of steel or cardboard. This point, M2, can be computed directly from the coordinates of the polygon vertices in a similar manner to that of calculating the polygon area, *A*, provided in Section 4.2.1. Indeed, it requires computation of *A* as an input. If the polygon is a triangle, which is a widely used form in spatial analysis, the center of gravity lies at the mean of the vertex coordinates, which is located at the intersection of straight lines drawn from the vertices to the mid-points of the opposite sides (Figure 4-8).

*Figure 4-8 Triangle centroid*

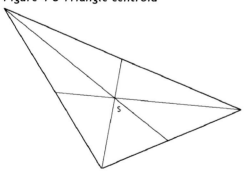

For general polygons, using the same notation as before, the formulas required for the *x*- and *y*-components are ($y > = 0$):

$$M2_x = \sum_{i=1}^{n-1} (x_{i+1}y_i - x_iy_{i+1})(x_i + x_{i+1}) / 6A$$

$$M2_y = \sum_{i=1}^{n-1} (x_{i+1}y_i - x_iy_{i+1})(y_i + y_{i+1}) / 6A$$

The formula arises as the weighted average of the centroids of triangles in a standard triangularization of the polygon, where the weights correspond to the triangle areas.

*Figure 4-9 Polygon centroid (M2) and alternative polygon centers*

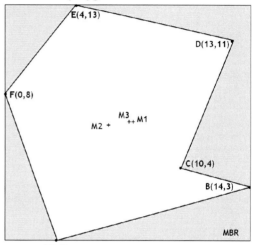

Mean centre: M1=(7.33,6.50)
Centre of gravity: M2=(5.82,6.33)
MBR centre: M3=(7.00,6.50)

Figure 4-9 shows a sample polygon with 6 nodes or vertices, A-F, together with the computed locations of the mean center (M1), centroid (M2) as defined by the center of gravity, and the center (M3), of the Minimum Bounding Rectangle (or MBR) which is shown in gray.

Each of these three points fall within the polygon boundary in this example, and are fairly closely spaced. The MBR center is clearly the fastest to compute, but is not invariant under rotation and is the most subject to outliers — e.g. a single vertex location that is very different from the majority of the elements being considered. For example, if point B had (valid or invalid) coordinates of B(34,3) then we would find M1=(10.67,6.5), M2=(8.67,5.36) and M3=(17,6.5). M3 is now well outside of the polygon, M1 is close to the polygon boundary and M2 remains firmly inside. None of these points minimizes the sum of distances to polygon vertices.

Despite the apparent robustness and widespread use of M2, with a polygon of complex shape the centroid may well lie outside of its boundary. In the example illustrated in Figure 4-10 we have generated

centroids for a set of polygons using the X-Tools add-in for ArcGIS, and these produce slightly different results from those created by ArcGIS itself. ArcGIS includes a function, Features to Points, which will create polygon centers that are guaranteed to lie inside the polygon if the option INSIDE is included in the command. Manifold includes a Centroids|Inner command which performs a similar function.

*Figure 4-10 Center and centroid positioning*

## Census tracts and centroids

Combined centroid of the two selected census tracts

This centroid lies in a lake - no census data apply to this polygon so it must be excluded in subsequent computations

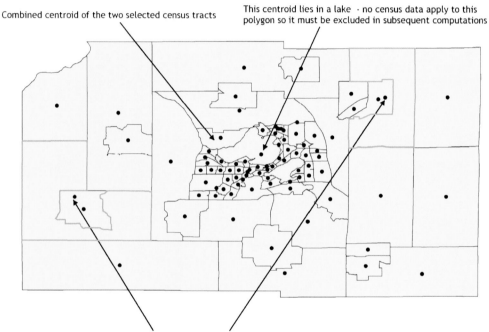

These centroids relate to the census tracts that are highlighted, in both cases being outside of their own tracts and inside another tract

An alternative to using the MBR is to find the smallest circle that completely encloses the polygon, taking the center of the circle as the polygon center (Figure 4-11, M4). This is the default in the Manifold GIS (viewable simply by selecting the menu option to View|Structure|Centroids) and/or using the Transform function "Centroids". This procedure suffers similar problems to that of using the MBR. Yet another alternative is to find the largest inscribed circle, and take its center as the polygon center (Figure 4-11, M5).

This approach has the advantage that the center will definitely be located inside the polygon, although possibly in an odd location, depending on the polygon shape. If the polygon is a triangle then M5 and M2 will coincide. Manifold supports location of centers of types M2, M3 and M4.

As we can also see in Figure 4-10 multiple polygons may be selected and assigned combined centers. In this example the combined center appears to have been computed from the MBR of the two selected census tracts, but different packages and toolsets may provide alternative procedures and thus positions. In such cases the center may be nowhere near any of the selected features, and if it is important to avoid such a circumstance the GIS may facilitate selection of the most central feature (e.g. the most central point or polygon) if one exists. In some instances the combined center calculation may be weighted by the value of an attribute associated with each polygon. This procedure will result in a weighted center whose location will be pulled towards regions with larger weights. However, in such cases the distribution of polygons used in the calculation may produce unrepresentative results.

This is apparent again in Figure 4-10 where a polygon center calculation for all census tracts in the western half of the region, weighted by farm revenues, would be pulled strongly to the east of the sub-region where many small urban tracts are found, even though these may have relatively low weights associated with them.

*Figure 4-11 Polygon center selection*

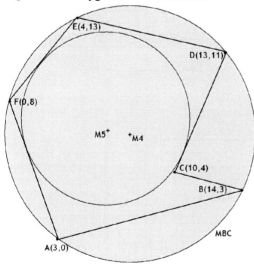

### 4.2.5.2 Point sets

If $(x_i, y_i)$ are the coordinate pairs of a point set then the Mean Center, $M1(x_0, y_0)$, is simply the average of the coordinate values, as we saw earlier:

$$M1(x_0, y_0) = \left( \sum_i w_i x_i \Big/ \sum_i w_i , \sum_i w_i y_i \Big/ \sum_i w_i \right)$$

In this version of the expression for M1 there is an additional (optional) component, $w_i$, representing weights associated with the points included in the calculation. For points sets the weights might be the number of crimes recorded at a particular location, or the number of beds in a hospital; for multiple polygons, where these are represented by their individual centers or centroids, the weights would typically be an attribute value associated with each polygon. Clearly if all weights=1 the formula simplifies to a calculation that is purely based on the coordinate values, with the number of points, $n = \Sigma w_i$.

M1 in this case is the center of gravity, or *centroid*, of the point set assuming the locations used in the calculation are treated as point masses. M1 is the location that minimizes the sum of (weighted) *squared distance* to all the points in the set, is simple and fast to compute, and is widely used. However, it is not the point that minimizes the sum of the (weighted) *distance* to each of the points. The latter is known sometimes as the (bivariate) "median center" (although Crimestat, for example, uses the term median center to be simply the middle values of the *x*- and *y*-coordinates). It is best described as the MAT point (the center of Minimum Aggregate Travel, M6). This point may be determined using the following iterative procedure, with M1 as the initial pair $(x_0, y_0)$ and $k=0,1...$:

$$x_{k+1} = \sum_{i=1}^{n} w_i x_i / d_{i,k} \Bigg/ \sum_{i=1}^{n} w_i / d_{i,k}$$

$$y_{k+1} = \sum_{i=1}^{n} w_i y_i / d_{i,k} \Bigg/ \sum_{i=1}^{n} w_i / d_{i,k}$$

In this expression $d_{i,k}$ is the distance from the $i^{th}$ point to the $k^{th}$ estimated optimal location. It is usual to adjust distances in this, and similar formulas involving division by interpoint distances, by a small increment and/or to apply code checks to avoid divide-by-zero or close to zero situations. For this particular problem testing the numerically estimated surface derivative and curvature, in addition for checking for division by zero, has been shown to be an effective approach to avoiding overshooting the true optimum (see Ostresh's WEBER algorithm, in Rushton *et al.*, 1973). Iteration is continued until the change in the objective function (the cumulative distance) or both coordinates is less than some pre-specified small value. These formulas for M1 and M6 can be derived by taking the standard equation for distance, $d_E$, or distance squared, $d_E{}^2$, and partially differentiating first with respect to $x$ and then with respect to $y$, and finally equating the results to 0 to determine the minimum value. An extension to this type of weighted mean is provided by the Geographically Weighted Regression (GWR) software package, and is described further in Section 5.6.3. With the GWR software it is possible to compute a series of locally defined (geographically weighted) means, and associated variances, which may then be analyzed and/or mapped.

The positions of M1, M3 and M6 are illustrated in Figure 4-12, using the same set of coordinates as for the vertices A-F of the polygon described in subsection 4.2.5.1.

*Figure 4-12 Point set centers*

Mean centre/Centre of gravity: M1=(7.33,6.50)
MAT: M6=(8.58,5.61)
MBR centre: M3=(7.00,6.50)

Note that M1=M2 in this case, and for both M1 and M3 (the MBR center) their position is unchanged from the polygonal case. Also note that if we move point B to B′ the position of M6 is unchanged (although the cumulative distance will be greater). This observation is true for each of the points A-F — they can be moved away from the MAT point to an arbitrary distance along a line connecting them to M6, and the position of M6 will be unaffected. This would not generally be the case with M1 or M3.

The locations described for different types of center, both here and in subsection 4.2.5.1, often assume that all points (or polygons) are weighted equally. If the set of weights, $w_i$, are not all equal, the locations of M1 and M6 will be altered, but M3 will be unchanged. The effect of unequal weights is to "pull" the location of M1 and M6 towards the locations with higher weights. For example, if point B in our previous example had a weight of 3, M1 would be moved to (9.00,5.63) just to the right of M6 in Figure 4-12, M3 would be unaltered, and M6 would be altered to (10.41,4.29) which is very close to point C. Any weights in the dataset that are zero or missing will generally result in the point being removed from the calculation. Such occurrences require checking to ensure valid data is not being discarded due to incomplete information or errors.

There is no difference between weighted calculations where the weights are integer values and the standard calculations for unit weights if some points in a set are co-located. For example, if point B is recorded in a dataset 3 times, its effective weight would be 3, and instead of 6 points there would be 8 to consider. Co-located point recording is very common, especially in crime and medical datasets where each incident is associated with a nominal rather than precise location. Examples of co-located data might be the closest street intersection to an incident, the nominal coordinates of a shopping mall, the location of the doctor's surgery where a patient is registered, or a location that recurs because incidents or cases have been rounded to the nearest 50 meters for data protection reasons. It is often a good idea to execute queries looking for duplicate and unweighted locations before conducting analyses of this type, since mapped datasets may not reveal the true underlying patterns. Likewise it is important to check that co-located data are meaningful for the analysis to be undertaken – surgery location is not generally a substitute for a patient's home address.

The preceding calculations have all been carried out using the standard Euclidean metric, $d_E$. As previously stated, this is the standard for GIS packages, but other metrics may be more appropriate depending on the problem at hand (see further, Section 4.4.1). Specialist packages like LOLA and Crimestat support a range of other metrics. Using the city block metric ($L_1$) and the minimax metric ($L_\infty$) the MAT point, M6, is no longer guaranteed to be unique – all points within a defined region may be equally close to the input point set (Crimestat only provides a single location, so LOLA or similar facilities are preferable for such computations). For example, the point set in Figure 4-12 with $L_1$ metric has an MAT solution point set (a rectangle) bounded by (4,4) and (10,8). Clearly, if the point set lay on a network the location of M6 would again been different.

To add to the confusion of the above Crimestat provides three further measures of centrality for point sets. Each involves variations in the way the mean is calculated (see further, Table 1-3): the geometric mean (the $x$- and $y$-coordinates are calculated using the sum of the logarithms of the coordinates, averaging and then taking antilogs); the harmonic mean (the $x$- and $y$-coordinates are calculated using the reciprocal of the coordinates, averaging and then taking the reciprocal of the result); and the triangulated mean (a Crimestat "special"). The first two alternative means are less sensitive to outliers (extreme values) than the conventional mean center, whilst the latter measure is claimed to represent the directionality of the data better. The Crimestat manual, Chapter 4, provides more details of each measure, with examples. Note that the harmonic mean is vulnerable to coordinate values which are 0 or close to 0.

### 4.2.5.3  Lines

In the case of a line (single segment, polyline or curve) the common notion of the center is simply the point on the line that is equidistant from the two endpoints. This provides both the (intrinsic) center of gravity and the mean center, although when a polyline is viewed as embedded in a plane its "center" should be considered to lie in the plane and not on the line.

For collections of lines there is no generally applied formula and a common central point might be selected from the centers or centroids of the individual elements, or from the MBR, or utilizing a central feature if one exists. Combinations of points, lines and polygons are treated in a similar manner. Because lines and line segments have a well-defined orientation, labeling tools that utilize line or segment centroids may also use the orientation of that element to align associated labels.

### 4.2.6  Point (object) in polygon (PIP)

One of the most basic of spatial operations is that of determining whether a given point lies inside a polygon. More generally the problem extends to the case of multiple points and polygons, with the problem being to assign every point to the correct polygon. Related problems include line in polygon and polygon in polygon tests. A fast initial screening approach is to check whether a point (or line, polygon) lies in the polygon's MBR. However, the standard algorithm for determining PIP in the vector model (known as the *semi-line algorithm*) is to extend a line vertically upwards (or horizontally, e.g. to the right) and then count the number of times this line crosses the polygon boundary. If the line crosses the boundary an odd number of times it lies inside the polygon. This is true even when the polygon is concave or contains holes. A number of special cases need to be considered, as illustrated in Figure 4-13. These include points that lie on the boundary or at a vertex, and points that lie directly below a vertical segment of the polygon boundary. A useful discussion of PIP algorithms and related procedures is provided in Worboys and Duckham (2004, pp 197-202).

If the given point lies on the boundary or at a vertex of the polygon there is a further difficulty, since a unique assignment rule could prevent the point from being allocated to any polygon. Solutions to such cases include: assigning the point to the first polygon tested and not to any subsequent polygons; randomly assigning the point to a unique polygon from the set whose boundary it lies on; reporting an exception (non-assignment); assigning a weight value to the point (e.g. 0.5 on a boundary or $1/n$ at a vertex, where $n$ is the number of polygons meeting at that vertex).

*Figure 4-13 Point in polygon — tests and special cases*

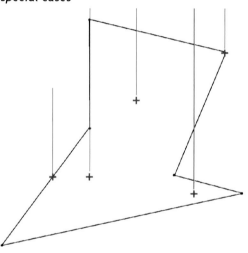

Where the PIP process is one of overlaying, the procedure within a GIS will typically append attribute data from the polygon to the point, although this may be in accordance with user-selectable transfer rules (e.g. sum or average a particular field). ArcGIS includes two PIP-related topology rules: (i) point must be properly inside polygon; and (ii) point must be covered by boundary of polygon (i.e. must be exactly on the boundary). These are two of 16 main vector topology rules supported within ArcGIS for combinations of point, line and polygon features.

A second PIP algorithm of similar computational complexity, but requiring trigonometric operations in its standard form (so more processor intensive) is known as the *winding number* method. In this procedure a line is extended to each vertex of the polygon from the sample point in turn (traversing anticlockwise). If the sum of the angles from the point to the vertices, $v_i$, is 0 the point lies outside the polygon, otherwise it lies inside or on the polygon. To clarify this procedure, let the polygon have $n$ vertices $v_i=v_1,v_2,v_3,... v_n=v_0$ and consider a unit vector from a sample point, $p$, to each vertex in turn. Define the (signed) angle at $p$ between the vectors $v_i$ and $v_{i+1}$, as $\theta_i$. Then compute the winding number:

$$wn = \sum_{i=0}^{n-1} \theta_i \text{ , or}$$

$$wn = \sum_{i=0}^{n-1} \cos^{-1}\left( \frac{\mathbf{pv}_i \cdot \mathbf{pv}_{i+1}}{\|\mathbf{pv}_i\|\|\mathbf{pv}_{i+1}\|} \right)$$

If $wn=0$ the point lies outside the polygon, otherwise it lies inside or on the polygon boundary. With some adjustment the algorithm can avoid calculating the angle and result in a computation that is as fast, or faster than crossing methods (tests suggest 20-30% faster for many non-convex polygons). It is also more general, in that it applies to cases where polygons are not simple, i.e. self-crossing of the polygon boundary is permitted.

The above addresses the issue for the case of a single polygon and for multiple non-overlapping contiguous polygons. With overlapping polygons, which is supported for example within the Manifold GIS, then unique allocation is not assured. Furthermore, if the sample region is not completely covered by polygons sample points may fall into no polygon. Similar issues arise with raster representation of points and polygons (as zones of continuous fields) but the problem of locating points inside zones is far simpler, whilst the allocation issues remains.

## 4.2.7 Polygon decomposition

Polygons may be divided into smaller sections in many different ways, for a wide variety of reasons. Most vector GIS packages support some decomposition procedures, through overlay of a template or *cookie cutter* polygons (e.g. the Clip operation in ArcGIS) and/or through the provision of explicit decomposition procedures. For example, complex polygons with convoluted boundaries may be divided up into a series of non-overlapping convex polygons. These polygons will have centers (e.g. centers of gravity) that are guaranteed to lie inside the original polygon. The multiple centers thus generated may then be used to assist labeling or in assigning data in spatial overlay operations. Polygons can also be divided into non-overlapping triangles, in a variety of different ways. Manifold, for example, provides commands to perform both such decompositions: Transform|Decompose to convex parts, and Transform|Decompose to triangles. A (simple) polygon with *n* vertices or nodes can be triangulated into *n*-2 triangles using a procedure known as diagonal triangulation. This form of triangulation utilizes existing polygon vertices, but other triangulations are possible if additional internal vertices are permitted. With *m* such internal vertices (or Steiner points) a total of *n*+2*m*-2 triangles will be generated.

A polygon can also be *skeletonised*, providing an additional view of its form and key internal points. In Figure 4-14 bands of increasing distance in constant steps from the external boundary are shown. These terminate in a single central point and generate one intermediate point. Connecting these internal points to the polygon nodes creates a skeleton of lines known as the *medial axis* of the polygon. The medial axis is not necessarily comprised of straight line segments. In practice skeletonization is carried out using algorithms known generically as *medial axis transforms*, and may be computed in linear time (i.e. as a linear function of the number of polygon vertices). The single central point in the example shown in Figure 4-14 is the center of the largest inscribed circle.

Applications of skeletonization include label placement, especially useful for complex polygons which are concave and/or contain holes, and polygon generalization/smoothing, which has been applied to closed polygons and to open regions such as contour maps — see for example Gold and Thibault (2001). The reverse process, "given a skeleton (e.g. stream pattern) reconstruct a landscape", has also been the subject of much research. Furthermore, the dual of skeletonization is one form of polygon decomposition, although not generally the version implemented within currently available GIS software. Neither does such software tend to provide skeletonization facilities, but asymmetric buffering (see Section 4.4.4), which is a commonly available feature, enables first-stage skeletonization to be carried out.

*Figure 4-14 Skeletonised convex polygon*

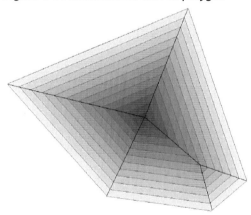

Raster-based spatial analysis makes limited use of region centers, where they occur mainly in connection with patch analysis. Patches are typically collections of contiguous cells that have the same or similar attribute values, although in some instances a patch may include holes. The commonest notion of center in such cases is the unweighted or weighted mean value of the cell coordinates of the patch under consideration. In cases where cell values (weights) are counts of points falling in each cell the weighted mean can be regarded as equivalent to the simple mean value (minimum of squared Euclidean distances) for point patterns.

## 4.2.8 Shape

A number of the sections in this Guide have touched on the issue of polygon shape: how this affects where the center lies; how compactness of polygon form may be related to standard shapes such as a circle or rectangle; and how polygons may be decomposed into simpler shapes, such as triangles. In practice defining some form of shape measure that provides an adequate description is difficult and many indices and procedures have been proposed. Shape measures may be applied to polygon forms or to grid patches (sets of contiguous grid cells that have common or similar attributes or are regarded as being a patch for analytical purposes). Measures relating to grid structures are described in Section 5.3.4, Landscape Metrics. The comments in this latter section apply equally well to shape measures for polygonal (vector) regions:

*"The most common measures of shape complexity are based on the relative amount of perimeter per unit area, usually indexed in terms of a perimeter-to-area ratio, or as a fractal dimension, and often standardized to a simple Euclidean shape (e.g., circle or square). The interpretation varies among the various shape metrics, but in general, higher values mean greater shape complexity or greater departure from simple Euclidean geometry."*

Vector-based GIS software packages do not normally provide shape index measures directly — it is up to the user to create index values. In many instances such values are functions of the area and perimeter of the polygon, and may be generated as a new calculated field from these (intrinsic or explicit) attributes. If we define $A_i$ as the Area of polygon $i$, and $L_i$ as its perimeter length, and $B_i$ as the area of a circle with perimeter $L_i$, then example measures include:

**Perimeter/Area ratio (P1A):**

$$P1A_i = \frac{L_i}{A_i}$$

Note that this ratio is unsatisfactory for most applications as its value changes with the size of the figure (i.e. irrespective of resolution issues).

**Perimeter²/Area ratio (P2A):**

$$P2A_i = \frac{L_i^2}{A_i}$$

This second ratio was used in the UK 2001 census Output Area generation exercise (see further, Section 4.2.11). If preferred, this index, or its square root may be adjusted so that its value equals 1 when applied to a circle of the same area as $A_i$.

**Shape Index or Compactness ratio (C):**

$$C_i = \sqrt{\frac{A_i}{B_i}}$$

Note that this ratio is dimensionless (i.e. not affected by the size of the polygon) and has a value of 1 for a circular region and a range of [0,1] for all plane shapes. Note that sometimes this index is computed as $(1-C_i)$. Grid-based packages (e.g. Idrisi, CRATIO command) and specialized pattern-analysis software (e.g. Fragstats) may compute ratios of this type as inbuilt functions.

**Related bounding figure (RBF):**

$$RBF_i = 1 - \frac{A_i}{F_i}$$

where $F_i$ is the area of a bounding figure. Typically the bounding figure will be the minimum bounding circle, but could equally well be the MBR or convex hull. In each case the ratio lies in the range [0,1], with 0 being the value if the polygon matches the bounding figure. When index values of this type are computed for multiple polygons (e.g. as a new column in an attribute table) a *shape distribution* is created, that may be examined with conventional univariate statistics (e.g. mean, median, standard deviation, range etc.) and/or graphically examined as a histogram.

More complex shape measures, such as those based on multiple characteristics of polygon form (e.g. the length of the major and minor internal axes, or the set of possible straight lines computable within the polygon) are more difficult to compute. At present all such measures typically require separate programmed computation, either within a GIS environment or externally.

Shape measures may also be computed for other vector objects, such as sets of points or lines. In the case of point sets the common procedure is to compute an RBF-type measure, i.e. essentially generating a polygon such as the convex hull of a cluster of points and analyzing its form. The standard deviational ellipse (see further, Section 4.5.3 and Section 5.4) also provides an option for point-set shape analysis, utilizing the ellipse area and major and minor axes.

For linear objects or collections of linear objects, many options exist, a number of which are directly supported within standard GIS packages, particularly those with hydrological analysis components (e.g. providing ratios such as stream length/basin area). Many such measures are indirect measures of linear component shapes. Perhaps the simplest measure for individual polylines is to compute the ratio of polyline length to the Euclidean (or spherical) distance between start and end points. This kind of measure is highly dependent on scale, line representation, generalization and point pair selection.

A *circuity index* (devised by Kansky) for transport networks based on this kind of idea involves comparing the inter-vertex network distance, $N$, with the Euclidean distance, $E$:

$$I = \frac{1}{V} \sum_{i=1}^{n} (N_i - E_i)^2$$

where $V$ is the number of vertices in the network and $n$ is the number of distinct pairwise connections, i.e. $n=V(V-1)/2$. This overall index can be disaggregated into separate indices for each vertex, providing separate measures of vertex based circuity. If information is available on user preferences for travel between vertex pairs, then so-called "desire lines" can be utilized in index computations of this kind (e.g. as weightings). As with many of the other measures described in this subsection the computation of index components and totals must utilize generic calculation facilities within the GIS or be computed externally.

## 4.2.9 Overlay and combination operations

Overlay operations involve the placement of one map layer (set of features) $A$, on top of a second map layer, $B$, to create a map layer, $C$, that is some combination of $A$ and $B$. $C$ is normally a new layer, but may be a modification of $B$. Layer $A$ in a vector GIS will consist of points, lines and/or polygons, whilst layer $B$ will normally consist of polygons. All objects are generally assumed to have planar enforcement, and the resulting object set or layer must also have planar enforcement. The general term for such operations is topological overlay, although a variety of terminology is used by different GIS suppliers, as we shall see below. In raster GIS layers $A$ and $B$ are both grids, which should have a common origin and orientation — if not, resampling is required.

- The process of overlaying map layers has some similarity with point set theory, but a large number of variations have been devised and implemented in different GIS packages. The principal operations have previously been outlined as the spatial analysis component of the OGC simple features specification (Table 4-2). The open source package, GRASS, is a typical example of a GIS that provides an implementation of polygon overlay which is very similar to conventional point set theory (Figure 4-15).

*Figure 4-15 GRASS overlay operations, v.overlay*

*Source: http://grass.itc.it/screenshots/vector.php*

Functions provided by GRASS include:

- *Intersection*, where the result includes all those polygon parts that occur in both *A* and *B*

- *Union*, where the result includes all those polygon parts that occur in either *A* or *B*, so is the sum of all the parts of both *A* and *B*

- *Not*, where the result includes only those polygon parts that occur in *A* but not in *B* (sometimes described as a Difference operation), and

*Exclusive or* (XOR), which includes polygons that occur in *A* or *B* but not both, so is the same as (*A* Union *B*) minus (*A* Intersection *B*)

TNTMips provides similar functionality and uses much the same terminology as GRASS (AND, OR, SUBTRACT, XOR) under the heading of vector combinations rather than overlay operations, and permits lines as well as polygons as the "operator" layer.

Note: (a) these operations may split up many of the original polygons (and/or lines) to create a new set of features, each with their own (inherited and derived) attributes (lengths, areas, perimeters, centroids, and associated attributes from *A* and/or *B*). New composite regions (with associated combined attribute datasets) are often the desired end result, in which case borders between adjacent polygons may be dissolved and datasets merged in order to achieve this end result; (b) operations are not generally symmetric, i.e. *A*<operation>*B* is not necessarily the same as *B*<operation>*A*, both from a point of view of the geometry and associated attribute data held in tables.

In ArcGIS operations of this type are known by the general term "Overlay", whilst in Manifold the ArcGIS Overlay operations are described as *Topological Overlays* to distinguish these composite operations from the more component based operations that Manifold describes as *Spatial Overlays*. Other vector GIS packages use descriptions such as *cookie cutters* (or EXTRACT operations) and *spatial joins*, and without doubt the terminology is confusing — the exact consequences of such operations applied using any particular GIS package will be different and should be examined very carefully. The ArcGIS implementation provides four main Overlay functions: Intersection and Union, which are essentially similar to those illustrated in Figure 4-15, and two additional operations: Identity, which splits up the elements in *B* based on the position of elements in *A*; and Update, which amends those parts of *B* that intersect with *A* such that in these regions *B*'s geometry and associated data reflects those of *A*.

The Manifold GIS generalizes the notion of overlay to include spatial proximity, for example lines that touch areas, and areas that are adjacent to (immediate neighbors of) other areas. The full set of permitted methods is shown in Table 4-3.

*Table 4-3 Spatial overlay methods, Manifold GIS*

|          | Contained | Containing | Intersecting | Boundary | Touching | Neighboring |
|----------|-----------|------------|--------------|----------|----------|-------------|
| Areas, A | A,L,P     | A          | A,L          | P        | A,L      | A,L         |
| Lines, L | L,P       | A,L        | A,L          | P        | A,L      | A,L         |
| Points, P|           | A,L        |              |          | P        | A,L         |

Manifold also permits polygons within a layer to be overlapping, which can result in more complex output patterns. In all cases the Manifold Spatial Overlay process transfers data (fields) from a source object (set of features of the same type) to a target object (also a set of features of the same type) according to transfer rules. These rules specify how the data fields are to be transferred (e.g. copied, summed) conditional upon the spatial overlay method. As such they are rather like an SQL "Update table" or "Create table" command, subject to "Where" conditions.

Polygon-on-polygon overlay, which is a relatively common procedure, frequently results in the creation of very small thin polygons known as *slivers*. These may be the genuine result of an overlay operation (i.e. valid objects and data) or they may be artifacts, created as a result of differences in the original data capture, manipulation or storage process associated with A and B, even though they should exactly match in places. Such slivers may be removed automatically during the overlay operation, usually by setting tolerance levels, or by post-processing, e.g. removing all polygons with a width less than a tolerance value and replacing these with an arc along the sliver centerline or assigning them to the largest adjacent polygon (e.g. in ArcGIS use the ELIMINATE function in ArcToolbox; in Manifold use the Normalize Topology function).

Overlays involve operations where two distinct sets of spatial object are combined in particular manner, visualized as overlaying one upon the other. Many other forms of combination are possible. For example, with a single layer of polygons, boundaries between polygons could be removed (*dissolved*) if the polygons are adjacent/share a common boundary and meet certain criteria. The attributes of the newly formed polygon will be the sum or some other measure of the component parts. If a new map layer is created by this process rather than an existing layer modified the process is sometimes described as *merging* rather than dissolving.

Manifold permits the use of the Dissolve operation on lines and points as well as polygons. In the case of lines, multiple line segments are replaced with a single line segment, whilst with points multiple points are replaced by a single center point. The attribute used to guide the dissolve process may be transferred to the new object(s) as: Blank (i.e. do not transfer values for this field); Average; Count; Maximum; Minimum; Sample (randomly chosen value from the

original object); or Sum. Other fields are transferred according to transfer rules set for each field.

ArcGIS supports two additional composite operations: Erase and Symmetric difference. In the Erase operation objects in A overlaid on B result in the removal of those parts of B that intersect with A (essentially the NOT operation of GRASS). Symmetric difference is similar to Erase, but those parts of A that do not intersect with B are included in the output set also (essentially the XOR operation we described earlier for GRASS). In addition ArcGIS supports operations such as Split, Append (a merge operation) and Integrate, which combine or separate features according to well-defined rules. Collectively within ArcGIS these various facilities are described as Geoprocessing Tools, and in ArcGIS V8 were available via a "Geoprocessing Wizard" but in ArcGIS V9 are provided in ArcToolbox as separately identified functions.

## 4.2.10 Areal interpolation

The polygon-on-polygon overlay process highlights an important problem: "how should attributes be assigned from input polygons to newly created polygons whose size and shape differ from the original set?" This is a specific example of a closely related problem, that of re-districting. Suppose that we have a set of non-overlapping polygons that represent census tracts, and a second set of polygons that represent hospital service districts, generated (for example) as simple Voronoi polygons around each hospital (see further, Section 4.2.14.3). We wish to estimate the population numbers and age/sex mix for the service districts. Based on this information we might assign budgets to the hospitals or iteratively adjust the service districts to provide a more even set of service areas (see further, Section 4.2.11).

In a simple overlay procedure we calculate the proportion of each census district that intersects with each separate service zone (by area) and then assign this proportion of the relevant attribute to the hospital in question. This assumes that the distribution of each attribute is constant, or uniform, within each census tract while also ensuring that the total counts for each attribute remain consistent with the census figures (so-called volume-preserving or *pycnophylactic* assignment). The standard intersection operator in many GIS packages will not carry out such proportional assignment, but simply carry over the source attributes to the target polygons. Assuming the source attribute table includes an explicit area value, and the intersected target provides an explicit or intrinsic measure of the intersection areas, then the proportional allocation procedure may be carried out by adding a calculated field containing the necessary adjustments. Note that this discussion assumes spatially extensive attributes (see Section 2.2.2) whereas with spatially intensive attributes alternative procedures must be applied (for example, initially using kernel density estimation – see Section 4.3.4 for more details).

Figure 4-16 and Figure 4-17 illustrate this process for test UK census Output Areas in part of Manchester. The population totals for each source area are shown in Figure 4-16, together with the area of overlap with a sample 1 km square region and a selected source polygon intersection (highlighted in red).

*Figure 4-16 Areal interpolation from census areas to a single grid cell*

Figure 4-17 shows the result of applying area-based proportional assignment to the square region in question. The region highlighted in red in the Figure 4-16 has its population estimate of 173 reduced to 32 in this case, with the sum of these proportional assignments (1632) providing the estimated total population for the entire square.

Variants of this procedure attempt to correct for the often unrealistic assumption of uniformity in the spatial distribution within polygons. If data are available for smaller sample regions (e.g. unit postcode areas in the above example) then this may be utilized in a similar manner to that already described. Another alternative is to model the distribution of the variable of interest (e.g. population) as a continuous surface. Essentially this procedure assigns the attribute value of interest to a suitable polygon center and then calculates the attribute value over a fine grid within the polygon by taking into account the values of the attribute at adjacent or nearby polygon centers.

*Figure 4-17 Proportionally assigned population values*

For example, if the source attribute values were much higher east of the target polygon than west, the values assigned within the source polygon might be assumed to show a slope from east to west rather than be distributed uniformly. Having estimated values for the *source* polygons on the fine grid, these values are then summed for each target polygon and adjusted to make sure that the totals match those for the original polygon. The individual grid cells may then be re-assigned to the *target* polygons (the hospital service areas in our example) giving a hopefully more accurate picture of the attribute values for these service areas. Current mainstream GIS packages do not tend to support the latter procedure, although simple sequences of operations, scripts or programs can be written to make such field assignments.

The SURPOP online software utility is an example of such a program. Details of the algorithm applied and software may be obtained from the SURPOP page and via the UK Census Dissemination Unit (CDU). In this instance the population, $P_i$, of each grid cell is approximated as:

$$\hat{P}_i = \sum_{j=1}^{N} w_{ij} P_j$$

where $P_j$ is the population of "centroid" $j$, and $w_{ij}$ is the weight applied to centroid $j$ for grid cell $i$. The number $N$ is determined by the windowsize used, i.e. the size of a moving $N$x$N$ grid cell region. The weights distribute a proportion of each centroid's population value to the cells within the window and are determined as a form of distance decay function (see also, Section 4.4.5) with a decay parameter, $\alpha$:

$$w_{ij} = \left( \frac{d^2 - s_{ij}^2}{d^2 + s_{ij}^2} \right)^{\alpha}$$

where $d$ is the average inter-centroid distance within the sampled window, and $s_{ij}$ is the distance between cell $i$ and centroid $j$. As a result of tests on UK enumeration districts, typically $a=1$ in this model. The values chosen for the grid resolution, windowsize and decay parameter, together with the selection of centroid locations, all affect the resulting surface model produced.

The above, adjusted volume-preserving assignment approaches, have significant drawbacks where the geography of the study region is highly variable and/or where attributes do not vary in a similar manner (do not exhibit strong positive covariance). For example, population is typically concentrated in urban areas and not spread evenly across arbitrary zones. In urban-rural borders and rural areas with distinct settlements a far better approach would be to utilize ancillary information, such as land-use, road network density (by type) or remote sensed imagery, to adjust attribute allocation. This ancillary data, which is often selected on the basis that it is readily available in a convenient form for use within GIS packages, can then be used as a form of weighting. Recent tests (see for example, Hawley and Moellering, 2005) have shown that the quality of areal interpolation can be substantially improved by such methods.

### 4.2.11 Districting and re-districting

A common analysis problem involves the combination of many small zones (typically stored as polygons) into a smaller number of merged larger zones or districts. This merging process is usually subject to a set of spatial and attribute-related constraints. Spatial constraints might be:

- districts must be comprised of adjacent (coterminous) regions

- districts must be sensible shapes e.g. reasonably compact

Attribute constraints might be:

- no district may have less than 100 people

- all districts must have a similar number of people (e.g. within a target range)

Several GIS packages now facilitate the automatic or semi-automatic creation of districts, or the re-organization of existing districts. These operations have many applications, from the designation of service areas to the definition (and re-definition) of census and electoral districts. For example, within Manifold (with the Business Tools extension) there are facilities to enable an existing set of districts to be re-assigned automatically to one of N new districts, such that each new district has a similar (balanced) value by area (an intrinsic attribute) or by a selected attribute (optionally weighted). This automated process may yield unsatisfactory results (for example, very convoluted districts) and an alternative, visual interface facility, is provided to enable the user to make manual alterations and see the results in terms of the attribute or attributes of interest. In the case of ArcGIS Districting is provided as a free downloadable add-in, and is essentially a manual operation supported by map and statistical windows. The CommonGIS package (current version) includes a districting facility as part of its newly integrated Library of Optimization Algorithms for Geographical Information Systems (LOGIS).

Districting and re-districting are generally processes of agglomeration or construction. The initial set of regions is reduced to a smaller set, according to selected rules. Automating this process involves a series of initial allocations, comparison of the results with the constraints and targets, and then re-allocation of selected smaller regions until the targets are met as closely as possible. As with many such problems, it may not be possible to prove that a given solution is the best possible (i.e. is optimal), but only that it is the best that has been found using the procedures adopted. An ArcGIS-compatible automated zone design system, ZDES, has been developed at the University of Leeds and may be downloaded from the associated web site (see details of web site addresses at the end of this Guide).

Creating new districts can be a confusing process. In addition to the kinds of issue we have already discussed there are two important affects to be aware of: scale (*grouping* or *statistical*) effects; and zoning (*arrangement*) effects.

The first of these issues, scale effects, are best understood through the use of a simple example. Consider the employment statistics

shown in Table 4-4. Areas A and B both contain a total of 100,000 people who are classified as either employed or not. In area A 10% of both Europeans and Asians are unemployed (i.e. equal proportions), and likewise in Area B we have equal proportions (this time 20% unemployed). So we expect that combining areas A and B will give us 200,000 people, with an equal proportion of Europeans and Asians unemployed (we would guess this to be 15%), but it is not the case — 13.6% of Europeans and 18.3% of Asians are seen to be unemployed! The reason for this unexpected result is that in Area A there are many more Europeans than Asians, so we are working from different total populations. This kind of problem is widespread in spatial datasets and is best addressed by the use of multiple scales of analysis, if possible and appropriate, as part of the initial research process (e.g. using variance/semi-variance analysis techniques, fractal analysis, or creating optimized districts with specified attributes as discussed above).

*Table 4-4 Regional employment data — grouping affects*

|  | Employed (000s) | Unemployed (000s) | Total (000s) (Unemployed %) |
|---|---|---|---|
| **Area A** | | | |
| European | 81 | 9 | 90 (10%) |
| Asian | 9 | 1 | 10 (10%) |
| **Total** | 90 | 10 | 100 (10%) |
| **Area B** | | | |
| European | 40 | 10 | 50 (20%) |
| Asian | 40 | 10 | 50 (20%) |
| **Total** | 80 | 20 | 100 (20%) |
| **A and B** | | | |
| European | 121 | 19 | 140 (13.6%) |
| Asian | 49 | 11 | 60 (18.3%) |
| **Total** | 170 | 30 | 200 (15%) |

The second issue is due to the way in which voting and census areas are defined — their shape, and the way in which they are aggregated, affects the results and can even change which party is elected. This is not to say that a particular arrangement *will* have such effects, but that it is possible to deliberately produce a districting plan that meets specific criteria, at least for a single attribute. This question (with or without reference to scale effects) is often referred to by the awkward name Modifiable Areal Unit Problem, or MAUP, as described by Openshaw (1997, 1984) and more recently discussed in some detail by Wong (2008).

Figure 4-18 illustrates this issue for an idealized region consisting of 9 small voting districts. The individual zone, row, column and overall total number of voters are shown in diagram A, with a total of 1420 voters of whom roughly 56% will vote for the first party listed/the red party (R) and 44% for the second

party listed/ the blue party (B). With 9 voting districts we expect roughly 5 to be won by the reds and 4 by the blues on a "first past the post" voting system (majority in a voting district wins the district in this example), as is indeed the case in this example. However, if these zones are actually not the voting districts themselves, but combinations of adjacent zones are used to define the voting areas, then the results may be quite different. As diagrams B to F show, with a first-past-the-post voting system then we could have a result in which every district was won by the reds (case C), to one in which 75% of the districts were won by the blues (case F). Note that the solutions shown are not unique, and several arrangements of adjacent zones will give the same voting results.

*Figure 4-18 Grouping data — Zone arrangement effects on voting results*

So it is not just the *process* of grouping that generates confusing results, but also the *pattern* of grouping, which is of great interest to those responsible for defining and revising electoral district boundaries. And this is not just a problem confined to voting patterns. For example, if the information being gathered relates to the proportions of trace metals (for example lead and zinc) in the soil, similar issues arise. Samples based on different field boundaries would show that in some arrangements the proportion of lead exceeded that of zinc, whilst other arrangements would show the opposite results. Similarly, measures of inter-zonal flows and spatial autocorrelation statistics (see further, Section 5.5.2) are significantly affected by scale and pattern aspects of grouping zones.

In practice the problem of zones arrangements may not be as significant an issue as it might appear. As Professor Richard Webber, the noted expert on geodemographics has remarked (private communication): "I have yet to come across any real world example of a conclusion being invalidly reached as a result of this hypothetical possibility". A wise strategy is to examine the data at various levels of aggregation, including the lowest (finest level) possible, and check that scale and zoning effects are understood and are unlikely to distort interpretations. Automated zoning was used to create the current UK 2001 Census of Population areas — see further Martin (2000) and Openshaw (1977). The procedure (known as AZP) was based on a 7-step approach, as follows:

- **Step 1:** Start by generating a random zoning system of *N* small zones into *M* regions, *M<N*

- **Step 2:** Make a list of the *M* regions.

- **Step 3:** Select and remove any region *K* at random from this list

- **Step 4:** Identify a set of zones bordering on members of region *K* that could be moved into region *K* without destroying the internal contiguity of the donor region(s)

- **Step 5:** Randomly select zones from this list until either there is a local improvement in the current value of the objective function or a move that is equivalently as good as the current best. Then make the move, update the list of candidate zones, and return to step 4 or else repeat step 5 until the list is exhausted

- **Step 6:** When the list for region *K* is exhausted return to step 3, select another region, and repeat steps 4-6

- **Step 7:** Repeat steps 2-6 until no further improving moves are made

In the UK case the initial small zones were taken as unit postcodes, which identify roughly 10-14 addresses. Unfortunately these individual addresses are stored as a list of georeferenced point data (nominal centers) rather than postcode areas, so the first stage of the analysis involved generating Voronoi polygons from these points, for the whole of the UK. These initial polygons were then merged to form unit postcode areas (Figure 4-19), based on the generated polygons and road alignments. Once these basic building blocks had been constructed the automated zoning process could begin. This is illustrated as a series of assignments in Figure 4-20, starting with an arbitrary assignment of contiguous unit postcode areas (Figure 4-20a), and then progressively selecting such areas for possible assignment to an adjacent zone (e.g. the pink regions in Figure 4-20b and Figure 4-20e). Assignment rules included target population size and a measure of social homogeneity, coupled with a measure of shape compactness and enforced contiguity. This process was then applied to a number of test areas across the UK, as is illustrated in the two scenarios, A and B, for part of Manchester, shown in Figure 4-21 (computed zones are shown with colors assigned on a 'unique values' basis). These scenarios were as follows:

- A: Threshold population=100; Target population=150; Shape constraint P2A=(perimeter squared)/area; no social homogeneity constraint applied

- B: Threshold population=100; Target population=250; Shape constraint

P2A=(perimeter squared)/area; social homogeneity constraint = tenure and dwelling type intra-area correlations

If scenario B is modified to exclude the shape constraint the assignment of areas is broadly similar, with detailed variations resulting in less compact final areas. and just 5% containing 40-99 households. Based on this methodology the Great Britain Ordnance Survey developed a full set of Output Areas

(OAs) with a target population of 125 households with a minimum of 40. These OAs were used for the 2001 census enabling OA data and postcodes to be linked, and providing a set of OAs that can be grouped into higher level units, such as wards and counties, as required. A total of 175,434 OAs were created in this manner, with 37.5% containing 120-129 households, 79.6% containing 110-139 households,

*Figure 4-19 Creating postcode polygons*

*Figure 4-20 Automated Zone Procedure (AZP)*

*Figure 4-21 AZP applied to part of Manchester, UK*

| A. Target population 150 | B. Target population 250 |
| --- | --- |
|  | |

## 4.2.12 Classification and clustering

"Classification is, perhaps, *the* basic procedure by which we impose some sort of order and coherence upon the vast inflow of information from the real world." Harvey (1969)

Harvey provides a very useful background to the field of classification, especially in a spatial context, but for the basics of classification within a GIS context Mitchell (1999, pp 46-55) and Longley *et al.* (2005, and in the forthcoming 3rd edition) are probably more useful and up-to-date starting points. These latter works address the question of how to classify and map attribute data associated with polygonal regions or provided as continuous fields. The manuals and online help facilities of the main GIS and image processing packages are also a good source of material for deciding which scheme might be the most appropriate for the dataset you have. Most of these schemes provide a range of standard alternatives for classifying univariate attributes, for example mapping population density by census tract. The attributes selected may be transformed in advance, for example: by producing spatially intensive variables such as densities rather than population totals; and/or by mathematically

transforming data, e.g. by classifying log transformed data rather than the original dataset; and/or by normalizing datasets (as discussed in Section 4.3.3). Alternatively the classification procedure selected may impose some form of normalization on the untransformed data (e.g. standard deviation based classification).

Classification needs to be seen in terms of purpose as well as method. However, GIS software places almost no constraints upon a user's selection of classification method, so it is the responsibility of the analyst to choose appropriate procedures and settings that are fit for purpose. Classification is by no means a peculiarly spatial problem, and most methods apply to almost any kind of data, i.e. there is rarely a specific spatial aspect, such as a contiguity condition, applied. Such facilities are more likely to be found in the spatial autocorrelation and pattern analysis features of GIS toolsets.

### 4.2.12.1 Univariate classification schemes

Within GIS software, univariate classification facilities are found as tools to: aid in the production of choropleth or thematic maps; explore untransformed or transformed datasets; analyze (classify and re-classify) image data (see further, Section 4.2.12.3); and display continuous field data. In the majority of cases these procedures perform classification based purely on the input dataset, without reference to separate external evaluation criteria.

In almost all instances the objects to be classified are regarded as discrete, distinct items that can only reside in one class at a time (sometimes referred to as *hard* classification). Separate schemes exist for classifying objects that have uncertain class membership (*soft* or *fuzzy* classification) and/or unclear boundaries (as discussed briefly in Section 4.2.13.4), or which require classification on the basis of multiple attributes (see Section 4.2.12.2). Typically the attributes used in classification have numerical values that are real or integer type. In most instances these numeric values represent interval or ratio-scaled variables. Purely nominal data are effectively already classified (see, for example, Figure 4-21 in which each zone has been assigned a unique color from a pre-selected palette; and see Section 2.2.2 for

a brief discussion of commonly used scales). Of course, there is always the option to apply no predefined classification procedure, but instead when mapping such data to apply a continuous gradation of grey tones or colors, using a linear or non-linear (e.g. ogive) scaling of the data values (see further Tobler, 1973 and Cromley and Ye, 2006).

Table 4-5 provides details of a number of univariate classification schemes together with comments on their use. Most of the main GIS packages provide classification options of the types listed, although some (such as the box and percentile methods) are only available in a limited number of software tools (e.g. GeoDa). A useful variant of the box method, known as hybrid equal interval, in which the inter-quartile range is itself divided into equal intervals, does not appear to be implemented in mainstream GIS packages. Schemes that take into account spatial contiguity, such as the so-called minimum boundary error method described by Cromley (1996), also do not appear to be readily available as a standard means of classification.

*Table 4-5 Selected univariate classification schemes*

| Classification scheme | Description/application |
|---|---|
| Unique values | Each value is treated separately, for example mapped as a distinct color |
| Manual classification | The analyst specifies the boundaries between classes required as a list, or specifies a lower bound and interval or lower and upper bound plus number of intervals required |
| Equal interval, Slice | The attribute values are divided into $n$ classes with each interval having the same width=Range/$n$. For raster maps this operation is often called *slice* |
| Defined interval | A variant of manual and equal interval, in which the user defines each of the intervals required |
| Exponential interval | Intervals are selected so that the *number* of observations in each successive interval increases (or decreases) exponentially |
| Equal count or quantile | Intervals are selected so that the number of *observations* in each interval is the same. If each interval contains 25% of the observations the result is known as a quartile classification. Ideally the procedure should indicate the exact numbers assigned to each class, since they will rarely be exactly equal |
| Percentile | Percentile plots are a variant of equal count or quantile plots. In the standard version equal percentages (percentiles) are included in each class. In GeoDa's implementation of percentile plots (specifically designed for exploratory spatial data analysis, ESDA) unequal numbers are assigned to provide classes that |

| Classification scheme | Description/application |
|---|---|
| | contain 6 intervals: <=1%, 1% to <10%, 10% to <50%, 50% to <90%, 90% to <99% and >=99% |
| Natural breaks/Jenks | Widely used within GIS packages, these are forms of variance-minimization classification. Breaks are typically uneven, and are selected to separate values where large changes in value occur. May be significantly affected by the number of classes selected and tends to have unusual class boundaries. Typically the method applied is due to Jenks, as described in Jenks and Caspall (1971), which in turn follows Fisher (1958). See Figure 4-22 for more details. Unsuitable for map comparisons |
| Standard deviation | The mean and standard deviation of the attribute values are calculated, and values classified according to their deviation from the mean (z-transform). The transformed values are then mapped, usually at intervals of 1.0 or 0.5 standard deviations. Note that this often results in no central class, only classes either side of the mean and the number of classes is then even. SD classifications in which there is a central class (defined as the mean value +/-0.5SD) with additional classes at +/- 1SD intervals beyond this central class, are also used |
| Box | A variant of quartile classification designed to highlight outliers, due to Tukey (1977, Section 2C). Typically six classes are defined, these being the 4 quartiles, plus two further classifications based on outliers. These outliers are defined as being data items (if any) that are more than 1.5 times the inter-quartile range (IQR) from the median. An even more restrictive set is defined by 3.0 times the IQR. A slightly different formulation is sometimes used to determine these box ends or *hinge* values. Box plots (see Section 5.2.2.2) are implemented in GeoDa and STARS, but are not generally found in mainstream GIS software. They are commonly implemented in statistics packages, for example the MATLab Statistics Toolbox |

Brewer and Pickle (2002) examined many of these methods, with particular attention being paid to ease of interpretation and comparison of map series, e.g. mapping time series data, for example of disease incidence by health service area over a number of years. They concluded that simple quantile methods were amongst the most effective, and had the great advantage of consistent legends for each map in the series, despite the fact that the class interval values often vary widely. They also found the schemes that resulted in a very large central class (e.g. 40%+) were more difficult to interpret.

In addition to selection of the scheme to use, the number of breaks or intervals and the positioning of these breaks are fundamental decisions. The number of breaks is often selected as an odd value: 5, 7 or 9. With an even number of classes there is no central class, and with a number of classes less than 4 or 5 the level of detail obtained may be too limited. With more than 9 classes gradations may be too fine to distinguish key differences between zones, but this will depend a great deal on the data and the purpose of the classification being selected. In a number of cases the GIS package provides linked frequency diagrams with breaks identified and in some cases interactively adjustable. In other cases generation of frequency diagrams should be conducted in advance to help determine the ideal number of classes and type of classification to be used.

For data with a very large range of values, smoothly varying across a range, a graduated set of classes and coloring may be entirely appropriate. Such classification schemes are common with field-like data and raster files. Continuous graded shading of thematic maps is also possible, with some packages, such as Manifold's Thematic Formatting facilities providing a wide range of options that reduce or remove the dependence on formal class boundaries. The Jenks method, as implemented in a number of GIS packages such as ArcGIS, is not always well-documented so a brief description of the algorithm is provided in Figure 4-22. This description also provides an initial model for some of the multivariate methods described in subsection 4.2.12.2.

---

### Figure 4-22 Jenks Natural Breaks algorithm

Step 1: The user selects the attribute, $x$, to be classified and specifies the number of classes required, $k$

Step 2: A set of $k-1$ random or uniform values are generated in the range $[\min\{x\},\max\{x\}]$. These are used as initial class boundaries

Step 3: The mean values for each initial class are computed and the sum of squared deviations of class members from the mean values is computed. The total sum of squared deviations (TSSD) is recorded

Step 4: Individual values in each class are then systematically assigned to adjacent classes by adjusting the class boundaries to see if the TSSD can be reduced. This is an iterative process, which ends when improvement in TSSD falls below a threshold level, i.e. when the within class variance is as small as possible and between class variance is as large as possible. True optimization is not assured. The entire process can be optionally repeated from Step 1 or 2 and TSSD values compared

---

Positioning of breaks may be pre-determined by the classification procedure (e.g. Jenks Natural breaks), but these are often manually adjustable for some of the schemes provided — this is particularly useful if specific values or intervals are preferred, such as whole numbers or some convenient values such as 1000s, or if comparisons are to be made across a series of maps. In some instances options are provided for dealing with zero-valued and/or missing data prior to classification, but if not provided the data should be inspected in advance and subsets selected prior to classification where necessary. Some authors recommend that

maps with large numbers of zero or missing data values should have such regions identified in a class of their own.

#### 4.2.12.2 Multivariate classification and clustering

Harvey (1969, p.346) describes the key steps of multivariate classification as follows:

- quantitative analysis of the inter-relationships among the attributes or among the objects

- transformation or reduction of the correlations to a geometric structure with known properties (usually Euclidean)

- grouping or clustering of the objects or attributes on the basis of the distance measured in this transformed space, and once the classes have been firmly identified

- the development of rules for assigning phenomena to classes

Important additional steps to those listed by Harvey are in-process and post-process analysis of the quality of classification achieved. In-process quality analysis attempts to use multiple classification approaches (typically *soft classifiers* — see further, below) to evaluate the robustness and strength of the classes that have been defined. Alternatively or additionally, random samples of classified data (e.g. pixels) are taken and compared with the ground truth, by field survey (using new or previously collected data).

Classification of datasets based purely on attribute information (i.e. ignoring spatial relationships) can readily be conducted using general purpose statistical and mathematical toolsets. Some techniques, such as clustering based on multivariate analysis of variance, require that input datasets be Normally distributed, but many methods make no such assumptions. Most statistical and mathematical libraries provide a range of tools to facilitate classification and assignment. These typically include:

- facilities that can be used to reduce the complexity (dimensionality) of the source datasets, such as *factor analysis, principal components analysis* and *multidimensional scaling*

- facilities to identify clusters within the dataset, either on a single level for a fixed number of clusters (e.g. *K*-means clustering) or on a hierarchical basis (typically techniques that rely on some form of linkage function, usually based on a function of the simple *n*-dimensional Euclidean distance between points within separate clusters); and

- facilities for optimally assigning new observations to existing classes (e.g. *linear discriminant analysis*)

Before we examine the application of such methods to the analysis of multi-band image data (the main application area for such methods within GIS and remotely-sensed image processing packages), we first summarize the *K*-means and linear discriminant analysis procedures mentioned above.

*K*-means clustering attempts to partition a multivariate dataset into *K* distinct (non-overlapping) clusters such that points within a cluster are as close as possible in multi-dimensional space, and as far away as possible from points in other clusters. The input dataset can be viewed as a set of objects with an associated set of *n* (typically real-valued) measures or attributes. Each object can then be viewed as a single point or vector $x=\{x_1, x_2, x_3..., x_n\}$ in *n*-dimensional space. The cluster procedure is then as follows:

- The method starts with a set of *K* initial cluster centers. These might be assigned: (i) as *K* random locations in *n*-space within the observed data ranges; (ii) as *K* uniformly sited locations within the observed data ranges; (iii) as a user-defined set of *K* locations; (iv) by selecting *K* datapoints at random from the observed set as cluster centers; or (v) as a set of *K* locations obtained by clustering a small subset of the data using random or uniform allocation. A minimum separation distance for starting points may be specified

- The distance between every point and each of the *K* means is computed, based on some prior defined metric (often using squared Euclidean, $L_2{}^2$, or City block, $L_1$, as these are both fast to compute — see further, Section 4.4.1). The Idrisi software package, for example, uses Euclidean distances and the general expression:

$$d_{ik} = \sum_n \sqrt{\left|X_{in} - C_{kn}\right|^2}$$

where $d_{ik}$ defines the distance from the $i^{\text{th}}$ pixel in an image to the $k^{\text{th}}$ centroid, $X_{in}$ is the *n*-element (band) vector of the $i^{\text{th}}$ pixel, and $C_{kn}$ is the *n*-element vector of the $k^{\text{th}}$ centroid

- Points are assigned to the nearest center (i.e. it is a locally optimizing *greedy heuristic*; see further, Section 7.2.2.1). Any entirely empty clusters may be discarded and (optionally) a new start point added

- The location of the center of each cluster is then re-computed based on the set of points allocated to that center, and the previous step is then repeated. This sequence is iterated until no further reassignments occur, or a preset number of iterations have been completed, or no cluster center is moved by more than a pre-specified small amount. The total distance (DSUM) of all points to the centers of the *K* clusters to which they have been assigned is calculated

- Each point is then re-examined in turn (Phase 2 of the process) and checked to see if DSUM is reduced if the point is assigned to another cluster. If DSUM is reduced the point is reassigned to the cluster that results in the maximum overall reduction

- Stopping criteria may be determined by setting a limit to the number of iterations of the process (e.g. 50), or the level of change in DSUM, or the number or percentage of data points that continue to be re-allocated (e.g. 1%), or a combination of these options

- Special consideration may be given to the re-allocation of data items where the cluster membership is very small (e.g. contain less than 1% of the data). The option to remove low membership clusters and re-allocate their members (i.e. consolidating the clusters to provide a smaller number of larger clusters) is quite common

- The entire process may then be repeated with a different choice of starting points. This may result in an overall reduction in the objective function, DSUM, since the algorithm is not guaranteed to provide an optimal partitioning

- Generic clustering algorithms, such as K-means, may result in many spatially isolated pixels or zones, which may be members of a well-represented class (>>1%). In some instances a smoothing filter can consolidate such occurrences with their surrounding zones, but must be applied with care since the resultant classification will knowingly contain mixtures

- It is often also the practice to assign different weights to clusters when finalizing the classes, in accordance with *a priori* interpretation of the resulting outcomes. The benefits of so doing should be set out in a clear and transparent manner in order to aid interpretation of the results by third parties

Linear Discriminant Analysis (LDA), as applied within Idrisi, assumes we have $P$ classes and $P$ linear discriminant functions. These functions, which are rather like linear regression equations, are computed by analysis of training site data comprised of $m$ image bands. Having computed the weights for each of these linear functions, a set of $P$ weighted sums is then calculated for each pixel in the target image and the sum that has the highest value or score, $S_i$, is taken as the class to which the pixel is to be assigned. The sum is of the form:

$$S_i = c_i + \sum_{j=1}^{m} w_{i,j} x_j$$

where $c_i$ is a constant for class $i$, $x_j$ is the observed pixel value in class $j$, and $w_{i,j}$ is the pre-computed weight applying to band $j$ and class $i$. Hence with $m=7$ spectral bands there would be a set of 7+1 associated weights for each discriminant function. If there were $P=5$ such functions (i.e. 5 classes), there would be a matrix, **W**, of 40 weight values, and each pixel would be assigned to one of the 5 classes.

Most GIS packages, such as such as TNTMips, Idrisi, GRASS and ArcGIS Spatial Analyst, include a range of multivariate classification procedures. As noted earlier, these are principally for image classification and pixel assignment, as are those provided within the specialized image processing suites, ERDAS and ENVI. The most commonly provided include K-means, ISODATA, and Maximum Likelihood procedures. More details, with specific reference to multi-band and hyperspectral image analysis, are provided in Sections 4.2.12.3 and 4.2.12.5, below. Details of image classification techniques that use artificial neural network (ANN) methods are provided in Section 8.3. Details of many of the traditional methods described may be found in Tou and Gonzales (1974, Chapter 3), Ball and Hall (1965), Richards (1986) and Burrough and McDonnell (1998, Ch.11).

### 4.2.12.3 Multi-band image classification

In this subsection we provide a brief description of many of the multi-band classifier procedures generally available, with special reference to those provided within one of the main raster-focused GIS packages, Idrisi. Other packages, notably ENVI, also provide many of these facilities.

Within GIS and remotely-sensed image processing software multivariate classification methods are almost exclusively applied to image datasets — typically multi-band image files. The objective is to identify distinct areas or features (collections of pixels or cells) such as forest, water, grassland and buildings and assign all occurrences of such features to distinct classes. This is either performed semi-automatically (supervised, requiring training site data) or automatically (unsupervised).

Supervised classification (S) involves the manual analysis of selected images to identify features of interest and assign polygonal regions to user-defined classes. The statistical characteristics of these regions within and across rasters, sometimes described as *signatures*, can then be used to guide subsequent classification. Special toolsets are generally provided for signature development. It may also be necessary to normalize the datasets (to ensure the range of values in each band is similar) and/or to (dimensionally) transform the datasets in some way before proceeding to the formal clustering and assignment processes (for example using techniques such as principal components analysis, PCA, or factor analysis, FA – see further, CATMOGs 7 and 8).

Unsupervised classification (U) either does not require training data to be specified in advance, or performs a form of automated selection from the input images. With these techniques it is often helpful to specify more clusters than you would ultimately like or expect and then to combine some of those produced if they seem essentially the same in terms of your own objectives rather than purely computational factors. For example separate clusters may be produced for deciduous and coniferous vegetation cover, but if the objective is to classify areas as woodland without separating these by type, post classification combination may be effective. Most of the more sophisticated raster-based GIS packages provide such facilities, for example TNTMips (see the TNTMips Image Classification Guide) and Idrisi (see the Idrisi Guide to GIS and Image Processing), as well as the more generic ArcGIS Spatial Analyst toolset and the specialized image processing suites, ERDAS and ENVI. Several of these packages refer to Richards (1986) as a primary source for many of the standard procedures they adopt for classification and interested readers are recommended to refer to this volume for more information.

Each pixel of a multi-band image to be classified can be regarded as being comprised of a vector $\mathbf{x}=\{x_1, x_2, x_3..., x_m\}$ of data values, one per band. Typically the data are real-valued and positive. In so-called remotely-sensed *multi-band image processing* the number of bands is generally not very large, typically 7 or fewer. In such multi-band images it is often the case that most of the useful information is contained in just two or three bands, for example the red, near infra-red and middle infra-red bands, and in some instances these may be used rather than the full set. *Hyperspectral images*, on the other hand, are comprised of a very large number of finely divided spectral bands, from 10s to 100s of such bands. A third type of multi-band image is one in which the images are co-registered but are not all derived from remote-sensing — some of the bands or raster layers may be derived from other forms of survey and/or be computationally derived (e.g. rasters generated by rasterizing zonal, linear or point vector data). An example involving the analysis of such data using artificial neural network (ANN) methods is provided in Section 8.3.3.2.

Table 4-6 summarizes the principal set of so-called *hard classifiers* (H), some of which also provide soft classification as an option. Hard classifiers assign every pixel in the target image to one of *n* classes, or to a null class (usually coded as 0). *Soft classifiers* (S) assign pixels to classes with a value that indicates their *degree of membership* of that class. This may be expressed as a probability value, $p_k$, with the sum over all $k=1..P$ classes being 1 (or 100%), or may be a value that is not regarded as a probability and may not sum to 1 (typically summing to less than 1). Display of soft classified images is often as a series of separate layers, one per class, with the pixels being color- or gray-scale coded to indicate their degree of membership. The output of soft classifiers can be *hardened*, in a variety of ways. One approach is to take the output from a soft classification and generate a set of classification maps that provide the first (most likely/highest scoring), second etc. class assignments as separate displays. Another approach is to utilize ancillary data, such as (buffered) GIS vector data that is overlaid on the classified results. For example, this may assist in identifying classes that are or are not built-up land (i.e. increasing the strength of evidence for specific classes) based on the known distance from roads. Yet another approach is to utilize prior geostatistical analysis of higher resolution remotely-sensed imagery obtained from a smaller area, or field survey data, to provide enhanced guidance for the classification process.

Most of the classification procedures described in Table 4-6 are non-hierarchical, i.e. they classify pixels in the target image into distinct classes that are not grouped into levels. Some do provide a tree-like structure (e.g. CTA). In this case, conceptually one might imagine high level groups such as Built, Wetland, Forest, Grass, and Rock. Forest, for example, might be divided into deciduous and evergreen. Deciduous might be further divided into species-type subgroups. In Table 4-6 the H/S

column identifies whether the classification is hard or soft, with some classifiers providing both options. The S/U column identifies whether the procedure is essentially supervised (S) or unsupervised (U). In addition, and not described in detail here, are *mixture analyses*, in which pixels may be allocated to one or more than one class simultaneously. For example, a pixel might be assigned to two different kinds of woodland or two different kinds of soil type, thus regarded as being of explicitly mixed rather than single class membership. Mixture assignments are usually on an hierarchical basis, e.g. with 3 classes [A], [B] and [C] the 7 possible mixtures would be [A], [B], [C], [A,B], [A,C], [B,C], and [A,B,C]. Clearly there may be a very large number of mixture class combinations, so this approach must be applied with caution.

*Table 4-6 Image classification facilities – Selected classifiers*

| Classifier (Idrisi function shown in CAPS) | S/U | H/S | Description |
|---|---|---|---|
| Simple one-pass clustering | U | H | A technique that generates up to *P* clusters by assigning each input cell to the nearest cluster if its Euclidean distance is less than a given threshold. If not the cell becomes a new cluster center. It principal merit is speed, but its quality of assignment may not be acceptable (see also, PIPED, below) |
| Parallelepiped (PIPED) | S | H | Based on a set of *lower and upper threshold* values determined for a signature on each band. To be assigned to a particular class, a pixel must exhibit values within this range (absolute limits or standard deviation, for training dataset) for every band considered. Non-unique assignment with no assignment (Class=0) if a pixel lies outside the threshold for all signatures. Very fast, but generally not recommended for use because the class 'boxes' defined by the thresholds typically overlap, meaning that pixel assignment to specific classes is arbitrary in these regions |
| Minimum distance to mean (MINDIST) | S | H | Essentially the same as simple one-pass clustering but cluster centers are pre-determined by analysis of a training dataset, using the *mean* values on each band for a signature. Pixels are assigned to the class with the mean closest to the value of that pixel. Applied when the number of pixels used to define signatures is very small or when training sites are not well defined. No assignment (Class=0) is made if a pixel lies outside a maximum search distance set by the user for all signatures. Data may be raw values or pre-normalized. Use in preference to MAXLIKE if training sites are not well defined in terms of classes. Fast, often performing well, but does not account for the variability between classes since it uses mean values only – MAXLIKE (below) is generally a preferable approach (see also ISOCLUST) |
| Maximum likelihood | S | H | A method that uses statistical analysis (variance and covariance) of a training dataset (class signatures) whose contents are assumed to be |

| Classifier (Idrisi function shown in CAPS) | S/U | H/S | Description |
|---|---|---|---|
| (MAXLIKE) | | | Normally distributed (prior transformation of the input dataset may therefore be advisable). It seeks to determine the probability (or likelihood) that a cell should be assigned to a particular cluster, with assignment being based on the computed Maximum Likelihood value. MAXLIKE operates in a similar manner to MINDIST but takes account of correlation between bands. Pixels are assigned to the most likely class based on a comparison of the posterior probability that it belongs to, each of the signatures being considered (i.e. Bayesian). Prior probabilities may be set in various ways, including uniform (all classes equally likely) or using separate knowledge of some or all classes, e.g. 30% is expected to be woodland, 20% grassland, etc, where the labels woodland and grassland correspond to specific signatures. Unique assignment — no assignment (Class=0) is made if a pixel lies outside a pre-specified probability level (e.g. 1%, 5%, i.e. less than x% likelihood of belonging to any of the signature classes). Requires number of pixels >10 times number of bands. Limitations (Idrisi): number of bands <65; number of signatures<256. Quality heavily affected by homogeneity of training sites. Relatively fast (see also ISOCLUST) |
| (Stepwise) Linear Discriminant (FISHER) | S | H | This is essentially a Linear Discriminant Analysis (LDA) method (see Section 4.2.12.2), which attempts to compute linear functions of the dataset variables that best explain or *discriminate* between values in a training dataset. With the stepwise variant new linear functions are added incrementally, orthogonal to each other, and then these functions are used to assign all data points to the classes. The criterion function minimized in such methods is usually Mahalanobis distance, or the $D^2$ function. Linear Discriminant Analysis of the training site data is used to form a set of linear functions that express the degree of support for each class. The assigned class for each pixel is then that class which receives the highest support after evaluation of all functions. In the Idrisi implementation there are as many classification functions as there are classes. Each function allows classification scores to be computed for each pixel for each class. Limitations (Idrisi): number of bands <65; number of signatures<256. Unique assignment. All pixels are assigned to classes. Relatively fast |
| *K*-nearest neighbors (KNN) | S | H,S | In this procedure the Euclidean distance is calculated for each pixel in an input image to all sampled training pixels in all classes. Then, for the specified *k*, only those *k*-nearest neighbors are examined in determining an image pixel's class or degree of membership to a class. For the hard classification output, the class that dominates the *k*-nearest neighbors is assigned to that pixel. For the soft classification output, the proportion for each category among the *k*-nearest neighbors is evaluated. For each class an image is produced with each pixel assigned its respective proportion. Variable speed of operation, depending on parameters, especially size of *k*-value |
| Histogram clustering (CLUSTER) | U | H | CLUSTER uses a histogram peak technique of cluster analysis. This is equivalent to looking for the peaks in a one-dimensional histogram, where a peak is defined as a value with a greater frequency than its neighbors on either side (see Figure 4-23). Once the peaks have been identified, all possible values are assigned to the nearest peak and the divisions between classes fall at the midpoints between peaks. In Idrisi a maximum of 7 image bands can be used as input, and pixels are assigned to a |

| Classifier (Idrisi function shown in CAPS) | S/U | H/S | Description |
|---|---|---|---|
| | | | maximum of 255 classes. A 1-dimensional to 7-dimensional histogram is used to find the peaks. A peak is a class where the frequency is higher than all of its non-diagonal neighbors (broad level), or higher than all but one of its non-diagonal neighbors (fine level). Input images are pre-processed into 256 gray-scale values, generally with the tails of the histograms cut off (e.g. 2.5% at each end). CLUSTER can be used to develop class signatures that may then be applied to supervised classification systems like MAXLIKE. Fast |
| ISOdata/ISOcluster (Iterative Self-Organizing) (ISOCLUST) | U | H | Similar to the $K$-means procedure but at each iteration the various clusters are examined to see if they would benefit from being combined or split, based on a number of criteria: (i) combination — if two cluster centers are closer than a pre-defined tolerance they are combined and a new mean calculated as the cluster center; (ii) if the number of members in a cluster is below a given level (e.g. 20) the cluster is discarded and the members re-assigned to the closest cluster; and (iii) separation — if the number of members, or the standard deviation, or the average distance from the cluster center exceed pre-defined values then the cluster may be split. ISOCLUST is an automated procedure that combines the CLUSTER operation with the MAXLIKE cluster assignment process, applied iteratively — both are described above. It is similar to the ISODATA procedure (see Dunn, 1973). CLUSTER is used to generate initial cluster centers (seed locations) and these define the signatures which are then used by MAXLIKE to determine cluster assignments. Restrictions are as per CLUSTER and MAXLIKE. The procedure is quite slow, depending on the complexity of the images and the number of clusters, but is claimed to produce very strong cluster assignment. |
| $K$-means (KMEANS) | U | H | The classical $K$-means algorithm has been described earlier in this Guide (Section 4.2.12.2). Limitations (Idrisi): $n<65$ image bands and $K<256$ clusters. Very dependent on selection of number of clusters and their initial center locations (seed locations). This is a heuristic, greedy algorithm for minimizing SSE (Sum of Squared Errors) hence it may not converge to a global optimum. Three options are provided in Idrisi for seed locations: random partitioning — each pixel is assigned at random to one of $K$ clusters and the cluster centers are computed from the assigned points; random centers — randomly selects $K$ pixels as the initial centers and assigns other pixels to these; and diagonal values — the range of pixel data values in $n$-space is computed and values assigned at even spacing along this [min] to [max] $n$-vector. Relatively fast |
| Fuzzy $c$-means (FCM) | U | H/S | Similar to the $K$-means procedure, originally developed by Dunn (1973) but uses weighted distances rather than unweighted distances. Weights are computed from prior analysis of training data for a specified number of classes. These cluster centers then define the classes and all cells are assigned a membership weight for each cluster. The process then proceeds as for $K$-means but with distances weighted by the prior assigned membership coefficients (see also, Section 4.2.13.4) |
| Minimum distribution angle (MDA) | U | H | An iterative procedure similar to $K$-means but instead of computing the distance from points to selected centers this method treats cell centers and data points as directed vectors from the origin. The angle between the data point and the cluster center vector provides a measure of similarity of attribute mix (ignoring magnitude). This concept is similar to |

| Classifier (Idrisi function shown in CAPS) | S/U | H/S | Description |
|---|---|---|---|
| | | | considering mixes of red and blue paint to produce purple. It is the proportions that matter rather than the amounts of paint used. See also, Spectral angle clustering in Section 4.2.12.5 |
| Multi-level perceptron (MLP) | S/U | H/S | A neural network technique. Described in detail in Section 8.3.1 *et seq* with a worked example. Fairly slow |
| Self organizing maps (SOM) | S/U | H | A neural network technique based on Kohonen (1990). Described in detail in Section 8.3.3 *et seq*. With the unsupervised model variant *K*-means is generally used to locate the initial clusters. Moderate speed of clustering |
| Fuzzy ARTMAP | S/U | H | ART stands for Adaptive Resonance Theory, a form of neural network model. Fuzzy ART is a clustering algorithm that operates on vectors with fuzzy input patterns (real numbers between 0.0 and 1.0) and incorporates an incremental learning approach which allows it to learn continuously (remembering previous learned states). The MAP part of the name refers to the use of an additional MAP layer in the neural network model when used in supervised mode. For more details see Mannan and Roy (1998), or Fischer (2006, Ch.11) |
| Classified tree analysis (CTA) | S | H/S | A univariate hierarchical data splitting procedure, that progressively divides the training dataset pixels into two classes based on a splitting rule, and then further subdivides these two classes (i.e. a binary tree structure). Division (splitting) may be achieved using the entropy statistic or similar measures (e.g. gain ratio, Gini statistic). See further, Zambon *et al.* (2006) and Idrisi's focus paper describing the technique |

*Figure 4-23 SPOT Band 1 image histogram — distinct peaks highlighted (CLUSTER)*

### 4.2.12.4 Uncertainty and image processing

Uncertainty is an intrinsic feature of remotely-sensed image data for several reasons, including:

**Resolution**: the resolution of a remotely-sensed image defines the area represented by a single pixel. If a pixel represents a 100m by 100m region it is almost certain that its contents will be of mixed landcover types, and hence will generate data that reflects this mixture. Specific techniques (generally based on soft classifiers such as Idrisi's UNMIX, BAYCLASS and FUZCLASS functions) are available for analyzing within-cell spectral variation, often described as sub-pixel classification

**Temporal variables:** time of day and season affect both the landcover (e.g. growth stages) and illumination patterns (e.g. lighting of slopes, vegetation surfaces, moisture levels) resulting in additional variations within and between image datasets and bands

**Spectral response:** remote-sensing may not measure the spectral response band or bands on which the particular surface provides maximum response. The response data may therefore be weak or mixed/easily confused with other surface responses

Soft classification procedures can provide an image displaying the *degree of uncertainty* of the classification. For example, for every soft classification image one pixel or set of contiguous pixels (region) may have the same or very similar degree of class membership, hence no one class is clearly favored. This may be contrasted with a hard classification process in which the winning class, i.e. the one with slightly higher probability or degree of membership, would be selected in preference to any other. An uncertainty map illustrates the degree to which one class (from a total of $P$ classes) stands out from the rest for each pixel in the image. Definition of uncertainty could be based on Shannon's information statistic (entropy) statistic or variations thereof, or on an application-specific measure. Idrisi adopts the latter approach, using an uncertainty measure, $U$, of the form:

$$U = 1 - \frac{m - s/P}{1 - 1/P}$$

Here, $m$ is the maximum degree of membership recorded for the pixel in question, and $s \le 1$ is the sum of the degree of membership for that pixel. Thus, with $P=10$ classes and $m=0.3$ and $s=1$, say, we have $U=1-0.22=0.78$ whilst with $m=0.1$ we have $U=1$ (complete uncertainty) and with $m=1$ $U=0$ (complete certainty).

### 4.2.12.5 Hyperspectral image classification

*Hyperspectral images* are comprised of a large number of finely divided spectral bands, from 10s to 100s of such bands. The following analysis utilizes a hyperspectral dataset produced by the NASA AVIRIS (Airborne Visible/Infrared Imaging Spectrometer) project. As noted previously, hyperspectral imagery is become increasingly available and is essentially the same as multi-band imagery but with far more bands provided. It has particular application in geological work, both terrestrial and for planetary/lunar data analysis.

The dataset we use in this subsection is comprised of 224 contiguous spectral bands in the range 400nm (nanometers) to approximately 2500 nm at 10 nm intervals. The raster image files cover 512x614 cells of 20m squares and relate to a mining region (Cuprite) in western Nevada, USA (hence c.10km by 12km in area). This dataset is available for download via the data section of the AVIRIS website and from the TNTMips web site as one of their tutorial datasets. It is discussed in more detail at the USGS spectral lab site: http://speclab.cr.usgs.gov, from which reference spectra may be obtained. The layers of raster datasets of this type are spatially matched and highly correlated. This means that storage of such data as 224 raster objects would be extremely inefficient and hence of much more compact (compressed) 3D object variant is stored by TNTMips which they describe as a *hypercube*. Figure 4-24 shows two alternative 2D representations of the region, where 3 spectral layers have been chosen to represent the red/green/blue (RGB) components of the image for display purposes. This provides a strong visual impression of the data, but each image is based on just 3 of the 224 layers and depends for its interpretation upon the choice of the three spectral bands and color scheme applied. There are a number of alternative representations for datasets of this type. The 3D hypercube described above can be displayed and layers selected systematically or as desired (Figure 4-25). This is essentially a visualization tool that enables closer inspection of the data and highlights the correlated nature of the information, but does not provide a direct route to analysis. Several software packages support analysis of this type of dataset, including Idrisi (the HYPERSAM and HYPERMIN facilities, and the new Earth Trends Modeler) and the TNTMips spectral angle mapping facility, which we have used in the current example. Each pixel of the 3D hypercube has a spectral value for the ordered set of frequencies (i.e. across the depth of the cube). This ordered set can be viewed as a graph or spectrogram and can be compared with reference spectrograms (e.g. ground survey reference samples) or using laboratory sets obtained from prior research for different surface materials and minerals. Similarity of (normalized) spectral plots to the image spectral plot provides a means of classifying individual pixels and hence the region as a whole.

*Figure 4-24 2D map of Cuprite mining district, Western Nevada, USA*

| Bands: R=207, G=123, B=36 | Bands: R=12, G=6, B=1 |

*Figure 4-25 3D hypercube visualization of Cuprite mining district, Western Nevada, USA*

Laboratory-generated reference spectra are available from various sources, including the USGS spectral analysis laboratory cited above. It should be noted, however, that laboratory-generated reference spectra will differ from remotely-sensed spectra owing to many factors, including non-uniform atmospheric distortions. Special facilities (e.g. the hyperspectral PROFILE facility in Idrisi) are available to identify and, where necessary, eliminate those bands that are subject to particularly high atmospheric distortion. As noted above, the analysis of hyperspectral images can be undertaken by regarding each cell or pixel as a single point in 224-dimensional space. The recorded value for each spectral band is then the coordinate value for this pixel for the selected dimension. The single point in $n$-space can be seen as a vector from the spectral origin, **0**, with the full pixel set (512x614 pixels) being seen as clouds of points in $n$-space. The *direction* of these vectors is more important than their *magnitude*, since the latter are affected by average brightness. Simple *spectral angle mapping* (SAM) consists of comparing a known (reference) spectrum, which has its own characteristic $m$-dimensional vector, with those in the sample image. Pixels that have an angular proximity to the reference vector below a user-specified value are assigned to that class (cf. Table 4-6, minimum distribution angle method). Every pixel in the source hypercube can be compared with the reference vectors in $m$-space and the angle between the pairs of vectors computed. The resulting set of scalar values can then be mapped as a form of "angular distance" raster (fuzzy, or soft class assignment) or just those values that are below a given angular distance threshold can be mapped (absolute, or hard class assignment). Figure 4-26 shows an absolute (hard) class assignment for a single spectrum overlaid on Figure 4-24B above (blue area).

*Figure 4-26 Single class assignment from spectral angle analysis*

## 4.2.13 Boundaries and zone membership

The definition and selection of boundaries is often a difficult, but nevertheless essential element in many areas of spatial analysis. One group of problems where this is especially important is in the analysis of point patterns — sets of points in the plane representing cases of a particular disease, or the location of ancient artifacts, or a particular species of plant. If the density of points (frequency of occurrence per unit area) is required then the total area under examination needs to be defined. Definition of this area, $A$, requires identification of a boundary, although there is now a variety of special procedures (known as kernel density methods) available for computation of densities without pre-defined fixed boundaries (see further, Section 4.3.4).

A further problem relates to the process of modeling the real world with abstracted linear forms (i.e. polylines and polygons). There are a variety of ways of modeling linear forms — mathematical, statistical, fractal, zonal — and each of these models will have implications for analysis. Data recorded in a GIS database, either as vector or grid elements, have already been modeled and to some extent the kinds of analyses that may be carried out are pre-determined. For example, most GIS packages do not provide facilities for analyzing the complexity or "texture" of modeled lines and surfaces, although some, such as Idrisi and Fragstats do support such analyses by examining grid datasets at various scales and/or using variable sized windows. The ArcGIS add-in, Hawth's Tools, provides a *line metrics* tool for generating measures of estimated fractal dimension and sinuosity of stored polylines. For fractal dimension this software computes, for each polyline:

$$D_c = \frac{\log(n)}{\log(n) + \log\left(\dfrac{d}{L}\right)}$$

where $n$ is the number of line segments that make up the polyline, $d$ is the distance between the start and end points of the polyline, and $L$ is the total length of the polyline, i.e. the cumulative length of all polyline segments. *Sinuosity* is computed as a simple ratio: $d/L$, for each polyline. In both cases the results are added as new fields to the feature attribute table.

### 4.2.13.1 Convex hulls

For point sets in the plane a simple and often useful boundary is the convex hull (Figure 4-27). This is taken as the convex polygon of smallest area that completely encloses the set (it may also be used for line and polygon sets).

*Figure 4-27 Convex hull of sample point set*

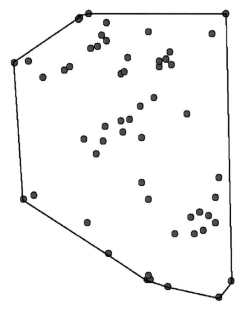

If the data you are working with consist solely of a single point set then the convex hull of this set encloses all the information you have available, even though you may know that the data extend beyond these limits.

The convex hull may also be useful in the analysis of optimum location and networking problems. For example the center of gravity of a set of points in the plane will always lie inside or on the convex hull of the point set, and the sequence of points which comprises the convex hull form part of the solution to certain network routing problems (systematic minimal tours of a set of locations). However, it is important to note that the convex hull of a set of objects (points, lines etc.) is affected markedly by extreme values, so outliers and/or errors can have a substantial impact on the shape, area, perimeter length and centroid of a convex hull. For example, one or two extreme values can substantially increase the area enclosed by the convex hull. Typically, however, convex hulls under-estimate area for many applications and hence will over-estimate densities if computed using an area measure based upon this hull.

By definition the convex hull includes a number of points as part of its boundary. For some problems this may be satisfactory whilst for others it may not be suitable. For example, when analyzing the distribution of points in a study region it may be preferable to minimize the potential distortions to sample statistics by avoiding points that lie on or close to the convex hull. Creating an inner buffer of the convex hull and analyzing the subset of points lying within the core of the region, with or without consideration of points lying in the buffer zone, may be preferable. Alternatively the convex hull may be uniformly increased (buffered) in size, for example by a given percentage of area or by a specified distance such as half the mean distance to the nearest-neighbors of enclosed points.

### 4.2.13.2 Non-convex hulls

The computation of convex hulls is a fast and useful facility, but does not necessarily match the requirements of the analyst attempting to define a region enclosing a set of objects. We have already noted, for example, that the method is strongly affected by the location of outliers, and as a result may enclose large regions that are of no interest or relevance to the analysis. Whilst the convex hull of a point set in the plane is unique, any number and variety of non-convex hulls may be generated. Such alternative hulls may meet certain pre-defined application-related criteria. Examples might include: the hull must be a polygon; the polygon must be as near convex as possible; the polygon must have the smallest possible area enclosing the set as possible; the polygon must reflect the density of points in the sample; the polygon must assign each point its own nominal region and include all points.

There are three principal methods for generating non-convex polygonal hulls (NCPHs) that meet specified criteria. These are: (a) expansion; (b) contraction; and (c) density contouring. Some of these methods may be implemented using most GIS packages, but the majority require some programming. TNTMips includes facilities for computing several of the variants described within its Polygon Fitting facility. These algorithms were originally developed to help identify animal "home ranges" but may be utilized in many areas — see for example, Harvey and Barbour (1965), White and Garrott (1990, pp 145-82, "Home range estimation") and Mitchell (2006).

**Case (a) expansion:** in this case the non-convex hull is created by assigning each point a surrounding region and then growing this region until all points are covered and a continuous external hull is obtained. This may be achieved in several ways. One method is to compute Voronoi polygons for all the points and use the external boundary of the (finite) set as the NCPH (see for example Figure 4-33B). This leaves the problem of how to treat the points that make up the convex hull. An alternative non-polygonal approach is to buffer all the points and increase the buffer width until a single merged zone is formed. This process may highlight the need to consider the benefits of using several sub-regions rather than a single region — for example, in cases where many of the observations lie near the region boundary with a large central region containing few observations. Yet another alternative is to overlay the study region with a rectangular grid and define the NCPH with reference to this (for example, requiring that the grid includes every point and a minimum number of cells surrounding every point). Where necessary interstitial gaps in the grid are grown to ensure a contiguous overall region is achieved without necessarily growing the external boundary.

**Case (b) contraction:** this case involves reduction of the convex hull according to selected rules. The simplest of these is a systematic area minimization procedure. First the area of the convex hull is computed. Next a point on the convex hull is removed and the new convex hull recomputed. The area of this new region is calculated and stored. The process is repeated for all points on the original convex hull and the point that results in the greatest decrease in area is permanently removed. The procedure then iterates until only a pre-defined percentage of the original points remain (e.g. 90%) or the area has been reduced by a given percentage. The result is a convex hull of an optimized subset of the original points. A second procedure, which results in a NCPH, involves a form of shrinkage of the convex hull around the point set, rather like a plastic bag full of small balls having the air removed. In this method the longest linear segment of the convex hull is selected and replaced with two segments connecting the original two end points via an intermediate point that is the closest to the original line — almost the reverse of point-weeding (Section 4.2.4). The process continues until the overall area enclosed has been reduced by a pre-determined amount, or a number of iterations have been reached — 10 is a typical number to use. Hybridization of this method with the preceding method is possible.

Note that in the majority of contraction and expansion methods the result is either a grid or polygon form, with the latter having straight line edges. Procedures also exist in which the restriction of convexity, connectedness and/or to straight edges is relaxed, e.g. forming so-called *alpha hulls* or *alpha shapes* where concavities and unconnected sets are permitted. Consider a circle or disc of radius 1/alpha. When alpha is small (close to zero) the disc radius is large (infinite at 0). With a large enough radius the disc can be placed over any given point set such that the set is fully enclosed and precisely two points from the set lie on its boundary (Figure 4-28A). These are then typically connected by a straight line, and a complete hull can thus be generated. Figure 4-28B to D illustrate the results obtained by varying alpha, as explained below.

*Figure 4-28 Alpha hulls*

a. alpha>0

b. alpha>0, increasing positive

c. alpha<0

d. alpha<0, increasing negative

In Figure 4-28B, with larger alpha the disc radius is reduced and only a limited number of circles can be drawn that enclose the point set and have a pair of points from the set on their boundary. The resulting alpha shape excludes many of the original points. Figure 4-28C and Figure 4-28D illustrate the shapes formed as alpha becomes increasingly negative. In this case the complement of the positive disc shapes are used. Some have likened this process in 3D to using an ice-cream scoop of a given radius to extract the 3D solid surrounding the immovable point set — smaller scoops can remove more material until the form becomes increasingly convex and starts to break up.

Specialized tools exist for constructing such hulls in 2D and 3D and are of particular application in visualization of environmental and similar datasets. The images shown in Figure 4-28 were generated using the interactive Java applet developed by François Bélair whilst at the Computational Geometry Laboratory of McGill University.

**Case (c) density contouring**: this last of the three cases involves overlaying the study region with a (fine) grid and then computing an estimated point density at each grid point. There are several ways in which the density can be estimated, but the most widely used, within GIS and related packages, is kernel estimation (discussed in some detail in Section 4.3.4). Once a density value has been assigned to each intersection or cell, the region taken for the NPCH may be determined by specifying a threshold density and using the grid directly, or by contouring the grid. The final result may then be used directly or converted to polygonal form, depending on the requirement.

### 4.2.13.3 Minimum Bounding Rectangles (MBRs)

One difficulty with convex hulls is that they are slightly awkward shapes to work with, and in many cases it is simpler to deal with a boundary that is a regular shape, such as a circle or rectangle. Rectangles that align with the coordinate system and enclose selected features compactly are known as Minimum Bounding Rectangles, or Minimum Enclosing (or Envelope) Rectangles (MBRs or MERs).

In most instances it is very fast to determine whether the MBR for one feature or set of features is completely contained within a study region or within the MBR of another set of features. Identifying where the center of an MBR lies is also very simple and thus they are useful for first-stage identification of simple overlays and membership.

MBRs and convex hulls provide an indication of the limits to the area over which you can reliably interpolate values and many GIS packages take one or other of these boundaries as the limit for procedures such as interpolation, generation of contour lines or the creation of triangulated irregular networks (TINs). Figure 4-29 shows the result of interpolating income per capita data to a fine grid using the census map shown earlier in Figure 4-10 (darker areas have higher per capita income). In this case the ArcGIS Spatial Analyst facility has been used, and as can be seen the interpolation process extends to the MBR of census tract centers and no further.

We can also see, in this example:

- the interpolation process replaces census tracts with a grid surface of values, comprising around 250x500 cells, which we have classified into 9 groups for display purposes

- the generated surface pattern is closely tied to the designated centroid locations; and

- interpolation has occurred for our rogue locations, including those that should have been screened out as being lakes (no data) *prior* to interpolation, and two small polygons which are classified as land but for which no census data are provided.

*Figure 4-29 Interpolation within "centroid" MBR*

*Data source: US Census Bureau*

Another problem with hulls (MBRs, convex polygons or more general hull forms) is that by definition they enclose the points for which you have data, and you may be aware of other points, which could or should be taken into consideration, but which lie outside this region. For example, the nearest tree to one on the boundary may actually be in the adjacent field and not within the pre-defined boundary (Figure 4-30).

*Figure 4-30 Point locations inside and outside bounding polygon*

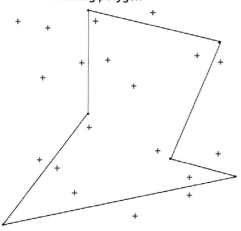

MBRs and other simple shapes are provided as options for feature enclosure in many GIS packages and in more specialized toolsets such as Crimestat (which is concerned with point events). Frequently the aim is to select a boundary which is reasonable and meaningful for subsequent analysis, often analyses that involve statistical calculations that rely on knowing the point density in advance. As boundaries are altered, the area, $A$, is changed and this can have a dramatic influence on the analytical results. This may distort analysis, for example giving poor interpolation results near to the region boundary or under-estimating the average distances between sampled points.

### 4.2.13.4 Fuzzy boundaries

A number of GIS packages include special facilities for identifying, selecting and analyzing boundaries. These may be the borders of distinct zones or areas, within which values on one or more attributes are relatively homogeneous, and distinct from those in adjacent areas, or they may be zones of rapid spatial change in more continuously varying attribute data. Amongst the tools available for boundary determination are raster-based GIS products, like Idrisi, and the more specialized Terraseer family of spatial analysis tools. Indeed Terraseer has a specific product, Boundaryseer, for boundary detection *and* analysis, using techniques such as overlap and sub-boundary statistical analysis (the pattern analysis software, PASSaGE, provides similar facilities). The problem these products seek to address is that of identifying where and how boundaries between different zones should be drawn and interpreted when the underlying data varies continuously, often without sharp breaks. For example, soil types may be classified by the proportion of sand, clay, organic matter and mineral content. Each of these variables will occur in a mix across a study region and may gradually merge from one recognized type to another.

In order to define boundaries between areas with, for example, different soil types, clear polygon-like boundaries are inappropriate. In such cases a widely used procedure is to allocate all grid cells to a set of *k* zones or classes based on *fuzzy membership* rather than binary or 0/1 membership. The idea here is to assign a number *between* 0 and 1 to indicate how much membership of the zone or class the cell is to be allocated, where 0 means not a member and 0.5 means the cell's *grade of membership* is 50% (but this is not a probabilistic measure). If a zone is mapped with a fuzzy boundary, the 50% or 0.5 set of cells is sometime regarded as the equivalent to the boundary or delimiter (cross-over point) in a crisp, discrete model situation. Using this notion, crisp polygon boundaries or identified zone edges in raster modeled data may be replaced with a band based on the degree of zone membership. Alternatively grid datasets may be subjected to fuzzy classification procedures whereby each grid cell acquires a membership value for one of *k* fuzzy classes, and a series of membership maps are generated, one for each class (see further, the discussion on soft classifiers in Section 4.2.12.4). Subsequent processing on these maps may then be used to locate boundaries.

Several fuzzy membership functions (MFs) have been developed to enable the assignment

process to be automated and to reflect expert opinion on the nature and extent of transitional zones. Burrough and McDonnell (1998, Ch.11) provides an excellent discussion of fuzzy sets and their applications in spatial classification and boundary determination problems. The GIS product Idrisi, which utilizes some of Burrough's work, provides four principal fuzzy MFs:

**Sigmoidal or (double) s-shaped functions**, which are produced by a combination of linear and $cos^2()$ functions in Idrisi's case, or as an algebraic expression of the form $m=1/(1+a(z-c)^2)$ where *a* is a parameter that varies the width of the function, *z* is the property being modeled (e.g. proportion of clay) and *c* is the value of this proportion at the function midpoint (see Figure 4-31; here membership values of >0.5 are regarded as being definitely members of the set *A*)

**J-shaped functions**, which are rather like the sigmoidal MFs but with the rounded top sliced off flat over some distance, *x* (if *x*=0 then the two sides of the J meet at a point). The equation used in this case is of the form: $m=1/(1+((z-a)/(a-c))^2)$

**Linear functions**, which are like the J-shaped function but with linear sides, like the slope of a pitched roof, and are thus simple to calculate and have a fixed and well-defined extent, and

**User-defined functions**, which are self-explanatory. In most applications MFs are symmetric, although monotonic increasing or decreasing options are provided in Idrisi

An alternative to using MFs as spreading functions is to apply a two-stage process: first, use a (fuzzy) classification procedure to assign a membership value ($m_{ik}$=0.0-1.0) to each grid cell, *i*, for each of *k* classes. This value is based on how similar the cell attributes are to each of *k* (pre-selected) attribute types or clusters. These may then be separately mapped, as discussed earlier.

*Figure 4-31 Sigmoidal fuzzy membership functions*

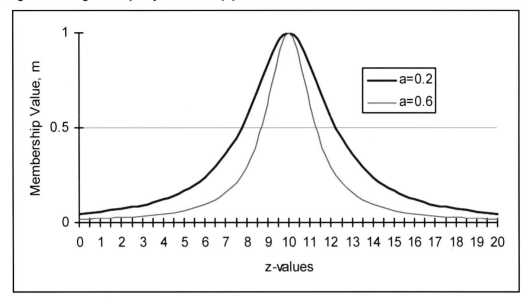

Having generated the membership assignments boundaries are then generated by a second algorithm. Boundaryseer provides three alternative procedures:

- Wombling (a family of procedures named after the author, W H Womble, 1951)

- Confusion Index (CI) measures, which are almost self-explanatory, and

- Classification Entropy (CE) based on information theoretic ideas

Wombling involves examining the gradient of the surface or surfaces under consideration in the immediate neighborhood of each cell or point. Typically, with raster datasets, this process examines the four cells in Rook's or Bishop's move position relative to the target cell or point — boundaries are identified based on the rate of change of a linear surface fitted through these four points, with high or sudden rates of change being the most significant. Wombling methods can be applied to vector and image datasets as well as raster data. Wombling edge-detection is provided in a number of other software products, including the SAM and PASSaGE macroecology packages.

The Confusion Index (CI) works on the presumption that if we compute the ratio of the second highest membership value of a cell $i$, $m_{i2}$, to the highest, $m_{i1}$, then any values close to 1 indicate that the cell could realistically be assigned to either class, and hence is likely to be on the boundary between the two classes.

Finally, Classification Entropy, devised by Brown (1998), creates a similar value to the CI measure, again in the range [0,1], but this time using the normalized entropy measure:

$$CE = \frac{\sum_{i=1}^{k} m_{ij} \ln(m_{ij})}{\ln(k)}$$

where the summation extends over all the $k$-classes and the measure applies to each of the $j$ cells or locations. This latter kind of measure is used in a number of spatial analysis applications (see further, Section 4.6).

Fuzzy procedures are by no means the only methods for detecting and mapping boundaries. Many other techniques and options exist. For example, the allocation of cells to one of k-classes can be undertaken using purely deterministic (spatially constrained) clustering procedures or probabilistic methods, including Bayesian and belief-based systems. In the latter methods cells are assigned probabilities of membership of the various classes. A fuller description of such methods is provided in the documentation for the Boundaryseer and Idrisi packages. As is apparent from this discussion, boundary detection is not only a complex and subtle process, but is also closely related to general-purpose classification and clustering methods, spatially-constrained clustering methods and techniques applied in image processing.

As noted earlier, boundaries may also be subject to analysis, for example to test hypotheses such as: "is the overlap observed between these two boundaries significant, and if so in what way, or could it have occurred at random?"; "is the form of a boundary unusual or related to those of neighboring areas?" Tools to answer such questions are provided in Boundaryseer but are otherwise not generally available.

### 4.2.13.5 Breaklines and natural boundaries

Natural boundaries, such as coastlines, rivers, lake shores, cliffs, man-made obstacles, geological intrusions and fault lines are widespread and are frequently significant in terms of understanding spatial processes. When conducting spatial analysis it is often important to examine datasets for the existence of such features, and to take explicit account of their impact where appropriate. A large number of structures and arrangements may be encountered, and the standard analytical tools provided within your preferred GIS package may not handle these adequately for your purposes. For example, simply masking out regions, such as lakes, areas of sea, regions where the underlying geology is not igneous etc., is often misleading, if all this procedure does is to hide those areas which are covered. Ideally the analytical procedure applied should be able to take account of the breakline or natural boundary in a meaningful manner. In the case of breaklines there are three different types that tend to be supported, principally in connection with

surface analysis and modeling (see further, Chapter 6).

Terminology usage varies here, so we shall use the form provided within ArcGIS 3D Analyst for convenience:

- Case 1: hard breaklines, which are well-defined surface structures, whose shape and heights are known and fixed, and which mark a significant change of surface continuity — for example, indicating a road, a stream, a dam or a major change of slope which has been surveyed along its length (e.g. a ridge). Such breaklines are usually specified as a set of triples $\{x,y,z\}$ and intermediate values are usually determined by simple linear interpolation

- Case 2: soft breaklines are similar to hard breaklines, but do not imply a change in surface continuity. They indicate that the known values along the breakline should be maintained, for example when creating a TIN of the surface, but no sharp change in the continuity of the underlying surface is implied

- Case 3: faults are more complex, in that they often have a spatial extent due to displacement and not just a simple linear form

The surface analysis package, Surfer, models breaklines as 3D polylines and faults as 2D polylines or polygons, reflecting their variable form. ArcGIS models breaklines as 3D polylines and faults as 2D polylines. Software packages treat these types of boundary in very different ways. Cases (1) and (2) take into account all data points provided, although in Case (1) z-values computed for the linear breakline take precedence over points that may lie on the other side of the line from the point being analyzed. Case (3) is quite different, since fault lines and zones are treated as barriers. In ArcGIS data values beyond a barrier are not included in computations, where the notion of beyond is defined by visibility from the source point; in Surfer linear barriers are treated as obstacles, which may be skirted around (involving considerable additional distances and extra processing), whilst polygonal faults are treated more like self-contained regions, with interpolation inside and outside the polygonal regions being treated separately.

## 4.2.14 Tessellations and triangulations

A region may be divided into a set of non-overlapping areas in many ways. As we noted in Table 1-1 a (regular or irregular) tessellation of a plane involves the subdivision of the plane into polygonal tiles that completely cover it. Within GIS regular tiles are almost always either square or rectangular, and form a (continuous) grid structure. Regular triangular and hexagonal grids are also possible in the plane but are rarely implemented in software packages. GIS does make extensive use of irregular triangular tessellations, both for division of plane regions and as an efficient means of representing surfaces.

### 4.2.14.1 Delaunay Triangulation

Given a set of points in the plane, $P$, lines may be drawn between these points to create a complete set of non-overlapping triangles (a triangulation) with the outer boundary being the convex hull of the point set. It has long been known that triangulation provides a secure method for locating points on the Earth's surface by field survey. It has also been found that a desirable characteristic of such triangulations is that long thin triangles with very acute internal angles are to be avoided in order to provide the best framework for measurement and analysis.

To ensure the triangulation will have the best chance of meeting the characteristics desired, a construction rule was devised by the mathematician Delaunay. This states that three points form a Delaunay Triangulation if and only if (*iff*) a circle which passes through all three points contains no other points in the set. Figure 4-32 illustrates this process for a set of spot height locations in a small area south of Edinburgh in Scotland (GB Ordnance Survey tile NT04). Each location is represented by an $(x,y)$ pair. Many programs support the creation of the triangulation required, for example the delaunay(**x,y**) function in MATLab

where **x**, and **y** are $n$x1 vectors containing the coordinates of all the points, or (as here) the Grid Data operation in Surfer, using the option to export the triangulation used as a base map. The red circles illustrate how the circle circumscribing each triangle has no other points from the set within it. Worboys and Duckham (2004, pp 202-207) provide a useful discussion of triangulation algorithms.

A number of other observations should be made about this process:

- this triangulation is unique in the sense that it is the only triangulation of the point set that satisfies the rule described above. However, with some point set arrangements (e.g. four points at the corners of a square or rectangle) multiple Delaunay triangulations are possible, hence to this extent it is not unique

- long thin triangles with acute angles do occur using this procedure, although the number and severity of these is minimized compared to other triangulations

- the center of the circumscribing circle (marked with an x here) may lie outside the triangle in question, as is the case with the smaller circle illustrated

- this procedure is by no means the only, or necessarily the best method of triangulation for all purposes. For example, when modeling a surface there may be important breaks of surface continuity or surveyed transects which it is highly desirable to include within the dataset, which are not captured by simple Delaunay-type procedures (as noted in Section 4.2.13.5)

If all points included in the Delaunay triangulation of a set $P$ also lie on the convex hull of $P$ the result is known as a furthest point Delaunay triangulation. The set of lines (edges) that belongs to all possible furthest site Delaunay triangulations is known as a *Delaunay diagram*, and has important applications in network analysis (see further, Chapter 7).

*Figure 4-32 Delaunay triangulation of spot height locations*

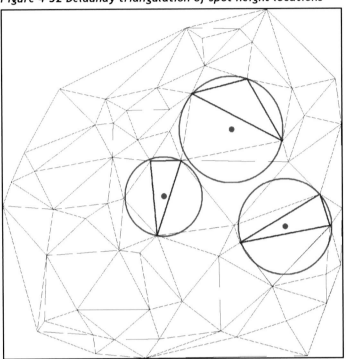

### 4.2.14.2 TINs – Triangulated irregular networks

Regular lattices such as grids provide a very inefficient means of storing details of surface topography. Areas that have similar slope could be better represented and stored using a series of inter-connected triangles forming an irregular mesh or network (a TIN). The nodes or vertices of these triangles can be placed closer together where landscape detail is more complex and further apart where surfaces are simpler. TINs may be designed or derived. Designed TINs arise in engineering and surveying models, whereas derived TINs are typically programmatically generated from grid-based datasets (digital elevation models or DEMs).

Although such TINs could be generated by selecting vertices using key feature extraction and surface modeling, a simpler and faster approach is to systematically divide the entire region into more and more triangles based on simple subdivision rules. For example, if you

start with a rectangular region and define vertices at each of the four corners, two triangulations are possible: (i) a line connecting the NE-SW corners creates one pair of triangles; or (ii) a line connecting the NW-SE corners creates a second pair. For each triangle a statistic can be computed, such as the maximum deviation in elevation of the triangle from the original DEM. The arrangement that produces the smallest maximum absolute deviation (a minimax criterion) can then be selected as the preferred triangulation. Each of the two initial triangles can then be subdivided further. For example, a point can be placed at the centroid of each triangle which creates a further three triangles, or 6 in total. The minimax criterion test can be applied for each of the subdivisions of the two original triangles and the process proceeds iteratively until the minimax criterion is less than a pre-defined threshold value (e.g. 5 meters) or the number of triangles generated has reached a maximum value, also pre-defined. This kind of procedure is used in many GIS packages — for example TNTMips describes this process as *adaptive densification*. TINs and DEMs are discussed in more detail in Chapter 6 (see for example, Figure 6-5).

### 4.2.14.3 Voronoi/Thiessen polygons

Given a set of points in the plane, there exists an associated set of regions surrounding these points, such that all locations within any given region are closer to one of the points than to any other point. These regions may be regarded as the *dual* of the point set, and are known as proximity polygons, Voronoi polygons or Thiessen regions. These various terms are equivalent, as is the term Dirichlet cell, all being derived from the names of their proponents: Dirichlet (in 1850); Voronoi (in 1909); and Thiessen (in 1912). Detailed explanations and discussion of Voronoi polygons is provided in Boots (CATMOG 45) and Okabe *et al.* (2000).

Figure 4-33A shows an example of Voronoi region creation, in this case using ArcGIS. The point set from which the map was generated is also shown and as can be seen, points are frequently close to polygon edges. Indeed, in some applications it may be desirable to exclude points that are closer together than some predefined tolerance level. Note that in this example Voronoi regions at the edges of the sample extend to infinity, and are shown as bounded (e.g. by the MBR of the point set plus 10%). Figure 4-33B shows the same point set plus the associated Delaunay triangulation once more, created within the MATLab mathematical modeling package, which (correctly) limits the set of regions generated to those that can be unambiguously computed. Figure 4-33B enables us to see exactly how Voronoi regions are created. There are two steps: the first is the triangulation process, connecting the point set as described in subsection 4.2.14.1; and the second is bisection of the triangulation lines of adjacent points to define Voronoi polygon boundaries.

There are many reasons an analyst may wish to generate Voronoi polygons from a point set,

but a common requirement is to assign values to regions or cells based on the attributes of the point set. The most common assignment is that of the individual point, or nearest-neighbor model. Other options are offered by some GIS packages in much the same way as is applied to grid and image files (in which each cell is surrounded by 4 or 8 immediate neighbors, depending on the model used). Note that the MATLab implementation does not extend to the MBR or other bounding region (e.g. rectangle) defined by the user. A selection of (a) MATLab and (b) GRASS functions that support operations discussed in this section is shown in Table 4-7.

*Table 4-7 Selected MATLab/GRASS planar geometric analysis functions*

| Function | Description |
|---|---|
| (a) convhull<br>(b) v.hull | Compute the convex hull of a point set, optionally providing its area |
| (a) delaunay<br>(b) v.delaunay | Delaunay triangulation |
| (a) dsearch | Nearest point search of Delaunay triangulation. Identifies the vertex of a Delaunay triangle that is closest to a specified point |
| (a) inpolygon | True (1) for points inside polygonal region, False (0) for points outside, and assigned 0.5 if points lie on the boundary |
| (a) polyarea<br>(b) area_poly2.c | Area of a polygon |
| (a) rectint | Area of intersection for two or more rectangles |
| (a) tsearch | Closest triangle search. Identifies the Delaunay triangle that includes a specified point |
| (a) voronoi<br>(b) v.voronoi | Voronoi diagram creation |

*Figure 4-33 Voronoi regions generated in ArcGIS and MATLab*

A. ArcGIS

B. MATLab

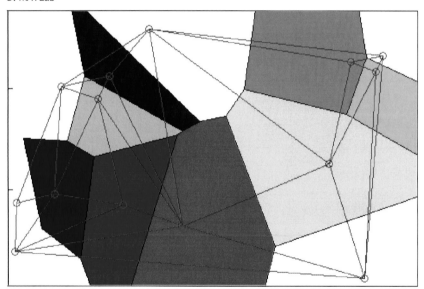

Assignment facilities provided within ArcGIS include: local mean value — the cell is assigned the average value of the cell and its direct neighbors; and local modal value — determined by computing the frequency distribution of all adjacent cells in 5 classes and then assigning the cell the class value from this set that is the most common amongst the cell and its immediate neighbors. These assignments represent local smoothing procedures. Local variation rather than values may also be computed. For example:

- local entropy value (equivalent to Shannon's Landscape Diversity Index, SHDI — see Section 5.3.4) — in this model the adjacent cells are again grouped into 5 sets (smart quantiles or natural breaks classes) and the number in each class is represented as a proportion of the total, $p_i$, $i$=1-5, from which Shannon's entropy statistic is computed (Table 1-3) and this value is assigned to the cell — values will range from 0 to $\log_2(5)$; and

- local standard deviation and local inter-quartile range — these statistics are computed for the cell and its immediate neighbors and the value assigned to the selected cell

Voronoi polygons may also be generated in grid or raster datasets (perhaps better described as Voronoi patches). Since the definition of a Voronoi polygon in the plane is that it consists of all locations closer to selected points than to any other points, such regions can be generated by a form of spreading algorithm. In this case we start with a number of points (the source points, sometimes called the target points) and spread outwards in all directions at a constant rate, like ripples spreading across the surface of a pond when a stone has been thrown into the middle. The process stops when the ripple (spreading) from another point is encountered. The rectangular grid structure and the number of search directions (typically 8) affect the form of the resulting cells (Figure 4-34).

With the raster representation Voronoi patch shape and boundary definition are not as clear cut as in vector operations. Within GIS packages processing activities of this type are usually carried out using techniques described as cost distance, or accumulated cost distance tools (e.g. in ArcGIS Spatial Analyst). In image processing the procedures adopt a somewhat different set of algorithms, based on scanning rather than spreading, which are known as distance transforms. The latter may be exact (in Euclidean distance terms) or approximate (see further, Section 4.4.2.2). Furthermore, with both approaches the space across which the scan or spread procedure is conducted may be homogenous (i.e. treated as uniform in all directions and at all points) or non-homogenous, containing areas of varying

difficulty to traverse, varying cost, and/or including obstacles.

*Figure 4-34 Voronoi cells for a homogeneous grid using a 3x3 distance transform*

Okabe and colleagues have also developed a software package, SANET, which can be installed as an ArcGIS add-in for "Spatial Analysis on a Network". The SANET software includes a network-based Voronoi tool, very similar to some of the network analysis tools provided in ArcGIS itself and in network-oriented packages such as TransCAD and Cube. An illustration of its facilities is shown in Figure 4-35. In this example, showing the Shibuya district of Tokyo, the point set (off-network sites which are Bank premises) have been linked to the nearest network edge, and then a *non-directed* network Voronoi regions generated from these locations (new network nodes) using shortest path distances. If one-way streets are taken into account separate inward- and outward-directed Voronoi regions are computed (see Okabe and Satoh, 2008, for more details). In each case these regions derived using unweighted calculations. Weighted calculations, for example taking into account the cost or time of travel across network links results in additional region definitions.

*Figure 4-35 Network-based Voronoi regions — Shibuya district, Tokyo*

*Data courtesy: Profs A Okabe, K Okunuki and S Shiode (University of Tokyo, Japan)*

# 4.3 Queries, Computations and Density

## 4.3.1 Spatial selection and spatial queries

As with many other terms, the expression "spatial query" means different things to different suppliers. In the majority of cases it refers to the process of *selecting* information (features and associated attribute data in tables) by some form of query operation that includes a spatial constraint. For example: SELECT all features WITHIN a specified radius of a specified point; or SELECT all point objects that fall WITHIN a specific polygon. For most (all) GIS packages this selection process can be achieved by a point-and-click visual interface, subject to certain selection rules. In parallel there is the option to execute a single command or series of commands as a script or program, or as a form of extended SQL query. The result of such queries may be a new table and feature set, which can be viewed, analyzed further or saved for additional analysis. Raster-based GIS packages do not generally support spatial query operations, although they may support standard SQL queries on attribute data. The various approaches are best understood by describing a number of specific implementations:

ArcGIS provides full support for standard SQL SELECT queries, such as: SELECT <all polygons in a given layer> WHERE <attribute table field> EQUALS <value>. It does not appear to support other forms of SQL query, such as MAKE TABLE, UPDATE or DELETE. It supports JOIN and RELATE operations between attribute tables based on specific fields, but it also provides spatial extensions to the JOIN and RELATE process enabling tables to be joined and queried based on their relative locations. Where joins are based on spatial location, data from one set of features are incorporated into the attribute table of the other set of features according to selectable rules. The ArcMAP visual interface provides a "Select by location" facility with selection qualified by a variety of spatial conditions (applicable to point, line and polygon features where meaningful): Intersect;

Are within a distance of; Completely contain; Are completely within; Have their center in; Share a line segment with; Touch the boundary of; Are identical to; Are crossed by the outline of; Contain; Are contained by. Each of the options may be further modified by selecting a tolerance level (a buffer — see further Section 4.4.4) around the points, lines or polygons in question.

Manifold provides support for specific spatial extensions to the standard SQL syntax. This enables a very large range of operations to be carried out, including so-called Action Queries (e.g. queries that CREATE, UPDATE and DELETE table data). Example spatial extensions that result in true or false being returned include: Adjacent, Contains, Intersection, IsArea/IsLine/IsPoint and Touches. These operations may be combined with other spatial operations (such as distance and buffer functions) to select records, and may also be combined with operators that generate spatial objects (e.g. a triangulation or convex hull of a point set) rather than simply selecting or amending existing objects. As such many of Manifold's spatial query functions are an extension of its "Transform" facilities, performing geometrical processing on the selected data as well as simply selecting items.

MapInfo, like ArcGIS, provides a range of SQL SELECT facilities and support for spatial joins. Spatial join operators supported include: Contains (A contains at least the other object, B's centroid), Contains Entire (A contains whole object B), Within (as per Contain, but A and B roles are reversed), Entirely within, and Intersects (A and B have at least one point in common). These operators enable attribute tables to be JOINed without sharing a common field (i.e. a spatial join only).

## 4.3.2 Simple calculations

Almost all GIS packages provide a wide range of calculation facilities. By simple calculations we mean arithmetic operations and standard functions applied to: (a) tabular data; (b) within queries and similar operations; and (c) applied to map layers (see further, Section 4.6). As with spatial queries, there are many different implementations of simple calculation operations and these are widely used, readily understandable, and applied as often to raster datasets as to vector data. A number of examples help to clarify the range of facilities provided:

(a) ArcGIS provides a field level calculator within attribute tables by right-clicking on any field (existing or newly added). This enables basic operations such as +, -, x and / to be performed, plus a range of standard functions such as cos(), exp(), log(), abs() etc. Operations are applied to one or more fields, e.g. current $field=(field1+field2*100)/field3$, and this process either updates the values for all records in the table selected or, if a subset have been pre-selected, updates records in just that subset. In addition an "Advanced" option is provided enabling Visual Basic for Application (VBA) commands to be entered and executed. Such commands are often needed in ArcGIS in order to add or update intrinsic data (as explicit fields in the attribute table) such as the area of a polygon or the $(x,y)$ coordinates of a polygon centroid. Manifold implements such operations through its extended SQL query facilities and using the Query toolbar facility it provides.

(b) Simple calculations and expressions are extensively used in SQL queries and in association with spatial extensions to standard SQL. Again, the common arithmetic operators are used (extended in some cases to facilitate integer division, modulo arithmetic etc.) combined with comparison operators (e.g. =, >, < etc.) and Boolean operators (e.g. AND, OR, NOT, XOR). Since queries often involve non-numeric fields additional operators are provided to enable the use of strings, dates and times. Note that it is often possible, and sometimes simpler, to perform calculations outside of the GIS framework using standard tools, such as spreadsheet or database programs.

(c) Within raster-based GIS, and in the raster processing facilities of general purpose GIS, there is a very large set of simple calculation facilities. Such facilities are a standard part of the set of operations provided in specifically raster-based GIS packages (e.g. Idrisi, PCRaster), but are often additional components in general purpose (vector-oriented) GIS. For example in ArcGIS the majority of such tools are provided in the Spatial Analyst extension whilst in Manifold they are provided in the Surface Tools extension.

The term *map algebra* is often used to describe operations that combine two or more grid layers according to a simple algebraic expression, e.g. $A+2*B+C/100$ where $A$, $B$ and $C$ are matching grid layers (Figure 4-36a). This is commonly the case with multi-band remote sensing data (e.g. 7 bands representing different spectral components of a single image). Map algebra may also be used where the grid resolutions do not match, in which case decisions have to be made (rules applied) on how resolution differences are to be accommodated. The example in Figure 4-36b show how grid $C$, being lower resolution, determines the resolution of the result grid. The general term for this kind of process is *resampling*.

If distinct raster layers have different resolutions (cell sizes) then one or more must be resampled to ensure their resolutions match. The normal practice is to adjust the layers of finest resolution to match the coarsest, and to use simple nearest-neighbor interpolation to estimate values. By nearest-neighbor is meant that values are assigned based on the position of the center of the output grid relative to the centers of finer resolution input grids. Grids do not have to consist entirely of square zones, nor do they have to align precisely, but if they do not then resampling and some form of localized interpolation is inevitable.

However, map algebra refers to a far broader set of operations, extending to functions that operate on individual grid cells, blocks of grid cells or entire grid layers (often described as *local, focal or neighborhood, zonal*, and *global* analysis) as we shall see in Section 4.6 and Chapter 6. In this Section we restrict our consideration to operations that apply on a cell-by-cell or point-by-point basis (the term *local* is generally used for such operations).

*Figure 4-36 Cell-by-cell or Local operations*

a. Matching grids

b. Grid resampling

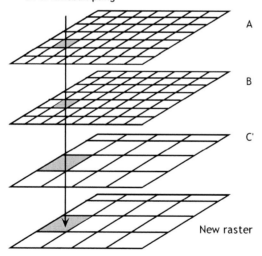

In Idrisi, for example, pairs of images (grids of pixels) may be combined using the operators: +, -, x, /, ^ (power), maximum, minimum, and cover. These operators combine images *A* and *B* on a pixel by pixel basis, for example adding each pixel in image *B* to each matching pixel in image *A*. Operations such as maximum and minimum identify a value from corresponding positions in image *A* or *B* as appropriate, whilst the cover function creates an image just containing pixels from *A* except where these are zero, in which case the pixels of *B* are taken (showing through the "holes" in *A*). With the exception of + and -, all other operations are non-symmetric, i.e. *A*<operator>*B* is not equal to *B*<operator>*A*. An example application of operations of this kind would be the algebraic expression:

$$C=(A-B)/(A+B)$$

where *C* is the output raster, *A* and *B* are input raster maps (e.g. remote sensed images or image bands) of vegetation cover, with pixels in *C* being taken as a vegetation index (with values being in the range -1 to +1). Note that a check is required to ensure that if *A*=*B*=0 for a pixel location then the calculation gives the result 0.

Many GIS packages allow the creation and saving of macros or scripts that implement regularly used map algebra expressions. For example TNTMips and ENVI include numerous pre-built combination formulas of this type. TNTMips holds such formulas as scripts that may be modified or augmented. For example, its two-band transformed vegetation index (TVI) script is of the form:

$$C = 100\left(\sqrt{\frac{A-B}{A+B}}\right), A - B \geq 0, A + B \geq 0$$
$$C = 0 \text{ if } A - B < 0$$

Here *A* might be the near infra-red band (Figure 4-37A) from a remote sensing image and *B* the red band image (Figure 4-37B), with the result being an index raster providing a measure of vegetation vigor (Figure 4-37C). The basic index has the range [0,100], and as elsewhere, checks for division by 0 are required.

*Figure 4-37 Map algebra: Index creation*

A. Near infra-red band

B. Red band

C. TVI

PCRaster, a non-commercial package designed specifically for manipulating raster data, provides a rich set of point operations, many of which have been derived from the work of Tomlin (1990). These include a similar set to those described above, i.e. arithmetic, trigonometric and logarithmic functions, coupled with Boolean and relational operators. Point operations are augmented by facilities for missing data detection and substitution, conditional expressions, data lookup and other facilities that mirror those provided in the extended SQL-type command structures described earlier.

Combination operations of this type are not confined to raster datasets. Polygon layers may be combined with raster layers, either by converting the polygon layers to rasters and then proceeding as above (the most common approach in GIS packages), or by direct support for such combinations within the GIS (as is the case with TNTMips for example).

### 4.3.3 Ratios, indices, normalization, standardization and rate smoothing

The vegetation index calculation we described in Section 4.3.2 were generated in a manner that ensured all output pixels (grid cells) would contain entries that lie in the range [-1,+1]; an index value of 0 indicates that matching pixel locations have the same value. There are many reasons for changing attribute data values in this manner before mapping and/or as part of the analysis of spatial datasets. One of the principal reasons is that if you create a map showing zones (e.g. counties) for a *spatially extensive* attribute, such as total population, it is very misleading — obviously a single total value (indicated perhaps by a color) does not apply throughout the zone in question. A more correct or meaningful view would be to divide by the area of the zone and show a *spatially intensive* attribute, the density of the population across the zone in this case. In this way zones of different size can be analyzed and mapped in a consistent manner.

The field of geodemographics, which involves the analysis of population demographics by where they live, involves the widespread use of index values — for a full discussion of this subject see Harris *et al.* (2005) and the "Geodemographics Knowledgebase" web site maintained by the UK Market Research Society (http://geodemographics.org.uk/).

In many instances, especially with data that are organized by area (e.g. census data, data provided by zip/post code, data by local authority or health districts etc.) production of ratios is vital. The aim is to adjust quantitative data that are provided as a simple count (number of people, sheep, cars etc.) or as a continuous variable or *weight*, by a population value for the zone, in a process known as *normalization*. This term, rather confusingly, is used in several other spatial contexts including statistical analysis, in mathematical expressions and in connection with certain topological operations. The context should make clear the form of normalization under consideration. Essentially, in the current context, this process involves dividing the count or weight data by a value (often another field in the attribute table) that will convert the information into a measure of intensity for the zone in question — e.g. cars owned per household, or trees per hectare. This process removes the effects associated with data drawn from zones of unequal area or variable "population" size and makes zone-based data comparable.

Three particular types of normalization are widely used: (i) averages; (ii) percentages; and (iii) densities. In the case of averages, an attribute value in each zone (for example the number of children) is adjusted by dividing by, for example, the number of households in each zone, to provide the average number of children per household, which may then be stored in a new field and/or mapped. In the case of percentages, or conversion to a [0,1] range, a selected attribute value is divided by the maximum value or (in the case of count data) the total count in the set from which it has been drawn. For example, the number of people in a zone registered as unemployed divided by the total population of working age (e.g. 18-65). The final example is that of densities, where the divisor is the area of the zone (which may be stored as an intrinsic

attribute by some software packages rather than a field) in which the specified attribute is found. The result is a set of values representing population per unit area, e.g. dwellings per square kilometer, mature trees per hectare, tons of wheat per acre etc. — all of which may be described as density measures.

The term *standardization* is closely related to the term normalization and is also widely used in analysis. It tends to appear in two separate contexts. The first is as a means of ensuring that data from separate sources are comparable for the problem at hand. For example, suppose that a measure of the success rate of medical treatments by health district were being studied. For each health district the success rates as a percentage for each type of operation could be analyzed, mapped and reported. However, variations in the demographic makeup of health districts have not been factored into the equation. If there is a very high proportion of elderly people in some districts the success rates may be lower for certain types of treatment than in other districts. Standardization is the process whereby the rates are adjusted to take account of such district variations, for example in age, sex, social deprivation etc. *Direct standardization* may be achieved by taking the district proportion in various age groups and comparing this to the regional or national proportions and adjusting the reported rates by using these values to create an age-weighted rate. *Indirect standardization* involves computing expected values for each district based on the regional or national figures broken down by mix of age/sex/deprivation etc., and comparing these expected values with the actual rates. The latter approach is less susceptible to small sample sizes in the mix of standardizing variables (i.e. when all are combined and coupled with specific treatments in specific districts).

The second use of the term standardization involves adjusting the magnitude of a particular dataset to facilitate comparison or combination with other datasets. Two principal forms of such standardization are commonly applied. The first is z-score standardization (see Table 1-3). This involves computing the mean and standard deviation of each dataset, and altering all values to a z-score in which the mean is subtracted from the value and the result divided by the standard deviation (which must be non-zero). This generates values that have a mean of zero and a standard deviation of 1. This procedure is widely used in the statistical analysis of datasets. The second approach involves range-based standardization. In this method the minimum and maximum of the data values are computed (thus the *range=max-min*), and each value has the min subtracted from it and is then divided by the range. To reduce the effect of extreme values range standardization may omit a number or percentage of the smallest and largest values (e.g. the lowest and highest 10%), giving a form of trimmed range. Trimmed range-based standardization is the method currently applied within the UK Office of National Statistics (ONS) classification of census areas (wards) using census variables such as demographics, housing, socio-economic data and employment.

Another way of looking at the process of dividing a count for a zone, e.g. population, by the zone area is to imagine the zone is divided into very many small squares. Each square will contain a number of people registered as living in that square. The total for the zone is simply the sum of the counts in all the little squares. But this form of representation is exactly that of raster or grid GIS, and hence raster representations generally do not require area-based normalization, since they are already in a suitable form. Of course, the process of generating a grid representation may have involved computation of values for each cell from vector data, either assuming a uniform model or some other (volume preserving model) as discussed in Section 4.2.10. Normalization is used with raster data for a variety of reasons, for example: (i) to change to set of values recorded in a single map layer to a [0,1] or [-1,1] range, e.g. by dividing each cell value, z, by the theoretical or observed maximum absolute value for the entire grid:

$z^* = z / z_{max},$ or using the transformation:

$$z^* = (z - z_{min}) / (z_{max} - z_{min})$$

and (ii) to combine two or more grid layers or images into a single, normalized or "indexed" value (sometimes this process is described as indexed overlay). In this latter case the overlay process may be a weighted sum, which is then normalized by dividing the resulting total by the sum of the weights. These various observations highlight a number of issues:

- the division process needs to have a way of dealing with cases where the divisor is 0

- missing data (as opposed to values that are 0) need to be handled

- if an attribute to be analyzed and/or mapped has already been normalized (e.g. is a percentage, a density, an average or a median) then it should not be further normalized as this will generally provide a meaningless result

- highly variable data can lead to confusing or misleading conclusions. For example, suppose one zone has a population of 10,000 children, and the incidence of childhood leukemia recorded for this zone over a 10 year period is 7 cases. The normalized rate is thus 0.7 per 1000 children. In an adjacent zone with only 500 children one case has been recorded. The rate is thus 2 per 1000 children, apparently far higher. Effects of this type, which are sometimes described as *variance instability*, are commonplace and cause particular problems when trying to determine whether rare illnesses or events occur with unexpectedly high frequencies in particular areas

- the result of normalization should be meaningful and defensible in terms of the problem at hand and the input datasets — using an inappropriate divisor or source data which are of dubious value or relevance will inevitably lead to unacceptable results

- obtaining an appropriate divisor may be problematic — for example if one is looking at the pattern of disease incidence in a particular year, census data (which in the UK are only collected every 10 years) may be an inadequate source of information on the size of the population at risk

GIS packages rarely emphasize the need for normalization. One exception is ArcGIS, where the Properties form for map layers includes a normalization field when quantitative data are to be classified and mapped (Figure 4-38).

*Figure 4-38 Normalization within ArcGIS*

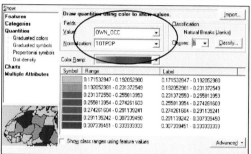

In this example we are normalizing the number of people who are categorized as owner occupiers (home owners, OWN_OCC) by a field called TOTPOP (total population). The normalization prompt is provided for graduated colors, graduated symbols and proportional symbols, but not for dot density representation as this already provides a spatially intensive representation of the data.

The result of normalization in such cases is a simple ratio. Assuming the field being normalized is a subset of the divisor (which it should be) the ratio will not exceed 1.0. Specialized spatial analysis software, like GeoDa, may provide a more extensive and powerful set of pre-defined normalization tools (see further, Section 5.2.1), although in this case the software does not support built-in user-definable calculation facilities. Many of GeoDa's facilities are designed to address problems associated with simple normalization, or in ESDA terminology, the computation of *raw rates*. The example of OWN_OCC/TOTPOP above would be a raw rate, which could be plotted as a percentile map in order to identify which zones have relatively high or low rates of owner occupancy, unemployment or some other variable of interest. As an illustration of this procedure, Figure 4-39 shows 100 counties in North Carolina, USA where the incidence of sudden infant death syndrome (SIDS, also known as "cot death") in the period 1st July 1974 to end June 1978 is mapped. This dataset has been normalized to form a *raw rate* by dividing the number of cases in each zone by the births recorded for the same period (BIR74). The resulting raw rates have been sorted, from the lowest to the highest, and divided into 7 groups (or quantiles), each containing approximately the same number of zones. The uppermost range is comprised of the zones in which the relative incidence or *rate* of SIDS is highest.

*Figure 4-39 Quantile map of normalized SIDS data*

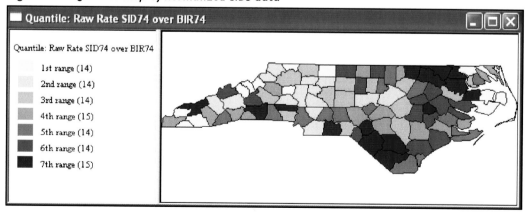

However, even raw rates can be misleading, as noted earlier, and various techniques have been devised for analyzing and mapping such data to bring out the real points of interest. One example will suffice to explain the types of procedure available. The ratio SID74/BIR74 is normally computed for every zone. However, one could compute this ratio for all zones first, based on the sum of the selected fields. This would give an average ratio or rate for the entire study area. This value could be regarded as the *expected rate* for each zone, $E$, say. We can then calculate the *expected number* of SIDS cases for each zone by multiplying the average rate $E$ by the relevant population in each zone, $i$: $E_i=E*BIR74_i$.

Now consider the ratio: $R_i=SID74_i/E_i$; this is a ratio with a value from $[0,n]$. It highlights those areas with higher than expected or lower than expected rates (Figure 4-40), i.e. *excess risk rates*. As can be seen, one zone in Figure 4-40 is picked out in red in the lower center of the mapped zones as appearing to have an unusually high SIDS rate, being at least 4 times the average for the region as a whole. This technique is one of a series of procedures, many of which are described as *rate smoothing*, that seek to focus attention on interesting data variations rather than artifacts of the way the zones are laid out or their underlying population size. As the GeoDa documentation states: "Using choropleth maps to represent the spatial distribution of rates or proportions represents a number of challenges. These are primarily due to the inherent variance instability (unequal precision) of rates as estimates for an underlying 'risk'." One approach proposed by Anselin to address this issue is their Empirical Bayes (EB) rate smoothing method (described in Anselin *et al.*, 2003 and supported in GeoDa). However, researchers should be aware that such smoothing is simply one form of 'reasonable' adjustment of the dataset that can introduce its own artifacts into subsequent data analyses.

*Figure 4-40 Excess risk rate map for SIDS data*

When attempting to develop explanatory models of such data (mortality data, disease incidence data, crime data etc.) it is the widely accepted practice to utilize the expected rate based on overall regional or national statistics as an essential component of the analysis. This issue is discussed further in Section 5.6.4.2 where the data illustrated here are re-visited — see also, Cressie and Chan (1989); and Berke (2004).

Single ratios provide the standard form of normalization, as described above, but more complex combinations of attributes, from one or more sets of spatial data, may be combined in a variety of ways in order to generate *index values*. One advantage of such procedures as that index values may be used as a guide for planning policy or as comparative measures, for example as a means of comparing crime rates and clear-up rates between different police forces. As the need to incorporate several factors in the construction of such indices becomes more important, simple weighting and ratio procedures will be found wanting, and more sophisticated methods (such as various forms of cluster analysis) will be required.

### 4.3.4 Density, kernels and occupancy

In Section 4.3.3 we noted that spatially extensive variables, such as total population, should not be plotted directly for zones under normal circumstances, but standardized in some manner. An exception to this general rule may be made where cartograms rather than conventional maps are produced (see Section 4.3.4.4). For such maps the areas are distorted in some manner to reflect the (positive) magnitude of an attribute of each region, whilst retaining a sense of the original areal-based map. Densities, with respect to the variable under consideration, thus become uniform in such maps.

For variables that are a subset of a total it is often useful to compute and map these data as a proportion of this total, but for totals themselves we will need to compute a density measure — dividing the total population, $N$, by the zone area, $A$. This yields a density value, $N/A$, for each zone, but assumes that population density is constant through the zone and then may suddenly change to some other value at the zone boundaries. In our discussions on boundaries and on areal interpolation we have already alluded to the inadequacies of simple density calculation, but it remains in widespread use. Conversion of the source dataset to a raster model using some form of intelligent interpolation may well provide a more satisfactory result. A good introduction to mapping density is provided in Mitchell (1999, Chapter 4). Techniques for computing density estimates, including so-called kernel density measures, are discussed in Sections 4.3.4.1 and 0.

#### 4.3.4.1 Point density

If the dataset we have is not zone-based but point- or line-based, alternative methods of determining density are required. The simplest measures apply some form of zoning and count the number of events in each zone, returning us to a zone-based dataset. For example, with data on thefts from cars (TFC events), each event may be geocoded and assigned to a unique zone such as a pre-defined 100mx100m grid (or *quadrat*) , or to city blocks, census blocks, or policing districts. The density of TFC events is then simply the event count divided by the area of the associated zone in which they are reported to have occurred.

A difficulty with this approach is that densities will vary substantially depending on how the zoning, grid or quadrat is selected, and on how variable are the size and associated attributes of each zone (e.g. variations in car ownership and usage patterns). Overall density calculation for all zones (e.g. a city-wide figure for the density of TFC events) suffers similar problems, especially with regard to definition of the boundary (such problems are generally known as *edge effects*, and methods to adjust for edge effects are known as *edge correction* or *edge bias correction* methods). Use of such information to compare crime event levels within or across cities is clearly fraught with difficulties. An alternative approach, particularly suited to ecological datasets, is to define zones based on a covariate of interest, for example the underlying geology and terrain slope. Each classified area can then be taken as a separate zone type and densities computed within these (polygonal) boundaries. This type of computation is supported within spatstat.

An alternative approach to density computation for two-dimensional point-sets is based on techniques developed in one-dimensional (univariate) statistical analysis. This is simplest to understand by looking at the example in Figure 4-41. We have a set of 5 events marked by crosses. They occur at positions 7, 8, 9, 12 and 14 along the line. We could argue that the point density across the entire 20-unit line length is 5/20=0.25 points per unit length and assign a value of 0.25 to each section, as shown on the gray line. We might equally well argue that if we divide the overall line into two halves, the density over the first half should be 0.3 per unit length and over the second, 0.2 per unit length, to reflect the variation in positioning of the 5 events.

There is clearly no single right answer or single method to assign the points to the line's entire length, so the method we choose will depend on the application we are considering. Important observations to notice about this problem include: the length of the line we start with seems to have an important effect on the density values we obtain, and since this may be arbitrary, some method of removing dependence on the line length is desirable; if

the line is partitioned into discrete chunks a sudden break in density occurs where the partition boundaries occur, which is often undesirable; depending on the number of partitions and distribution of points, areas may contain zero density, even if this is not the kind of spread we are seeking or regard as meaningful; the line is assumed to be continuous, and allocation of density values to every part is valid; and finally, if we have too many partitions all sections will only contain values of 1 or 0, which is essentially back to where we started from.

*Figure 4-41 Point data*

*Figure 4-42 Simple linear (box or uniform) kernel smoothing*

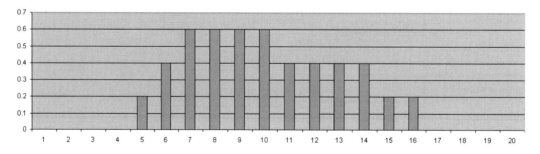

These observations can be dealt with by treating each point in the original set as if it was spread over a range, then adding together overlapping zones and checking that the total adds up to the original value. For example, choosing each point and smoothing it over 5 units in a uniform symmetric manner, we obtain the result shown in Figure 4-42. The rows in the diagram show the spreading of each of the 5 original points, with the total row showing the sums (densities) assigned to

each unit segment. These add up to 5, as they should, and a chart showing this distribution confirms the pattern of spread. This method still leaves us with some difficulties: there are no density values towards the edges of our linear region; density values still jump abruptly from one value to the next; and values are evenly spread around the initial points, whereas it might be more realistic to have a greater weighting of importance towards the center of each point. All of these concerns can be addressed by selecting a well-defined, smooth and optionally unbounded function, known as a *kernel*, and using this to spread the values. The function often used is a Normal distribution, which is a bell-shaped curve extending to infinity in each direction, but with a finite (unit) area contained underneath the bell (Figure 4-43).

*Figure 4-43 Univariate Normal kernel smoothing and cumulative densities*

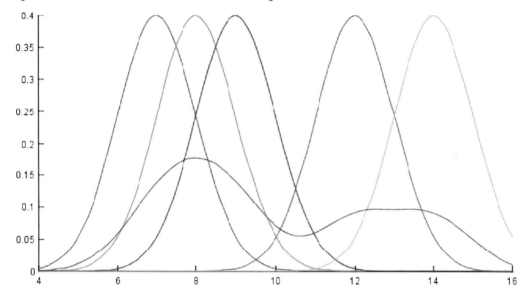

*Figure 4-44 Alternative univariate kernel density functions*

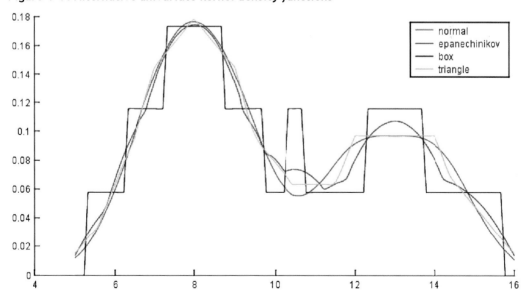

In Figure 4-43, for each point (7,8,9,12 and 14) we have provided a Normal distribution curve with central value (the mean) at the point in question and with an average spread (standard deviation) of 2 units. We can then add the areas under each of these curves together to obtain a (cumulative) curve with two peaks, and then divide this curve by 5 to adjust the area under the curve back to 1 giving the lower red curve shown. When adjusted in this way the values are often described as probability densities, and when extended to two dimensions, the resulting surface is described as a probability density surface, rather than a density surface. We now have a density value for every position along the original line, with smooth transitions between the values, which is exactly what we were trying to achieve.

There still remain some questions: why should we use the Normal distribution? could we not use almost any unimodal symmetric function with a finite area under it? and why did we choose a value of 2 units for the average spread? The answer to these questions is that the specific selections made are a matter of choice and experience, although in some instances a symmetric distribution with a finite extent (e.g. a box or triangular function) may be regarded as more suitable than one with an infinite possible extent. Figure 4-44 shows a selection of commonly used functions plotted for the same point set, using the MATLab Statistics Toolbox function ksdensity(). As may be seen from examining the various curves shown in Figure 4-44 the exact form of the kernel function does not tend to have a major impact on the set of density values assigned across the linear segment (or area in 2D applications). Of much greater impact is the choice of the spread parameter, or *bandwidth*. For further details on these and other functions used for smoothing and density estimation see Bowman and Azzalini (1997) and Silverman (1986).

All of this discussion so far addresses problems in one dimension (univariate density estimation). We now need to extend the process to two dimensions, which turns out to be simply a matter of taking the univariate procedures and adding a second dimension

(effectively rotating the kernel function about each point). If we were to use the Normal distribution again as our kernel function it would have a two-dimensional bell-shaped form over every point (Figure 4-45). As before, we place the kernel function over each point in our study region and calculate the value contributed by that point over a finely drawn grid. The grid resolution does not affect the resulting surface form to any great degree, but if possible should be set to be meaningful within the context of the dataset being analyzed, including any known spatial errors or rounding that may have been applied, and making allowance for any areas that should be omitted from the computations (e.g. industrial zones, water, parks etc. when considering residential-based data). Values for all points at every grid intersection or for every grid cell are then computed and added together to give a composite density surface.

*Figure 4-45 2D Normal kernel*

The resulting grid values may be provided as: (i) relative densities — these provide values in events per unit area (i.e. they are adjusted by the grid size, giving a figure as events per square meter or per hectare) — this is the default or only option in many GIS packages, including ArcGIS; (ii) absolute densities — these provide values in terms of events per grid cell, and hence are not adjusted by cell size. The sum of the values across all cells should equal the number of events used in the analysis; (iii) probabilities — as per (ii) but divided by the total number of events. Crimestat supports all three variants. Computed density values may then be plotted in 2D (e.g. as density contours) or as a 3D surface (as in Figure 4-46). In this latter case the kernel density procedure has been applied to a dataset of reported cases of lung cancer in part of Lancashire, England. This example is discussed further in Section 5.4.4, and fully in Diggle (1990) and more recently in Baddeley *et al.* (2005). The software used in this instance was Crimestat, with a Normal kernel function and average spread (bandwidth) determined from the point pattern itself. Map data were output in ESRI shape file format (SHP) and mapped in ArcGIS to produce a 2D map and in

ASCII grid format for visualization in 3D using Surfer. Other GIS packages support a variety of kernel functions and procedures. ArcGIS Spatial Analyst provides kernel density estimation for point and line objects, but only supports one kernel function, which it describes as a quadratic kernel (a bounded kernel) but which is often described as an Epanechnikov kernel (see further, Table 4-8).

*Figure 4-46 Kernel density map, Lung Case data, 3D visualization*

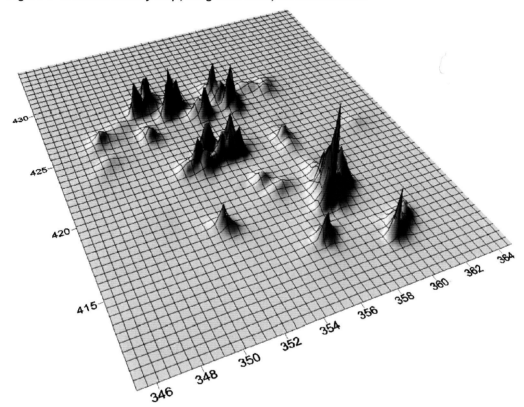

MapInfo's grid analysis add-on package, Vertical Mapper, includes kernel density mapping as do the spatial statistics packages SPLANCS and spatstat, and the crime analysis add-on for MapInfo, Hot Spot Detective (in the latter two cases based on quartic kernels). TransCAD/Maptitude supports what it describes as density grid creation with the option of count (simple), quartic, triangular or uniform kernels. Crimestat supports four alternative kernels to the Normal, all of which

have finite extent (i.e. typically are defined to have a value of 0 beyond a specified distance). These are known as the quartic, exponential, triangular and uniform kernels. If kernel density methods are applied in urban areas the use of network kernel density estimation should be considered (see Section 0), as Okabe *et al.* (2009) have shown that the use of planar KDEs can lead to erroneous conclusions regarding clustering for point events on networks.

The details of each of the main kernel functions used in various GIS and statistical packages are as shown in Table 4-8. The value at grid location $g_j$, at a distance $d_{ij}$ from an event point $i$, is obtained as the sum of individual applications of the kernel function over all event points in the source dataset. The table shows normalized functions, where the distances $d_{ij}$ have been divided by the kernel bandwidth, $h$, i.e. $t=d_{ij}/h$. Graphs of these functions are shown in Figure 4-47, where each has been normalized such that the area under the graph sums to 1.

Whether the kernel for a particular event point contributes to the value at a grid point depends on: (i) the type of kernel function (bounded or not); (ii) the parameter, $k$, if applicable, which may be user defined or determined automatically in some instances; and (iii) and the bandwidth, $h$, that is selected (a larger bandwidth spreads the influence of event points over a greater distance, but is also more likely to experience edge effects close to the study region boundaries). Event point sets may be weighted resulting in some event points having greater influence than others.

### Table 4-8 Widely used univariate kernel density functions

| Kernel | Formula | Comments. Note $t=d_{ij}/h$, $h$ is the bandwidth |
|---|---|---|
| Normal (or Gaussian) | $\dfrac{1}{2k}e^{-\frac{t^2}{2}}$ | Unbounded, hence defined for all $t$. The standard kernel in Crimestat; bandwidth $h$ is the standard deviation (and may be fixed or adaptive) |
| Quartic (spherical) | $\dfrac{3}{k}\left(1-t^2\right)^2, t \leq 1$ <br> $= 0, t > 1$ | Bounded. Approximates the Normal. $k$ is a constant |
| (Negative) Exponential | $Ae^{-k\lvert t\rvert}, \lvert t\rvert \leq 1$ <br> $= 0, t > 1$ | Optionally bounded. $A$ is a constant (e.g. $A=3/2$) and $k$ is a parameter (e.g. $k=3$). Weights more heavily to the central point than other kernels |
| Triangular (conic) | $1-\lvert t\rvert, \lvert t\rvert \leq 1$ <br> $= 0, t > 1$ | Bounded. Very simple linear decay with distance. |
| Uniform (flat) | $k, \lvert t\rvert \leq 1$ <br> $= 0, t > 1$ | Bounded. $k$=a constant. No central weighting so function is like a uniform disk placed over each event point |
| Epanechnikov (paraboloid/quadratic) | $\dfrac{3}{4}\left(1-t^2\right), \lvert t\rvert \leq 1$ <br> $= 0, t > 1$ | Bounded; optimal smoothing function for some statistical applications; used as the smoothing function in the Geographical Analysis Machine (GAM/K) and in ArcGIS |

Bandwidth selection is often more of an art than a science, but it may be subject to formal analysis and estimation, for example by applying kernel density estimation (KDE) procedures to sets of data where actual densities are known. An alternative to fixed bandwidth selection is *adaptive selection*, whereby the user specifies the selection criterion, for example defining the number of event points to include within a circle centered on each event point, and taking the

radius of this circle as the bandwidth around that point. A somewhat different form of adaptive density model is provided within the spatstat software. In this case a random sample of points (a fraction, $f\%$) is taken, and this is used to create a voronoi tessellation of the sample point set. The density of the remaining points ($1-f\%$) is then computed for each cell of the tessellation. The process is then replicated $n$ times and the average densities of all replicates computed.

*Figure 4-47 Univariate kernel density functions, unit bandwidth*

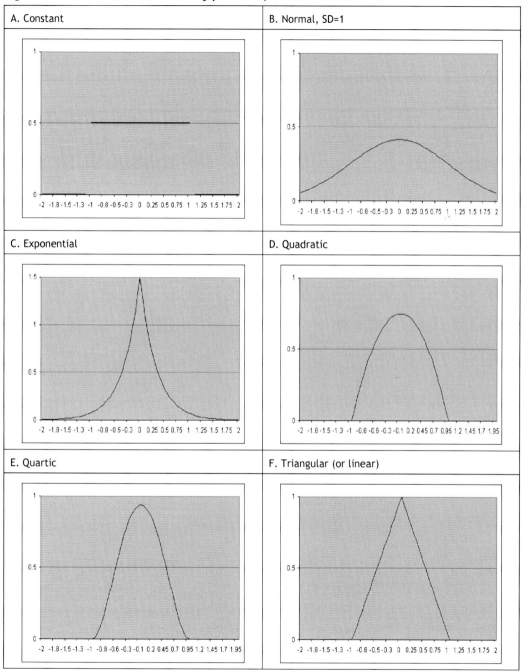

Kernel smoothing, or kernel density estimation methods (KDE methods) of the type described have a variety of applications: exploratory point data analysis; point data smoothing; creation of continuous surfaces from point data in order to combine or compare these with other datasets that are continuous/in raster form; probability distribution estimation; interpolation (although this terminology is confusing and not recommended; Crimestat is amongst a number of packages that use this terminology, which is essentially incorrect); and hot spot detection.

KDE can also be used in visualizing and analyzing temporal patterns, for example crime events at different times of day and/or over different periods, with the objective of understanding and potentially predicting event patterns. KDE can also be applied with more than one point set, for example a set of cases and a set of controls. The output of such "dual" dataset analysis is normally a ratio of the primary set to the secondary set (or ratio of the log transform of the variables), with the objective being to analyze the primary pattern with background effects being removed or minimized. Care must be taken in such cases that the results are not subject to distortion by very low or zero values in the second density surface, and that common bandwidths are used. Crimestat provides support for 6 alternative dual density outputs: simple ratio; log ratio; difference in densities (two variants, with and without standardization); and sum of densities (again, with and without standardization). Levine (2007, Chapter 8) provides an excellent discussion of the various techniques and options, including alternative methods for bandwidth selection, together with examples from crime analysis, health research, urban development and ecology.

The use of kernel functions as a form of point weighting enables the creation of local weighted means and variances. The locally weighted (kernel) statistics supported within the GWR software are defined as follows:

$$\bar{x}(u) = \frac{\sum_{i=1}^{n} w(u)_i \, x_i}{\sum_{i=1}^{n} w(u)_i}, \qquad \text{and}$$

$$\sigma^2(u) = \frac{\sum_{i=1}^{n} w(u)_i \left(x_i - \bar{x}(u)\right)^2}{\sum_{i=1}^{n} w(u)_i}$$

These are local statistics, based on locations, $u$, and weighting function $w()$ defined by a fixed or adaptive kernel function. The bandwidth in this case must be user-defined, and might be chosen on the basis of experience or could use an adaptively derived bandwidth (e.g. from an associated regression study) for comparison purposes.

### 4.3.4.2 Kernel density for networks

The preceding discussion is not readily applicable to the case of points on networks, such as accidents along roads or thefts in urban areas. In these instances one might attempt to compute the density by applying a two-dimensional kernel procedure as described in the preceding section, overlaying the network, and examining the density patterns along the network routes. However, this approach has been shown to produce biased density estimates (e.g. it suggests variable densities along routes when these are known to be uniform). To resolve this problem kernel density computations in situations where events occur along or adjacent to networks, should be calculated using shortest paths and adjusted kernel functions (the conventional functions described earlier are not suitable without modification. This question has been addressed by Okabe *et al.* (2009) and is being made available in a new release of their SANET software. They show that a non-continuous fixed bandwidth kernel function, which is unimodal and symmetric, can be used to compute unbiased kernel densities on large networks (e.g. the street network of Kashiwa, Japan, with 35,235 links, 25,146 nodes and 3109 point events). The function used is essentially a modified form of the linear or triangular kernel (Figure 4-47F), applied to networks which may divide into multiple segments at junctions, but for which the integral of the kernel function is held at unity. The authors suggest that for problems of the type they have investigated (i.e. dense, urban networks, the bandwidth should be 100-300metres.

### 4.3.4.3 Line and intersection densities

Density methods may be applied to linear forms as well as point forms. Some statistics of interest include:

- the number of line segments per unit area (sometimes called the *line frequency*, $\lambda$, rather than the density)

- the length of line segments (by type) per unit area. The equation $L_a = L_0 e^{-r/b}$ has been found to provide a good model of the distribution of urban road length with radial distance, $r$, from many city centers. $L_0$=the road density at the city center, which for London, UK is c.19.5 kms/km$^2$; $b$ is a parameter to be fitted from sample data. The inverse of this density measure is the average area associated with a unit of path length, sometimes called the *constant of path maintenance*

- the number of *line intersections* per unit area

- the number of line intersections per unit of length (the latter is known as the *intersection density*, $k$). This is a particular case of the density of points on lines, which may be subject to kernel density smoothing in the manner discussed earlier in this Section. It can be shown that if $\lambda$ is the line density (frequency) then for a random network of straight lines there will be an average of $k = \lambda^2 / \pi$ intersections per unit length. $K = k / \lambda^2$ is sometimes called the *crossings factor*, and experimental evidence suggests that the random model provides an upper limit to this measure, so $K$ has the range $[0, 1/\pi]$.

All these measures provide information that may be useful for analysis, including inter-regional comparisons. Applications include hydrology, ecology and road traffic analysis.

For further discussion of applications in these areas and statistical measures see Haggett and Chorley (1969, Chapter 2.II) and Vaughan (1987, Chapter 3). A number of GIS packages provide facilities for kernel density mapping of lines (i.e. not points on lines – this is covered at the end of Section 0, above) as well as points (e.g. ArcGIS Spatial Analyst, Density operations). Essentially these work in a similar manner to 2D point operations, spreading the linear form symmetrically according to a specified kernel function. ArcGIS provides two sets of point density and line density functions (for SIMPLE or KERNEL density operations), one set that results in a grid being generated and the other for use in map algebra environments (i.e. where a grid already exists). SIMPLE density operations generate a set of grid values based on a neighborhood shape (e.g. circular, annular, rectangular, or polygonal) and size (e.g. radius). Similar facilities do not appear to be available with most other mainstream GIS packages. The GRASS open source package include a vector processing function v.kernel (formerly s.kernel) that now includes linear kernel generation (i.e. a 1D kernel) in addition to its generation of 2D raster grids from vector point sets with a Normal (Gaussian) kernel.

### 4.3.4.4 Cartograms

A cartogram is a form of map in which some spatially extensive variable such as population size or gross national product is substituted for land area. The geometry or space of the map is distorted (transformed) in order to convey the information of this alternate variable. The end result is a map or diagram in which the density of the variable under consideration is uniform throughout the map; variation in values are represented by variations in the size of mapped regions. Cartograms may be created use a variety of algorithms. One simple approach, due to Dorling (1995, CATMOG 59), is to associate the centroid of each mapped zone with the value of the variable to be mapped, and then to construct a circle around this point with area proportional to the magnitude of the variable. The size of the circles are typically scaled so that the largest is some fraction of a bounding rectangle encompassing all the original zones.

Generally these circles will overlap, as illustrated for Zurich cantons in Figure 4-48A. By systematically moving and rescaling the circles overlapping can be minimized whilst retaining approximate contiguity of the mapped regions (Figure 4-48B).

Dorling (1995, p32) describes the algorithm, for which sample code is provided, as follows:

*Each region ... is treated as an object in a gravity model which is repelled by other circles with which it overlaps, but is attracted to circles which were neighboring regions on the original map. Forces akin to forces of gravity are calculated, including velocity and acceleration, and the whole process is acted out as if it were occurring in treacle, to avoid any circles moving too quickly (as can occur when small objects orbit too close to large objects in the original gravity models).*

This example illustrates a procedure that seeks to represent the variable 'population' by the areas of the circles, whilst retaining the approximate relative positions and contiguity of the communes whilst avoiding overlap. It results in a discontinuous map with no attempt to retain any of the original region shapes. This form of cartogram is supported in several GIS and mapping packages, including MAPresso (Java-based), MapViewer and GeoDa.

If the objective is to create a cartogram that retains full contiguity, then the original area-based map needs to be stretched, or 'rubber-sheeted', in some way. Many algorithms have been proposed for such cartograms, commencing with Tobler's work on map transformations, Tobler (1963). More recently continuous transformation cartograms have been implemented using the rubber-sheeting algorithms of Dougenik *et al.* (1985) and the diffusion-based algorithm of Gastner and Newman (2004) – see Figure 4-49B (Zurich cantons), Figure 4-50 and Figure 4-51B (which uses the North Carolina dataset) discussed in several sections of this Guide.

It is important to note that within-zone variation is not represented in this technique,

hence representation of highly concentrated datasets (such as population) will provide a very particular view of the dataset. If zoned or gridded data is available within zones it may be useful to consider using such information when generating catrograms.

*Figure 4-48 Cartogram creation using basic Dorling algorithm*

A. Zurich Canton, Switzerland. 171 communes, population mapped as proportional circles

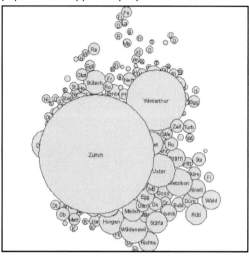

B. Cartogram creation using Dorling algorithm

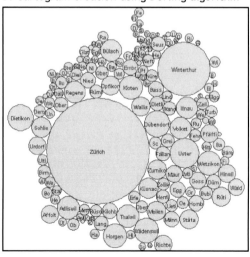

Created using MAPresso (Adrian Herzog)

*Figure 4-49 Cartogram creation using Dougenik, Chrisman and Niemeyer algorithm*

A. Zurich Canton, Switzerland. 171 communes, population mapped thematically

B. Cartogram creation using Dougenik, Chrisman and Niemeyer algorithm

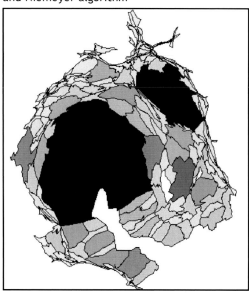

Created using MAPresso (Adrian Herzog)

*Figure 4-50 World Population as a Cartogram*

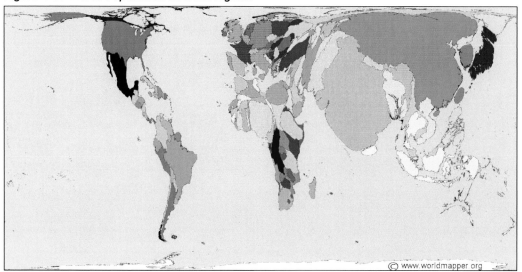

*© Copyright 2006 SASI Group (University of Sheffield) and Mark Newman (University of Michigan).*

The Gastner-Newman technique commences with the source map with its varying 'population' density and conceptually allows the individual members of this population to diffuse from higher density zones to lower density zones until such time as density is uniform. Zone boundaries are progressively moved during the diffusion process such that the net flow through them is zero, until they reach a stable position. It is important to note that here, as with many software implementations of geospatial algorithms, the final cartograms may differ depending upon the software package used to generate them and the parameters used or selected. For example, Dorling cartograms are produced very rapidly by GeoDa, with no option for parameter selection, and with some residual overlapping of the circular regions (Figure 4-51C). If the MapViewer software is chosen with the same dataset the results are markedly different for almost all parameter selections (Figure 4-51D). Of course, as another alternative, the shape of regions could be retained and their size altered to reflect the mapped variable if they are sufficiently well separated (i.e. a form of 'explosion' or multipolygon representation of the original mapped regions – see Figure 4-51E).

A final cartogram procedure that warrants attention involves identifying a zoning of the original source data in which the population is approximately equal (e.g. census areas, electoral districts). These zones, which will generally be of varying sizes, are then replaced with equal-sized hexagons and re-arranged into a lattice that approximates the source map. This procedure provides a contiguous mapping of the source data, retaining some of the overall form of the conventional map, whilst eliminating most of the variations due to underlying population levels. The Atlas of mortality in Britain by Shaw *et al.* (2008) uses this approach for all of its maps (see for example, Figure 4-52) – these show the cause of death for roughly 15 million cases over a 24 year period.

*Figure 4-51 Cartograms of births data, 1974*

A. Source data

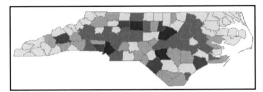

B. Glastner-Newman diffusion algorithm (ArcGIS 9 Cartogram Geoprocessing tool)

C. GeoDa's Dorling cartogram

D. MapViewer's Dorling cartogram

E. MapViewer's non-contiguous 'explosion' cartogram

*Figure 4-52 Hexagonal cartogram showing*
*UK mortality data, age group 20-24*

*Note: in this diagram each hexagon is divided into two halves which may have different principal causes of death within a given district, for this age group*

# 4.4 Distance Operations

Fundamental to all spatial analysis is the use of distance calculations. If our model of the world (mapped region under investigation) is regarded as a flat plane (2D Euclidean space) or a perfect sphere, then we can use the simple distance formulas $d_E$ and $d_S$ provided in Section 4.2 to compute distances between point pairs. These provide the basic building blocks for many forms of spatial analysis within most GIS packages. However, these two formulas are too limiting for certain forms of analysis and additional distance measures are required. In some cases these alternative measures (or metrics) can be computed directly from the coordinates of input point pairs, but in others computation is an incremental process. In fact incremental methods that compute length along a designated path (between a series of closely spaced point pairs) by summing the lengths of path segments, are the most general way of determining distance, i.e. the notions of distance and path are inextricably linked.

Figure 4-53 provides a simple cross-sectional illustration of the kind of issues that arise. We wish to determine the distance separating points A and B. If A and B are not too far apart (e.g. less than 10 kms) we could use a high precision laser rangefinder to establish the *slope distance* between A and B, assuming there is no atmospheric distortion. In practice there will be some distortion and the laser wave path will need to be adjusted in order to provide an estimated slope path distance. This in turn will require further adjustment if it is to be referenced to a common datum or a level terrain surface. In each case the distance recorded between A and B will be different.

From the diagram (Figure 4-53) it is clear that none of these distances corresponds to the actual distance across the terrain surface along a fixed transect, nor to a distance adjusted or computed to reflect the particular model of the Earth or region of the globe we are using. In some cases these differences will be small, whilst in other they may be highly significant.

*Figure 4-53 Alternative measures of terrain distance*

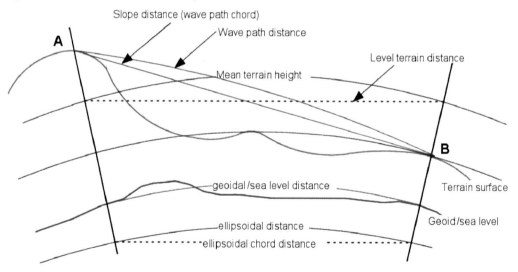

In general, simple Euclidean 2D (incremental) computations are satisfactory for many problems involving relatively smooth terrains extending over an area of perhaps 20km by 20km, even using suitably defined longitude and latitude coordinates (assuming these latter coordinates are not inside the Arctic or Antarctic regions). Closer to the poles the distortion of lines of latitude results in increasing errors in this formula and a variant known as the Polar Coordinate Flat-Earth formula may be used as an improved approximation:

$d = R\sqrt{A - B}$, where

$$A = (\pi/2 - \varphi_1)^2 + (\pi/2 - \varphi_2)^2$$
$$B = 2(\pi/2 - \varphi_1)(\pi/2 - \varphi_2)\cos(\lambda_2 - \lambda_1)$$

In this formula we are using polar coordinates ($\varphi, \lambda$) to represent latitude and longitude expressed in radians, and $R$ = the radius of the terrestrial sphere. With this formula the error is at most 20 meters over 20 kms even at 88°N or S. For example, the formula evaluates the distance between $A(70°N, 30°N)$ and $B(71°N, 31°N)$ as 117.6 kms (using the WGS84 ellipsoid), 112.8 kms 10° further north, and 111.4 kms at 87°N/88°N. One degree separation (ignoring longitude differences) would be 111.3 kms. However, for: (a) larger regions, or problems where *surface distance* is important; (b) problems involving networks; and (c) for problems involving variable costs; alternative procedures are required. Within mainstream GIS packages a range of tools exist to support such analysis, including the provision of support for Euclidean and Spherical distance (but not always ellipsoidal distance), network distance and cost distance (where cost is a generalized concept as we discuss in the subsections that follow).

Most software packages offer at least three categories of distance measure: (i) coordinate-based distance measures in the plane or on a sphere (which may be adjusted to a more close approximation of the Earth's shape); (ii) network-based measures determined by summing the stored length or related measure of a single link or multiple set of links along a specified route (e.g. shortest, quickest); and (iii) polyline-based measures, determined by summing the length of stored straight line segments (sequences of closely spaced plane coordinates) representing a given feature, such as a boundary. The first and third of these distance measures utilize the simple and familiar formulas for distance in uniform 2D and 3D Euclidean space and on the surface of a perfect sphere or spheroid. It is important to

check to see if distance computations provided represent true distances (e.g. in miles or kms) since Euclidean computations on raw latitude/longitude values produces incorrect results.

These formulas make two fundamental assumptions: (i) the distance to be measured is to be calculated along the shortest physical path in the selected space — this is defined to be the shortest straight line between the selected points (Euclidean straight lines or great circle arcs on the sphere); and (ii) that the space is completely uniform — there are no variations in terms of direction or location. These assumptions facilitate the use of expressions that only require knowledge of the coordinates of the initial and final locations, and thereby avoid the difficult question of how you actually get from $A$ to $B$.

In most cases measured terrestrial distances are reduced to a common base, such as the WGS84 reference ellipsoid. Note that the reference ellipsoid may be above or below the geoidal surface, and neither distance corresponds to distance across the landscape. Laser-based measurement is rarely used for distances of 50km or more, and increasingly DGPS measurements of location followed by direct coordinate-based calculations avoid the requirement for the wave path adjustments discussed above.

Whilst coordinate-based formulation is very convenient, it generally means that a GIS will not provide true distances between locations across the physical surface. It is possible for such systems to provide slope distance, and potentially surface distance along a selected transect or profile, but such measures are not provided in most packages. A number of packages do provide the option to specify transects, as lines or polylines, and then to provide a range of information relating to these transects. Examples include the Cross Section facility in MapInfo's Vertical Mapper, the Grid|Slice command procedures in Surfer, the Profiles and Elevations facilities in Manifold (Surface Tools) and the Profile facility in ArcGIS 3D Analyst. In addition to path profiles (elevations, lengths and related transect statistics) such paths may be linked with volumetric cut-and-fill analyses (see further Sections 6.2.3 and 6.2.6).

For problems that are not constrained to lie on networks it is possible to derive distances from the surface representation within the GIS. For example this can be achieved using a regular or irregular lattice representation along whose edges a set of links may be accumulated to form a (shortest) path between the origin and destination points. For the subset of problems concerned with existing networks, such questions could be restricted to locations that lie on these networks (or at network nodes) where path link lengths have been previously obtained. Both of these approaches immediately raise a series of additional questions: how accurate is the representation being used and does it distort the resulting path? which path through the network or surface representation should be used (e.g. shortest length, least effort, most scenic)? how are intermediate start and end points to be handled? are selected paths symmetric (in terms of physical distance, time, cost, effort etc.)? what constraints on the path are being applied (e.g. in terms of gradient, curvature, restriction to the existing physical surface etc.)? is the measure returned understandable and meaningful in terms of the requirements? how are multi-point/multi-path problems to be handled? Answers to some of these questions are discussed in Section 4.4.2, but we first discuss the notion of a metric.

### 4.4.1 Metrics

#### 4.4.1.1 Introduction

The term metric in connection with spatial analysis normally refers to the form of distance calculation applied, although it has a number of other meanings (e.g. the metric system of weights and measures; in the Manifold GIS package it means the sequence of coordinates that defines a vector object). Here we stick to its use in connection with distance computation. The essential features of the notion of distance are:

- a finite or infinite set of distinct, definable objects, and

- a rule or set of rules for determining the degree of separation of object pairs (a "measure").

From a mathematical perspective a metric $d_{ij}$, denoting a measure of separation between points $i$ and $j$, should satisfy a number of specific conditions. These are:

$d_{ij} > 0$ if $i \neq j$  (distinction or separation)

$d_{ij} = 0$ if $i = j$  (co-location or equivalence)

$d_{ij} + d_{jk} \geq d_{ik}$  (triangle inequality)

$d_{ij} = d_{ji}$  (symmetry)

The standard formulas $d_E$ and $d_S$ we discussed earlier in this Guide meet all four of these requirements, but there are many situations in which one or more of these conditions fails to be met. Particularly common are cases in which either the triangle inequality or symmetry conditions fail. Typically these occur in transport networks, where one-way routing systems apply or where there are variable tariffs or traffic flow asymmetries. Circular routes, such as the inner and outer circuits of Glasgow's "Clockwork Orange" underground system (Figure 4-54) provide an example of asymmetry. This service operates one clockwise and one anti-clockwise route, each of length 10.4 kms and transit time of 24 minutes. On a given circuit, the journey-time from Kelvinbridge to Hillhead, for example, which is 2 to 3 minutes, is clearly not the same as Hillhead to Kelvinbridge (over 20 minutes), and between stations it is not possible to change circuits.

*Figure 4-54 Glasgow's Clockwork Orange Underground*

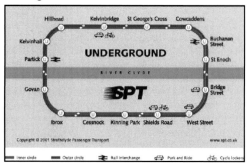

Asymmetry is also a characteristic of a number of telecommunications networks, where some modem standards and some broadband internet technologies (e.g. ADSL) operate in this way — information is generally received at a faster rate than it can be transmitted. A similar situation applies in many hybrid broadcast/telecommunications systems, such as satellite, coax or fiber-optic downstream and copper/cable upstream, and in some mobile network architectures. Pure broadcast technologies, such as terrestrial television and radio, are strictly one-way and only facilitate two-way communication via completely separate media (such as post, telephone or email). This kind of asymmetry also reflects a fundamental human characteristic — our ability to receive and process information is far greater than our ability to respond to it in an active manner.

If the triangularity constraint is not met we have the possibility that $d_{ij} + d_{jk} < d_{ik}$ which offends our notion of "between-ness" and thus of conventional notions of distance and space. For example, this would suggest that the "distance" from London to Madrid plus the "distance" from Madrid to Lima might be *less than* (cheaper than, faster than) the direct "distance" from London to Lima. A similar pattern can be found with railway and other transport timetables, where express trains and stopping trains in combination may reach a destination faster than a direct stopping train, even though the rail distance travelled may be greater. It may not be possible to draw a time- or space-consistent map of such data, but this does not mean that the measure used is not valuable. Indeed, in such cases non-cartographic representations (e.g. GIS internal representation, to/from matrices) of the data are often more meaningful and useful in optimization and routing problems, and as such are explicitly supported in GIS-T packages such as TransCAD and Cube.

#### 4.4.1.2 Terrestrial distances

Most GIS software uses the standard Euclidean formula, $d_E$, when computing distances between plane coordinate pairs and for calculation of "local" distances, as in the case of the vector buffer operator (see further, Section 4.4.4.1). It is important to check to see if distance computations provided represent true distances (e.g. in miles or kms) since Euclidean computations on raw latitude/longitude values produces incorrect results. Some packages, such as MapInfo, provide the option of using spherical distance, $d_S$, as a default. Manifold computes distances either using Euclidean or Ellipsoidal methods (supported via its functions Distance() and DistanceEarth(), and in its Tracker facility).

The MATLab Mapping Toolbox provides a range of distance and associated mapping functions, which help to illustrate some of the differences that apply on larger scale maps. Figure 4-55 shows a map of the North Atlantic on a Mercator projection, with the great circle path and the line of constant bearing, or *rhumb line* between Boston, Mass. and Bristol, England. The MATLab function distance() will compute the length of each path, taking the latitude and longitude of Boston and Bristol as inputs, and optionally a geoid parameter. The GRASS module geodist.c provides similar functionality. In the example shown the great circle distance is computed as 5105.6 kms based on its default terrestrial radius of 6371 kms; the Haversine formula we gave in Section 4.2.1 produces the same result, whilst the rhumb line distance is 5283.4 kms.

*Figure 4-55 Great circle and constant bearing paths, Boston to Bristol*

The geoid parameter, rather confusingly named, provides the option to select a model of the Earth which has an ellipsoidal form, specified by a two element vector: (i) the length of the major semi-axis of the ellipsoid and; (ii) its eccentricity or flattening coefficient. If these parameters are not specified it is assumed that the two semi-axes are equal, and thus provide a spherical or great circle measure. If geoid (ellipsoid) values are provided then an approximation method is used to calculate distances. It first treats the two terrestrial coordinates as if they were Cartesian coordinates in three dimensions and calculates the Euclidean distance between them. This value, which is the chord length of an elliptical section, is then adjusted by a correction factor to produce the final estimate of ellipsoidal distance. In our example this gives a revised distance of 5110.4 kms, a few kilometers longer than the great circle distance, as expected. Finally, yet another alternative is to use the more accurate Vincenty (1975) algorithm to obtain the ellipsoidal distance, which gives a figure of 5119.7 kms for the matching ellipsoid in this example.

### 4.4.1.3 Extended Euclidean and $L_p$-metric distances

Euclidean distance is the most widely used GIS metric. In 2D space (planar or projected space) the Euclidean distance between points $a(x_1,y_1)$ and $b(x_2,y_2)$ is a special case of the $n$-dimensional Euclidean metric. Within GIS this extended Euclidean metric is used to determine 3D distances (across surfaces and within solid structures) and in multi-dimensional analyses such as clustering. For 3D problems using $\{x,y,z\}$ as our coordinate representation the measure is simply:

$$d(a,b) = \left( \left(x_1 - x_2\right)^2 + \left(y_1 - y_2\right)^2 + \left(z_1 - z_2\right)^2 \right)^{1/2}$$

More generally we may represent our points $a$ and $b$ using subscripts to represent the dimensions 1,2,...$n$. Thus we have $a=(a_1,a_2)$ and $b=(b_1,b_2)$ for the 2D case. The general form of the Euclidean metric in $n$-space then becomes:

$$d(a,b) = \left( \sum_{i=1}^{n} \left(a_i - b_i\right)^2 \right)^{1/2}$$

This formula is processor-intensive to compute for very large number of point pairs and dimensions, mainly due to the square root operation. For some applications, such as $K$-means clustering (see Section 4.2.12.2) and line generalization (see Section 4.2.4) the square root is not taken, which breaks its metric behavior, but remains suitable for these specific purposes. In other areas, such as incremental grid operations, approximations to the Euclidean metric are taken to avoid such problems (see further, Section 4.4.2.2).

The formula above also arises, with some modifications, in the analysis of statistical datasets. The standard Euclidean metric in $n$-space takes no account of the average variation of the data points. However, it can be normalized (made scale free) by calculating the variance of the point set components, $\sigma_i^2$, and using these as a divisor:

$$d(a,b) = \left( \sum_{i=1}^{n} \frac{(a_i - b_i)^2}{\sigma_i^2} \right)^{1/2}$$

This is known as the *normalized Euclidean metric* (see also, Section 4.3.3) and is essentially the same as the Euclidean metric if the variances of point set components (the average variation of values or attributes of each dimensional component are equal. Pre-normalizing the attributes of input datasets (e.g. raster files) and then computing conventional $n$-dimensional Euclidean distances will produce the same result. This expression is also closely related to a more general measure, introduced by P C Mahalanobis in 1936 and named after him, which is used to determine the similarity of an unknown sample set to a known one. In addition to the variances of the components *Mahalanobis distance* takes into account the covariances that may exist. This more general measure is used in a number of GIS packages in connection with the analysis of remote sensing data.

For applications that require network distance measures between locations, Euclidean distance is generally inadequate and computing large numbers of (shortest) network distances may be impractical or inappropriate. In order to obtain more useful measures of inter-location distance many authors have suggested that the standard Euclidean distance formula be amended in various ways. The most frequently used modifications are based on replacing the use of the square and square root operations — i.e. replacing the powers of 2 and 1/2 — with other values, typically $p$ and $1/p$, estimated from sampling the network to be analyzed. We shall refer to such modifications as the family of $L_p$ metrics or $p$-norms, with $L_2$ being the standard Euclidean measure. They are amongst a range of alternative metrics supported by the Locational Analysis package, LOLA, which provides output in ArcGIS shape file format (SHP) as an option (see further, Section 7.4.1 et seq.).

The distance between two points in the plane: $a(x_1,y_1)$ and $b(x_2,y_2)$ with this metric is defined as $d_p(a,b)$, where:

$$d_p(a,b) = \left( \left| x_1 - x_2 \right|^P + \left| y_1 - y_2 \right|^P \right)^{1/P}$$

Figure 4-56 plots "circles" using various values for $p$, with the case $p=2$ (the Euclidean metric) giving a perfect circle — the only value which provides a rotationally invariant distance measure. The lines show the position of a point at a fixed distance from the center using the simple $p^{th}$ power/$p^{th}$ root model.

*Figure 4-56 p-metric circles*

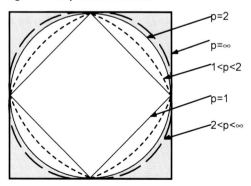

In geographic literature the case $p=1$ is variously called the Manhattan, Taxicab, Rectilinear or City block metric, and is supported in a number of software packages, including LOLA and the Crimestat package (in the latter instance with both Plane and Spherical computations). With $p=2$ we have the standard Euclidean metric and with $p=\infty$ we have the so-called minimax or Chebyshev metric used in a number of optimization problems. Note that the shape of the "circle" for $p=1$ is a square at a 45 degree angle, and this is the same as the shape for $p=\infty$.

Values for $p$ of approximately 1.7 have been found by many studies to approximate road distances within and between towns, and such estimates may be used in place of direct-line distance (where $p=2$) in problems such as locational analysis and the modeling of travel patterns — see for example, Love et al. (1972) and (1988). An alternative is to use a simple *route factor* (typically around 1.3) as a multiplier and to continue using Euclidean distances, but inflated by this route factor. Note that if $p<1$ the triangle inequality no longer holds, i.e. it is possible for the distance (or time) from A to B plus the distance from B to C to be *less than* the distance (or time) from A to C. This characteristic is quite common in transport infrastructures, where one-way systems, timetabled routes and traffic congestion alter the expected paths significantly. Numerous variations on the simple $L_p$ metric model have been studied, including using a mixture of powers for the $x$- and $y$-directions ($p$ and $q$), adding weighting factors for the two directions, including a different power, $s$, for the root etc. Most of these variations provide modest improvements in estimation of transport route distances at the expense of increased complexity in determination of the parameters. A summary of the possible values for $p$ in the $L_p$ metrics and their interpretation is provided in Table 4-9.

One of the most striking features of the $L_p$ metric diagram (Figure 4-56) is that for every value of $p$ except 2 the "circles" show rotational bias — maximized at 45 degrees. Similar bias exists if other variants of the $L_p$

metric family are plotted. This highlights the fact that a distance value obtained by measurement and application of any of these modified formulas will change if the reference frame is rotated. If this seems a bit obscure, imagine measuring the distance between two points randomly located on a rectangular street network oriented north-south/east-west. In general this will involve finding the length of a route in the north-south direction and adding the length of a route in the east-west direction. If, however, we could ignore the physical network and rotate and translate the pattern of streets about one of the points until the two points both lay along one road (a rotated north-south route), the length measured would be shorter. This comment applies equally to grid files, where distances (and many other measures) are often calculated in an incremental manner which is affected by the grid orientation.

*Table 4-9 Interpretation of p-values*

| | |
|---|---|
| $0 < p < 1$ | The $L_p$ formula does not yield a metric because the triangle inequality no longer holds — for example, construction of minimal spanning trees on the basis of progressively connecting nearest-neighbors is not valid. Routes in cities may have values of $p < 1$ indicating that routes are complex — a value of $p = 2/3$ indicates that distances are effectively twice as far as direct line estimates would suggest. The locus of points in this case is concave |
| $1 < p < 2$ | The distance, $d$, is a metric which is intermediate between the Manhattan grid-like street pattern and the normal Euclidean metric, and is thus applicable to more complex city street networks |
| $p > 2$ | As $p$ increases greater weight is given to the largest components of distance in the network. Consider the distance from $(0,0)$ to $(1, 1-E)$ where $0 < E < 1$. For $p=1$ $d = 2-E$; for $p=2$ and $E << 1$ $d \approx \sqrt{2}\sqrt{(1-E)}$ and as $p$ increases, $d \to 1$. In all cases as $p \to \infty$ then $d = \max(|x_1 - x_2|, |y_1 - y_2|)$ |

The above observations on rotational relationships can be used in problem solving —

for example, in some cases it may be possible to solve selected problems by applying the sequence of actions:

- rotate the problem coordinate frame

- solve the problem using the metric appropriate to the rotated frame, and then

- rotate the frame back to its original position.

For example, Okabe *et al.* (2000, Section 3.7) show that in order to determine the Voronoi diagram for a set of planar points under the $L_\infty$ metric, the set of points may be rotated by an angle of $+\pi/4$ radians and the regions computed using the $L_1$ metric, with the resulting diagram rotated back by $-\pi/4$ radians to produce the final solution.

Although the *p*-metric family provides real value in analytic studies, this lack of rotational invariance is undesirable in the context of distance measurement. Clearly it would be simple for suppliers to include such distance expressions in their GIS packages, but the estimation of the parameters and the interpretation of their results require considerable care. In practice the advent of more powerful hardware and software, and greatly improved network datasets, has meant that many problems can be tackled by explicit network analysis rather than the application of alternative metrics (see further, Chapter 7).

### 4.4.2 Cost distance

The term cost distance is widely used within GIS and in this context has a dual meaning: (i) the notion of an alternative family of distance metrics; and (ii) a procedure for determining least cost paths across continuous surfaces, typically using grid representations

Within GIS the term is distinct from the computation of varying costs or times of travel across a network. The term cost in this connection is also a generic idea, not necessarily implying financial cost, but some composite measure that varies (i.e. is not constant) across the study region, and which needs to be taken into account when computing paths and distances.

An example serves to clarify this notion. Suppose that we wish to construct a section of road between two points, $A(0,2)$ and $B(4,2)$, where costs are constant over the region of interest. In this case the distance is simply 4 units and the path involved is a straight line in the plane (Figure 4-57, bold line). Construction costs will simply be $4k$ units, where $k$ is some constant (the cost per unit length of path construction). Now suppose that construction costs also depend on the cost of land acquisition, and that land costs vary in our study region in a simple manner — greater to the "north" of our region than to the "south". In this situation it is cheaper to construct our road with a curve in it, taking advantage of the fact that land costs are lower to the south (nearer the x-axis in our model).

*Figure 4-57 Cost distance model*

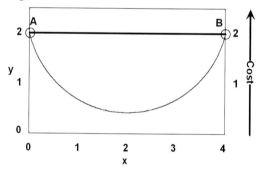

If costs increase in a precisely linear manner, the optimal (least cost) path will have a smooth curve form of the kind shown by the thinner line (a shape like a chain hanging between two posts). This case turns out to be solvable mathematically, as are cases where costs vary in radially symmetric manner (e.g. around a city center), whereas almost every other example of varying costs cannot be solved precisely and we need to resort to computational procedures to find the least cost path.

### 4.4.2.1 Accumulated cost surfaces and least cost paths

Within GIS packages solutions to such problems are found using a family of algorithms known as Accumulated Cost Surface (ACS) methods — for a fuller discussion of ACS methods and representational accuracy see Douglas (1994) and Eastman (1989). The ACS procedure is applied to raster datasets, in which the primary input surface is a complete grid of generalized costs, i.e. every cell is assigned an absolute or relative cost measure, where costs must be (positive) ratio-scaled variables. In Figure 4-58 we show a hypothetical cost grid for the same example as shown in Figure 4-57. Values increase linearly away from the x-axis, from 0.5 to 2.5. This essentially a much simplified representation of the function $f(x,y)=y$, so $f(x,y)=0$ when $y=0$ for all $x$ and increases steadily so at $y=2$ $f(x,y)=2$. In practice cost functions should rarely if ever have zero-valued sections, so this example should be considered illustrative!

Providing a gridded representation of the cost surface highlights the importance of using a sufficiently fine representation of the surface, since the solution path must be computed by adding up the costs along alternative paths. If the grid resolution is quite coarse, as in Figure 4-58, the solution path will not have the curved form of the optimal path, but will simply be a very blocky stepped line of cells approximating the curve. Amending the grid resolution (halving the cell size to 0.25 units) as shown in Figure 4-59A improves both the cost surface representation and the possible solution paths that are considered.

*Figure 4-58 Cost surface as grid*

*Figure 4-59 Grid resolution and cost distance*

(a) Cost surface

(b) Queen's moves steps

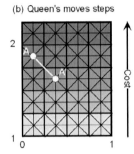

If we look at a path in Figure 4-58 that starts at $A(0,2)$ and goes diagonally down towards $C(2,0)$ and then back up to $B(4,2)$ we have cell costs of 2+1.5+1+.5+.5+1+1.5+2=10 units (times cell size of 0.5 gives a cost distance of 5 units). But this path is longer than the sum of the steps – all the diagonal steps are $\sqrt{2}$ (1.414... units) longer than horizontal and vertical steps, so the total cost must be increased for such steps by this factor, giving a final cost distance of 6.85 units. This is less than the cost of 8 units that would be incurred for a straight line path from $A$ to $B$. But can we be sure this is the best route possible for this problem and is the calculation "correct"?

ACS provides a systematic procedure for answering this question. With this algorithm we start at $A$ and sum up the costs in all directions, step by step, choosing the least cost increment at each step. Eventually, when we arrive at $B$, we will have the overall least cost of getting to $B$, and if we have kept track of our route (the steps we have taken) we will have the least cost path from $A$ to $B$. Thus ACS is a form of spread algorithm, with values increasing in all directions depending on the grid resolution, cost surface and algorithmic implementation. Almost all GIS implementations of ACS use immediate neighbors in calculating values (i.e. queen's moves, to the 8 adjacent cells) but some facilitate calculation to neighbors further away. GRASS, for example, offers the option in the r.cost function, of using knight's move neighbors (one step up and one diagonal) in its calculations. Distance transform methods (see further Section 4.4.2.2) utilize a much wider

range of neighbors, and hence are not restricted to 8-directional cost surfaces and path alignments, and thus do not exhibit the common directional bias and computational errors of ACS distance models.

As we start to consider the ACS idea more closely we see that a number of additional issues need to be addressed. The first is that in a GIS-enabled grid structure cells (or more specifically cell centers) are frequently used as references rather than grid lines. Thus our starting point $A$ cannot be (0,2) exactly but must be a cell center and our end points will also all be cell centers. For example, see Figure 4-59B where $A(0,2)$ is approximated on the grid by the point $A(0.125, 1.875)$. For the best results we should estimate the value of the cost function at cell centers if possible, rather than at cell edges or grid lines. In the example we are using we have ignored this latter factor, which will often be the case since finer detail for within cell estimation may not be available (although could be obtained by interpolation).

A second issue is that if we take grid cell centers as our reference point, the start point will be half way across the first cell, and the next point will be half way across an adjacent cell, so it can be argued that the cell values (costs) should be allocated 50:50 over this one step, and likewise for steps 2, 3 etc. This can be seen in Figure 4-59B where the starting point for $A$ is shown as a selected cell center and the step to $A'$ in the diagonally adjacent cell lies 50% in a cell with cost 2 and 50% in a cell with cost 1.75. This 50:50 division of costs is the normal approach used in GIS packages. The averaged cost from $A$ to $A'$ is then (2+1.75)/2=3.75/2 and thus the incremental cost distance is $\sqrt{2}*0.25*3.75/2$ units (adjusting for the diagonal path using $\sqrt{2}$ and for the cell size of 0.25 units in this example).

We now have all the basic elements we need in order to compute accumulated costs and identify the least cost path from $A$ to $B$. Using our example cost grid, with a cell size of 0.25 units, we need to carry out the following operations using a typical GIS:

- Create a source grid that contains a 0 in the cell in which our starting point A lies, and some other value (e.g. -1, 1, 9999) for all other grid cells. This can be done with a text editor and converted to a GIS compatible grid format if necessary

- Create a cost grid in the same manner, exactly the same size and the same resolution as the source grid, but containing the costs associated with each cell position (i.e. similar to the cells in Figure 4-59a)

- Run the cost distance facility within the GIS on these two input grids, requesting the output as a cost distance (ACS) grid, and also requesting (if necessary) that a direction or tracking dataset is generated that can be subsequently used to identify least cost paths

- Finally, to create the least cost paths, a target grid is required, which contains the target or destination points (again as 0s or a similar cell identifier for the target points). The least cost path facility in the GIS is then run using the target grid, ACS grid and tracking grid

A sample result for our test problem is shown in Figure 4-60. Each grid cell has been separately colored and a series of additional destination points (cells) have been included in the least cost path finding stage. The least cost path from A to B, corresponding to our original problem, hugs the bottom of the diagram as it seeks to take advantage of the low cost first row (cells with a value of only 0.25 units). Routes to other cells may share common paths for parts of their route and may not be unique, as indicated by the two routes to the cell diagonally below point A to the right. If the cost surface had been flatter, for example $f(x,y)=y/4+1$, the ACS model with the cell resolution illustrated would fail to select the correct path, but would show a horizontal path from A to B. To obtain a more accurate estimate of the correct path and cost distance a much finer grid would be required. For this latter example the true path is a gentle curve with a minimum value at around y=1.65 and total cost of 5.88 units.

*Figure 4-60 Accumulated cost surface and least cost paths*

This simple example provides a flavor of cost distance computation, but this procedure (or family of procedures) has far more to offer. The first and perhaps most important point to note is that the source and target features do not need to be single points. They can be multiple distinct points (cells), lines (linear groups of cells), or regions (clusters of adjacent cells). In all such cases the ACS procedure computes the lowest total distance to a target cell from its nearest source cell. If requested the GIS may also produce an allocation raster, which identifies which source each cell in the grid is closest to (typically by giving each cell a unique integer identifier). Obstacles (e.g. lakes, cliffs etc.) may be included in these models by setting cells in the cost raster to very high values or by the GIS explicitly supporting unavailable (masked) cells (e.g. in Idrisi, coding barrier cells as -1).

The input cost raster may be, and often is, a composite grid created from a number of other (normalized) input grids by simple map algebraic operations. The final cost grid may also be normalized to provide an indication for each cell of the relative cost, difficulty or *friction* of crossing that cell. Figure 4-61 illustrates the result of such a process, which has been applied to determining possible alternative routes for a main road in part of South-East England. The map shows the existing road (the A259T) from Hastings in the south-west to Brenzett in the north-east. Three alternative routes, identified here by arrows, were generated by ACS methods.

These routes were generated from cost surfaces that included different weighted values for a series of inputs: land-use (grade and type of land); SSSIs (Sites of special scientific interest); areas of designated Ancient Woodland; the slope of the land across the study area (derived from a DEM); existing (buffered) built-up areas (many of which are conservation areas) and ancient monuments; National Trust land; and existing (buffered) road and rail routes. The final route alternatives were then computed from the composite ACS surface and smoothed to reduce the effects of the gridding of all the datasets and output paths. This information was then provided as input to a public consultation exercise.

This is a relatively simple example of a general class of problems categorized as corridor planning — selection of alternative routes for roads, rail lines, power lines or other purposes frequently requires the involvement of many parties, and formal multi-criteria decision support systems, such as AHP and ANP, have been extensively used in this field — see, for example, Azis (1990), Bailey (2003) and Piantanakulchai (2005).

*Figure 4-61 Alternative route selection by ACS*

The above examples are based on the procedures utilized in ArcGIS, Spatial Analyst.

Many other packages offer similar facilities. For example, Idrisi offers two alternative algorithms: one, called the *pushbroom* algorithm, is similar to the distance transform procedures described in Section 4.4.2.2, and is fast but not suitable for use with more complex problems (for example truly implementing barriers); a second Idrisi procedure, *costgrow*, is much slower but does facilitate complex friction patterns and fixed barriers. Idrisi also allows for anisotropy in the cost modeling process, with some directions (e.g. downhill) being preferable to others (e.g. uphill). SAGA, GRASS and PCRaster provide similar functions, with inputs optionally including a friction surface (with relative friction values and absolute barriers) and a physical surface, with movements restricted to uphill, downhill and either stopping at or crossing flat areas. Such procedures are clearly targeted at hydrological and related studies, so whilst being well suited to these environments are not readily generalized. Many such programs, particularly those with an environmental sciences and remote sensing background, perform the path finding stage using a form of steepest descent procedure (often described as a *drainage* procedure) applied to the ACS. This approach is not guaranteed to provide the correct shortest path — tracked paths should be used. This is illustrated in Figure 4-62, where local Euclidean grid distances and 50:50 splitting of costs between the cells shaded in gray has been used to generate the ACS grid, Figure 4-62B. The steepest path from the target cell back to the source cell (Figure 4-62C) is not the least cost path, as its total accumulated cost is 13.726. The correct least cost path is shown in Figure 4-62D. ACS procedures are subject to a number of other problems, for example: becoming trapped in localized plateaus or pits; inadequate handling of multiple equivalent paths; or failing when input and/or output datasets are specified to operate in integer rather than float mode.

A number of GIS packages incorporate extensions to the standard cost distance/ACS model. For example, ArcGIS provides a variant of the ACS procedure which it describes as Path Distance. This is essentially the same as

ACS but includes options such as inclusion of surface distance (using a surface raster or DEM), and vertical and horizontal movement rasters that are utilized in adjusting the optimum path computation. TNTMips also includes a path analysis procedure that takes into account the physical surface form, but the authors are cautious about its optimality.

*Figure 4-62 Steepest path vs tracked path*

A. Cost surface

| 1 | 5 | 5 | 5 | 1 |
|---|---|---|---|---|
| 1 | 5 | 5 | 5 | 1 |
| 1 | 5 | 5 | 5 | 1 |
| 1 | 5 | 5 | 1 | 1 |
| 1 | 1 | 1 | 1 | 1 |

B. Accumulated cost surface (ACS)

| 4.414 | 7.414 | 12.414 | 8.828 | 5.828 |
|---|---|---|---|---|
| 3.414 | 6.656 | 11.656 | 8.07 | 4.828 |
| 2.414 | 5.656 | 6.656 | 5.414 | 3.828 |
| 1.414 | 3 | 4.242 | 2.414 | 3.414 |
| 1 | 0 | 1 | 2 | 3 |

C. ACS Steepest descent path

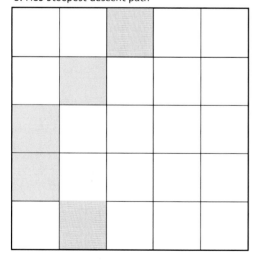

D. ACS Least cost path

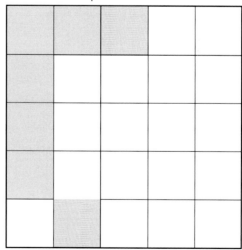

Idrisi provides a similar facility, Disperse, designed to provide a simple force-based model of anisotropic object dispersal (SAGA provides comparable facilities). In this case the inputs are a set of four grid files: (i) the location of the target and source features (non-zero entries are targets, zeros are sources); (ii) and (iii) two grids, one containing the magnitude and the other containing the direction (azimuth) of the anisotropic force field, i.e. a vector field modeled using a pair of grids; and (iv) an output grid. The notion of the magnitude of the force field in this implementation is as the inverse of a friction field, $F$, force=$1/F$ where $F$ in this case is taken to be greater than 1. The anisotropic dispersal model is either user specified or utilizes an inbuilt cosine function that modifies the stated friction field:

$$F'=F^*f, \text{ where } f = \frac{1}{\cos^k \alpha}$$

$\alpha$ is an angular difference between the angle being considered and the stated friction angle, and $k$ is a parameter ($k$=2 is the default). The process may be modeled as a series of steps (time periods) by pre-specifying a maximum dispersal distance at each stage.

#### 4.4.2.2 Distance transforms

In the image processing world a procedure similar to ACS (Section 4.4.2.1) has been developed in connection with work on pattern recognition. The procedure is known as a Distance Transform (DT), and is typically implemented on binary images in a scanning manner rather than the spreading approach of ACS. Extremely efficient algorithms have been developed to generate exact Euclidean DTs and excellent approximations to exact Euclidean DTs (EDTs) on large images. Some of these procedures have even been implemented within hardware chipsets for real-time applications. GIS vendors do not generally utilize DT methods, but they are included in many image processing toolsets and packages, including the MATLab Image Processing Toolkit: e.g. see the bwdist() function, which provides a variety of metrics for black and white images, including City Block and exact Euclidean. A second example with more direct links with GIS is the product suite, ERDAS.

Using DTs, distances over the image or grid are calculated in an incremental manner based entirely on the distance to *nearby* (not necessarily *adjacent*) cells. The standard algorithm involves a two-pass scan of a square or rectangular lattice: a forward scan from top left (NW corner) to bottom right (SE corner),

and then a backwards scan from bottom right to top left (i.e. SE→NW corner). The scan commences by placing the forward scan mask over the first available cell in the grid to be transformed – in a 3x3 scan mask ($M$x$M$ cells, where $M$=3) this will be grid cell (row 2, col 2). A basic DT 3x3 mask is illustrated in Figure 4-63, where 5 values are used based on the two-value (3,4) integer mask. (3,4) is useful as it is extremely fast to process, and dividing through by 3 at the end yields direct steps of 1 and diagonal steps of 1.33... giving a reasonable approximation to *local* Euclidean measure (1.414...) and within 6% of exact *global* Euclidean measure.

*Figure 4-63 3x3 Distance transformation – scan elements*

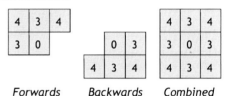

*Forwards     Backwards     Combined*

Typically the underlying grid to be transformed is an array in which unreached cells are initially assigned a large number (e.g. 999) and target or source cells are assigned a value of 0. Cells that act as barriers or restricted areas (e.g. buildings) can be coded with even larger numbers (e.g. 9999), in which case they are never altered. On completion of the two-pass scan each cell in the resulting lattice will contain the distance to the *nearest point* in the set of source points. If barriers are included they must be in blocks of at least ($M$-1)x($M$-1) cells, and accessible areas should consist of at least ($M$+1)x($M$+1) cells. In addition, two scan pairs: (NW→SE/SE→NW) and (SW→NE/NE→SW), with one or more iterations, are required to ensure full scanning of the grid. On completion of the scan each cell in the resulting lattice will contain the distance to the *nearest point* in the set of source points. The pushbroom algorithm described by Eastman (1989) and used in Idrisi for their cost distance modeling is very similar to this approach.

The central function in this algorithm is of the form: $d0=\min\{d+D(i),d0\}$, where $d0$ is the current value at the central point (0) of the template, $D(i)$ is the local distance to the $i^{th}$ element of the template, and $d$ is the current value at $(r,c)$. The basic algorithm involves $O(Mn^2)$ computations where $n$ is the maximum dimension of the grid. Details of DT procedures are provided in the references cited, and code samples in MATLab and Python are available from: www.desmith.com/MJdS/DT1.htm.

*Table 4-10 3x3 Chamfer metrics*

| Case | Description | Adjacency matrix | | |
|------|-------------|------|------|------|
| 1 | Distances are determined by the $L_1$ or 'city-block' metric and paths correspond to the "rook's move" in chess parlance. <br><br> Maximum error: 29.29% | 2 | 1 | 2 |
| | | 1 | 0 | 1 |
| | | 2 | 1 | 2 |
| 2 | Distances are defined as case 1 for *any* immediate neighbor, i.e. horizontal or diagonal ("rook's move" and "bishop's move"). <br><br> Maximum error: 41.41% | 1 | 1 | 1 |
| | | 1 | 0 | 1 |
| | | 1 | 1 | 1 |
| 3 | As per 2 but with diagonal distances determined by the Euclidean metric applied locally – sometimes referred to as Octagonal or Local Euclidean metric. <br><br> Maximum error: 7.61% | √2 | 1 | √2 |
| | | 1 | 0 | 1 |
| | | √2 | 1 | √2 |
| 4 | Chamfer (3,4)/3 metric. This uses integer values to provide a better estimate of Euclidean distance than Cases 1 or 2. <br><br> Maximum error: 6.07% | 4 | 3 | 4 |
| | | 3 | 0 | 3 |
| | | 4 | 3 | 4 |
| 5 | Fractional chamfer (Borgefors, 1986) – non-integer values for both rook's move and bishop's move directions (revised after Butt and Maragos, 1998). <br><br> Maximum error: 3.96% | 1.36039 | 0.96194 | 1.36039 |
| | | 0.96194 | 0 | 0.96194 |
| | | 1.36039 | 0.96194 | 1.36039 |

A selection of 3x3 masks is shown in Table 4-10. These are known as *chamfer metrics* because the locus of the metric generates a figure similar to a cross-section of a piece of wood with chamfered or beveled edges. The generic form of such masks is defined by the two unique mask values (a,b), e.g. (2,1) or (3,4). The maximum error percentages shown in Table 4-10 provide the *global* maximum errors for the metric as compared with global Euclidean measure. The use of 3x3 local metrics is fast and simple, but results in directional bias in the resulting DT. These show the familiar 4- or 8-direction patterns seen in many GIS processes that rely on 3x3 neighborhoods (see, for example, Figure 4-34).

This problem can be considerably reduced by extending the neighborhood to a 5x5 mask ($M=5$), in which case 3 values define the mask: (a,b,c) as shown in Figure 4-64. Amongst the best integer values for this mask size are the triple (5,7,11), dividing all cell values by 5 at the end to give (1,1.4,2.2). The best fractional values are (0.9866, 1.4141, 2.2062). Use of the integer values above ensures that every grid cell distance computed (i.e. *global* values) is within 2% of the exact Euclidean distance and within 1.36% for the fractional masks. This compares with global errors of up to 7.6% with a pure *local* Euclidean metric.

### Figure 4-64 5x5 DT mask

| 2b | c | 2a | c | 2b |
|----|---|----|---|----|
| c  | b | a  | b | c  |
| 2a | a | 0  | a | 2a |
| c  | b | a  | b | c  |
| 2b | c | 2a | c | 2b |

Figure 4-65A provides the simplest test case for the DT procedure. This shows a uniform region with a single target point in the center (originally coded as 0, with all other grid cells coded 999). This figure shows the *best* non-exact DT possible using a fractional-valued 5x5 scanning template. The exact Euclidean distance transform (EDT) of this uniform space yields a perfectly circular set of filled contours around the central point. The vector equivalent would be a multi-ring buffer operation. When applied to multiple points (e.g. as part of a point-pattern analysis exercise) the set of computed distances, $F()$, is known as the *empty space function*.

If a simple barrier is introduced, e.g. representing a river with a bridge point, shortest paths appear *diffracted* through the gap (Figure 4-65B). In this example the target point has been set as (2,50). With a complex barrier, as in Figure 4-65C, a single extra iteration has been used to ensure full convergence. In all cases shortest paths to target points can be drawn as orthogonal to the distance bands, but are best constructed using tracking of the selected steps, as described further in the examples below. Although the DT approach may seem somewhat divorced from practical GIS analysis, DT procedures have been extended and developed by: Ratti *et al.* (architecture and the built environment; 2001, 2004); de Smith (transport routes; 2004, 2006), Ikonen and Toivanen (image processing; 2005); and Kristinsson *et al.* (geothermal pipelines, 2005) to provide a new and fast family of ACS-like procedures for solving many grid-related distance problems.

### Figure 4-65 Distance transform, single point

A. 5x5 DT, no constraints, target (50,50)

B. 5x5 DT, barrier – target (2,50)

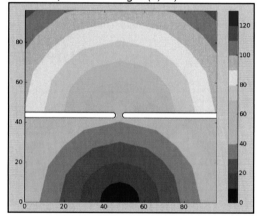

C. 5x5 DT, complex obstacle – target (50,90)

We limit discussion here to a small sample of applications. The first deals with radially symmetric models of traffic in cities — see Angel and Hyman, Urban Fields (1976, pp 15-16 and 159) for a full discussion of the models involved. The second example examines pedestrian movement within urban areas, whilst the third set of examples address questions of optimal road and pipeline location under a range of constraints.

Figure 4-66 shows the result of applying a least 'cost' distance transform (LCDT) to a city with traffic speeds symmetrically varying from almost 0kph in the center (where the crossed lines meet) to much higher levels (e.g. 50kph+) at the city edge. The cost field in this case is traffic speed (i.e. a velocity field) and the curved lines show contours of equal travel time (isochrones) to or from a point due South of the city center.

*Figure 4-66 Urban traffic modeling*

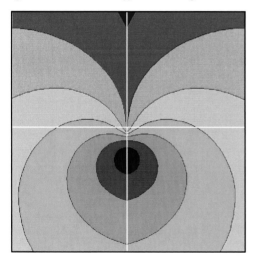

The central function in the DT procedure in this instance is of the form:

$$d0 = \min\{d+D(i)^*COST(r,c), d0\}$$

where $d0$ is the current value at the central point (0) of the mask, $D(i)$ is the local distance to the $i^{th}$ element of the mask, $d$ is the current value at $(r,c)$ and $COST(r,c)$ is the (averaged) cost function at row $r$, column $c$. As can be seen, the velocity field distorts the distance

bands. Shortest (quickest) paths across this transformed surface may be plotted by following routes to or from the source point in any given direction, remaining at right angles (orthogonal) to the equal time contours, or by tracking of the computed quickest paths. Hence the quickest route from the start point due South of the center to locations North of the city center would curve around (East or West) the center to avoid congestion (low traffic speeds). In this particular example these curve form log spirals (Wardrop, 1969).Angel and Hyman applied models of this type to the analysis of traffic flows in Manchester, UK. Distance transform methods enable such models to be calibrated against known analytical results and then applied to more realistic complex velocity and cost fields, for example to examine the possible effects of introducing central zone congestion charging.

A second example of this procedure is shown in Figure 4-67. This shows a section of the Notting Hill area of central London, with the annual Carnival route shown in white and areas in dark gray being masked out (buildings etc.). Colors indicate increasing distances (in meters) from the Carnival route along nearby streets.

*Figure 4-67 Notting Hill Carnival routes*

Although this example has been created by a DT scanning procedure the result is sometimes described as a "burning fire" analogy, with the fire spreading from the source locations (in this case a route) outwards along adjacent streets and squares (for true fire spread models see www.fire.org and Stratton, 2004). The same techniques can be applied in public open spaces and even within building complexes such as shopping malls, galleries and airports. This illustrates the ability of DT methods to operate in what might be described as complex friction environments.

Distance transforms are very flexible in their ability to incorporate problem-specific constraints. For example, in a typical ACS procedure variable slopes are modeled by regarding steeper slopes as higher cost, rather than relating the spreading process to slope directly (other than some uphill/downhill constrained implementations). The selection of a route for a road, railway or pipeline is affected by slope, but primarily in the direction of the path rather than the maximum slope of the physical surface (although this does have a bearing on construction cost).

Figure 4-68 illustrates the application of a gradient-constrained DT (GCDT) to the selection of road routes through a hilly landscape. The most northerly two routes (upper right in the diagram) were constrained to a 1:12 and 1:11 gradient (before engineering grading) whilst the most southerly two represent routes found using less restrictive 1:9 and 1:8 gradient constraints.

With minor modifications the GCDT procedure described above has been utilized with a high resolution (10meter) DEM to locate alternative pipeline routes for the Hellisheiði 80MW geothermal power station in Iceland (Kristinsson, Jonsson and Jonsdottir, 2005). In this case additional constraints were applied giving the maximum and minimum heights permitted for the route and differential directional constraints that permitted limited flow uphill, which is possible for these kinds of two-phase pipelines (Figure 4-69A,B).

*Figure 4-68 Alternative routes selected by gradient constrained DT*

*Figure 4-69 Hellisheiði power plant pipeline route selection*

A. Overview of power plant area

B. Alternative solution paths A, B1, B2 and C for Well 3

### 4.4.3    Network distance

Network distance, as the name suggests, is the distance (or cost, time etc.) involved in traversing a network. In most instances the term refers to the lowest value distance measure between pairs or lists of points (generally network nodes or points upstream and/or downstream in hydrological applications). Typically the network is a logical collection of linked polylines, joined at network nodes (or vertices), and possessing a network topology (sometimes called a geometry). Network links and nodes may have additional explicit attributes, such as type of link, weights applied to links and nodes, rules governing behavior of flows (e.g. link directionality, permitted turns, barriers) etc., and intrinsic attributes (e.g. position and segment lengths). When network distances are computed by a GIS the procedure takes into account the various explicit and intrinsic attributes of the network and the rules applied for the problem selected. Thus network distance will vary in meaning according to the problem at hand. A variety of hybrid concepts exist, which may be modeled within some GIS packages, but generally only in a limited manner. These include multi-modal networks (thus seeking routes that may combine road, rail and bus for example), and mixed network/cost distance situations, in which sources or targets may not lie on the network, but for which sections of optimal routes (or network building programme) need to utilize existing network infrastructures.

Most GIS packages have not historically included extensive networking tools as part of their standard offering, but may provide limited functionality in this area (e.g. ArcGIS Utility Network Analyst and Linear Referencing tools). This situation is now changing: Manifold does include a range of network analysis tools via its Business Tools extension; ArcGIS V9 now ships with the new Network Analyst option as part of the main distribution kit; TNTMips now includes a network analysis module with a wide range of facilities; and the open source GIS, GRASS, includes a range of network analysis tools in its core modules for vector processing, with functions such as v.net.path generating shortest paths and outputting

associated attribute data such as distances and times in linked attribute tables. A rather different tool, SANET, is specifically designed to carry out certain types of spatial analysis on a network (e.g. statistical analysis), and is provided as an ArcGIS add-in. TransCAD and Cube also differ from most GIS products as they are essentially "GIS for transportation" (GIS-T) offerings. TransCAD is built on a general purpose GIS engine, Maptitude and Cube is built on ArcGIS. Figure 4-70 illustrates the use of network distance within the TransCAD shortest path facility, utilizing least distance (heavy line shown in blue) and least time (heavy line shown in green) with a single intermediate node. Such algorithms are widely used in web-based GIS providing routing and traffic advice (see for example, Google maps, www.mapquest.com). Output from these systems is in a variety of forms, including tabulation of section-by-section network distance/time and cumulative distance and/or time.

*Figure 4-70 Shortest and least time paths*

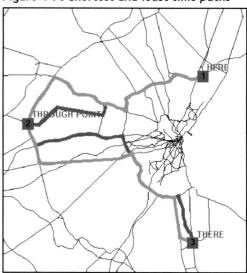

Depending on the GIS package, for large networks with potentially complex routing it is often advisable to compute link lengths as an explicit field or table and work with this data rather than expecting the GIS to re-compute such information dynamically from an intrinsic field. For more details see Chapter 7.

### 4.4.4 Buffering

#### 4.4.4.1 Vector buffering

Buffering is the process of creating one or more zones around selected features, within a pre-specified distance (almost always Euclidean distance) from these features. The resulting buffer is an area object or series of area objects (typically polygons) that may be automatically merged (dissolved) where they overlap. In many cases the buffer regions are created from a combination of straight lines and circular arcs centered on the vertices of the convex hull. In Figure 4-71A simple symmetric buffers generated using the GRASS v.buffer operation are shown, whilst in Figure 4-71B the result of applying a 100metre buffer to sections of road network is shown, without buffer segment merging (selected segment highlighted). Buffers may be applied to:

- point, line or polygon objects, or to cells in a grid dataset

- they may be symmetric, i.e. spreading outwards from lines and polygon boundaries in both directions (left and right or inside and out), or

- they may be asymmetric, spreading inwards or outwards only (see for example the buffering used in polygon skeletonization, Figure 4-14)

- buffers may also be applied differentially, for example larger buffers applied to major roads and smaller buffers applied to minor roads, as part of a pollution analysis exercise (air-borne, noise, vibration etc.)

- buffers may be applied incrementally, progressively increasing and/or reducing in size

Although the idea of buffering appears very straightforward, and has many applications, different GIS packages implement the facility in a variety of ways. In ArcGIS extensive support is provide in ArcToolbox for buffer creation of selected features, with facilities to select buffering: to the left, right or both sides of polylines and polygons; to select whether linear feature buffers are terminated with rounded or squared-off ends; and to select features which may have their buffered regions combined (dissolved together) and optionally a selected attribute (field) to be used for determining whether dissolve operations should be performed. An additional buffer tool is provided to generate *multiple buffer rings* in a single operation. MapInfo provides a similar facility, which it calls "Concentric ring buffers".

### Figure 4-71 Simple buffering

A. v.buffer in GRASS

*http://grass.itc.it/screenshots/vector.php*

B. Buffer tool, line element, ArcToolbox

*Figure 4-72 Manifold: Buffer operations*

A. Selected polygon

B. Border buffer

C. Inner buffer

polygonal area provides a buffer that extends outside the polygon plus the entire polygon internal area, effectively growing the entire polygon. To limit the buffer zone to the boundary of a polygon the Border buffer zone operation must be used (Figure 4-72B). An additional operation, Inner buffer zone is provided which selects the inner part of a polygon, comprising all areas at least the buffer distance from the boundary (Figure 4-72C). Repeated buffering operations may be applied, either to the original feature or to the resulting buffered entity itself. Buffer features may also by modified, e.g. by clipping operations or intersection, to generate new or modified zones, as required. The Buffers operation in Manifold creates distinct buffer zones (Figure 4-73A), whilst an alternative function, 'Common buffers' creates merged zones (Figure 4-73B).

*Figure 4-73 Manifold: Buffering options*

A. Buffer

B. Common buffer

Manifold's principal buffering facility is invoked via the Transform toolbar, and the standard Buffers operation when applied to a

Once a buffer has been created, or as part of the creation process, a new map layer containing the buffer polygons will be generated. This map layer will have an associated attribute table, and if not already generated, attributes such as polygon areas can be computed. The new layer may, in turn be combined with other layers (e.g. via an Intersect overlay) to analyze attribute data within the buffer zone.

### 4.4.4.2 Raster buffering

Buffering may also be applied in raster GIS, whereby cells are classified according to their distance from one or more target cells (grid distance, Euclidean distance or a more complex, cost-related distance). For example, in Idrisi by default target cells are coded as 1, buffer cells as 2 and other cells as 0, and the buffer width to apply is specified in reference system units (based on true Euclidean distances or grid-based cost distances). The process of generating a buffer in this environment is very similar to performing a standard image processing task, that of generating a distance transform of the (binary) input image, and then selecting from the resulting output image all those cells that have entries (distance values) less than or equal to the buffer width specified. These selected cells are then re-classified (RECLASS in Idrisi) as required (e.g. to a value of 2; see also, Section 4.4.2.2).

### 4.4.4.3 Hybrid buffering

Buffer operations within vector GIS generate regions, and distances within those regions meet the overall buffering criterion set. The use of multiple buffering does enable a degree of gradation within such buffer regions, but for more detail some form of hybrid buffering may be more appropriate. In this approach either hybrid buffering is directly supported by the GIS tool (e.g. as with MapInfo's Vertical Mapper, Grid buffer facility) or the relevant vector objects will require conversion to grid format and then grid buffering applied. The latter may be achieved using cost distance (ACS) methods or distance transforms (DTs), as described in Section 4.4.2.

### 4.4.4.4 Network buffering

A simple buffer operation applied to a vector map of roads will create a set of merged or unmerged regions either side of the selected roads. An alternative form of buffering for such networks is a time or distance buffer from a point source or sources with respect to the network. In the case of roads, this form of buffer generates travel-distance or drive-time zones. The Manifold GIS Business Tools option provides for such buffering. In their model drive times are computed to all network points in one or more time zones, plus a distance buffer (speed related) for off-road travel (e.g. walking). This is a very processor intensive operation. TransCAD and ArcGIS Network Analyst provide similar functionality via their "drive time" analysis facilities (see, for example, Figure 7-18). AccessionGIS is a more advanced toolset, built using ArcGIS components, which incorporates multi-modal travel and timetables.

## 4.4.5 Distance decay models

Almost by definition, spatial modeling makes extensive use of distance measures. In many instances a suitable metric is selected and used directly, but for many other situations some generalized function of distance is used. Typically these models involve the assumption that the strength of relationships between locations, or the effect one location has upon another, diminishes as separation increases. There are a wide range of GIS analysis techniques that make use of this concept — we describe a number of these briefly below, and address them separately in a number of the later chapters of this Guide. There are, of course, many situations in which such models are not appropriate, such as in the context of telecommunications links and in situations where time-distance computations are more relevant (e.g. single- or multi-modal network travel modeling, discussed further in Section 7.1 *et seq.*).

The most widely used distance decay models are those in which distance is introduced as an inverse function to some power, typically 1 or 2. Thus the value of some variable of interest, $z$, at location $j$, $z_j$, might be modeled as some function, $f()$, of attribute values, $z_i$, associated with other locations, $i$, weighted by the inverse of the distance separating locations $i$ and $j$, $d_{ij}$ raised to a power, $\beta$:

$$z_j = \frac{f(\{z_i\})}{d_{ij}^{\beta}}, \beta \geq 0$$

The exponent, $\beta$, has the effect of reducing the influence of other locations as the distance to these increases. With $\beta=0$ distance has no effect, whilst with $\beta=1$ the impact is linear. Values of $\beta \gg 1$ rapidly diminish the contribution to the expression from locations that are more remote.

One of the commonest applications of this kind of model is in surface interpolation. Most GIS and surface analysis packages provide support for such operations (see further, Section 6.6.1). However, inverse distance weighting (IDW), as it is known, is used in many other situations. An example is the study by Draper *et al.* (2005) referred to in Section 3.1. The distance of cancer cases and controls from overhead power lines was calculated and the inverse and inverse squared distances were then used as weights in modeling the observations. The idea behind this approach was to take into account the fact that electromagnetic radiation intensity diminishes with distance from the source.

Inverse distance modeling is one of the main techniques used in the fields of transportation, travel demand modeling and trade area analysis. The propensity to travel between pairs of locations is often assumed to be related to the separation between the locations and some measure of the size of the source and destination zones. The basic model is derived from analogies with the force of gravity:

$$I_{ij} = \alpha \frac{M_i M_j}{d_{ij}^{\beta}}$$

Here the interaction (e.g. number of trips) between zones $i$ and $j$ is taken to be some measure of the mass, $M$, at each location,

divided by the distance between the zones. As before, $\alpha$ and $\beta$ are parameters to be estimated. The general form of such 'spatial interaction' models is:

$$T_{ij} = A_i B_j O_i D_j f(d_{ij})$$

where $T_{ij}$ is the number of trips between zones $i$ and $j$, $O_i$ is a measure of the size of the origin location $i$ (e.g. the total number of trips to commuters in zone $i$), $D_j$ is a measure of the size of the destination zone (e.g. the total number of work places in zone $j$), and $f(d_{ij})$ is some appropriate function of the distance or degree of separation of zones $i$ and $j$. $A_i$ and $B_j$ are balancing factors of the form:

$$A_i = 1/\sum_j B_j D_j f(d_{ij}), \; B_j = 1/\sum_i A_i D_j f(d_{ij})$$

These latter expressions are designed to ensure that the modeled row and column totals add up to the total number of trips from and to each zone (i.e. a so-called doubly-constrained model, which assumes that the totals are correct and not subject to sampling error). Note that by taking logarithms the model is transformed into a (weighted) linear sum, and is often analyzed in this form. In this case the weights are powers applied to the origin, destination and distance variables that must be estimated from sample data.

For a fuller discussion and background to such modeling see CATMOG 2 and CATMOG 4, Roy (2004) which provides a very complete and up-to-date book on the subject, Miller and Shaw (2001, Ch.8), Wilson (1967), and Fischer (2006, chapter 3, reprinted from a paper of 2000). Fischer's paper describes both the basic spatial interaction model outlined above and alternative methods for model calibration, including least squares, maximum likelihood, and in Parts II and IV of the same volume, neural network methods. Common variants of this type of model are the origin-constrained and destination-constrained versions, in which case either the $A_i$ or the $B_j$ are determined by balancing, but not both. In the case of trade area modeling, gravity models or Huff models (which are origin constrained) are often used.

The former typically use inverse distance power models coupled with measures of location attraction, such as retail square footage. Vertical Mapper, for the MapInfo product, is an example of GIS software that provides such facilities. Typical models for $f(d_{ij})$ include: simple inverse distance models (as above); negative exponential models; and combined or Gamma models. All three types (plus others) are supported by TransCAD as impedance functions within its trip distribution modeling facility. Crimestat incorporates similar functions within its trip distribution modeling component. The statistical models within GeoBUGS provide for a generalized powered exponential family of distance decay models of the form:

$$f(d) = e^{-(\varphi d)^{k}}, \ k \in [0,2], \ \varphi > 0$$

where $\varphi$ is the principal decay parameter relating the decay pattern to the effective range of correlations that are meaningful. Note that the parameter $k$ acts as a smoothing factor and with $k=2$ this is essentially a Gaussian distance decay function. Geographically Weighted Regression (GWR) utilizes similar decay functions (the authors describe these as kernel functions – see further, Section 5.6.3), this time of the form:

$$f(d) = e^{-d^2/2h^2}, \text{ or } f(d) = e^{-d/h}, \text{ or}$$

$$f(d) = \left(1 - \frac{d^2}{h^2}\right)^2, d < r, \ f(d) = 0 \text{ otherwise}$$

In these functions the parameter, $h$, is also known as the *bandwidth*. A small bandwidth results in very rapid distance decay, whereas a larger value will result in a smoother weighting scheme. The Gaussian model is an unbounded function, and as an alternative GeoBUGS provides the following bounded or disk model of distance decay:

$$f(d) = \frac{2}{\pi}\left[\cos^{-1}\left(\frac{d}{\alpha}\right) - \left\{\left(\frac{d}{\alpha}\right)\left(1 - \left(\frac{d}{\alpha}\right)^2\right)\right\}^{1/2}\right], d < \alpha$$

With $f(d)=0$ otherwise. This model decays slightly more rapidly than a straight line over the interval $[0,\alpha)$, especially over the initial part of the interval. The parameter, $\alpha$, here has a similar role to that of the bandwidth parameter in the GWR expressions above.

All such models may suffer from problems associated with clustering – for example where a number of alternative (competing) destinations are equidistant from an origin zone, but may be located either in approximately the same direction or in very different directions. Such clustering has implications for modeling, since competition and even interaction *between* destination zones is inadequately represented. Most GIS and related software packages do not provide direct support for analysis of such factors, and it is up to the user to specify and implement an appropriate modeling framework to address these issues.

These are all models based on a mathematical function of distance. In addition to such models other models or measurements of impedance are extensively used, typically in the form of origin-destination (O-D) matrices. The latter may be derived from measurements or from alternative distance-related models such as intervening opportunities, see Stouffler (1940), or lagged adjacencies (e.g. see the spatial weights modeling options in GeoDa, and Section 5.5.2.3). Distance, $d$, in this instance is a free-space or network-related measure of impedance to interaction (e.g. network distance, time, cost or adjacency). The most widely implemented distance impedance expressions are of the form:

$$\alpha/d^{\beta}, \ \alpha e^{-\beta d} \text{ and } \alpha e^{-\gamma d}/d^{\beta}$$

where $\alpha$, $\beta$ and $\gamma$ are parameters to be selected or estimated. Figure 4-74 and Figure 4-75 illustrate the first two of these models, in each case standardized with an $\alpha$ value to provide a value of 10 at $d=0.1$ units and a range of values for $\beta$. The Gamma model provides curves that are intermediate between the two sets shown, depending on the specific values of $\gamma$ and $\beta$ chosen or fitted from sample data.

*Figure 4-74 Inverse distance decay models, $a/d^\beta$*

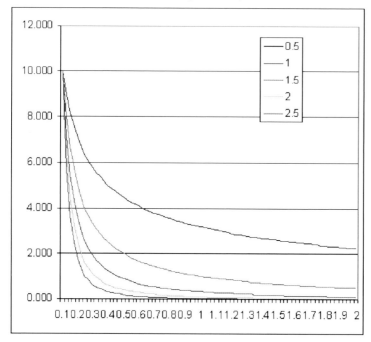

*Figure 4-75 Exponential distance decay models, $\alpha e^{-\beta d}$*

Pure inverse distance models (and the Gamma model) have a (serious) problem when distances are small, since the expression will tend to infinity as $d$ tends to 0. A partial solution to this problem is to include a small distance adjustment to such formulas, such that $d=d+\varepsilon$ where $\varepsilon>0$, or to exclude distances that are below a given threshold from the inverse distance calculations (possibly defining a fixed value for the function in such cases). These approaches stabilize computations but are essentially arbitrary. The exponential model has the advantage that it tends to 1 as $d$ tends to 0, so may be preferable if observations are known to be very closely placed or even coincident.

Models of this kind may be constrained in various ways: by limiting the maximum range to be included in computations; by limiting the maximum number of locations to be considered; by restricting the range of values the parameters may take; and by explicitly taking account of barriers (e.g. inaccessible regions). More sophisticated analysis would take into account aspects of the dynamics and uncertainty associated with the interactions or flows being modeled. Somewhat different models of distance decay are incorporated into radial basis interpolation and geostatistical analysis (see further, Sections 6.6.4 and 6.7).

The analysis of data variation by distance or distance bands (e.g. variograms and correlogram analysis) is designed to identify overall patterns of variation in a measured variable with linear (Euclidean) distance. In such instances a maximum distance or range is identified if possible, and the pattern of variation in the measured variable is modeled to reflect the diminishing associations observed as distance increases. Here the models effectively treat distance as an independent variable and the observations (generally averaged by distance band) as a form of dependent variable.

# 4.5 Directional Operations

### 4.5.1 Directional analysis — overview

Directional analysis is perhaps less well known and well used than other forms of spatial analysis. It primarily deals with the analysis of lines, points sets and surface orientation, sometimes from different time periods, examining patterns in order to identify and utilize information on specific directional trends. Researchers In the fields of geology, sedimentology and geomorphology utilize directional analysis to examine fault lines and fracture systems, glacial striations, particulate distributions and lithography patterns; in ecology it is used to study patterns of wildlife movement and plant dispersal; in hydrology and other forms of flow analysis directional considerations are paramount; in wildfire management directional analysis is used to predict local (30metre-100metre) wind flows as a function of local topography; and directional analysis can be used when studying patterns of disease incidence or the distribution of particular crime events.

If a particular dataset exhibits no discernable variation in direction across a study region it is described as *isotropic*. Whilst such situations may be regarded as unusual in the real world, it is frequently the starting assumption for many forms of analysis. Variations that have a particular directional bias are known as *anisotropic*. In some areas of GIS analysis, for example geostatistics, examination of anisotropy is a fundamental part of the modeling and prediction process (see further, Section 6.7). For an introduction that includes a discussion of hypothesis testing for directional data, and a review of applications of these techniques to spatial datasets, see Gaile and Burt (1980) CATMOG 25. It should be noted that when comparing and analyzing directional datasets computed with projected (plane) coordinate systems, there may be introduced directional bias. Comparisons should be made between datasets that have been generated using the same projections and approximate scale, or by utilizing spherical coordinates where necessary. For small areas (under 100kmx100km) the problems for most applications should be minor.

### 4.5.2 Directional analysis of linear datasets

Directional analysis applied to linear forms (line segments, polylines, or smooth curves) is sometimes known as *alignment analysis* or *lineament analysis*. Line elements within a GIS are normally directed, in the sense that they have a start and end point determined during data capture. This directed aspect of the line may or may not be relevant, and if relevant may be incorrect for the analysis you are considering. Hence all such datasets need to be examined carefully before proceeding with analysis.

In addition to line-based data from which orientation is derived, the same types of analysis may be applied to point datasets with an associated directional attribute or attributes. For example, these might be: recordings of the initial migration direction of birds of various types from a small area of woodland; the dispersal pattern of seeds from a tree; the wind direction recorded at a series of meteorological stations at hourly intervals; or the direction of a particular type of crime event in a city with respect to a given reference point. As such this is simply a particular application of such statistics to a defined dataset. However, if such data are stored within a GIS as attributes in a table associated with a point set, then conventional descriptive statistics such as mean and variance should not be used. Similar concerns apply to any form of modulo or cyclic data, for example fields containing temporal data recording the time of day in minutes from midnight or numeric day of week associated with events recorded over a number of weeks.

Data with directional information is essentially of two types: directed (or vector) data, where the direction is unique and specified as an angle in the range $[0°,360°]$ or $[0,2\pi]$ using radian measure; and oriented or bi-directional data, often referred to as *axial* data, where only the orientation is defined. Axial data are normally doubled, and converted to a 360°

range using modulo arithmetic, processed and the results are then re-converted to a [0°,180°] or [0,π] range.

Determination and processing of line direction within a GIS is problematic for a number of reasons:

- the way in which a line is represented, the level of detail it portrays, and the extent to which real world features are generalized

- the data capture process and composite form of line representation (polylines) — where is the true start and end of the line for directional analysis purposes?

- the nature of circular (or cyclic) measure: the orientation of an undirected line at 90 degrees to the vertical is indistinguishable from one at 270°; furthermore the difference between 280° and 90° is not taken to be 280°-90°=190°, but 360°-280°+90°=170°. Similarly the mean direction of 3 lines at 280° (or -80°), 90° and 90° is not sensibly calculated as (280°+90°+90°)/3=186.7° or as (-80°+90°+90°)/3=16.7°, but a consistent and meaningful definition of such an average is needed. With two angles, 350° and 10° from due north this is even more obvious, as a mean direction of 180° (i.e. due South) does not make sense

We treat each of these issues in turn. If the source data of forms are suspected of being fractal in nature, across a very wide range of scales, then in theory they may exhibit no reliable tangents (directions) at any point. In practice the process of data capture accepts that our model within a GIS has involved simplification of the real world, and that the data may be represented as a collection of non-fractal discrete elements (polylines or pixels). Assuming this representation is acceptable and meaningful for the problem being investigated, analysis of the captured data can proceed. Particular attention should be given to the location of the initial and final points (end nodes) in such cases, as these may offer more acceptable point pairs for the analysis of broader directional patterns than any of the intervening line segments.

More problematic is the issue of generalization. Subsequent to data capture, feature representation within the GIS may be subject to some form of generalization as discussed earlier (Section 4.2.3). These processes significantly alter the direction of linear forms, especially the component parts (segments) of polylines. For these reasons, when performing directional analysis on polylines, a range of alternative ways of describing the line direction may be needed. Examples include: end node to end node; linear best fit to all nodes; disaggregated analysis (treating all line segments as separate elements); and weighted analysis (treating a polyline as a weighted average of the directions of its component segments, e.g. weighted by segment length). Smooth curves (e.g. contours) may be treated in a similar manner, approximating these by polylines and applying the same concepts as for standard polylines. A GIS package that supports such selection facilities is TNTMips — most other packages have more limited facilities.

These approaches address the first and second bullet points above. One way to address the third bullet point is to treat the lines or line segments as vectors (i.e. having an origin, a magnitude and a direction with respect to that origin) and then to use trigonometric functions of the directions rather than the directions themselves to perform the computations. This will give us the direction (and optionally magnitude) of the *resultant vector,* **r** (the mean effect of each vector "pulling" in its own direction). For example:

- let the set of $N=i+1$ points determining a polyline define a set of $i$ directions $\{\theta_i\}$ from a given origin with respect to a predefined direction (e.g. grid north)

- compute the two vector components (northing and easting): $V_n=\Sigma\cos\theta_i$ and $V_e=\Sigma\sin\theta_i$

The resultant vector, **r**, has mean or preferred direction $\tan^{-1}(V_e/V_n)$. For example, using our earlier example with three vectors at -80°, 90° and 90° from horizontal the resultant mean direction is +80.3°; with the two vectors 350° and 10° the resultant is 0° (due north). The directional mean by itself is of limited value unless the underlying data demonstrate a consistent directional pattern that one wishes to summarize. If a set of vectors show an arbitrary or random pattern the mean direction could be almost any value, which is of little use.

The length or *magnitude* of the resultant vector if all *N* component vectors have unit magnitude or are simply provided as angular measurements is simply:

$$|\mathbf{r}| = \sqrt{V_n^2 + V_e^2}$$

If $\{\theta_i\}=0$ for all *i*, all the $V_n$ components will be 0 and all the $V_e$ components will be 1, hence $|\mathbf{r}|=N$ where $|\mathbf{r}|$ denotes the vector magnitude of **r**. Dividing through by *N* standardizes $|\mathbf{r}|$ such that the length of the mean vector, $r^*=|\mathbf{r}^*|$, lies in the range [0,1]. Larger values *suggest* greater clustering of the sample vectors around the mean.

The *circular variance* is simply var=1-$|\mathbf{r}|$/$N$, or var=1-$r^*$, and again lies in the range [0,1]. The *circular standard deviation* is defined as:

$$sd = \sqrt{-2\ln(r^*)}$$

If the point set for analysis includes the vector length, $v_i$, then the expression for the directional mean can be generalized (weighted by length) as $V_n=\Sigma v_i\cos\theta_i$ and $V_e=\Sigma v_i\sin\theta_i$. The resultant vector magnitude in this case will no longer lie in the range [0,1] if normalized by the number of vectors.

Assuming that we have a suitably encoded dataset consisting of distinct or linked polylines (e.g. a stream network), we can explore directional trends in the entire dataset or subsections of the data. This process is illustrated in Figure 4-76 for a sample stream network in the Crowe Butte region of Washington State, using tools from the TNTMips package.

*Figure 4-76 Directional analysis of streams*

A. Hydrology, Crow Butte region

B. Direction roses: end point and segment versions

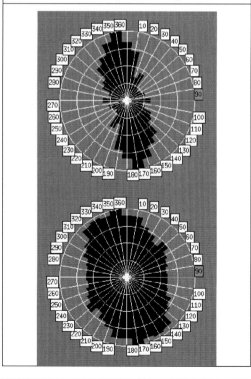

The two direction rose diagrams show the number of stream segments having orientations in 10 degree groupings (i.e. rather like a circular frequency diagram or histogram). The pattern is completely symmetric since in this case lines are regarded as undirected.

Any given section of the rose diagram can be selected, and the number of components (frequency of the sample) will be displayed. Higher frequencies are shown as longer segments, although some software provides the option of using areas to indicate frequency variations rather than lengths on rose diagrams. Furthermore the line elements that contribute to specific directional bands can be identified on the associated map, shown here in red (a form of linking, familiar to most users of GIS packages). The directional data for all lines in this case were treated as end node to end node. The lower rose diagram shows the results when all component parts of polylines are included in the analysis, showing a much more even spread of orientations. As with almost all forms of GIS analysis, it is important to observe and take account of the effects of the region selection process, and as can be seen here, many of the streams are arbitrarily dissected by the boundary, which may impact the interpretation of results.

Similar functionality is provided within ArcGIS, in its Linear Directional Mean facility. Whilst this does provide a choice of metric (Euclidean or Manhattan) and selection of directed or non-directed computation, selection of alternative modes of interpreting polylines (as described above) is not provided so polylines would need to be segmented (or combined) as required prior to analysis.

For a more complete set of tools, including distributional analysis, specialized software such as Oriana from Kovach Computer Services is required. This facilitates analysis of point-like datasets or datasets that have been extracted from a GIS in this form. Input is in tabular form (text, csv, Excel etc.), and graphing and distributional analysis of single or multiple datasets is supported. Oriana may be unable to process large datasets (such as grid

outputs in column format), in which case the use of generic programs such as MATLab and the Surfer-related program Grapher may be more effective. Those wishing to use license-free software, there are a number of options, including the Python language charting and graphing suite, Matplotlib. The formulas used by Oriana follow those provided in Fisher (1993) and Mardia and Jupp (1999). Measures are provided which compare the observed distribution to a uniform distribution and/or the distribution due to von Mises that is the circular equivalent of the Normal distribution. Graphically the von Mises distribution with a mean at π is essentially identical to the Normal distribution with the $x$-axis being in the range $[0,2\pi)$. The general form of the von Mises distribution is:

$$p(x) = \frac{e^{\kappa \cos(x-\alpha)}}{2\pi I_0(\kappa)}$$

where $\alpha$ is the mean direction of the distribution in the range $[0,2\pi)$, and $\kappa > 0$ is a shape parameter known as the concentration (effectively equivalent to the standard deviation). $I_0(\kappa)$ is the modified Bessel function of the first kind, of order 0 (see Section 1.4.2.8). The circular variance of this distribution is:

$$\sigma^2 = 1 - \frac{I_1(\kappa)}{I_0(\kappa)}$$

This modified Bessel function is relatively straightforward to compute for integer orders, although it requires summation of an infinite series:

$$I_0(\kappa) = \sum_{i=0}^{\infty} \frac{(-1)^i (\kappa/2)^{2i}}{(i!)^2} \text{ , and}$$

$$I_1(\kappa) = \frac{\kappa}{2} \sum_{i=0}^{\infty} \frac{(-1)^i (\kappa/2)^{2i+1}}{i!(i+1)!}$$

Several types of spatial dataset consist of multiple components that incorporate directional information. For example: wind direction and speed over time for a specific location or set of locations; single grid files of derived gradient data (slope, or gradient magnitude and aspect, or direction of maximum gradient — see further, Section 6.2); dual grid files containing either direction and magnitude data (polar information) in separate grids, or Cartesian data (x and y components) in each grid, for example simple optimal path tracking data (see further, Section 4.4.2.2). Plotting such data may utilize a variety of display methods.

For temporal data a variant of the rose diagram can be utilized that provides stacked histogram functionality in the radial direction in addition to the circular histogram facility provided by a standard rose diagram. The Grapher program, available from the same providers as Surfer, is an example of a package that supports such displays, as do Oriana and Matplotlib, but many statistical graphing packages provide similar functionality. This kind of diagram is illustrated in Figure 4-77, where the radial extent shows the frequency of measured wind speeds (hourly intervals) separated into speed categories in knots (with zero speed values removed). The black arrow shows the mean vector (direction and speed) for the entire dataset of almost 4500 records.

*Figure 4-77 Two-variable wind rose*

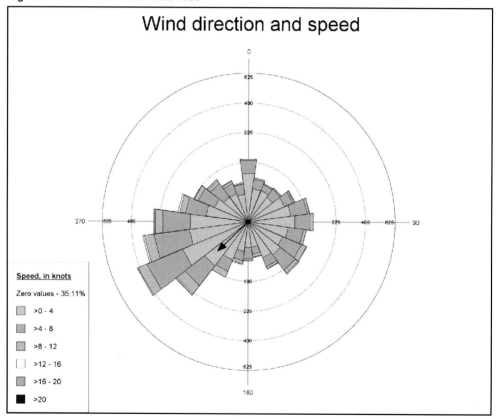

In some instances smoothed contour plots of wind direction are created rather than stacked histograms. This enables multiple plots to be superimposed, as is the case for selected sites in the London Air Quality network. In this case the plots show pollution levels, by type, as the magnitude and average wind direction over a selected time period as the directional component.

### 4.5.3 Directional analysis of point datasets

A somewhat different form of directional analysis is used within many packages to summarize the distribution of point sets around a mean center. The average variation in the distance of points around the mean can be viewed as a circle or set of circles at a set of standard distances (like standard deviations in univariate statistics). In addition, separate variations in x- and y-coordinate values may be used to generate a standard distance ellipse, with major and minor axes reflecting the directional variation of the point pattern.

Figure 4-78 illustrates this for the location of churches on Romney Marsh in SE England. The two ellipses are set at one and two standard deviations respectively. Determination of the standard deviations in x and y are not made using the original data, but using transformed coordinates selected by minimizing the squared deviations from the point set to transformed (rotated) x and y axes. This is similar to the process of computing a linear regression on the (x,y) coordinate pairs and using the slope of the best fit line in angular measure to calculate the adjusted standard deviations.

The formula for the angle of (clockwise) rotation of the y-axis is somewhat lengthy:

$$\theta = \tan^{-1}\left(\frac{\sum(x_i - \bar{x})^2 - \sum(y_i - \bar{y})^2 + \sqrt{C}}{2\sum(x_i - \bar{x})(y_i - \bar{y})}\right)$$

where

$$C = \left(\sum(x_i - \bar{x})^2 - \sum(y_i - \bar{y})^2\right)^2 + 4\sum\left((x_i - \bar{x})(y_i - \bar{y})\right)^2$$

Using this value the two standard deviations can then be computed in much the same way as for conventional standard deviations, but with the degrees of freedom in this case being n-2, where n is the number of points in the sample (for n large the divisor will be close to n, as per the common formulation of standard distance).

The formulas cited are those used within Crimestat, which have been adjusted to ensure the ellipse axes are the correct length and the formula is consistent if the standard deviations in x- and y- are equal:

$$SD_x = \sqrt{\frac{2\sum\left((x_i - \bar{x})\cos\theta - (y_i - \bar{y})\sin\theta\right)^2}{n-2}}$$

$$SD_y = \sqrt{\frac{2\sum\left((x_i - \bar{x})\sin\theta - (y_i - \bar{y})\cos\theta\right)^2}{n-2}}$$

Software packages may provide information on the rotational angle and other attributes of the standard deviational ellipse. For example, Crimestat includes the angle of rotation and the individual standard deviation values, together with the area of the standard deviational ellipse (which is simply $A=SD_xSD_y\pi$; the lengths of the two ellipse axes are $2SD_x$ and $2SD_y$). For the data illustrated in Figure 4-78 the clockwise rotation of the y-axis is 53.2 degrees and the ratio of major to minor axis length, or *coefficient of eccentricity*, is 1.76.

*Figure 4-78 Standard distance circle and ellipses*

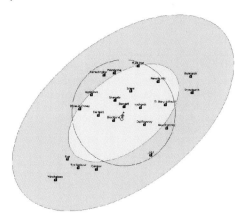

Crimestat includes directional data in another technique, Correlated Walk Analysis (CWA). CWA is an analytical procedure based on examining a sequence of events (e.g. crimes, animal movements) in terms of location, bearing (direction from a given point) and time lapse. Its objective is to predict where subsequent events, e.g. burglaries, may occur. Random walks, of various types (see further below), may be used as part of such analysis. For more details of these methods and their applications see the Crimestat manual, Chapters 4 and 9.

An essential part of such analyses is the examination of patterns in the distribution of point data as the distance and direction of examination is varied. A simple Correlated Random Walk (CRW) simulation facility is provided with Hawth's Tools for ArcGIS that enables model paths to be generated and saved as features (Figure 4-79). This facility highlights the impact of model parameters on the resulting path form (in this example using CRW as the basic model, but other models such as pure random/Brownian motion and so-called persistent random walks are also supported).

Graphs that plot the average difference in values for pairs of points in a region, over given blocks of distance, optionally grouped into different blocks of directions, are known as correlograms or variograms. If the region is isotropic there will be no significant differences between the variograms drawn for one direction (e.g. 0-30 degrees) or from another (e.g. 60-90 degrees), whereas with significant anisotropy the shapes of these variograms will differ. Hence if modeling is to utilize such information, different models or model parameters may be required to accommodate these directional differences (these issues are covered in greater detail in Section 6.7.1.11).

*Figure 4-79 Correlated Random Walk simulation*

A. 500 step CRW, variable (random uniform) step length, directional model N(0,1) degrees

B. 500 step CRW, variable (random uniform) step length, directional model N(30,15) degrees

### 4.5.4 Directional analysis of surfaces

There are many applications of directional analysis relating to surfaces. These include: analyzing and mapping surface *aspect* (e.g. the d.rast.arrow function in GRASS, the aspect generation tools of Landserf, SAGA, TAS, ArcGIS and TNTMips), which is defined as the direction of the surface gradient (as opposed to the magnitude of the gradient — see Figure 4-80); analyzing and modeling flow directions and *friction* as part of hydrological and similar studies (e.g. local drainage directions such as the lddcreate function in PCRaster, the Flow function in Idrisi, and the FlowDirection function in the ArcGIS Spatial Analyst hydrology toolset); and analyses relating to the lighting of surfaces, as part of solar energy analysis, lighting for visualization, and for visibility analysis (e.g. in the ArcGIS 3D Analyst and Spatial Analyst toolsets). Each of these topics is discussed in some detail in Chapter 6.

In general the representation of direction in such instances is strongly affected by the underlying model or representation of the surface — for example, with grid (raster) surfaces there is often directional bias as a result of the limited range of directions available in immediate neighborhoods (e.g. only 8 directions in a 3x3 neighborhood).

For vector-like grid data (single or dual-grid source data) a vector plot may be informative. An example of such a plot is shown in Figure 4-80 where gradient vectors have been plotted using Surfer for a sample grid file of the Mt St Helens volcano. In this case color has been used to indicate vectors of greater magnitude (from white through blue to red). Similar mapping of simulated wind directions is performed by software tools such as WindWizard and WindNinja designed for use in conjunction with wildfire modeling and management (Figure 4-81). In this example wind flow has been modeled for the OS NT04 DEM (Pentland Hills area) with 100 meter output grid resolution and input direction of 230 degrees and speed 50 mph. Output here is displayed using Google Earth (.KML file) .

*Figure 4-80 Slope and aspect plot, Mt St Helens data, USA*

Figure 4-81 Wind flow grid simulation using WindNinja

# 4.6 Grid Operations and Map Algebra

In this Section we provide an introduction to grid analysis methods, including an overview of the kind of facilities available in raster analysis packages and toolsets. Many of the facilities relate to operations on surfaces (e.g. computation of gradient and aspect) and field-like datasets (e.g. interpolation and prediction techniques). These topics are covered in detail in Chapter 6.

## 4.6.1 Operations on single and multiple grids

Grid or raster data files typically have a single attribute associated with each cell position. Datasets of this type can be thought of as triples $(x,y,z)$ where $x$ and $y$ are the cell coordinates and $z$ the attribute values. $z$-values might be: a color code in the case of image data; a binary value, for example in the case of converted vector data (without additional attributes); a cell classification number, such as the type of vegetation cover associated with that location; or a measured or calculated data value, such as an interpolated figure for soil heavy metal content in parts per million (ppm), the height of a surface in meters, or the estimated average level of noise from a given source type (e.g. roads). In all instances the set of values observed in a single grid of size $M$-rows and $N$-columns is limited, either by the coding or classification procedure adopted, or by the fact that ultimately only $MxN$ values can possibly be recorded.

This set of values may be summarized and analyzed using basic univariate statistics (non-spatial analysis) and many GIS packages provide a wide number of simple single-grid measures. These include many of the basic statistics described in Table 1-3, including the arithmetic mean, max, min, count, sum, variety, minority, majority, range, mid-range, variance and standard deviation. Each of these operations applies to the set of individual cells of a single grid and may be described as *local* statistics.

Simple statistical operations may be applied to groups of cells, for example the immediate 8 cell neighborhood (or window) of each cell or to individual cells across multiple grids (see also, Section 5.3). Where regular neighborhoods of cells are involved such operations are termed *focal*, or if the neighborhoods are defined using pre-defined (irregular) zones, then the operations are described as *zonal*.

There are a large number of basic grid operations supported for image and general raster files. These include local, focal and zonal operations depending on the scope of the operation. Such operations may be applied to a single grid, or to a number of input grids, depending on the operation in question. The set of possible operations of this type are often referred to as *map algebra*. Originally this term was introduced by Tomlin (1983) as the process of map combination for co-registered layers with rasters of identical size and resolution. Combinations involved arithmetic and Boolean operations. A typical example would be the addition of separate grids for an area, where each grid cell represented the level of noise, $L$, due a particular source such as A: road, B: aircraft, measured or computed in the same manner. The total noise level for each cell would then be computed as the sum of the individual grid datasets, i.e. A+B+C+.., as described in Section 4.3.2 and Figure 4-36A. This is how grids such as that illustrated in Figure 3-4 (Noise map, Augsburg) have been created. However the term map algebra is now used more widely by many suppliers. For example, ArcGIS describes the set of all operations performed using its Spatial Analyst option as "map algebra". More specifically it divides such functions into five main categories:

- Local functions, which include mathematical and statistical functions, reclassification, and selection operations

- Focal functions, which provide tools for neighborhood analysis

- Zonal functions, which provide tools for zonal analysis and the calculation of zonal statistics

- Global functions, which provide tools for full raster layer or raster dataset analysis, for example the generation of Cost Distance rasters

- Application functions, specific to tasks such as hydrology and geometric transformation

Similar facilities are provided in many of the mainstream raster-based GIS packages, such as PCRaster, TNTMips and Idrisi, and in the raster-processing toolsets of more generic packages such as GRASS and the Vertical Mapper facility for MapInfo. Many of these are described in greater detail in Chapter 6.

The map algebra concept is capable of being extended in several ways. One example is extension to explicitly handle the time domain coupled with 1, 2 or 3-dimensional spatial datasets. Mennis *et al.* (2005A, 2005B) have developed such a model and implemented a set of Java classes for handling what they describe as *multidimensional map algebra* (mma). Performance issues are one of the principal barriers to widespread use of such concepts, but as improved data structures and processing architectures emerge for spatio-temporal datasets, concepts of this kind are likely to be more widely applied. A second example of extension to map algebra ideas is *map calculus*, put forward by Haklay (2004, 2006). Haklay proposes retaining the functional form of surfaces to be combined, wherever possible, and performing operations on these forms rather than the resultant grids. For example, instead of generating a high resolution grid from a point dataset using some interpolation function, F(), one could retain the functional form F() and only generate the resulting grid as an output when required. This has the potential to provide a more manageable approach to spatio-temporal modeling than the *mma* procedure in some instances.

### 4.6.2 Linear spatial filtering

The term spatial filtering is principally associated with digital image processing, although such methods may be applied to almost any type of grid or image. The term is also used, in a related manner, in the area of spatial statistics (see further, Section 5.6.5).

Most GIS packages provide simple grid filtering functions, whilst those that have a bias towards image processing and grid file handling (e.g. TNTMips, Surfer, Idrisi) tend to provide a broader range of functions. The most commonly provided functions are so-called low-pass and high-pass spatial filters. These are focal functions whose operation is determined by a kernel or neighborhood of *NxN* cells around each pixel or grid position. Grid cells "covered" by the kernel are multiplied by the matching kernel entry and then the weighted average is calculated and assigned as the value for the central cell, *G*. A 3x3 symmetric kernel might look something like:

$$\begin{bmatrix} a & a & a \\ a & b & a \\ a & a & a \end{bmatrix} \text{ or perhaps } \begin{bmatrix} c & a & c \\ a & b & a \\ c & a & c \end{bmatrix}$$

In the first of these examples *a* and *b* are positive numbers, typically integers. If *a*=*b*=1 then the kernel provides a simple averaging or smoothing operation, whereas if *a*=1 and *b*=4 more weight would be applied to the grid cell being filtered. In both cases the weighted average is divided by the sum of the kernel elements. No divisor is applied in cases where the kernel sums to 0 or 1. Filters of this type are sometimes described as *low-pass spatial filters*. For example, consider the filter:

$$\begin{bmatrix} 1 & 1 & 1 \\ 1 & 4 & 1 \\ 1 & 1 & 1 \end{bmatrix} \text{ and grid section } \begin{bmatrix} 98 & 176 & 200 \\ 90 & 187 & 188 \\ 124 & 170 & 175 \end{bmatrix}.$$

The value at the central grid position $G(2,2)=187$ is replaced by the weighted average of itself (assigned a weight of 4) and the surrounding 8 cells (each assigned a weight of 1). The adjusted value is 164 after rounding. In the second example if *a*, *b* and *c* are positive with *b*>*a*>*c* the kernel is described as Gaussian, being symmetric but center-weighted, for example:

$$\begin{bmatrix} 1 & 2 & 1 \\ 2 & 4 & 2 \\ 1 & 2 & 1 \end{bmatrix}$$

With the same data grid as above the filtered value is $G=162$. More generally, if $\{C_i\}$ is the set of coefficients of an $m=N \times N$ kernel matrix and $\{P_i\}$ is the set of source grid values within this kernel neighborhood, then the filtered grid value, $G$, is defined as:

$$G = \sum_{i=1}^{m} C_i P_i \bigg/ \sum_{i=1}^{m} C_i + B$$

The extra term, $B$, here is often set to 0. It is a bias factor that increases or decreases the resulting filter value by a fixed amount.

*High-pass spatial filters* emphasize the difference between the central point of the kernel and the values in its immediate neighborhood. Typically the entries in such kernels have a mix of positive and negative values, but the entries still add up to 1:

$$\begin{bmatrix} -a & -a & -a \\ -a & +b & -a \\ -a & -a & -a \end{bmatrix}$$

Values are often used to provide image sharpening prior to further processing. Table 4-11 provides examples and a summary of typical linear spatial filters used in GIS and image analysis. Basic linear image filtering operations fall into a number of categories:

- Sharpening — for which the kernel matrix elements sum to 1 and the matrix is symmetric. Matrix elements are a mix of positive, negative and zero entries

- Blurring — also known as a smoothing, averaging or low-pass filtering, since this reduces or removes extreme values. In this case the kernel matrix elements sum to >1, entries are normally all positive and the matrix is symmetric

- Edge detection — for which the kernel matrix elements sum to 0 and the matrix

exhibits some symmetry. As with sharpening, matrix elements are a mix of positive, negative and zero entries

- Embossing — for which the kernel matrix elements sum to 0 as per edge detection, but the matrix is asymmetric. It is usual to compute the embossed version of an image on a grayscale version, which is obtained by finding the average value of the bands, e.g. red (r), green (g) and blue (b) components, as $x=(r+g+b)/3$ for each pixel, and assigning the resulting values in the range [0,255] to a gray scale (where 0=black and 255=white)

A number of general characteristics of this type of filtering should be noted:

- if the range of values permitted within the grid are limited (e.g. RGB values in the range [0,255]) then computed values that fall outside of this range must be truncated to the range limits. This generates some computational (as opposed to user defined) bias in the processing

- multi-band image data filters are applied to each band separately. Hence a sharpening filter applied to an RGB image, for example, would be applied to the R, G and B components

- filtering may be conducted more than once (single pass or multi-pass). Each pass re-applies the same filter or filters to the target grid or image (layer or band)

- user-defined kernels are widely supported, both in image processing packages and within GIS software. Users may be able to select a pre-defined filter and modify this to suit their requirements, or to create their own $N \times N$ kernel

- all of the examples described involve simple linear operations, essentially weighted averaging (sometimes described as *linear convolution*). Non-linear filtering is also widely available and is described in more detail in Section 4.6.3

*Table 4-11 Linear spatial filters*

| Filter type | Filter | Sample 3x3 kernels | Description |
|---|---|---|---|
| Low-pass (symmetric) | Averaging | $\begin{bmatrix} a & a & a \\ a & b & a \\ a & a & a \end{bmatrix}, \begin{bmatrix} 0 & a & 0 \\ a & b & a \\ 0 & a & 0 \end{bmatrix}$ | Smoothing, noise reduction or blurring filter (focal mean) |
| | Gaussian | $\begin{bmatrix} c & a & c \\ a & b & a \\ c & a & c \end{bmatrix}$ | Smoothing, noise reduction or blurring filter (focal weighted mean) |
| High-pass (symmetric) | Sharpening | $\begin{bmatrix} -a & -a & -a \\ -a & +b & -a \\ -a & -a & -a \end{bmatrix},$ $\begin{bmatrix} 0 & -a & 0 \\ -a & +b & -a \\ 0 & -a & 0 \end{bmatrix}$ | Mean effect removal/sharpening filter (focal sum). Provides limited edge detection. Typically entries sum to 1 but may be greater. 3x3 Laplacian kernels typical add to 1. Larger Laplacian kernels (e.g. 7x7) may be more complex and sum to >1 |
| Gradient (asymmetric) | Edge detection | $\begin{bmatrix} a & b & a \\ 0 & 0 & 0 \\ -a & -b & -a \end{bmatrix}, \begin{bmatrix} -a & 0 & a \\ -b & 0 & b \\ -a & 0 & a \end{bmatrix}$ | Applied singly or as a two-pass process. These kernels highlight vertical and horizontal edges. When used in combination they are known as Gradient or Order 1 derivative filters. Typically $a=1$ and $b=1$ or 2 and entries sum to 0. A variant known as the Roberts method has row 3 all zero and column 1 zero for the first pass and column 3 zero for the second pass (i.e. a 2x2 filter) |
| | Embossing | $\begin{bmatrix} 0 & +a & +a \\ -a & +a & +a \\ -a & -a & 0 \end{bmatrix}$ | Edge detecting filters that enhance edges in a selected compass direction to provide an embossed effect. The example here shows a sample north-east kernel |
| | Directional | $\begin{bmatrix} -1 & 1 & 1 \\ -1 & -2 & 1 \\ -1 & 1 & 1 \end{bmatrix}, \begin{bmatrix} 1 & 1 & 1 \\ 1 & -2 & 1 \\ -1 & -1 & -1 \end{bmatrix}$ $\begin{bmatrix} 1 & 2 & 1 \\ 0 & 0 & 0 \\ -1 & -2 & -1 \end{bmatrix}$ | Simple computation of gradient in one of 8 compass directions. east and north directional derivatives are illustrated in the first two examples here. Note that the third example shown corresponds to Horn's method of derivative calculation for the north/south component ($dz/dy$) as described in Section 6.1.3. Compares with Edge detection filtering. A non-linear variant of this procedure is to compute all 8 values and select the maximum absolute value of these as the output |

It should be noted that at image or grid edges it is not possible to apply the kernel symmetrically. This effect is more pronounced for larger kernels, but applies in every instance. There are many options for resolving such effects. Common procedures include: leaving the edge pixels unaltered; blanking edge pixels (which causes the grid to shrink); using an asymmetric (i.e. partial) kernel, which can generate artifacts; and mirroring, where grid values inside the kernel are used as surrogates for the missing values outside the kernel

In addition to filters that operate in the spatial domain, pure frequency domain filters may also be applied. These operate on the set of grid values within an image without reference to the spatial pattern. Frequency domain filtering (for example Fast Fourier Transforms or FFTs) is provided in some GIS packages such as TNTMips and Idrisi, but such procedures are not described in this Guide. FFTs are used, for example, to removing striping effects from remotely-sensed imagery.

## 4.6.3 Non-linear spatial filtering

With linear filtering the value at each grid position, G, is altered using a simple kernel as a weights matrix. With non-linear filtering kernels are not generally used. Instead the value at G is determined by some procedure other than weighted averaging. For example, G may be determined by a statistical measure (other than the mean) based on an NxN neighborhood of G. NxN is typically 5x5 or greater, and almost any basic statistic (as listed in Table 1-3) may be used. Typical examples might be the minimum value in the neighborhood, or the cell value that is most common (occurs in the majority) within the neighborhood. Other measures commonly supported included variance, standard deviation, coefficient of variation and inter-quartile range. In each case the computations are based on the defined neighborhood.

ArcGIS describes such operations as Neighborhood operations involving Focal or Block statistics, with neighborhoods defined more generally than in typical filtering software (e.g. as rectangles, rings or wedges).

Most other packages stick with the image processing terminology of filtering and square or rectangular neighborhoods. ArcGIS also provides a special function to handle the Majority case (MajorityFilter) with integer-valued grids that incorporates an additional spatial contiguity constraint. The rule applied is that either half or at least half of the cell values in the 3x3 neighborhood must be the same as the value at G, and these must satisfy a rook's move (4-way) or queen's move (8-way) contiguity constraint. Multiple passes of this filter can be made and will stabilize to a fixed pattern.

Several non-linear filters examine local deviations in grid values. In addition to standard statistical measures, median deviation and threshold averaging may be applied (see also, Section 6.7.2.6 on median-polishing). In median deviation filtering the value at G is replaced by G-B, where B is the local median. This emphasizes outliers. With thresholding averaging the value at G is retained if it is within a defined absolute value of the local mean (calculated excluding the value at G itself), otherwise it is replaced with this local average. The effect is to remove outliers. This is a form of "noise reduction", a procedure that is supported in many image processing packages and in some GIS software. TNTMips, for example, provides 6 noise reduction filters, all of which utilize local statistics to adjust the resulting dataset or image. These are principally based on the local median or mode value (variously computed), but also include a form of trimmed mean (the Olympic filter) in which 1 or more values at the upper and lower end of the local ranked set of values is dropped and the mean of the subset calculated as the selected output value.

Simple hillshading may be achieved using a form of non-linear filter. In this case horizontal, vertical or diagonal difference filtering is applied. The procedure subtracts all the values in row 1 say, from row 2 and assigns a value of -1, 0 or 1 for example to the outcome, depending on the sign of the result. A color-graded map of the output grid provides the hillshading effect.

### 4.6.4 Erosion and dilation

*Erosion* and *dilation*, in the context of grid operations, refer to morphological operations applied to binary and grayscale images. These are terms commonly used within image processing but only arise in a small number of GIS packages in this context. Erosion involves the removal (alteration) of pixels at the edges of regions, for example changing binary 1 values to 0, whilst dilation is the reverse process with regions growing out from their boundaries. Buffering is a form of dilation.

These two processes are often carried out using a form of kernel known as a structural element. A structural element is an *NxN* kernel with entries classified according to a binary scheme, typically as 0 or 1. If all entries are coded 1 then the structural element is a solid square block, the center of which is laid over each pixel in the source image in turn. Pixels that are coded as 1 in the structural element and extend beyond the boundary of a shape in the source image result in that element being extended or dilated. The shape of the structural element may vary, for example as a vertical bar, horizontal bar, cross shape or a user-defined pattern.

To illustrate this process we have taken a small section of a USGS DEM file and then applied dilation and erosion processes to this source. The results are shown in Figure 4-82. If dilation is followed by erosion the process is described as a *Closing* operation, whilst Erosion followed by dilation is known as *Opening*. These processes are not symmetric, and thus are generally not reversible. Opening eliminates small and thinner features, resulting in smoother edged regions, whilst Closing also smoothes shapes but makes thin narrow features larger and eliminates small holes and narrow gaps. These changes are the result of deliberate morphological modification of the source data files. However, similar effects may be observed as a result of transformation operations performed manually or automatically for other purposes — for example resampling (changing resolution), rotation, multiple overlay, or map algebra operations.

*Figure 4-82 Dilation and erosion operations*

A. Source DEM section

B. Dilation: 9x9 structural element, 9x3 vertical bar

C. Erosion: 9x9 structural element, 9x3 vertical bar

# 5 Data Exploration and Spatial Statistics

## 5.1 Statistical Methods and Spatial Data

This chapter of the Guide focuses on a range of exploratory data analysis techniques and statistical methods that have been implemented in widely available GIS and GIS-related software packages. Initially we describe a range of simple statistical facilities that are provided within GIS packages, notably those supporting descriptive statistical measures and special facilities relating to spatial sampling.

Section 5.2 then addresses the question of exploratory data analysis in an explicitly spatial context and describes a range of tools currently available that support such analysis as a precursor to further investigation and modeling. Aspects of these methods have been touched upon in elsewhere in this Guide, notably in Section 4.3.

Sections 5.3, 5.4 and 5.5 then examine three of the main areas of spatial pattern analysis: Grid-based analysis; point sets and distance statistics; and spatial autocorrelation. Each area is covered in some detail, although a truly comprehensive coverage of tools and techniques lies beyond the space available here. Readers are recommended to refer to the many references and toolsets cited in the text for a more complete picture of each area, especially in relation to software that has been for specific disciplines such as epidemiology, spatial econometrics or ecological analysis.

Finally, in Section 5.6, building on the material in Section 5.5, we make a brief foray into the field of statistical modeling using regression techniques. We describe and illustrate some of the main approaches that have been developed to tackle the specific difficulties that arise with spatial datasets.

The "R Spatial" project, a part of the overall R Statistics OpenSource software programme, includes many facilities for spatial data handling, display and statistical analysis. As such it provides perhaps the most complete collection of software tools for analysts. These include facilities for:

- Point pattern analysis

- Geostatistics

- Disease mapping and analysis

- Spatial regression, and

- Ecological analysis

Details of the main routines that are available via this project are listed in the "R-Project spatial statistics software packages" Appendix at the end of this Guide. As will be seen, the functionality provided incorporates many of the core statistical methods that are discussed in the Sections that follow.

Many of the techniques of spatial analysis described elsewhere in this Guide make use of statistical measures and methods. These include the contextual discussion in Section 2.4, listing of univariate statistical measures in Table 1-3, and directional analysis in Section 4.5.1. Statistical procedures with specific spatial extensions are described in this chapter and in Section 6.7. In each case ideas and methods from mainstream statistics have been extended and developed in order to address the specific needs of spatial datasets. The nature of these extensions is different from the ways in which multivariate statistics are derived from their univariate counterparts because of the ways in which they depend upon the fundamental organizing concepts of distance, direction, contiguity and scale. In many instances classical hypothesis testing and inferential procedures cannot be applied to spatial problems (or at least, not without reservations and/or the use of specialized modeling techniques). This may be because the datasets do not satisfy classical independence or distributional requirements and/or because the sampling framework is unknown or unsuitable.

The result of research in this field over the past 50 years or so has been the development of a collection of core statistical procedures for spatial analysis. Many of these procedures are descriptive and/or exploratory. Such methods are not without the support of strong statistical foundations, but recognize that the requirements and assumptions of classical statistics are often not strictly met. However, recent advances in spatial modeling and estimation procedures, inferential methods, and associated software tools mean that it is now possible to model relatively complex, fine structured, large spatial datasets using a wide range of methods.

Cressie (1993) proposed a taxonomy of spatial statistics based on the underlying model of the dataset being considered. The three main topics he identified using this approach are:

- **point pattern analysis:** corresponding to a location-specific view of the data (discussed here in Sections 5.4 and 5.6)

- **lattice or regional analysis:** corresponding to zonal models of space, notably planar enforced sets of regions (such as administrative or census districts — discussed here in Sections 5.2, 5.3, 5.5 and 5.6), and

- **geostatistical modeling:** applying to a continuous field view of the underlying dataset — core issues relating to spatial modeling are discussed in Section 5.5, and geostatistical methods as applied to interpolation of field data in Section 6.7

Cressie's basic taxonomy has been revised and developed further by Anselin (2002, p.14). He summarizes key aspects associated with the object/field distinction in spatial data models and their implications as shown in Table 5-1. This analysis highlights not only the more obvious differences between the two main data models, but also the implications of these in terms of the analytical approaches implied. It also identifies the focus on interpolation and infill in the case of fields, versus extrapolation and domain expansion (spatial and temporal prediction) in the case of vector structures.

The distinctions between the various groupings are not always clear, and methods applied in one area are often carried across in part to others. For example, a grid may represent a field view, a lattice view or an aggregated point set view of underlying data. Some aspects of this issue are described in Section 5.3, which deals with grid-based statistical analysis.

*Table 5-1 Implications of Data Models*

|  | Object | Field |
|---|---|---|
| GIS | vector | raster |
| Spatial Data | points, lines, polygons | surfaces |
| Location | discrete | continuous |
| Observations | process realization | sample |
| Spatial Arrangement | spatial weights | distance function |
| Statistical Analysis | lattice | geostatistics |
| Prediction | extrapolation | interpolation |
| Models | lag and error | error |
| Asymptotics | expanding domain | infill |

In the field of ecological data analysis, Perry *et al.* (2002) provide an excellent review of spatial pattern analysis and statistical methods. Their 'guidelines' paper includes recommendations and examples of many of the techniques discussed in the subsequent sections of this chapter. Although their commentary applies primarily to ecological data (e.g. entomology, animal and plant distribution, forestry), which has an emphasis on one-dimensional (transect) analysis and sampled rectangular zones (quadrats) , much of their discussion may equally be applied to spatial data derived from other application areas. A version of the summary table they include in their paper is provided as Table 5-2.

Table 5-2 Description of methods for analysis of spatial data in ecology

| Method | Type of data | A | B | C | D | E | F | G |
|--------|-------------|---|---|---|---|---|---|---|
| Ripley's K and L | Point (x,y) | n | y | y | (y) | n | 1,2 | y |
| Quadrat variance methods* | Point (x,y) | n | (n) | y | n | n | 1 | n |
| Block quadrat variance methods* | Point with attributes (x,y,z) | n | (n) | y | (y) | n | 2 | n |
| Correlograms, Moran's I, Geary C etc. | Point with attributes (x,y,z) | n | y | y | y | n | 1,2 | y |
| Geostatistics — variograms | Point with attributes (x,y,z) | n | n | y | y | n | 1,2 | y |
| Geostatistics — Kriging | Point with attributes (x,y,z) | y | y | y | y | n | 1,2 | y |
| Angular correlation* | Point with attributes (x,y,z) | n | y | n | y | n | 2 | y |
| Wavelets* | Point with attributes (x,y,z) | n | n | y | n | y | 1,2 | n |
| SADIE: spatial analysis by distance indices* | Point with attributes (x,y,z) | n | y | n | n | y | 1,2 | y |
| Landscape metrics | Area with attributes (A,z) | (n) | (n) | n | (n) | n | 2 | y |
| Variance-mean (Morisita, Taylor etc.)* | Non-spatial (attributes only) | n | n | n | n | n | 1,2 | y |
| Nearest neighbor | Point (x,y) | n | n | n | n | n | 1,2 | y |

Key: A: Model based? B: Allows hypothesis tests? C: Information available at multiple scales? D: Information available on anisotropy? E: Information available on local pattern? F: 1- or 2-dimensions or both 1 and 2 dimensions? G: Irregularly spaced units allowed? n=no, y=yes, (n)=rarely, (y)=possible; * technique not currently covered in this Guide but is supported in ecological analysis software such as SAM and PASSaGE. For more details see Perry et al. (2002)

## 5.1.1 Descriptive statistics

Almost all GIS packages provide a range of facilities for computing simple univariate statistical measures on tabular attribute data associated with vector objects. Many of the basic statistics listed in Table 1-3 are provided, either directly by opening an attribute table and selecting a column for analysis, or by executing some form of simple calculation facility. In addition to these basic measures, tools are often provided that display frequency histograms of data, with or without data transformation. Such facilities may be stand-alone or may be embedded in related functionality, such as map classification and symbology tools.

For image or grid datasets many packages provide a wide range of non-spatial and spatial statistical facilities. Purely non-spatial facilities include the same type of statistical measures as for vector objects, where the attributes are grid cell values rather than attribute table columns. In addition, many packages provide a range of statistical tools designed for multiple grid analysis. A number of these go beyond data description to provide facilities such as data reduction (examining data redundancy) and modeling (e.g. simple regression techniques). Some of these are described in the following subsections.

Much of the subject commonly described as "Spatial Statistics" deals with vector datasets, and many of the tools and techniques that have been developed apply (directly or indirectly) to point rather than line or area-based data. Increasingly, however, integrated tools such as GeoDa, PySal and SAM have become available that facilitate the direct exploration, analysis and modeling of zone-based data and small area (local) patterns.

## 5.1.2 Spatial sampling

Principles and methods of spatial sampling have been described briefly in Section 2.3.8 and some of the general concepts are explored in more detail in Dixon and Leach (1977, CATMOG 17) and more recently in Delmelle (2008). In this subsection we focus on 2D sampling, but similar concepts apply to 1-D (transect) and 3D (volumetric) sampling. When spatial samples are subsequently analyzed, many factors have to be taken into consideration, such as: sample size; how representative the sample is; whether the sample might be biased in any way; whether temporal factors are important; to what extent edge effects might influence the sample and the subsequent analysis; whether sampled data has been aggregated; how the data measurements were conducted (procedures and equipment); whether sampling order or arrangement is important; to what extent can the measured data samples be regarded as being from a population? In short, the full range of classical sampling issues must be considered coupled with some specifically spatial factors.

Amongst the most commonly applied sampling schemes are those based on point sampling within a regular grid framework. Figure 5-1 illustrates a number of the simplest schemes based on 100 sample points. The first (Figure 5-1A) shows a set of regularly spaced sample points in a sample square region. Systematic sampling of this type, and variants such as that shown in Figure 5-1D in which the start points of each sequence are selected with a random offset, suffer from two major problems: (i) the sampling interval may coincide with some periodicity in the data being studied (or a related variable), resulting in substantial bias in the data; and (ii) the set of distances sampled is effectively fixed, hence important distance-related effects (such as dispersal, contagion etc.) may be missed entirely. Purely random sampling, as illustrated in Figure 5-1B has attractions from a statistical perspective, but as can be seen, marked clustering occurs whilst some areas are left without any samples at all. A number of solutions to these problems are used, often based on combining the coverage benefits of regular sampling with the

randomness of true random selection. Figure 5-1C illustrates this class of sampling schemes, with each sample point being selected as a random offset from the regularly spaced (x,y) coordinates shown by the + symbols. The degree of offset determines how regular or how random the sampled points will be. Note that some clustering of samples may still occur with this approach. In each of these examples the point selection is carried out without any prior knowledge of the objects to be sampled or the environment from which the samples are to be drawn. If ancillary information is available, it may alter the design selected. For example, if samples are sought that represent certain landscape classes (e.g. grassland, deciduous woodland, coniferous woodland, etc.), then it is generally preferable to stratify the samples by regions that have been separated identified as forming these various classes. Likewise, if 100 samples are to be taken, and it is known that certain parts of the landscape are much more varied than others (in respect of the data to be studied) then it makes sense to undertake more samples in the most varying regions.

In addition to fixed sampling schemes, adaptive schemes can be applied which may offer improvements in terms of estimating mean values and reducing uncertainty (providing lower variances). Typically an adaptive scheme will involve four steps: apply a coarse resolution fixed scheme (e.g. as per Figure 5-1C ) to the study area; record data at each sampled location; compute decision criteria for continued sampling; and extend sampling in the neighborhood of locations that meet the decision criteria. For example, if recorded values of Cadmium in soil samples at certain locations exceeds a pre-defined threshold, then additional samples might be taken radially around the initial threshold locations. Alternatively, the initial values at each location might be used to compute an experimental variogram (see Section 6.7.1.7), from which estimates values and variances of these values can be computed using Kriging methods (see Section 6.7.2). Locations with high Kriging variance (i.e. poorly represented) could then be identified and additional sampling designed to reduce this uncertainty.

*Figure 5-1 Point-based sampling schemes*

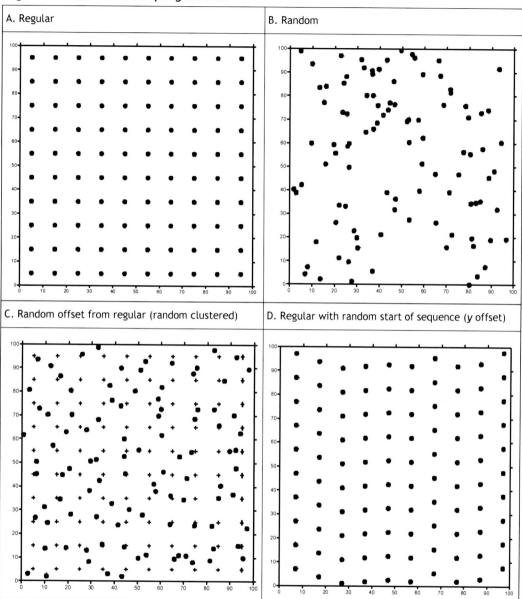

A. Regular

B. Random

C. Random offset from regular (random clustered)

D. Regular with random start of sequence (*y* offset)

### 5.1.2.1 Sampling frameworks

GIS toolsets and related software incorporate few facilities that directly address issues of sampling and sample design. Most commonly the terms *sampling* and *resampling* in GIS are used to refer to the frequency with which an existing dataset (raster image or in some cases, vector object) is sampled for simple display or processing purposes (e.g. when overlaying multiple data layers, or computing surface transects). These operations are not directly related to questions of statistical sampling. Two aspects of statistical sampling are explicitly supported within several GIS packages. These are: (i) the selection (sampling) of specific point or grid cell locations within an existing dataset; and (ii) the removal of spatial bias from collected datasets, using a procedure known as declustering. We describe each of these in subsections 5.1.2.1 and 5.1.2.2.

A number of GIS software packages, such as TNTMips, ENVI, Idrisi and GRASS provide tools to assist in the selection of sample points, grid cells or regions of interest (ROI) from input datasets. Often these datasets are remote-sensing images, which may or may not have been subjected to some form of initial classification procedure. Examples of the facilities provided are listed below:

ENVI — takes a raster image file as input and provides three types of sampling, which it describes as:

- Stratified random sampling, which may be proportionate or disproportionate. In the former case random samples are made from each class or ROI in proportion to the class or region size. Disproportionate sampling essentially requires users to specify the sample size, although the elements will still be randomly selected from each class or ROI

- Equalized random sampling, which selects an equal number of observations at random from each class or ROI

- Random sampling, which ignores classes or ROIs and simply selects a predefined number of cells or points at random

The selected points or cells (which may be output as a separate georeferenced list or table) are then used in post-classification analysis — comparing classifications with *ground truth* in each case (obtained from field survey or other independent data sources).

Idrisi offers similar facilities to ENVI via its SAMPLE function, providing random, systematic or stratified random point (cell) sampling from an input image (grid). The selection process for stratified random simply involves regarding the input image as being constructed from rectangular blocks of cells, and then sampling random cells within these larger blocks.

GRASS provides simple random sampling which may be combined with masking to create forms of stratified random samples. This facility may be somewhat cumbersome to implement. GRASS also provides a facility to generate random sets of cells that are at least $D$ units apart, where $D$ is a user-specified buffer distance. This can result in a more stratified than random sample and it is suggested that $D$ should be derived with reference to observed levels of spatial autocorrelation (cf. Sections 5.5 and 6.7).

TNTMips supports a range of point sampling facilities to be used within vector polygons (e.g. field boundaries, Figure 5-2). These provide the more familiar form of statistical sampling frameworks that would precede field studies, and have application for research into areas such as soil composition (e.g. for precision farming), groundwater analysis, geological studies, or ecological research. However, they could equally well be applied to urban environments, as a precursor to environmental monitoring or even household surveys. The software provides for a two-stage process: (i) the creation of grids within the polygonal regions to be studied; and (ii) the selection of points within these grid structures. Grids are of user-definable size (edge length or area), shape (triangular, hexagonal, square, linear strips or random rectangles), and orientation (angle of rotation). A series of sample generated grids are shown in Figure 5-2.

*Figure 5-2 Grid generation examples*

| A. Square grid | B. Hexagonal grid | C. Random rectangular grid, 60° |
|---|---|---|

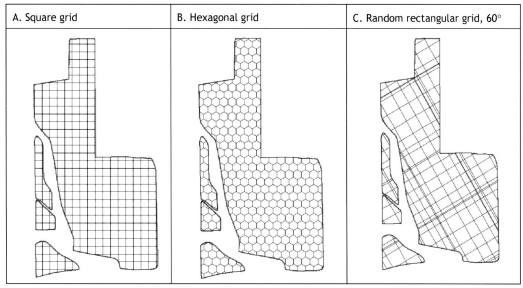

*Figure 5-3 Grid sampling examples within hexagonal grid, 1 hectare area*

| A. Regular (cell center) | B. Systematic (random offset) | C. Random, no center bias |
|---|---|---|

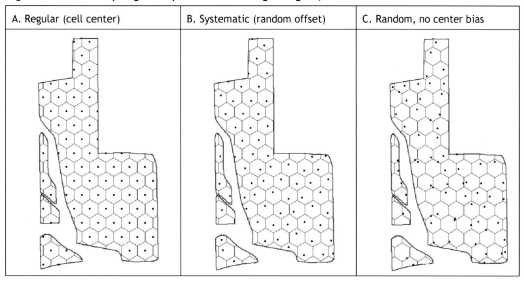

Where a regular cell framework has been generated the software then supports creation of sampling points *within* each cell — single points in this example. The methods supported are regular (center of cell, Figure 5-3A); systematic unaligned (Figure 5-3B) in which the first cell point is selected with random $x,y$ coordinates and subsequent points are selected using the same $x$ or $y$ coordinate as the previous cell, but with one of the two coordinates selected at random, alternating on a column-by-column basis); and random (Figure 5-3C). In the latter two cases a weighting factor is provided that biases selection towards the center of the cell (100= no bias, 1=maximum bias). Selected sample points that nominally fall inside a cell but outside of the polygon boundary are excluded.

With general purpose GIS packages it is straightforward to generate a random, regular or partially randomized point set (within or externally to the GIS), and then to compute the intersection of this set with pre-defined polygons or grid cells. With this approach simple point-sampling schemes may be created, although precise matching to polygon forms, sample numbers or attribute weightings may be difficult. Purpose-built add-ins, such as Hawth's Tools for ArcGIS, provide a range of tailored sampling facilities. These include: (i) generation of random points, with a range of selection options (including use of raster or polygon reference layers — see Figure 5-4A, Mississippi, USA); (ii) random selection from an existing feature set (points, lines, polygons — see Figure 5-4B, 200 radio-activity monitoring sites in Germany. Random sample of 30 (red/large dots)<100 units of radiation and 30 (crosses)>=100 units of radiation); and (iii) conditional point sampling, designed for case-control analysis and similar applications. The latter facilitates a variety of random point generation methods in a region surrounding specified source points.

Random points in the plane may be used as sampling points or in connection with modeling — for example as part of a Monte Carlo simulation of a probability distribution. Random points can also be generated on a network. Naturally the distribution of such points will be affected by the distribution of the network links in the plane, and may thus appear clustered with respect to the plane (excluding the network). The corollary of this observation is that a clustered point pattern in the plane that is, in fact, a set of points on a network, may actually be a random uniform distribution when shortest network path distances are used rather than Euclidean planar distances. For example, the set of 100 points in Figure 5-5A (Tripolis, in Greece) appears to be far from random, but in fact this is a random uniform (Poisson) point set on a network, as shown in Figure 5-5B. This example was generated using the SANET software, which also provides a wide range of tools for analyzing observed point patterns on or almost on networks such as that illustrated (see further, Section 5.4.1).

The term *quadrat sampling* is applied to schemes in which information on all static point data (e.g. trees, birds' nests etc.) is collected using an overlay of regular form (e.g. a square or hexagonal grid). Collected data are then aggregated to the level of the quadrat, whose size, orientation and internal variability will all affect the resultant figures (e.g. counts). Very small quadrats will ultimately contain 0 or 1 point objects, whilst very large quadrats will contain almost all the observations and hence will be of little value in understanding the variability of the data over space. An alternative to procedures based on lattices of quadrats is to "drop" quadrats onto the study area at random. Such quadrats may be of any size or shape, but circular forms have the advantage of being directionally invariant. A disadvantage with this approach is that some areas may be repeat sampled unless precautions are taken to exclude areas once sampled.

*Figure 5-4 Random point generation examples – ArcGIS*

| A. Random sample points, 5 per county | B. Stratified random selection, 30% of each stratum |
|---|---|

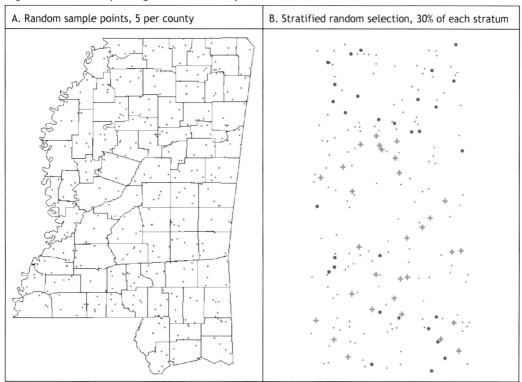

*Figure 5-5 Random point samples on a network*

| A. Point set in the plane | B. Random point set on a network |
|---|---|

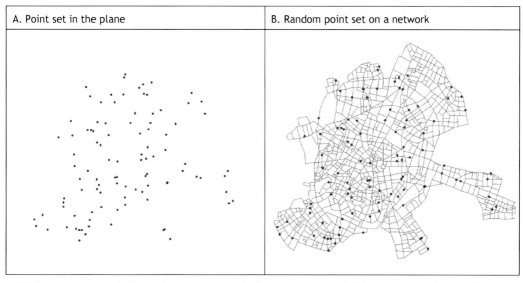

*SANET software: Prof A Okabe et al; Network data (Tripolis, Greece): S Sirigos; see also Figure 7-16*

## 5.1.2.2 Declustering

Point samples may be unduly clustered spatially, for a variety of reasons. For example, samples from rivers, boreholes and wells may provide the basis for a chemical analysis of groundwater supplies, and the distribution of these is often clustered. Geological, hydrological and hydrographic surveys frequently involve intensive data collection in localized areas, with sparsely sampled areas elsewhere. Practical constraints, such as access in built-up or industrialized zones, may also dictate sampling schemes that exhibit strong clustering. And of course, there may be clustering as a feature of the sampling design (e.g. stratified sampling, repeat sampling in small areas to obtain a representative measure of selected attributes). The latter may have been designed to ensure that different regions of interest (ROIs) are represented adequately, or that suspected areas of greater local variation are sampled in more detail than areas that are suspected of being more uniform.

Measured attributes in such instances may not be representative of population (whole region) attributes because observations in close proximity to one another may exhibit strong positive spatial autocorrelation — neighboring measurements often have very similar attributes (see further Section 5.5.1). This results in attributes within these regions having undue weight in subsequent calculations. In the extreme, almost all observations may have been taken in a small region with consistently high or low attribute values, whilst very few have been taken from all remaining parts of the study area. Assuming spatial autocorrelation is present, clustering has the effect that measures such as the calculation of mean values, the estimation of regression parameters, or the determination of confidence intervals may be substantially biased.

A partial solution to problems of this kind is known as spatial declustering. Essentially this involves removing or reducing the known or estimated adverse effects of clustering in order to obtain a more representative picture of the underlying population data and/or to ensure techniques such as feature extraction and surface modeling operate in an acceptable and useful manner. There are several approaches that may be adopted, each of which involves adjusting the sample values prior to further analysis. One of the simplest procedures for declustering involves defining a regular grid over sampled points (rather as per the grid generation procedure described in the Section 6.5.2). The grid cell size is selected such that it is meaningful for the problem at hand (e.g. feature extraction) and/or ensures that the average number of points falling in a grid cell is 1 (typically). Cells which contain many sample points may then be regarded as clustered or possibly over-sampled, and a statistic such as the median value of the measured attribute(s) across all sampled points in that cell may then be used as the single assigned cell (center) value. Another commonly provided declustering technique based on this grid-overlay approach is to use the density of points as a weighting function. For example, cells with 0 points have zero weight, cells with 1 point have a weight of 1, and cells with $n$ points have each point weighted $1/n$ (hence in effect this is a simple averaging procedure). In reality both of these procedures amount to a kind of stratification of already sampled locations subsequent to their selection. It is important to note that procedures of this kind present no substitute for randomness in the selection of locations to be sampled and can amount to very dubious practice if the intention is subsequently to build an inferential statistical model using the observations that are retained.

In a similar vein, and as an alternative to count-based weighting, area-based weighting is provided as an option in several packages. This involves generating a set of Voronoi regions around each sample point, which results in small areas for closely spaced points and large areas for sparsely arranged sample points. The weights applied are then directly related to these areas. This method is simple but needs to have some justification and/or validation in terms of the problem under consideration, and may suffer from serious edge-effect problems, depending on how the Voronoi regions are computed (e.g. to the edge of the mapped region, or to the MBR or convex hull of the sample point set). Hybridized variants of area-based weighting (e.g. by adjusting the weights using known physical boundaries and/or nearest neighbor distances) have been shown to substantially reduce mean absolute error (MAE) and RMSE in some instances, e.g. see Dubois and Saisana (2002). Revised point-weighting schemes of this kind can be generated within GIS packages and then applied to the target attributes prior to further analysis. The scheme proposed by Dubois and Saisana, for example, which they tested on DEM data for Switzerland, was of the form:

$$w_i = \frac{s_i}{s_m} \times \frac{d_i^2}{s_m}$$

where $w_i$ is the weight applied to the $i^{th}$ sample point, $i=1,2,...n$; $s_i$ is the area of the $i^{th}$ Voronoi region; $s_m$ is the average area of all the Voronoi regions (i.e. study area/$n$); and $d_i^2$ is the squared distance of the $i^{th}$ sample point to its nearest neighbor. Models of this type do not have universal application, and selection of appropriate declustering procedures requires careful analysis of the sample data, sub-sampling and cross-validating against some form of ground truth where necessary, and then applying adjustments in a manner appropriate to the problem and dataset to hand.

# 5.2 Exploratory Spatial Data Analysis

## 5.2.1  EDA, ESDA and ESTDA

Much of the groundwork in spatial statistics is concerned with the description and exploration of spatial datasets. The generic term for such methods is exploratory data analysis (EDA), or in the context of spatial and spatio-temporal analysis, ESDA and ESTDA respectively. Such methods are by no means exclusively statistical in nature, and for ESDA special forms of data mapping are of considerable importance. In the past EDA or *data mining* tools have not offered 'spatial' visualization, although there are tools now available, such as those providing 'network' spatialization and visualization (e.g. Gephi), and neural network mapping (SOM Toolbox).

The simplest form of EDA involves the computation of basic statistics, and in the context of spatial data, statistical summaries of attribute tables and grid values. Useful online references on EDA include the NIST e-Handbook (EDA section), CATMOG 49 (an early monograph that deals with ESDA), and especially for ESDA, the GeoDa workbook and GeoViz toolkit documentation. Graphical analysis of such data tend to be histograms, pie charts, box plots and/or scatter plots. None of these provides an explicitly spatial perspective on the data. However, where such facilities are dynamically linked to mapped and tabular views of the data they can provide a powerful toolset for ESDA purposes. The selection of objects through such linking may be programmatically defined (e.g. all values lying more than 2 standard deviations from the mean) or user defined, often by graphical selection. The latter is known as *brushing*, and generally involves selection of a number of objects (e.g. points) from a graphical or mapped representation (Figure 5-6, Columbus, Ohio). Selected features are automatically highlighted (*linked*) in the other views of the dataset (histogram, map and attribute table in the example illustrated).

*Figure 5-6 Brushing and linking, GeoDa*

Facilities of this type are implemented in a number of GIS packages, notably in ArcGIS V9 (with a range of tools for different data types, but limited to a fixed number of points for selected ESDA tools such as semivariance analysis) and in the stand-alone package GeoDa. The latter has been built using ArcGIS objects and reads and writes ArcGIS shape files. It limits its attention to *lattice data*, by which is meant discrete spatial units (zones/areas) rather than point sets or point samples from a continuous surface.

A wide range of ESDA tools, which include brushing and linking as core functionality, have been implemented in GeoVista Studio and the somewhat more accessible Java version, the GeoViz toolkit (which also reads SHP files).

These focus on the exploration of multivariate datasets, and include the visualization tool known as the parallel coordinate plot, or PCP. In the example illustrated in Figure 5-7 five variables are included: house values, income levels, crimes recorded (residential burglaries and vehicle thefts), open space and the percentage of housing with deficient plumbing. Each variable is shown with a [min, max] vertical scale and a linking line that corresponds to the case (census tract). Lines are colored according to a user-chosen single variable and classification rule. By selecting a single line, such as that shown, the variable values are displayed and all the other visualization windows, such as various forms of maps and graphs, show the selected object highlighted.

*Figure 5-7 Parallel coordinate plot*

Other visualization facilities of this type include star plots and star plot maps, which show multivariate data as a star of values (Figure 5-8).

*Figure 5-8 Star plot*

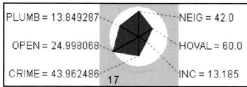

In this type of chart each variable is plotted in a separate direction, with the length of the star arm being proportional to the variable magnitude. Each mapped region will have an individual star plot, which can be mapped as an overlay onto a classified base map to provide a start plot map.

Extensions to a number of these techniques to the spatio-temporal domain (ESTDA) have recently been made available in a number of software packages. These include: the STARS open source project; BioMedware's (commercial) Space-time Intelligence System (STIS); and the National Cancer Institute's

(NCI) SaTScan software, available free of charge, from http://www.satscan.org/. The NCI's GIS website is an excellent source of information and guidance as regards the mapping and analysis of epidemiological datasets. In conjunction with the NCI the GeoVista team at Penn State University have recently developed ESTAT, their Exploratory Spatio-Temporal Analysis Toolkit, a Java-based implementation of several of the ESDA tools provided within GeoVista augmented by linked time-series plots. The latter are similar in format to the PCP display, but with the horizontal axis providing fixed time periods (e.g. years) and the data plotted being a single variable, e.g. the morbidity rate for a particular form of cancer. Individual lines again correspond to the spatial entities (e.g. counties, states).

A recent publication, with a specific focus on spatial and spatio-temporal EDA is Andrienko and Andrienko's "Exploratory Analysis of Spatial and Temporal Data". The authors are associated with the CommonGIS Java-based software project that enables ESTDA to be delivered over the Internet — interactive Java-based examples from Andrienko *et al.* (2003) are included on the CommonGIS web site. They view the purpose of ESDTA as providing a data focus in which:

- peculiarities of the data can be revealed and an appreciation obtained as to how the data should be further processed (e.g. filtered, transformed, split, combined, ...)

- hypotheses can be generated for further testing (e.g. using statistical methods), and

- proper methods can be selected for in-depth analysis of the data

They make the case that space and time must be seen as complementary views of the same data. This leads on to need for systematic analysis of: (i) the evolution of spatial patterns in time; and (ii) the distribution of temporal behaviors in space. Because spatio-temporal datasets are complex and often incomplete and inconsistent they recommend that such data are divided up and explored by slices and subsets (species, age groups, countries, years etc.), and that care is taken to examine outliers and unexpected patterns. This approach is especially important for data obtained from non-governmental sources, e.g. much of the data obtained via the Internet.

## 5.2.2 Outlier detection

One of the areas ESDA tools focus on is outlier detection, as there are many instances in which so-called outliers are of great interest. In the present context these are spatial objects whose value on one or more attributes is markedly different from others in the set under consideration. The data in question may be correct or may be the result of some form of error (measurement, coding, representation etc.). Such data are of interest since they may represent the most important items in an investigation (e.g. mineral concentrations, a pollution source, an unexpectedly high incidence of a particular disease). Or they might represent data that need to be removed or adjusted (e.g. smoothed) if either the information is known or suspected to be incorrect, or if its retention will adversely affect the results obtained from the application of a particular analytical technique.

### 5.2.2.1 Mapped histograms

One of the simplest methods of highlighting possible outliers is to create a histogram of the data, typically using a fine class division, and then to examine the extreme classes. Where this facility is linked to a map of the data, the location of the object(s) may be identified and examined (Figure 5-9). The upper figure shows the histogram and basic statistics for the attribute OWN_OCC (the number of Owner Occupiers, i.e. property owners) within 86 census districts (test census Output Areas, OAs, for part of Manchester, UK). The districts with the highest data values have been selected on the histogram window, and are simultaneously highlighted in the map window (lower figure). The same approach may be applied for other vector object types, such as point data.

*Figure 5-9 Histogram linkage*

*Source: UK 2001 Census Test Output Areas (OAs)*

Data items that lie at the upper or lower limits of a dataset range may be described as *global outliers*. This term refers to values that are extreme compared to the dataset as a whole. However, within the dataset there may be values that are "relatively extreme" and these are referred to as *local outliers*. A local outlier is a value that is markedly different from (spatially) neighboring values. An example of this might be a set of measurements taken along a transect, with a value part of the way along the transect that is very different from those immediately before or after, but still well within the overall range of the data

recorded on the entire transect. Some ESDA software packages, such as ArcGIS Geostatistical Analyst, provide tools for displaying local as well as global outliers for selected data types.

### 5.2.2.2  Box plots

Box plots (or box-whisker plots) are a form of EDA provided in many data analysis and graphing packages (e.g. Minitab, SPSS, STATA, Grapher, Matplotlib, Mondrian, WinBUGS, GeoXP). Together with distribution plots and scatter plots they provide one of the three main ways in which statistical data are examined graphically. Because box plots are less familiar to many, and of particular use in examining outliers, we describe them in some detail (see Figure 5-10).

*Figure 5-10 Simple box plot*

A box plot consists of a number of distinct elements. The example in Figure 5-10 was generated using MATLab Statistics Toolbox and we provide definitions below that apply to this particular implementation:

- The lower and upper lines of the "box" in the center of the plot window are the 25th and 75th percentiles of the sample. The distance between the top and bottom of the box is the inter-quartile range (IQR)

- The line in the middle of the box is the sample median. If the median is not centered in the box it is an indication of skewness

- The *whiskers* are lines extending above and below the box. They show the extent of the rest of the sample (unless there are outliers). Assuming no outliers, the maximum of the sample is the top of the upper whisker. The minimum of the sample is the bottom of the lower whisker. By default, an outlier is a value that is more than 1.5 times the IQR away from the top or bottom of the box (a *hinge* value of 1.5), so with outliers the whiskers show a form of trimmed range, i.e. excluding the outliers (n.b. the term *hinge* is also used in statistics to refer to locations within the main data range, in some instances matching the upper and lower quartile values)

- A symbol, e.g. a small circle, at the top and/or bottom of the plot is an indication of an outlier in the data. This point may be the result of a data entry error, a poor measurement or perhaps a highly significant observation

- The notches in the box are a graphic confidence interval about the median of a sample. A side-by-side comparison of two notched box plots is sometimes described as the graphical equivalent of a *t*-test. Box plots do not have notches by default

The box plots in Figure 5-10 are for a set of radioactivity observations made at 1008 sites in Germany on one day in 2004. The plot on the left consists of 200 of the records, with whiskers extending to 1.5 times the IQR. Some packages allow user specification of the hinges, or provide an alternative set value (e.g. GeoDa 3 times IQR; WinBUGS 2.5% and 97.5% limits). The plot on the right shows a further 808 locations and their readings (see also Figure 5-13). Three values in sample 1 were deliberately altered for this plot, e.g. simulating measurement or coding errors. One, for example, involved recording a measured value of 106.0 as 16.0. The plot picks out each of these outliers. Box plots with a link to zone-based spatial datasets are supported within GeoDa. Figure 5-11 illustrates the technique, again using the Manchester area test census Output Areas described earlier in this section.

*Figure 5-11 Mapped box plot, GeoDa*

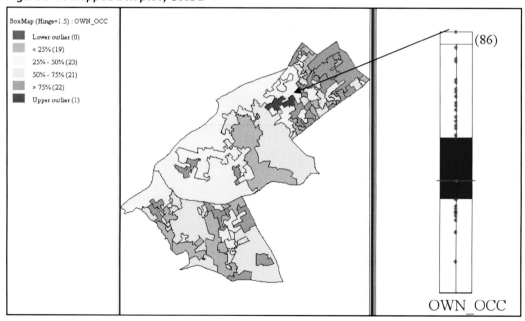

The census variable Owner Occupier has been selected for mapping, and a conventional box plot of the data is also illustrated. In the GeoDa implementation each data item that lies outside the box but within the whiskers is shown with a *, and the sole "true" outlier OA appears at the very top of the box plot above the upper whisker. The mapped box plot shows the OAs that fall into the various data quartiles (and the number of OAs in each), plus upper and lower outlier OAs — in this case just the one upper OA of rather complex shape, the same as that identified in Figure 5-9.

### 5.2.3 Cross tabulations and conditional choropleth plots

Mapped zonal data typically consist of a single variable, or a ratio of two variables, one of which is acting as a normalization factor, e.g. mapping the ratio

$r$=persons_in_employment/total_population

Separate maps may be created for each variable or ratio of interest, but these are typically independent entities that may be difficult to compare and interpret. It would be relatively straightforward to create a series of maps of a particular variable of interest, for example the reported rate of lung cancer by health district where each map showed the rate for areas where the proportion of smokers was high, medium or low. This would be a form of control or "conditioning" on the information shown. This simple approach can be implemented within any GIS. The approach can be extended further to two (or more) variables by crosstabulating the source data. If the crosstabulation is carried out on categorical data (e.g. sex, racial grouping) then once again a series of maps may be generated for each cell in the crosstabulation. However, with unclassified continuously varying data it is useful to examine the effect of specific levels of such data on the spatial distribution. Specialized visualization tools have been developed recently to support operations of this type, including CCMaps and extensions to GeoDa (derived from the ideas developed in the CCMaps project). They are known as interactive *Conditional Choropleth* mapping tools and may be dynamically linked

to other visualizations such as box plots, histograms and scatterplots. The aim of such software, in the words of the original authors, is to:

- Stimulate analytical reasoning

- Detect the unexpected

- Discover the unexpected, and

- Stimulate hypothesis generation

Figure 5-12 illustrates this procedure using data on lung cancer mortality rates, by county, for the USA — see Carr *et al.* (2000, 2002) for a brief description of the method and this particular dataset. There are 9 maps in total. The colored bar at the top shows how the counties have been classified, with for example 34% in the blue (low) category, corresponding to 63.7-375 deaths per 100,000. The breakpoints on this scale may be dragged to provide alternative classification levels, the effects of which are dynamically updated in the map windows. Each map row represents one level of the percentage of the population below the USA designated poverty level (right hand slider scale) and each map column represents one level of the recorded annual precipitation level. The region in South-East of the USA (top right in the set of map windows) appears to have a high incidence of lung cancer mortality and a high score for both conditioning variables.

The figures in the top right of each mapped window show the weighted mean mortality rate, and the $R$-squared value in the lower right corner shows the percentage of the overall variability accounted for by these weighted means. By adjusting the two conditioning variable sliders (which are actually a form of box plot) or by using a built-in search facility (described as *cognostics*) a combination of slider values that maximize $R^2$ can be obtained — in this example to a value of just below 43%. For more details regarding the application of CCmapping and associated linked visualizations (e.g. conditional box-plots and conditional scatterplots) please refer to the CCMaps and/or GeoDa documentation and referenced articles.

## Figure 5-12 Conditional Choropleth mapping

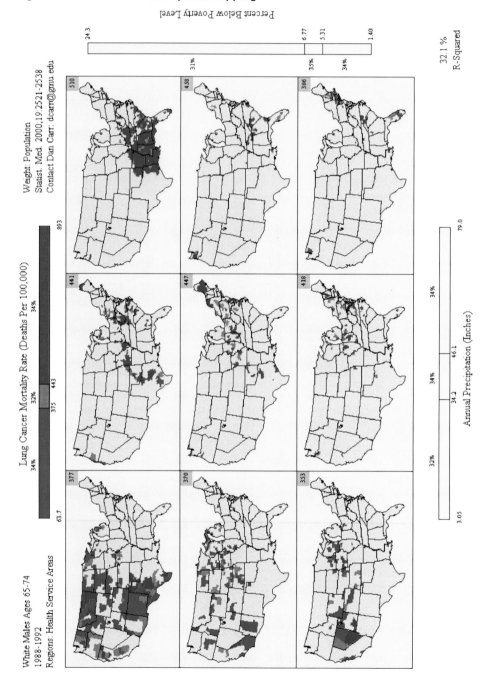

## 5.2.4 ESDA and mapped point data

Figure 5-13 illustrates a number of alternative methods for exploring variations in mapped point-based datasets with associated weights or continuously variable attributes. As in Figure 5-10 the (Sample 1) dataset consists of location information for 200 radioactivity monitoring stations in Germany, together with the levels of radiation recorded on a single day in 2004. A simple ESDA approach is to map the data and apply symbology to reflect the data values recorded. In Figure 5-13A and B this is illustrated by the use of variable symbol size and/or color to reflect underlying values. In Figure 5-13C a more sophisticated analysis has

been conducted. In this case a semivariogram scatterplot ((see further, Section 6.7.1.15) of the dataset was generated (using ArcGIS Geostatistical Analyst) and the set of points on the scatterplot with the highest semivariance values were selected by brushing. Since these points in the scatterplot represent data pairs the linked map highlights the pairings. As can be seen the most extreme semivariance values are all related to just two of the original 200 source points in the lower right of the map. It may be that these latter points are of special interest (have unusually high or low radioactivity measurement) or that the data are incorrect and require adjustment or removal of selected values.

*Figure 5-13 Exploratory analysis of radioactivity data*

| A. Variable point size | B. Variable color | C. Semivariogram pairs | D. Voronoi analysis, cluster |
|---|---|---|---|

The last of the four images shown, Figure 5-13D, shows a rather different form of ESDA. Voronoi polygons (see Section 4.2.14.3) have been generated for the MBR of the entire point set and the radioactivity data mapped based on cell adjacencies. A set of 5 classes has been defined and cells that fall into a different class interval from all of their immediate neighbors are colored gray, otherwise they are colored by class interval. Note that these outliers are

determined spatially, and will not in general correspond to extreme data values — they are local spatial outliers. Other Voronoi region statistics available as an alternative to this cluster approach include: mapping actual radioactivity values (described as "simple" mapping); using a local neighborhood mean or median for all cells; allocation based on a local neighborhood entropy statistic (see Table 1-3);

and spread-based statistics, such as standard deviation and range-based mapping.

*Table 5-3 Voronoi-based ESDA*

| Local Smoothing | Mean, Mode, Median |
|---|---|
| Local Variation | Standard deviation<br>Inter-quartile range<br>Entropy |
| Local Outliers | Cluster |
| Local Influence | Simple |

A summary of the interpretation of each of these choices is provided in Table 5-3 (these may be compared with some of the grid analysis methods described in Section 4.6).

### 5.2.5 Trend analysis of continuous data

A somewhat different approach to ESDA for continuous data represented as a point set with z-values is to examine whether any simple trends are present. For the radioactivity point set illustrated in Figure 5-13 a simple 3D trend analysis is shown in Figure 5-14.

*Figure 5-14 Trend analysis of radioactivity dataset*

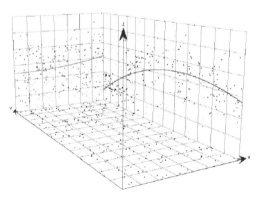

This diagram shows the point set mapped in the *XY*-plane, with the radioactivity levels (z-values) projected onto the *XZ*- and *YZ*-planes. Simple low-order (2nd degree) polynomial trend curves have then been fitted to these

projected datasets, providing a useful pre-analysis visualization of possible trends. Again, as with the forms of ESDA described earlier, points in this visualization may be brushed and associated representations highlighted through linking. Trend analysis of the kind illustrated here uses the basic methods of curve fitting applied in regression modeling (see further, Section 5.6).

### 5.2.6 Cluster hunting and scan statistics

Cluster hunting is the term used to apply to a family of techniques that involve computationally intensive search procedures for point- and zone-based cluster identification. They aim to identify clusters based on the spatial arrangements of incidents combined with basic information on the background population. They then search for clusters (areas of unexpectedly high incidence) by exhaustively examining all possible locations on a fine grid covering the study area. One of the most well-known of these techniques, GAM, is best described in the authors' own words (from the GAM web site):

*"The Geographical Analysis Machine (GAM) is an attempt at automated exploratory spatial data analysis of point or small area data that is easy to understand. The purpose is to answer a simple practical question; namely given some spatial data of something interesting where might there be evidence of localized geographic clustering if you do not know in advance where to look. [This may be] due to lack of knowledge of possible causal mechanisms, or if prior knowledge of the data precludes testing more hypotheses on the same database. Or more simply put, you send GAM a geographically referenced point or small area referenced database and it will indicate where there is evidence of localized clustering and how strong it is"*

A Java version of GAM can be downloaded from the University of Leeds CCG web site. This is a working version of the software but is, unfortunately, not the subject of ongoing support or development at present. The Java version of GAM takes as an input a text file of the form:

ID,easting,northing,incidence_count,population_count

The incidence_count value contains the variable of interest, e.g. disease incidence, and the population_count variable contains the population variable, e.g. the population at risk. Frequently the location data will be taken as the centers of small area statistics zones, and the population variable will be the total applicable value for that zone (e.g. census output area or tract). The study area is then divided into a grid, and circles are placed at every grid intersection. The number of incidents falling inside these circles are counted and checked to see if they are, by some measure, excessive. The notion of excessive could be user-specified (e.g. more than a certain number/rate of incidents, or pre-computed variable levels for each location) or can be computed by the program based on an expected level defined as the population at risk times the mean incidence rate.

The steps in the analytical procedure are as follows:

- Step 1. Read in $X$ (easting), $Y$ (northing), a variable of interest, and data for the population at risk

- Step 2 Identify the MBR containing the data, identify starting circle radius, and degree of overlap. If $R$ is the radius of a circle of area equal to the MBR, then starting radius might be $r=R/100$ with increment $dr=R/100$

- Step 3 Generate a grid covering this rectangle so that circles of current radius overlap by the desired amount — a range of radius values $r$ will be used, varying over a user-specified range of distances

- Step 4 For each grid-intersection generate a circle of radius $r$

- Step 5 Retrieve two counts for the population at risk and the variable of interest

- Step 6 Apply some "significance" test procedure — a variety of alternative procedures, including Monte Carlo simulation) and bootstrap methods are

supported. The latter is a form a sampling with replacement, similar to jackknifing in some respects — see further, Section 6.7.2.2 and Efron (1982) and Efron and Tibshirani (1997)

- Step 7 Keep the result if significant

- Step 8 Repeat Steps 5 to 7 until all circles have been processed

- Step 9 Increase circle radius by $dr$ and return to Step 3 else go to Step 10

- Step 10 Create a smoothed density surface of excess incidence for the significant circles using a kernel smoothing procedure and aggregating the results for all circles (this step uses the Epanechnikov kernel function, Table 4-8)

- Step 11 Map this surface and inspect the results

GAM with kernel smoothing is generally referred to as GAM/K, and it is in this form that is currently used. It is by no means the only method of cluster hunting, but has been found in tests on synthetic data to be one of the most effective at locating genuine clusters in large test datasets, and also one of the least subject to finding false clusters. Further discussion relating to this topic is provided in Section 5.4.4.

GAM has been the subject of considerable controversy over the years and alternative methods are often used in preference, in particular the spatial scan statistic due to Kulldorf (1997) and provided in the SaTScan software. Again, using author's own description of the facilities provided, "SaTScan is designed to:

- Perform geographical surveillance of disease, to detect spatial or space-time disease clusters, and to see if they are statistically significant

- Test whether a disease is randomly distributed over space, over time or over space and time

- Evaluate the statistical significance of disease cluster alarms

- Perform repeated time-periodic disease surveillance for early detection of disease outbreaks

SaTScan uses either a Poisson-based model, where the number of events in a geographical area is Poisson-distributed, according to a known underlying population at risk; a Bernoulli model, with 0/1 event data such as cases and controls; a space-time permutation model, using only case data; an ordinal model, for ordered categorical data; an exponential model for survival time data with or without censored variables; or a normal model for other types of continuous data. The data may be either aggregated at the census tract, zip code, county or other geographical level, or there may be unique coordinates for each observation. SaTScan adjusts for the underlying spatial inhomogeneity of a background population. It can also adjust for any number of categorical covariates provided by the user, as well as for temporal trends, known space-time clusters and missing data. It is possible to scan multiple data sets simultaneously to look for clusters that occur in one or more of them."

SaTScan has been applied in a very wide range of application areas, many of which are listed and viewable as downloadable articles. These cover many medical topics (notably cancer research and the study of infectious diseases), together with studies in fields ranging from criminology to demography, history, and accidental poisoning. Many of the papers can be selected from the SaTScan bibliography: http://www.satscan.org/references.html.

# 5.3 Grid-based Statistics

## 5.3.1 Overview of grid-based statistics

In the earlier discussion of local, focal, zonal and global analysis of grids (Section 4.6.1) we described how basic statistical measures may be obtained from grid datasets. These measures are similar to those applied to univariate attribute data, but may operate at various levels of spatial grouping of a single grid or may be applied across grids. As an example, many of Idrisi's statistics facilities, which are a rather mixed collection provided under a single menu item, are listed in Table 5-4.

*Table 5-4 Sample statistical tools for grid data — Idrisi*

| Facility | Description |
|---|---|
| Histo | Single grid — create histogram on $n$ classes from cell values. Classes may cover a spatial subset of the grid (e.g. by masking), have excluded values (e.g. 0, -999), have user defined boundaries etc. |
| Pattern | Single grid — generate selected Landscape metrics (e.g. richness, dominance, diversity, fragmentation) — as discussed in Section 5.3.4 |
| Center | Computes the weighted mean center of an input image (grid) where cells are regarded as point counts or weights (see also, Section 4.2.5.2). This function also generates the standard distance radius (see Section 4.5.3) for the point set, and the *Coefficient of Relative Dispersion* (CRD) which is the ratio of the standard distance measure to the radius of a circle having the same area as the study region, expressed as a percentage |
| Crosstab | The standard form of Crosstab compares two classified images, typically matching in spatial extent (e.g. time slices of the same region, images of adjacent zones of the same size and resolution), each with up to 127 classes. The principal output is a crosstabulation table, showing each class in image 1 as the rows, each class of image 2 as the columns, and counts of values in the table. Hence if image 1 contains 234 cells classified as A and image 2 contains 370 cells classified as A, then *at most* 234 cells will appear in row A column A of the output table. For common classification schemes (with square crosstabs) the diagonal of this crosstab matrix shows matching (e.g. unchanged) grid values. Potentially up to $MxN$ combinations of classes are possible (taking AB as different from BA). Class combinations may be mapped providing a spatial representation of the crosstabulation that is a form of spatial overlay (AND) operation. Two measures of association (correlation) between the images are provided: Cramer's V and the Kappa index (described in more detail in Section 5.3.2). The latter requires that the classification scheme for both images match |
| Quadrat | Quadrat (grid based) point pattern analysis. In this case each grid cell is regarded as a separate quadrat with cell values corresponding to point counts. Masking may be applied, and may well be desirable. Standard statistical measures are provided, with the variance/mean $(V/M)$ ratio being used as an indicator of spatial clustering. Values of $V/M$=1 may indicate a random pattern, assuming an underlying independent, homogeneous random process, whilst $V/M$<1 suggests more uniform patterns under this model. These interpretations are not valid if the process is not stationary. Note that the results are significantly affected by quadrat (grid cell) size and overall sampling area. If $D$=study area/number of points, ideal quadrat sizes are suggested as being in the range $[D,2D]$ |
| Regress Multireg Logisticreg | Provides regression modeling between multiple image files or attribute files, with or without image masking. Interpretation of image (grid) file regression may be difficult, since spatial autocorrelation within images is almost always strong (and may even have been generated by resampling or other interpolation methods), resulting in misleading values for degrees of freedom and associated statistical measures |

Within many GIS packages statistical tools that apply to grid datasets are grouped together with other, non-statistical facilities, or embedded within application-specific functionality, such as image classification. For example, in ArcGIS the majority of these tools are located in the Spatial Analyst (Neighborhood analysis and Multivariate analysis subsections); in ENVI statistics facilities are located under the Basic Tools|Statistics menu and the Basic Tools|Spatial Statistics menu, the latter providing global and local spatial autocorrelation measures of the types described in Section 5.5.3. In the following subsections we examine a number of these tools in greater detail.

## 5.3.2 Crosstabulated grid data, the Kappa Index and Cramer's V statistic

The creation and analysis of crosstabulated data is a familiar process in many fields and often the subject of simple statistical analysis, principally through the use of Chi-square tests. These are covered in all basic statistics texts, but for completeness we will include a brief description here, before showing how such methods may be applied to specifically spatial problems (see further, O'Brien, CATMOG 51, which describes both simple 2-way tables and more complex analysis applied to 2-way and multi-way, incomplete and asymmetric tables).

A common crosstab arrangement is a table of rows, representing distinct treatments (e.g. A=no soil improvement, B=organic manure treatment, and C=non-organic treatment) tabulated against responses (R) or outcomes (e.g. classified levels of crop production, or presence/absence of a given pest or disease; Table 5-5). Tabulated cell values are counts of events, e.g. the number of treated plots falling into each response category. This kind of 2-way presentation of data is often analyzed to identify whether the observed frequencies in each cell are significantly different from those that might be expected under the assumption that the outcomes are independent of the treatments — i.e. the row and column classifications are independent.

Let X be an $N$-row by $M$-column crosstabulation of frequency counts, $x_{ij}$, with overall total $\Sigma x_{ij}=x..=T$ (the subscript dots indicate that we have summed across all subscript values — see Table 5-5, sometimes summation subscripts use a + symbol rather than a dot, as in $x_{i+}$). Now let $p=p_i$. be the proportion of the overall total $T$ found in row $i$, and $q=p._j$ be the proportion of $T$ found in column $j$, then the expected frequency in cell $(i,j)$ under the assumption of independence, i.e. the treatments do not affect the responses, is simply $Tpq$.

*Table 5-5 Simple 2-way contingency table*

|   | R1 | R2 | R3 | Totals |
|---|---|---|---|---|
| A | $x_{11}$ | $x_{12}$ | $x_{13}$ | $x_1.$ |
| B | $x_{21}$ | $x_{22}$ | $x_{23}$ | $x_2.$ |
| C | $x_{31}$ | $x_{32}$ | $x_{33}$ | $x_3.$ |
| Totals | $x._1$ | $x._2$ | $x._3$ | $x..=T$ |

The difference between the observed ($O$) and expected ($E$) frequencies provides a measure of how close the observations are to a pattern that might arise assuming the rows and columns are independent. To remove the sign of these differences the values are squared, and then are standardized by dividing through by the expected frequencies, and finally summed. This provides an overall measure of differences that under a broad range of conditions follows the Chi-square ($\chi^2$) distribution with $(N-1)(M-1)$ degrees of freedom. The computation of the statistic is often shown in the form:

$$\chi^2 = \sum \frac{(O-E)^2}{E}, \text{ or}$$

$$\chi^2 = \sum_{i=1}^{N} \sum_{j=1}^{M} \frac{\left(x_{ij} - x_{i.}x_{.j}/T\right)^2}{x_{i.}x_{.j}/T}$$

If the computed value is large then it is less likely that the rows and columns are independent than if it is small. The probability that a particular computed value might have arisen by chance, given the size of the table (as represented by the degrees of freedom) can be obtained from tables of the Chi-square distribution or computed using built-in functions in many software packages, including Excel. Results in this analysis are also adversely affected by small counts and as a rule of thumb no more than 20% of cell values should be less than 5. In such cases it may be desirable to aggregate columns or rows (if such aggregation remains meaningful), or to adopt an alternative test procedure (e.g. simulation/permutation tests).

Within spatial analysis this approach to studying crosstabulated datasets has been utilized to provide an insight into classified spatial datasets — either matching pairs of images that are timeslices, or remote sensing imagery and ground truth datasets. The proportion, $p$, of cells in image 1 that match those in image 2, is the principal measure of interest. If $p$ is close to 1 then the two images are likely to be very similar. The detailed pattern of differences can be interpreted from the crosstabulation of the classes and/or by generating a new image in which either every classification combination is presented, or binary coding is used to indicate the location of matching/unchanged cells (0) and non-matching/changed cells (1).

The crosstabulation (or cross-classification procedure) described in Table 5-4, results in a potentially large table comprising rows representing the classification of the cells in image 1 and columns showing corresponding classifications in image 2. Cell entries are then counts of observed combinations for co-located cells. In the context of automated classification using training data this crosstab is sometimes referred to as a *confusion matrix* and the diagonal elements as a proportion of the row totals provide an indicator of the amount of confusion (100% would imply no confusion).

The cross-classification table may also be used to generate an index that describes the overall (global) similarity between the two images (a form of correlation measure). The two index values that are commonly computed (e.g. in

Idrisi, ENVI and similar software) are the Kappa Index of Agreement and Cramer's V index. Both have a range of values that typically range from 0 to 1, with 1 indicating perfect agreement and 0 indicating a pattern arising by chance. Negative values are possible and occur where the proportion of matching cells is low. Both index measures are calculated using procedures developed from the Chi-square analysis of standard contingency tables.

The Kappa Index of Agreement (also known as KIA), is of the form:

$$\kappa = \frac{O - E}{1 - E}$$

where $O$ is the observed accuracy or *proportion* of matching values (the matrix diagonal) and $E$ is the expected proportion of matches in this diagonal assuming a model of classification independence derived from the observed row and column totals. Hence $O$ is simply the sum of the diagonal elements divided by the overall total, $T$, and $E$ is computed in a similar manner to the expected values for a Chi-square calculation, with each element being summed. Thus $E$ is the sum for each diagonal cell of the row total times the column total divided by the overall total squared. If $x_{ij}$ represents the observed entry in row $i$, column $j$, then row totals are given by $x_{i.}$, column totals are given by $x_{.j}$ and the overall total is given by $T = x_{..}$. Thus the expected values are obtained from the row and column proportions, $p_{i.} = x_{i.}/T$ and $p_{.j} = x_{.j}/T$, giving $e_{ij} = p_{i.}{}^*p_{.j}$

The Kappa index may be disaggregated into class or "per category" components by examining the row-wise expectations:

$$\kappa_i = \frac{O_{ii} - E_{ii}}{O_{i.} - E_{ii}}$$

Cramer's V statistic is similar to the Kappa index and is derived directly from the Chi-square statistic computed for a given crosstabulation (or contingency table). As with the Kappa statistic its value is reported in the range [0,1], with the same interpretation, but in this instance the source table can be an $MxN$ array, thus the classification schemes do not have to be identical. The statistic is computed as:

$$V = \sqrt{\frac{1}{T} \frac{\chi^2}{\min\{(M-1),(N-1)\}}}$$

### 5.3.3 Quadrat analysis of grid datasets

As noted earlier, quadrat sampling is the term used to describe a procedure of sampling and recording point-based data within regularly shaped regions (typically a grid of square cells; see further, Thomas (1977, CATMOG 12). Since grid data are already in this form, it is possible to analyze grids where the contents of grid cells (or blocks of cells) are regarded as counts of point objects (Figure 5-15). In the example illustrated a 5x5 grid has been used to collect data on point events shown by the symbol x. The event distribution has then been coded as counts in the grid below. Simple statistics may then be computed, such as the mean number of points per cell/cell block (4 in this example), and the variance of this measure (4.59 in this case).

If the distribution of points across the set of grid cells is random, it can be modeled using the Poisson distribution. The Poisson distribution is applicable where events (points in our case) are independent, there are a large number of events (typically 100+), and the probability of an individual event occurring (e.g. a point falling in any particular location) is small and uniform. It is derived as an approximation to the Binomial distribution by applying these conditions.

As noted in Table 1-3, the Poisson distribution has the form:

$$f(x) = \frac{m^x}{x!} e^{-m} \; ; \; x=0,1,2,...$$

where $m$ is the mean and $x$ is the count of events. In our example the (sample) mean is 4, so the individual terms of the distribution may be computed (i.e. for $x=0,1,2,3...$) and used as

a set of "expected" values, under the null hypothesis that the observed frequency distribution is random. The set of $n$ observed frequency values may then be compared to the set of expected values using a simple Chi-square test, to obtain an estimate of the probability that the data reflects a random distribution of events.

*Figure 5-15 Quadrat counts*

| 3 | 2 | 6 | 2 | 2 |
|---|---|---|---|---|
| 2 | 4 | 3 | 7 | 3 |
| 2 | 6 | 6 | 9 | 4 |
| 5 | 6 | 3 | 5 | 5 |
| 3 | 7 | 3 | 2 | 0 |

For the example shown above a frequency analysis of the form shown in Table 5-6 may be drawn up. The *sum* row shows the total number of observations made (grid cells) and the value of the $\chi^2$ statistic. The degrees of freedom (DF) in this case are 11-1-1=9, because there are 11 frequency classes, the total count is known (-1DF), and the mean ($m$) has been estimated from the sample (-1DF). The 5% probability level from tables or computed value of the Chi-square distribution is $\chi^2_{0.05,9}$=16.9, thus a value of 9.3 is well within the expectation for a random pattern and thus we cannot reject the null hypothesis on the basis of this information.

*Table 5-6 Simple Chi-square frequency table computation*

| Freq | Obs, O | Exp, E | |O-E| | $|O\text{-}E|^2/E$ |
|------|--------|--------|-------|-------------|
| 0 | 1 | .5 | .5 | 0.64 |
| 1 | 0 | 1.8 | 1.8 | 1.83 |
| 2 | 6 | 3.7 | 2.3 | 1.49 |
| 3 | 6 | 4.9 | 1.1 | 0.25 |
| 4 | 2 | 4.9 | 2.9 | 1.7 |
| 5 | 3 | 3.9 | .9 | 0.21 |
| 6 | 4 | 2.6 | 1.4 | 0.75 |
| 7 | 2 | 1.5 | .5 | 0.18 |
| 8 | 0 | .7 | .7 | 0.74 |
| 9 | 1 | .3 | .7 | 1.35 |
| 10 | 0 | .1 | .1 | 0.13 |
| Sum | 25 | | | $\chi^2$=9.3 |

Aggregating rows to ensure most table cell counts are greater than 5 — e.g. by grouping frequencies into four classes (0,1), (2,3), (4,5) and (6+) — gives a $\chi^2$ statistic of 4.6 with 3 degrees of freedom, and $\chi^2_{0.05,2}$=6, confirming the previous result. This kind of test is supported within the spatstat software, although the authors point to an important weakness of the test as providing only an indication of whether or not the pattern appears to be drawn from an homogenous

Poisson process, rather than providing additional information (e.g. in what way does a pattern depart from the null hypothesis?). Furthermore, a close match of a sample to a Poisson frequency distribution does not, of itself, guarantee that the sample is truly random. Consider the case of a sample collected along a transect which has the following observed sequence of values (e.g. counts of a particular insect or plant in each 1 meter section of the transect):

0,1,1,2,2,2,2,3,3,3,3,3,4,4,4,4,4,5,5,5,5,6,6,6,7,7,8,9

This sequence has frequencies for classes 0,1,2, 3... etc of: 1,2,4,5,5,4,3,2,1,1 and these are the frequencies one would expect from a Poisson distribution with mean 4, as per Table 5-6. However, the data clearly shows a linear trend in observed values and thus departs strongly from a random pattern. Similar issues may arise in 2D samples in which bilinear or other trends exist (see, for example, Figure 5-27). The assumption in many analytical techniques is that the underlying probability of occurrence is homogeneously distributed across the sample region — if it can be shown that this is not the case, then simple models will give misleading results. Software such as spatstat does enable non-stationary Poisson process models, such as those with a trend or a variation in process intensity that depends upon a covariate such as soil conditions, to be fitted using maximum likelihood methods. Essentially a stationary process is one that is invariant under Euclidean translation.

The observed and expected frequency distributions can also be compared by computing the maximum absolute difference in their cumulative probability distributions and then applying the Kolmogorov-Smirnov (KS) test statistic. The KS procedure is in some respects a more powerful and flexible approach than the Chi-square test. Testing procedures of this type are rarely supported directly within GIS and related packages, other than specialized tools such as spatstat, where it is provided as the kstest() function. In this instance, the kstest() function may be applied to datasets divided on the basis of some covariate of interest, such as terrain slope. KS procedures are widely supported in statistical packages such as Minitab, SPSS and STATA and may be readily computed programmatically or by use of a generic tool such as Excel. Note that KS tests should really be reserved for expected distributions and covariates that are continuous as there may be difficulties in estimation of the appropriate mean value for the expected distribution and tied values can weaken its applicability.

### 5.3.4 Landscape Metrics

There are many software packages that provide methods for analyzing patterns observed in remote sensed image files and raster grids. Some of these focus on the process of classifying pixels or grid cells, in order to identify land-use and vegetation cover. A second and often related procedure is that of describing and analyzing the observed patterns. For example, it has been found that the quality of classification of forested regions can be considerably improved through the use of texture analysis (Zhang *et al.*, 2004), which may utilize measures of the kind described below or a range of other forms of surface variability analysis.

As we have seen in the preceding subsections, descriptive statistics may be simple summaries of the frequencies of particular classification values or categories, which are non-spatial attributes of the dataset, or they may provide spatial measures or *landscape metrics*. A substantial number of such metrics have been devised over the last 50 years, principally in the field of landscape ecology, and a number of software packages and toolkits developed to undertake such analysis. The most well-known package, Fragstats, provides much of the background for other packages, such as Fragstats for ArcView, Patch Analyst (which provides both vector and raster-based patch analysis). Pattern analysis facilities of this kind are also to be found in SAGA, SAM and PASSaGE. The TEXTURE set of image transform operators in Idrisi supports several such measures, and we start by using this facility to clarify the operation of some of these metrics. TEXTURE actually supports four separate sets of image texture analysis: variability; fractal analysis; class frequency; and edge analysis.

These analyses are typically performed on integer-valued image files only.

Figure 5-16 illustrates the range of measures provided for the first of the categories, variability. The input is a single image file and the output is again an image file, this time with each pixel representing the computed (i.e. transformed) value computed from the input image. Note that a kernel of pixels is used for each calculation, in this case selectable from 3x3, 5x5 or 7x7 pixel blocks. These operations are essentially pre-defined map algebra focal operations, as described in Section 4.6. The second category of texture analysis functions, fractal dimension analysis takes a single input image provides the source data and the output is a generated fractal dimension image based on estimated pixel dimension values using a 3x3 kernel. The fractal dimension is itself computed using the estimated slope (or reflectance value equivalent if a remotely-sensed image) over the kernel (see also, Section 6.7.1.16).

The various texture measures that are supported are as follows:

**Relative Richness:** $R=n/nmax*100$, where $n$=the number of different classes present in the kernel, $nmax$=maximum number of classes in entire image

**Diversity:** $H=-\Sigma(p*\ln(p))$, where $\Sigma$=the sum over all classes in the entire image, and $p$=proportion of each class in the kernel

**Dominance:** $D=Hmax-H$, where $H$=Diversity, $Hmax$=maximum diversity=$\ln(n)$ and $n$=number of different classes present in the kernel

**Fragmentation:** $F=(n-1)/(c-1)$ where $n$=number of different classes present in the kernel, $c$=number of cells considered (9, 25 or 49)

**NDC**=number of different classes in each 3 x 3, 5 x 5, or 7 x 7 neighborhood (ranges from 1-9, 1-25, 1-49)

**CVN**=number of cells different from the center cell in each 3x3, 5x5, or 7x7 neighborhood (ranges from 0-8, 0-24, 0-48)

**BCM**=number of different pairs in each 3x3, 5x5, or 7x7 neighborhood

*Figure 5-16 Texture analysis — variability*

The remaining two sets of texture analysis provided in Idrisi, *class frequency* and *edge analysis* are fairly self-explanatory. The class frequencies are computed for each pixel for a pre-specified class over a 3x3, 5x5 (quasi-octagonal) or 7x7 (quasi-octagonal) neighborhood and then mapped. For a given class, 40 say, most pixels will show a frequency of 0, some will show 1, 2... etc. up to the possible maximum of *nxn* where *n* is the kernel size. Edge analysis is effectively edge enhancement or filtering, as described in Section 4.6.2, i.e. operations applied using a kernel to every pixel, with one of 8 directional 3x3 filter kernels applied (derived from Pratt, 1991, and Jain, 1989), e.g. North filter:

row 1: 1  1  1
row 2: 1 -2  1
row 3: -1 -1 -1

Below, we provide summary details of both the non-spatial and spatial metrics based on an edited version of the Fragstats documentation (with their kind permission). As noted above, these metrics cover a wide range of measures, many of which are closely correlated, and only a subset of which are implemented in widely available software packages.

The common usage of the term "landscape metrics" refers exclusively to indices developed for categorical map patterns. Landscape metrics are algorithms that quantify specific spatial characteristics of patches, classes of patches, or entire landscape mosaics. A plethora of metrics has been developed to quantify categorical map patterns. These metrics fall into two general categories: those that quantify the composition of the map without reference to spatial attributes, and those that quantify the spatial configuration of the map, requiring spatial information for their calculation (McGarigal and Marks 1995, Gustafson 1998).

Although a large part of landscape pattern analysis deals with the identification of scale and intensity of pattern, landscape metrics focus on the characterization of the geometric and spatial properties of categorical map patterns represented at a particular scale (grain and extent). Thus, while it is important to recognize the variety of types of landscape patterns and goals of landscape pattern analysis, Fragstats focuses on landscape metrics as they are applied in landscape ecology... Landscape is not necessarily defined by its size; rather, it is defined by an interacting mosaic of patches relevant to the phenomenon under consideration (at any scale).

**P: Patch-level metrics** are defined for individual patches, and characterize the spatial character and context of patches. In most applications, patch metrics serve primarily as the computational basis for several of the landscape metrics, for example by averaging patch attributes across all patches in the class or landscape; the computed values for each individual patch may have little interpretive value.

**C: Class-level metrics** are integrated over all the patches of a given type (class). These may be integrated by simple averaging, or through some sort of weighted-averaging scheme to bias the estimate to reflect the greater contribution of large patches to the overall index. There are additional aggregate properties at the class level that result from the unique configuration of patches across the landscape.

**L: Landscape-level metrics** are integrated over all patch types or classes over the full extent of the data (i.e., the entire landscape). Like class metrics, these may be integrated by a simple or weighted averaging, or may reflect aggregate properties of the patch mosaic. In many applications, the primary interest is in the pattern (i.e., composition and configuration) of the entire landscape mosaic.

### 5.3.4.1 Non-spatial landscape metrics

Composition [of a grid map] is easily quantified and refers to features associated with the variety and abundance of patch types within the landscape, but without considering the spatial character, placement, or location of patches within the mosaic. Because composition requires integration over all patch types, composition metrics are only applicable at the landscape-level. There are many quantitative measures of landscape composition, including the proportion of the landscape in each patch type, patch richness, patch evenness, and patch diversity. Indeed, because of the many ways in which diversity can be measured, there are literally hundreds of possible ways to quantify landscape composition. Unfortunately, because diversity indices are derived from the indices used to summarize species diversity in community ecology, they suffer the same interpretative drawbacks. It is incumbent upon the investigator or manager to choose the formulation that best represents their concerns. The principal measures of composition are:

**Proportional Abundance** of each Class: One of the simplest and perhaps most useful pieces of information that can be derived is the proportion of each class relative to the entire map

**Richness:** Richness is simply the number of different patch types

**Evenness:** Evenness is the relative abundance of different patch types, typically emphasizing either relative dominance or its complement, equitability. There are many possible evenness (or dominance) measures corresponding to the many diversity measures. Evenness is usually reported as a function of the maximum diversity possible for a given richness. That is, evenness is given as 1 when the patch mosaic is perfectly diverse given the observed patch richness, and approaches 0 as evenness decreases. Evenness is sometimes reported as its complement, dominance, by subtracting the observed diversity from the maximum for a given richness. In this case, dominance approaches 0 for maximum equitability and increases >0 for higher dominance

**Diversity:** A composite measure of richness and evenness and can be computed in a variety of forms (e.g., Shannon and Weaver 1949, Simpson 1949), depending on the relative emphasis placed on these two components

### 5.3.4.2 Spatial landscape metrics

Spatial configuration [of a grid map] is much more difficult to quantify and refers to the spatial character and arrangement, position, or orientation of patches within the class or landscape. Some aspects of configuration, such as patch isolation or patch contagion, are measures of the placement of patch types relative to other patches, other patch types, or other features of interest. Other aspects of configuration, such as shape (see also, Section 4.2.8) and core area, are measures of the spatial character of the patches. There are many aspects of configuration and the literature is replete with methods and indices developed for representing them.

Configuration can be quantified in terms of the landscape unit itself (i.e., the patch). The spatial pattern being represented is the spatial character of the individual patches, even though the aggregation is across patches at the class or landscape level. The location of patches relative to each other is not explicitly represented. Metrics quantified in terms of the individual patches (e.g., mean patch size and shape) are spatially explicit at the level of the individual patch, not the class or landscape. Such metrics represent recognition that the ecological properties of a patch are influenced by the surrounding neighborhood (e.g., edge effects) and that the magnitude of these influences is affected by patch size and shape. These metrics simply quantify, for the class or landscape as a whole, some attribute of the statistical distribution (e.g., mean, max, variance) of the corresponding patch characteristic (e.g., size, shape). Indeed, any patch-level metric can be summarized in this manner at the class and landscape levels. Configuration also can be quantified in terms of the spatial relationship of patches and patch types (e.g., nearest-neighbor,

contagion). These metrics are spatially explicit at the class or landscape level because the relative location of individual patches within the patch mosaic is represented in some way. Such metrics represent recognition that ecological processes and organisms are affected by the overall configuration of patches and patch types within the broader patch mosaic.

A number of configuration metrics can be formulated either in terms of the individual patches or in terms of the whole class or landscape, depending on the emphasis sought. For example, perimeter-area fractal dimension is a measure of shape complexity (Mandelbrot 1982, Burrough 1986, Milne 1991) that can be computed for each patch and then averaged for the class or landscape, or it can be computed from the class or landscape as a whole by regressing the logarithm of patch perimeter on the logarithm of patch area. Similarly, core area can be computed for each patch and then represented as mean patch core area for the class or landscape, or it can be computed simply as total core area in the class or landscape. Obviously, one form can be derived from the other if the number of patches is known and so they are largely redundant; the choice of formulations is dependent upon user preference or the emphasis (patch or class/landscape) sought. The same is true for a number of other common landscape metrics. Typically, these metrics are spatially explicit at the patch level, not at the class or landscape level.

The principal aspects of configuration and a sample of representative metrics are:

**Patch size distribution and density:** The simplest measure of configuration is patch size, which represents a fundamental attribute of the spatial character of a patch. Most landscape metrics either directly incorporate patch size information or are affected by patch size. Patch size distribution can be summarized at the class and landscape levels in a variety of ways (e.g., mean, median, max, variance, etc.), or, alternatively, represented as patch density, which is simply the number of patches per unit area.

**Patch shape complexity:** Shape complexity relates to the geometry of patches--whether they tend to be simple and compact, or irregular and convoluted. Shape is an extremely difficult spatial attribute to capture in a metric because of the infinite number of possible patch shapes. Hence, shape metrics generally index overall shape complexity rather than attempt to assign a value to each unique shape. The most common measures of shape complexity are based on the relative amount of perimeter per unit area, usually indexed in terms of a perimeter-to-area ratio, or as a fractal dimension, and often standardized to a simple Euclidean shape (e.g., circle or square). The interpretation varies among the various shape metrics, but in general, higher values mean greater shape complexity or greater departure from simple Euclidean geometry. Other methods have been proposed: radius of gyration (Pickover 1990); contiguity (LaGro 1991); linearity index (Gustafson and Parker 1992); and elongation and deformity indices (Baskent and Jordan 1995), but these have not yet become widely used (Gustafson 1998).

**Core Area:** Core area represents the interior area of patches after a user-specified edge buffer is eliminated. The core area is the area unaffected by the edges of the patch. This "edge effect" distance is defined by the user to be relevant to the phenomenon under consideration and can either be treated as fixed or adjusted for each unique edge type. Core area integrates patch size, shape, and edge effect distance into a single measure. All other things equal, smaller patches with greater shape complexity have less core area. Most of the metrics associated with size distribution (e.g., mean patch size and variability) can be formulated in terms of core area.

**Isolation/Proximity:** Isolation or proximity refers to the tendency for patches to be relatively isolated in space (i.e., distant) from other patches of the same or similar (ecologically friendly) class. Because the notion of "isolation" is vague, there are many possible measures depending on how distance is defined and how patches of the same class

and those of other classes are treated. If $d_{ij}$ is the nearest-neighbor distance from patch $i$ to another patch $j$ of the same type, then the average isolation of patches can be summarized simply as the mean nearest-neighbor distance over all patches. Alternatively, isolation can be formulated in terms of both the size and proximity of neighboring patches within a local neighborhood around each patch using the isolation index of Whitcomb et al. (1981) or proximity index of Gustafson and Parker (1992), where the neighborhood size is specified by the user and presumably scaled to the ecological process under consideration. The original proximity index was formulated to consider only patches of the same class within the specified neighborhood. This binary representation of the landscape reflects an island biogeographic perspective on landscape pattern. Alternatively, this metric can be formulated to consider the contributions of all patch types to the isolation of the focal patch, reflecting a landscape mosaic perspective on landscape patterns.

**Contrast:** Contrast refers to the relative difference among patch types. For example, mature forest next to younger forest might have a lower-contrast edge than mature forest adjacent to open field, depending on how the notion of contrast is defined. This can be computed as a contrast-weighted edge density, where each type of edge (i.e., between each pair of patch types) is assigned a contrast weight. Alternatively, this can be computed as a neighborhood contrast index, where the mean contrast between the focal patch and all patches within a user-specified neighborhood is computed based on assigned contrast weights. Relative to the focal patch, if patch types with high contrast lead to greater isolation of the focal patch, as is often the case, then contrast will be inversely related to isolation (at least for those isolation measures that consider all patch types).

**Dispersion:** Dispersion refers to the tendency for patches to be regularly or contagiously distributed (i.e., clumped) with respect to each other. There are many dispersion indices developed for the assessment of spatial point patterns, some of which have been applied to categorical maps. A common approach is based on nearest-neighbor distances between patches of the same type. Often this is computed in terms of the relative variability in nearest-neighbor distances among patches; for example, based on the ratio of the variance to mean nearest-neighbor distance. Here, if the variance is greater than the mean, then the patches are more clumped in distribution than random, and if the variance is less than the mean, then the patches are more uniformly distributed. This index can be averaged over all patch types to yield an average index of dispersion for the landscape. [*Guide editors note: this class of measure is not recommended as it is dimensionally inconsistent — V/M ratios are appropriate for count-based or quadrat data but not for distance-based measures*]. Alternative indices of dispersion based on nearest-neighbor distances can be computed, such as the familiar Clark and Evans (1954) index.

**Contagion and Interspersion:** Contagion refers to the tendency of patch types to be spatially aggregated; that is, to occur in large, aggregated or "contagious" distributions. Contagion ignores patches per se and measures the extent to which cells of similar class are aggregated. Interspersion, on the other hand, refers to the intermixing of patches of different types and is based entirely on patch (as opposed to cell) adjacencies. There are several different approaches for measuring contagion and interspersion. One popular index that subsumes both dispersion and interspersion is the contagion index based on the probability of finding a cell of type $i$ next to a cell of type $j$ (Li and Reynolds 1993). This index increases in value as a landscape is dominated by a few large (i.e., contiguous) patches and decreases in value with increasing subdivision and interspersion of patch types. This index summarizes the aggregation of all classes and thereby provides a measure of overall clumpiness of the landscape. McGarigal and Marks (1995) suggest a complementary interspersion/juxtaposition index that increases in value as patches tend to be more evenly interspersed in a "salt and pepper" mixture. These and other metrics are generated from the matrix of pairwise adjacencies between all patch types, where the elements of the matrix are the proportions of edges in each pairwise type. There are alternative methods for calculating class-specific contagion using fractal geometry (Gardner and O'Neill 1991). Lacunarity is an especially promising method borrowed from fractal geometry by which contagion can be characterized across a range of spatial scales (Plotnick *et al.* 1993 and 1996, Dale 2000). The technique involves using a moving window and is concerned with the frequency with which one encounters the focal class in a window of different sizes. A log-log plot of lacunarity against window size expresses the contagion of the map, or its tendency to aggregate into discrete patches, across a range of spatial scales.

**Subdivision:** Subdivision refers to the degree to which a patch type is broken up (i.e., subdivided) into separate patches (i.e., fragments), not the size (per se), shape, relative location, or spatial arrangement of those patches. Because these latter attributes are usually affected by subdivision, it is difficult to isolate subdivision as an independent component. Subdivision can be evaluated using a variety of metrics already discussed; for example, the number, density, and average size of patches and the degree of contagion all indirectly evaluate subdivision. However, a suite of metrics derived from the cumulative distribution of patch sizes provide alternative and more explicit measures of subdivision (Jaeger 2000). When applied at the class level, these metrics can be used to measure the degree of fragmentation of the focal patch type. Applied at the landscape level, these metrics connote the graininess of the landscape; i.e., the tendency of the landscape to exhibit a fine- versus coarse-grain texture. A fine-grain landscape is characterized by many small patches (highly subdivided); whereas, a coarse-grain landscape is characterized by fewer large patches.

**Connectivity:** Connectivity generally refers to the functional connections among patches. What constitutes a "functional connection" between patches clearly depends on the application or process of interest; patches that are connected for bird dispersal might not be connected for salamanders, seed dispersal, fire spread, or hydrologic flow. Connections might be based on strict adjacency (touching), some threshold distance, some decreasing function of distance that reflects the probability of connection at a given distance, or a resistance-weighted distance function. Then various indices of overall connectedness can be derived based on the pairwise connections between patches. For example, one such index, connectance, can be defined on the number of functional joinings, where each pair of patches is either connected or not. Alternatively, from percolation theory, connectedness can be inferred from patch density or be given as a binary response, indicating whether or not a spanning cluster or percolating cluster exists; i.e., a connection of patches of the same class that spans across the entire landscape (Gardner *et al.*, 1987). Connectedness can also be defined in terms of correlation length for a raster map comprised of patches defined as clusters of connected cells. Correlation length is based on the average extensiveness of connected cells. A map's correlation length is interpreted as the average distance one might traverse the map, on average, from a random starting point and moving in a random direction, i.e., it is the expected traversibility of the map (Keitt *et al.*, 1997).

# 5.4 Point Sets and Distance Statistics

The aggregation of point-based observations into quadrats results in a substantial loss of information regarding the underlying distribution of events. The procedure is also highly susceptible to issues relating to the shape, size, orientation and contiguity of the quadrats. By retaining the specific locations of the original points, assuming that this information is available, more detailed analysis can be undertaken. Typically this form of spatial analysis examines the variations in *density* or *intensity* of observed points over the study region, and the distances between point pairs — either between events, or between events and random or control points. Distances are typically computed as Euclidean, but spherical distances may also be provided by some packages. Network-based analyses are rarely if ever provided (the SANET software being an important exception), other than indirectly through the use of the $L_1$ metric or other $L_p$-type measure (e.g. such metrics are supported in Crimestat and LOLA).

For analysis of this type of data, events should be distinct objects (possibly weighted) and not the result of computations (e.g. zone or point set centroids). All events in a meaningful delimited study region (incorporating areas in which events *are* observed and also *are not* observed) are normally included in an analysis — analysis of subsets of the data (samples) should be undertaken with caution. If point events include associated attribute data, such as the type of tree, or the time of an event, they are said to be *marked*. Several attributes may be associated with each point, in which case the marking is multivariate. Analyses of the relationship between a given point pattern and a separate, usually continuous *explanatory* variable defined over the same region, may yield an improved understanding of the pattern and processes at work. Such explanatory variables are usually described as *covariates*.

For more complete discussions of basic point pattern analysis see O'Sullivan and Unwin (2003, Ch.4), Mitchell (2005, Ch.3) and the free and extensive Crimestat Manual (most chapters). More specialized books covering this subject area include Cressie (1993), Diggle (1983) and Bailey and Gatrell (1995). With the increasing importance of the R-Spatial programme, many tools and techniques for spatial point pattern analysis have been incorporated into the R-Spatial library, notably within spatstat (see also, www.spatstat.org and the reference article by the authors, Baddeley and Turner, 2005). Spatsat supports five main functional areas:

- Creation, manipulation and plotting of point patterns

- Exploratory data analysis, including density mapping

- Simulation of point processes

- Parametric model fitting, and

- Hypothesis tests, residual plots and diagnostics

In addition to the 500-page manual on spatstat, an excellent 200 page coursenotes document based on spatstat has been developed by the authors which is downloadable from the CSIRO website: http://www.csiro.au. In the sections that follow, we can only touch upon some of the more common problems and issues involved in point-pattern analysis – interested researchers are strongly recommended to work through the literature cited, particularly the Crimestat and spatstat documents, for a broader understanding of the topic and the tools and techniques now available.

## 5.4.1 Basic distance-derived statistics

With point data a range of core global statistics can be computed. Commonly produced measures of central tendency and spread include: identification of the location of the center of the point set (typically arithmetic mean, but optionally harmonic and geometric mean centers); identification of the median center (with or without weights and constraints); and standard distance, weighted standard distance and standard deviational ellipses. Each of these measures has been described earlier in Sections 4.2.5 and 4.5.3. A further measure, provided within some packages, is a table of all pairs of inter-point distances. This matrix is typically symmetric and completely specifies the arrangement of points — i.e. given this distance matrix the point set can be re-constructed, subject only to simple Euclidean transformations (translation, rotation and reflection).

Note that here we are describing Euclidean distance matrices — many other forms of distance matrix are possible and useful, although in general will not conform to the invariance characteristics of a Euclidean distance matrix. Examples including distance matrices that are computed using alternative metrics, such as squared Euclidean or Manhattan distance; non-symmetric distances matrices (e.g. based on transport infrastructure, routing and timetables); and proximity-based measures, such as similarity of genetic make-up or biomass. In cases where a matching distance matrix and proximity matrix are both available, Mantel tests (see Section 5.4.5) may be used to investigate the correlation between the two sets of measurements.

## 5.4.2 Nearest neighbor methods

In many disciplines the distance between events (e.g. trees, cases of a disease, bird's nests) reflects an underlying process, for example competition for food or nutrients, birth and dispersal processes, infection or contagion. Particular attention is therefore focused on the nearest event to a particular other event or point of interest. This nearest event is known as the nearest neighbor (NN) or first-order nearest neighbor. The second nearest event is then the second-order nearest neighbor and so forth to $k^{th}$-order NN. A global (whole area) measure of a point pattern is the mean distance to the $k^{th}$-order nearest neighbor, and more typically for $k=1$.

The steps involved in computing this measure are as follows:

- Input coordinates of all points $\{x_i, y_i\}$

- Compute the (symmetric) distances matrix **D** between every pair of points

- For each $i$, sort the distances to identify the $1^{st}$, $2^{nd}$,...$k^{th}$ nearest values

- Compute the mean of the observed $1^{st}$, $2^{nd}$, ...$k^{th}$ nearest values

- Compare this mean with the expected mean under Complete Spatial Randomness (CSR or Poisson) model

To undertake the last step in this sequence the expected mean under the CSR hypothesis is needed. The distribution of NN distances can be obtained from the terms of the Poisson distribution (see Section 1.4.2.6) using the information in Figure 5-17. In this we envisage the point under consideration as lying at the center of a circle, radius $r$.

Assume that the overall density of points in the study region is a constant value, $m$. Then the expected number in a circle of radius $r$ is simply $m\pi r^2$, which is where this term comes from in the expressions shown below. The model examines the probability that there are no other points within this circle of radius $r$, $p(r,0)$, but there is exactly one, $p(dr,1)$, in the thin yellow annular region shown, i.e. in the interval between $r$ and $r+dr$ from the original point. We can now use this information, as $dr \to 0$ to obtain the distribution of nearest neighbor distances under CSR, and hence the moments of this distribution, including the mean and variance.

*Figure 5-17 Nearest Neighbor distribution*

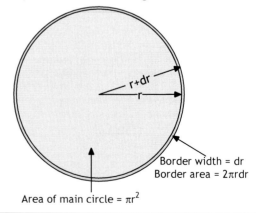

Area of main circle = $\pi r^2$

Border width = dr
Border area = $2\pi r dr$

The steps for deriving the first-order NN distribution are shown below, together with the first three central moments:

$$p(r,0) = (m\pi r^2)^0 e^{-(m\pi r^2)} / 0! = e^{-(m\pi r^2)}$$

$$p(dr,1) = (m2\pi rdr)^1 e^{-(m2\pi rdr)} / 1! \approx m2\pi rdr$$

$$p(r) = p(r,0).p(dr,1) = 2m\pi re^{-(m\pi r^2)}dr$$

Let $x=m\pi r^2$ then $dx=2m\pi rdr$ and $r=(x/m\pi)^{1/2}$, hence $p(r)=e^{-x}dr$, thus the mean, $\mu$, may be obtained as the first moment, $\mu_1$ or $\mu$, by integration:

$$\mu = \int_0^\infty re^{-x}dx = \frac{1}{\sqrt{m\pi}}\int_0^\infty x^{1/2}e^{-x}dx$$

$$\mu = \frac{1}{\sqrt{m\pi}}\Gamma(3/2) = \frac{1}{2\sqrt{m}}$$

where $\Gamma()$ is the Gamma function (see Section 1.4.2.8). The variance, $\mu_2$ or $\sigma^2$, can be obtained in a similar manner, giving the result:

$$\mu_2 = \frac{(4-\pi)}{4\pi m}$$

The mean distance to NN under CSR is thus a simple function of the density, $m$. For a uniform (completely dispersed) distribution of points the expected mean distance to NN is simply double the CSR value. Assuming that the density can be estimated reliably (a significant issue in itself) then a simple index of global spatial randomness can be obtained by taking the ratio of the observed mean, distance to NN, $\bar{r}_o$, divided by the expected mean distance, $\mu$ or $\bar{r}_e$ :

$$R = \bar{r}_o / \bar{r}_e$$

Values of $R<1$ suggest greater clustering (closer spacing) than would be expected under CSR, whilst values of $R>1$ suggest a more even distribution. The significance of the observed value can be tested, assuming we have a fairly large number of points, e.g. $n>100$. Using the z-transform (based on the standard error

rather than the variance, as we are comparing mean values), we have:

$$z = (\bar{r}_o - \bar{r}_e)/\sigma_e \sim N(0,1), \text{ where}$$

$$\sigma_e = \mu_2/\sqrt{n} = 0.261358/\sqrt{mn}$$

Programs such as Crimestat provide index values and significance estimates, whilst ArcGIS Spatial Statistics toolbox simply provides index information. The general expression for the crude moments, $\mu_\alpha$, $\alpha =1,2,3...$, of the $k^{th}$-order nearest neighbor distribution in $D$-dimensions ($D=1,2,3..$) with population density, $m$, is:

$$\mu_\alpha(_D r_k) = \frac{1}{(k-1)!(m\Phi)^{\alpha/D}}\Gamma\left(\frac{kD+\alpha}{D}\right)$$

where $\Phi$ is the volume of a unit hypersphere:

$$\Phi = \frac{\pi^{D/2}}{\Gamma\left(\frac{D}{2}+1\right)},$$

and $\Gamma(x)$ is the standard Gamma function. In 2D this expression for the mean ($\alpha=1$, $D=2$) simplifies to:

$$\mu_k = \frac{\left(k-\frac{1}{2}\right)!}{(k-1)!\sqrt{m\pi}}$$

Hence for $k=1$ this simplifies further to:

$$\mu_1 = \frac{(1/2)!}{\sqrt{m\pi}} = \frac{1}{2\sqrt{m}}, \text{ as above}$$

A number of comments about this form of basic point-pattern analysis need to be made. The first is that the statistic depends heavily on the parameter, $m$. This is usually estimated by dividing the study area, $A$, by the number of points, $N$, i.e. $m=A/N$. However, deciding on the appropriate study area may alter the results substantially (Table 5-7 and Figure 4-78). In this example three alternative region boundaries have been selected: SDC — standard distance circle; 2SDE — an ellipse of size 2 standard deviations; and the MBR of the point set — Minimum Bounding Rectangle. These three regions result in substantially different ratio values and z-scores for the point set, primarily as a result of their different areal extents.

**Table 5-7 NN Statistics and study area size**

| Region | SDC | 2SDE | MBR |
|--------|-------|-------|-------|
| R-index | 1.798 | 0.97 | 1.337 |
| Z | 7.163 | 0.267 | 3.026 |
| Area, km² | 176 | 605 | 318 |

One solution to this problem is to be very careful about the boundary specification, ideally using a user-defined polygon that corresponds to a meaningful boundary (e.g. a physical habitat boundary), or possibly the convex hull of the point set plus a buffer zone (see below). Most available software does not support such boundary specification, although add-ins have been developed to facilitate this kind of region definition.

A related problem to that of region definition is that of edge-related errors (boundary effects). If the NN to a selected event is actually outside the study region the apparent NN found will be further away than the true value, leading to over-estimation of mean distances (see, for example, Figure 4-30). This problem is most severe with low numbers of points and higher order NN analyses. It can be minimized by careful selection of the study boundary, the application of edge correction factors (e.g. as provided within Crimestat and spatstat), by applying a boundary guard zone (e.g. a inner or outer buffer), by remapping the space onto a torus (e.g. so each of four MBR edges are treated as if they wrap onto the opposite pair) and lastly, by applying NN analysis only where the number of events is quite large and the NN order of analysis is not too high. If there are very good reasons to assume that the event distribution is truly random with uniform density over a particular study region, then the formula for the mean distance to NN can be inverted to obtain an estimate of the point density, $m$:

$$\mu = \frac{1}{2\sqrt{m}}, \text{ hence } m = \frac{1}{4\mu^2} \approx \frac{1}{4\bar{r}_o^2}$$

First-order NN analysis provides a simple global approach to point pattern analysis, but is of limited use for most real-world problems. Frequently real or apparent clustering is observed, and we may wish to consider questions such as:

- Is the observed clustering due to natural background variation in the population from which the events arise?

- Over what spatial scales does clustering occur?

- Are clusters a reflection of regional variations in underlying variables?

- Are clusters associated with some feature of interest, such as a refinery, waste disposal site or nuclear plant?

- Are clusters simply spatial or are they spatio-temporal?

These questions demand tools that are more exploratory in nature rather than strictly descriptive. Many tools have been developed to assist with answering such questions. The simplest, perhaps, is to plot the value of the $k^{th}$ order NN index against the order level, $k$. This option is supported with the Crimestat package, amongst others. A rather better approach (making greater use of the underlying data, particularly with larger point sets) is to examine the observed *frequency distribution* of nearest neighbor distances. This can be achieved by dividing the observed nearest neighbor distances into evenly spaced distance bands, $0\text{-}d_1$, $d_1\text{-}d_2$, $d_2\text{-}...$ and then comparing these frequencies (expressed as proportions of the total) to the expected distribution under CSR. Comparison is usually carried out on the cumulative probability distribution, $G(r)$, which may be obtained by integration of the expression for $p(r)$ above:

$$G(r) = \int_0^r m2\pi r e^{-m\pi r^2}\, dr = 1 - e^{-m\pi r^2}$$

Typically both the observed and expected cumulative distributions are plotted and visually compared. A variation on this arrangement is to select random points in the study area and compute the distance from these to the nearest event. The observed cumulative distribution in this case is denoted $F(r)$, or commonly with a ^ (hat) symbol above the $F$ to indicate that it is an estimate based on the observed data (sometimes referred to as Fhat). It has an expected cumulative distribution as per $G(r)$. However, if the sample pattern is more clustered than random the observed $F(r)$ plot will differ from the observed $G(r)$ plot, rising far more slowly. Support for $F(r)$ and $G(r)$ computation and associated Monte Carlo simulation (see below) is not provided within most GIS and related packages, but it is provided in the SPLANCS package (S-Plus and R-Plus implementations — FHAT and GHAT functions) and $G(r)$ is provided within the spatstat package. It is also relatively straightforward to generate these functions programmatically.

In principle, a measure of the difference between the observed and expected cumulative distributions can be computed (e.g. the Kolmogorov-Smirnov test statistic), and its significance determined. However, the set of nearest neighbor distance does not represent a set of independent samples — almost by definition NN distances are non-independent and frequently are reflexive — i.e. the NN of event $A$ is event $B$ and the NN of event $B$ is event $A$. Even under CSR such reflexivity occurs for over 62% of first order neighbors. For these and related reasons (e.g. edge effects) significance testing involves Monte Carlo simulation. For example, with $N$ observed events in a study area $A$, one can simulate a set of $N$ purely random events within the same region and compute the cumulative distribution for this set. The maximum absolute difference between the simulated cumulative distribution and the theoretical cumulative distribution can then be calculated and the value recorded. The process in then repeated a large number of times (e.g. $T$=999 times). Let $X$ be the number of times the recorded difference was larger than that between the observed pattern and

the expected cumulative distribution. Then $p=(1+X)/(1+T)$ is the estimated probability of observing a difference of the magnitude found. Thus if $X$=99 and $T$=999 we would have $p$=0.1 or 10%.

### 5.4.3 Pairwise distances

A similar and in many ways more powerful approach, known as Ripley's K (or L) function, is supported within several packages, including Crimestat, SPLANCS and spatstat. Ripley's procedure utilizes a larger set of event-event distances, not just nearest neighbor distances.

*Figure 5-18 Ripley's K function computation*

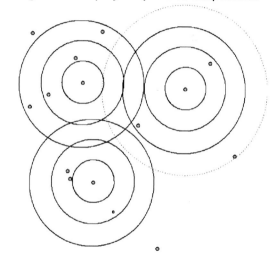

It operates as follows (see Figure 5-18):

- Construct a circle, radius $d$, around each point (event), $i$ ($d$ rather than $r$ is generally used for the circle radius in this technique)

- Count the number of other events, labeled $j$, that fall inside this circle

- Repeat these first two stages for all points $i$, and then sum the results

These steps equate to computing the sum:

$$K(d) = \frac{A}{N} \sum_i \sum_j \frac{I(d_{ij})}{N}, i \neq j$$

where $I(d_{ij})=1$ if the distance, $d_{ij}$, from $i$ to $j$ is less then $d$ otherwise $I(d_{ij})=0$

- Increment $d$ by a small fixed amount (e.g. $R/100$, where $R$ is the radius of a circle of area equal to the study area, $A$)

- Repeat the computation, giving values of K($d$) for a set of distances, $d$

The function K($d$) can then be plotted against distance, $d$, in a manner similar to that described in Section 6.7 for correlograms and variograms. The graph of the (transformed) K($d$) function provides an excellent insight into localized clustering, with characteristic graphs reflecting particular observed patterns. Computation of (the transformed) K($d$) function for a mapped dataset is supported in both SPLANCS, spatstat, and Crimestat and in all cases Monte Carlo simulation of confidence envelopes is provided.

As noted earlier, under CSR the expected number of events within a circle of radius $r$ or $d$ is simply the event density (sometimes referred to as the *intensity*), $m$, times the circle area. With $m$ estimated as the overall number of events divided by the study area, $N/A$, we have

$$E(\# < d) = \frac{N}{A}\pi d^2$$

The observed K($d$) function minus the expected value above has an expected value of L($d$)=0 for a given $d$. L($d$) measures the difference between the observed pattern and that expected under CSR. It is generally computed and plotted with $d$ subtracted from the expectation:

$$L(d) = \sqrt{\frac{K(d)}{\pi}} - d$$

If the component $d$ is not subtracted (as per Ripley's original formulation of this method) then the L($d$) plot against $d$ for a truly random distribution will be a line at 45 degrees (i.e. L($d$)=$d$ whereas with $d$ subtracted it will be approximately 0 for all $d$. This transformed expression is the form in which the $K$-statistic

is analyzed within Crimestat. The sampling distribution of L($d$) is unknown, but may be approximated by Monte Carlo simulation, as described earlier. Crimestat produces its simulations based on a rectangular region of area $A$ and shape matching the MBR, whilst SPLANCS utilizes a user-specified polygon, which is more satisfactory in most cases. Figure 5-19 shows the L($d$) plot for the lung cancer point set shown in Figure 5-21 (998 observations). The envelope shown provides the maximum and minimum L($d$) curves generated from 300 simulation runs. The observed plot falls outside this envelope over shorter distances, confirming the visually observable short-range clustering patterns. As $d$ is incremented the behavior of the L($d$) statistic becomes increasingly subject to border effects. Ideally the number of points utilized should be large (well in excess of 100 if possible) and where necessary edge correction procedures should be adopted. Simple edge correction can be implemented by weighting circular regions that lie partially outside the study boundary by the proportion lying within the study region.

The ideas behind the production of the standard K($d$) statistic and associated Monte Carlo simulations can be used to provide additional measures that are often more useful. For example, instead of comparing the observed pattern to CSR, alternative models could be examined. SPLANCS and spatstat, for example, support comparison with Poisson Cluster Processes (PCP) rather than a simple Poisson (CSR) process. PCP is similar to a simple Poisson process in that it starts with a random point set. These are regarded as "parents". Each parent then produces a random number of offspring, and these are located at random around the parent according to a bivariate distribution function, $g(x,y)$, for example a circular Normal with variance (spread), $\sigma^2$:

$$g(x,y) = \frac{1}{k}e^{-(x^2+y^2)/k}, \text{ where } k = 2\pi\sigma^2$$

The parents are then removed from the set and the PCP consists of the set of all offspring (Figure 5-20).

*Figure 5-19 Ripley K function, shown as transformed L function plot*

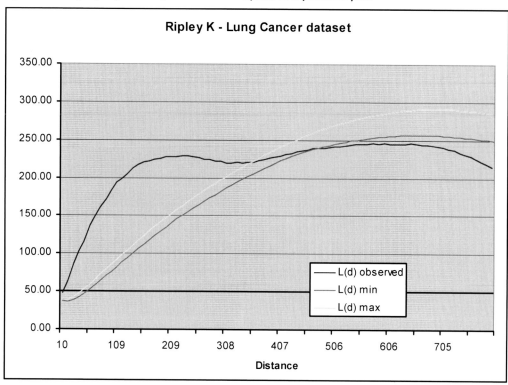

**Ripley K - Lung Cancer dataset**

SPLANCS implements this kind of model with three parameters: RHO: intensity (density parameter, $\rho$) of the parent process; M: the average number of offspring per parent; and S2: the variance of location of offspring relative to their parent (the $\sigma^2$ value in the expression above). By generating many PCP simulations for a given study region, an alternative probability envelope can be computed and plotted against the observed K- or L-function. There are many possible Poisson Cluster Processes; spatstat for example, implements the PCP process described above, which it refers to as a *Thomas process*. Other PCP processes supported in spatstat include: the Matérn PCP, in which $g(x,y)$ is defined as a uniform disc of radius r around each parent; the *Gauss-Poisson* PCP in which each cluster is a single point or pair of points; and a very general PCP known as the *Neyman-Scott* process, of which the Thomas process is a specific instance.

*Figure 5-20 Thomas Poisson Cluster Process (20 clusters, SD=0.03, mean=5)*

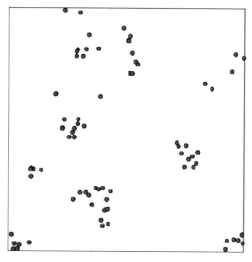

*Source: Simulation generated using spatstat*

A second important variant of the K(d) function involves treatment of two or more point (event) patterns within the same region. For example, one set of points might represent disease cases and a second set might be matched cases (controls) selected at random from the background population. Similar procedures may be used for spatio-temporal analysis, for example comparing crime patterns or disease incidence over time. If both datasets exhibit similar clustering we would expect the plots for both to be similar, or the difference between the computed functions, $D=K_1(d)-K_2(d)$, to be approximately zero for all d. Where background data are only available at an aggregated level (e.g. census Output Areas), it may be acceptable to assign the second set of points to the OA centroids together with a weighting factor reflecting the zone population. Crimestat supports such weighting as an option in order to assist in studies with background variation.

Another variant of the K(d) function, supported within SPLANCS and in SANET for a network-based variant, is the bivariate model (or Cross-K function). With the Cross-K function the relationship between two separate point patterns is being examined. For example, in an ecological study this might involve examining collaborative or competitive behavior between two species, or an analysis of infected trees and the "at risk" population. In this instance the K(d) function measures the number of events in set B that lie within distance d of events A. The SPLANCS function K12Hat supports this model together with supporting simulation functions to provide an estimated probability envelope for the function. A network-based equivalent, supported within the SANET software, might be used to examine the relationship between reported crime incidents and the location of railway stations (see Okabe et al., 2006a, 2006b, and Okabe and Satoh, 2008).

Readers may have noticed the similarity between the procedures involved in generating Ripley's K, and the generation of kernel density maps (Section 4.3.4.1). The latter involves assigning a proportion of each event or point to a circular neighborhood, and then summing and normalizing the weighted surface at grid intersection points. This provides a continuous density surface rather than a linear model, and can be used to highlight local clustering. However, with case/control data or case/background variation data, separate surfaces may be computed for each dataset and then these may be combined, e.g. by taking the difference or the ratio of the case surface/control surface (for densities greater than some minimum value) to provide a comparison surface. Values of 1 on the ratio surface represent matching densities, whilst values greater than 1 represent locations where the cases occur in higher densities than the controls or background data.

As noted earlier, the majority of these distance-based statistics are computed using the Euclidean or similar analytical metrics. Where the observations lie on a network, for example an urban street network, it is often preferable to perform computations using a metric determined from the network, typically using shortest path calculations (see also, Figure 5-5). Network-based statistical techniques implemented within the SANET package (see Okabe et al. 2006a, 2006b for more details) include: nearest neighbor analysis; conditional nearest neighbor analysis (in which the location of a related point set is incorporated into the model, see Okabe and Miki, 1984); Ripley's K-function; and Ripley's Cross-K function. If the observed points are not georeferenced to network nodes they can be assigned by SANET as additional nodes placed on the closest network link and then network variants of the statistical methods may be run. In these models distances are computed using shortest paths (which may be regarded as a reasonable behavioral assumption or approximation) and probability distributions (mean values and probability envelopes) are computed by Monte Carlo simulation.

It is worth concluding this subsection with some general observations (cautionary notes) regarding point pattern analysis:

- The classical statistical model of CSR is inappropriate for many spatial datasets, but does provide a starting point for analysis and simulations in many instances

- A close examination of the source data is always advisable, checking questions such as: how the data were collected; how locations and attributes were recorded; when data were recorded; what data (e.g. true or surrogate) information is represented; what overall measurement error is associated with the data; etc. Examining the underlying dataset for duplicates or near-duplicates is often an importance exercise

- Multiple analytical approaches, including visualization techniques (1D, 2D, 3D) are advisable since initial impressions and single approaches may be misleading. Density (intensity) modeling and mapping are often useful exploratory techniques that aid understanding of the patterns observed

- The variables selectable in analyzing point patterns (e.g. sample region, weights, order neighbor, maximum distance, clustering model, kernel function and bandwidth etc.) can yield very different results depending on the values and models chosen

- Borders, area definitions, metrics, background variation, temporal variation and non-spatial data issues are of major significance in describing and modeling point patterns

- Analysis of rare events presents particular problems — the small numbers involved may result in very low densities of events in large parts of a study region, if only by chance. Calculations based on zone counts are particularly subject to extremes and problems computing ratios

- Analysis should be seen as exploratory, and a part of an overall in-depth analysis process

- Analyses of this kind will not provide meaningful cause-effect or process-realization models — in general pattern analysis tells us very little about process, although it may enable us to exclude

certain processes from consideration. Many processes can result in the same or similar observed patterns, and different patterns can generate the same or very similar statistical measures, such as K(d) functions

- Model fitting is often a challenging process, although recent toolsets make this process a great deal easier than in the past. Examination of the goodness of fit and sophisticated residuals analysis now form an important part of this type of spatial analysis

### 5.4.4  Hot spot and cluster analysis

Identifying that clustering exists in spatial and spatio-temporal datasets does not provide a detailed picture of the nature and pattern of clustering. It is frequently helpful to apply simple hot-spot (and cold spot) identification techniques to such datasets. For example, Figure 5-21 shows the location of almost 1000 recorded lung cancer cases in part of Lancashire, UK, over the period 1974-83.

*Figure 5-21 Lung cancer incidence data*

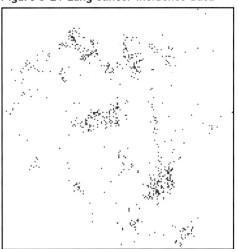

Visual inspection suggests that several clusters of different types and sizes exist, but the initial inspection of the mapped data is somewhat misleading. Examining the source dataset shows that roughly 50% of the dataset consists of duplicate locations, i.e. points are geocoded to the same coordinates — in several instances coincident locations with 5+ events. This is a very common feature of some types of event dataset and may occur for several reasons: (i) rounding to the nearest whole grid reference; (ii) measurement error and/or data resolution issues; (iii) genuinely co-located events — for example, in the infamous Dr Harold Shipman murder cases, 8 of the murders took place at the same nursing home; (iv) allocation of events to an agreed or surrogate location — for example, to the nearest road intersection or to the location at which an incident was reported rather than took place (e.g. a police station or a medical practice) or to a nominal address (e.g. place of birth); (v) deliberate data modification, e.g. for privacy or security reasons... the list is extensive and mapping the data as uniform sized points does not reflect this. In this particular dataset, Figure 5-21, the observed clustering is essentially a reflection of population density, or more specifically the *population at risk*.

Very closely located events may also be difficult to detect, depending on their separation and the symbology used. ArcGIS incorporates a "collect events" tool that combines such duplicate data and creates a new "count" field containing the frequency of occurrences. The attribute table applies to a new feature with fewer elements in the new table. The count field may then be used as a weight and rendered as variable point sizes — although this may exacerbate overlap problems. The MapInfo add-in, HotSpot Detective, provides similar functionality.

Assuming the point set is unweighted, and exhibits marked clustering, it is then useful to identify factors such as: (i) where are the main (most intensive) clusters located? (ii) are clusters distinct or do they merge into one another? (iii) are clusters associated with some known background variable, such as the presence of a suspected environmental hazard (e.g. a power station, a smoke plume from a chemical facility) or reflecting variations in land-use (farmland, urban areas, water etc.), or variations in the background population or other regional variable? (iv) is there a common size to clusters or are they variable in size? (v)

do clusters themselves cluster into higher order groupings? (vi) if comparable data are mapped over time, do the clusters remain stable or do they move and/or disappear? Again, there are many questions and many more approaches to addressing such questions.

Crimestat, Clusterseer and several other packages provide a very useful range of facilities to assist in answering some of these questions. Here we use Crimestat to illustrate a number of these. The first is identification and highlighting of the top *N* duplicate locations. In order to deal with possible uncertainty in georeferencing, a fuzzy variant of this facility is provided in Crimestat, enabling common locations to be regarded as those falling within a specified range of each other (e.g. within 10 meters). Having conducted this initial analysis Crimestat then provides a range of spatial clustering and hot-spot identification methods, as described in subsections 5.4.4.1 to 5.4.4.3. Note that in general such techniques are based on static patterns, and for some problems (such as analyzing certain types of disease incidence) spatio-temporal techniques are preferable (see, for example, Jacquez and Meliker, 2008, for a discussion of one approach to addressing such questions).

### 5.4.4.1 Hierarchical nearest neighbor clustering

Crimestat provides a general purpose form of clustering based on nearest neighbor (NN) distances. This form of clustering can be single-level or multi-level hierarchical (NNh) and is of particular applicability if nearest neighbor distance is believed to be of relevance to the problem being considered. Events are considered to be a member of a level 1 cluster if they lie within the expected mean distance under CSR plus or minus a confidence interval value obtained from the standard error plus a user-definable tolerance. These parameters effectively define a search radius within which point pairs are combined into clusters. A further constraint can be applied, specifying the minimum number of events required to constitute a cluster. The mean center and standard deviational ellipses for these clusters are calculated and may be saved in various GIS file formats. These mean centers are then regarded as a new point set, and are subjected to the same type of clustering in order to identify and generate second order and ultimately higher orders of clustering. Clearly the number of points in the initial sample and the degree of clustering have a major bearing on the way in which such clusters are identified. Figure 5-22 illustrates the results of applying this process for the lung cancer data shown earlier.

Crimestat also provides a variation on this clustering procedure to account for background or "baseline" variation. It describes the procedure as a risk adjusted NNh method, or RNNh. The background data is represented as a fine grid using kernel density estimation, and this is used to adjust the threshold distance for clustering the original point set, on a cell-by-cell basis (see also, Section 5.4.4.3). Note that with both NNh and RNNh not all events are assigned to clusters, and each point is assigned to either one cluster at a given hierarchical level or none at all.

*Figure 5-22 Lung cancer NNh clusters*

### 5.4.4.2  *K*-means clustering

A conceptually different clustering approach is point-set partitioning. Essentially this procedure is a form of *K*-means clustering, as described in Section 4.2.12.2 on classification. The user specifies the value *K*, and a set of *K*

random points are placed in the study region as *seed points*. Each point in the dataset is then allocated to the nearest seed point. The set of points assigned to each seed point is then used to create a new set of seed points comprised from the centers of these initial groupings. The procedure continues until the sum of distances (or squared distances) from each point to its cluster center seed cannot be reduced significantly by further iterations. Some implementations run the procedure multiple times, with differing initial seeds, selecting the final result from the solution that minimizes overall cluster dispersion. Another widely used option, particularly with large datasets and many variables (dimensions), involves 'training' the selection by analyzing the clusters for a subset of the data and then using the best solution set as the starting point for the entire dataset. Crimestat, working on 2-dimensional pointset clustering, attempts to identify very good starting points for the initial seeds by a form of simple density analysis (placing a grid over the point set and identifying distinct areas of point concentrations).

Unlike NNh clustering, the *K*-means procedure assigns all events to a unique cluster and clusters do not form hierarchical groupings. Its dependence on the user selection of the *K*-value and the underlying sub-optimal algorithm used are distinct weaknesses. Dependence on *K* can be reduced by systematically increasing *K* from 1,...*K* and examining the weighting of cluster centers on the problem variables and plotting the total and average cluster dispersion values as *K* increases.

### 5.4.4.3  Kernel density clustering

Kernel density estimation (KDE) may also provide an informative (exploratory) tool for hot-spot and cool-spot identification and analysis. Although not strictly a form of clustering, assignment of points to cells that have greater than a pre-determined density value provides a form of clustering in this case. Figure 5-23A illustrates the use of KDE for the same point dataset as in Section 5.4.4 (lung and larynx cancer cases in the Chorley-Ribble area of Lancashire) using a quartic (finite extent) KDE model. Note that this dataset is included as one of the test sets distributed with the spatstat R software.

The pattern shown is largely a reflection of the distribution of population and associated infrastructure (roads etc.) in the region. The density grid illustrated has been overlain with the point set and an ellipse showing the possible relationship between the high density area in the south of the study area with an old incinerator plant (dot in lower left of ellipse) and hypothetical smoke plume. The principal interest in this particular dataset was in the relationship between the incinerator location and another, far rarer, form of cancer, affecting the larynx (Figure 5-23B). A small apparent cluster (4 events identified located very close to the incinerator site in Figure 5-23B) had been observed and the research sought to establish whether this was a real or apparent relationship. The incidence of lung cancer in this instance was being used as a form of control dataset, on the hypothesis that these data represented an estimate of the distribution of the underlying population at risk, and assuming that there was no relationship between lung cancer incidence and incinerator location (a working assumption only). See Diggle (1990), Baddeley et al. (2005) and related papers for more details.

As can been seen from Figure 5-23, the overall pattern of the larynx cancer cases seems to follow the pattern exhibited by the lung cancer cases, i.e. to be largely a reflection of underlying variation in the at-risk population. Whether there is a real and unexpected cluster in the neighborhood of the old incinerator is difficult to determine. Diggle's model and tests suggest that the cluster does appear to be significant. But he also notes the sensitivity of the model to the low number of cases — with deletion of just one of these cases there is a reasonable chance the result could have arisen by chance. He also notes the problem of formulating hypotheses based on examining specific apparent clusters. A wide range of comparable regions should be studied, without pre-conceptions, since clusters may well be observed which may or may not be associated with particular facilities (see also the earlier

discussion of exploratory *cluster hunting* in Section 5.2.6).

### Figure 5-23 KDE cancer incidence mapping

A. Lung cancer incidence (978 controls)

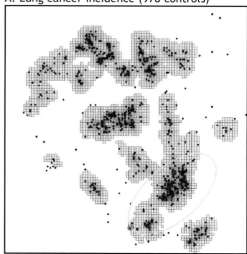

B. Larynx cancer incidence (58 cases)

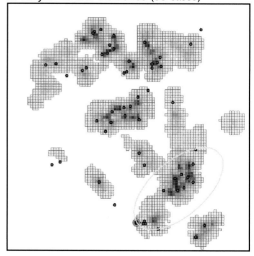

#### 5.4.4.4 Spatio-temporal clustering

It is often the case that event data, such as disease incidence, has associated temporal information, for example: the date of birth; the date of death; the date of diagnosis. In such cases it is often of interest to determine whether there is evidence of spatio-temporal clustering. The question was initially raised by Knox (1964) when investigating cases of childhood leukemia in a region of NE England. Knox proposed a simple means of testing for such clustering, or space-time interaction. He suggested that each case, $i$, one could compute the (Euclidean) distance to every other case, $j$, and record this in a table or matrix as the set $\{x_{ij}\}$. Likewise one could compute the separation in time between each of these events, and produce a second set $\{y_{ij}\}$. For the data under consideration Knox then sought to identify a critical distance, $D$, and critical time interval, $T$, that appeared to be meaningful for the problem being examined. Using these critical values, the data could then be classified into a 2x2 contingency table, with the suspected spatio-temporal cluster being the count of events that fell in the first cell, i.e. the cell with $x_{ij}<D$ and $y_{ij}<T$. Knox has 96 cases and hence there were 96(95)/2=4560 pairs to consider. Of these there were 152 close pairs in time and 25 close pairs in space, with 5 being close in both space and time. The expected number can be estimated as per normal contingency tables using the marginal totals, i.e. as 152 x 25/4560=0.8333. The question then arises as to how to test whether the observed value of 5 is significantly greater than the expected value which is <1. At the time Knox proposed using the Poisson distribution with mean 0.8333 as the basis for significance testing, which suggested that a value of 5 was highly significant.

Subsequently many statisticians examined Knox's approach and ideas, highlighting a number of problems with the method and suggesting a range of modifications and developments. Of particular interest in the paper by Mantel (1967) , in which he develops Knox's ideas and which has led to not only tests for spatio-temporal clustering, but also a more general methodology that has been adopted widely in spatial ecology (see further, Section 5.4.5, below). Mantel proposed using a test statistic of the form:

$$Z = \sum_{i,j} x_{ij} y_{ij}, \ i \neq j$$

This measure has the advantage of including the actual distance and time measures, rather than discarding this information. Knox's test can be seen as a special case of Mantel's $Z$ statistic if the $x_{ij}<D$ are coded as 1 and $y_{ij}<T$ are also coded as 1, and otherwise entries are coded as 0. The Mantel statistic then simply counts the number of close pairs. Note that, depending on how the summation limits are defined, it may be necessary to divide the result by 2, and that in this form distances are treated as symmetric.

To test the significance of the observed Z-value Mantel proposes using a Monte Carlo simulation approach. A simple procedure is to randomly permute the rows and columns of one of the matrices, typically the locations matrix. After each permutation the Z-statistic is computed. A set of, say 1000 permutations are performed, generating a probability distribution for $Z$ under the assumption that the space-time matching is random. The observed Z-value can then be compared with this computed probability distribution to obtain an estimate of the significance of the observed result.

If the Mantel Z-statistic is amended slightly, normalizing it to fall in the range [-1,1], it can be seen to be form of product moment correlation coefficient. This is achieved by adjusting the data values by subtracting the mean value in each table and dividing by the observed standard deviation (i.e. a z-transform), and then adjusting for the number of pairs: n(n-1)/2 less 1 to obtain the degrees of freedom:

$$r(XY) = \frac{1}{n(n-1)2-1} \sum_{i,j} \left( \frac{x_{ij} - \bar{x}}{s_x} \right) \left( \frac{y_{ij} - \bar{y}}{s_y} \right), \ i \neq j$$

Several issues may make the analysis of such data more difficult than appears at first sight. Some of these issues include: is the examination of pairwise data sufficient? (are 3-way interactions important for example); are there any factors in the determination of the temporal data that may bias the results (for example, how close are onset of a disease and diagnosis? are cases detected because they are being looked for especially or defined as cases where they were not so defined in the past/elsewhere in the study region?; how are critical time and distance values to be determined (for Knox tests), and is it reasonable to assume this distance is constant when underlying population densities may vary considerably?; if one examines a region in which an unexpectedly large number of cases have been reported, testing for space-time clustering may show no significant spatio-temporal effects, which is actually the result of region pre-selection rather than failure to detect a spatio-temporal effect; changes in the underlying population distribution in the study region over time may have occurred, which will affect the results; the distance measure applied may not be appropriate — Mantel suggested that for contagious diseases in particular a reciprocal transform be used to adjust for the overly strong influence of large distances and times on the results (with a constant included to avoid the distortions apparent with very small times and distances).

Jaquez (1996) proposed using *k*-nearest neighbors (*k*-NN) rather than an explicit distance measure. This test is similar to those described above, but does not rely on distance directly — instead he defines the *k*-nearest neighbors as the set of cases as near or nearer to a given case that the $k^{th}$ NN. He then defines a similar expression to the basic Mantel or Knox statistic:

$$J_k = \sum_{i,j} x_{ijk} y_{ijk}, \; i \neq j$$

In this statistic the variables are taken as binary values as per the Knox model, so the totals are counts. As with Mantel's test he proposes permuting one or other table to generate a suitable reference distribution (he suggests permuting the rows of the time matrix). In a range of tests Jaquez demonstrated that the *k*-NN approach was more powerful than the standard Mantel and Knox methods and is less susceptible to several of the issues described above. The value of *k* chosen may be varied to test the sensitivity of the results to the value chosen.

Kulldorf and Hjalmars (1999) sought to address another of the weaknesses of the Knox test, that of population shift bias. They showed that if one has the background population data over time, and therefore information on population growth or decline in the various parts of the study region, this element of bias can be removed. This is achieved by randomly assigning cases to a given region and timeslot in proportion to the actual population (or population at risk) in that region at that time. Computations and tests then proceed much as per Mantel and Jaquez describe. The difficulty with this approach, is that it requires access to data that may not be readily available.

A range of spatial and spatio-temporal cluster analysis tools are provided in the National Cancer Institute's (NCI) SaTScan software, which is available free of charge, from http://www.satscan.org/. These include purely spatial scanning statistics (as described further in Section 5.2.6), the scanning version of permutation-type models described above, and the space-time scan statistics developed by Kulldorf (1997). The latter extends the spatial scanning approach to include a time dimension, with the scan being a cylinder (the spatial scan being the cylinder radius and the time scan as the height). A key feature of this software is the identification of both the existence of significant clusters (by size) and where these clusters are located.

### 5.4.5 Proximity matrix comparisons

In many instances data are collected from a series of point-like locations and recorded with both location and attribute information. A distance matrix can then readily be constructed from the location data, and in some instances, a similar matrix of 'proximity' can be constructed from the attribute data. For example, at each location the genetic make-up of species may be recorded and a measure derived enabling the 'distance' (proximity, similarity) between these genetic measures to be calculated for each pair of locations. The result is two (or more) square matrices of matching dimensions. Typically these matrices are symmetric and the researcher is interested in examining whether there is any correlation between the proximity data matrix and the spatial matrix, bearing in mind that we might expect nearby locations to be non-independent on attribute measures, which contradicts classical correlation statistics requirements.

The Mantel test, which is widely used in spatial ecology, is one approach to addressing this issue. The test, devised by Mantel (1967) for analysis of spatio-temporal datasets (see Section 5.4.4.4) computes a form of product moment correlation statistic, $r$, between matching pairs of entries in each distance matrix. The null hypothesis is that this correlation is zero. Only the upper or lower triangles of the two matrices are required for the computation as the entries are symmetric. The resulting correlation coefficient is then tested against a simulated probability distribution computed by randomly permutating the rows and columns of either one of the matrices and then computing the value of $r$ under this permutation. Repeated random permutations (1000+) and computations of $r$ will yield an ordered set of values which will include the original $r$-value within their spread. Suppose the proportion of permuted values that are larger than the observed value is 7% — this suggested that there is roughly a 7% chance of seeing a correlation as large as the observed value or greater, i.e. the observed value is quite high (despite its absolute value often not being very large), which might be regarded as a significant result indicating that spatial factors (or *spatial autocorrelation* — see further, Section 5.5.2) in the data are important. The test can be extended in a number of ways, for example by grouping the Euclidean distances into distinct classes and then computing separate correlation coefficients for each distance class, thereby generating a Mantel correlogram. For more details Urban (2003) provides an excellent summary.

Many GIS and non-GIS software packages, especially those designed for use in spatial ecology, support computation of Mantel tests. These include packages such as PASSaGE, the R-Project (see the Spatial topic page and specifically the ade4 package), and purely statistical packages such as XLStat (for Excel).

Related techniques that involve matrix comparisons include the work of Hubert and Golledge (1982) and the grid-based methods described in Section 5.3.2. This latter section describes a range of statistics that are used to compare grid datasets, especially remote-sensed data, including the use of Chi-Square statistics, the Kappa Index and Cramer's V statistic. Hubert and Golledge address the case in which two rectangular matrices represent data on the same $n$ objects (e.g. cities) and the same $m$ attributes (e.g. crime rates, by type, in consecutive years). The authors devise an index that measures the degree to which both matrices are similar, together with a significance testing strategy that takes into account the possible dependency among the $m$ attributes. Spatial dependence issues remain, and an approach to addressing these through a measure of spatial association due to Tjøstheim (1978) is discussed. As an alternative, with more direct recognition of spatial effects, autocorrelation-based regression techniques (see Section 5.6.4) may be a preferred approach to the analysis of this type of dataset.

# 5.5 Spatial Autocorrelation

### 5.5.1 Autocorrelation, time series and spatial analysis

The term spatial autocorrelation owes its origins to work in a related field, time series analysis (TSA), and in turn to the notion of correlation in univariate statistics. Since spatial autocorrelation follows these concepts so closely we will introduce the subject using these more familiar origins. Readers may also wish to refer to Cliff and Ord (1981), Goodchild (1986, CATMOG 47), or Fortin and Dale (2008). Throughout this discussion it is important to recognize that correlation may *suggest*, but does not *imply*, causation; it is extremely easy to make erroneous assumptions regarding cause-effect relationships from correlation data, but such results should be examined in great detail before suggesting any causation.

As we saw in Table 1-3, if we have a sample set $\{x_i, y_i\}$ of $n$ pairs of data values the correlation between them is given by the ratio

of the covariance (the way they vary jointly) to the square root of the variance of each variable. This is effectively a way of standardizing the covariance by the average spread of each variable, to ensure that the correlation coefficient, $r$, falls in the range [-1,1]. The formula used for this ratio is:

$$r = \frac{\sum_{i=1}^{n}(x_i - \bar{x})(y_i - \bar{y})}{\sqrt{\sum_{i=1}^{n}(x_i - \bar{x})^2}\sqrt{\sum_{i=1}^{n}(y_i - \bar{y})^2}}$$

Now suppose that instead of a set of data pairs $\{x_i, y_i\}$ we have a set of $n$ values, $\{x_t\}$, which represent measurements taken at different time periods, $t=1,2,3,4,...n$, for example daily levels of rainfall at a particular location, or the closing daily price of a stock or commodity. Figure 5-24 shows a typical stock price time series: the blue line is the closing stock price on each trading day; the red and black looped lines highlight the time series for 7 and 14 day intervals or 'lags', i.e. the sets $\{x_t, x_{t+7}, x_{t+14}, x_{t+21}, ...\}$ and $\{x_t, x_{t+14}, x_{t+28}, x_{t+42}, ...\}$.

*Figure 5-24 Time series of stock price and volume data*

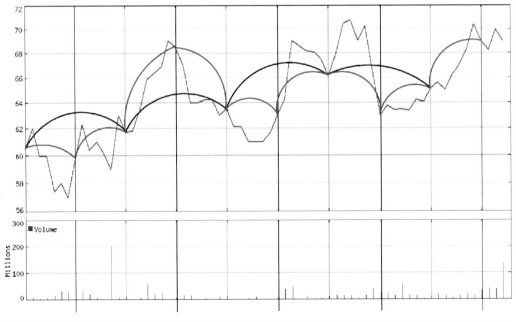

The pattern of values recorded and graphed might show that rainfall, or commodity prices, exhibits some regularity over time. For example, it might show that days of high rainfall are commonly followed by another day of high rainfall, and days of low rainfall are also often followed by days of low rainfall. In this case there would be a strong positive correlation between the rainfall on successive days, i.e. on days that are one step or *lag* apart. We could regard the set of "day 1" values as one series, $\{x_{t,1}\}$ $t$=1,2,3...$n$-1, and set of "day 2" values as a second series $\{x_{t,2}\}$ $t$=2,3...$n$, and compute the correlation coefficient for these two series in the same manner as for the $r$ expression above. Each series has a mean value, which is simply:

$$\overline{x}_{.1} = \frac{1}{n-1}\sum_{t=1}^{n-1} x_t \text{ and } \overline{x}_{.2} = \frac{1}{n-1}\sum_{t=2}^{n} x_t$$

Using these two mean values we can then construct a correlation coefficient between our two series. This is essentially the same formula as for $r$:

$$r_{.1} = \frac{\sum_{t=1}^{n-1}(x_t - \overline{x}_{.1})(x_{t+1} - \overline{x}_{.2})}{\sqrt{\sum_{t=1}^{n-1}(x_t - \overline{x}_{.1})^2}\sqrt{\sum_{t=1}^{n-1}(x_{t+1} - \overline{x}_{.2})^2}}$$

If $n$ is reasonably large then the value $1/(n$-1) will be very close to $1/n$, and the values of the two means and standard deviations will be almost the same, so the above expression can be simplified under these circumstances to:

$$r_{.1} = \frac{\sum_{t=1}^{n-1}(x_t - \overline{x})(x_{t+1} - \overline{x})}{\sum_{t=1}^{n}(x_t - \overline{x})^2}$$

This expression is known as the *serial correlation coefficient* for a lag of 1 time period. It may be generalized for lags of 2, 3, ...,$k$ steps as follows:

$$r_{.k} = \frac{\sum_{t=1}^{n-k}(x_t - \overline{x})(x_{t+k} - \overline{x})}{\sum_{t=1}^{n}(x_t - \overline{x})^2}$$

The term *autocorrelation* coefficient has been used since the 1950s to describe this expression, rather than serial correlation coefficient. The top part of this expression is like the covariance, but at a lag of $k$, and the bottom is like the covariance at lag of 0. These two components are sometimes known as the *autocovariance* at $k$ and 0 lags. In time series analysis it is usual for the time spacing, or "distance", to be in equal steps. The set of values $\{r_{.k}\}$ can then be plotted against the lag, $k$, to see how the pattern of correlation varies with lag. This plot is known as a *correlogram*, and provides a valuable insight into the behavior of the time series at different lags or "distances".

For a random series the values for the $r_{.k}$ will all be approximately 0 — in fact they are distributed as N(0,1/$n$). If there is short term correlation, as in our rainfall example, the $r_{.k}$ will start high (close to +1) and decrease to roughly 0 when the number of lags exceeds the length (or range) of this correlation. It is possible of course, that the overall pattern of rainfall shows a steady increase over time, in which case the correlograms will not tend to zero in the manner expected. In this case the series is described as *non-stationary* (see further, Section 6.7.1.8) and before carrying out such analysis an attempt to remove the trend component should be undertaken. Typically this involves fitting a trend curve (e.g. a best fit straight line) to the original data points and subtracting values for this curve from the original dataset at lags 1,2,3... before carrying out the analysis. The original data may also contain outliers, which if left in may distort the analysis, so inspection of the source data and outlier adjustment or removal (e.g. of data errors) may be advisable. Having identified these factors, adjusted the data if necessary, and computed the correlograms, the next step is to examine the results and attempt to interpret the observed patterns. Unfortunately, as is the case with many patterns observed in time or space, more than one process can generate an identical pattern. However, modeling an observed pattern may provide an effective means of estimating missing or sparse data, or predicting values beyond the observed range, despite the fact that the process generating the model may not be unique.

These comments apply to series which follow a clear sequence of steps in a single dimension, time. At first sight such methods do not translate easily to spatial problems, since there is no obvious single direction to follow. Of course one could select a single transect and take measurements at fixed intervals to produce a well-ordered series, which could then be analyzed in exactly the manner described. But more general procedures are needed if a wide range of practical spatial problems are to be subjected to such analysis. These procedures need to model space in a manner that results in well-ordered data series, ideally in evenly spaced steps, using the general notion of proximity bands (see further, Section 5.5.2).

## 5.5.2 Global spatial autocorrelation

The procedures adopted for analyzing patterns of *spatial* autocorrelation depend on the type of data available. There is considerable difference between:

a) a set of 100 values obtained for a 10x10 grid of (100mx100m) squares which covers a 1000mx1000m region;

b) a set of values obtained for 100 contiguous but arbitrarily shaped polygons which again cover the same region;

c) a set of nominal values (classes) for 100 contiguous but arbitrarily shaped polygons which again cover the same region; and

d) a set of data values obtained from 100 arbitrarily distributed sample points in our study region

Each case warrants a slightly different approach, but each utilizes the notion of proximity bands as a means of imposing some form of serial behavior to the data. The idea is then to examine the correlation between areas

or points at given levels of separation, to obtain a similar measure to that used within time series analysis. Initially we examine the case of nominal-valued data (Section 5.5.2.1), which helps identify the key concepts involved and focuses our attention on a set of questions regarding such analysis that we examine in more detail in Sections 5.5.2.2 *et seq.*

### 5.5.2.1 Join counts and the analysis of nominal-valued spatial data

Consider a regular grid of cells that completely covers a sampled region with a value associated with each grid square. The set of values in this case could be binary, e.g. presence/absence; or they could be classified into one of $k$ classes (see Dacey, 1968, for a full discussion of this case); or $k$ classes could be re-classified back into two classes, one class from $k$ and the remaining $k$-1 classes. Typically this latter kind of data is nominal-valued, i.e. the cell or zone values can be regarded as categories, such as woodland, grassland, sandy desert etc. rather than ordered values.

If we assume the data are binary, perhaps representing the presence or absence of a particular species of insect or plant variety in sample quadrats, a range of possible patterns might be observed (Figure 5-25A-D). In Figure 5-25A all the observed values for presence are in one half of the 6x6 grid (strong positive autocorrelation), whilst in Figure 5-25B they are perfectly evenly distributed (strong negative autocorrelation). Figure 5-25C gives a particular case of a random pattern (of which there are many). In each case 50% of the cells show presence, but this value could easily be 10% or any other value depending on the data being studied. Figure 5-25D is an example of a real-world dataset showing the presence or absence of desert holly in a 16x16 cell sample region. Note that in each instance our comments refer to autocorrelation at the scale of the cell, i.e. between cells; within cells autocorrelation is typically strongly positive.

One way of analyzing these patterns is to ask "what is the chance that a particular pattern could occur at random?" In each of the three sample patterns shown we can look at the spatial equivalent of one time step or lag, the patterns observed at one cell step, i.e. adjacent cells. If steps are restricted to rook's moves we can count the number of instances of 1-1, 0-0, 1-0 and 0-1 occurring, and compare these to the number we might expect if the pattern was random. These numbers are referred to as *join counts* (sometimes erroneously described as 'joint counts'). For smaller regions edge effects will be significant, so calculations need to be adjusted to reflect the fact that along the borders not all of the four directions are possible. For example, only two adjacent cells exist for the four corner positions, and only three adjacencies for other border cells.

*Figure 5-25 Join count patterns*

A. Completely separated pattern (+ve)

| 1 | 1 | 1 | 0 | 0 | 0 |
|---|---|---|---|---|---|
| 1 | 1 | 1 | 0 | 0 | 0 |
| 1 | 1 | 1 | 0 | 0 | 0 |
| 1 | 1 | 1 | 0 | 0 | 0 |
| 1 | 1 | 1 | 0 | 0 | 0 |
| 1 | 1 | 1 | 0 | 0 | 0 |

B. Evenly spaced pattern (-ve)

| 1 | 0 | 1 | 0 | 1 | 0 |
|---|---|---|---|---|---|
| 0 | 1 | 0 | 1 | 0 | 1 |
| 1 | 0 | 1 | 0 | 1 | 0 |
| 0 | 1 | 0 | 1 | 0 | 1 |
| 1 | 0 | 1 | 0 | 1 | 0 |
| 0 | 1 | 0 | 1 | 0 | 1 |

C. Random pattern

| 0 | 0 | 1 | 1 | 0 | 1 |
|---|---|---|---|---|---|
| 0 | 1 | 1 | 0 | 1 | 0 |
| 1 | 0 | 1 | 1 | 0 | 0 |
| 0 | 0 | 0 | 0 | 0 | 1 |
| 1 | 1 | 1 | 1 | 0 | 0 |
| 1 | 0 | 1 | 1 | 0 | 1 |

D. Atriplex hymeneltrya (desert holly)

Row and column totals for the adjacencies, or joins, are shown in Figure 5-26 with the overall total being 120/2=60 joins. For our patterns, with 50% occupancy, we might expect 15 of these to be 1-1 joins, 15 to be 0-0 joins and the remaining 30 to be 0-1 or 1-0 joins. We can count up the number of each type of join and compare this to our expected values to judge how special (significant) or not our patterns are. In Figure 5-25A there are 27 1-1 joins, 27 0-0 joins and only 6 0-1 or 1-0 joins — this seems very unlikely, and is indeed most unlikely. Similar calculations can be undertaken for cases B and C, and as expected for case B all 60 joins are of type 1-0 or 0-1, which is again extremely unlikely to occur by chance. Case C has 35 1-0/0-1 joins compared with perhaps 30 expected, with 1-1 joins being 13 and 0-0 being 12, as against perhaps 15 in each case.

## Figure 5-26 Join count computation

| 2 | 3 | 3 | 3 | 3 | 2 | 16 |
|---|---|---|---|---|---|----|
| 3 | 4 | 4 | 4 | 4 | 3 | 22 |
| 3 | 4 | 4 | 4 | 4 | 3 | 22 |
| 3 | 4 | 4 | 4 | 4 | 3 | 22 |
| 3 | 4 | 4 | 4 | 4 | 3 | 22 |
| 2 | 3 | 3 | 3 | 3 | 2 | 16 |
| 16 | 22 | 22 | 22 | 22 | 16 | 120 |

A test for the significance of the results we have observed can be produced using a Normal or z-transform of the data. In practice three separate z-transforms are needed, one for the 1-1 case, one for 0-0, and one for 0-1 and 1-0. These transforms evaluate expressions of the form $z=(O-E)/SD$ where $O$ is the observed number of joins of a given type, $E$ is the expected number based on a random model, and $SD$ is the expected standard deviation. The procedure and formulas can be implemented in software scripts for use within mainstream GIS packages or data may be externally analyzed using specialized software and then the results mapped within a GIS; for example, using the Rookcase Excel add-in produced by Sawada (1999) and obtainable from the University of Ottawa, Laboratory for Paleoclimatology and Climatology. Results for the four examples given in Figure 5-25A-D generated using the Rookcase add-in are shown in Table 5-8 ("B" and "W" here refer to Black and White, rather than 1 or 0; "Rand." refers to the randomization model, which is discussed further below; and # means the number (of joins). Table 5-9 provides details of the principal formulas used in these computations.

## Table 5-8 Join count analysis results

A. Positive autocorrelation

| | BW Joins | BB Joins | WW Joins |
|---|---|---|---|
| # of Joins | 6 | 27 | 27 |
| z-Rand. statistic | -6.58 | 5.80 | 5.80 |
| Variance Rand. | 14.26 | 4.59 | 4.59 |
| Expected # of Joins | 30.86 | 14.57 | 14.57 |
| Number of Observations | # of B's | # of W's | Total Joins |
| 36 | 18 | 18 | 60 |

B. Negative autocorrelation

| | BW Joins | BB Joins | WW Joins |
|---|---|---|---|
| # of Joins | 60 | 0 | 0 |
| z-Rand. statistic | 7.72 | -6.80 | -6.80 |
| Variance Rand. | 14.26 | 4.59 | 4.59 |
| Expected # of Joins | 30.86 | 14.57 | 14.57 |
| Number of Observations | # of B's | # of W's | Total Joins |
| 36 | 18 | 18 | 60 |

C. Random model — no discernable autocorrelation

| | BW Joins | BB Joins | WW Joins |
|---|---|---|---|
| # of Joins | 35 | 13 | 12 |
| z-Rand. statistic | 1.10 | -0.73 | -1.20 |
| Variance Rand. | 14.26 | 4.59 | 4.59 |
| Expected # of Joins | 30.86 | 14.57 | 14.57 |
| Number of Observations | # of B's | # of W's | Total Joins |
| 36 | 18 | 18 | 60 |

D. A. hymeneltrya — positive BB autocorrelation

| | BW Joins | BB Joins | WW Joins |
|---|---|---|---|
| # of Joins | 173 | 39 | 268 |
| z-Rand. statistic | -1.14 | 2.00 | 0.24 |
| Variance Rand. | 70.67 | 17.69 | 22.97 |
| Expected # of Joins | 182.57 | 30.59 | 266.84 |
| Number of Observations | # of B's | # of W's | Total Joins |
| 256 | 65 | 191 | 480 |

Two features of the results in Table 5-8 should be noted: (i) the expected number of joins is not 30,15,15 as we suggested earlier, but 30.86, 14.57,14.57 these being adjusted values to take account of what is known as non-free sampling (i.e. sampling without replacement); and (ii) the z-statistic in Table 5-8B shows a large positive value for BW joins, and large negative values for BB and WW joins (absolute values of >1.96 would be significant at the 5% probability level). This mixed pattern can be confusing, especially if one or two of the z-scores shows a significant value whilst others do not, as in Table 5-8D.

The join counts method has been utilized in a variety of application areas including: ecological data analysis; to analyze patterns of voting (for example voting for one of two political parties or individuals); for analysis of land-use (e.g. developed or undeveloped land); and for examination of the distribution of rural settlements. However, the complexity of computing the theoretical means and variances in more realistic spatial models, the difficulty of interpreting the multiple z-scores, coupled with the availability of alternative approaches to analysis, have meant that join count procedures are not widely used and are rarely implemented in mainstream GIS packages. Support for this kind of analysis is provided in the *joincount* functions of the R-Project spatial package, spdep and within the PASSaGE software. Metrics based on these concepts are provided in Fragstats and similar packages (see further, Section 5.3.3 and Section 5.3.4), for example in the computation of Connection and Contagion indices.

The standard form of the join counts statistical analysis makes a number of assumptions regarding the observation data. These include (under free sampling) that the distribution of BB and WW joins is asymptotically Normal (Gaussian) and that the data is first-order homogeneous. To clarify this latter point, we use an example from Kabos and Csillag (2002) who have investigated relaxing this assumption. They give the example of two simulated images with same B/W distribution (50%B and 50%W), but with different first-order effects. Their first pattern was simulated with first-order homogeneity. i.e., $p_b$, the probability of any cell being black was 0.5 for all cells (Figure 5-27 lefthand image). Their second pattern was simulated by setting $p_b=0.6$ for half of the image and $p_b=0.4$ for the other half, so the overall probability $p_b$ remained at 0.5 but was no longer homogeneously distributed across the image (Figure 5-27, righthand image). They found that that the join count statistics (JCS) using $p_b=0.5$ accepted the null hypothesis of spatial randomness for the first image, but rejected it for the second. Using unmodified JCS, they have thus demonstrated that we would erroneously (but understandably) conclude that there is significant spatial autocorrelation in the second image.

*Figure 5-27 Homogeneous and non-homogenous probability images*

*Table 5-9 Join count mean and variance formulas*

| Mean | Variance | Sampling hypothesis |
|---|---|---|
| Same color case (e.g. black-black or white-white) | | |
| $\mu_F = \dfrac{1}{2}S_0 p_b^2$ | $\sigma_F^2 = \dfrac{1}{4}\left(S_1 p_b^2 + (S_2 - 2S_1)p_b^3 + (S_1 - S_2)p_b^4\right)$ | F: Free sampling (re-sampling or 'without replacement') |
| $\mu_R = \dfrac{1}{2}S_0 \dbinom{n_b}{2}\Big/\dbinom{n}{2}$ | $\sigma_R^2 = \dfrac{1}{4}\left( \begin{array}{l} S_1 \dbinom{n_b}{2}\Big/\dbinom{n}{2} + \\[2mm] (S_2 - 2S_1)\dbinom{n_b}{3}\Big/\dbinom{n}{3} + \\[2mm] (S_0^2 + S_1 - S_2)\dbinom{n_b}{4}\Big/\dbinom{n}{4} \end{array}\right) - \mu_R^2$ | R: Non-free sampling (randomization or 'with replacement') |
| Different color case (e.g. black-white) | | |
| $\mu_f = S_0 p_B p_W$ | $\sigma_f^2 = \dfrac{1}{4}\left( \begin{array}{l} 2S_1 p_b p_w + (S_2 - 2S_1)p_b p_w (p_b + p_w) \\[2mm] +4(S_1 - S_2)p_b^2 p_w^2 \end{array}\right)$ | f: Free sampling (re-sampling or 'without replacement') |
| $\mu_r = S_0 \dbinom{n_b}{2}\dbinom{n_w}{2}\Big/\dbinom{n}{2}$ | $\sigma_r^2 = \dfrac{1}{4}\left( \begin{array}{l} 2S_1 n_b n_w \Big/\dbinom{n}{2} + \\[2mm] (S_2 - 2S_1)n_b n_w (n_b + n_w - 2)\Big/\dbinom{n}{3} + \\[2mm] 4(S_0^2 + S_1 - S_2)\dbinom{n_b}{2}\dbinom{n_w}{2}\Big/\dbinom{n}{4} \end{array}\right) - \mu_r^2$ | r: Non-free sampling (randomization or 'with replacement') |

*where:* $p_b$, $p_w$ = probability of the category of interest occurring in a cell or lattice zone (e.g. probability of black or white zones in the case of binary datasets); note that where probabilities are estimated from the lattice then $p_b = n_b/n$ and $p_w = n_w/n$ but probabilities might be estimated from a related variable (e.g. proportion of votes cast) or from a broader sample (regional or national data);

$n_b$ = number (count) of the category of interest occurring in a cell or lattice zone (e.g. number of black zones in the case of binary datasets);

**W**=$\{w_{ij}\}$ is a spatial weights matrix, the basic version being a binary weights matrix in which $w_{ii}=0$ and $w_{ij}=1$ if zones $i$ and $j$ are adjacent, else $w_{ij}=0$. The formulas below simplify considerably with binary weights; and

$$\binom{n}{r} = \frac{n!}{(n-r)!\,r!}, \quad S_1 = \frac{1}{2}\sum_i \sum_j (w_{ij} + w_{ji})^2, \quad S_2 = \sum_i \left(\sum_j w_{ij} + \sum_i w_{ji}\right)^2 \text{ and } S_0 = \sum_i \sum_j w_{ij}, \ i \neq j$$

Additional questions might reasonably be asked about this analytical procedure that point the way to more powerful extensions and developments of these ideas. Key questions, which we discuss below and in Section 5.5.2.2 include:

- how sensitive is this technique (and, of course, many other techniques) to the particular size of grid cell used and the number of cells?

- if there are k classes rather than just two, how might this kind of data be analyzed?

- why choose rook's moves — why not permit queen's moves, which would extend the idea of contiguity but increase the complexity of computation?

- why restrict the notion of contiguity to directly adjacent cells (a lag of 1) — why not examine longer range effects, i.e. higher order spatial lags? Indeed, with separate analyses for different lags or distance bands one could produce a form of *correlogram* of autocorrelation effects

- why should every cell have the same level of importance or weight — why not permit cells to have differing weights, depending on the kind of model of spatial association we are considering?

- should the analysis be restricted to regular grids, or could it be extended to irregular grids, polygonal regions and even pure point data?

- is a single statistic for a whole area meaningful, or should separate statistics be computed for sub-regions or individual cells and then plotted, giving a Local Indicator of Spatial Autocorrelation (LISA) measure, which would highlight clustering effects?

- if the data in the study cells are integer or real-valued, why restrict analysis (lose valuable information) by ignoring the *levels* in regions?

- how should we determine the cell probabilities, e.g. $p_B$? Is it sufficient to always derive the probability estimate from the observed proportions of cells of type B, or are there other approaches that might be more appropriate?

We briefly comment on the first two of these questions in the discussion below. The remaining questions in the list, notably those relating to cases where the data values in the grid, lattice or point-set are integer or real-valued, are discussed in Section 5.5.2.2 *et seq.*

*Figure 5-28 Grouping and size effects*

A. 2x2 grouping of Atriplex hymeneltrya grid

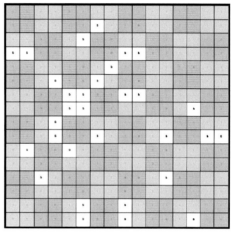

B. 128x128 grid of Calluna vulgaris presence

The first point raised above can be examined directly by reviewing our example in Figure 5-25D. If the grid had been sampled at half the frequency in each direction there would be

8x8=64 cells rather than 16x16=256 cells, and in this instance only one new larger cell contains no data, i.e. a 0, all others showing a desert holly plant present (Figure 5-28A, empty 2x2 cell shown in white). So we immediately see that such techniques may be highly sensitive to grid resolution, or, with irregular lattices, to the particular density, shape and connectivity of individual areas.

Furthermore, with large grids, e.g. 128x128 cells, the z-scores may become huge, raising doubts over the sensitivity and interpretation of the technique as the resolution of sampling or the size of the area covered is increased; in Figure 5-28B there are 16384 cells and all three z-scores are over 160. A critical question here is whether the data in such cases reflect the result of direct observation, or whether they represent results from re-sampling or similar computational procedures. In the latter instance test scores may not be valid. At the other extreme scores may be suspect where the number of cells or regions is small (less than 30) or the category selected only occurs in a small percentage of areas.

The second question deals with the k-class case. There are several ways of dealing with this situation. Perhaps the first question to ask is whether the classes are genuinely nominal-valued (e.g. distinct species of tree); or whether the classes have been created from a set of underlying data that are themselves, integer or real-valued. In the latter instance it is sensible to examine the underlying data separately using more powerful techniques, such as Moran's I (see Section 5.5.2.2). It is also possible to tackle each of the k classes in turn, treating these as B=Black say, and regarding all other classes as W=White, and proceeding as described earlier. Alternatively one can examine all the k classes simultaneously by identifying all instances of the same class being found in adjacent areas. This pattern of occurrences can then be compared with the expected pattern assuming the zones are labeled in a spatially random manner, and/or using a pseudo-probability distribution generated using random permutations of the known values.

Support for this form of 'multi-colored map' analysis is to be found in the R-Project package, spdep, *joincount* functions and the join counts option of the PASSaGE software. Note that for some of the analyses performed it is assumed that the spatial weights matrix, **W**, is symmetric, or can be adjusted to be symmetric; this excludes the use of some, more complex, neighborhood relations.

### 5.5.2.2  Moran *I* and Geary *C*

Many of the remaining questions from the preceding subsection relating to join count procedures can be addressed by considering a more general case than presence/absence data, with a region that is not a regular lattice. We start with a simple incomplete rectangular lattice, shown in Figure 5-29 as an arrangement of 10 cells with real-valued entries. Note that although this is shown with rectangular edges it is topologically equivalent to any set of planar regions that exhibit the same adjacency pattern, however irregular in form.

*Figure 5-29 Irregular lattice dataset*

| | +4.55 | +5.54 |
|---|---|---|
| +2.24 | -5.15 | +9.02 |
| +3.10 | -4.39 | -2.09 |
| | +0.46 | -3.06 |

Instead of displaying this data as an irregular lattice, it can be recast as a table of (x,y,z) triples, where rows are numbered 1,2... from the top and columns are likewise numbered 1,2... from the left, as shown in Table 5-10. This coordinate based description of the data immediately suggests a generalization that may be applied to point datasets, with the (x,y) pairs providing the coordinate information. These (x,y) pairs could be well-defined points, or grid cells, or even polygon centroids.

*Table 5-10 Tabulated lattice data*

| x | y | z |
|---|---|---|
| 1 | 2 | 4.55 |
| 1 | 3 | 5.54 |
| 2 | 1 | 2.24 |
| 2 | 2 | -5.15 |
| 2 | 3 | 9.02 |
| 3 | 1 | 3.1 |
| 3 | 2 | -4.39 |
| 3 | 3 | -2.09 |
| 4 | 2 | 0.46 |
| 4 | 3 | -3.06 |

This tabular form loses information, in that cell adjacencies are not explicitly captured. Figure 5-30 provides this missing adjacency information for the sample lattice as a binary matrix using rook's move definitions. In this example cells in the original dataset are numbered from 1 to 10, starting with the first cell being in row 2 column 1 of the source data and continuing down the rows and across the columns.

*Figure 5-30 Adjacency matrix, W*

|    | 1 | 2 | 3 | 4 | 5 | 6 | 7 | 8 | 9 | 10 |
|----|---|---|---|---|---|---|---|---|---|----|
| 1  | 0 | 1 | 0 | 1 | 0 | 0 | 0 | 0 | 0 | 0  |
| 2  | 1 | 0 | 0 | 0 | 1 | 0 | 0 | 0 | 0 | 0  |
| 3  | 0 | 0 | 0 | 1 | 0 | 0 | 1 | 0 | 0 | 0  |
| 4  | 1 | 0 | 1 | 0 | 1 | 0 | 0 | 1 | 0 | 0  |
| 5  | 0 | 1 | 0 | 1 | 0 | 1 | 0 | 0 | 1 | 0  |
| 6  | 0 | 0 | 0 | 0 | 1 | 0 | 0 | 0 | 0 | 1  |
| 7  | 0 | 0 | 1 | 0 | 0 | 0 | 0 | 1 | 0 | 0  |
| 8  | 0 | 0 | 0 | 1 | 0 | 0 | 1 | 0 | 1 | 0  |
| 9  | 0 | 0 | 0 | 0 | 1 | 0 | 0 | 1 | 0 | 1  |
| 10 | 0 | 0 | 0 | 0 | 0 | 1 | 0 | 0 | 1 | 0  |

This matrix can be thought of as a specific example of a spatial weights matrix, $\mathbf{W}=\{w_{ij}\}$, indicating elements of computations that are to be included or excluded. In this example $w_{ij}=1$ if two cells are adjacent (joined) and

$w_{ij}=0$ otherwise. This matrix is symmetric and binary, but these features are not pre-requisites. For example, one might choose to create a matrix $\mathbf{W}$ in which rook's move adjacencies were given a weight of 0.9 and bishop's moves (the diagonal connections) a weight of 0.1. More generally, if the source dataset was polygonal, e.g. well-defined agricultural tracts, then adjacency weights might be chosen to reflect the relative lengths of shared boundaries.

We now have a set of values $\{z_i\}$ and a set of weights $\{w_{ij}\}$. We are looking for some way of combining this information using a function, $f()$, which satisfies the following criteria:

- If the pair $(z_i, z_j)$ are both +ve or both -ve $f(z_i, z_j)>0$
- If the pair $(z_i, z_j)$ are a mix of +ve and -ve $f(z_i, z_j)<0$
- If the pair $(z_i, z_j)$ are both large values $f(z_i, z_j)$ is large
- Patterns of adjacency reflected in the matrix $\mathbf{W}$ must be accounted for in the computation

One of the simplest ways to fulfill these criteria is to multiply the zone values together, optionally adjusting for the overall mean value for all zones and including the adjacency information, which gives:

$$\sum\sum z_i z_j$$

or with mean adjustment and weights included:

$$\sum\sum w_{ij}(z_i - \bar{z})(z_j - \bar{z})$$

As noted above, assuming the weights $w_{ij}$ are binary, they simply identify which elements of the computation are to be included or excluded in the calculation. This expression looks quite like the covariance of the selected data. To adjust for the number of items included in this sum, and produce a covariance value, we need to divide through by the sum of the weights used, i.e.

$$\frac{\sum_i \sum_j w_{ij}(z_i - \bar{z})(z_j - \bar{z})}{\sum_i \sum_j w_{ij}}$$

To standardize this covariance expression we divide it by the variance of the data, which is simply:

$$\frac{\sum_i (z_i - \bar{z})^2}{n}$$

The ratio of these two expressions gives us an index, known as Moran's I, and has values that typically range from approximately +1, representing complete positive spatial autocorrelation, to approximately -1, representing complete negative spatial autocorrelation:

$$I = \frac{1}{p} \frac{\sum_i \sum_j w_{ij}(z_i - \bar{z})(z_j - \bar{z})}{\sum_i (z_i - \bar{z})^2}, \text{ where}$$

$$p = \sum_i \sum_j w_{ij} / n$$

The upper and lower limits of this index may vary depending on the configuration of the weights used. It is the spatial equivalent of the correlation coefficient, $r$, and very similar to the (unweighted) time series autocorrelation coefficient, $r_{.1}$ derived in Section 5.5.1:

$$r_{.1} = \frac{\sum_t (x_t - \bar{x})(x_{t+1} - \bar{x})}{\sum_t (x_t - \bar{x})^2}$$

If the observations, $z_i$, are spatially independent Normal random variables, the expected value of Moran's I is:

$$E(I) = -\frac{1}{n-1}$$

Hence for large $n$ the expected value is approximately 0.

The variance of $I$ under these conditions is shown below (compare this to the formulas in Table 5-9):

$$Var(I) = \frac{n^2(n-1)S_1 - n(n-1)S_2 - 2S_0{}^2}{(n+1)(n-1)S_0{}^2}, \text{ where}$$

$$S_1 = \frac{1}{2} \sum_i \sum_j \left(w_{ij} + w_{ji}\right)^2, i \neq j$$

$$S_2 = \sum_i \left(\sum_j w_{ij} + \sum_i w_{ji}\right)^2, \text{ and}$$

$$S_0 = \sum_i \sum_j w_{ij}, i \neq j$$

The variance of $I$ under the assumption of randomization (i.e. randomly re-distributed over the support, without replacement) is yet more complicated, but is provided in a number of software packages. From the expected values and variances z-scores and significance levels for $I$ can then be computed under the alternative sampling assumptions.

The computation of Moran's I for the sample dataset provided in Figure 5-29 illustrates the procedure. First we compute the matrix of unadjusted variance- and covariance-like quantities (Figure 5-31A). There are 10 cells, and values for each cell are shown together with their deviations from the overall mean value, 1.022, in the column and row bounding the 10x10 matrix of computed values, **C**. The diagonal of the 10x10 matrix gives the variance-like quantities whilst the off-diagonal components give the covariance-like quantities. The weight-adjusted matrix (Figure 5-31B) includes only the off-diagonal elements, and only those for which adjacencies have been included. The total of these values is 16.19, compared with the sum of the diagonal values which is 196.68. The computation of Moran's I requires one final element, adjustment by $1/p$, which in this case is the number of cells (10 in our case) divided by the sum of the elements in **W**, which is 26, giving: $I = 10 \times 16.19/(26 \times 196.68)$ so $I = 0.0317$. If this value is close to 0 there is very little spatial autocorrelation, which is what we have found in this example.

### Figure 5-31 Moran's I computation

**A. Computation of variance/covariance-like quantities, matrix C**

| Var/Covar matrix | | | 1 | 2 | 3 | 4 | 5 | 6 | 7 | 8 | 9 | 10 | Diagonal values: |
|---|---|---|---|---|---|---|---|---|---|---|---|---|---|
| | z(I) | z(I)-mean | 1.22 | 2.08 | 3.53 | -6.17 | -5.41 | -0.56 | 4.52 | 8.00 | -3.11 | -4.08 | (z(I)-mean)^2 |
| 1 | 2.24 | 1.22 | 1.48 | 2.53 | 4.30 | -7.52 | -6.59 | -0.68 | 5.50 | 9.74 | -3.79 | -4.97 | 1.48 |
| 2 | 3.10 | 2.08 | 2.53 | 4.32 | 7.33 | -12.83 | -11.25 | -1.17 | 9.39 | 16.62 | -6.47 | -8.48 | 4.32 |
| 3 | 4.55 | 3.53 | 4.30 | 7.33 | 12.45 | -21.77 | -19.09 | -1.98 | 15.94 | 28.22 | -10.98 | -14.40 | 12.45 |
| 4 | -5.15 | -6.17 | -7.52 | -12.83 | -21.77 | 38.09 | 33.40 | 3.47 | -27.89 | -49.36 | 19.21 | 25.19 | 38.09 |
| 5 | -4.39 | -5.41 | -6.59 | -11.25 | -19.09 | 33.40 | 29.29 | 3.04 | -24.45 | -43.29 | 16.84 | 22.09 | 29.29 |
| 6 | 0.46 | -0.56 | -0.68 | -1.17 | -1.98 | 3.47 | 3.04 | 0.32 | -2.54 | -4.49 | 1.75 | 2.29 | 0.32 |
| 7 | 5.54 | 4.52 | 5.50 | 9.39 | 15.94 | -27.89 | -24.45 | -2.54 | 20.41 | 36.13 | -14.06 | -18.44 | 20.41 |
| 8 | 9.02 | 8.00 | 9.74 | 16.62 | 28.22 | -49.36 | -43.29 | -4.49 | 36.13 | 63.97 | -24.89 | -32.65 | 63.97 |
| 9 | -2.09 | -3.11 | -3.79 | -6.47 | -10.98 | 19.21 | 16.84 | 1.75 | -14.06 | -24.89 | 9.68 | 12.70 | 9.68 |
| 10 | -3.06 | -4.08 | -4.97 | -8.48 | -14.40 | 25.19 | 22.09 | 2.29 | -18.44 | -32.65 | 12.70 | 16.66 | 16.66 |
| Mean | 1.02 | | | | | | | | | | | SSD | 196.68 |
| SD | 4.67 | | | | | | | | | | | | 4.67 |

**B. C*W: Adjustment by multiplication of the weighting matrix, W**

| | 1 | 2 | 3 | 4 | 5 | 6 | 7 | 8 | 9 | 10 | |
|---|---|---|---|---|---|---|---|---|---|---|---|
| 1 | 0.00 | 2.53 | 0.00 | -7.52 | 0.00 | 0.00 | 0.00 | 0.00 | 0.00 | 0.00 | -4.99 |
| 2 | 2.53 | 0.00 | 0.00 | 0.00 | -11.25 | 0.00 | 0.00 | 0.00 | 0.00 | 0.00 | -8.72 |
| 3 | 0.00 | 0.00 | 0.00 | -21.77 | 0.00 | 0.00 | 15.94 | 0.00 | 0.00 | 0.00 | -5.84 |
| 4 | -7.52 | 0.00 | -21.77 | 0.00 | 33.40 | 0.00 | 0.00 | -49.36 | 0.00 | 0.00 | -45.25 |
| 5 | 0.00 | -11.25 | 0.00 | 33.40 | 0.00 | 3.04 | 0.00 | 0.00 | 16.84 | 0.00 | 42.04 |
| 6 | 0.00 | 0.00 | 0.00 | 0.00 | 3.04 | 0.00 | 0.00 | 0.00 | 0.00 | 2.29 | 5.34 |
| 7 | 0.00 | 0.00 | 15.94 | 0.00 | 0.00 | 0.00 | 0.00 | 36.13 | 0.00 | 0.00 | 52.07 |
| 8 | 0.00 | 0.00 | 0.00 | -49.36 | 0.00 | 0.00 | 36.13 | 0.00 | -24.89 | 0.00 | -38.12 |
| 9 | 0.00 | 0.00 | 0.00 | 0.00 | 16.84 | 0.00 | 0.00 | -24.89 | 0.00 | 12.70 | 4.66 |
| 10 | 0.00 | 0.00 | 0.00 | 0.00 | 0.00 | 2.29 | 0.00 | 0.00 | 12.70 | 0.00 | 15.00 |
| | | | | | | | | | | Covar SS | 16.19 |

If we rearrange the cell values the index value will change accordingly. For example, if the negative values in our example are swapped with the positive values in column 3, so that column 2 is entirely positive and column 3 entirely negative (Figure 5-32) the index value computed is I=0.26 (see Figure 5-37 for the significance test of this index value).

### Figure 5-32 Revised source data

| | +4.55 | -5.15 |
|---|---|---|
| +2.24 | +5.54 | -4.39 |
| +3.10 | +9.02 | -2.09 |
| | +0.46 | -3.06 |

Moran's I is one of the most frequently implemented statistics within GIS packages, including ArcGIS Spatial Statistics Toolbox, the AUTOCORR function in Idrisi, and in most other spatial analytical tools. This is in part due to its ease of computation across a range of datasets and weightings, and because of its relationship to well-understood measures used in univariate statistics and time series analysis. It is also readily extended in a number of ways that increase its application and usefulness. These extensions include: adjustment for differences in underlying population size; treatment of spatial point data utilizing distance bands rather like time lags; and computation of local Moran I values rather than a single whole map or global Moran I value. We examine each of these in turn.

Oden (1995) proposed an adjustment to Moran's I for zonal data where population size data (e.g. population at risk) is available. This statistic is supported within Clusterseer, but is not generally provided in other packages. Under this adjusted version the null hypothesis is that measured rates (e.g. disease rates, crime rates) in adjacent areas are independent, with the spatial variation observed simply reflecting the spatial variation in the underlying population. The computation of this statistic is quite involved, but essentially utilizes the difference between the proportion of cases or incidents in a given zone (i.e. as a proportion of the total cases in the study region) and the expected proportion in the population at large (again, computed as the population in zone $i$/total population at risk). The expected value for the adjusted statistic is similar to that for the standard statistic, being $E(I_{pop})=-1/(N-1)$ where $N$ is now the total population at risk. This statistic is not independent of population size, but can be readily standardized by dividing the computed value by the overall incidence rate for the study region.

We now turn to treatment of spatial point data rather than zoned or lattice data. Suppose that instead of zones we had a set of points $(x,y)$ with associated data values, $z$ (which could be values assigned to zone centroids). We could then compute:

$$I(h) = N(h) \frac{\sum_i \sum_j z_i z_j}{\sum_i z_i^2}$$

where $N(h)$ is the number of points in a distance band of width $d$ and mean distance of $h$; $z_i$ is the (standardized) value at point $i$; and $z_j$ is the (standardized) value at a point $j$ distance $h$ from $i$ (in practice within a distance band from $h-0.5d$ to $h+0.5d$). The summations apply for all point pairs in the selected band. Hence the adjacency matrix $W$ is replaced by distance, $h$, and by using a number of bands a set of $I$ values can be computed and plotted against $h$. This form of graph or diagram showing correlation information, as noted earlier, is known as a *correlogram*. To be meaningful the width of distance bands, $h$, should be greater than the minimum inter-point distance in the dataset, and the initial band should commence at $0.5d$ in order to give a better representation to values near the origin.

For example, the GS+ demonstration dataset comprises 132 separate spatial measurements of lead and aluminum levels in soil samples. An extract of the first 10 records is shown in Figure 5-33A with missing values being blank entries (coded on input in this case as -99). Note that missing values are not the same as zero values, and recorded zero values may actually be a reflection of the limitations of the measuring device rather than a true zero value. In such instances it may appropriate to adjust zero values to the minimum recordable value. Figure 5-33B shows a map of the point set for the selected $z$-variable (Pb, lead), with separate symbols indicating the four quartiles of the overall dataset that each point lies within (the triangular shape is the upper quartile, the square is the lower quartile). There are well over 10,000 possible point pairings in this sample dataset, but when grouped into distance bands only a subset of pairings is considered (Figure 5-33C). For example, in the first band, lag class 1, there are 226 point pairs, the average distance between pairs is 5.77 units, the bandwidth, $h$, is fixed for all lags at 8.21 units (defaulted to the maximum pairwise distance/10), and the Moran I value is 0.4179. This value decreases for the first few lags and then becomes closer to 0 and somewhat random. These values may be plotted, as shown in Figure 5-33D. Spatial autocorrelation (positive) as measured by this function, appears to be present for separation distances up to around 20-25 meters.

Each square on the graph in Figure 5-33D represents an index value generated from a large number of point pairs, and the individual contributions to the covariance can be plotted as a cloud of (in this case) 226 values (Figure 5-34). For example, the largest value in this cloud (see arrow) has a value of 0.4276 and is derived from points 100 and 115, whose separation distance is 6.44 units, and whose data values are 0.17 and 1.25 respectively. Now $(0.17-1.25)^2$ is not 0.4276, so we must look rather more carefully at what GS+ is doing with the data. The input dataset, like many such samples, is strongly left skewed — there are many small values recorded and only a few larger ones, with 1.25 being the maximum $z$-value. By default GS+ automatically transforms the data to make it more Normal, using the log transform $z^*=\ln(z+1)$. This gives the values: $z^*_{100}=0.157$ and $z^*_{115}=0.811$ and thus $(0.157-0.811)^2=0.4276$

*Figure 5-33 Sample dataset and Moran I analysis*

| A. Dataset, first 10 records | | | | B. Coordinates of data points |

| X-Coor | Y-Coor | Z | |
|---|---|---|---|
| m east | m north | Pb | Al |
| 4.50 | 11.90 | 0.42 | 0.42 |
| 2.70 | 29.40 | 0.60 | 0.45 |
| 1.60 | 32.60 | 0.60 | 0.08 |
| 4.10 | 44.50 | 0.43 | |
| 0.60 | 64.00 | 0.51 | 0.14 |
| 2.40 | 71.80 | 0.34 | 0.32 |
| 7.80 | 3.50 | 0.37 | 0.12 |
| 6.70 | 10.20 | 0.61 | |
| 6.70 | 16.30 | 0.46 | 0.49 |
| 6.50 | 27.20 | 0.44 | 0.07 |

C. Moran I statistics, by lag

D. Isotropic Correlogram

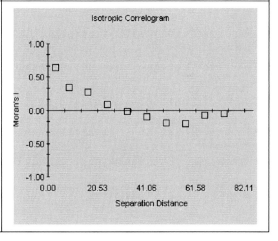

| Lag Class | Average Distance | Moran's I | Pairs |
|---|---|---|---|
| 1 | 5.77 | 0.4179 | 226 |
| 2 | 12.74 | 0.3691 | 675 |
| 3 | 20.74 | 0.1321 | 979 |
| 4 | 28.69 | 0.0616 | 1174 |
| 5 | 37.00 | -0.0772 | 1214 |
| 6 | 45.15 | -0.1483 | 1174 |
| 7 | 53.27 | -0.1997 | 989 |
| 8 | 61.37 | -0.1907 | 785 |
| 9 | 69.42 | 0.0037 | 553 |
| 10 | 77.39 | -0.0237 | 241 |

The correlogram shown is isotropic, i.e. it has been calculated for all points, irrespective of direction. Spatial patterns may well exhibit directional bias and hence it may be of interest to divide the circular lag regions into sectors and investigate the correlograms for each sector. Due to symmetry only half the possible bearings need to be considered. Taking a sector window of, say, 45 degrees (i.e. $X$ +/- 22.5 degrees) results in a set of 4 possible sectors to be analyzed. The choice of initial bearing, $X$, can be selected by reference to the problem at hand, or by examining the dataset to locate the orientation of the principal axis of the standard deviational ellipse. Software packages often identify this for the user and then generate a set of anisotropic correlograms to enable the data to be examined sector-by-sector. If all are broadly similar it is likely that directional effects are small. Again, looking at this sample dataset, the principal axis is at 130 degrees, and the four anisotropic correlograms do not differ greatly.

*Figure 5-34 Moran I (co)variance cloud, lag 1*

One alternative to the Moran I form of computation involves returning to the original set of criteria for a suitable function. Instead of computing the product sum:

$$S1 = \sum\sum z_i z_j$$

We could equally well have computed the sum of squared differences:

$$S2 = \sum\sum (z_i - z_j)^2$$

Or the absolute differences:

$$S3 = \sum\sum |z_i - z_j|$$

since these have similar desirable properties.

These expressions once again can be standardized by dividing by the variance and adjusted for the ratio of zones or point pairs sampled. If the expression S2 above is used the resulting measure is known as the Contiguity ratio or Geary's C ratio:

$$C = \frac{1}{p}\frac{\sum\sum w_{ij}(z_i - z_j)^2}{\sum(z_i - \bar{z})^2}$$

$$p = 2\frac{\sum\sum w_{ij}}{n-1}$$

This expression may be compared to the formula for Moran I provided earlier. Unfortunately this ratio is not particularly easy to interpret: its values vary around 1, which indicates no spatial autocorrelation; to values as low as 0, which indicate positive autocorrelation; and values greater than 1 which indicate negative autocorrelation. Perhaps for this reason it is rarely implemented in GIS packages in this form, but expression S2 turns out to be extremely useful in what is known as semivariance analysis as we shall see in our discussion on geostatistics (see Section 6.7).

Due to the inconvenience of working with absolute values, expression S3 is rarely used, but it is applied in semivariance analysis and is less sensitive to extreme values than computations based on S2. In this case the correlograms are known as Madograms — for more details see Deutsch and Journel (1992) and Goovaerts (1997).

### 5.5.2.3 Weighting models and lags

Our discussion on correlograms highlights the way in which distance bands can be used to generate data series in a manner similar to the lags used in time series analysis and Ripley's K function. Weighting matrices that incorporate values other than 0 and 1 were introduced by Cliff and Ord (1973). One way in which distance-based weighting is applied is to use the actual distances, rather than distance bands, as the means by which data pairs are "ordered". The usual approach (for example that adopted within the Crimestat package) is to use inverse distance, so that pairs that are further apart contribute less to the overall index value than those that are close together. The distance weighted Moran's I is then given by:

$$I = \frac{1}{p} \frac{\sum \sum \left[ \left( z_i - \bar{z} \right) \left( z_j - \bar{z} \right) \right] / \left( d_{ij} + \varepsilon \right)}{\sum \left( z_i - \bar{z} \right)^2} \text{, where}$$

$$p = \frac{1}{n} \sum \sum 1 / \left( d_{ij} + \varepsilon \right)$$

The $\varepsilon$ here represents an increment applied to the distance to ensure that when $d_{ij}$ is small, results are not overly distorted or overflow. Other software packages implement a range of such distance weightings. For example, ArcGIS includes: inverse distance; inverse distance squared; and specified distance bands amongst its options.

With datasets that represents zones rather than points, as in our earlier examples, GIS tools may be used to map the data and compute spatial weights. Amongst the most

extensive facilities available at present for conducting such calculations are provided by the GeoDa and ArcGIS packages, so we will use these to illustrate the range of facilities that have been implemented in readily available software.

Simple rook's move and queen's move contiguity weights are supported within GeoDa for polygonal regions. Typically these will be first order contiguity values, but $2^{nd}$ or higher order weights can also be generated. Secondly, distance-based weights can be generated based on polygon centroid locations or using a defined $(x,y)$ pair falling within the selected polygon. This requires a threshold value to be set, and all points (representing polygons) within this distance band are included within the weighting (as per ArcGIS distance bands). ArcGIS also supports a combination of fixed distance bands and distance decay, which it calls *zone of indifference weighting*. Distance computations in both GeoDa and ArcGIS are based on projected (Euclidean) distance, plus a second option: in GeoDa's case unprojected (approximate arc distance); and in the case of ArcGIS, city block calculations ($L_1$ metric).

A further method, based on the number of nearest-neighbors, is also supported in GeoDa. This requires the number of neighbors to be included as a parameter, and then varies the distances to reflect the value set (i.e. an adaptive method). The GeoDa code uses the Approximate Nearest Neighbor (ANN) software library developed at the University of Maryland to determine such neighborhood relations.

The advantage of this nearest-neighbors approach is that the spatial weights for tightly packed small zones will be more similar to those of larger zones within the same study region, which tends not be the case with pure distance-based selection. Finally, a user-defined spatial weights matrix may be defined and read into either of these two packages — of course this requires very careful construction to ensure the weights matrix reflects the topology and weighting patterns intended. Neither of these packages explicitly supports weights based on shared boundary lengths. With initial "point set data" weights could be determined by construction of Voronoi polygons and computing the lengths of shared boundaries, but facilities to perform such operations directly are not provided within existing GIS and related software. Information from the Delaunay triangulation and/or Voronoi polygon creation could be used to generate a spatial weights file, which ArcGIS and GeoDa, for example could import. In this case, and by modifying or augmenting a program-generated standard weights file, weights with closer application-specific meaning may be created, for example based on measured interactions or flows between the sampled regions.

Idrisi supports simple autocorrelation computations for raster datasets using Moran's I. Its weights matrix options include rook's move and king's move (we would call this queen's move), with weights of 1 and 0.7071... for the direct and diagonal moves respectively. A form of support for higher order lags is indirectly supported in Idrisi by resampling the grid.

### 5.5.3 Local indicators of spatial association (LISA)

If we look more closely at the Moran I index we see that it can be disaggregated to provide a series of local indices. We start with the standard formulation we provided earlier:

$$I = \frac{1}{p} \frac{\sum_i \sum_j w_{ij}(z_i - \overline{z})(z_j - \overline{z})}{\sum_i (z_i - \overline{z})^2}, \text{ where}$$

$$p = \sum_i \sum_j w_{ij} / n$$

Examining the computation of this "global" index provided earlier in Figure 5-31B, we can see that each row in the computation contributes to the overall sum (Figure 5-35A), with the covariance component being 16.19 and overall Moran I value 0.03167. Each row item could be standardized by the overall sum

of squared deviations and adjusted by the number of cells, $n$, as shown. The total of these local contributions divided by the total number of joins, $\Sigma\Sigma w_{ij}$, gives the overall or Global Moran I value. These individual components, or Local Indicators of Spatial Association (LISA), can be mapped and tested for significance to provide an indication of clustering patterns within the study region (Figure 5-36). The calculations require some adjustment in order to provide Global Moran I and LISA values in their commonly used form. The first adjustment is to the weights matrix. It is usual to standardize the row totals in the weights matrix to sum to 1. One advantage of row standardization is that for each row (location) the set of weights corresponds to a form of weighted average of the neighbors that are included, which also enables different models to be readily compared. Row standardization may also provide a computationally more suitable weights matrix. This procedure alters the Global Moran I value when rows have differing totals, which is the typical situation. For the example above the effect is to increase the computed Moran I to 0.0736. The second adjustment involves using $(n-1)$ rather than $n$ as the row multiplier, and then the sum is re-adjusted by this factor to produce the Global index value. These changes are illustrated in Figure 5-35B and Figure 5-36 and correspond to the computations performed within GeoDa, R and SpaceStat (Anselin, personal communication). ArcGIS offers the option to have no weights matrix standardization, row standardization (dividing rows by row totals) or total weights standardization (dividing all cells by the overall cell total). The Geary $C$ contiguity index may also be disaggregated to produce a LISA measure, in the same manner as for the Moran I. Another measure, known as the "G" statistic, due to Getis and Ord (1992, 1995), may also be used in this way. The latter is supported within ArcGIS as both a global index and in disaggregated form for identifying local clustering patterns, which ArcGIS considers this as a form of hot-spot analysis.

*Figure 5-35 Local Moran I computation*

**A. C*W:** Adjustment by multiplication of the weighting matrix, **W**

| | 1 | 2 | 3 | 4 | 5 | 6 | 7 | 8 | 9 | 10 | Row sum, S | R=S/SSD | I(i)=nR | |
|---|---|---|---|---|---|---|---|---|---|---|---|---|---|---|
| 1 | 0.00 | 2.53 | 0.00 | -7.52 | 0.00 | 0.00 | 0.00 | 0.00 | 0.00 | 0.00 | -4.99 | -0.03 | -0.25 | |
| 2 | 2.53 | 0.00 | 0.00 | 0.00 | -11.25 | 0.00 | 0.00 | 0.00 | 0.00 | 0.00 | -8.72 | -0.04 | -0.44 | |
| 3 | 0.00 | 0.00 | 0.00 | -21.77 | 0.00 | 0.00 | 15.94 | 0.00 | 0.00 | 0.00 | -5.84 | -0.03 | -0.30 | |
| 4 | -7.52 | 0.00 | -21.77 | 0.00 | 33.40 | 0.00 | 0.00 | -49.36 | 0.00 | 0.00 | -45.25 | -0.23 | -2.30 | |
| 5 | 0.00 | -11.25 | 0.00 | 33.40 | 0.00 | 3.04 | 0.00 | 0.00 | 16.84 | 0.00 | 42.04 | 0.21 | 2.14 | |
| 6 | 0.00 | 0.00 | 0.00 | 0.00 | 3.04 | 0.00 | 0.00 | 0.00 | 0.00 | 2.29 | 5.34 | 0.03 | 0.27 | |
| 7 | 0.00 | 0.00 | 15.94 | 0.00 | 0.00 | 0.00 | 0.00 | 36.13 | 0.00 | 0.00 | 52.07 | 0.26 | 2.65 | |
| 8 | 0.00 | 0.00 | 0.00 | -49.36 | 0.00 | 0.00 | 36.13 | 0.00 | -24.89 | 0.00 | -38.12 | -0.19 | -1.94 | |
| 9 | 0.00 | 0.00 | 0.00 | 0.00 | 16.84 | 0.00 | 0.00 | -24.89 | 0.00 | 12.70 | 4.66 | 0.02 | 0.24 | |
| 10 | 0.00 | 0.00 | 0.00 | 0.00 | 0.00 | 2.29 | 0.00 | 0.00 | 12.70 | 0.00 | 15.00 | 0.08 | 0.76 | |
| | | | | | | | | | | Covar S | **16.19** | | **0.82** | 0.03167 |

**B. C*W1:** Adjustment by multiplication of the row-adjusted weighting matrix, **W1**

| | 1 | 2 | 3 | 4 | 5 | 6 | 7 | 8 | 9 | 10 | Row sum, S | R=S/SSD | I(i)=(n-1)R | |
|---|---|---|---|---|---|---|---|---|---|---|---|---|---|---|
| 1 | 0.00 | 1.27 | 0.00 | -3.76 | 0.00 | 0.00 | 0.00 | 0.00 | 0.00 | 0.00 | -2.49 | -0.0127 | -0.1141 | |
| 2 | 1.27 | 0.00 | 0.00 | 0.00 | -5.62 | 0.00 | 0.00 | 0.00 | 0.00 | 0.00 | -4.36 | -0.0222 | -0.1994 | |
| 3 | 0.00 | 0.00 | 0.00 | -10.89 | 0.00 | 0.00 | 7.97 | 0.00 | 0.00 | 0.00 | -2.92 | -0.0148 | -0.1335 | |
| 4 | -1.88 | 0.00 | -5.44 | 0.00 | 8.35 | 0.00 | 0.00 | -12.34 | 0.00 | 0.00 | -11.31 | -0.0575 | -0.5177 | |
| 5 | 0.00 | -2.81 | 0.00 | 8.35 | 0.00 | 0.76 | 0.00 | 0.00 | 4.21 | 0.00 | 10.51 | 0.0534 | 0.4810 | |
| 6 | 0.00 | 0.00 | 0.00 | 0.00 | 1.52 | 0.00 | 0.00 | 0.00 | 0.00 | 1.15 | 2.67 | 0.0136 | 0.1221 | |
| 7 | 0.00 | 0.00 | 7.97 | 0.00 | 0.00 | 0.00 | 0.00 | 18.07 | 0.00 | 0.00 | 26.04 | 0.1324 | 1.1915 | |
| 8 | 0.00 | 0.00 | 0.00 | -16.45 | 0.00 | 0.00 | 12.04 | 0.00 | -8.30 | 0.00 | -12.71 | -0.0646 | -0.5814 | |
| 9 | 0.00 | 0.00 | 0.00 | 0.00 | 5.61 | 0.00 | 0.00 | -8.30 | 0.00 | 4.23 | 1.55 | 0.0079 | 0.0710 | |
| 10 | 0.00 | 0.00 | 0.00 | 0.00 | 0.00 | 1.15 | 0.00 | 0.00 | 6.35 | 0.00 | 7.50 | 0.0381 | 0.3431 | |
| | | | | | | | | | | Covar S | 11.48 | | 0.6625 | 0.073612 |

*Figure 5-36 LISA map, Moran I*

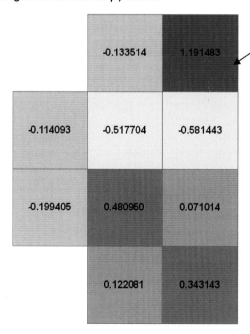

The ArcGIS implementation of the G statistic facilitates the use of simple fixed Euclidean distance bands (threshold distances) within binary weights (as described below), but also permits the use of the Manhattan metric and a variety of alternative models of contiguity such as: inverse distance; inverse distance squared; so-called Zones of Indifference (a combination of inverse distance and threshold distance); and user-defined spatial weights matrices. Unlike the Moran I and Geary C statistics, the Getis and Ord G statistic identifies the degree to which high or low values cluster together.

The standard global form of the Getis and Ord G statistic is:

$$G = \frac{\sum_i \sum_j w_{ij} z_i z_j}{\sum_i \sum_j z_i z_j}, i \neq j$$

whilst the local variant is

$$G_i = \frac{\sum_j w_{ij} z_j}{\sum_j z_j}, i \neq j$$

The weights matrix, **W**, is typically defined as a symmetric binary contiguity matrix, with contiguity determined by a (generalized) distance threshold, $d$. A variant of this latter statistic, which is regarded as of greater use in hot-spot analysis, permits $i=j$ in the expression (so includes $i$ in the summations, with $w_{ii}=1$ rather than 0 in the binary weights contiguity model) and is known as the $G_i^*$ statistic rather than $G_i$. Note that these local statistics are not meaningful if there are no events or values in the set of cells or zones under examination.

The expected value of $G$ under Complete Spatial Randomness (CSR) is:

$$E(G) = \frac{\sum_i \sum_j w_{ij}}{n(n-1)} = \frac{W}{n(n-1)}, i \neq j$$

where $n$ is the number of points or zones in the study area and $W$ is the sum of the weights, which for binary weights is simply the number of pairs within the distance threshold, $d$. The equivalent expected value for the local variant is:

$$E(G_i) = \frac{\sum_j w_{ij}}{(n-1)} = \frac{W_i}{(n-1)}$$

where $n$ is the number of points or zones within the threshold distance, $d$, for point/region $i$. Closed formulas for the variances have been obtained but are very lengthy. They facilitate the construction of z-scores and hence significance testing of the global and local versions of the G statistics. For the local measure both computed values and z-scores may be useful to map.

The Rookcase add-in provides support for all three LISA measures with variable lag distance and number of lags. Further discussion of these methods is provided in several other sections of this Guide: in Section 5.2 covering exploratory spatial data analysis (ESDA); in Section 5.6.5 in the context of regression modeling; and in Sections 4.6 and Chapter 6 relating to grid files, since there are parallels between several of the concepts applied.

### 5.5.4 Significance tests for autocorrelation indices

As noted in the preceding sections and in Table 5-9, the various global and local spatial autocorrelation coefficients discussed can be tested for statistical significance under two, rather different, model assumptions. The first is the classical statistical assumption of Normality, whereby it is assumed that the observed value of the coefficient is the result of the set $\{z_i\}$ of values being independent and identically distributed drawings from a Normal distribution, implying that variances are constant across the region. The second model is one of randomization, whereby the observed pattern of the set $\{z_i\}$ of values is assumed to be just one realization from all possible random permutations of the observed values across all the zones.

Both models have important weaknesses, for example as a result of underlying population size variation and lack of homogeneity of probabilities, but are widely implemented in software packages to provide estimates of the significance of observed results. In the case of the randomization model many software packages generate a set of $N$ random permutations of the input data, where $N$ is user specified. For each simulation run index values are computed and the set of such values used to provide a pseudo-probability distribution for the given problem, against which the observed value can be compared. A z-transform of the coefficients under Normality or Randomization assumptions is distributed approximately N(0,1), hence this may be compared to percentage points of the Normal distribution to identify particularly high or low values.

The Rookcase add-in for Excel computes both values, for the global Moran I and Geary $C$, and the summary results in Figure 5-37 illustrate this for the revised test dataset shown in Figure 5-32. Note that these results are calculated using overall weight adjustment rather than row-wise adjustment. The results suggest the observed index value of 0.26 could reasonably be expected to have occurred by chance. With the local variant of Moran's I the same procedures as for the Global statistic can be adopted.

Crimestat provides the option to compute z-scores for this statistic but notes that it may be very slow to calculate, depending on the number of zones. GeoDa uses random permutations to obtain an estimated mean and standard deviation, which may then be used to create an estimated z-score.

The local variants of these statistics utilize values in individual cells or zones over and over again. This process means that the values obtained for adjacent neighbors will not be independent, which breaches the requirements for significance testing, a problem exacerbated by the fact that such cells are also likely to exhibit spatial autocorrelation. There are no generally-agreed solutions to these problems, but one approach is to regard each test as one of a multiple set. In classical statistics multiple tests of *independent* sets (the members of which are not correlated) are made using a reduced or corrected significance level, $\alpha$. The most basic of these adjustments (known as a Bonferroni correction, after its original protagonist) is to use a significance level defined by $\alpha/n$, where $n$ is the number of tests carried out, or in the present case, the number of zones or features being tested. If $n$ is very large the use of such corrections results in extremely conservative confidence levels that may be inappropriate. Monte Carlo randomization techniques that seek to estimate the sampling distribution may be more appropriate in such cases.

*Figure 5-37 Significance tests for revised sample dataset*

| Summary: Moran's I and Geary's C | | | | |
|---|---|---|---|---|
| Moran's I = | 0.26 | | Geary's C = | 0.82 |
| z-Normal I = | 1.63 | | z-Normal C = | 0.72 |
| Var. Normal I = | 0.05 | | Var. Normal C = | 0.06 |
| z-Random I = | 1.57 | | z-Random C = | 0.74 |
| Var. Random I = | 0.06 | | Var. Random C = | 0.06 |
| | | | | |
| # Obs | Mean | SD | # Neighbours | |
| 10 | 1.02 | 4.67 | 13 | |

# 5.6 Spatial Regression

## 5.6.1 Regression overview

Regression analysis is the term used to describe a family of methods that seek to model the relationship between one (or more) *dependent* or *response* variables and a number of *independent* or *predictor* variables. A typical (linear) relationship might be of the form:

$$y = \beta_0 + \beta_1 x_1 + \beta_2 x_2 + \beta_3 x_3 + ..., \text{ or}$$
$$y = \mathbf{x}\boldsymbol{\beta}$$

where $\boldsymbol{\beta}$ is a column vector of $p$ parameters to be determined and $\mathbf{x}$ is a row vector of independent variables with a 1 in the first column. It should be noted that the expression shown below is also described as linear since it remains linear in the coefficients, $\boldsymbol{\beta}$, even if it is not linear in the predictor variables, $\mathbf{x}$, e.g.:

$$y = \beta_0 + \beta_1 x_1 + \beta_2 x_1^2 + \beta_3 x_2 + \beta_4 x_1 x_2 + ...$$

If $y=\{y_i\}$ is a set of $n$ observations or measurements of the response variable, with corresponding recording of matching values for the set of independent variables, then a series of linear equations of the type shown above can be constructed. However, typically the number of observations will be greater than the number of coefficients (the system is said to be *over-determined*). One approach to this problem is to seek a best fit solution, where best fit is taken to mean a solution for the vector $\boldsymbol{\beta}$ that minimizes the difference between the fitted model and observed values at these data points. In practice the procedure most widely applied seeks to minimize the sum of squared differences, hence the term *Least Squares*. Each linear expression requires an additional "error" component to allow for the degree of fit of the expression to the particular data values. If we denote these error components by $\varepsilon_i$, the general form of the expression above now becomes:

$$y_i = \beta_0 + \beta_1 x_{1i} + \beta_2 x_{2i} + \beta_3 x_{3i} + ... + \varepsilon_i, \text{ or}$$
$$y = \mathbf{X}\boldsymbol{\beta} + \boldsymbol{\varepsilon}$$

where $\mathbf{X}$ is now a matrix with 1's in column 1, and $\boldsymbol{\varepsilon}$ is a vector of errors that in conceptual terms is assumed to represent the effects of unobserved variables and measurement errors in the observations. Typically we assume that the expected value of these errors is zero, $E(\varepsilon)=\mathbf{0}$, and the variance, $E(\varepsilon\varepsilon)=\sigma^2\mathbf{I}$, is constant. Here $\mathbf{0}$ is a column vector of zeros and $\mathbf{I}$ is the identity matrix.

This set of $n$ equations in $p$ unknowns ($n>p$) is typically solved for the vector $\boldsymbol{\beta}$ by seeking to minimize the sum of the squared error terms, $\varepsilon\varepsilon^T$ (*Ordinary Least Squares*, or *OLS*). The solution for the coefficients using this approach is obtained from the matrix expression:

$$\hat{\boldsymbol{\beta}} = \left(\mathbf{X}^T\mathbf{X}\right)^{-1}\mathbf{X}^T\mathbf{y}, \text{ and } var(\hat{\boldsymbol{\beta}}) = \sigma^2\left(\mathbf{X}^T\mathbf{X}\right)^{-1}$$

where the hat (^) symbol denotes concern with sample estimates of population parameters and the sample estimates of the population error ($\varepsilon$) terms are described as 'residuals'.

The variance for such models is usually estimated from the residuals of the fitted model, using the expression:

$$\hat{\sigma}^2 = \frac{\sum_{i=1}^{n}\left(y_i - \hat{y}_i\right)^2}{n - p}$$

Methods such as these may be used in the context of spatial description and mapping, as part of a process of data exploration, or for explanatory and/or predictive purposes.

The broad principles of regression analysis and modeling, as described in basic statistics texts, also apply to spatial datasets. In a spatial context one is seeking to model the variation in some spatially distributed dependent variable, for example house prices in a city, from a set of independent variables such as size of property, age of property, distance from transport facilities, proportion of green space in the region etc. (see further Table 5-11, *hedonic regression*). Spatial coordinates might be explicitly or implicitly incorporated into such models, for example including the coordinates of the centroid of a census tract or event location into the modeling process, or by taking account of the pattern of adjacency of neighboring zones.

Similar methods are also widely supported in raster-based packages, with the dependent variable being taken as one grid from a set of matching layers or bands, and the independent variables being taken as the matching grids. Grid cell entries are treated as the sample values (responses) and the measured predictor values. In most packages this technique is used to aid grid combination, but others suggest that it may be used for predictive purposes (e.g. predicting crop yield from a series of measured grids that provide details of soil structure and chemical makeup). This kind of modeling is generally unsafe due to the high degree of spatial autocorrelation between nearby cells in each grid (possibly generated by interpolation or resampling).

Ideally in regression analysis the form of the chosen model should be as simple as possible, both in terms of the expression employed and the number of independent variables included — these are sometimes referred to as the *simplicity* and *parsimony* objectives. In addition, the proportion of the variation in the dependent variable(s), **y**, explained by the independent variables, **x**, should be as high as possible, and the correlation between separate independent variables should be as low as possible. These criteria form part of a *strength of evidence* objective. If some, or all, of the **x** are highly correlated (typically having a correlation coefficient above 0.8) the model almost certainly contains redundant information and may be described as being *over-specified*. If a strong relationship exists between selected independent variables and is also broadly linear, the variables are said to exhibit *multi-collinearity*. There are a number of standard techniques for reducing multi-collinearity, including: applying the so-called centering transform (deducting the mean of the relevant independent variable from each measured value); increasing the sample size (especially if samples are quite small); removing the most inter-correlated variable;

and combining inter-correlated variables into a new single composite variable (e.g. using principal components analysis, PCA, or other data reduction techniques). The latter procedures can be viewed as forms of model re-specification.

With higher-order spatial trend analyses, multi-collinearity is to be expected since various combinations of the coordinates are themselves the independent variables. Technically, imperfect multi-collinearity does not result in the OLS assumptions being violated, but does lead to large standard errors for the coefficients involved, also referred to as *variance inflation* (VI). This limits their usefulness. As a rule of thumb, if the measure known as the Multi-collinearity Condition Number, MCN, is greater than 30 this problem is quite serious and should be addressed. The MCN is derived from the ratio of the largest to the smallest eigenvalue of the matrix $X^TX$. Generally the square root of this ratio is reported, but it is important to check this for any specific software package (if no square root is taken values greater than 1000 are taken as significant).

When fitting a model using OLS it is generally assumed that the errors (residuals for sample points) are identical and independently distributed (denoted *iid*). If the spread of errors is not constant, for example if in some parts of the study area the residuals are much more variable than in others these errors are said to exhibit *heteroskedasticity*. If the latter is the case (which may be detected using a range of standard tests) the estimated variance under OLS will be biased, either being too large or too small (it is not generally possible to know which direction the bias takes). As a result the specification of confidence intervals and the application of standard statistical significance tests (e.g. F tests) will not be reliable.

Many (most) spatial datasets exhibit patterns of data and/or residuals in which neighboring areas have similar values (*positive spatial autocorrelation*) and hence violate the core assumptions of standard regression models. One result of this feature of spatial data is to greatly over-estimate the effective sample size, and hence the degrees of freedom that may be indicated (for example in multiple grid regressions) will be stated as being far higher than they should be. One possible (partial) solution to this problem, in the case of grids, is to take (stratified or equalized) random samples from the response grid and apply regression to the subset of grid cells that correspond to these samples in the predictor grids. This approach is sometimes (rather confusingly) referred to as resampling.

A common additional requirement for standard regression modeling, as noted above, is that the distribution of the errors is not only identical but also Normal, i.e.

$\varepsilon \sim N(0, \sigma^2 I)$

If the distribution of the errors is Normal and the regression relationship is linear, this equates to the response variable being Normally distributed, and vice versa, i.e.

$y \sim N(X\beta, \sigma^2 I)$ , or setting the vector $\mu = X\beta$

$y \sim N(\mu, \sigma^2 I)$

The assumption of Normality permits the analytical derivation of confidence intervals for the model parameters and significance tests on their values (against the null hypothesis that they are zero). In order to satisfy the Normality conditions required in many models it is common to transform (continuous valued) response data using Log, Square Root or Box-Cox functions (Table 1-3) prior to analysis where this can be shown to improve the approximation to the Normal. It is also advisable to examine and, where appropriate, remove outliers even if these are not errors in the dataset but represent valid data that would otherwise distort the modeling process. Exclusion must be made explicit and separate investigation of any excluded data carried out. An alternative to exclusion is to weight observations according to some rule. Spatial declustering (see Section 5.1.2.2) is an example of such weighting applied to spatial datasets.

If spatial autocorrelation has been detected (see Section 5.5.1 *et seq.*) a more reasonable assumption is:

$y \sim N(\mu, C)$

where $C$ is a positive definite covariance matrix. Typically $C$ would be defined in such a way as to ensure that locations that are close to each other are represented with a high value for the modeled covariance, whilst places further apart have lower covariance. This may be achieved using some form of distance-decay function or, for zoned data, using a contiguity-based spatial weights matrix. This kind of arrangement is similar to *Generalized Least Squares* (GLS), which allows for so-called second-order effects via the inclusion of a covariance matrix. The standard form of expression for GLS is:

$y = X\beta + u$

where $u$ is a vector of random variables (errors) with mean 0 and variance-covariance matrix $C$. The GLS solution for $\beta$ is then:

$$\hat{\beta} = \left(X^T C^{-1} X\right)^{-1} X^T C^{-1} y, \ \operatorname{var}(\hat{\beta}) = \left(X^T C^{-1} X\right)^{-1}$$

In spatial analysis this kind of GLS model is often utilized, with the matrix $C$ modeled using some form of distance or interaction function. Note that $C$ must be invertible, which places some restrictions on the possible forms it may take. Simple weighted least squares (WLS) is a variant of GLS in which the matrix $C$ is diagonal and the diagonal values are not equal (hence the errors are heteroskedastic). In this case the weights are normally set to the inverse of the variance, thereby giving less weight to observations which have higher variance.

In addition to regression on dependent variables that take continuous values, similar methods have been developed for binary and count or rate data. In the case of binary data the data typically are transformed using the logit function (see Table 1-3). The central assumption of this model is that that the probability, $p$, of the dependent variable, $y$, taking the value 1 (rather than 0) follows the logistic curve, i.e.

$$p = prob\langle y = 1|\mathbf{x}\rangle = \frac{e^{\beta x}}{1 + e^{\beta x}}$$

This model can be linearised using the logit transform, $q = \ln(p/(1-p))$. The regression model then becomes

$$q_i = \beta_0 + \beta_1 x_{1i} + \beta_2 x_{2i} + \beta_3 x_{3i} + \ldots + \varepsilon_i, \text{ or}$$
$$\mathbf{q} = \mathbf{X\beta} + \mathbf{\varepsilon}$$

As with standard linear regression the errors in this model are assumed to be *iid* and the predictor variables are assumed not to be co-linear. The parameters in such models are determined using non-linear (iterative) optimization methods, involving maximization of the likelihood function. With count or rate data Poisson regression may be applicable. The model is similar in form to the binary logit model, but in this case the response variable, $y$, is count (integer) data (hence non-continuous). The basic model in this case is of the form:

$$y = Ae^{\beta x}$$

where $A$ is an (optional) offset or population-based value (e.g. the underlying population at risk in each modeled zone). This model may be linearised, as per the logit model, but this time by simply applying a log transform: $q = \ln(y)$. The regression model then becomes:

$$q_i = (\ln(A) + \beta_0) + \beta_1 x_{1i} + \beta_2 x_{2i} + \beta_3 x_{3i} + \ldots + \varepsilon_i, \text{ or}$$
$$\mathbf{q} = \mathbf{X\beta} + \mathbf{\varepsilon}$$

There are many variants of linear and non-linear regression analysis and a wealth of associated terms applied in this field — a number of these are summarized in Table 5-11. In some instances the techniques are not always described as regression analysis *per se*, but share many underlying statistical assumptions and associated tests.

Choosing between alternative models presents a particular challenge. Each additional parameter may improve the fit of the model to the sample dataset (or data set), but at the cost of increasing model complexity. Model building should be guided by the principal of *parsimony* — that is the simplest model that is fit for the purpose for which it is built. Overly complicated models frequently involve a loss of information regarding the nature of key relationships. Drawing on this *information content* view of modeling, an information theoretic statistic is often used as a guide to model selection. The most common statistic now used is known as the Akaike Information Criterion (AIC) and is often computed in its small-sample corrected version (AICc) since this is asymptotic to the standard version. The measures are defined as:

$$AIC = -2\ln(L) + 2k$$
$$AICc = -2\ln(L) + 2k\left(\frac{n}{n-k-1}\right)$$

where $n$ is the sample size, $k$ is the number of parameters used in the model, and $L$ is the likelihood function. It is recommended that the corrected version be used unless $n/k > 40$. If the errors are assumed to be Normally distributed then the standard expression can be re-written as:

$$AIC = n(\ln(2\pi\sigma^2) + 1) + 2k$$

The AIC measure is utilized in several of the software packages described in this Section and elsewhere in this Guide (e.g. in the point pattern analysis software, spatstat). For example GeoDa uses the version above in OLS estimation, whilst Geographically Weighted Regression (GWR, see further Section 5.6.3) uses a variant of the version corrected for small sample sizes. Both packages use appropriate alternative expressions in cases where the likelihood functions are different from the Normal model. A wide range of regression models, including OLS and GWR, and several autocorrelation models (see below) are supported by the SAM package (which also supports AIC-based model selection). Although SAM has been designed for and by macroecologists, it can equally well be applied in other fields of spatial research.

*Table 5-11 Selected regression analysis terminology*

| Form of model | Notes |
|---|---|
| Simple linear | A single approximately continuous response (dependent) variable and one or more predictor variables related by an expression that is linear in its coefficients (i.e. not necessary linear in the predictor variables). Note the similarity to weighted averages and geostatistical models |
| Multiple | This term applies when there are multiple predictor variables and all are quantitative |
| Multivariate | Regression involving more than one response variable. If, in addition, there are multiple predictor variables the composite term multivariate multiple regression is used |
| SAR | Simultaneous autoregressive models (SAR is also used as an abbreviation for Spatial Autoregression). A form of regression model including adjustments for spatial autocorrelation. Many variants of SAR model have been devised |
| CAR | Conditional autoregressive models — as per SAR, a form of regression model including adjustments for spatial autocorrelation. Differs from SAR in the specification of the inverse covariance matrix. In this model the expected value of the response variable is regarded as being conditional on the recorded values at all other locations |
| Logistic | Logistic regression applies where the response variable is binary, i.e. of type 1/0 or Yes/No. Typically this involves use of the logit transform (Table 1-3), with linear regression being conducted on the transformed data. Variants on the basic binary model are available for response variables that represent more than two categories, which may or may not be ordered |
| Poisson | Poisson regression applies where the response variable is a count (e.g. crime incidents, cases of a disease) rather than a continuous variable. This model may also be applied to standardized counts or "rates", such as disease incidence per capita, species of tree per square kilometer. It assumes the response variable has a Poisson distribution whose expected value (mean) is dependent on one or more predictor variables. Typically the log of the expected value is assumed to have a linear relationship with the predictor variables. An excess of zeros in many sample datasets may present problems when attempting to apply this form of regression |
| Ecological | The term ecological regression does not relate directly to the subject of ecology, but to the application of regression methods to data that are aggregated to zones (lattices) , as is often the case with census datasets and information collected by administrative districts. The related issue of the so-called *ecological fallacy* (referred to in Section 3.3.1) concerns the difficulty of making inferences about the nature of individuals within an aggregated region on the basis of statistics (data values, parameters, relationships) that apply to the aggregated data |
| Hedonic | The term hedonic regression is used in economics, especially in real estate (property) economics, to estimate demand or prices as a combination of separate components, each of which may be treated as if it had its own market or price. In the context of regression these separate components are often treated as the independent variables in the modeling process |
| Analysis of variance | Applies if all of the predictors are either qualitative or classified into a (small) number of distinct groups. Analysis of variance methods are often used to analyze the significance of alternative regression models under the Normality assumption for the distribution of errors |
| Analysis of covariance | Applies if some of the predictors are qualitative and some are quantitative. Analysis of covariance methods are also widely applied in spatial modeling, where the covariance of observations at pairs of locations is examined |

A second information theoretic measure, which places greater weight on the number of parameters used, is often also provided. This is known as the Bayesian Information Criterion or BIC, or sometimes as the Swartz Criterion. It has the simpler form:

$$BIC = -2\ln(L) + k\ln(n)$$

### 5.6.2 Simple regression and trend surface modeling

Simple regression techniques have been widely applied in spatial analysis for a very long time. The general form of model employed can be represented by the expression:

$$y = f(x_1, x_2, \mathbf{w})$$

where: $y$ is the (possibly transformed) observed value of some continuous dependent variable $y$ at location $(x_1, x_2)$; $f()$ is a general function to be defined, but often a linear expression in the coefficients; and $\mathbf{w}$ is a vector of attributes measured at $(x_1, x_2)$. For example, if $f()$ is simply modeled as a linear function of the coordinates we can write

$$y = \beta_0 + \beta_1 x_1 + \beta_2 x_2$$

Model performance can be assessed using a number of statistics that are discussed in standard statistical text books. One such statistic, which will be referred to in our subsequent discussion, is the correlation coefficient squared (or $R^2$) statistic. This statistic records the proportion of variation in the data that is explained by the model. A modification this statistic, adjusted $R^2$, takes into account the complexity of the model in terms of the number of variables that are specified.

With a set of $n$ observations made at different locations in the study area, $y_i(x_{1i}, x_{2i})$, a series of $n$ equations can be set up and solved for the $p=3$ unknown parameters using OLS. This is simply a linear trend or best fit linear surface through the point set, $\{y_i\}$. A set of differences between the observed values and the best fit surface can then be computed:

$$\varepsilon_i = \hat{y}_i - y_i$$

where the $y$ hat values (the estimated values) are obtained by evaluating the trend surface at each point $i$. Assuming the value of $n$ is reasonably large and provides a representative coverage of the complete set of locations in the study area, these residuals may be treated as samples from a continuous surface and mapped using simple contouring or filled contouring procedures. If, on the other hand, the sample points represent centroids of zones (pre-defined regions or generated zones, e.g. Voronoi polygons) the visualization of residuals is generally applied to these zones as a choropleth map. Plotting the residuals using a combination of the fitted surface and stick/point display in 3D may also be helpful but is less common within GIS packages.

Whichever approach is adopted the fitting of a trend surface and mapping of residuals is a form of exploratory spatial data analysis (ESDA — see further, Section 5.2) and is supported in many GIS and related packages. Within GIS packages such residual maps may be overlaid on topographic or thematic maps with a pre-specified transparency (e.g. 50%) enabling spatial associations between large positive or negative residuals to be visually compared to potential explanatory factors.

With higher order polynomials or alternative functions (e.g. trigonometric series) the fit of the trend surface to the sample data *may* be improved (the sum of the squared residuals reduced) but the overall utility of the procedure may well become questionable. This may occur for many reasons including the increased difficulty in interpreting the fitted surface (e.g. in terms of process), and increased volatility of the surface close to and immediately beyond the convex hull of the sample points and/or in sparsely sampled regions. Higher order polynomial trend surfaces are usually limited to second order equations, although in some applications 3rd order or above have been shown to be useful — for example, Lichstein *et al.* (2002) fit a full 3rd order polynomial trend equation to the spatial coordinates of bird species sightings. They then proceed to analyze the distribution of bird species by modeling habitat + trend (large scale spatial pattern) + spatial autocorrelation (small scale spatial pattern) in order to identify separate factors that might be used to explain observed distribution patterns by species. Note that any analysis of trends in this way will result in a fitted surface whose form is heavily dependent upon the set of specific locations at which measured values of *y* are available and the scale factors operating for the problem being examined. Frequently data locations are not the result of selections made by the analyst but are pre-determined survey locations that may reflect convenience for data gathering (e.g. proximity to a forest path, access to quarry sites, location of wells) rather than an ideal sampling frame for analytic purposes.

The most common measure of the quality of fit of a trend surface or similar regression is the *coefficient of determination*, which is the squared coefficient of (multiple) correlation, $R^2$. This is simply a function of the squared residuals with standardization being achieved using the sum of squared deviations of observations from their overall mean:

$$R^2 = 1 - \frac{\sum \varepsilon_i^2}{\sum (y_i - \bar{y})^2}, \; R^2 \in [0,1]$$

Under appropriate conditions, e.g. $\varepsilon \sim N(0, \sigma^2 I)$ the significance of this coefficient can be evaluated in a meaningful way, with values close to 1 generally being highly significant. Frequently, however, the statistical significance of the measure cannot be determined due to distribution conditions not being met, and the value obtained should be seen as no more than an indicator of goodness of fit.

Trend surface and residuals analysis is essentially a form of non-statistical ESDA — it is not necessary to state how significant the fit of the model is or what confidence limits might be placed around the values of the estimated coefficients and the fitted surface. For inferential analysis the standard pre-conditions that apply are extremely unlikely to be met in the context of spatial analysis.

Conditions that may apply for statistical purposes include:

- the set $\{y_i\}$ is comprised of independent (uncorrelated) observable random variables. This set does not have to be drawn from a Normal distribution but it is often helpful or necessary that they are at least asymptotically Normal (possibly after transformation)

- the set $\{\varepsilon_i\}$ is comprised of independently and identically distributed (iid) unobservable random variables with mean 0 and constant variance, $\sigma^2$, where $\sigma^2$ is not a function of $\beta$ or x

- the set $\{\varepsilon_i\}$ is Normally distributed — this condition is not a pre-requisite but is a requirement for inference on finite sets (as previously noted, this condition is directly connected to the first bullet point above)

- the model applied is appropriate, complete and global. This assumption incorporates the assumption that the independent variables, **x**, are themselves uncorrelated, and the parameters $\beta$ are global constants

Tests for the Normality of the observations and the residuals are commonplace (the first and third conditions above), and a variety of tests for heteroskedasticity (resulting in failure to meet the second condition) have been implemented in a several GIS-related packages. Note that heteroskedasticity may or may not be associated with positive spatial autocorrelation. As discussed in Section 5.5.2.2, testing for (global) spatial autocorrelation using the Moran I statistic is a useful starting point for such analyses. A spatial weights matrix, **W**, is required in order to generate the Moran I statistic. As shown earlier this statistic has the form:

$$I = \frac{1}{p} \frac{\sum \sum w_{ij}(y_i - \bar{y})(y_j - \bar{y})}{\sum (y_i - \bar{y})^2}, \text{ where}$$

$$p = \sum \sum w_{ij} / n$$

This measure is the spatial equivalent of the standard product moment correlation coefficient. The weighting terms, $w_{ij}$, are defined either from patterns of zone adjacency or using some form of distance-decay function. A value of Moran's I=1 indicates perfect positive spatial autocorrelation, whilst a value of I very close to 0 indicates no spatial autocorrelation. A value such as I=0.2 indicates some positive spatial autocorrelation, although this may or may not be significant — with large spatial datasets small positive I-values are very often technically identified as significant, although the value of this interpretation may not be great.

Assuming that significant spatial autocorrelation is identified several options exist for continued analysis using regression methods:

- proceed with the analysis ignoring the observed spatial autocorrelation (particularly if it is small) accepting that the drawing of confidence intervals and determination of significance levels will not be possible, or if computed may be misleading

- drop the requirement that the parameters β are global constants and allow these to vary with location. Effectively this involves fitting a series of regression surfaces to the dataset in such a way as to ensure a continuous prediction surface is created. One procedure for achieving this objective is known as Geographical Weighted Regression (GWR), and is described in Section 5.6.3; or

- include additional elements into the regression model that take explicit account of the observed pattern of spatial autocorrelation, as described in Section 5.6.4.1

### 5.6.3 Geographically Weighted Regression (GWR)

GWR is the term introduced by Fotheringham, Charlton and Brunsdon (1997, 2002) to describe a family of regression models in which the coefficients, β, are allowed to vary spatially. GWR uses the coordinates of each sample point or zone centroid, $t_i$, as a target point for a form of spatially weighted least squares regression (for some models the target points can be separately defined, e.g. as grid intersection points, rather than observed data points). The result is a model of the form:

$$y = X\beta(t) + \epsilon$$

The coefficients β(t) are determined by examining the set of points within a well-defined neighborhood of each of the sample points. This neighborhood is essentially a circle, radius $r$, around each data point (anisotropic modeling is not currently supported). However, if $r$ is treated as a fixed value in which all points are regarded as of equal importance it could include every point (for $r$ large) or alternatively no other points (for $r$ very small). Instead of using a fixed value for $r$ it is replaced by a distance-decay function, $f(d)$, as described earlier (Section 4.4.5). This function may be finite or infinite, much as with kernel density estimation (Section 4.3.4). The functions utilized in the GWR software package are of the form:

$$f(d) = e^{-d^2/2h^2}, \text{ or } f(d) = e^{-d/h}, \text{ or}$$

$$f(d) = \left(1 - \frac{d^2}{h^2}\right)^2, d < r, \ f(d) = 0 \text{ otherwise}$$

In these functions the parameter, $h$, also known as the *bandwidth*, is the key factor determining the way in which the weighting schemes operate. A small bandwidth results in very rapid distance decay, whereas a larger value will result in a smoother weighting scheme. This parameter may be defined manually or alternatively by some form of adaptive method such as cross-validation minimization, e.g. jackknifing — see further, Section 6.7.2.2 and Efron (1982) and Efron and Tibshirani (1997), or minimization of the Akaike Information Criterion (AIC). The use of a kernel function also raises the possibility of generating additional descriptive statistics, as have been described earlier.

Using a selected kernel function and bandwidth, $h$, a diagonal weighting matrix, $\mathbf{W}(t)$, may be defined for every sample point, $t$, with off-diagonal elements being 0. The parameters $\beta(t)$ for this point can then be determined using the standard solution for weighted least squares regression:

$$\hat{\boldsymbol{\beta}}(t) = \left(\mathbf{X}^T\mathbf{W}(t)\mathbf{X}\right)^{-1}\mathbf{X}^T\mathbf{W}(t)\mathbf{y}$$

or, letting $\mathbf{D} = \left(\mathbf{X}^T\mathbf{W}(t)\mathbf{X}\right)^{-1}\mathbf{X}^T\mathbf{W}(t)$

$\hat{\boldsymbol{\beta}}(t) = \mathbf{D}\mathbf{y}$ , and $\operatorname{var}\left(\hat{\boldsymbol{\beta}}(t)\right) = \mathbf{D}\mathbf{D}^T\sigma^2$

The standard errors of the parameter estimates can be computed as the square root of these variances and used in $t$-tests to obtain estimates of the significance of the individual components. In this model the variance component, $\sigma^2$, is defined by the normalized residual sum of squares (RSS) divided by the degrees of freedom. The latter are defined by the number of parameters, $p$, in a global model, or the *effective number of parameters* in the GWR model. This value is approximated by the authors as the trace of a matrix $\mathbf{S}$, $\operatorname{tr}(\mathbf{S})$ (the sum of the diagonal elements of $\mathbf{S}$) defined by the relation: $\hat{\mathbf{y}} = \mathbf{S}\mathbf{y}$

A set of such equations is solved for all points, $t$. The fit of the model may be examined in the usual manner, although it is to be expected that the fit in terms of variance explanation will almost always be an improvement over global methods, if only because there are far more parameters fitted to the dataset. For this reason comparisons should be made on additional criteria, for example the AIC measure which takes account of the model complexity. As with conventional regression, the modeled surface and (standardized) residuals may be mapped for exploratory purposes, but additionally the parameters $\beta(t)$ and their estimated standard errors may also be mapped since these also vary spatially. Within GWR standardized residuals are determined as the sum of squared residuals, $\varepsilon\varepsilon^T$, divided by the degrees of freedom,

$n$-$\operatorname{tr}(\mathbf{S})$. The authors recommend examining any values for these residuals >3.

To illustrate this process we shall use an example dataset comprising educational attainment by county in the state of Georgia, USA (the dependent or response variable, Table 5-12). This dataset lists the percentage of University graduates by county together with a range of social data that might act as independent variables to be used in predicting the dependent variable. The data have been assigned to a set of 159 point locations (county centroids) and show an overall average of 19% of the population recorded as being graduates, with an average per county of 10.9% (i.e. not population weighted). The range by county is from 4.2% to 37.5%. Table 5-12 shows the predictor variables and the global regression parameters estimated by OLS, which collectively account for around 63% of the variance. Also shown are the GWR parameter estimates, expressed as a range of values that have been computed. In the diagnostics section of this table note the drop in residual sum of squares, the increase in the adjusted $R^2$, and a modest fall in the AICc statistic. The authors suggest that a fall of 3 or more in the AICc value warrants examination as demonstrating a meaningful improvement in model fit. Note that differences in the method of calculation of the AIC statistic can easily result in differences of greater than 3, so caution is required when comparing alternative software packages on this measure. As mentioned above, the standardized residuals from the GWR predictions can be mapped in order to identify any prediction outliers. Figure 5-38A shows this mapped dataset, with the dark blue and red counties illustrated being those with the highest and lowest deviations. These counties may then be examined to try and ascertain if there are any special characteristics of these cases that might explain the large residuals. By definition the GWR modeled parameters falling within the range shown in Table 5-12 include a value for every county. Hence each parameter can also be mapped, as shown in Figure 5-38B. In this case the map highlights a distinct pattern of variation, with higher values in the north and lower values in the south.

Table 5-12 *Georgia dataset — global regression estimates and diagnostics*

| Predictor variables | Global parameter estimate | GWR parameter estimates |
|---|---|---|
| Total population, $\beta_1$ | $0.24 \times 10^{-4}$ | $0.14$ to $0.28 \times 10^{-4}$ |
| % rural, $\beta_2$ | -0.044 | -0.06 to -0.03 |
| % elderly, $\beta_3$ | -0.06 (not signif.) | -0.26 to -0.06 |
| % foreign born, $\beta_4$ | 1.26 | 0.51 to 2.42 |
| % poverty, $\beta_5$ | -0.15 | -0.20 to -0.00 |
| % black, $\beta_6$ | 0.022 (not signif.) | -0.04 to 0.08 |
| Intercept, $\beta_0$ | 14.78 | 12.62 to 16.49 |
| **Diagnostics** | | |
| Residual SS | 1816 | 1506 |
| Adjusted $R^2$ | 0.63 | 0.68 |
| Effective parameters | 7 | 12.81 |
| AICc | 855.4 | 839.2 |

Figure 5-38 *Georgia educational attainment: GWR residuals map, Gaussian adaptive kernel*

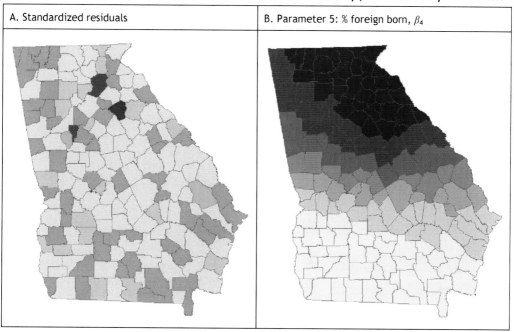

| A. Standardized residuals | B. Parameter 5: % foreign born, $\beta_4$ |
|---|---|

As Fotheringham *et al.* (2005) have noted: "In some instances ... it is difficult to justify why some relationships should be allowed to vary spatially. In others, empirical results may suggest that some relationships are stationary over space while others vary significantly. In these instances, 'mixed' GWR models, where some relationships are allowed to vary spatially while others are held constant, would seem to be more appropriate." For such cases the authors are planning to release a Version 4 of the GWR software which will provide specific support for mixed models.

The same kind of GWR analysis can be carried out on count data, using Poisson regression (GWPR), and on binary data, using Logistic regression (GWLR). The GWR V3 program supports both models. The standard Poisson and Logistic regression models described in Table 5-11 are utilized, but with the coefficients $\beta(t)$ varying with location, $t$, as before. As an example, GWPR has been applied to counts of disease incidence amongst a particular age/sex grouping, recorded by health district. In such models an *offset* value is applied to the model based on a matching count variable, such as the total number of people in that district in the selected age/sex cohort. For example, Nakaya *et al.* (2005) applied GWPR to mortality rates in Tokyo. The dependent variable in this instance was based on the standardized mortality ratio (SMR) for each of 262 municipality zones. The SMR is defined as the observed number of deaths, $O_i$, in a specified time period (e.g. 1990) in a given zone $i$, divided by the expected number, $E_i$, for that zone based on national or regional mortality rates (i.e. by demographic grouping). In the GWPR model the $O_i$ became the response variable and the $E_i$ provided the offset values. The study was able to examine relationships between the dependent variable and a number of independent variables at the local level, highlighting particular relationships that global models may not have identified. In fact the best model the authors were able to produce included a mix of global and local parameter estimates, with the proportion of older people (64+) and of house-owners taken as globals and the proportion of professional and technical people and the proportion of unemployed people being allowed to vary regionally.

For Logistic GWR one might have true presence/absence data, or recoded continuous data based on some critical threshold value. For example, with the Georgia dataset the dependent variable could be recoded as 1 if the percentage of graduates is above the state average and 0 otherwise. This is rather an artificial example, but recoding of this type is often applied in decision-making — for example coding land as contaminated (1) if, say, the average measured cadmium level in the soil exceeds a certain number of parts per million (ppm) and not contaminated (0) with respect to this trace element if below this threshold level.

Both Poisson and Logistic GWR require model fitting using a technique known as iteratively reweighted least squares (IRLS). The analysis is carried out in much the same manner as previously described, but the computation of the Akaike Information Criterion (AIC) and AICc differs from the OLS expressions.

The ready availability of GWR V3 software, supporting Gaussian, Poisson and Logistic models, together with a companion book and materials, has resulted in an upsurge in interest in the technique. This includes its consideration by spatial econometricians, medical statisticians and ecologists amongst others (GWR support has recently been included in the R-spatial collection as spgwr and in the SAM ecology package, as well as in the latest versions of ESRI's ArcGIS). It has the attraction of accepting the non-stationarity of most spatial datasets (see further, Section 6.7.1.8), and proceeding to create models with improved information characteristics and amenable to further exploratory analysis. For large-scale problems the processing overheads of GWR may become prohibitive, but the technique is well-suited to parallel or grid-enabled processing, as has recently been demonstrated by Harris *et al.*, 2006 and others.

### 5.6.4 Spatial autoregressive and Bayesian modeling

#### 5.6.4.1 Spatial autoregressive modeling

Many of the techniques that are briefly described in this final subsection originate from time series analysis and were subsequently developed from the mid-1950s within the discipline known as spatial statistics. They have been applied and substantially extended in the last 25 years, notably by econometricians, geographers and medical statisticians. Additional disciplines that have made extensive use of these techniques include the actuarial, ecological and environmental sciences. Detailed discussion of the methods and underlying theory may be found in Cressie (1993), Bailey and Gatrell (1995), Anselin (1988), Anselin and Bera (1998), Anselin (2002) and Haining (2003). Haining (2003) discusses the various forms of model that may be appropriate for the statistical analysis of spatial data. He notes the choice of a particular modeling approach often reflects the data types, preferences and experience within the disciplines involved, with social sciences, earth sciences and medical researchers all tending to focus on different approaches.

The procedures have been implemented in: SpaceStat; S-Plus; the R-Spatial project; MATLab Spatial Statistics Toolbox (Pace *et al.*); WinBUGS; SAM; PySal; and GeoDa packages, amongst others. A number of these have been specifically developed to deal with large (and often sparse) matrix difficulties that arise with detailed regional and national datasets.

A pure spatial autoregressive model simply consists of a spatially lagged version of the dependent variable, **y**:

$$\mathbf{y} = \rho \mathbf{W} \mathbf{y} + \boldsymbol{\varepsilon}$$

As can be seen this is similar to a standard linear regression model where the first term is constructed from a predefined $n$ by $n$ spatial weighting matrix, **W**, applied to the observed variable, **y**, together with a spatial autoregression parameter, $\rho$, which typically has to be estimated from the data. Anselin (2008, p257) describes spatial lag models as "a formal representation of the equilibrium outcome of processes of social and spatial interaction". Essentially a spatial lag model is expressing the notion that the value of a variable at a given location is related to the values of the same variable measured at nearby locations, reflecting some kind of interaction effect. The spatial weights matrix, **W**, is almost always standardized such that its rows sum to 1, hence it is effectively including a weighted average of neighboring values into the regression equation. Note that in this case **W** is not necessarily symmetric (compare this with the symmetry requirements on conditional autoregressive, or CAR, models that are discussed in Section 5.6.4.2).

For an individual observation the basic spatial lagged autoregression equation is simply:

$$y_i = \rho \sum_j w_{ij} y_j + \varepsilon_i$$

Note the similarity of this model to a series of simultaneous equations (hence the description of such models as simultaneous autoregressive, or SAR, models). The model can also be compared with a simple time series autoregressive model, from which it owes its origins:

$$y_t = \rho y_{t-1} + \varepsilon_t$$

Since the dependent variable, **y**, appears on both sides of the expression:

$\mathbf{y} = \rho \mathbf{W} \mathbf{y} + \boldsymbol{\varepsilon}$ it can be re-arranged to give:

$$\mathbf{y} = (\mathbf{I} - \rho \mathbf{W})^{-1} + \boldsymbol{\varepsilon}$$

from which we can obtain an expression for the variance of **y** as:

$$\mathrm{var}(\mathbf{y}) = E(\mathbf{y}\mathbf{y}^{\mathsf{T}}) = (\mathbf{I} - \rho \mathbf{W})^{-1} E(\boldsymbol{\varepsilon}\boldsymbol{\varepsilon}^{\mathsf{T}})(\mathbf{I} - \rho \mathbf{W}^{\mathsf{T}})^{-1}$$

hence

$$\text{var}(\mathbf{y}) = E(\mathbf{y}\mathbf{y}^T) = (\mathbf{I} - \rho\mathbf{W})^{-1}\mathbf{C}(\mathbf{I} - \rho\mathbf{W}^T)^{-1}$$

where $\mathbf{C}$ is the variance-covariance matrix.

This derivation has made no distributional assumptions regarding the response variable or the errors. In this model the spatial weights matrix, $\mathbf{W}$, is effectively raised to the power 1, so only first-order neighbors are included in the autoregressive function, and for this reason this model is therefore sometimes described as having a 'first-order' specification.

Although widely used, Wall (2004) has pointed out significant weaknesses in the interpretation of the spatial structure of commonly applied SAR and CAR spatial weighting schemes. These models were originally designed for use on infinite regular lattices, rather than finite irregular lattices (which have edges and variable numbers of neighbors per zone) and in this latter context are less well behaved. She recommends considering use of geostatistical models as an alternative or additional approach when analyzing lattice (zonal) datasets, since in this approach the covariance function is modeled directly. Of course, the use of geostatistical methods also have their weaknesses in this context, notably the need to use zone centroids or similar arbitrary points rather than the zones themselves when constructing the experimental variogram (see further, Sections 6.7.1 and 6.7.1.15).

If we add additional predictor variables, $\mathbf{x}$, to the pure spatially lagged autoregression model described earlier we have a *mixed regressive spatial autoregressive* model (*mrsa*):

$$\mathbf{y} = \mathbf{X}\mathbf{\beta} + \rho\mathbf{W}\mathbf{y} + \mathbf{\varepsilon}$$

As can be seen this is the same as a standard linear regression model with the addition of the autoregressive component (the SAM software refers to this formulation as a 'lagged response model'). As before we can re-arrange this expression to solve for $\mathbf{y}$:

$$\mathbf{y} = (\mathbf{I} - \rho\mathbf{W})^{-1}\mathbf{X}\mathbf{\beta} + (\mathbf{I} - \rho\mathbf{W})^{-1}\mathbf{\varepsilon}$$

The design of this kind of mixed model incorporates spatial autocorrelation together with the influence of other (aspatial) predictor variables. The objective of this revised approach is to obtain a significant improvement over a standard OLS model. The level of improvement will depend on how well the revised model represents or explains the source data, and to an extent this will vary depending on the detailed form of the weighting matrix, $\mathbf{W}$.

Theoretical analyses have shown that this type of model can be derived from a variety of different processes, including direct processes such as spatial diffusion, certain forms of spatial interaction (including spillover and gravity or potential-type process models), and indirect processes such as resource distribution. This lack of a well-defined link between process and form is commonplace in spatial analysis, and is well-documented in fields such as point set clustering and fractal analysis. That is also applies here, in spatial regression modeling, should come as no surprise.

A second approach to SAR modeling is known as the spatial error model. This model is applied when there appears to be significant spatial autocorrelation, but tests for spatial lag effects do not suggests that inclusion of the latter would provide a significant improvement. A decision diagram for selecting the appropriate model based on a set of additional diagnostics (Lagrangian multiplier test statistics) is included in GeoDa (see the tutorial materials for a discussion of their use). The spatial error model (from GeoDa) is defined as:

$$\mathbf{y} = \mathbf{X}\mathbf{\beta} + \mathbf{\varepsilon}, \text{ where } \mathbf{\varepsilon} = \lambda\mathbf{W}\mathbf{\varepsilon} + \mathbf{u}$$

Hence the basic model is as per the standard linear model, but now the error term is assumed to be made up of a spatially weighted error vector, $\lambda\mathbf{W}\mathbf{\varepsilon}$, and a vector of *iid* errors, $\mathbf{u}$. We can re-arrange the expression for $\mathbf{\varepsilon}$, above, to obtain:

$$\mathbf{\varepsilon} = (\mathbf{I} - \lambda\mathbf{W})^{-1}\mathbf{u}$$

hence the error variance-covariance matrix, **C**, in this case is given by:

$$E(\boldsymbol{\varepsilon\varepsilon}) = \sigma^2 \left[ (\mathbf{I} - \lambda\mathbf{W})^T (\mathbf{I} - \lambda\mathbf{W}) \right]^{-1}$$

The Georgia, USA educational attainment dataset used to illustrate GWR in Section 5.6.3 and Table 5-12 can be analyzed in a similar manner using spatial autoregressive methods. If this is conducted within GeoDa the OLS results match those within GWR (although the AIC values differ slightly owing to the differences in the detailed expressions applied). However, to apply a spatial autoregressive model a spatial weights matrix is required. In the following example we have set the spatial weights to be defined by simple first-order rook's move contiguity (adjacent edges), and then examined the GeoDa diagnostics to determine which form of regression model seems most appropriate to apply. In this instance the spatial error model was identified as the most appropriate and the regression re-run using this model. The results are summarized in Table 5-13, which is simply an extended version of the Table 5-12, including the new autoregressive parameter estimates.

*Table 5-13 Georgia dataset – comparative regression estimates and diagnostics*

| Predictor variables | Global parameter estimate | Spatial error model parameter estimates | GWR parameter estimates |
|---|---|---|---|
| Total population, $\beta_1$ | 0.24 x10$^{-4}$ | 0.24 x10$^{-4}$ | 0.14 to 0.28 x10$^{-4}$ |
| % rural, $\beta_2$ | -0.044 | -0.046 | -0.06 to -0.03 |
| % elderly, $\beta_3$ | -0.06* | -0.099* | -0.26 to -0.06 |
| % foreign born, $\beta_4$ | 1.26 | 1.196 | 0.51 to 2.42 |
| % poverty, $\beta_5$ | -0.15 | -0.145 | -0.20 to -0.00 |
| % black, $\beta_6$ | 0.022* | 0.013* | -0.04 to 0.08 |
| Intercept, $\beta_0$ | 14.78 | 15.46 | 12.62 to 16.49 |
| lambda, $\lambda$ | | 0.313 | |
| **Diagnostics** | | | |
| Residual SS (RSS) | 1816 | 1708 | 1506 |
| Adjusted $R^2$ | 0.63 | 0.67 | 0.68 |
| Effective parameters | 7 | 7 | 12.81 |
| AIC / AICc | 855.4 | 846.0 | 839.2 |

* not significant

Although the RSS value in Table 5-13 is not as low as with GWR, the model is intrinsically far simpler and enables a more global view of the relationship between variables. There is an argument for utilizing both global regression and GWR approaches when analyzing datasets of this type, since they provide different perspectives on the data, and different insights into the use of such data for predictive purposes. The spatial error model applied in this example was defined above as:

$$\mathbf{y} = \mathbf{X\beta} + \boldsymbol{\varepsilon}, \text{ where } \boldsymbol{\varepsilon} = \lambda\mathbf{W\varepsilon} + \mathbf{u}.$$

Observing that: $\boldsymbol{\varepsilon} = \mathbf{y} - \mathbf{X\beta}$ we have:

$y = X\beta + \lambda W(y - X\beta) + u$, or

$y = X\beta + \lambda Wy - \lambda WX\beta + u$

Hence this expression models the dependent variable $y$ as a combination of a general (global) linear trend component, $X\beta$, plus a pure spatial autocorrelation component, $\lambda Wy$, plus a (negative) neighboring trend or predictor component, $\lambda WX\beta$, plus a set of *iid* random errors, $u$ (the SAM software refers to this formulation as a 'lagged predictor model')

Comparing this to the *mrsa* model above:

$y = X\beta + \rho Wy + \varepsilon$

we see that the spatial error model can be viewed as a form of mixed spatial lag model with an additional spatial component, the neighboring trend, $\lambda WX\beta$.

These types of model can be generalized still further (Haining, 2003, p355), for example as:

$y = \alpha 1 + X\beta + \rho Wy + WX\delta + (I - \varphi W)^{-1} \varepsilon$

where the scalars $\alpha$, $\rho$, and $\varphi$, and the vectors $\beta$ and $\delta$ are all parameters to be estimated, and the final term represents spatial autocorrelation on the errors. Clearly one could proceed from the generalized model to the particular, or vice versa. Likewise one could progressively increase or decrease the set of explanatory variables in the model.

Given the considerable complexity of spatial phenomena, Haining suggests a data-driven approach to statistical modeling, which can be seen as fitting comfortably within the Data and Analysis components of the PPDAC framework described in Section 3.1 and Figure 3-3. His approach commences with ESDA, proceeds to model specification for the current data, and then progresses to an iterative cycle of selection and implementation of parameter estimation, assessment of model fit and re-specification where necessary.

## 5.6.4.2 Conditional autoregressive and Bayesian modeling

A somewhat different conceptual model, which in practice may produce similar results, is known as conditional autoregressive modeling (CAR). The essential idea here is that the probability of values estimated at any given location are conditional on the level of neighboring values. The standard or 'proper' CAR model for the expectation of a specific observation, $y_i$, is of the form:

$$E\left(y_i \mid all\ y_{j \neq i}\right) = \mu_i + \rho \sum_{j \neq i} w_{ij}\left(y_j - \mu_j\right)$$

where $\mu_i$ is the expected value at $i$, and $\rho$ is a spatial autocorrelation parameter that determines the size and nature (positive or negative) of the spatial neighborhood effect. The summation term in this expression is simply the weighted sum of the mean adjusted values at all other locations $j$ — this may or may not be a reasonable assumption for a particular problem under consideration.

In the standard CAR model spatial weights are often computed using some form of distance decay function. The range of this function may be unbounded or set to a value beyond which the weights are taken as 0. This range might be determined from some *a priori* knowledge relating to the problem at hand, or perhaps estimated from a semivariogram or correlogram (see further, Section 6.7.1.15).

In the CAR model the covariance matrix is of the form:

$var(y) = (I - \rho W)^{-1} M$

and if the conditional variances of $y$ are assumed constant this simplifies to:

$var(y) = (I - \rho W)^{-1} I \sigma^2$

Requirements on the specification of the weighting matrix, $W$, and conditional variance matrix, $M$, include: (i) $M$ is an $n$ by $n$ diagonal matrix with $m_{ii} > 0$; (ii) to ensure symmetry of the variance-covariance matrix $w_{ij} m_{ji} = w_{ji} m_{ij}$;

and (iii) $0 > \rho > \rho_{max}$ (typically) where $\rho_{max}$ is determined from the largest eigenvalues of $\mathbf{M}^{-1/2}\mathbf{W}\mathbf{M}^{1/2}$.

In the study by Lichstein et al. (2002), cited in Section 5.6.2 above, they chose to use CAR following the recommendation of Cressie (1993) and because they felt it to be more appropriate for their study. They found no real difference in the results obtained with the CAR model from those achieved using SAR modeling of the type described in the previous section. Wall (2004) likewise found little difference between CAR and SAR models in her analysis of educational data across USA states.

A range of CAR models are supported by the GeoBUGS extension to the WinBUGS package. This software is specifically designed to support Bayesian rather than frequentist statistical modeling, and uses computationally intensive techniques (Markov Chain Monte Carlo or MCMC simulation with Gibbs sampling) to obtain the fitted parameter estimates and confidence intervals. An ArcGIS tool (Adjacency for WinBUGS) is available from the USGS to generate the spatial adjacency matrix required for WinBUGS CAR models. The application in this case is for modeling and mapping avian abundance, especially for migratory bird species whose conservation is of concern.

Haining (2003) discusses the use of such Bayesian models, in which additional (prior) information (for example, national or regional crime survey data) is used to strengthen the modeling process and reduce bias in local estimates. The Bayesian approach treats the unknown parameters (e.g. the vector $\boldsymbol{\beta}$) as a set of random variables, just like the data, to which may be associated prior distributions. The prior guesses for these parameters (possibly 'borrowed' from spatially adjacent and/or regional or national information) are then combined with the likelihood of the observed data to obtain posterior distributions for the parameters, from which inferential analysis proceeds. Essentially this provides a broader range of modeling approaches than pure (classical) frequentist analysis, and has been shown to result in substantial

improvements over using simple rate data such as standard mortality ratios (SMRs); see for example, Yasui et al. (2000) for a fuller discussion of this question. These kinds of model have mostly been applied in epidemiological studies, for both mapping and modeling purposes, but have also been applied to other forms of spatial data (e.g. see Li et al., 2007).

In the so-called proper CAR model (WinBUGS function car.proper) the variance-covariance matrix is positive definite. The example values given in the WinBUGS manual for $\mathbf{M}$ and $\mathbf{W}$ based on expected counts, $E_i$, are of the form:

$m_{ii}=1/E_i$

$w_{ij}=(E_j/E_i)^{1/2}$ for neighboring areas $i,j$ or

$w_{ij}=0$ otherwise

This particular example relates to the Sudden Infant Death Syndrome (SIDS) data described in Section 4.3.3 and in Cressie and Chan (1989) and more recently revisited by Berke (2004). Here the definition of neighboring area was not based on adjacency but on distance between county seats ($d<30$ miles), a value determined from an examination of an experimental variogram (an estimate of a variogram based on sample data). The specific model applied in this case was actually of the form:

$$w_{ij} = \left\{ C(k)d_{ij}^{-k} \right\} \left( E_j / E_i \right)^{1/2}$$

where the term in curly brackets is a (Euclidean) distance decay function, with $k$ selected as 0, 1 or 2, and $C(k)$ is a constant of proportionality to ensure results are easily compared across different values of $k$. In this study the authors chose $k=1$ as this provided the best results when considered from a likelihood perspective, hence their weights were of the form:

$$w_{ij} = \left( E_j / E_i \right)^{1/2} 1/d_{ij}$$

Edge effects in this model are quite significant, since over a third of counties lie on the State boundary and clearly States do not represent closed systems for many (most) applications.

In this example the 'proper' (or autoGaussian) model fitted for this dataset was not applied to the full raw dataset, but to a Freeman-Tukey variance-stabilizing square root transform of the data (see Table 1-3 and Freeman and Tukey, 1950) with Anson County omitted as an outlier. This county is the one picked up as an outlier in Figure 4-40, the "Excess risk rate map for SIDS data".

Cressie and Chan had looked for non-spatial explanatory variables based on population density, percentage urban, number of hospital beds per 100,000 population, median family income and non-white live-birth rate. They then extended their analysis to include spatial patterns, but even after doing so could not adequately explain the observed variations in the data for this period, or for the subsequent 5 year period. It remains the case that the causes of SIDS are not fully understood, but medical research has shown that the placement of very young children on their back when sleeping, the use of pacifiers (dummies) and avoidance of overheating, all help to reduce the risks involved substantially. It is reasonable to suggest that the spatial variations observed and their changes over time might have been, in part, a reflection of cultural and social factors (such as advice given to mothers by local medical staff). These factors were not explicitly picked up by the non-spatial explanatory variables. Although such factors may be related to race-specific customs, it is likely that the spatial variations observed and modeled *may* have reflected variations in these advisory and behavioral factors. Certainly it would have warranted a very close examination of such factors in counties with unusually high and low death rates in each time period.

An *intrinsic* version of the CAR model (IAR or ICAR) is also supported, in which the variance-covariance matrix is not positive definite, but is semi-definite (WinBUGS functions *car.normal* and the robust variant *car.l1*). The intrinsic version (applied initially in an image processing context) is based on pairwise differences between the observed values (similar to the computations used in variogram analysis, from which it originates — see Matheron (1973) and Künsch (1987) for a detailed mathematical treatment) and is now a more popular choice of CAR model for many researchers. Intrinsic models are a generalization of the standard conditional autoregressive models to support certain types of non-stationarity. The example values given in the WinBUGS manual for **M** and **W** for the intrinsic CAR model, based on Besag *et al.*, (1991) and Besag and Kooperberg (1995) are of the form:

$$m_{ii}=1/n_i$$

where $n_i$ is the number of areas adjacent to $i$, and

$w_{ij}=1$ for neighboring areas $i, j$ $(i \neq j)$ or

$w_{ij}=0$ otherwise

The use of simple 1/0 weighting schemes for CAR models is not really appropriate for finite irregular lattices, and frequently a row-adjusted scheme of the form $\mathbf{W^*}=\{w_{ij}^*\}$ is used, where $w_{ij}^*=w_{ij}/w_{i.}$ (often written within this field as $w_{ij}/w_{i+}$). Hence the expected conditional means, for example, refer to an average rather than a summation. The symmetry requirement for CAR models cited earlier, i.e. $w_{ij}m_{ji}=w_{ji}m_{ij}$ implies that the conditional variances should be proportional to $1/w_{i+}$.

Having fitted the chosen model to the sample data, the residuals may be examined by mapping and/or by using the Moran I correlogram, $I(h)$, to identify any remaining patterns. If the residuals appear to show little or no spatial pattern it supports the view that the fitted model provides a good representation of the observed spatial patterns. However, as noted earlier, different models with fundamentally different interpretations may provide equally good fits to the data, hence drawing inferences from such models is difficult. Detailed examinations of the likely processes that apply for the particular dataset under consideration are vital for such analyses.

In the examples cited in this subsection, the response variable, $y$, has been assumed to be continuous. As with GWR, autoregressive models have been developed to handle discrete and binary data, for example autoLogistic and autoPoisson models — see Haining (2003, Chapters 9 and 10) for more details. Haining (2003, p.367 *et seq*) provides examples of the use of WinBUGS for Bayesian autoregressive modeling of burglaries in Sheffield, UK, by ward (Binomial logistic model) and children excluded from school (Poisson model). He includes sample code and data for these examples, together with maps of the results and provisional interpretations.

Griffith (2005) tested six alternative spatial regression models using data on cases of West Nile Virus (WNV) in the USA, by State (for current mapping of cases see: http://diseasemaps.usgs.gov). These tests included SAR, CAR and spatial filtering specifications (see further, Section 5.6.5). He concluded that none of the models provided an ideal specification for the observed data, but a number of general lessons could be learnt to assist analysts in determining the best approach to use in disease map modeling:

- switching between alternative model specifications should yield similar intercept values – if markedly different values are obtained an analyst should be suspicious and ascertain why

- non-Normal data (such as the WNV cases) are best described with non-Normal probability models

- it appears from the tests on WNV data that spatial filtering models (see Section 5.6.5) can be used to explore the nature of spatial autocorrelation effects (positive and negative effects) more quickly and effectively than SAR and CAR models

### 5.6.5 Spatial filtering models

Conceptually the spatial lag models and spatial error models are substantially different, yet the results from their use on a given dataset may be similar. Furthermore, both are related to a process known as *spatial differencing* which is a form of *spatial filtering*. This is similar to simple differencing methods applied in time series analysis, but instead of analyzing values at each time slot, $y_t$, one examines the differences between sequential time slots (i.e. first differences), $y_t$-$y_{t-1}$. In the spatial context the expression:

$$y = X\beta + \varepsilon$$

can be written with a first-order spatially autocorrelated difference as:

$$y - \rho Wy = X\beta - \rho WX\beta + \varepsilon, \text{ or}$$
$$y(I - \rho W) = (I - \rho W)X\beta + \varepsilon, \text{ hence}$$
$$y = X\beta + (I - \rho W)^{-1}\varepsilon$$

Thus a model with a spatially autoregressive error term is a form of standard regression equation (OLS) on spatially filtered data. The term:

$$(I - \rho W)^{-1}$$

is the spatial filter in this instance. Similarly the mixed spatial lag model, *mrsa*, described earlier:

$$y = \rho Wy + X\beta + \varepsilon$$

can be written with a first-order spatially autocorrelated difference as:

$$y - \rho Wy = X\beta + \varepsilon, \text{ or}$$
$$y(I - \rho W) = X\beta + \varepsilon$$

Hence, once again the model can be seen as a form of spatial filter where in this case only the dependent variable is filtered.

A somewhat different approach has been pioneered by Getis and Griffith (2002). They apply spatial filtering to potential independent variables in a regression equation using one of two procedures: (i) using the $G_i$ statistic described in Section 5.5.3 to transform the source data (Getis method); or (ii) decomposition of the Moran I statistic into orthogonal and uncorrelated map pattern components (Griffith). The approach of Getis is the most straightforward to describe and apply, since it involves a simple transformation of the original data values.

Let $G_i(d)$ be the local Getis and Ord spatial autocorrelation statistic applying to observation (point) $i$:

$$G_i(d) = \frac{\sum_j w_{ij}(d)x_j}{\sum_j x_j}, i \neq j$$

where $d$ is the estimated range of observed spatial autocorrelation. This expression is the *observed* value of the statistic for location $i$. The *expected value* of the statistic for location $i$ is of the form $W_i/(n\text{-}1)$. The filtering transformation of the observed data values $x_i$ applied is then:

$$x_i{}^* = x_i \frac{E_i}{O_i}, \text{ i.e.}$$

$$x_i{}^* = x_i \left( \frac{W_i}{n-1} \right) \Big/ G_i(d)$$

where $W_i$ is the sum of the binary weights, $w_{ij}$, within a distance $d$ of $i$, and $n$ is the number of observations. The original dataset can then be viewed as being comprised of a spatial component, $x_{sp}=\{x_i\text{-}x_i{}^*\}$, and a non-spatial (filtered) component, $x_f=\{x_i{}^*\}$. These two components are then used in standard linear OLS as dependent variables and analysis proceeds as described earlier. Hence for each filtered dependent variable there will be two additional terms in the regression equation.

Getis and Griffith (2002) applied unfiltered OLS, standard spatial autocorrelation, Getis filtered OLS and Griffith filtered OLS to sample US state expenditure data (observation taken as applying to state centroids). For OLS, standard spatial autocorrelation and the Getis filtering the coefficient of determination was found to be 75%, whilst with the Griffith method a slightly higher value of 80% was obtained. The authors conclude that both filtering methods provide a more appropriate specification of the regression model, facilitating meaningful interpretation of all of the regression coefficients, with the advantage of not requiring formal specification of an appropriate spatial autocorrelation model. Overall the Griffith approach appears somewhat more powerful, but the Getis approach is simpler to apply, although it does require that the filtered variables are positive and have a natural origin (i.e. are positive ratio-scale variables).

# 6 Surface and Field Analysis

## 6.1 Modeling Surfaces

### 6.1.1  Test datasets

The analysis of physical surfaces and fields is a topic that is best explored using tangible examples. To this end, this part of the Guide uses a number of common datasets to illustrate the various forms of analysis that may be readily carried out. Our first dataset comprises eight sub-tiles from the GB Ordnance Survey 10m digital elevation model (DEM), taken from tiles TQ81, TQ82, TQ91 and TQ92. Detailed analysis is conducted on one of the tiles, TQ81NE. Each DEM tile contains

approximately 250,000 cells, and the mosaic-ed (combined) 8-tile region is thus roughly 2 million cells. A 3D visualization of tile TQ81NE is shown in Figure 6-1. This was created in Surfer. Comments on artifacts associated with this dataset appear later in this chapter. The data files referred to may be obtained from the Ordnance Survey directly or via the EDINA data download service (for academic use only — see the Web links: "Selected national and international data and information sources" Section at the end of this Guide for details).

Each main tile (e.g. TQ81) is made up of 4 sub-tiles (in this example TQ81NE, NW, SE and SW). These sub-tiles are 5000mx5000m, and the TQ81NE tile has a modest maximum height of around 70m. The tiles consist of a number of ridges, separated by relatively broad very flat valleys, and border on the English Channel.

*Figure 6-1 East Sussex test surface, OS TQ81NE*

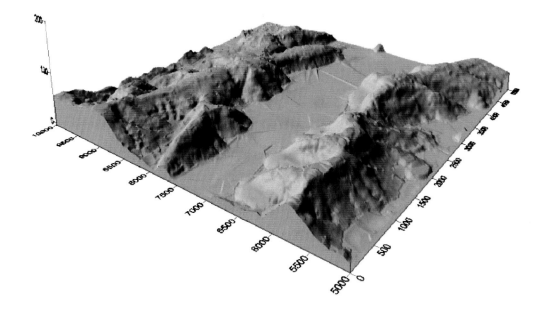

A separate dataset representing a much more rugged landscape is also used, both in the present chapter (notably in the section covering interpolation methods) and elsewhere in this Guide. This covers part of the Pentland Hills area to the south of Edinburgh in Scotland.

*Figure 6-2 Pentland Hills test surface*

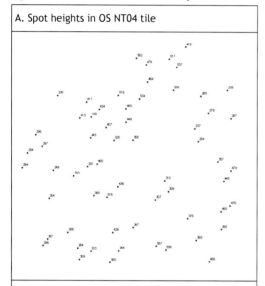

A. Spot heights in OS NT04 tile

B. Relief map: 25m DEM for NT04 tile

The principal OS tile used in this case is NT04. It has already been used in our discussion of

Delaunay triangulations and Voronoi polygons (Section 4.2.14.3).

### 6.1.2 Surfaces and fields

The test datasets described in Section 6.1.1 are representations of physical surfaces. For every location in the set {x,y} there is a single scalar value z representing the height of the surface at that point. There is no reason however to restrict the set of z-values to be heights — they could equally well be some other variable, such as the cost of land or the level of a soil trace element. The range of values that {z} may take would typically be the set of (positive) real numbers, although only integer values may be recorded depending on the dataset in question.

In some instances a number of z-values are associated with each (x,y) location. This is the case, for example, with multi-spectral remote sensing data, where separate spectral bands are coded for each pixel of an image. In this case each band can be considered as a distinct surface, and is typically stored as separate layers within an image folder. Frequently such data are integer-coded color values, so have a well-defined and limited range, e.g. [0,255]. Another example is the case of spatial datasets (surfaces) that are recorded over a number of time periods — for example atmospheric pressure or temperature at a specified altitude, recorded at hourly intervals.

In all of these examples the recorded information is a single interval or ratio-scaled value. Spatial datasets of this type are considered as surfaces or (scalar) *fields* within GIS. Datasets in which multiple values for the same variable are recorded for a single location and time (e.g. geological borehole data) and/or have a directional component (e.g. wind speed and direction), are typically excluded from the set of objects described as surfaces or fields, or are re-cast where possible to fit such a model (e.g. as multiple layers). The term *vector field* is used to refer to fields that include both a magnitude and a directional value at every point.

Having defined the kind of datasets that qualify, the question of how such information is obtained and stored becomes central to the process of analyzing and interpreting such data. A very large proportion of data that describes the physical world (terrain, vegetation, land-use etc.) is obtained from one of two sources (possibly both) — national mapping agencies and sample surveys.

National agencies provide details of topography; land-use; geology etc.; derived from a mixture of terrestrial, aerial and satellite surveys. Traditionally such data were analyzed and then recorded on paper maps, although this has now been largely superseded by digital encoding and storage, with paper maps as one of a range of possible output forms. For terrain data, output consisted largely of contour maps with spot heights, and the great majority of current digital terrain datasets, including those available in grid or raster format, have been derived from such contour maps. One result of this process has been to make available grid datasets or *digital elevation models* (DEMs) for many areas of the world. However, since these have been programmatically generated there is a tendency for artifacts to appear, such as small ridges, troughs and hollows, and these can be seen even in the most carefully produced national datasets, including the GB Ordnance Survey and United States Geological Survey (USGS) datasets. For example, the test dataset for the OS tile TQ91SW includes an area of sea, which the file records as having a range of values from 0 to -3m! The same issue applies to conversion utilities built-in to many GIS packages — converting input contour datasets to grid format, or grid data to contours or TIN format.

Another principal source of field-like data is from sample surveys. In this case one or more sample values are known for a set of distinct (point-like) locations. These might be soil samples, radioactivity data, meteorological station data or some other variable that is known to be spatially continuous. Values at unsampled locations, typically defined as a fine grid, are estimated from the measured data using a variety of interpolation and prediction methods. Hence again grid data

may be subject to artifacts and additional estimated or unknown errors of modeling.

In each of these examples the surface or grid can be thought of as a single valued function $z=f(x,y)$. Mathematically derived functions that apply to an entire region or to sub-sections of regions may be used to create grid datasets. For example the surface shown in Figure 6-3 is a representation obtained by fitting a linear regression surface of the form $z=ax+by+c$ to the set of spot heights provided by the GB Ordnance Survey for tile NT04.

*Figure 6-3 Linear regression surface fit to NT04 spot heights*

More complex mathematical models are frequently used to generate and analyze surface datasets. Many of those available in modern GIS packages and related software (notably geostatistical packages) are described in the subsections that follow.

### 6.1.3 Raster models

A raster, grid or image file may be thought of as a rectangular array of identical square cells, each of which has an associated value (which may be zero or a code for "missing value"). The array therefore comprises a number of rows and columns. In some instances (as in mathematics) rows run from 1 to $n$ from the top and from 1 to $m$ from the left, whilst in others (including standard geographic referencing) the rows may be in the reverse order, i.e. the first row is actually the bottom of the array, or most southerly position, with subsequent rows representing successive steps to the north (northings). Columns in this model correspond to east-west location, and may be referred to as eastings. In Cartesian coordinates eastings correspond to $x$-values and northings to $y$-values. The contents of cells are then considered as field values or surface heights, and conventionally referred to by the letter $z$. A raster grid is thus an array of $n$ rows and $m$ columns $\{x,y,z\}$. Where multiple bands or values exist for each $(x,y)$ location a series of triples $\{x,y,z_1\}$, $\{x,y,z_2\}$, $\{x,y,z_3\}$ ... are recorded, and typically treated as a set of separate (associated) surfaces. Collections of grid datasets that are adjacent are often called tiles, and separate tiles may be processed independently or may first require combining into a single larger grid before analysis takes place. This process is known as creating a *mosaic* in some GIS packages, or a combination operation in others. When such datasets are combined there may be user-selectable rules on how any small overlaps of edges should be treated — typically these default to a First model, i.e. the values in the first grid to be processed take precedence, but other options might include averaging, taking the largest or smallest values etc. The advantage of combining grids as a mosaic is that analysis is conducted on the entire dataset (region) of interest, taking into account all of the recorded values, and minimizing edge effects; the main disadvantage is that such datasets can become extremely large and thus very cumbersome and slow to process.

We can describe the 2-step (Moore von Neumann, or MvN) neighborhood of a single cell of a grid structure in (at least) two separate ways, depending on the referencing system applied (Figure 6-4).

*Figure 6-4 Raster file neighborhoods*

A. NSEW          B. OFFSET

Here we have illustrated referencing for cells using compass-type notation and using

numerical offset notation. Both may be extended to cells further away from $z^*$, but the numerical system is simpler as it remains in the same format (2 values) as more distant cells are included.

Using either of the notational forms we can define operations on raster grids. For example, the rate of change in the $x$-direction and $y$-direction about $z^*$ (the first-order partial derivatives) can be estimated as:

$$\frac{\partial z}{\partial x} \approx \frac{z_E - z_W}{2\Delta x}, \frac{\partial z}{\partial y} \approx \frac{z_N - z_S}{2\Delta y} \text{ or}$$

$$\frac{\partial z}{\partial x} \approx \frac{z_{1,0} - z_{-1,0}}{2\Delta x}, \frac{\partial z}{\partial y} \approx \frac{z_{0,1} - z_{0,-1}}{2\Delta y}$$

where the $\Delta x$ and $\Delta y$ values are determined by the grid resolution. These are the formulas used by the Surfer and Idrisi packages, amongst others. Basic second order differentials, required for curvature calculations, follow a similar format:

$$\frac{\partial^2 z}{\partial x^2} \approx \frac{z_E - 2z^* + z_W}{\Delta x^2},$$

$$\frac{\partial^2 z}{\partial y^2} \approx \frac{z_N - 2z^* + z_S}{\Delta y^2},$$

$$\frac{\partial^2 z}{\partial x \partial y} \approx \frac{z_{NE} - z_{NW} - z_{SE} + z_{SW}}{4\Delta x \Delta y}$$

An alternative approximation, first introduced by Horn (1981) uses all 8 immediate neighbors of $z^*$. ArcGIS is an example of a GIS package that uses this method for some of its calculations: for the $x$-direction the directly east and west positions are weighted 2 whilst the remaining 4 directions (NE, NW, SE, SW) are weighted 1; for the $y$-direction the directly north and south points are weighted 2 and the remainder weighted 1. The result is a slightly more complicated pair of formulas for the first-order differentials that have been found to be better than many alternatives, especially for rough surfaces. Using these approximations both slope and aspect can be estimated for each point of a grid (see further, Section

6.2.1). The formulas are based on standard finite difference expressions:

$$\frac{\partial z}{\partial x} \approx \frac{(z_{1,1} + 2z_{1,0} + z_{1,-1}) - (z_{-1,1} + 2z_{-1,0} + z_{-1,-1})}{8\Delta x}$$

$$\frac{\partial z}{\partial y} \approx \frac{(z_{1,1} + 2z_{0,1} + z_{-1,1}) - (z_{1,-1} + 2z_{0,-1} + z_{-1,-1})}{8\Delta y}$$

Surface curvature measures (including plan, profile and tangential curvature) require second order derivatives, and again these may use relatively simple formulas or more complex variants. ArcGIS uses a method of estimation based on fitting a partial fourth-order polynomial to the 3x3 window in which $z^*$ sits, whilst Surfer applies simpler differential approximations. Both approaches are described in more detail in Section 6.2. Landserf uses a different method from those described above for all of its main surface analysis facilities. The method is based on a quadratic surface approximation at each grid cell, using the immediate 8-cell neighborhood (i.e. a 3x3 window) as standard. It also provides the option to use a larger window size and a distance decay function for weighting cells that are more distant (such functions are described in Section 4.4.5).The quadratic fitted surface is of the form:

$$z = ax^2 + by^2 + cxy + dx + ey + f$$

where $a$, $b$, $c$, $d$, $e$ and $f$ are constants to be estimated. The fitted quadratic can be analytically differentiated, the components equated to 0, and the slope, aspect and curvature components derived directly from this process. The result is a set of very simple expressions in terms of the constants for the main surface characteristics: *aspect* is simply computed as:

$$A = \tan^{-1}(e/d),$$

and *slope* as:

$$S_t = \tan^{-1}(e^2 + d^2)$$

It should be noted that the question of determining the coefficients remains, and since there are only 6 of these and potentially 9 cell values to utilize, a level of redundancy exists permitting a range of choices or procedures for coefficient selection, with least squares fitting being one such choice.

An alternative, devised by Zevenbergen and Thorne (1987), is to fit a 9 parameter function that is of quartic ($4^{th}$) order but only quadratic in $x$ and $y$:

$$z = ax^2y^2 + bx^2y + cxy^2 + dx^2 + ey^2 + fxy + gx + hy + i$$

This function has the advantage that all its parameters are uniquely determined from the values of the cells in the 3x3 window, and the function passes exactly through each data point, including the central point. The coefficients $a$, $b$, $c$ and $i$ are not used in computations of slope, aspect or curvature, so may be ignored for these measures. The coefficient $i = z^*$, the value at the central point of the 3x3 window ($z_{0,0}$). The coefficients $g$ and $h$ turn out to be identical to the simple expressions used by Surfer and others as estimates of first order derivatives, and these determine both slope and aspect computations so the method reduces to simple finite differences for these measures. The expressions for plan and profile curvature are more complex, and use all of the coefficients $d$-$h$. This quartic model is the one used by ArcGIS as described above, SAGA (as its default option) and in the RiverTools facility Extract|Finite difference grid. The terms $d$-$h$ are also determined in exactly the same manner as for the second-order derivatives used by Surfer, as defined above. The derivation and use of these expressions is discussed in more detail in Moore *et al.* (1991, 1993), Wood (1996) and Zevenbergen and Thorne (1987). Useful analyses of alternative algorithms and the associated issues of errors and uncertainty analysis are provided by Jones (1998), Zhang and Goodchild (2002, Chapter 5) and Zhou and Liu (2004).

Surfaces represented by grids suffer a number of disadvantages. These include:

- very large requirements for data storage, processing and display — the test grid TQ81NE that will be used for illustrative purposes here is 1.4Mbytes as an NTF file, 1.7Mbytes as an ASCII or Surfer grid, and less than 150kbytes as an ArcGIS TIN file and only 33kbytes as a 500-vertex Landserf TIN file (albeit with some degree of information loss). Image files are often far larger — a single USGS High Resolution Orthoimage covering approximately 4.5kmx4.5km in color at 0.3m resolution requires 660Mbytes of memory to load (40Mbytes when compressed with no information loss)

- a fixed grid size and orientation that does not reflect variations in underlying surface complexity

- lack of clarity regarding linear and point-like features

- use of 3x3 windows (8-cell neighborhoods) can result in strong directional bias in some surface computations. Larger window sizes and more sophisticated local models can alleviate some of these difficulties

On the other hand grids are extremely convenient for data manipulation, combination and display, which explains their widespread popularity.

### 6.1.4 Vector models

The most common vector-based models of surfaces are contours and TINs. Source data may be provided in either of these formats, or may be converted to these formats from DEM files. Typically they are far more compact than DEMs, but less suitable for analytical methods, and TINs may result in a significant loss of information unless the underlying surface is of triangular form. TINs are widely used in engineering modeling (they are the principal form of surface model in Autodesk's Land Desktop package for example). Since DEMs may well have been generated from contour datasets, reversing the process may not result in the same pattern of contours, depending on the algorithms used in each case. Contour creation is described in Section 6.5.3.

Figure 6-5A-C shows the test area source DEM together with derived contour and TIN representations, created using the Landserf

package for the TQ81NE test region. The TIN example is based on a program selected set of 500 vertices, resulting in approximately 1000 triangular regions. The representation is not unique, and a similar computation using another package (e.g. TNTMips, which uses a similar method that it calls adaptive densification) may result in a different pattern of triangles. Note that representation of flat regions with the TIN model can be problematic. The generated models may be used to re-generate an approximation to the source DEM as shown in Figure 6-5D — the differences between the TIN-generated DEM and the original DEM can be plotted as a grid, as shown in Figure 6-5E. The darkest reds are the areas of maximum "error" — in this case up to 10m. The error map can be improved (the quality of the TIN representation enhanced) by increasing the number of vertices. Note that this is not the same as the difference between the TIN and the true surface, which in principle can be computed everywhere.

TIN creation from DEMs benefits from a level of feature extraction in order to produce the most efficient description of the surface (i.e. with minimum surface error and inclusion of key surface features, such as peaks, pits and ridge lines). However, such facilities are rarely provided in TIN-generation algorithms as noted earlier (Section 4.2.14.2). Pure feature-based vector models, which are essentially networks of polylines or curves linking peaks, pits and passes or saddles along ridges or channels are sometimes computable as output from GIS analysis tools, but are not provided as a standard form of vector representation (see Rana and Wood (2000) and Rana (2004a) for further discussion of this topic). Figure 6-5F shows feature network extraction from the source DEM. The level of network connectivity, and hence surface representation, obtained by such methods will vary depending on the values of user-definable parameters that are set, and on the nature of the surface itself. The factors are in addition to the computational problems we have alluded to.

*Figure 6-5 Vector models of TQ81NE*

| A. Source raster | B. Contour - derived | C. TIN - derived |
| --- | --- | --- |
| D. TIN derived raster | E. TIN derived raster - errors | F. Derived feature network |

## 6.1.5 Mathematical models

We have previously noted that a surface or grid can be thought of as a single valued function $z=f(x,y)$. Mathematical models of surfaces typically assume that the function $f(x,y)$ has certain distinctive properties: (i) single valued — i.e. there is only one $z$ value for each $(x,y)$ pair; (ii) continuous — in broad terms this means that a value exists for every $(x,y)$ pair; and (iii) twice differentiable — first and second differentials can be computed at (almost) all locations. The mathematical surface model is then a single function or a piecewise function that satisfies these requirements. Piecewise functions are continuous functions over some interval or region (e.g. a 3x3 grid of cells) but which have breaklines at the edges of the region. Piecewise continuous functions are widely used in surface modeling and interpolation, where particular conditions are set on behavior of the function at the edges (for example that the gradient matches that of the adjacent regions).

Single function mathematical models are typically used to approximate real-world surfaces, often using least squares methods to provide best fit parameter estimation. As such they are described as approximating or non-exact models. Piecewise models are typically exact, but inexact or smoothing variants of such models are also provided within some software packages. In most cases models used are algebraic functions with powers limited to linear, quadratic or cubic expressions in $x$ and $y$. Example surfaces of orders 1-3 are shown in Figure 6-6 — each of these examples was generated as a grid using the Surfer Grid menu, Functions option. Some software tools talk about quadric or quartic functions (i.e. in 4th powers), but these are typically limited to terms of power 2 in x and y, i.e. expressions like $ax^2y^2$. Quintic functions (i.e. in 5th powers) are also used occasionally, for example TNTMips provides the option for quintic polynomial fit to individual triangles in a TIN network (deriving the parameters from the triangle itself and its immediate neighbors). This is then used in interpolation within the selected triangles. Quintic functions, with all 21 parameters, are the minimum degree of polynomials needed to ensure zero, first and second-order continuity across triangle edges.

In principle, mathematical models, which are scale-independent compact representations of surfaces, could be used in place of alternative vector and grid models. At present this idea, which has been described as *Map Calculus* by Haklay (2004, 2006), has not been implemented in commercial GIS packages. Haklay provides a simple demonstration of this approach using Manifold, and it is possible that such models will be incorporated into GIS packages in the future.

*Figure 6-6 First, second and third order mathematical surfaces*

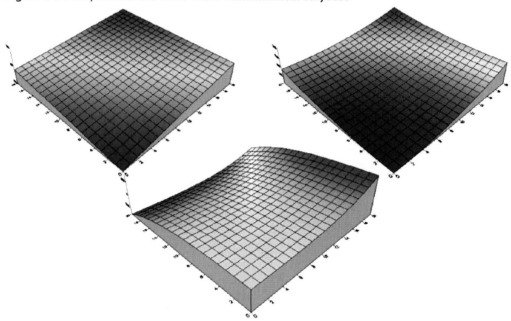

### 6.1.6   Statistical and fractal models

Several GIS packages facilitate the creation of grids or surfaces using statistical functions rather than just mathematical functions. The generated surfaces may then be combined with existing surfaces or mathematically defined surfaces to create new grids which may be used for a variety of purposes: uncertainty modeling; providing reference grids for comparison or residuals analysis purposes; for the generation of idealized terrains; or for statistical analyses. ArcGIS provides a function for creating raster files whose entries are uniform random values in the range [0,1] or Normally distributed random z-values with mean=0 and standard deviation=1, i.e. $z\sim N(0,1)$. The resulting grids can be modified (e.g. multiplied by a constant, adding an offset or trend) when generated or subsequent to generation. GRASS (r.random.surface function) provides similar functionality, but also facilitates a user-specified level of spatial dependence, implemented using a simple distance decay function with filtering.

## Figure 6-7 Random and fractal grids

A. Random Uniform [0,1]

B. Random Normal(0,1)

C. Ridged multi-fractal

Figure 6-7A and B illustrates the ArcGIS functionality, where a 250x250 grid with cell size 1 unit has been generated. Each cell is given a value independently as a random value from the chosen distribution. In the random uniform case all values will lie in the range [0,1] whilst in the Normal case values may take any value, but will typically fall within the bounds [-5,+5], with just over 95% of values (the paler colors) falling in the range [-2,2].

Figure 6-7C shows a markedly different pattern, which has been generated by a hybrid random process designed to yield a surface with known fractal dimension, $D_C>2$, and surface characteristics that are more terrain-like than purely random. GIS software packages do not appear to provide models for artificial terrain generation, although this is an area that may be developed in future. This particular example was created using the Fractal Terrains package, which provides a range of fractal generation methods, from simple Brownian motion to various ridged multi-fractal procedures. In principle such methods could be implemented within many of the popular grid-oriented GIS packages using scripting or object-based programming, but there appear to be few examples of this at present. For more details on this area see Hanrahan *et al.* (2003, notably Chapter 16).

A slightly different approach, based on random perturbation of mathematical surfaces, is illustrated in Figure 6-8. In this instance a simple linear surface has been modified by random perturbation of each cell. In the upper example a 5x5 grid and a random uniform function has been used; in the lower case a 20x20 grid and a random Normal function has been applied. Both examples were generated using the Grid|Functions facility in Surfer, followed by using the Map facility for the 3D surface visualization and wireframe overlay. The wireframe lines in this case are simply straight line connections between the grid values taken in *x*- and *y*-directions separately.

*Figure 6-8 Pseudo-random surfaces*

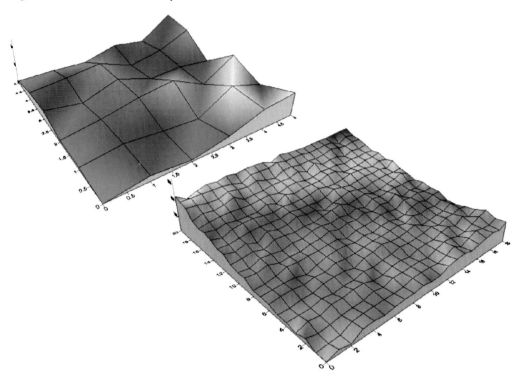

# 6.2 Surface Geometry

## 6.2.1 Gradient, slope and aspect

The term gradient refers to a vector quantity, i.e. an object that has both magnitude and direction. The magnitude or size of the gradient is the slope, whilst the direction in which the maximum value of this magnitude occurs is known as the aspect. Slope is one of the most widely used of surface attributes so understanding how it is generated and what alternatives exist is extremely important.

### 6.2.1.1 Slope

The common notion of the slope of a surface or terrain, $t$, is the amount of rise (e.g. change in elevation) over run in some direction, usually the direction for which the rise over run is greatest, i.e. the steepest path up or down the surface. In practice we would specify some distance over which the slope is to be calculated, such as the amount of rise over a 10 meter distance *in the plane*. If this was 2 meters, for example, the rise over run would be $S=2{:}10$ or $1{:}5$ or $0.2$ or 20%. This ratio is actually the tangent function: $S=\tan(S_t)$ where $S_t$ is the terrain slope in radians. If the run were taken as the surface distance rather than the plane distance then we would have $S=\sin(S_t)$. For gentle slopes (less than 1:4) this ambiguity in the definition of slope is not serious, but in general the tan() version is preferred.

The normal use of the term slope within GIS packages is the tan() value $S_t$, usually reported in degrees from the horizontal (11.3° in this example). To convert between the two one would use an expression such as:

$$S_t=\text{degrees}(\tan^{-1}(S))=360\tan^{-1}(S)/2\pi$$

For an analytical surface, $F(x,y)$, slope is defined as the magnitude of the first derivative of the surface function:

$$S=\sqrt{\left(\frac{\partial F}{\partial x}\right)^2+\left(\frac{\partial F}{\partial y}\right)^2}$$

This formula is not based on a rise-over-run calculation over a fixed interval, but rather assumes that a plane surface can be placed at any point on the surface $F(x,y)$ in such a way that it only just touches the surface — it is a tangential plane and relies on the notion of infinitesimally small distances. It is closely related to the formula for Euclidean distance, and simply shows how much the surface $F$ rises with a small fixed increment in $x$ and $y$. However, surfaces within GIS are rarely if ever represented by analytic functions — typically they will be modeled as TINs or grids, with a finite resolution. Hence slope calculations will use approximations to the formula above depending on the surface model used, which is itself an approximate representation of the true surface. In almost all instances software packages apply grid-based computation, with TINs being first converted to grid format. Strictly speaking such conversion is not necessary, since TINs can provide interpolated surface values at every point, and use of a suitable (generally non-linear) function could then provide slope (and aspect) values directly.

The slope of a line crossing the surface (e.g. a road or pipeline) is dependent on the direction of the line relative to the underlying surface — it is always less than or equal to the slope of the surface. If the direction in question is an angle $\alpha$ we need to adjust the gradient vector by taking a dot product with a unit vector in the direction of interest. This enables slope values to be computed in any path direction. Such values are known as *directional derivatives* (see further, subsection 6.2.3). If the differential components for gradient and curvature have been calculated for a surface (e.g. a grid) then directional derivatives can be computed with very little further computation.

Using the grid model described in Section 6.1.3 we have surface values represented by triples $\{x,y,z\}$, and can compare this with the mathematical formulation above to see that $z(x,y)$ is equivalent to $F(x,y)$. We have described this as an equivalence, but it should not be assumed that this is strictly true — the set of values $z(x,y)$ is a particular representation of a non-mathematical surface or field at a pre-defined set of locations.

With a grid model slope can be determined at any particular location $z^*$ by simple approximation methods using the rook's move or NSEW values for $z$ at that point:

$$S = \sqrt{\left(\frac{z_E - z_W}{2\Delta x}\right)^2 + \left(\frac{z_N - z_S}{2\Delta y}\right)^2}$$

and $S_t$ computed as before. This is the approach used by Surfer, as described in Section 6.1.3. Within ArcGIS the 8-cell method due to Horn (1981), described in Section 6.1.3 is used.

Methods based on fitting a plane surface to the unweighted 8-cell neighborhood of $z^*$ and using its slope as the surface slope estimate have been found to be less satisfactory. Even less acceptable are slopes computed by examining the maximum difference in cell values in the 8-cell neighborhood in the $x$- and $y$-directions and across the diagonals (suitably adjusted for cell size and diagonal length where appropriate).

Vertical Mapper for MapInfo uses yet another approach. It computes the slope and aspect of the 8 triangles defined by the mid-points of the 3x3 window centered on $z^*$ (Figure 6-9). It then averages these to provide its estimates for slope and aspect at the point $z^*$, in a similar manner to one of the methods for computing surface area (as illustrated in Figure 4-5). The result is a measure that is less susceptible to directional bias, providing a full range of directions (infinitely many are possible). The 8 individual triangles of this local neighborhood each have distinct slope values and aspect (directions). These individual directions can be examined to see which is the steepest, and this slope value used in determining drainage flows across the surface. This approach, with the added element of assigning flows to two adjacent "downslope" cells, provides the basis for the method described by Tarboton (1997) as the D-infinity drainage method (see further, Section 6.4). ERDAS uses yet another method, based on the average of the 3 east-west and 3 north-south differences for the estimates of $dz/dx$ and $dz/dy$ and then utilizes these as above for slope and aspect calculation.

*Figure 6-9 8-triangle slope computation*

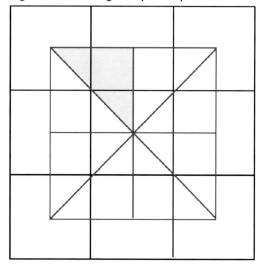

It will be apparent that these computations are extremely sensitive to scale. Larger grid intervals will result in smoothing of slope values, which may be desirable in some situations — in others it will be problematic. The availability of suitable datasets and the purposes to which the slope computations are to be put should be the basis of selection of method and resolution.

Some of these issues are illustrated in Figure 6-10. Here the jagged black line represents the surface we are analyzing, which has some periodicity in its form. A grid resolution represented by the vertical green lines would always result in a slope estimate that was fairly constant and steep, whilst halving the interval (doubling the resolution) would give a rapidly alternating picture of the slopes. However, it may be that for the purposes of analysis a broader picture is required, as illustrated by the straight line, which would be generated if the underlying grid were smoothed (e.g. by a local averaging process) or if a much larger grid spacing were used.

*Figure 6-10 Gradient and sampling resolution*

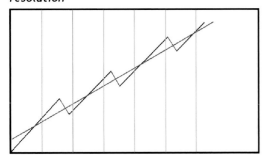

Figure 6-11B shows the result of computing slope values in degrees for the source map displayed in Figure 6-11A. The red and yellow areas are those of highest values (up to 65 degrees). The source raster has a resolution of 10 meters, and as the resolution is reduced/cell sizes for analysis are made larger, the maximum slope computed from this particular dataset falls to roughly 50 degrees with a 20m resolution and under 30 degrees with a 100m resolution. Slope computation is also affected to a greater or lesser degree by grid orientation, since it relies on grid values in particular directions.

## 6.2.1.2 Aspect

Aspect is defined as the directional component of the gradient vector and is the direction of maximum gradient of the surface at a given point. As with slope, aspect is calculated from estimates of the partial derivatives:

$$\frac{\partial z}{\partial x}, \text{ and } \frac{\partial z}{\partial y}$$

Aspect is computed in degrees from due north, i.e. as an azimuth in degrees not radians. The expression required is:

$$A = 270 - \frac{360}{2\pi} \tan^{-1}\left(\frac{\partial z}{\partial x}, \frac{\partial z}{\partial y}\right)$$

where the inverse tan function applies to both components — this function is often described, and implemented in software, using the notation atan2($a,b$). Since the function is equivalent to atan($b/a$) for $a>0$ the standard

inverse tan function may be used if preferred for $a>0$.

*Figure 6-11 Slope computation output*

A. Source terrain map

B. Slope map

As with the calculation of slope, Surfer uses simple finite differences for aspect calculation whereas ArcGIS uses the more complex 8-point formulas of Horn. This does not avoid problems of directional bias resulting from the computational procedure, grid structure and/or errors in or rounding of grid values.

Figure 6-12A shows the frequency distribution produced by the ArcGIS Aspect facility when applied to the terrain shown in Figure 6-11A. Strong peaks in this distribution can be observed at approximately 45° intervals, which of course does not reflect the true frequency distribution of landscape aspect. Landserf analysis of aspect for a subset of the region covered by Figure 6-11A is shown in Figure 6-12B (with zero values excluded). There are still discernable peaks, especially in the 8 major compass-point directions, but the computations appears to be smoother overall. Computations of aspect suffer from edge effects, resulting in zero or undefined values for boundary cells. Zero values are also generated wherever there are flat areas, and these can dominate frequency diagrams and associated analyses. Different packages treat flat areas in different ways, and these should be checked before relying too heavily on the results generated. Exclusion of zeros may be desirable in any further analysis of such data, and checks on the treatment of 360° should also be made, although these do not seem to be a particular problem with most packages.

n Figure 6-12C we have generated a circular frequency histogram of the set of aspect values again with zeros excluded. This is a more appropriate way of examining the data but is not available in most GIS packages. In this case the diagram was generated using the rose() function in MATLab with 60 intervals. Note that 0° and 360° in Figure 6-12C are in the usual position for mathematical analysis, i.e. horizontal, and the $\log_{10}$ of frequencies rather than frequencies themselves have been plotted in order to reduce the effect of isolated peaks at certain frequencies.

Clearly there are some problems with this computational process, since areas of sea to the lower right of the output (Figure 6-13A-C) are shown as having variable aspect — these are linear artifacts or ghost lines, which arise due to artifacts in the underlying source DEM.

*Figure 6-12 Frequency distribution of aspect values*

A. ArcGIS Spatial Analyst: Aspect

B. Landserf: Analyse|Surface parameter|Aspect

C. Landserf Aspect data — Rose diagram (MATLab), Log freq.

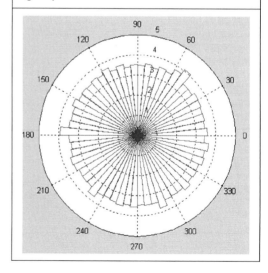

*Figure 6-13 Aspect computation output*

| A. Source terrain map | B. Aspect - classified |
| C. Aspect — graduated colors | D. Aspect — NSEW classification |

If a graduated color scale is used to represent this data, as in Figure 6-13C, the pattern appears clearer, with high values shown in purple in this example, but the circular nature of the data means that this representation is misleading. A more appropriate visualization is one in which categories and colors reflect the circular nature of the data, as in Figure 6-13D. Here the range 325°- 45° (broadly north-facing) has been colored pale orange, east-facing yellow, west-facing blue and southerly pale green.

## 6.2.2 Profiles and curvature

### 6.2.2.1 Profiles and cross-sections

Many GIS packages provide tools for examining the profile of a surface along a selected straight line or series of straight line segments (a polyline). The form of the profile reflects: the number of observations taken along the selected line (with only two sampled points, at the start and end, the profile will be a straight line showing the slope between the two points, and as the number of observations is increased the surface will be represented in greater detail); the direction(s) of the selected line segments; and the nature of the surface itself, as represented in the surface model being utilized.

Figure 6-14 shows a profile from south to north of the test surface TQ81NE along its westerly edge (the edge shaded gray in Figure 6-1), in this case produced using Landserf — similar functionality is provided in many packages (e.g. TAS, ArcGIS).

*Figure 6-14 Profile of NS transect, TQ81NE*

The vertical extent is clearly exaggerated, but the profile shown does provide an indication of the slope and curvature of the surface *along the selected line*. The important point to note here is that the selected line does not represent the direction of maximum gradient, so values for slope and curvature apply solely to the direction chosen and will differ from calculations of slope and curvature for the surface as a whole.

In addition to single profile computation multiple-slice profiling can be performed using some packages, such as TNTMips. Figure 6-15 illustrates this procedure using the TQ81NE dataset once more, with a selection of slices taken at 50 grid cell intervals (500m intervals as this is a 10m DEM). The profile averages for the *entire* input raster object are shown as the baselines against which the curve-filling is generated. In this example we have rotated the output (profiles plus relief map backdrop) through 90 degrees for clarity of viewing.

*Figure 6-15 Multiple profile computation*

### 6.2.2.2 Curvature and morphometric analysis

As with slope, curvature values depend upon the line or plane along which such calculations are made. There are several alternative measures of surface curvature. The three most frequently provided within GIS software are profile curvature, plan curvature and tangential curvature. Additional terms and measures include longitudinal curvature, cross-sectional curvature, maximum and minimum curvature, and mean curvature.

In order to clarify these various terms we have drawn some illustrative details on part of test tile TQ81NE (Figure 6-16).

*Figure 6-16 Surface morphology*

At the sample location $(x,y)=(600,5400)$ a straight line has been drawn to indicate the slope and arrows indicates the direction in which the slope has been computed (the aspect). At this point a vertical plane (i.e. a plane drawn in the $Z$-direction) could be constructed that is oriented in the direction of the aspect and passes through $(x,y,z)$. It is the plane in which gravitational processes are maximized, so is of great interest in problems of hydrology, soil movement and geomorphological analyses. A plane constructed at right angles (orthogonal) to this vertical plane, i.e. a plane passing through the target point and slicing the surface horizontally (parallel to the $XY$-plane) maps out a line on the surface that is effectively a contour at that point. This second plane is the one for which gravitational effects are minimized. *Profile and plan convexity* (or curvature) is defined in terms of these two planes (see further, subsections 6.2.2.3 and 6.2.2.4). A slice through the surface could also be drawn in the $YZ$-plane, also passing through (x,y,z). This would again generate a line where it intersected with the surface, and the somewhat confusingly named *tangential curvature* is defined in terms of this arrangement.

To provide an additional level of complexity and confusion to the above terms, there are a further set of curvature values that correspond to those used in the mathematical analysis of surfaces (see for example, do Carmo (1976) and/or the Mathworld web site for more details). The slope and aspect of a surface at any given point are computed by imagining that a plane can be drawn that just touches the surface. The direction this tangential plane faces (not to be confused with the YZ plane described above) defines the aspect, and the slope is the magnitude of the gradient in this direction. But the tangential plane is not aligned with the *XY*-plane, the *YZ*-plane or the *ZX*-plane. It sits at an angle to all three. If a pole were constructed attached to this tangential plane at the point (x,y,z) at right angles to the surface it would point in a direction known as the Normal to the surface (as shown in Figure 6-16, white arrow). As with the three coordinate planes *XY*, *XZ*, and *YZ* we can now construct three planes that are orthogonal to each other based on the tangential plane and the surface Normal. One of these three is the tangential plane itself, the second is a plane through the surface Normal and in the direction of the aspect, and the last is a plane at right angles to both of these. These last two planes will cut the surface at an angle that is neither horizontal nor vertical. Where they cut the surface they will generate a line, whose curvature can be calculated. The Normal plane produce a line whose curvature at (x,y,z) is known as the *longitudinal curvature*, and the plane at right angles to the Normal generates a line with curvature at (x,y,z) known as the *cross-sectional curvature* (see further, subsection 6.2.2.6). Perhaps the simplest way of understanding the difference between the mathematical expressions of curvature and those commonly used in landscape analysis is to compare lines of latitude on a globe, which are formed by the intersection of a horizontal plane with the surface of a sphere, with great circles, which are formed by the intersection of a plane Normal to the surface, passing through the center of the sphere. The latter (corresponding to the mathematical view of a tangent plane and Normal) will always be larger circles, so have a greater radius of curvature, r, and thus a lower curvature value than the former, which correspond to the contour or landscape perspective.

Curvature is conventionally described using the Greek letter kappa, $\kappa$, so we use this in conjunction with subscripts to define each form of curvature. The main expressions provided are based on those provided by Surfer, which in turn are based on Moore *et al.* (1991, 1993). For quadratic surface modeling as used in Landserf, expressions are based on Evans (1979) cited in Wood (1996). GIS packages, such as ArcGIS, may multiply curvature values by -100 for convenience, as recommended by Zeverbergen and Thorne (1987), to give values in the approximate range [-1,1] with a sign that ensures that positive curvature equates to convex forms and negative curvature equates to concave forms. The value $r=1/\kappa$ is the radius of curvature, hence $\kappa$ can be viewed as directly related to the size of a circle or a sphere that just touches the surface at sampled points.

Wood (1996) uses the signs of the measured slope, and the curvature measures: cross-sectional, maximum and minimum curvature, to characterize surface features, i.e. to help identify peaks, ridges, passes, planar regions, channels and pits. The simplified relationships he defines are shown in Table 6-1, where blanks indicate the value or sign of the measure has no relevance, and if a second line of conditions is included it relates to the immediate 3x3 neighborhood of the target point. Thus these various curvature measures have applications in both process modeling and feature extraction, and as such may be applied not only to physical surfaces but in some cases, other types of surface data or fields. Readers are referred to Rana and Wood (2000) and Rana (2004a) for a fuller discussion of this area and the problems associated with trying to carry out such analyses on real-world surfaces.

*Table 6-1 Morphometric features — a simplified classification*

| Feature | Slope | Curvature | | |
|---------|-------|-----------|---------|---------|
| | | Cross-sectional | Maximum | Minimum |
| Peak | 0 | | + | + |
| Ridge | 0 | | + | 0 |
| | + | + | | |
| Pass | 0 | | + | - |
| Plane | 0 | | 0 | 0 |
| | + | 0 | | |
| Channel | 0 | | 0 | - |
| | + | - | | |
| Pit | 0 | | - | - |

*after Wood (1996, Table 5.3). + and - indicate positive or negative curvature, 0 indicates no curvature, blank indicates not relevant*

### 6.2.2.3  Profile curvature

The labeled red line in Figure 6-16 indicates the *profile curvature* which is the shape of the surface in the immediate neighborhood of the sample point contained within the vertical plane described in Section 6.2.2.2. It represents the rate of change of the slope at that point in the vertical plane, and is negative if the shape is concave, positive if the shape is convex and zero if there is no slope. Profile curvature is defined as:

$$\kappa_{pr} = \frac{\dfrac{\partial^2 z}{\partial x^2}\left(\dfrac{\partial z}{\partial x}\right)^2 + 2\dfrac{\partial^2 z}{\partial x \partial y}\dfrac{\partial z}{\partial x}\dfrac{\partial z}{\partial y} + \dfrac{\partial^2 z}{\partial y^2}\left(\dfrac{\partial z}{\partial y}\right)^2}{pq^{3/2}},$$

$$p = \left(\frac{\partial z}{\partial x}\right)^2 + \left(\frac{\partial z}{\partial y}\right)^2, q = 1 + p$$

Surfer implements the above expression using the approximations provided in Section 6.1.3. Both ArcGIS and Landserf utilize mathematical models fitted to the surface using the 3x3 window surrounding the target point z*, in

order to obtain estimates of profile curvature. These result in expressions that are defined in terms of the coefficients of the surface functions provided earlier.

For Landserf (quadratic surface model) we have:

$$\kappa_{pr} = \frac{-200\left(ad^2 + be^2 + cde\right)}{\left(e^2 + d^2\right)\left(1 + d^2 + e^2\right)^{3/2}}$$

For ArcGIS (fourth order surface model) we have:

$$\kappa_{pr} = \frac{200\left(dg^2 + eh^2 + fgh\right)}{\left(g^2 + h^2\right)}$$

where the coefficients *d-h* are computed in the manner described in Section 6.1.3.

### 6.2.2.4  Plan curvature

The *plan curvature* is the shape of the surface viewed as if a horizontal plane has sliced through the surface at the target point (the labeled green line in Figure 6-16). It is essentially the curvature of a contour line at height z and location (x,y). The differential expression for plan curvature is similar to that for profile curvature:

$$\kappa_{pl} = \frac{\dfrac{\partial^2 z}{\partial x^2}\left(\dfrac{\partial z}{\partial x}\right)^2 - 2\dfrac{\partial^2 z}{\partial x \partial y}\dfrac{\partial z}{\partial x}\dfrac{\partial z}{\partial y} + \dfrac{\partial^2 z}{\partial y^2}\left(\dfrac{\partial z}{\partial y}\right)^2}{p^{3/2}}$$

$$p = \left(\frac{\partial z}{\partial x}\right)^2 + \left(\frac{\partial z}{\partial y}\right)^2$$

Surfer implements the above expression using the approximations provided in Section 6.1.3. Both ArcGIS and Landserf utilize mathematical models fitted to the surface using the 3x3 window surrounding the target point z* in order to obtain estimates of profile curvature. These result in expressions that are defined in terms of the coefficients of the surface functions provided earlier.

For Landserf (quadratic surface model) we have:

$$\kappa_{pl} = \frac{200\left(bd^2 + ae^2 - cde\right)}{\left(e^2 + d^2\right)^{3/2}}$$

For ArcGIS (fourth order surface model) we have a similar looking formula, although the coefficient values will differ from those of the quadratic model:

$$\kappa_{pl} = \frac{-200\left(dh^2 + eg^2 - fgh\right)}{\left(g^2 + h^2\right)}$$

The coefficients $d$-$h$, which are different for the quadratic and quartic models, are computed in the manner described in Section 6.1.3.

Note that ArcGIS also defines a general term which it describes as *curvature*, defined as the difference between the plan and profile curvatures, which simplifies to $\kappa = -200(d+e)$

### 6.2.2.5 Tangential curvature

Tangential curvature is again closely related to plan and profile curvature, and also to the slope, $S_t$. The differential formula is:

$$\kappa_{tg} = \frac{\dfrac{\partial^2 z}{\partial x^2}\left(\dfrac{\partial z}{\partial x}\right)^2 - 2\dfrac{\partial^2 z}{\partial x \partial y}\dfrac{\partial z}{\partial x}\dfrac{\partial z}{\partial y} + \dfrac{\partial^2 z}{\partial y^2}\left(\dfrac{\partial z}{\partial y}\right)^2}{pq^{1/2}}$$

$$= \kappa_{pl}\left(\frac{p}{q}\right)^{1/2}, \text{ where}$$

$$p = \left(\frac{\partial z}{\partial x}\right)^2 + \left(\frac{\partial z}{\partial y}\right)^2, \text{ and } q = 1 + p$$

Surfer implements the above expression using the approximations provided in Section 6.1.3. ArcGIS and Landserf do not provide this function.

### 6.2.2.6 Longitudinal and cross-sectional curvature

Landserf provides these additional curvature measures based upon approximation of the surface using a local quadratic. The formulas used for each are as follows, where the letters $a$-$e$ refer to the coefficients of the quadratic form described in Section 6.1.3:

$$\kappa_{lon} = \frac{-200\left(ad^2 + be^2 + cde\right)}{\left(e^2 + d^2\right)}$$

$$\kappa_{cro} = \frac{-200\left(bd^2 + ae^2 - cde\right)}{\left(e^2 + d^2\right)}$$

### 6.2.2.7 Mean, maximum and minimum curvature

Mean curvature is a term used in a variety of ways. In some instances it is defined as the difference between the plan and profile curvature, or as a measure of the average curvature for specific cells (the average of the maximum and minimum curvature for that cell), or even the mean value over all cells in a grid. Likewise maximum and minimum (profile) curvatures can be defined in both local and global terms. Within Landserf local formulas for the mean, maximum and minimum values are provided based on the quadratic model used throughout the package. These again are drawn from Evans (1979) as cited by Wood (1996) and are as follows:

$$\kappa_{min} = -a - b + \sqrt{(a - b)^2 + c^2}$$

$$\kappa_{max} = -a - b - \sqrt{(a - b)^2 + c^2}$$

Hence

$$\kappa_{mean} = (\kappa_{max} + \kappa_{min})/2$$

### 6.2.3 Directional derivatives

As noted earlier, once the components for gradient and curvature calculations have been estimated (first and second differentials) the computation of similar functions for other directions, $\alpha$, is relatively straightforward. In these computations a step in the chosen direction is defined as having length $ds$, so the first directional derivative is obtained as follows:

$$\frac{dz}{ds} = \frac{\partial z}{\partial x}\cos(\alpha) + \frac{\partial z}{\partial y}\sin(\alpha)$$

If $\alpha=0$ or a multiple of $\pi$ this reduces to the x-component of the vector, whilst if $\alpha=\pi/2$ or a similar multiple it reduces to the y-component (although the sign may change). In a similar manner the second derivative is defined as:

$$\frac{d^2 z}{ds^2} = \frac{\partial^2 z}{\partial x^2}\cos^2(\alpha) + 2\frac{\partial^2 z}{\partial x \partial y}\cos(\alpha)\sin(\alpha)$$
$$+ \frac{\partial^2 z}{\partial y^2}\sin^2(\alpha)$$

Surfer provides computation of both of these derivatives based on a user-defined angle input. This angle applies to every grid cell, so will almost always differ from the values obtained by the kind of terrain modeling computations described in Section 6.2.2. Curvature computations based on the mathematical view of tangential curvature are also provided. Collectively these computations show how the surface changes in terms of gradient and curvature *in a particular constant direction*.

If the selected direction is a major compass point (NSEW) one of the sin or cos terms will be zero and the other =+1 or -1. The first directional derivative for the directions due north or due east would then be:

East: $\dfrac{\partial z}{\partial x} \approx \dfrac{z_E - z_W}{2\Delta x}$, North: $\dfrac{\partial z}{\partial y} \approx \dfrac{z_N - z_S}{2\Delta y}$

These simple expressions are those described in Section 6.1.3 and also, in the context of filtering, in Section 4.6.2.

### 6.2.4 Paths on surfaces

A path crossing a surface may be modeled in various ways. Simple cross-sectional profiles or transects, as we have previously seen, are typically modeled by sampling the line at a given frequency, or constructing the profile directly from the height of cells representing the surface across which the line passes. In general paths on surfaces are assumed to lie exactly on the surface and are modeled as polylines, smooth curves or sets of adjacent cells in the plane. Strictly speaking a curve crossing a surface is a form of space (3D) curve rather than a plane curve, and could be modeled as such. In practice the planar form is modeled and smoothed where necessary, with horizontal and vertical profiles treated separately. A path, $P$, may be modeled using incremental distance, $t$, along its length as a parameter: $P=\{x(t),y(t)\}$ or for a space curve $P=\{x(t),y(t),z(t)\}$. As $t$ increases from 0 (the start point) to $T$ (the end point, defined by the total length of the path) the set of points $\{x(t),y(t),z(t)\}$ map out the precise route of the path.

Incremental path slope, direction and curvature in plan or profile views may be computed using simple finite difference expressions based on the point set, or by calculating the relevant differentials using smooth curve approximations to the point set. For example, using spline curve modeling, as described in de Smith (2006), paths may be constructed across surfaces that meet specific engineering design requirements in terms of the minimum radius of curvature acceptable in vertical and plan profiles. Such paths will not necessarily remain on the surface, but will pass above or below the original surface at various points. Construction of these paths then requires a degree of cut-and-fill and/or bridging and tunneling.

Path curvature, $\kappa$, at point $t$, is defined by the expression shown below — see for example, do Carmo (1976, Ch.1) or the Mathworld website entry for curvature for more details:

$$\kappa(t) = \|\gamma'(t) \times \gamma''(t)\| / \|\gamma'(t)\|^3$$

where $\gamma(t)$ is the parameterized space curve, $\gamma'(t)$ and $\gamma''(t)$ are the first and second differentials of the curve, $\times$ is the 3D vector cross product and $\|x\|$ is the Euclidean Norm of $x$. This expression may be written in the form we have provided earlier as:

$$\kappa(t) = \frac{\dfrac{\partial x}{\partial t}\dfrac{\partial^2 y}{\partial t^2} - \dfrac{\partial y}{\partial t}\dfrac{\partial^2 x}{\partial t^2}}{\left(\left(\dfrac{\partial x}{\partial t}\right)^2 + \left(\dfrac{\partial y}{\partial t}\right)^2\right)^{3/2}}$$

As noted earlier, the radius of curvature is simply $r=1/\kappa$. Sample computation of $\kappa$ for use within MATLab is described in de Boor (2003, p. 2-31).

Vertical profile path smoothing using spline functions is illustrated in Figure 6-17. This shows the profile of an initial path (dotted line) across a surface that was designed to meet maximum slope constraints but did not meet horizontal curvature requirements. The vertical profile of the horizontally smoothed version of this path is shown as a solid line, which shows greater variation in profile than the original path. The new path has then been smoothed again (bold line) to meet vertical curvature and slope constraints.

*Figure 6-17 Path smoothing — vertical profile*

### 6.2.5 Surface smoothing

Surfaces may be smoothed in a variety of different ways. Many of the interpolation methods described in Sections 6.6 and 6.7 may be described as surface smoothing functions, since they provide estimates that do not pass exactly through the point sets provided. More generally, however, the term smoothing for surfaces refers to procedures that amend an existing grid. This is achieved through one of three main methods: (i) resolution increase (this may be the main objective of the procedure); (ii) grid recalculation, which if the grid has fewer rows and columns than the original is sometimes described as thinning; and (iii) filtering or kernel smoothing, involving operations on NxN windows or kernels. Smoothing operations that are terrain-specific (e.g. filling pits in a surface) are discussed separately in Section 6.2.6.

Smoothing a grid by resolution increase involves increasing the number of nodes or cells and then fitting an exact smoothing interpolator through these points and the original set. Typically the function used will be a bicubic spline. Figure 6-18A shows a low resolution grid (with 6x6 nodes — the same as that illustrated in Figure 6-8, upper diagram). In Figure 6-18B this surface has been spline smoothed to provide a 16x16 grid that passes exactly through the original point set, but is also a much smoother surface model.

Smoothing a grid by recalculation involves defining the number of grid rows and columns required, and then computing the result by interpolation to this resolution whilst again honoring the original point set. If a recalculated grid has the same number of rows and columns as the original grid no recalculation is carried out. If it is defined as the same resolution as in case (i), the result is an identical grid to that shown in Figure 6-18B.

Applying a filter or kernel to a grid can result in a wide range of effects, one of which is smoothing. Figure 6-18C illustrates this process for the same source grid, using a 3x3 kernel in which the central weight is 4, the NSEW position weights are 2, and the diagonal weights 1 (as described in Section 4.6.2). The total weighting is thus 16, so the result is divided by 16 after each grid position has been adjusted using this kernel.

*Figure 6-18 Grid smoothing*

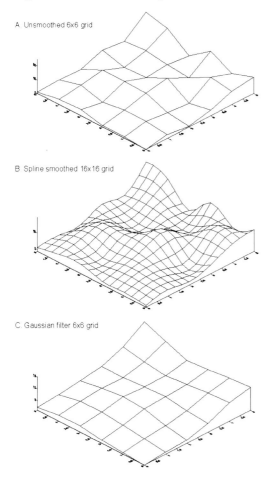

A. Unsmoothed 6x6 grid

B. Spline smoothed 16x16 grid

C. Gaussian filter 6x6 grid

This is a form of simple weighted average, in this case often described as a Gaussian kernel owing to the general symmetric, center-weighted kernel form applied. This procedure is very similar to operations that are standard in image processing, such as edge detection and de-blurring.

## 6.2.6 Pit filling

Grid models of terrains often contain individual cells or groups of cells that are surrounded by cells with larger (higher) values. Pits are uncommon features of natural terrains, except in karst landscapes and some types of desert, so in many instances observed pits arise from errors in data capture and subsequent modeling of the surface. Pit filling is thus primarily of form of error correction procedure.

For hydrological analysis pits can be assumed to fill with water during flow and it is often convenient to remove them prior to analysis. This is an application-specific form of smoothing, but may be applied to any grid file, assuming that the result is meaningful for the problem at hand. GIS software such as Landserf, SAGA, PCRaster, GRASS, ArcGIS and Idrisi all provide such functionality as standard (e.g. see the *lddcreatedem* and related functions in PCRaster, the specialized procedures provided in ANUDEM and similar functions in other packages). Some of these implementations involve simple pit removal working on the assumption that such pits are likely to be minor errors in modeling the landscape, whilst many adopt a broader view of the hydrology. These programs attempt to distinguish between errors or artifacts, and true hydrological depressions. They then seek to remove selected pits (generally by filling) using an iterative process in order to correctly generate local drainage directions and from these, a completely connected drainage network. Several programs, including GRASS and Idrisi implement the algorithm developed by Jenson and Domingue (1988), whilst ArcGIS utilizes their work and also the work of Tarboton *et al.* (1991) and Hutchinson (1989).

Implementations vary depending upon the number of cells to replace, the conditions applied and the value used for replacement. The simplest condition is that all 8-neighbor cells must contain values greater than a single central cell and the replaced value is the minimum of those surrounding the central cell. Output will consist of a new, pit-less grid file and in some cases, a grid file showing the removed pits and their values. Variants of this operation include masked fill in which a pre-defined sub-region is subject to pit removal, and depression removal in which multi-cell pits (depressions) are removed based on hydrological flow and the depth of fill required. ANUDEM applies a more complex procedure, as described briefly in Section 6.6.14

### 6.2.7 Volumetric analysis

Surface-related volume calculations are usually performed on: (i) a single grid (which we call here the "upper" surface) with respect to a reference plane (i.e. z=constant, which we call the "lower" surface), rather as per the surface area computations described in Section 4.2.3.1; or (ii) on a pair of grids. In the latter case the difference in volumes is computed assuming that the first grid represents the upper surface and the second represents the lower surface, even though the two may intersect. The result of the computations is an estimated positive volume (upper surface volume that is above the lower surface) and an estimated negative volume (where the lower surface is above the upper surface). If the upper surface is always above the lower then all values will be positive. Some packages require an additional reference surface to be defined, e.g. as an absolute base value.

For example, using our test surface TQ81NE, with a reference plane of z=0, the entire surface is above sea level so the total volume reported is entirely positive with a value of roughly 570 million cubic meters, i.e. around $0.57km^3$. Note that this figure includes adjustment to allow for a 10m x 10m grid size. Using a reference plane at z=30m the positive (solid matter) volume is around $0.13km^3$ and the negative (air space) around $0.3km^3$. At 22.5m the two volumes are approximately equalized at c.$0.2km^3$, i.e. cut=fill if one were trying to level out this region using the available materials.

Volumes are calculated by numerical integration procedures, similar to those described earlier for determining the area of a polygon. With very small grid sizes the accuracy of volume estimation is, in theory, better, but this will depend on the way in which the surface is modeled. Surface roughness affects the results, especially where the surface is complex in form, the differences between upper and lower surface are small, and the computational method simplistic. The simplest procedure (which appears to be that adopted by ArcGIS) involves use of the trapezoidal rule (see also, Section 4.2.1), first in the x-direction across all grid nodes or cells, for the first row in the grid, and then for each subsequent row. This creates a set of slices with areas $A_1, A_2, ...A_n$. The slices times the grid resolution in the y-direction provides an estimate of volume. The first and last elements in each row may be weighted 1, with all other elements weighted 2, and then the sums divided by 2 to adjust for double counting. Although this provides a fairly crude and clearly biased estimate of the surface form at the top of each DEM cell, it is quite effective – the difference between this approach and more complex procedures, such as the extended Simpson's rule and variants of this which are provided in Surfer for example, is minimal in the test example we have cited (a tiny fraction of a percent).

Engineering-oriented packages, such as Autodesk's Land Desktop product, and civil engineering extensions to this, offer a wider range of options including volume estimation from surface point data and cross-sectional slices. ArcGIS includes volume computation from TIN surface representations, which one would presume is exact with respect to this surface model. Mathematical packages, such as MATLab perform surface integration in much the same way as described above, although the input is typically a mathematical function rather than a terrain model. This enables the numerical integration procedure to meet precise tolerances (accuracy levels) based on using successively finer steps (i.e. similar to utilizing an arbitrarily fine grid model).

# 6.3 Visibility

The visibility of points in a landscape from one or more locations has many applications. These include studies of scenic quality, sound reduction, urban design, civil and military observation needs and telecommunications planning, amongst others. Many GIS packages offer visibility analysis, with varying degrees of functionality. Two principal functions are provided: line of sight, which is essentially a point-to-point operation; and viewshed, which is typically a point or point set to surface operation. Packages such as ArcGIS with Spatial or 3DAnalyst and MapInfo with Vertical Profiler provide a broad set of facilities, whilst programs such as TNTMips, Idrisi and Manifold provide a subset of these functions. Typically these operations are performed on grid files, but a similar, vector-based procedure known as Isovist analysis has been developed by Rana (2004b). This includes an add-on "Isovist Analyst" for ArcView (see further, Section 6.3.3).

For large distances the curvature of the Earth and optical refraction may be important, and packages often provide options to automatically adjust for these factors. For radio-wave modeling, Earth curvature tends to have an enlarged effect, which is generally modeled as 4/3 times the basic Earth curvature effect (possibly adjusted for different wavelengths). Other radio-wave modeling factors, such as Fresnel and non-linear signal decay effects (attenuation, interference, reflection, refraction) are not provided for, but may be incorporated as application-specific models using the programming facilities of the package.

An additional and in many ways more important issue is the question of offsets from the surface. Lines of sight are rarely if ever made from the surface itself — the observer's height and/or a structure (such as a radio mast) provide the vertical position from which computations should be made (the same question may arise for target points, such as communication or observation towers). A further and very important factor requiring consideration is the impact of surface uncertainty and obstructions (such as vegetation, road embankments, signs and buildings) on such computations. Lines of sight and viewsheds are highly susceptible to such factors, principally because of the low angles involved. For example, with zero offset from a surface, visibility is equivalent to shining a powerful light beam from the observation point and scanning around in a full circle. Any small rise or obstruction, such as a 1 meter high mound of earth or a bush, especially if close to the observation point, will cast a very large shadow behind it. Scaling this problem up to include larger objects over a range of distances and variable curvature of the landscape highlights the need to view results with caution. Raising and lowering the offset height of the observation point(s), moving the observation points and inspecting the results is one way to evaluate the sensitivity of results to such factors. Another is to increment and/or decrement the surface where known obstructions are understood to exist (e.g. by adding an estimated vegetation height and/or buildings height raster to a DEM).

## 6.3.1 Viewsheds and RF propagation

Viewsheds are regions of visibility observable from one or more observation points. Typically the inputs for viewshed analysis are:

- a surface raster or set of raster files that have been joined into a single file by a mosaic operation

- one or more observation points. In vector GIS these are typically points, sets of points or polylines, whilst in raster GIS these are generally a second raster containing non-zero values for viewpoint cells (thus may be any number, representing points, lines or polygons). For convenience we shall define the number of such observation points as $m$; and

- offset values for the observation points. The scope of the analysis may be limited by selecting: (a) a maximum (and in some cases, minimum) range for computations; and (b) horizontal and/or vertical limits (upper and lower) for angular computation

Executing the computation produces an output raster with the same extent as the input raster and a typical coding scheme of 0 for not visible, and $1>=n>=m$ for a count of the frequency with which the cell in question may be observed from the $m$ source points. Mapping this raster for values that equal $m$ will identify those parts of the landscape visible from all observation points (in Manifold this is a separate selectable option). Several GIS packages use the term Radiate rather than Viewshed for this type of analysis. Because of the sensitivity of viewshed computations (algorithmic and surface detail uncertainties) some packages and algorithms provide a level of uncertainty built into the procedure, for example dividing the regions into: (i) almost certainly visible; (ii) possibly visible; (iii) possibly invisible; and (iv) almost certainly invisible.

As an example we shall consider the case of preliminary selection of sites for mobile radio masts. The first step is to obtain a DEM for the study region, with the finest resolution available. In this case GB Ordnance Survey 10m DEMs were used. The second step is to identify potential locations for masts based on areas that are known to be poorly serviced or not serviced at all. The mast height is an important factor, as may be issues of access, land ownership, power availability, security, proximity to schools and houses etc. All of these are readily accounted for within GIS packages. Figure 6-19 illustrates this process for a sample region covering 10kmx10km in Southern England (the lower left corner is the TQ81NE tile we have used elsewhere).

Figure 6-19A shows the topography of the region, with the dark blue area in the lower right corner being the sea. Figure 6-19B and Figure 6-19C show two different viewshed rasters, based on 10m high masts located where indicated, with the pink areas being non-visible locations and green areas as visible. The different "shadows" cast by local topographic features are clearly illustrated.

*Figure 6-19 Viewshed computation*

A. Topography

B. Viewshed 1

C. Viewshed 2

This analysis is simplistic for radio transmission analysis since it does not take into account the characteristics of radio wave propagation. Visibility may not be sufficient to determine signal quality. Other factors to be considered include: the frequency of the transmitter; the power of the transmitter (or gain); and the terrain surface in the neighborhood of the transmission path, all of which affect the strength of the signal at the receiving site (the signal loss or attenuation). For example, trees and buildings that rise above the land surface but are not in the direct line of sight may produce signal attenuation and a zone of clearance around/above such obstacles is required in order to obtain a satisfactory received signal.

Special purpose software packages exist for performing such computations, many including mapping and profile analysis facilities, and a number using GIS format files (e.g. .SHP, USGS DEM) for input and optionally output. Examples of such software include Nokia's NETACT, ATDI's ICS Telecom and Softwright's Terrain Analysis Package (TAP). Software built upon GIS platforms includes programs such as Cellular Expert which runs as an ArcGIS application (Figure 6-20, ArcScene visualization) and RCC's ComSiteDesign suite.

*Figure 6-20 3D Urban radio wave propagation modeling using Cellular Expert and ArcGIS*

*Figure 6-21 Radio frequency viewshed*

| A. Topography, Swansea area, South Wales | B. Predicted signal strength Viewshed |
| --- | --- |
|  |  |

Figure 6-21 illustrates this process using the (now superseded) HerTZ Mapper software for a sample DEM in South Wales. A test site for a mast has been placed at the location marked B. This was specified as an 8m high mast, with transmission frequency 1800MHz and 34dB gain (typical of GSM mobile phone masts designed for small cell operations). Figure 6-21B shows the predicted signal strength based on a Bullington-Fresnel propagation model, with colors indicating the difference signal strengths. As noted earlier, these kinds of computations can be developed as programmed extensions to mainstream GIS packages, such as ArcGIS.

In addition to software providers and consultancies, a number of telecommunications operators and service providers have adopted this approach and produced their own internal systems built on GIS platforms (e.g. the US operator, Teligent, again using ArcGIS software). A significant advantage of this approach is that a vast range of fundamental and associated data are available and managed within GIS frameworks, enabling pure engineering modeling to be combined with customer and service area analysis, facilities management, and environmental and planning considerations.

## 6.3.2   Line of sight

Line of sight computations provide point-to-point information on visibility by means of: (a) mapped lines — variable coloring of a line drawn on the map between the source and target points; (b) tabulated data for the selected transect; and (c) profiles. Lines of sight may be computed from a single point to multiple destinations at regular angular intervals, providing a simplified picture of overall visibility from an observation point. However, for a more detailed picture complete viewsheds should be computed.

Using the example provided in Figure 6-19A (OS TQ81NE tile) can might examine the line of sight from the proposed mobile phone mast in Figure 6-19B to a sample point on the coast. The result is illustrated in Figure 6-22, where the source point has an offset of 10m. Locations highlighted in red are not visible from the source or target along this line. Again, as discussed in Section 6.3.1, with telecommunications modeling specific line-of-sight profile analysis tools are required. These include the ability to insert surface *clutter* such as trees, water areas and buildings, and to observe the effect of these on the signal strength and the Fresnel zones.

*Figure 6-22 Line of sight analysis*

Some modeling packages, such as MATLab, provide a number of functions for line of sight and viewshed computation that can be combined in a variety of ways and displayed as 3D visualizations. This approach has the advantage of flexibility of both display and access to the computational details and results. An example is illustrated in Figure 6-23, where visible areas are shown in dark blue visible lines of sight in yellow (white) and invisible line profiles in dotted red. The computations are based on an offset from the surface of 20 meters.

*Figure 6-23 Viewsheds and lines of sight on a synthetic (Gaussian) surface*

### 6.3.3   Isovist analysis and space syntax

#### 6.3.3.1  Isovists

Analysis of visibility within urban landscapes (external and/or internal visibility) raises additional questions and problems. With buildings and streets represented as 2D polygons, rather than 3D grids, a first level of visibility analysis can be carried out – this kind of analysis is generally described as isovist analysis (Benedikt, 1979). Applications of such analysis include questions such as where to place CCTV cameras or security guards in order to ensure all points are visible from the selected locations. This in turn involves an NP-hard optimization problem (see further Section 7.1.4), that of determining the minimum number of such points to ensure complete coverage. The problem also extends in a natural manner to 3D environments.

Rana (2004b) has developed efficient heuristic procedures for solving such problems based on a combination of systematic evaluation of visibility from a fine grid of initial observer positions, and then reducing this set by a ranking rule (Ranking and Overlap Elimination, or ROPE procedure). By stochastically iterating this procedure using randomly selected observer positions (S-ROPE) the final count of observer points may be reduced and thus approach optimality. An ArcView add-on

(Isovist Analyst) is available to perform this operation. The procedure is illustrated in Figure 6-24 for an area of central London (Aldwych). A sample isovist region is shown in green (street areas), based on one of the initial test observer locations shown as a red dot symbol. The blue dotted box symbols indicate the 27 locations identified by the program using the S-ROPE algorithm with around 8000 starting points as the (approximately) optimal positions for surveillance cameras, ensuring 100% coverage. Restricting the initial solution set to medial axis regions determined by simple distance transform methods (as described in Section 4.4.2.2) shows an immediate further improvement of these results (Rana, 2006). It is interesting to consider how difficult it would be for architects, surveillance specialists or traffic monitoring units to perform such analysis manually.

*Figure 6-24 Isovist analysis, Street network, central London*

### 6.3.3.2 Space syntax

Closely related to isovist analysis is the much broader topic known as *space syntax*. This research area was developed initially by Hillier *et al.* (1993) in the context of architectural design and movement behavior in small-scale regions of the built environment, but has been extended to apply to much larger urban areas.

The earliest work in this field focused on so-called *axial lines*. These lines are defined as the longest visibility lines (or 'lines of direct movement') in the 2D public urban space. By analyzing the geometry of streets, open spaces and buildings the $1^{st}$, $2^{nd}$, $3^{rd}$ etc. longest lines of visibility can (in principle) be identified and drawn. A set of such lines covering an entire area will contain many lines and many intersections of these lines. Together they define an 'axial map'. The axial lines with the highest number of intersections are said to have high 'connectivity'. Figure 6-25 illustrates these basic elements using part of the streetscape of the town of Gävle, in Sweden. Here the axial lines with the highest connectivity are colored red, with the lowest being colored blue.

*Figure 6-25 Axial lines and connectivity*

*Source: Axwoman software, Dr B Jiang*

A set of additional measures can be computed once a network of axial lines has been constructed. These include examining the hierarchy of axial lines, for example determining the number of other axial lines within a given number of steps (e.g. 3 steps) distance – this is known as the *depth* of the axial map. However, the computation of axial lines and maps is complex, slow and not an exact process. It also focuses on spatial elements that are not incorporated as standard objects within GIS datasets. For this reason Jiang and Claramunt (2002) proposed identifying 'characteristic points' within urban GIS data, and then using the connectivity of these key points to derive similar urban morphology measures to those produced using the space syntax approach. These characteristic points are relatively simple to identify (e.g. road intersections/network nodes, combined with additional vertices included to handle curved routes). Once identified it is then possible to construct a set of urban morphology measures that are strongly correlated with many of those produced using axial lines. The example in Figure 6-25 was generated using Jiang's Java-based axial line software; ArcGIS extensions for urban morphology analysis (Axwoman) and axial line generation (Axialgen) are also available from Prof Jiang.

The concepts behind space syntax and isovist analysis are combined in Turner's Depthmap software (Turner, 2004). This uses a similar approach to that of Rana (2004b) described in the preceding subsection (Section 6.3.3.1). First, a vector file (e.g. a DXF file) of the building or street layout to be analyzed is loaded. Then a fine grid of points/cells is overlain on the parts of the diagram or map that is to be analyzed. The program computes the Euclidean inter-visibility between each pair of points in the set (essentially a *visibility graph*) and from this can, for example, color code each cell in a raster view of the map according to the number of other points it is visible from (a form of global visibility ranking). With this starting point, a range of visibility and connectivity measures can be computed. Furthermore, using a similar starting point with a greedy algorithm, Depthmap can also automatically generate an axial map and related measures. Figure 6-26 provides simple illustration of these concepts. This shows the internal space of an art gallery with its rooms and connecting doors. Locations that have the highest levels of overall visibility are colored red and yellow, and the computed axial lines, with color coding, are also displayed.

*Figure 6-26 Depthmap — Gallery space visibility map*

# 6.4 Watersheds and Drainage

## 6.4.1 Overview of watersheds and drainage

Many GIS programs support analysis of surface water hydrology and hydrological processes. In almost all cases the data input is a grid file of surface elevations (a DEM file) rather than a TIN, plus optional seed or *pour points*, and output is a number of vector and grid files. Programs with a focus on grid processing such as SAGA, PCRaster, Idrisi, GRASS, TNTMips and ANUDEM provide a wide range of facilities for this type of analysis. Vector-oriented programs with strong grid support, such as ArcGIS and Manifold (V6.5 onwards) provide similar facilities. The central (pragmatic) notion is that of a uniform pattern of raindrops falling throughout the study region, creating water flows from location to location down the locally steepest path, combining with other paths and accumulating the total of upstream flows in the process. Where flows in adjacent cells are away from each other it suggests that a local watershed exists. As streams combine larger and larger regions which drain into these streams are determined, and these regions are described as *stream basins* with boundaries known as *watersheds*.

## 6.4.2 Drainage modeling

There are many assumptions made in the basic drainage model, but it has proven to be of considerable value. These assumptions include: (i) uniform precipitation; (ii) flows take place entirely across surfaces, which they do not alter, and are unaffected by absorption (notably different soil or rock types) or groundwater; (iii) flows grow as a linear function with distance and are not altered by the slope values, just by the direction; (iv) there are no barriers to flow; and (v) the study region is complete and meaningful in the context of the analysis. Several GIS packages provide facilities and options that allow many of these assumptions to be relaxed or explicitly modeled. The facilities for generating streams and watersheds within most GIS packages are separated into several

functions, whilst in TNTMips and Manifold integrated tools are provided to carry out many of the procedures required. Within this Section we shall utilize the terminology and procedures applied in TNTMips, but these are very similar to those used by all packages. A good description of the methods involved is given in Burrough and McDonnell (1998, Ch.8).

The core steps in this kind of analysis are:

- Creation of an amended initial DEM with pits or depressions removed, as described in Section 6.2.6. This ensures that flows will be continuous across the surface, depending on the parameters selected (in some cases the GIS program may force fill pits until continuous flows can be generated)

- Systematic examination of the entire grid to identify flow directions. This is similar in concept to the creation of an *aspect* raster (some programs, such as GRASS, utilize an aspect grid as input). Most GIS implementations use the so-called *D8 algorithm*, which involves examining a 3x3 window of cells for the locally steepest direction (rise over run) and then coding each cell to indicate which one direction (of the 8 available) the flow is to follow (e.g. coded as 1,2,...8 or 1,2,4,...128). Some packages, such as RiverTools from RIVIX, SAGA and the TAUDEM add-in for ArcGIS from Tarboton, implement the Tarboton (1997) D-infinity algorithm (Section 6.4.3 and Figure 6-27). SAGA provides a wide range of flow algorithms, from the simple deterministic D8 and D-infinity to stochastic D8 and ray-tracing methods. RiverTools also implements an enhanced procedure known as the Mass Flux Method (MFM). Both D-infinity and MFM provide improved modeling since they handle divergent as well as convergent flows, but nonetheless they retain grid-related directional bias. The output from these procedures is often described as an *ldd* or local drainage direction grid. In some GIS implementations the 3x3 window is expanded if all surrounding cells have the same slope. In this case the neighborhood is enlarged until a unique direction can be chosen. GRASS and several other packages also consider all possible directions, avoiding problems of significant directional bias (zigzag and parallel lines)

- Identification of flat areas and local extrema (peaks and pits)

- Computation of hypothetical stream paths and accumulated flows. This is typically carried out by accumulating the number of uphill cells (counting rook's moves as 1 unit and diagonal flows as longer — either 1.414... units or approximated as 3/2 units for speed of computation by working in integer arithmetic for most of the calculations) to obtain an accumulated value per cell. There may be a minimum value required or user-specified before accumulations are considered to constitute a stream, and hence be included in generated stream networks. SAGA and PCRaster, for example, include an extensive set of options relating to flow patterns

- Merging streams into topologically consistent networks and calculating simple stream-order statistics, e.g. Strahler, Horton and Shreve order values — see Haggett and Chorley (1969) or similar texts for more details on branching networks

- Identification of the upstream limits of different stream systems, in order to determine watersheds and compute watershed-related statistics

- Identification of basins within these watersheds, typically representing the watersheds of secondary streams (first level tributaries) from the main stream within the watershed

- Optional specification of points within the grid file that may be examined for the downstream impact of introduced flows, e.g. spillovers or pollutants entering the system, and/or the upstream flows that may impact upon a downstream location

- Computation of statistics relating to the various elements generated, for example details of stream lengths, basin and watershed areas, membership lists (streams within watersheds), estimation of sediment transport amounts etc. and computation of estimated soil loss using the Universal Soil Loss Equation (USLE)

### 6.4.3  D-infinity model

The D-infinity flow assignment model is illustrated in Figure 6-27. Flows are assigned to two cells or pixels (colored here in yellow) based on the direction of maximum gradient of the 8 triangular facets illustrated. The proportions assigned to each pixel are determined by the two ratios:

$$p_1 = \frac{\alpha_1}{\alpha_1 + \alpha_2}, p_2 = \frac{\alpha_2}{\alpha_1 + \alpha_2}$$

where $\alpha$ is defined in radians or degrees, as measured as in mathematics (i.e. from due east).

*Figure 6-27 D-Infinity flow assignment*

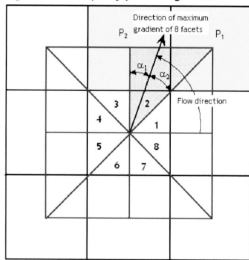

In the D-infinity model, if the steepest slope vector angle illustrated lies outside of a facet (a special case that may well occur) then the direction vector is taken along the steepest edge of the facet.

### 6.4.4 Drainage modeling case study

In the following discussion we use the Pentland Hills NT04 test DEM to illustrate the procedures involved. If a relatively flat and/or poorly bounded region is selected, with integer height values, the output from hydrological modeling may be ambiguous, so here we have selected a more mountainous test dataset.

#### 6.4.4.1 Flow accumulation

Figure 6-28A shows the Pentland Hills source DEM as a hillshaded relief map. This version of the relief has been pre-processed to remove small pits in the surface, as described in Section 6.4.2. Using this amended grid file as input, a local drainage direction (ldd) grid has been generated (Figure 6-28B), which is similar to, but not precisely the same as, the aspect map in this case. This is because it is based on the simple D8 algorithm rather than more complex computations used in aspect determination. With the ldd map as input, flow accumulation modeling can proceed. Figure 6-28C shows a close-up of a part of the NT04 grid after the accumulation process has been run. Lighter pixels are those with higher accumulation values, and the pixelated nature of the accumulations and the boundary between accumulation zones can be clearly seen.

#### 6.4.4.2 Stream network construction

The flow accumulation grid provides the basis for stream network construction, typically marking all accumulation values greater than some pre-defined figure (e.g. 10) as being streams or potential streams. This process is illustrated in Figure 6-29A. Note that an assignment rule (e.g. proximity) is required for flat regions. Figure 6-29B shows those regions of the source DEM (prior to pit-filling) that may warrant closer attention. This may be because their values indicate that they are either flat (shown here in yellow) or local extrema (maxima in red, minima in blue, saddles in green). Each stream is identified by coloring the appropriate pixels; in this case without making allowance for accumulation value in the number of pixels colored (i.e. unlike Figure 6-28C).

*Figure 6-28 Flow direction and accumulation*

A. Source DEM after pit removal

B. ldd grid — D8 algorithm

C. Flow accumulation — selected area

*Figure 6-29 Stream identification*

| A. Streams |
|---|
|  |

| B. Flat areas and extrema |
|---|
|  |

*Figure 6-30 Watersheds and basins*

| A. Watersheds |
|---|
|  |

| B. Stream basins |
|---|
|  |

### 6.4.4.3   Stream basin construction

Surrounding collections of streams are the upstream limits of flow, which identify the watersheds, as shown in Figure 6-29A and without the stream overlay in Figure 6-30A. Figure 6-30B illustrates the construction of stream basins. These are shown here as yellow/white polygons, and are subdivisions of the main watershed polygons. The stream branching patterns shown and the identification of stream basins are both determined by flow threshold parameters, e.g. by setting the parameter lower a larger number of smaller stream basins will be identified, whilst increasing this parameter will reduce the number of such basins within each watershed.

# 6.5 Gridding, Interpolation and Contouring

## 6.5.1 Overview of gridding and interpolation

The term gridding refers to the process of generating a grid of data values from an existing set (generally of the form $\{x,y,z\}$ triples) using two-dimensional (spatial) interpolation methods. These interpolation methods assume that the attributes being modeled, $z$, are continuous or piecewise continuous across the study region, i.e. that $z=f(x,y)$ exists and is single-valued for all $(x,y)$ except where regions are explicitly masked off (i.e. excluded from modeling).

Interpolation methods often assume data points are correct (exact), but they may assume they are subject to error (generally of known or estimated extent). The models used may be exact (go precisely through the sample data points) or inexact (approximate the values at the data points). If the data points are relatively sparse and irregular, interpolation needs to be more sophisticated (subtle) than for dense, regularly spaced data. However, regularly spaced data may be subject to bias due to intrinsic frequencies in the data (spacing and/or directional effects). An interesting example cited by Burrough and McDonnell (1998) is that of soil samples taken in a field that had previously been ploughed, with values recorded being affected by the furrow patterns. Sparse datasets are typical of many applications in which data are costly or time-consuming to collect, for example using boreholes, meteorological stations, soil sampling or radiation measures.

There have been a many studies that compare the effectiveness of alternative interpolation techniques, using a wide range of different test datasets and conditions. Overall it has been found that a number of well-defined factors have a major influence on the quality of interpolation: data measurement accuracy; data density; data distribution; and spatial variability. These are fairly predictable findings, but prior examination of each of these elements may assist in choosing the most appropriate technique for the problem at hand and/or be used in guiding sampling of new or supplementary datasets. Interpolation quality can often be substantially improved through the use of ancillary information, such as remote sensing data or additional environmental information (e.g. location of stream networks).

Having obtained the best possible dataset, within budget and time constraints, achieving the maximum usage and value is very important — hence the need for interpolation procedures that assist in estimating values at unsampled locations. More generally, spatial interpolation is required:

- to convert a sample of data points to a complete coverage (set of values) for the study region

- to convert from one level of data resolution or orientation to another (resampling). Usually resolution is reduced to the coarsest in a set, but resolution can be increased using a suitable interpolator, such as an simple or incremental bicubic spline (stair interpolation)

- to convert from one representation of a continuous surface to another, e.g. TIN to grid or contour to grid

Grid files may be pre-generated (as for example, with elevation grid datasets from national mapping agencies), or may be generated from an input dataset of $\{x,y,z\}$ form. In the latter case values of $z$ are estimated for unsampled points, typically a square grid of pre-specified resolution. This generated grid may then be analyzed in order to identify its statistical attributes, its approximation or fit to the input dataset and/or other information available for validation of its quality. It may then be mapped in a variety of forms, e.g. contour, filled contour, shaded relief, wireframe, perspective 3D surface. Grids may also be generated in a number of other ways: from remote sensing datasets (e.g. hyperspectral images); as a result of conversion of vector datasets (e.g. contour to grid conversion); as representations of mathematical functions (e.g. as a output from a mathematical expression, with or without random or fractal perturbations); or as a result of map algebra, resampling and/or overlay operations.

Grid generation using local interpolation functions, of whatever type, is typically a process based on weighted averages of values at nearby points. The assumption is that each grid cell or intersection is likely to be similar to other values in its neighborhood. Most such models are of the general form:

$$z_j = \sum_{i=1}^{n} \lambda_i z_i$$

where $z_j$ is the z-value to be estimated for location $j$, the $\lambda_i$ are a set of estimated weights (proportional contributions that sum to 1) and the $z_i$ are the known (measured) values at points $(x_i, y_i)$. Assuming that $\lambda_i > 0$ for all $i$, then

$$\min\{z_i\} \le z_j \le \max\{z_i\}$$

i.e. $z_j$ will always lie within the range of observed data values. If one imagines $z_j$ being a point on a small hilltop surrounded by observations that are below it such estimators will generate a flat surface in the neighborhood of $z_j$ at the height of or slightly below the maximum observed value.

The size and shape of the search neighborhood is usually selectable. The size is taken either as a static value (e.g. a specific radius) or is determined in an adaptive manner (e.g. requiring a minimum number of observations to be used in any calculation). The shape of the neighborhood or search area may be circular, elliptical, or segmented variants of these forms. A number of packages facilitate the inclusion of known breaklines, exclusion zones and/or missing values as part of the gridding process. Most GIS packages provide a wide range of facilities for gridding, many of which are described in Section 6.5.2. Surfer provides amongst the most extensive set of options and offers suggestions as to their selection and use. Recommendations based on

those of Surfer and similar GIS-related facilities are summarized in Table 6-2.

Generating a grid from a (global) function does not require separate interpolation, merely definition of the maximum and minimum values for the x and y components and either the grid increment (size) or number of rows and columns to be generated. An example of such a function might be:

$z = ax + by + c + 100^* \text{rnd}()$

where $a$, $b$ and $c$ are constants and rnd() is a random number generator providing numbers in the range [-1,1]. Another example is the Gaussian surface plotted in Figure 6-23.

## 6.5.2 Gridding and interpolation methods

Examples of each of 10 methods for generating the grids described in Table 6-2 are plotted in Figure 6-31C-L. The source data in this case is a set of 62 spot heights from the GB Ordnance Survey NT04 tile, which covers part of the Pentland Hills area to the south of Edinburgh. Also shown is the source OS vector file of contours for this region at 20m contour intervals. Each of the plotted maps has been generated with a 20m contour interval using the methods listed and taking their default parameter settings as provided within the Surfer package.

If the input $\{x,y,z\}$ dataset is already a complete or nearly complete set of grid values, little or no interpolation is required — simple nearest-neighbor methods are typically used for filling in missing values in such cases.

There are several key points to note about these maps and the data used to generate them:

- all the derived contour maps shown have been generated by first creating a grid file using the interpolation procedure in question, and then contouring applied using linear grid interpolation (as described in the Section 6.5.3)

- with a highly variable surface such as this, 62 data points are insufficient to re-create the source data, despite the relatively small size of the region in question

- two of the interpolation methods (natural neighbor and triangulation plus linear interpolation) limit their extent to the convex hull of the input point set

- some methods, including moving averages, nearest-neighbor and triangulation produce very unsatisfactory-looking results with this dataset

- several methods generate very similar looking results, notably natural neighbor and Kriging, and minimum curvature and modified Shepard (see further, Sections 6.6 and 6.7)

- interpolation methods based on profiles tend to produce much better results, since these use contour data as their primary input, from which they generate a grid

- interpolation methods based on some arrangements of data points (e.g. points selected *along* contour lines) can easily result in misleading or erroneous results

*Table 6-2 Gridding and interpolation methods*

| Method | Speed | Type | Comments |
|---|---|---|---|
| Inverse distance weighting (IDW) | Fast | Exact, unless smoothing factor specified | Tends to generate bull's eye patterns. Simple and effective with dense data. No extrapolation. All interpolated values between data points lie within the range of the data point values and hence may not approximate valleys and peaks well |
| Natural neighbor | Fast | Exact | A weighted average of neighboring observations using weights determined by Voronoi polygon concepts. Good for dense datasets. Typically implementations do not provide extrapolation |
| Nearest-neighbor | Fast | Exact | Most useful for almost complete datasets (e.g. grids with missing values). Does not provide extrapolation |
| Kriging - Geostatistical models (stochastic) | Slow/ Medium | Exact if no nugget (assumed measurement error) | Very flexible range of methods based on modeling variograms. Can provide extrapolation and prediction error estimates. Some controversy over aspects of the statistical modeling and inference. Speed not substantially affected by increasing number of data points. Good results may be achieved with <250 data points |
| Conditional simulation | Slow | Exact | Flexible range of techniques that use a fitted variogram as a starting point. Effective as a means of reproducing statistical variation across a surface and obtaining pseudo-confidence intervals |
| Radial basis | Slow/ Medium | Exact if no smoothing value specified | Uses a range of kernel functions, similar to variogram models in Kriging. Flexible, similar in results to Kriging but without addition assumptions regarding statistical properties of the input data points |
| Modified Shepard | Fast | Exact, unless smoothing factor specified | Similar to inverse distance, modified using local least squares estimation. Generates fewer artifacts and can provide extrapolation |

| Method | Speed | Type | Comments |
|--------|-------|------|----------|
| Triangulation with linear interpolation | Fast | Exact | A Delaunay triangulation based procedure. Requires a medium-large number of data point to generate acceptable results. |
| Triangulation with spline interpolation | Fast | Exact | A Delaunay triangulation based procedure, with bicubic spline fitting rather than plane surface fitting. Generates very smooth surfaces. Widely used in computer-aided design |
| Profiling | Fast | Exact | A procedure that converts contour data to grid format. Similar to linear interpolation methods used in generating contour data (see subsection 6.5.3). See also, Topogrid, subsection 6.6.14 |
| Minimum curvature | Medium | Exact/Smoothing | Generates very smooth surfaces that exactly fit the dataset |
| Spline functions | Fast | Exact (smoothing possible) | Available as a distinct procedure and incorporated into a number of other methods. Bicubic and biharmonic splines are commonly provided (see for example, Sandwell, 1987) |
| Local polynomial | Fast | Smoothing | Most applicable to datasets that are locally smooth |
| Polynomial regression | Fast | Smoothing | Provides a trend surface fit to the data points. Most effective for analyzing 1$^{st}$-order (linear) and 2$^{nd}$-order (quadratic) patterns, and residuals analysis/trend removal. Can suffer from edge effects, depending on the data. See also, Section 5.6 |
| Moving average | Fast | Smoothing | Uses averages based on a user-defined search ellipse. Requires a medium-large number of data points to generate acceptable results |
| Topogrid/Topo to Raster | Slow/ Medium | Not specified | Based on iterative finite difference methods. Interpolates a hydrologically "correct" grid from a set of point, line and polygon data, based on procedures developed by Hutchinson (1988, 1989, 1996). Requires contour vector data as input. Available in ArcGIS based on Hutchinson's ANUDEM program |

In Figure 6-31 a series of contour plots are provided, in each case based on the set of GB Ordnance Survey spot heights shown in Figure 6-31A (Pentland Hills, OS NT04). The first plot, Figure 6-31B, shows the GB Ordnance Survey contour map for the same region, as a base for comparison purposes. The subsequent contour maps show the results obtained using a variety of interpolation techniques that have been applied to the source spot heights. These are each discussed in more detail in Sections 6.6 and 6.7.

*Figure 6-31 Contour plots for alternative interpolation methods — generated with Surfer 8*

Contour plots for alternative interpolation methods — 1

A. Source data — spot heights, OS NT04

B. Source data — contours, OS NT04

C. Inverse distance weighting, $1/d^2$

D. Natural neighbor

Contour plots for alternative interpolation methods — 2

E. Nearest-neighbor

F. Kriging — linear variogram

G. Radial basis — quadric function

H. Modified Shepard

## Contour plots for alternative interpolation methods — 3

### I. Triangulation with linear interpolation

### J. Minimum curvature

### K. Radial basis — bicubic spline, no smoothing

### L. Local polynomial — linear

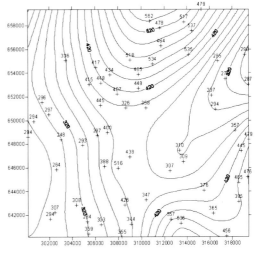

### 6.5.3 Contouring

Contour maps of surfaces (topographic or other) can be derived from grid, DEM or TIN representations, or may be sourced from vector datasets such as those produced by national mapping agencies. Contours are lines of equal value on a surface and are thus level sets — lines that may be generated by flooding a surface to a specified level or by slicing a surface horizontally. Where contours are generated from grid data they tend to be interpolated linear segments or smoothed segments derived from linear interpolation. If grid data are viewed as a set of grid lines rather than cells, the line intersections or grid nodes have values. A straight line segment of constant value (e.g. 480m) can be constructed from pairs of NS and EW nodes by simple linear interpolation (Figure 6-32). The result is a polyline with vertices at each grid line intersection and a constant value (e.g. elevation estimate).

*Figure 6-32 Linear interpolation of contours*

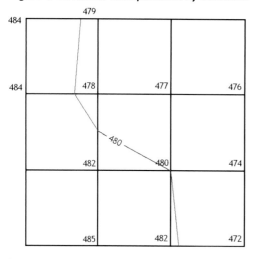

The polylines so generated may then be smoothed in a variety of ways — the most common being to fit a spline function to the straight line segments and interpolate a denser set of points that may be plotted to provide a smooth set of contours. Note that independently smoothed contours can result in separate contours crossing, so the procedure needs to be carried out with care. Alternatively input grids may be resampled to provide a finer resolution input or pre-smoothed using mathematical or map algebra operations with contouring conducted on the resultant revised dataset. For TIN datasets linear interpolation is typically the only choice, with post-computation polyline smoothing as an option.

Figure 6-33 illustrates the standard process using the sample TQ81NE region represented as a DEM and using TNTMips software. As noted earlier, there appear to be artifacts (linear forms) represented in the flat regions of the source data. Figure 6-33B shows contours generated using simple linear interpolation, with a close-up of a section of the surface provided in Figure 6-33C. The angular form of some line elements is reduced in Figure 6-33D using the iterative thresholding procedure provided as a standard option in TNTMips. This is essentially a form of bicubic spline smoothing. A similar result, often with even smoother curves, is obtained if the input file is pre-smoothed using simple weighted average or Gaussian smoothing over a sample window, e.g. a 3x3 or 5x5 window, and then linear interpolation applied. ArcGIS recommends using pre-smoothing of grids with a 3x3 weighting matrix and the map algebra operation Focal Sum (Weight option) with a custom weight of 0.96 for the central cell and the remaining 8 cells weighted to 0.005.

*Figure 6-33 Contour computation output*

| A. Source terrain map | B. Contour map |
| C. Contour — linear close-up | D. Contour — bicubic iterative thresholding |

# 6.6 Deterministic Interpolation Methods

In Section 6.5 we noted that interpolation typically involves generating a fine rectangular grid covering the study region, and then estimation of the surface value or height for every grid intersection or cell. The estimation process involves the use of a simple linear expression in order to compute grid values:

$$z_j = \sum_{i=1}^{n} \lambda_i z_i$$

where $z_j$ is the z-value to be estimated for location $j$, the $\lambda_i$ are a set of estimated weights and the $z_i$ are the known (measured) values at points $(x_i,y_i)$. As $z_j$ is a simple weighted average an additional constraint is required ensuring that the sum of the weights adds up to 1:

$$\sum_{i=1}^{n} \lambda_i = 1$$

The interpolation problem is to determine the optimum weights to be used. If $\lambda_i=0$ for all $i$ except for the measured point closest to the grid intersection then this would represent a form of nearest-neighbor interpolation. If all $n$ points in the dataset were used and weighted equally every point would have weights $1/n$ and would be given the same z-value. In many cases, as per Tobler's First Law, measured points closer to $z_j$ are more likely to be similar to $z_j$ than those further afield and hence warrant weighting more strongly than observations that are a long way away. Indeed, there may be little to gain from including points that lie beyond a given radius, or more than $m<n$ points away, or points that lie in certain directions.

Each of the methods described has its own approach to computation of these weights. In each case the weights are determined by the choice of model, algorithm and user-defined parameters. This differs from the approach described in Section 6.7, where the structure of the input data is first analyzed and on the basis of this a model and preferred set of parameters are identified — i.e. these are not directly selected by the user. Despite this apparent distinction, all methods may be subjected to a procedure known as cross-validation, which can assist in the choice of model and parameters. The simplest form of cross-validation is systematic point removal and estimation. The procedure is as follows:

- the model and parameters are chosen

- one by one each of the original source points is removed from the dataset and the model is used to estimate the value at that particular point. The differences between the input (true) value and the estimated value is calculated and stored

- statistics are then prepared providing measures such as the mean error, mean absolute error, RMSE, the maximum and minimum errors, and whereabouts these occur

- the user then may modify the model parameters or even select another model, repeating the process until the error estimates are at an acceptable level

- the gridding process then proceeds and the data are mapped

There are variants of this procedure (for example selection of a random subset of the source data points for simultaneous removal — a technique known as jackknifing), and various alternative cross-validation methods. The latter include:

- re-sampling — obtaining additional data (as opposed to resampling the existing data)

- detailed modeling of related datasets (e.g. easy-to-measure variables) — examples might include distance from a feature such as a river or point-source of pollution, or measurement of a highly correlated variable, such as using light emission at night as a surrogate for human activity leading to increased $CO_2$ emissions

- detailed modeling incorporating related datasets — look at possible stratification, modeling non-stationarity, boundaries/faults

- comparison with independent data of the same variate (e.g. aerial photographs)

### 6.6.1 Inverse distance weighting (IDW)

Inverse distance weighting models work on the premise that observations further away should have their contributions diminished according to how far away they are. The simplest model involves dividing each of the observations by the distance it is from the target point raised to a power $\alpha$ :

$$z_j = k_j \sum_{i=1}^{n} \frac{1}{d_{ij}^{\alpha}} z_i$$

The value $k_j$ in this expression is an adjustment to ensure that the weights add up to 1. If the parameter $\alpha=1$ we have:

$$k_j = \sum_{i=1}^{n} \frac{1}{d_{ij}}$$

Many GIS packages provide this kind of inverse distance model for interpolation, as it is simple to implement and to understand. Often the model is generalized in a number of ways:

- a faster rate of distance decay may be provided, by including a power function of distance, $\alpha>1$, rather than simple linear distance. While any $\alpha$ value convenient for a given application may be used, common practice is to use distance ($\alpha=1$) or distance squared ($\alpha=2$)

- since it is possible that the grid intersection could coincide with a data point (especially likely at region corners or edges if MBRs have been used on the original point set), an explicit check or adjustment to the expression is needed to avoid computational errors (overflow). Typically the adjacent point weight is set to 1 (its value is copied) and the remaining weights are set to 0

- if a user-selectable adjustment to the minimum inter-point distance is specified,

this can result in smoothed rather than exact interpolation. This may be a simple incremental amount added to the distance, $t$, or an adjusted distance value such as $d_{ij}^{'}=\sqrt{(d_{ij}^{2}+t^{2})}$

- as with all methods, additional controls may be applied or available: limiting the number of points included; specifying the search directions and search shape; and limiting computations by excluding pre-defined regions, breaklines or faults

Figure 6-34 and Figure 6-35 provide illustrations of the method applied to the test data for Pentland Hills OS NT04. The surface plot shows how simple IDW with no smoothing and power 2 distance decay results in dips and peaks around the data points but is otherwise relatively smooth in appearance.

*Figure 6-34 IDW as surface plot*

Figure 6-35A shows the source data (spot heights and contours) with Figure 6-35B and Figure 6-35C illustrating the surface obtained using parameters of $\alpha=1$ and $\alpha=2$. Both exhibit the familiar bull's eye effect of standard IDW. Figure 6-35D is markedly different and seems much closer to the source contours. In this case we have selected $\alpha=3$, a smoothing factor of $t=2$, and an anisotropy (directional bias) of 45 degrees using an elliptical search region with a ratio of 2:1. The selection of these values was made after limited experimentation using simple cross-validation and comparison with additional information.

Some GIS products, such as the ArcGIS Geostatistical Analyst (but not the ArcGIS Spatial Analyst) attempt to select an optimal value for $\alpha$ automatically. The method adopted varies, but typically involves cross-validating the data for incremental values of $\alpha$, for example $\alpha=0(0.25)4$, and selecting the value (or locally interpolated value) that yields the minimum RMSE value for the surface as a whole. In the example illustrated ArcGIS estimates $\alpha=2.96$ and RMSE at approximately 5 meters, although the maximum absolute error is around 100 meters.

*Figure 6-35 Contour plots for alternative IDW methods, OS NT04*

## 6.6.2 Natural neighbor

Natural neighbor interpolation creates weights for each of the input points based on their assumed "area of influence". These areas are determined by the generation of Voronoi polygons around each input point. In principle every grid intersection created would be in one of these polygons and could be assigned the value of the point around which the polygon has been created. This would result in a step-like surface of patches. This is the kind of result that is obtained from Nearest Neighbor interpolation. A far more effective approach involves a development of this idea, as described below. The end result is a smooth surface with discontinuities at the input points (Figure 6-31D).

The first step in the process is to create a Delaunay triangulation of the $j=1$, 2...62 input data points (Figure 6-36A) as a preliminary stage in the creation of Voronoi polygons.

The second stage is to generate a set of Voronoi polygons for the study region (Figure 6-36B). Each of the points, $j$, in the source dataset has its own Voronoi polygon, which has an area $A_j$. In order to determine the estimated value at a sample point $P$ the point $P$ is temporarily added to the set (so there are now 63 points) and the Voronoi polygons are re-computed. Adding point $P$ results in a new Voronoi polygon and redefinition of those immediately surrounding it (Figure 6-36C). This new polygon has an area $A_p$.

Effectively this new point has "borrowed" some of the area of influence from each of the nearby points. This can be seen in Figure 6-36D, where the new region has been overlaid on the original set. There are $k=5$ original polygons that the new polygon has borrowed area from. Let us call these borrowed areas $A_{ip}$, $i=1,...k$ then the total area of $P$'s Voronoi polygon is:

$$A_p = \sum_{i=1}^{k} A_{ip}$$

and thus the proportion borrowed from each of the original points is:

$$\lambda_i = \frac{A_{ip}}{\sum_{i=1}^{k} A_{ip}}$$

These proportions are the weights used to compute the estimated value at $P$, based on the standard linear weighting equation:

$$z_p = \sum_{i=1}^{k} \lambda_i z_i$$

If the point $P$ coincides with one of the existing points its area of overlap with that point would be 100%, hence its weight would be 1, as required. If the Voronoi polygon for $P$ does not overlap a region the weight associated with that region is 0. One of the main advantages of this method of interpolation is that it requires no decision-making regarding the number of points to use, the radius or direction of search, or any other parameters. It is a surprisingly effective and straightforward technique that is widely used in many disciplines other than GIS.

The standard implementation of this method provides interpolated values for the convex hull of the input point set. However, one or two software packages extend this to enable limited extrapolation to the boundary of a rectangular region (the MBR). This is achieved by using a slightly enlarged MBR (e.g. increased by 10%). Within this enlarged region temporary points are added to the original set at each corner (and/or along the region boundary). z-values for these temporary points are estimated by simple IDW or a similar technique, and then the Voronoi regions computed for all points. The procedure continues as before, but on completion the temporary points are discarded and the MBR re-drawn based on the original point set.

*Figure 6-36 Natural Neighbor interpolation — computation of weights*

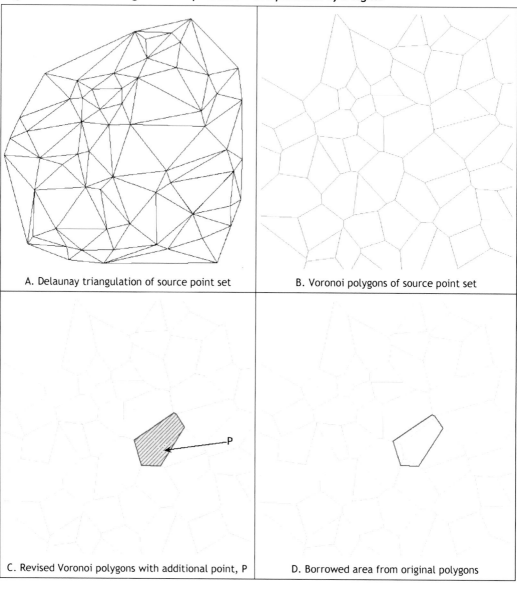

A. Delaunay triangulation of source point set

B. Voronoi polygons of source point set

C. Revised Voronoi polygons with additional point, P

D. Borrowed area from original polygons

### 6.6.3 Nearest-neighbor

This is a simple technique whereby each grid intersection is assigned the value of the nearest point in the input set, as illustrated in Figure 6-31E. The result is a stepped surface if applied to data such as the Pentland Hills, OS NT04 spot heights, but this is not the kind of situation in which the method is employed. The commonest applications are for: (i) evenly or near-evenly spaced input data that need to be converted to a grid file with similar spatial frequency; (ii) resampling grids or images, especially where no change to pixel/grid values is desirable; (iii) where there is a need to substitute missing values in a grid where most cells are complete; and (iv) where there is concern over the continuity of the underlying field and/or expectation that steps in the surface provide the most appropriate representation of the underlying data.

### 6.6.4 Radial basis and spline functions

Radial basis interpolation is the name given to a large family of exact interpolators. In many ways the methods applied are similar to those used in geostatistical interpolation (see Section 6.7), but without the benefit of prior analysis of variograms. On the other hand they do not make any assumptions regarding the input data points (other than they are not co-linear) and provide excellent interpolators for a wide range of data. See also Section 8.3.2 for an alternative (neural network) approach to modeling with radial basis functions.

A great deal of research has been conducted into the quality of these interpolators, across many disciplines. For terrain modeling and Earth Sciences generally the so-called multiquadric function has been found particularly effective, as have thin plate splines. The simplest variant of this method, without smoothing (i.e. as an exact interpolator) can be viewed as a weighted linear function of distance (or inverse distance) from grid point to data point, plus a "bias" factor, $m$. The model is of the form:

$$z_p = \sum_{i=1}^n w_i \varphi(r_i) + m$$

or the equivalent model, using the untransformed data values and data weights $\lambda_i$:

$$z_p = \sum_{i=1}^n \lambda_i z_i$$

In these expressions $z_p$ is the estimated value for the surface at grid point $p$; $\varphi(r_i)$ is the radial basis function selected, with $r_i$ being the radial distance from point $p$ to the $i^{th}$ data point; the weights $w_i$ and $\lambda_i$ and the bias value $m$ (or Lagrangian multiplier) are estimated from the data points. This requires solving a system of $n$ linear equations. Using the second of the two models above the procedure is then essentially the same as for Ordinary Kriging (see further, Section 6.7.2). For clarity we outline this latter procedure below as a series of steps using matrix notation:

- Compute the $n \times n$ matrix, $\mathbf{D}$, of inter-point distances between all $(x,y)$ pairs in the source dataset (or a selected subset of these)

- Apply the chosen radial basis function, $\varphi()$, to each distance in $\mathbf{D}$, to produce a new array $\mathbf{\Phi}$

- Augment $\mathbf{\Phi}$ with a unit column vector and a unit row vector, plus a single entry 0 in position $(n+1),(n+1)$. Call this augmented matrix $\mathbf{A}$ — see below for an illustration

- Compute the column vector $\mathbf{r}$ of distances from the grid point, $p$, to each of the source data points used to create $\mathbf{D}$

- Apply the chosen radial basis function to each distance in $\mathbf{r}$, to produce a column vector $\mathbf{\varphi}$ and then create the $(n+1)$ column vector $\mathbf{c}$ as $\mathbf{\varphi}$ plus a single 1 as the last entry

- Compute the matrix product $\mathbf{b} = \mathbf{A}^{-1}\mathbf{c}$. This provides the set of $n$ weights to be used in the calculation of the estimated value at $p$, plus the Lagrangian value $m$ using the linear equation cited earlier in this Section. The value $m$ is not used in calculating the estimate at $p$ in this formulation

In matrix form the system of linear equations being solved is of the form:

$$\begin{bmatrix} \Phi & 1 \\ 1' & 0 \end{bmatrix} \begin{bmatrix} \lambda \\ m \end{bmatrix} = \begin{bmatrix} \varphi \\ 1 \end{bmatrix}$$

i.e. **Ab=c** hence **b=A⁻¹c**.

A variety of different radial basis functions may be used. A selection of those commonly available follows. Where more than one functional form is cited by separate GIS software suppliers the name of the package has been included. The parameter $c$ in these expressions (not to be confused with the vector **c** above), which may be 0, determines the amount of smoothing. For an example implementation using a number of alternative Radial Basis functions on track (transect-like) data see Carlson and Foley (1991, 1992).

**Multiquadric:**

$$\varphi_1(r) = \sqrt{r^2 + c^2}$$

If the application of this function is restricted to some range, a, and we write $h=r/a$, then

$$\varphi_1(h) = \sqrt{h^2 + c^2}$$

is approximately linear over the range $[c,1]$ and approximately $c$ over the range $[0,c]$.

**Inverse multiquadric:**

$$\varphi_2(r) = \frac{1}{\sqrt{r^2 + c^2}}$$

**Thin plate spline:**

$$\varphi_3(r) = c^2 r^2 \ln(cr) \text{ (ArcGIS)}$$

$$\varphi_3(r) = (c^2 + r^2)\ln(c^2 + r^2) \text{ (Surfer)}$$

**Multilog:**

$$\varphi_4(r) = \ln(c^2 + r^2)$$

**Natural cubic spline:**

$$\varphi_5(r) = (c^2 + r^2)^{3/2} \text{ (Surfer)}$$

**Spline with tension:**

$$\varphi_6(r) = \ln(cr/2) + I_0(cr) + \gamma \text{ (ArcGIS)}$$

where $I_0()$ is the modified Bessel function and $\gamma \approx 0.5771...$ is Euler's constant. As noted earlier in this Guide (Table 1-3) the modified Bessel function of order 0 is given by:

$$I_0(cr) = \sum_{i=0}^{\infty} \frac{(-1)^i (cr/2)^{2i}}{(i!)^2}$$

**Completely regularized spline function:**

$$\phi_7(r) = \ln(cr/2)^2 + E_1(cr)^2 + \gamma \text{ (ArcGIS)}$$

where $E_1()$ is the exponential integral function and $\gamma$ is Euler's constant, as before. The exponential integral function is given by:

$$E_1(x) = \int_1^{\infty} \frac{e^{-tx}}{t} dt$$

In each of the above models the smoothing parameter $c$ remains to be determined. ArcGIS Geostatistical Analyst seeks to optimize $c$ by computing the RMSE of the prediction versus the data point values using simple cross-validation. Surfer selects a default value based on the diagonal length of the MBR of the data points and the number of points this MBR contains. This may then be modified to meet the user's requirements.

### 6.6.5 Modified Shepard

There are many variations on Shepard's original interpolation method, which is essentially the standard inverse distance (IDW) procedure. One variant introduced by Shepard involves the use of two separate powers: a lower value (generally 2) for nearby data points and a higher value (generally 4) for points further away. Another variant, implemented in some packages, adjusts the weights based on how far away the furthest point (in the entire set or within a given radius) is to be found. If this distance is $R$ then a revised IDW formula is:

$$z_j = k_j \sum_{i=1}^{n} \left( \frac{R - d_{ij}}{Rd_{ij}} \right)^{\alpha} z_i$$

The value $k_j$ in this expression is:

$$k_j = \sum_{i=1}^{n} \left( \frac{R - d_{ij}}{Rd_{ij}} \right)^{\alpha}$$

This is the form used in the Groundwater Modeling System (GMS) of Environmental Modeling Systems Inc.

Surfer uses a more complex procedure based on a local quadratic polynomial fit in the neighborhood of each data point. This is sometimes called the modified quadratic Shepard's method — for an example implementation see Carlson and Foley (1991, 1992). The procedure then continues as an inverse distance model using surface values obtained from the fitted quadratic surface rather than the original data points. The result is an IDW-type interpolator without the strong bull's-eye effect that simple IDW can suffer from. The method can be exact or approximate, depending on whether a smoothing factor is specified (see Figure 6-31H).

### 6.6.6 Triangulation with linear interpolation

The standard form of interpolation using triangulation of the data points is a widely available exact method. The Delaunay triangulation of the point set is first computed with the z-values of the vertices determining the tilt of the triangles. Interpolation is then simply a matter of identifying the value at each grid node by linearly interpolating within the relevant triangle.

Linear interpolation may be achieved, for example, using matrix determinants in a similar manner to those used in Section

4.2.3.1. A plane surface through three points $\{x_i, y_i, z_i\}$, $i=1,2,3$ has a formula in determinant form of:

$$\begin{vmatrix} x & y & z & 1 \\ x_1 & y_1 & z_1 & 1 \\ x_2 & y_2 & z_2 & 1 \\ x_3 & y_3 & z_3 & 1 \end{vmatrix} = 0$$

For example, consider a TIN element defined by the three coordinates: (0,10,10), (10,0,20), (0,0,5). Points in the planar triangle defined by the three (x,y) coordinates (including the vertices) may be interpolated from the above plane surface. In this case evaluating the determinant gives $z=5+3x/2+y/2$, from which all values may be computed.

### 6.6.7 Triangulation with spline-like interpolation

A number of other procedures exist for interpolation of smooth surfaces from TIN representations. Many of these have their origins in computer-aided geometric design (CAGD), with engineering and visualization applications. Some software packages, such as the groundwater modeling system, GMS from EMS-i, include CAGD interpolation methods, notably Clough-Tocher procedures. These involve fitting a piecewise two-dimensional cubic (i.e. a bicubic) function to each triangular patch, rather as per piecewise cubic spline interpolation on a regular grid. The fitted function may be regarded as being of the form:

$$f(x,y) = a_1 + a_2 x + a_3 y + a_4 x^2 + a_5 y^2 +$$
$$a_6 xy + a_7 x^2 y + a_8 xy^2 + a_9 x^3 + a_{10} y^3$$

The vertices of each triangle provide 3 values, $z=f(x,y)$, and the first-order partial differentials estimated at each vertex $z_y=f_y(x,y)$ and $z_x=f_x(x,y)$ provide a further 6, giving a total of 9 values from which the constants in the complete bicubic expression may be determined (Figure 6-37). However, there are 10 such constants, and at least one additional value is needed to uniquely determine the fitted function. In practice the original triangle is subdivided into three sub-triangles using the centroid of the main triangle. Each sub-triangle includes one edge from the original triangle and the first-order derivative of the Normal to the surface at the midpoint of this edge is used to provide the final parameter. Separate bicubic patches are then fitted to each of the three subtriangles, which collectively provide a continuous spline-like surface approximation at all points. This procedure is exact, fast and smooth, with interpolated values inside the triangle having values that may be above or below the maximum and minimum values of the vertex $z$-values.

*Figure 6-37 Clough-Tocher TIN interpolation*

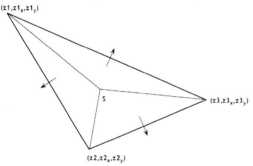

### 6.6.8 Rectangular or bi-linear interpolation

With a reasonably dense and uniform arrangement of data points (or with a grid image file) a number of simple and fast interpolation procedures can be performed. A common procedure for non-uniform data involves dividing the area around a grid point to be interpolated with a segmented circle enclosing a number of neighboring data points. The nearest data point in each of four segments or sectors of the circle is then selected and a 4-sided polygon defined connecting these points. This polygon can be used to define a weighted average for the grid point, either directly (e.g. using simple inverse distance weighting) or indirectly by assigning an adjusted value to each of the 4 grid cells that surround the sample point and taking the average of these. In either case a square or rectangle is determined which again may be used to assign a linearly interpolated value to

the central grid point. The cell-based version of this procedure is widely used in image processing, including re-scaling/resampling operations.

### 6.6.9 Profiling

This is a surface fitting procedure that utilizes elevation contours to create an interpolated grid surface. The standard form, implemented in TNTMips for example, is a simple linear interpolation based on the nearest pair of contour lines. Nearest is defined as the closest to the selected grid point in any one of 8 directions (i.e. four direction pairs). The resultant grid will provide an exact interpolation at contour locations but will be discontinuous across contour lines. This procedure will flatten ridges and "fill" valleys unless a non-linear interpolant is used. For terrain surfaces procedures that correctly model the hydrological structure of the landscape are preferable, e.g. Topogrid-type interpolation (see Section 6.6.14).

### 6.6.10 Polynomial regression

Polynomial regression provides interpolation by approximating the source data points using a best fit global polynomial expression. The surfaces are typically simple polynomial functions of order 1, 2 or 3, fitted to the point set by ordinary least squares. Such surfaces are described in Sections 5.6, 6.1.4 and 6.5.1 and illustrated in Figure 6-38). With linear regression the fitted surface has 3 constants, and is of the form:

$$z(x,y) = a_1 + a_2 x + a_3 y$$

whilst the bi-cubic model requires estimation of 10 constants and is of the form:

$$z(x,y) = a_1 + a_2 x + a_3 y + a_4 x^2 + a_5 y^2 +$$
$$a_6 xy + a_7 x^2 y + a_8 xy^2 + a_9 x^3 + a_{10} y^3$$

Typically global polynomial surface fitting is not used as a means of interpolation, but rather as a form of trend analysis, with further analysis being carried out on the residuals obtained when the fitted surface values are subtracted from those of the source.

*Figure 6-38 Regression fitting to test dataset OS NT04*

| A. Linear regression | B. Bicubic polynomial regression |
|---|---|

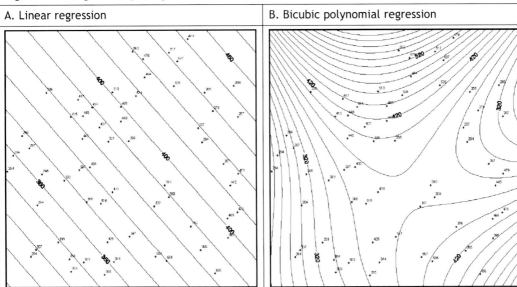

## 6.6.11 Minimum curvature

Minimum curvature is similar to bi-cubic spline fitting, in that the surface is modeled assuming that a smooth elastic-like membrane is used to approximate the surface. However, the interpolation is not exact, but close to exact, and is designed to ensure that the amount of surface curvature is as small as possible. This is achieved through a multi-stage process. As mentioned in Section 6.6.10 the first stage is simple linear regression and extraction of residuals. The procedure uses these residuals for interpolation rather than the original data points, but then it adds the regression surface data values back on completion. The interpolation process itself involves an iterative procedure that seeks to smooth the interpolated grid to a pre-specified parameter setting using a grid which is progressively made increasingly fine. The procedure is quite complex and is described in detail in Smith and Wessel (1990).

## 6.6.12 Moving average

This method of interpolation involves simple averaging using a moving window (usually a circle or ellipse). For each interpolated grid point a circle of specified radius (or an ellipse

defined with semi-major axis, semi-minor axis and orientation angle) is placed with its center at the grid point. All data points that lie within the window are averaged to produce the estimate at the grid point. If there are no data points within the window the selected point has no value assigned to it. The method is thus heavily dependent on the choice of window size and orientation, and the density of source data points. The resulting surface is simple and fast to generate, but may exhibit discontinuities.

## 6.6.13 Local polynomial

Local polynomial interpolation can be seen as a combination of (global) polynomial methods and the moving average procedure. As with global polynomials a least square polynomial fit to the data is applied, with options for Order 1, 2 or 3 equations. However, instead of fitting the polynomial to the entire dataset it is fitted to a local subset defined by a window, as in the moving average model. The size of this window needs to be large enough for a reasonable number of data points to be included in the process. One further adjustment is made to this procedure — a measure of distance-based weighting is included, so the least squares model is in fact a weighted least squares fit. The weights are computed using a power function of distance as a fraction of the window size. The simplest case is where the moving window is a circle, radius $R$. If the distance between grid point $(x_i, y_i)$ and a data point $(x, y)$ within the circle is denoted $d_i$, then the weight $w_i$ is defined as:

$$w_i = \left(1 - \frac{d_i}{R}\right)^p$$

where $p$ is a user definable power. The least squares procedure then involves minimizing the expression:

$$\sum_{i=1}^{n} w_i \left(f(x_i, y_i) - z_i\right)^2$$

If $p=0$ all the weights are 1. The default value for $p$ within Surfer is 2 and the maximum 20.

### 6.6.14 Topogrid/Topo to raster

This is a specific technique designed to facilitate conversion of vector surface data, in the form of contours, to hydrologically consistent DEM format. It is provided within ArcGIS and based directly on the work of Hutchinson (1988, 1989) and his ANUDEM (Australian National University DEM) program implementation. Surface interpolation uses a form of thin plate spline that is discretised to allow for discontinuities in the modeled surfaces (ridge lines, cliffs etc.). In order to ensure consistency in the drainage model it pre-fills any pits that it considers spurious (see further, Section 6.2.6 on pit filling and Section 6.4 on watersheds and drainage). Hutchinson describes ANUDEM as follows:

"ANUDEM ensures good shape and drainage structure in the calculated DEMs in five main ways by:

- Imposing a drainage enforcement condition on the fitted grid values that automatically removes spurious sinks or pits. This eliminates one of the main weaknesses of elevation grids produced by general purpose interpolation techniques. It

greatly improves the utility of the DEM for hydrological applications. It can also aid in the efficient detection of data errors

- Incorporating surface drainage constraints directly from input streamline data

- Delineating ridges and streams automatically from input contour line data. This is achieved by inserting curvilinear ridge and streamlines associated with corners of contour lines that indicate where these lines cross the elevation contours

- Breaking the continuity of the DEM over data cliff lines

- Ensuring compatibility of lake boundaries with the elevations of connecting streamlines and neighboring DEM points

The drainage enforcement algorithm is one of the principal innovations of ANUDEM. It has been found in practice to be a powerful condition that can significantly increase the accuracy, especially in terms of drainage properties, of digital elevation models interpolated from both sparse and dense elevation data... The essence of the drainage enforcement algorithm is to find for each sink point the lowest adjacent saddle point that leads to a lower data point, sink or edge and enforcing a descending chain condition from the sink, via the intervening saddle, to the lower data point, sink or edge (Hutchinson 1989). This action is not executed if a conflicting elevation data point has been allocated to the saddle. The action of the drainage enforcement algorithm is modified by the systematic application of two user supplied elevation tolerances."

For further details refer to the ANUDEM website.

# 6.7 Geostatistical Interpolation Methods

## 6.7.1 Core concepts

Geostatistical interpolation differs from the procedures described in Section 6.6 in that it assumes the data point values represent a sample from some underlying true population. By analyzing this sample it is often possible to derive a general model that describes how the sample values vary with distance (and optionally, direction). This model may be then used to interpolate, or *predict*, values at unsampled locations, in much the same way as with deterministic interpolation. If the samples meet various additional conditions it may also be possible to provide estimated confidence intervals for these predictions. Geostatistical interpolation methods attempt to address questions such as:

- how many points are needed to compute the local average?

- what size, orientation and shape of neighborhood should be chosen?

- what model and weights should be used to compute the local average?

- what errors (uncertainties) are associated with interpolated values?

A substantial number of specialist terms are used in the field of geostatistics and many of these are explained in subsection 6.7.1.1, before we proceed to describe specific geostatistical models. These include:

- Geostatistics

- Semivariance

- Sample size

- Support

- Declustering

- Variogram

- Stationarity

- Sill, range and nugget

- Transformation

- Anisotropy

- Indicator semivariance

- Cross-semivariance

- Comments on geostatistical software packages

- Semivariance

- Fractal analysis

- Madograms and Rodograms, and

- Periodograms and Fourier analysis

### 6.7.1.1 Geostatistics

We can define geostatistics as referring to "…models and methods for data observed at a discrete set of locations, such that the observed value, $z_i$, is either a direct measurement of, or is statistically related to, the value of an underlying continuous spatial phenomenon, $F(x,y)$, at the corresponding sampled location $(x_i,y_i)$ within some spatial region A." This definition is based on that drawn up by Professor Diggle and his colleagues at the University of Lancaster, Spatial Statistics Group. It emphasizes the fact that the term is particular to the analysis of continuous spatial phenomena, which is precisely the area that is of interest in 2D interpolation. It also highlights the statistical nature of the procedures involved, although rigid adherence to statistical requirements is not a pre-requisite for applying such techniques — rather it is a pre-requisite for interpretation of some of the results, especially those relating to statistical measures such as the estimation of prediction errors and confidence bands. As a more specific resource on geospatial analysis, in particular geostatistics and associated software packages, the European Commission's AI-GEOSTATS website (www.ai-geostats.org) is highly recommended.

For the purposes of the present Section we focus on the application of geostatistical methods to interpolation problems. As noted in Section 6.7.1, geostatistical interpolation differs from deterministic interpolation in that it assumes the source data points are a specific statistical sample or realization from some true underlying surface function, and this sample must first be analyzed in order to create a suitable model that will provide the best possible estimate of this underlying surface.

The initial analysis and modeling stage involves examining the dataset for outliers, and then for spatial autocorrelation, essentially using similar techniques to those described in Section 5.5.2.2. Of particular relevance here is the Geary C statistics which (ignoring weights for the present) is given by:

$$C = \frac{1}{2} \frac{\sum_i \sum_j (z_i - z_j)^2}{\sum_i (z_i - \overline{z})^2}$$

and the correlogram form of the Moran I statistic:

$$I(h) = N(h) \frac{\sum_i \sum_j z_i z_j}{\sum_i z_i^2}$$

where, as in Section 5.5.2.2, $N(h)$ is the number of points in a distance band of width $d$ or $\Delta$ and mean distance of $h$; $z_i$ is the (standardized) value at point $i$; and $z_j$ is the (standardized) value at a point $j$ distance $h$ from $i$ (in practice within a distance band from $h-\Delta/2$ to $h+\Delta/2$). The summations apply for all point pairs in the selected band.

### 6.7.1.2 Geostatistical references

There is an enormous volume of literature relating to geostatistics and geostatistical methods. Basic introductions in the GIS literature are provided in O'Sullivan and Unwin (2003) and Burrough and McDonnell (1998) amongst others. More advanced books include those by Goovaerts (1997, 1999), Deutsch and Journel (1992), Cressie (1993) and Isaaks and Srivastava (1989). The European Commission website devoted to Geostatistics (www.ai-geostats.org) is a useful starting point, as is the Center for Computational Geostatistics (CCG), a site that includes very useful course

material by Prof Deutsch and colleagues on Monte Carlo simulation with applications in the petro-chemicals industry. This site lists articles, books, courses and conferences, software products and datasets available within the field of spatial statistics in general and geostatistics in particular. There is also some controversy about the usage of geostatistics, as there is with many attempts to apply statistical methods to spatial phenomena.

### 6.7.1.3 Semivariance

The Geary and Moran ratios described in Section 6.7.1.1 are very similar to the functions used within geostatistics to understand the pattern of variation of observed surface values. These latter functions measure differences in observed values over a set of distance bands or *lags*. The function most commonly used is known as the (experimental) semivariance, and has the general form:

$$\hat{\gamma}(h) = \frac{1}{2N(h)} \sum_{d_{ij}=h-\Delta/2}^{d_{ij}=h+\Delta/2} (z_i - z_j)^2$$

where $h$ is a fixed distance or lag, say 1000 meters, $d_{ij}$ is the distance between points $i$ and $j$, and $\Delta$ is the width of a band whose center is at $h$, say 100m wide — hence in this case extending over the interval [950m,1050m]. The summation considers all pairs of observed data values whose spatial separation falls into the chosen band. There are $N(h)$ of these pairs, hence the expression measures the average squared dissimilarity between the data pairs in this band. Important and useful relationships exist between the variogram, the variance (Var) and the covariance (Cov):

$$2\gamma(\mathbf{h}) = Var\{z(\mathbf{u}+\mathbf{h}) - z(\mathbf{u})\}, \forall \mathbf{u}, \text{ and}$$
$$\gamma(\mathbf{h}) = Cov(0) - Cov(\mathbf{h}), \text{ where}$$
$$Cov(\mathbf{h}) = E\{z(\mathbf{u}+\mathbf{h})z(\mathbf{u})\} - E\{z(\mathbf{u})\}^2, \text{ and}$$
$$Cov(0) = Var(z(\mathbf{u}))$$

In these expressions the $\mathbf{u}$ vector is the set of locations at which the observations, $z(\mathbf{u})$, have been made, and **h** is a separation vector (i.e. with both distance and directional components). Cov(**h**) is the stationary variance and Cov(**u**+**h**) is the stationary covariance, for all **u** and **u**+**h**.

In practice, software implementations first compute the squared differences between all pairs of values in the dataset, and then allocate these to lag classes based on the distance (and optionally direction) separating the pair. This provides a set of semivariance values for distance lags, *h*, increasing in steps from 0 (or 0 plus some small increment) to a value somewhat less than the greatest distance between point pairs. When this set of values is plotted against the separation distance, *h*, it provides a graph known as a variogram (Figure 6-39).

*Figure 6-39 Sample variogram*

In this example the dataset consists of the 98 soil pollution data records provided in Burrough and McDonnell (1998, Appendix 3). The specific variable analyzed is the level of zinc in parts per million (ppm) in the samples taken. Lags are shown at 200 meter intervals. The first black square shows the semivariance which has been calculated using 207 of the data pairs, i.e. those that fall into the distance band [0,200] meters. The total number of possible pairs in this dataset is 98*97/2=4753. This dataset will be used to illustrate several of the geostatistical procedures described in the following subsections. Note that the worked example in Burrough and McDonnell (1998, p140-141) using this dataset contains computational errors.

### 6.7.1.4  Sample size

With very dense data points many interpolation techniques will give similar results. As the density falls and becomes less regular selection of interpolation method becomes more critical and careful examination of the dataset and any known characteristics of the underlying surface becomes increasingly important. If the number of data points is too small (the sample size is too low) the method may either be unworkable (for example there are insufficient data pairs in a given distance band to provide meaningful information) or may produce unusable results. Some authors have suggested that ideally there should be at least 150 data points in order to obtain satisfactory semivariance estimates, although fewer points may be used with some success, especially where ancillary information about the data is available. Others suggest that the number of grid points interpolated should not be more than 20-50 times the number of data points. In practice it is the variability of the underlying surface and the importance of capturing a given level of detail that provides the best guidance. Conversely, prior knowledge of the patterns of variation of spatial data may be used to direct subsequent sampling schemes (e.g. point spacing on a regular grid) to have the best chance of ensuring that prediction errors lie within predetermined bounds.

### 6.7.1.5  Support

This is the term used to describe the length, area or volume applying to each of the (physical) samples taken, even though these may be nominally assigned to a point for computational purposes. Predicted values at other locations based on such data apply to similar supports at these locations. If a series of observations have been made in a small area or block, and then combined to produce an averaged value, again assigned to a point, the support would be comprised of this combined or "upscaled" data.

### 6.7.1.6  Declustering

Source data points are often preferentially sampled, such that some areas are more densely sampled than others. Where this occurs the data may not provide a truly random sample from the hypothetical population of all possible values, and hence the distribution of sampled values will not be Normal even after simple transforms are applied. Some packages (e.g. ArcGIS Geostatistical Analyst, and those utilizing GStat) offer procedures for declustering the source data points by assigning weights to these points. One simple procedure for weighting is to use the area of the Voronoi polygon surrounding the point to adjust for clustering (this topic is also discussed in Section 5.1.2.2).

### 6.7.1.7 Variogram

If the observed pattern of variation with distance (the variogram) can be modeled using a relatively simple equation (some function of distance), then values at unknown locations can be estimated by applying the model to obtain weights that may be used in an interpolation process, much the same as those described in Section 6.6. Indeed, there is a strong similarity between the methods used in radial basis interpolation (Section 6.6.4) and some forms of geostatistical interpolation. The modeling of variograms and similar graphs is described in Section 6.7.1.15. The use of such models in interpolation is described in Section 6.7.2. These methods are generally described as different forms of Kriging, so-named after the South African mining engineer, Krige, who introduced the general procedures used. Variograms can be re-scaled using the sample variance of the input data. This process is useful where several variograms on different variates are to be compared.

### 6.7.1.8 Stationarity

The term stationarity originates in the analysis of random processes, in particular in connection with time series. In this context a stationary random process is one for which all of its statistical properties (e.g. mean, variance, distribution, correlations etc.) do not vary over time. In the context of spatial analysis a stationary process would be one that is stationary in space. Stationarity is often described in terms of first order, second order

etc. First order stationary processes must have a constant mean, irrespective of the spatial configuration of sampled points. Second order stationarity implies that the autocorrelation function depends solely on the degree of separation of the observations in time or space. A non-stationary process would be one where the process varies depending on when in time or where in space it is examined. Several techniques, including a number of those in regression modeling (e.g. GWR) accept that many spatial processes will be non-stationary and seek to model this characteristic explicitly.

### 6.7.1.9 Sill, range and nugget

The increase in the semivariogram values with increasing lags seen in Figure 6-39 diminishes with distance and levels off, in this example at around 1100 meters. This distance is known as the *range* or active lag distance, and is the approximate distance at which spatial autocorrelation between data point pairs ceases or becomes much more variable. At this range a plateau or *sill* in the semivariance values has been reached (Figure 6-40). Such variograms are called *transitive*. *Non-transitive variograms* are ones in which the sill is not reached within the region of interest. The term *practical range* is sometimes used and defined as the distance at which 95% of the sill is reached for an asymptotic variogram model (as in Figure 6-40), or for which variation around the sill is <5% for a wave/hole-effect model (see further, Figure 6-44K). When a curve is fitted to the set of points that lie within this range and sill the model used may have a zero or non-zero intercept with the y-axis. In Figure 6-40 a non-zero intercept is shown, which is known as the *nugget* or *nugget variance*, $C_0$, referring back to the original application of such methods to mineral exploration. The nugget is usually assumed to be non-spatial variation due to measurement error and variations in the data that relate to shorter ranges than the minimum sampled data spacing. The sill minus the nugget is sometimes known as the *partial sill* or *structural variance*, $C$. The values $C$ and $C_0$ often appear as parameters in fitted models.

*Figure 6-40 Sill, range and nugget*

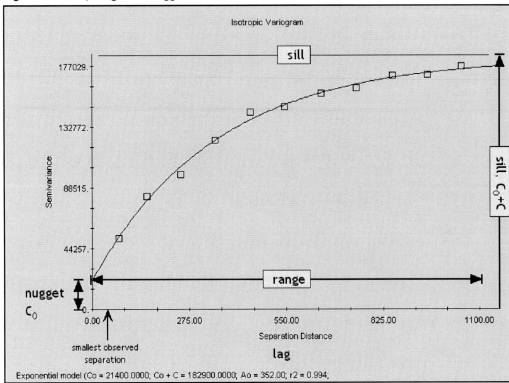

Isotropic Variogram

Exponential model (Co = 21400.0000; Co + C = 182900.0000; Ao = 352.00; r2 = 0.994;

## 6.7.1.10 Transformation

Because the techniques involved make assumptions about the statistical nature of the observed data values it may be necessary to transform these values prior to analysis, in order to achieve a closer approximation to Normality. Frequently this is performed via a log or Box-Cox transform (see subsection 1.4.2.7 for a range of data transformation functions). In Figure 6-41 we show a series of transformations of 301 Radon level measurements made in the are around Castleisland in South-West Ireland. These graphs and the associated test statistics were generated using the Minitab package. Three very large-valued outliers were removed from the original dataset prior to distribution analysis.

The raw data plotted in Figure 6-41A is clearly non-Normal, diverging substantially from the straight line which indicates a Normal distribution. In this case simple Log transformation of the data improves the fit to Normal but still diverges, even when corrections are made for background radiation (Figure 6-41C). In each of these three cases the Anderson-Darling test of fit to Normal fails, whereas for the Box-Cox transform (Figure 6-41D) with optimized parameter, $k$, the test passes and in this instance analysis proceeded using this specific transform. The Anderson-Darling test is a variation on the Kolmogorov-Smirnov test, again based on the cumulative distribution function, but is more sensitive to the tails of the distribution.

Figure 6-41 Data transformation for Normality

(a) Raw Radon Level

(b) Log$_e$ Raw Radon Level

(c) Log$_e$ Background Corrected Radon Level

(d) Box-Cox Transformed Radon Level

Source: F O'Sullivan (2005)

### 6.7.1.11 Anisotropy

In many instances the variogram is not of constant form in all directions. This feature is known as *anisotropy*, and the example shown in Figure 6-39 is of an isotropic variogram, i.e. one in which any directional variations are ignored. An alternative approach to the calculation of the semivariance would be to divide the lag band into a series of discrete segments, say at 45 degree intervals, and then calculate separate variograms for each direction. Since the directions are not oriented (i.e. directions such as 0 and 180 degrees are treated as equivalent) there would be four such variograms in this case at 0, 45, 90 and 135 degrees. More generally the variogram can be thought of as a function of two variables or

surface, $\gamma(\theta,h)$, that may or may not be radially symmetric.

The semivariance surface may be plotted as a 2D map (Figure 6-42) or 3D surface representation. The center of the map is the origin of the semivariogram, with a radially symmetric structure indicting that there is little or no anisotropy. If there is a strong directional bias, this can be regarded as the major axis of a directional ellipse, with a major axis providing the range in the primary direction, and the minor axis providing the range in the orthogonal direction. A single anisotropic model may be fitted to such datasets, or a series of separate models fitted to the data grouped into distinct directional bins. Note that the practical range may vary with direction in anisotropic modeling.

*Figure 6-42 Anisotropy 2D map, zinc data*

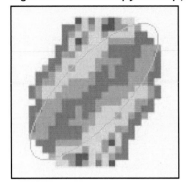

Not all software packages use radial sectors — some (including ArcGIS) use approximations to this form based on a grid structure. Other packages, such as Isatis, support more complex directional models and 3D variograms and anisotropy (e.g. for mineral deposit applications). They take into account the problem that simple directional sectors, which can be seen as cone-like regions in 2D and 3D, widen as distance from the selected point increases. To ensure that only points from a narrower band of directions are selected they provide for cylindrical and block-like anisotropic modeling.

### 6.7.1.12 Indicator semivariance

Some spatial variations of continuous datasets are less "smooth" than others. For example the concentrations of radioactive isotopes in soil samples is much lower than zinc or nickel, but may show marked peaks in some locations. Instead of using the z-values of the source data points directly in such cases, it may be more meaningful to record or transform the data as a binary set, with z-values above a pre-specified value as having a value of 1, and those below this threshold, $t$, having a value of 0 (or vice versa). The semivariogram formula is then applied, but this time to the $\{0,1\}$ values rather than the original values. These new values are called indicators, and are often denoted in the form $i(\mathbf{u},t)$. Indicator semivariance facilitates modeling of the probability that the variable of interest

exceeds a given threshold value, $t$, at unknown points.

As noted above, indicator semivariance analysis is a form of analysis on transformed variables, in this case thresholding to binary values. As with other variograms, indicator variograms may be calculated from the source data values transformed to binary, or re-scaled values using the variance of the sample data. Figure 6-43 illustrates both variants, using the same dataset as in Figure 6-40. Typically the re-scaled graph (Figure 6-43B) will show values in the range $[0,1]$. This scaling should be removed before proceeding with interpolation.

*Figure 6-43 Indicator variograms*

A. Simple indicator variogram of zinc dataset

B. Re-scaled indicator variogram of zinc dataset

### 6.7.1.13 Cross-semivariance

Spatial datasets that contain measurements on two or more variables may be analyzed in a similar manner to the procedures described for a single variate. Typically analysis is performed on pairs of variates, $\{z\}$ and $\{w\}$ say, where patterns of co-variation are of interest. Examination of such patterns may be of theoretical interest, for example in helping to understand underlying processes, or may assist in the prediction of one variate based on better information or more data that are available for another variate.

### 6.7.1.14 Comments on geostatistical software packages

The following (edited) observations on facilities provided in available geostatistical software (stand-alone or within/linked to GIS) are taken (with permission) from the AI-GEOSTATS (www.ai-geostats.org) prior to its recent re-implementation:

**Display of proportional/classed symbol maps:** often the first step in the analysis of geostatistical data. Showing symbols with a size that is proportional or characteristic of their attributed value can help the data analyst to identify outliers and trends.

**Moving windows statistics:** geostatistics assumes second order stationarity in the data: the mean has to exist and is constant and independent of location *within the region of stationarity*. The covariance has to exist as well, and is only dependent on the distance between any two values, and not on the locations. One way to evaluate second order stationarity is to divide the studied area into cells and compare the mean and the covariance between all cells. The moving windows technique uses an overlap of the cells as if a window was moving over the whole dataset.

**Sampling network analysis:** techniques used to quantify the degree of irregularity of the sampling network. These include the analysis of: Thiessen polygons; the fractal dimension of the sampling network; and the use of the Morishita Index. Nearest-neighbors statistics and many other tests can also be used to describe the spatial distribution of the measurements.

**Trend analysis:** An underlying trend may appear in the data and needs to be taken into account when applying Ordinary Kriging (Universal Kriging is supposed to take the drift

into account). The drift is frequently modeled with a simple linear or a quadratic model.

**Declustering:** When global estimations are desired one needs to obtain statistics that are representative of the whole area of interest. By attributing lower weights to clustered measurements one can reduce their influence and so limit the bias one would have obtained without a prior declustering. Two declustering techniques are frequently used: the cell and the polygonal declustering method.

**Variogram analysis:** The use of spatial autocorrelation being one of the main keys in a geostatistical case study, one would expect the GIS to provide at least the possibility to calculate the experimental semivariogram.

**Interactive variography:** The display of the experimental semivariogram is not enough to analyze the spatial autocorrelation. Prior to the modeling of the experimental semivariogram one needs to evaluate its robustness. Software packages such as Variowin and Isatis provide tools for the interactive analysis of the spatial autocorrelation. Their success comes from the high level of interactivity between pairs of samples, h-scatterplots, variogram clouds and the experimental variogram. Such interactivity is necessary in order to identify and remove outliers as well as to evaluate the impact of the choice of the distance of the lags.

Whilst many software packages provide automatic fitting functions of the experimental semivariograms, most practitioners still prefer to adjust their model by hand. As an example, the additional knowledge of a component of the nugget effect (e.g. documented measurement errors) will help to define a more realistic value of the nugget than the one that would have been calculated with an automatic fitting. Therefore, the interactivity during the variogram modeling still remains an essential requirement of a good package.

In many case studies a spatial structuring of the studied phenomenon appears in a particular direction. Not taking this anisotropy into account may strongly affect conclusions derived from the analysis of the spatial correlation or from the estimations.

**Models implemented**: Very often, spatial interpolation functions are implemented like black boxes in GIS or contouring software. It is even truer with geostatistical techniques that require the users to understand properly the underlying theory. The quality of the documentation of the available geostatistical functions should be a key for the GIS users willing to apply their tools to a geostatistical case study.

Additional interpolation/estimation functions are more than welcome since a geostatistical case study can be very time consuming, especially with very large datasets. On the other hand if one has the time to compare the efficiency of the various functions, one can expect to find that sometimes a non-geostatistical method has performed better, according to the user's criteria, than geostatistical techniques. Here again, clear documentation of the implemented functions is essential.

**Search strategies**: The search strategy of the neighboring measurements to use during the estimation/interpolation step has clearly a strong impact on the estimates. One should ideally have the possibility to select: the number of measurements to use; the maximum distance at which one should search; and the measurements according to their locations. For example, one should have the possibility to select few points in each quarter of the circle used to select the neighbors. As for the analysis of the spatial correlation, one should have the possibility to use an ellipse of search rather than a circle

**Masking**: When the studied area has an irregular shape, or when estimates are not desired at certain locations, one should have the option to prevent certain regions from being interpolated by defining inclusive or exclusive polygons.

### 6.7.1.15 Semivariance modeling

Assuming a dataset has been examined, outliers identified and removed or masked where appropriate, data transformed where necessary and semivariances computed, modeling of the variogram may proceed. A large variety of alternative models have been proposed over recent years, and many of the more popular models are incorporated into GIS packages and geostatistical software. Table 6-3 shows a selection of the principal models provided within such packages and Figure 6-44 provides sample graphs for each of those listed. The majority of these models are included within ArcGIS Geostatistical Analyst (which also includes a number of other models), Vertical Mapper for MapInfo and Surfer, and in packages that are based on or utilize GStat, such as Idrisi, PCRaster and GRASS. Other products, such as GS+, GSLIB and Variowin (a free, interactive variogram analysis tool) may provide a smaller range of models but offer considerable flexibility in the modeling and display process (see also, the R spatial projects page on the GeoDa website). In Table 6-3 the distance variable, $h$, is pre-scaled by the effective range, $a$. In much of the literature and product documentation sets this scaling is not shown, so where we show $h$ they may show $h/a$, $h/d$, or a similar ratio. Linear combinations of models are widely supported, for example: $p$*nugget + $q$*spherical1 + $r$*spherical2, but justifying, selecting and combining the component functions may be difficult.

Selecting and fitting variograms is something of an art rather than a science. Many packages provide a default model and attempt to find the best set of parameters to fit the dataset, whilst others apply this process for all models they support and select the one with the highest correlation coefficient or lowest residual sum of squares. Selecting only models that are asymptotic to the sill (i.e. to 1 in the diagrams shown) provides a useful first level of discrimination between functions. Both the selection of active lag distance to be considered, and the lag interval to be used, will affect the model fitted — the use of values that are too large in either case may result in over-large estimates of nugget variance. An example for which a combined model might be deemed appropriate is where multiple (nested) scales of spatial variation are observed.

Examining the profiles of these functions it is clear that the main differences between many of them applies in the first and last quarters of the effective range, hence close examination of the data within these ranges is advisable. Anisotropy may be automatically modeled or require selection, with attributes such as size and type of sectors being specified. Optimized selection of model and/or parameters under anisotropy may well alter the major axis of anisotropy identified to some extent, depending on the model selected. Most packages do not allow interactive alteration of

models and parameters (exceptions include Variowin and Isatis), but all will allow exploration by trial-and-error, re-calculating the model to user-defined specifications. One difficulty with these approaches is that it is very difficult to replicate results across packages, even when selected parameters are "forced" by the user.

*Table 6-3 Variogram models (univariate, isotropic)*

| Model | Formula | Notes |
|---|---|---|
| Nugget effect | $\gamma(0) = C_0$ | Simple constant. May be added to all models. Models with a nugget will not be exact |
| Linear | $\gamma(h) = C_1(h)$ | No sill. Often used in combination with other functions. May be used as a ramp, with a constant sill value set at a range, a |
| Spherical Sph() | $\gamma(h) = C_1\left(\dfrac{3h}{2} - \dfrac{1}{2}h^3\right), h < 1$ <br><br> $\gamma(h) = C_1, h \geq 1$ | Useful when the nugget effect is important but small. Given as the default model in some packages. |
| Exponential Exp() | $\gamma(h) = C_1\left(1 - e^{-kh}\right)$ | $k$ is a constant, often $k=1$ or $k=3$. Useful when there is a larger nugget and slow rise to the sill — see for example, Figure 6-40. |
| Gaussian | $\gamma(h) = C_1\left(1 - e^{-kh^2}\right)$ | $k$ is a constant, often $k=3$. Can be unstable without a nugget. Provides a more s-shaped curve. |
| Quadratic | $\gamma(h) = C_1\left(2h - h^2\right), \gamma(h) = C_1, h \geq 1$ | |
| Rational quadratic | $\gamma(h) = C_1\left(\dfrac{kh^2}{1 + kh^2}\right)$ | $k$ is a constant. ArcGIS uses $k=19$ |
| Power | $\gamma(h) = C_1 h^n$ | No sill. $0<n<2$ is a constant |
| Logarithmic | $\gamma(h) = C_1 \ln(h), h > 0$ | No sill. |
| Cubic | $\gamma(h) = C_1(7h^2 - 8.75h^3 + 3.5h^5 - 0.75h^7)$ | Compare to Gaussian — S-shaped curve with well-defined sill |
| Tetraspherical | $\gamma(h) = \dfrac{2C_1}{\pi}\left(\dfrac{\sin^{-1}(h) + h\sqrt{1 - h^2} +}{\dfrac{2h}{3}\left(1 - h^2\right)^{3/2}}\right), h \leq 1$ <br><br> $\gamma(h) = 1, h > 1$ | Similar to Circular with extra final term |
| Pentaspherical | $\gamma(h) = C_1(1.875h - 1.25h^3 + 0.375h^5)$ | |
| Wave hole effect | $\gamma(h) = C_1\left(1 - \dfrac{\sin(kh)}{kh}\right), h > 0$ | $k$ is a constant, often $2\pi$. Useful where periodic patterns in the data with distance are observed or expected. cos() rather than sin() function is sometimes used |
| Circular | $\gamma(h) = \dfrac{2C_1}{\pi}\left(\sin^{-1}(h) + h\sqrt{1 - h^2}\right), h \leq 1$ <br><br> $\gamma(h) = 1, h > 1$ | |

## Figure 6-44 Variogram models – graphs

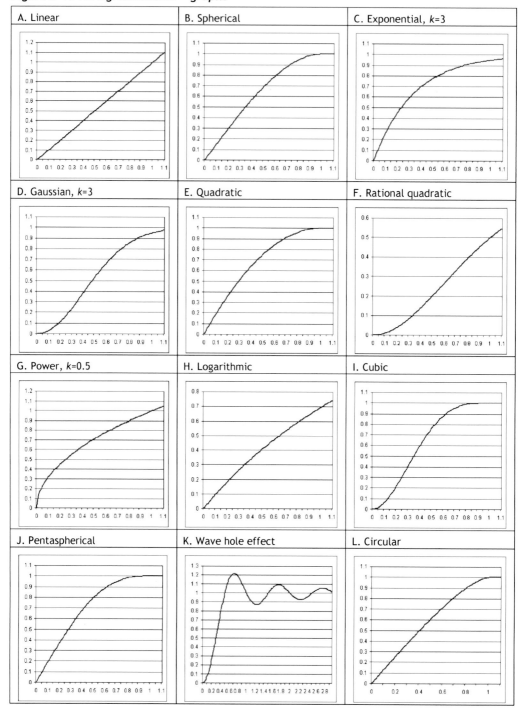

### 6.7.1.16 Fractal analysis

Determining the fractal dimension of terrain surfaces is a contentious process. In practice such analysis involves obtaining an estimate that is highly dependent on the way in which the data have been captured and stored, and the modeling choices made by the user, rather than simply being a reflection of the complexity of original surface. For many datasets the fractal dimension as computed in one program will differ from that computed by other programs, and may only apply across a limited scale range.

Figure 6-45 shows the result of fractal analysis of one of our test surfaces, OS tile TQ81NE, using the Landserf package. The fractal dimension in this example is computed by selecting a fixed interval lag and computing the standard variogram for the surface based on this lag, assuming an isotropic process, and then plotting the log of the lag against the log of the variogram. The best fit line $y=ax+b$ is then used to compute the fractal or capacity dimension, $D_C$, using the expression:

$$D_C = 3 - a/2$$

Hence in this example $D_C=2.2$. The Pentland Hills test dataset (tile OS NT04) has a higher value of 2.4, although interpretation of the computed differences is not straightforward. This approach yields a single measure of fractal dimension for the entire surface.

*Figure 6-45 Fractal analysis of TQ81NE*

Idrisi computes fractal values for an entire grid using a 3x3 window or kernel, based on the slope values computed for that window. If $s_{ij}$ is the slope value in degrees from 0 at location $(i,j)$ then the fractal dimension, $D_{C,ij}$ , is computed as:

$$D_{C,ij} = \frac{\log(2)}{\log(2) + \log\left(\sin\left(\frac{180 - s_{ij}}{2}\right)\right)}$$

where the logs can be in any base. This formula results in a linear (profile-like) fractal measure, providing an index of surface texture in the range [1,2].

### 6.7.1.17 Madograms and Rodograms

Madograms are computed in the same way as variograms, but the absolute values of lagged differences are calculated rather than the squared differences. Hence the equivalent expression to the semivariogram is:

$$\hat{\gamma}M(h) = \frac{1}{2N(h)} \sum_{d_{ij}=h-\Delta/2}^{d_{ij}=h+\Delta/2} |z_i - z_j|$$

The use of absolute values rather than squared differences reduces the impact of clustering and outliers, assisting in the determination of range and anisotropy for data with these characteristics. They may be seen as a supplement to variogram analysis and are not used subsequently in interpolation. Madograms should not be used for modeling nugget variance.

Rodograms are essentially the same as Madograms, and are used in a similar manner, but take the square root of the absolute values:

$$\hat{\gamma}R(h) = \frac{1}{2N(h)} \sum_{d_{ij}=h-\Delta/2}^{d_{ij}=h+\Delta/2} |z_i - z_j|^{1/2}$$

### 6.7.1.18 Periodograms and Fourier analysis

A surface represented as a grid, $z(x,y)$, may be analyzed to identify possibly two-dimensional periodicities in the data using a combination of sin() and cos() functions. Surfer for example, analyses the grid looking for frequencies that are integer multiples of $2\pi/k$, where $k$ represents the number of grid cells in the $x$ or $y$ directions. This form of analysis, whilst widespread in many disciplines, has only been applied in a few areas of spatial analysis, for example meteorological modeling.

### 6.7.2  Kriging interpolation

#### 6.7.2.1  Core process

Burrough and McDonnell (1998, p.155) describe Kriging as a multi-stage process of interpolation that builds upon calculation and modeling of the experimental variogram. Slightly modifying their summary we have the following stages:

- examine the data for Normality and trends — transform where necessary. Note that Kriging only requires Normality in order to create confidence intervals (probability maps). Whatever the data distribution, Kriging will provide a best unbiased predictor of values at unsampled points

- compute the experimental variogram and fit a suitable model. If the nugget value is very high then interpolation is not sensible

- check the model by cross-validation, and/or by the inclusion of a separate validation file (e.g. additional measurements not included in the modeling process). Examine the detailed validation results for both size and sign of deviations, and any unexpected patterns that these show (e.g. spikes, spatial bias)

- decide on whether to apply Kriging or conditional simulation (see further Section 6.7.2.12. The latter is becoming increasingly widely used, but is not supported in many geostatistical packages — GSLIB and GS+ and Isatis are exceptions). Kriging is effectively a smoothing interpolator whereas conditional simulation is not

- if using Kriging, then use the variogram model to interpolate sites onto a regular grid where the sites are either equal in size to the original sample (Point Kriging) or are larger blocks of land (Block Kriging). Block Kriging generates smoother surfaces — it estimates average values over a block. Kriging is not exact if a nugget is included

- display results as grid cell maps or contours, singly or draped over other data layers. Both predictions and standard deviations of predictions should be computed and mapped in most cases. If the random errors are Normally distributed and satisfy stationarity conditions then probability, quantile or confidence maps can be produced

The basic geostatistical interpolation procedure, assuming Ordinary Kriging (OK) for the time being, is essentially identical to that used in deterministic interpolation, notably interpolation using radial basis functions (see Section 6.6.4). The values at unsampled (grid) points are computed as a simple linear weighted average of neighboring measured data points, where the (optimal) weights are determined from the fitted variogram rather than determined by the user. For a specific grid point, $p$, we have:

$$z_p = \sum_{i=1}^{n} \lambda_i z_i$$

with the condition that the weights must add up to 1:

$$\sum_{i=1}^{n} \lambda_i = 1$$

In Kriging these weights may be positive or negative. The condition that the weights must sum to 1 is equivalent to a process of re-estimating the mean value at each new location. Hence Ordinary Kriging is essentially the same as Simple Kriging (see 6.7.2.3) with a *location-dependent mean*. Note that this allows for variation of the mean value from location to location, it is assumed that the mean value is fixed within the search window used for computations. If the mean values changes substantially over very short distances then it is described as *non-stationary* and alternative methods such as Universal Kriging should be considered (Section 0)

Kriging assumes a general form of surface model which is a mix of:

- a deterministic model $m(x,y)$, sometimes called the *structural component* of $z$ at locations $(x,y)$ — in OK this is assumed to be an unknown mean value, i.e. a constant, within a given neighborhood under consideration

- a regionalized statistical variation from $z(x,y)$, which we will denote $e_1(x,y)$ — in OK and other Kriging methods this regionalized variation is determined by modeling the semivariance and using the fitted function in the interpolation process

- a random noise (Normal error) component, with 0 mean, which we will denote $e_2(x,y)$ (actually two components, measurement error and random or "white" noise, which we cannot generally separate)

In equation form this model is of the form:

$Z(x,y)=m(x,y)+e_1(x,y)+e_2(x,y)$

or combining the two error terms and using Greek letter notation:

$Z(x,y)=\mu(x,y)+\varepsilon(x,y)$

If the vector s is used to represent the surface coordinates $(x,y)$ then the standard model is often written as:

$Z(s)=\mu(s)+\varepsilon(s)$

If there is no overall trend or *drift* present then $m(x,y)$ or $\mu(s)$ is simply the overall (local) mean value of the sampled data. If a marked trend is observed this may be removed before modeling in most packages (usually a linear or quadratic regression surface) and then added back in at the end of the process. The procedure for Ordinary Kriging is essentially the same as we provided earlier for radial basis interpolation (Section 6.6.4), but with the second step using the modeled

semivariances rather than a user-selected function. As before, the steps are:

- Compute the $n \times n$ matrix, D, of inter-point distances between all $(x,y)$ pairs in the source dataset (or a selected subset of these)

- Apply the chosen variogram model, $\varphi()$, to each distance in D, to produce a new array $\Phi$

- Augment $\Phi$ with a unit column vector and a unit row vector, plus a single entry 0 in position $(n+1),(n+1)$. Call this augmented array A — see below for an illustration

- Compute the column vector r of distances from a grid point, $p$, to each of the $n$ source data points used to create D

- Apply the chosen variogram model, $\varphi()$, to each distance in r, to produce a column vector $\varphi = \varphi(r)$ of modeled semivariances augmented with a single 1 as the last entry. Call this augmented column vector c — see below for an illustration

- Compute the matrix product $b=A^{-1}c$. This provides the set of $n$ weights, $\lambda_i$, to be used in the calculation of the estimated value at $p$, plus the Lagrangian value, $m$, which is utilized in the calculation of variances as described below

In matrix form the system of linear equations being solved is of the form:

$$\begin{bmatrix} \Phi & 1 \\ 1' & 0 \end{bmatrix} \begin{bmatrix} \lambda \\ m \end{bmatrix} = \begin{bmatrix} \varphi \\ 1 \end{bmatrix}$$

or more simply $Ab=c$, hence $b=A^{-1}c$.

The estimated value for point $p$ is computed using the $n$ weights, $\lambda_i$, (but ignoring the Lagrangian, $m$) in the normal manner:

$$z_p = \sum_{i=1}^{n} \lambda_i z_i$$

or using matrix notation:

$$z_p = \lambda' z$$

The estimated variance at point $p$ is then determined from the computed weights, times the modeled semivariance values, plus the Lagrangian, $m$:

$$\hat{\sigma}_p^2 = \sum_{i=1}^n \lambda_i c_i + m$$

or again using matrix notation:

$$\hat{\sigma}_p^2 = \lambda' \varphi + m = b' c$$

The variance estimates can be plotted directly and/or used to create confidence intervals for the modeled data surface under the (possibly risky) assumption that modeled random errors are distributed as Normal variates and are second-order stationary. Note that if the estimated points, $p$, lie on a fine grid, then average predicted values over discrete subsets of the grid (blocks) will be similar to those obtained by applying block Kriging to the same area, albeit with far more computation.

### 6.7.2.2 Goodness of fit

Having undertaken Kriging interpolation a variety of methods and procedures exist to enable the quality of the results, or goodness of fit, to be evaluated. These include:

Residual plots: (sometimes referred to as error plots) and standard deviation maps; maps of residuals from trend analyses

Crossvalidation: this typically involves removing each observed data point one at a time (leaving the model otherwise unaltered) and then calculating the predicted values at these points. Best fit models should minimize residuals (often referred to as errors) in these predictions: minimizing maximum residuals/errors; minimizing total sum of squared residuals/errors; removing extreme residual values (outliers/invalid results)…. Some packages allow the validation results to be exported for further examination and statistical analysis

Jackknifing: see Efron (1982) and Efron and Tibshirani (1997) for more details. This is essentially a form of cross-validation achieved by statistically re-sampling the source dataset. Typically one or more subsets consisting of x% of data points are removed at random (without replacement) and statistics of interest calculated on these subsets, which are then compared to the global value. Note that the term *bootstrapping*, often used alongside *jackknifing*, refers to procedures involving re-sampling with replacement

Re-sampling the source material (field data): an expensive or impractical option in many cases, but a realistic option in others

Detailed modeling of related datasets (e.g. easy to measure variables)

Detailed modeling incorporating related datasets: look at possible stratification of the source dataset (e.g. using underlying geological information); explicitly model non-stationarity, if appropriate; explicitly incorporate boundaries/faults or similar linear or areal elements that may substantive affect the results

Comparison with independent data (e.g. satellite data or other aerial imagery)

Examination of the fit for possible artifacts and bull's-eyes (a form of circular artifact) — these may be generated by the interpolation process and/or be a feature inherited from the underlying dataset

### 6.7.2.3 Simple Kriging

Simple Kriging assumes that the data have a known, constant, mean value throughout the study area (i.e. a global mean value, in practice 0, is a suitable assumed value for modeling purposes) and exhibits second order stationarity. These assumptions are overly restrictive for most problems and hence this method is rarely used. De-trending and z-score (Normal) transformation may help to remove some of these problems. Ordinary Kriging (OK) and its variants have more relaxed assumptions than Simple Kriging (subsection 6.7.2.4). OK is the mostly widespread procedure implemented in GIS packages.

### 6.7.2.4 Ordinary Kriging

Ordinary Kriging (OK), plus variants of OK, is the most widespread procedure of this type implemented in GIS packages. OK has been described in more detail at the start of Section 6.7.2. As with other forms of Kriging, OK methods may use point or block computations, the latter resulting in a smoothed surface and inexact interpolation. As noted earlier, if the vector **s** is used to represent the surface coordinates $(x,y)$ then the standard model is often written as:

$$Z(\mathbf{s}) = \mu(\mathbf{s}) + \varepsilon(\mathbf{s})$$

Figure 6-46 shows the result of applying Ordinary Kriging to the zinc dataset discussed earlier (Figure 6-39 and Figure 6-40; from Burrough and McDonnell, 1998, Appendix 3). Figure 6-46A provides a map of the predicted z-values, whilst Figure 6-46B shows the estimated standard deviations. In each of these the variogram model is based on the simple isotropic exponential formula shown earlier (Figure 6-40) and the analysis is based on untransformed data. The steps involved in generating Figure 6-46A are as follows:

- compute $\mathbf{D}=d(i,j)$, the inter-point distance matrix for all 98 sample points, **z**.

- Use these distances to compute matrix $\Phi=c_0+c_1(1-e^{-d/a0})$, the modeled variogram values. Augment $\Phi$ with unit column and row vectors plus 0 in the lower right hand corner to produce matrix **A**

- compute the inverse matrix $\mathbf{A1}=\mathbf{A}^{-1}$

- define a rectangular grid, 100x100 say, from min-max values of $(x,y)$ for interpolated values and mapping purposes

- for every grid point, $k$: compute $r(k)=d(i,k)$, the distance vector, **r**, from grid point $k$ to sample points, **z**; then compute modeled variogram values **r1** using $r1(k)=c_0+c_1(1-e^{-r/a0})$. These steps involve applying the chosen variogram model, $\varphi()$, to each distance in **r**, to produce a column vector $\mathbf{\varphi}=\varphi(\mathbf{r})$

- compute $w(k)=\mathbf{A1}*b1(k)$; these are the weights for point $k$

- then $est(k)=Sum(w(k)*z(i))$, i.e. the estimated value at point $k$ is a weighted sum of the original data values, **z**

*Figure 6-46 Ordinary Kriging of zinc dataset*

A. z-values (predictions)

B. Standard deviations

The predicted z-values appear as a smoothly varying map, whilst the predicted standard deviations appear somewhat as bull's-eyes around the original source data points. To the east of the region, where there are no source data points, uncertainty is much greater and the values of the results in this area are of little value. To the west of the region is a masked-off area, a facility which is explicitly supported within some packages. The fact that there are no data points in extensive parts of the sampled region presents problems, including issues of apparent anisotropy and questions as to the appropriateness of a broadly radial modeling approach. Substantial improvements to this approach (in terms of standard deviations) are reported by Burrough and McDonnell (1998, p.156) by the use of stratification (see further Section 6.7.2.10).

### 6.7.2.5 Universal Kriging

Also called 'Kriging with a trend', or KT Kriging, Universal Kriging (UK) is a procedure that uses a regression model as part of the Kriging process, typically modeling the unknown local mean values as having a local linear or quadratic trend. UK with no trend is the same as Ordinary Kriging (OK). Ordinary Kriging with a deterministic trend is often used in preference to UK as the modeling process is simpler and the results using the two approaches are often very similar.

### 6.7.2.6 Median-Polishing and Kriging

As an alternative to Universal Kriging (UK), which involves identification and removal of trends in the data, some packages (such as Manifold) support a technique known as median-polishing. This involves finding the median of observed (sampled) data values in a neighborhood (typically using a rectangular grid), generating row and column medians of these values in an iterative process ('polishing' the dataset). The median values are then subtracted from the original data points as local estimates of the mean value and Kriging of the residuals is carried out using either Ordinary Kriging (OK) or UK. For a discussion and application of such methods see Berke (2000, 2004).

### 6.7.2.7 Indicator Kriging

Indicator Kriging is essentially the same as Ordinary Kriging, but using the binary data generated using the thresholding procedure described in Section 6.7.1.15 and illustrated in Figure 6-43. Indicator Kriging can be used with a nugget effect, and Co-Kriging (Section 6.7.2.11) of indicator data is also possible and supported in some packages. In the latter

case, a second thresholding procedure is used and then both binary variables employed to predict values at unknown points for the first indicator variable. Note that the output does not provide a prediction of actual data values at grid points. The standard model for Indicator Kriging is often written as:

$$I(\mathbf{s}) = \mu + \varepsilon(\mathbf{s})$$

where $\mu$ is an unknown constant and $I(\mathbf{s})$ is a binary variable.

### 6.7.2.8 Probability Kriging

Like Indicator Kriging, Probability Kriging is a non-linear method employing indicator variables. It can be seen as a form of Co-Kriging in which the first variable is the indicator and the second variable is the original (un-transformed) data. As with Indicator Kriging the output does not provide a prediction of actual data values at grid points. With Probability Kriging the Indicator Kriging model is extended to the form:

$$I(\mathbf{s}) = \mu_1 + \varepsilon_1(\mathbf{s})$$

$$Z(\mathbf{s}) = \mu_2 + \varepsilon_2(\mathbf{s})$$

where $\mu_1$ and $\mu_2$ are unknown constants and $I(\mathbf{s})$ is a binary variable, as before. This procedure may be compared with that of Co-Kriging (see further, Section 6.7.2.11).

### 6.7.2.9 Disjunctive Kriging

Disjunctive Kriging is a non-linear procedure in which the original dataset is transformed using a series of additive functions, typically Hermite polynomials (see further, below). In this case the standard model is altered to the form:

$$F\left(Z(\mathbf{s})\right) = \mu(\mathbf{s}) + \varepsilon(\mathbf{s})$$

where $F()$ is the function in question. Indicator Kriging can be regarded as a special case of Disjunctive Kriging since the original data are transformed by the Indicator function. Disjunctive Kriging assumes pairwise bivariate Normality in the data, which is rarely verifiable in spatial datasets. A z-score (Normal) transformation of the data prior to Disjunctive Kriging is often desirable.

Hermite polynomials, $H_n(x)$, are a set of orthogonal polynomials that are most simply defined using the recurrence relation:

$$H_{n+1}(x)=2xH_n(x)-2nH_{n-1}(x)$$

with the first 3 terms being $H_0(x)=1$, $H_1(x)=2x$ and $H_2(x)=4x^2-2$. The range of $x$ is $[-\infty,+\infty]$, whereas most orthogonal polynomials have a more restricted range.

### 6.7.2.10 Non-stationary Modeling and Stratified Kriging

Variogram analysis and Kriging are often applied to a complete dataset as a single, global process. However, it may be desirable to sub-divide the study region into separate regions or strata, based on additional information. Stratification might be based on underlying geological formations, frequency of flooding, land and water regions, vegetation cover or other attributes that are of relevance to the problem at hand. In such cases the size and shape of sub-regions, and the effect of edges on the computed variograms, needs to be considered. Interpolated values using different models and parameters for each region will result in discontinuities at sub-region boundaries unless Kriging equations and/or the resulting surfaces are adjusted to support continuity. Currently, general purpose software does not support such procedures directly, but they may be implemented using standard facilities by manual stratification and re-combination of surfaces, albeit with problems of discontinuities to be resolved.

If non-stationarity of the semi-variogram is suspected, the study region can be subdivided into regularly shaped areas (assuming sufficient data is available) by using a moving window and/or systematic partitioning. Separate variograms can then be estimated for the subdivisions and 'local' rather than global Kriging models applied if appropriate. The resulting predictions (interpolations) may then show an improvement over the global model, at the cost of additional computational effort

and a considerable increase in the number of parameters used.

### 6.7.2.11 Co-Kriging

Many GIS packages support the analysis of a primary and secondary dataset, mapped across the same region, using a straightforward extension of standard Kriging techniques. With Co-Kriging the estimated value at an unsampled location is a linear weighted sum of all of the variables being examined (i.e. two or more). Co-Kriging extends the Ordinary Kriging model to the form:

$$Z_1(\mathbf{s}) = \mu_1(\mathbf{s}) + \varepsilon_1(\mathbf{s})$$

$$Z_2(\mathbf{s}) = \mu_2(\mathbf{s}) + \varepsilon_2(\mathbf{s})$$

where $\mu_1$ and $\mu_2$ are unknown mean values (constants) and $\varepsilon_1$ and $\varepsilon_2$ are random errors. Each of these sets of random errors may exhibit autocorrelation and cross-correlation between the datasets, which the procedure attempts to model. Co-Kriging uses this cross-correlation to improve the estimation of $Z_1(\mathbf{s})$. Co-Kriging can also be applied to models other than Ordinary Kriging (e.g. Indicator Co-Kriging, etc.).

### 6.7.2.12 Factorial Kriging

The term Factorial Kriging is used to refer to procedures in which the modeled variogram exhibits multi-scale variation. If these various scales of variation can be identified and extracted, Kriging may then be carried out using separate component parts of the variogram — for example, a spherical model component with range 2,000 meters, a similar model component with range 10,000 meters, and a separate drift component. Factorial Kriging is not widely supported in geostatistics packages at present — Isatis, a very powerful package, is one of the few that does provide support for such analysis.

### 6.7.2.13 Conditional simulation

This is an interpolation procedure that can be seen as a development of Kriging. However, unlike Kriging it exactly reproduces the global characteristics of the source data (notably the source data points, the histogram of input data values and covariances) and it creates multiple maps which collectively provide an estimate of local and global uncertainty. Conditional simulation also reflects patterns of local variability more satisfactorily than Kriging, since the latter tends to smooth data locally, especially where source data points are sparse. Conditional simulation is an exact interpolator and cross-validation of the type used in other interpolation methods is not applicable, although a secondary (conditioning) dataset may be used.

The most widely available procedure for conditional simulation is one of three such methods provided in the GSLIB geostatistical package (the others being *simulated annealing* and *sequential indicator simulation*). The technique is known as *Gaussian Sequential Simulation* (GSS) and involves creating a surface using a random (or *stochastic*) process, applied many times to the same initial dataset. The specifics of implementations vary from package to package (further development of conditional simulation is provided in packages such as GMS, GS+ and Isatis, and also in the Idrisi and ArcGIS GIS software), but we shall first summarize the general procedure and then illustrate the results with the zinc dataset referred to in previous subsections (from Burrough and McDonnell, 1998, Appendix 3).

The inputs to conditional simulation are similar to those for Simple or Ordinary Kriging — a set of scattered data points for which one or more measured z-values have been recorded. The standard algorithm is then a three step process:

- **Step 1 initialization:** analyze the input data for Normality, applying de-clustering and/or transformation if necessary; compute a best-fit experimental variogram model for the data; then define a fine grid (generally finer than is used for Kriging) over the entire study region. In some instances the definition of this grid is a multi-level process, starting with a relatively coarse grid and then progressively generating finer and finer

grids. This has the advantage of improved representation of longer distance effects as well as short-range variability

- **Step 2 random walk:** pick a random location on the grid, $X$, and perform step 3, below. Then move to another (unvisited) grid location at random and continue until all grid nodes have been visited. If a multi-level grid approach is applied then repeat this process with the finer grid, using the results from the previous stage plus the input data points as the set of source data values, $z^*(x,y)$. The use of random walks or similar procedures minimizes the risk of creating artifacts that have been found to occur if systematic grid search is utilized

- **Step 3 local search and conditional estimation:** identify all $z^*(x,y)$ that lie within a pre-defined radius of $X$ or locate the $N$ nearest neighboring $z^*(x,y)$ locations (e.g. $N$=16). Use the variogram model obtained in step 1 to provide a predicted (mean, $m$) value at $X$ and estimated standard deviation (sd) at $X$, as per Ordinary Kriging, i.e. as a linear weighted combination of the $N$ selected points (this is the conditional control applied); then, using the cumulative Normal distribution with mean $m$ and standard deviation $sd$, select a random value (i.e. a random Normal variate in this case), and assign this as the estimate at $X$

These steps result in a single instance of a simulated grid at a given resolution (single level or multi-level process). The entire process is then repeated $M$ times using a different random starting point and random number sequence. $M$ may be quite large (e.g. $M$=1000) in order to obtain improved estimates of the surface mean and uncertainty (confidence bands), together with a smoother resulting surface. Inevitably the process is very computationally intensive, particularly if $M$ is large, the grid resolution fine and/or multi-level processing is utilized.

Conditional simulation applied as an interpolation method on the zinc dataset yields results of the type shown in Figure 6-47.

The results illustrated are based on 100 iterations. Although Burrough and McDonnell (1998) recommend 500+ iterations, increasing the iterations with this dataset and modeling system (GS+) results in very minor alteration of the z-values — it has been suggested that this particular implementation may over-smooth the results.

Comparing this result with that obtained by Ordinary Kriging (Figure 6-46A) shows the resultant interpolations appear very similar, although the predicted data value range is greater in the conditional simulation model — Kriging tends to smooth and under-estimate the spatial variability of data as it is a form of weighted moving average. Predicted values in the unsampled areas are also often better behaved (smoother, less subject to artifacts) in the conditional simulation model. Figure 6-47B shows the standard deviation map, which is substantially different from that obtained by Ordinary Kriging (Figure 6-46B) — both the pattern and the range are altered, with the range being very much reduced. This is particularly apparent in regions where the initial data points are sparse or absent. Increasing $M$ results in minor alteration of the mapped patterns and value range, for the standard deviations in this example. A particular additional feature of conditional simulation lies in its generation of a set of individual realizations. These may be used, for example, to create a *distribution* of the areas above or below a given value, which is not the case with Kriging.

*Figure 6-47 Conditional simulation of untransformed zinc test dataset*

A. z-values, $M$=100 (predicted values)

B. Standard deviations, $M$=100

# 7 Network and Location Analysis

## 7.1 Introduction to Network and Location Analysis

### 7.1.1 Overview of network and location analysis

This chapter deals with two separate but closely related topics. The first involves questions regarding preferred routes, either traversing physical (transport) networks or by directly connecting pre-defined locations. The second topic covered involves the selection of locations and 'service areas' (principally within existing networks) that meet pre-specified criteria. Many GIS packages provide a limited set of functions designed to answer basic questions of this kind. Some packages provide more extensive tools using optional add-ins, such as ESRI's ArcGIS Network Analyst (now included in ArcGIS as standard), ESRI's ArcLogistics option and Manifold's Business Tools option. Other packages, such as Caliper's TransCAD (built using the Maptitude GIS platform) and Citilab's Cube suite (built using ArcGIS libraries), aim to provide a fully integrated GIS-T (GIS for Transportation) suite with an extensive range of routing and modeling facilities. As an illustration, TransCAD provides facilities for: network analysis (shortest paths, travelling salesman problems and network partitioning); transit analysis (designing and modeling the use of public transit networks and associated fare structures); transportation planning and travel demand modeling (trip modeling, modal split modeling and traffic assignment); vehicle routing and logistics (dispatching/collection problems, arc routing problems and flow-related problems); and territory management and site location modeling.

In many cases network analysis problems can be defined (*abstracted*) in terms that do not require a GIS for data manipulation, solution or presentation. For this reason algorithms for their exact or approximate solution are available as stand-alone code modules or as libraries providing solutions for generic problems, which then may be integrated into application suites with final output in map, list and/or table form. For example, problems involving the optimal selection of one or more locations in the plane (e.g. depots) given a set of point locations representing demand (e.g. customer sites) simply may require the relevant coordinate set (and associated demand levels) as input. The same observation applies to problems where a route traversing a set of points is required, but for which no explicit prior network has been defined. Likewise, assuming that a predefined network exists, many problems can be solved without detailed knowledge of the shape of links between network nodes – in general only their length or a related measure such as travel time in each direction is required, often provided as a shortest path or least-cost matrix. In this chapter, therefore, we discuss the solution to a range of network optimization problems using both GIS and non-GIS toolsets. Recommended reading to accompany this chapter includes: Tinkler (CATMOG 14), Scott (1971), Miller and Shaw (2001) "Geographic Information Systems for Transportation"; Ahuja et al. (1993) "Network flows: Theory, algorithms and applications"; Rodrigue et al. (2006) "The geography of transport systems"; and Daskin (1995) "Network and discrete location: Models, algorithms and applications". A software package, SITATION, to accompany Daskin's book, is available for free download.

### 7.1.2 Terminology

Table 7-1 provides a number of key definitions used within the discipline of network analysis. These terms are used within the various subsections of this chapter and widely within the cited references. The terms are all derived from abstract graph theory, itself part of the broader field of pure mathematics. Much work on graph theory bears little or no relation to the kind of spatial analysis discussed in this Guide, but nevertheless many of the results within this field are essential parts of the search for efficient (fast, high quality, compact, robust) solutions to many spatial problems.

*Table 7-1 Network analysis terminology*

| Term | Description |
|---|---|
| Vertex | A point location considered as a network node. Vertices are typically either distinct points or the end points or intersection points of lines or polylines. Note that intermediate points along a polyline are not generally vertices |
| Edge | A (directed or undirected) link between two vertices that are directly connected is called an edge. An undirected edge is determined by an unordered sequence of vertices, e.g. (3,8), which is the same as (8,3) whereas for a directed edge the order of the sequence matters, with (3,8) being from 3 to 8. An indirect link (via one or more other vertices) is not an edge. Edges are sometimes referred to as links or arcs |
| Degree (of a vertex) | In an undirected graph the number of edges meeting at a vertex. In a directed graph the degree usually refers to number of edges directed to a vertex (the *indegree*) minus the number of edges directed from a vertex (the *outdegree*) |
| Graph | A collection of vertices and edges constitutes a graph. Directed graphs are graphs that include one or more directed edges. If all edges are directed such graphs are known as *digraphs*. The mathematical study of the properties of graphs and paths through graphs is known as graph theory |
| Path | A (network) path is a sequence of connected edges between vertices |
| Connected graph | If at least one path exists between every vertex and every other vertex in a graph it is described as connected. A fully connected graph is one in which every vertex is directly connected to every other vertex. In such a graph, if there are $n$ vertices there are $n(n-1)/2$ edges, assuming all edges are undirected |
| Connectivity | Network connectivity is the minimum number of nodes or links that must fail in order to partition the network (or sub-network) into two or more disjoint networks. The larger the connectivity for a network the better the network is able to cope with failures. In the real world network nodes and links do fail (e.g. roads require maintenance or an accident may block a link or junction). When nodes or links fail the network should continue to function with reduced capacity. Network connectivity is a measure of the resiliency of a network and its ability to continue to support traffic flows despite such problems. |
| Planar graph | If a graph can be drawn in the plane (embedded) in such a way as to ensure edges only intersect at points that are vertices then the graph is described as planar |
| Network | A collection of vertices and edges together with associated attribute data that may be represented and analyzed using graph theoretic methods. A network is often defined as a graph that has at least one real-valued attribute or weight (e.g. length) associated with every edge |
| Diameter | The maximum number of links that must be traversed to reach any node along a shortest path. Networks with small diameters are generally faster to traverse |
| Cycle | A path from a given vertex to itself that traverses other vertices is a cycle. A graph that has no cycles is called *acyclic* |
| Tree | An $n$-vertex acyclic network or subnetwork in which every vertex is connected, for which the number of edges is $n-1$. A unique path exists between every pair of vertices in a tree |

The disciplines that have focused the greatest attention on applications of graph theory in a geospatial context are those of operations research and combinatorial geometry. Within both areas an enormous range of results has been obtained and these provide the building blocks for the facilities seen increasingly in GIS and related software packages.

Figure 7-1 illustrates a number of aspects of simple networks. Each network shown is comprised of seven nodes or vertices. In this example no information is provided on the values (e.g. length, cost) to be associated with links or edges, attention being focused instead simply on connectivity. From this perspective the first two diagrams are topologically equivalent, despite their apparent different arrangement in the plane. The third network is clearly different, with a number of one-way or 'directed' links, and a different pattern of connectivity. In each case these networks can be represented as a square binary connectivity matrix, where direct connections between nodes are indicated by 1, otherwise entries are set to 0. The first two networks in Figure 7-1 have identical connectivity matrices, which are symmetric, whilst the third will be different and asymmetric.

*Figure 7-1 Network topologies*

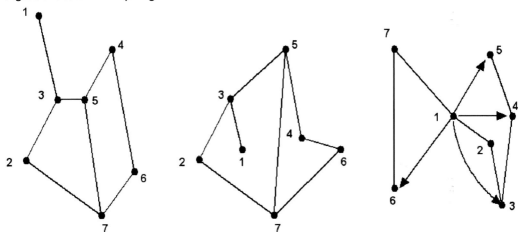

### 7.1.3 Source data

A set of line segments or polylines, such as a road or street map, does not typically constitute a network. In order to conduct many forms of network analysis it is necessary to ensure that a set of distinct nodes or vertices (V) exist and between each vertex one or more links to other vertices are defined. These links are referred to as edges (E). At the simplest level edges may be directed (e.g. one way) or undirected (two-way) and may have one or more attributes associated with them (e.g. name, length, travel time/cost, mode of transport).

Alternatively, one can simply start with a point set in the plane representing network vertices and no edges. In this case a set of links between vertices is to be constructed, typically using straight line (Euclidean) segments that satisfy certain criteria. This can be considered as a form of network construction problem or simply a routing problem that ignores the details of any underlying fine network structure.

Many polyline spatial datasets that appear to satisfy the requirements for network analysis in fact do not. This is often because the required vertices do not exist as objects and/or the set of lines are not precisely linked — the endpoint of one polyline does not precisely coincide with the start or endpoint of other polylines in the set. Furthermore, where segments of polylines cross the nature of the intersection needs to be defined — for example: is the intersection to be regarded as a vertex?; or should we regard one line as passing over or under the other? The simplest arrangement is one that assumes all such intersections constitute valid network vertices, and that all lines whose endpoints are closer to each other than some specified tolerance value (typically a small Euclidean distance measure) are, in fact, coincident and constitute a network vertex.

With these assumptions made (or variants of these) many GIS packages will convert a set of line data into a network, i.e. effectively imposing a network structure or topology on the dataset. Edge and/or vertex labeling may form part of this process, enabling subsequent routing plans to be referenced by route or street name and flow direction. Having done so, and/or as part of this process, attributes may assigned to edges and vertices individually, across selected subsets or globally. Examples include: (i) definition of turn attributes at intersections (permitted, not-permitted by link and any penalty, such as additional time or cost associated with such a turn); (ii) definition of U-turn permissions; (iii) definition of weights (or impedances) to be associated with edges (typically transition times, often defaulted to use edge length as a surrogate) — in some cases different definitions may be applied for each direction traversed along the edge, in others the link may be modeled as two separate edges, one for each direction of travel; (iv) definition of one-way edges and their direction; (v) specification of any permanent or temporary barriers, typically at vertices — links that are barred are often simply disabled or assigned a very high impedance value; and (vi) defining demand and capacity constraint levels (edge and/or vertex based).

Once such a network has been defined, attempts at optimal routing can be made — for example finding the shortest (or fastest) path between a given pair of vertices such as an accident location and an ambulance station or stand-by point. However, as noted earlier in this Guide, street network and similar physical

infrastructures do not necessarily satisfy the requirements of a full metric space, and it may be the case that some points are simply not reachable from others, or that optimal routing can only be approximated and/or remain difficult or impossible to prove to be optimal. Again, the criterion one adopts in such cases is fitness for purpose — best known approximations, which in some instances are provably within a certain closeness to optimal solutions, are often the options that have to be taken. These can then be evaluated against operational criteria (e.g. maximum acceptable time for an ambulance to arrive at an incident for 99.8% of call-outs) and the problem or criteria re-evaluated if such criteria cannot be met. One of the great advantages of many of the toolsets available is the ability to run 'what if' scenarios, experimenting with alternative constraints, flows, changes in demand or supply, etc., and evaluating the varying costs or times resultant on these variations. This information provides a form of sensitivity analysis, which may (for example) enable depot location decisions to be made taking into account variations in availability of suitable sites, access routes and labor, forecast temporal variations etc., within areas of broadly similar generalized costs.

With pure point-based data no pre-existing network is assumed, and problems relate to determining the form of network (set of edges) or path that connects the point set in some particular manner. This assumes that either no underlying physical network exists and travel between vertices is possible and uniform across the plane or that an underlying transport infrastructure exists and is sufficiently fine and direct to allow its specific form to be ignored for the problem at hand. This latter assumption may or may not be entirely realistic, but has the advantage of enabling difficult problems to be addressed without the need for the additional burden of large numbers of network-based computations. Finally, depending on the problem being addressed, neither point (location) nor line (network) data are required — a pre-computed inter-point distance or cost matrix may be sufficient. However, this is not generally sufficient to re-construct a unique map of the locations, nor will real-world routes chosen be represented – only the sequence of links and associated distances/costs will be available.

### 7.1.4 Algorithms and computational complexity theory

Most of the key problems addressed in location and network analysis can be classed as "optimization problems". As such, they are an important subset of a much broader set of problems. Understanding the computing resources required, in order to achieve solutions of standard optimization and decision-making problems, is extremely important.

In the case of networks, which typically consist of a set of $n$ vertices, V, and $m$ edges, E, the amount of time taken to compute an exact solution as a function of the number of these elements is vital. Typically this information is provided in so-called "big O" notation and is based on the total number of steps involved in the operation and the way in which these steps are processed. This provides a very crude measure of the order (approximate amount) of time and possibly space (memory, disc) required to complete a run of a particular algorithm, notably as the number of steps becomes large. The actual time required for any specific implementation will vary greatly, depending on the quality of the implementation and the size of the problem. As an example if the amount of time is stated as $O(n^k)$ where $k$ is some Real number $k>0$, then the time required grows as a simple power function (or polynomial function) of the number of elements, $n$, in the problem. This is generally a worst-case scenario. Example polynomial orders include $O(n^2)$ and $O(n\log n)$. Examples of non-polynomial order include $O(n!)$ and $O(2^n)$. Note that for $n>3$, ignoring any additional constant multipliers, the following relation holds:

$$O(\log n)<O(n)<O(n\log n)<O(n^2)$$

i.e. typically some polynomial orders involve far fewer operations than others. The same is true for non-polynomial algorithms, where for example $O(2^n)<<O(n!)$ for $n>3$.

Assuming the problem in question can be solved exactly by a well-defined *deterministic* algorithm in polynomial time, it is said to be of type P. An example of a problem that can be solved in polynomial time is finding the shortest path from a single source point through a planar Euclidean network. Polynomial time algorithms are sometimes denoted using the abbreviation PTAS or PTAs.

It is possible to identify problems for which a given solution can be checked for optimality in polynomial time, but for which no deterministic algorithm can be devised. A non-deterministic algorithm (or computer) would be one that either: (i) guesses the correct solution and then must verify it to check it is correct; or (ii) utilizes a computer that includes an infinite number of processors working in parallel to determine possible solutions that again must be verified. Non-deterministic Polynomial time or NP problems are the class of problems that can only be determined in this manner. It is clear that P⊆NP but as yet the hypothesis P=NP has not been proven or shown to be false (this hypothesis is the subject of one of the seven $1Million Millennium Math Prizes offered by the Clay Mathematics Institute: see www.claymath.org/millennium/P_vs_NP/ for more details).

An example of an NP networking problem is that of determining whether a given non-directional network has a simple cycle that contains every vertex. It is clearly easy to check whether the cycle passes through every vertex and is not self-crossing, but it is very difficult to compute a specific instance of such a circuit as $n$ increases. In fact this problem (known as the Hamiltonian Circuit Problem – HCP) is within the class NP. A specific, and even more challenging problem, related to the HCP, is the Travelling Salesman Problem (TSP). In this case one must find an HC for a network where each location may only be visited once and has minimum overall cost (or time/length).

A problem is described as being *NP-hard* if solving it would enable all problems in the class NP to be solved in polynomial time. Some

NP-hard problems are in the class NP and some are not. Those that are in NP are called *NP-complete* (or *NP-full*). Proving that a specific problem is NP-complete involves first showing that it is a member of the set NP and then finding a problem that is known to be NP-complete and seeing if one can reduce (re-define/re-work) this problem such that it becomes identical to the problem being considered. For example, to show that the TSP is NP-complete we could proceed as follows: (i) since HCP is known to be NP-complete we could seek to show first that TSP is a member of the set NP; and then (ii) we could seek to show that the HCP is reducible in polynomial time to the TSP. A central result in complexity theory is the proof that every NP-complete problem is inter-changeable with every other one. NP-hard problems that are not NP-complete are considerably harder to solve, since even their solutions cannot be checked in polynomial time, unlike those of NP-complete problems.

# 7.2 Key Problems in Network and Location Analysis

## 7.2.1 Overview — network analysis

Table 7-2 provides a brief list of some of the key (optimization) problems that are encompassed within our use of the term "network analysis". Solutions for many important practical problems are built upon these core optimization problems and the various procedures (algorithms) applied to them. Examples include: the production of optimal routing and vehicle loading plans; multi-modal transport problems; identification of drive-time zones; network partitioning and territory definition; facility location on a network; and travel demand analysis. For selected problems exact solution methods exist, but in some cases these may require an excessive amount of time to complete. Commonly applied exact procedures include linear programming, in some instances augmented with cutting planes where an integer solution is required, branch and bound procedures, and dynamic programming. More details on many of these topics may be found in standard works on algorithms and complexity, for example Cormen *et al.* (2001) or Daskin (1995).

In many instances provably optimal solutions to key problems of certain sizes are not achievable and solutions based on heuristics that achieve near optimality in most cases are the norm. The majority of these solution procedures are essentially static, but they can be applied to more dynamic or real-time environments if they are fast enough. Many heuristics involve some form of local search or swapping (interchange) procedure. So-called greedy algorithms make choices based on the progress of steps so far and selecting the next step by choosing the local optimum in the hope of reaching the global optimum, rather than seeking a global optimum directly (e.g. by exhaustive search). A typical example would be attempting to find the shortest tour of a set of cities (a travelling salesman

problem) by selecting one city at random as the start point and then selecting the next location to visit by choosing the closest city. The resulting tour will visit all the cities but will almost always be suboptimal. Some greedy algorithms, such as Dijkstra's procedure for finding shortest paths through a network (see Section 7.3.4), always yield exact (optimal) solutions. Interchange heuristics involve swapping one or more components in a current solution, thus changing the order or arrangement of the solution. If the objective function — the value we are trying to optimize — improves, the new arrangement is retained and the process proceeds to further interchanges according to some rule.

Tabu search methods are increasingly used in heuristic algorithms that adopt local searching. The term *tabu* (taboo) refers to the exclusion of certain options (e.g. adding or dropping a link in a network) based on options that have been recently searched. This has the effect of increasing the range of local searches and thus reducing the risk of solutions being trapped in local optima. There are several related methods such as simulated annealing, genetic algorithms and behavioral models (such as insect-based analogies) that have been shown to be effective in providing heuristics for some particularly difficult problems.

Many of the problems we describe can be modeled using one or more linear equations combined with a number of associated constraint expressions specified as equalities and/or inequalities. This form of standardized representation enables different problems to be compared within the discipline of the spatial sciences and across the broad discipline of optimization as a whole. In addition it enables many problems to be expressed in a form that is suitable for submission to specialized optimization packages such as LEDA, CPLEX, LP-solve and Xpress-MP. These provide source code sets and/or compiled libraries that offer optimal or heuristic solutions to a wide range of optimization problems, including linear programming (LP) and mixed integer programming (MIP) tasks. However, many algorithms for solving networking problems do not use linear programming or related techniques as these may be less efficient (i.e. slower) than specialized procedures, or the problems are not amenable to formulation as an LP or MIP problem. A good place to review such topics is the LP-solve website managed by Sourceforge:

http://lpsolve.sourceforge.net/5.5/

This site includes a useful Linear Programming FAQ page from which we have extracted the following explanatory quotation (with minor edits):

---

"In the context of linear programming, the term "network" is most often associated with the minimum-cost network flow problem (MCFP – see Table 7-2). A network for this problem is viewed as a collection of nodes (vertices or locations) and arcs (or edges or links) connecting selected pairs of nodes. Arcs carry a physical or conceptual flow of some kind, and may be directed (one-way) or undirected (two-way). Some nodes may be sources (permitting flow to enter the network) or sinks (permitting flow to leave).

The network linear programming problem is to minimize the (linear) total cost of flows along all arcs of a network, subject to conservation of flow at each node, and upper and/or lower bounds on the flow along each arc. This is a special case of the general linear programming problem. The transportation problem is an even more special case in which the network is bipartite: all arcs run from nodes in one subset to the nodes in a disjoint subset. A variety of other well-known network problems, including shortest path problems, maximum flow problems, and certain assignment problems, can also be modeled and solved as network linear programs.

Network linear programs can be solved 10 to 100 times faster than general linear programs of the same size, by use of specialized optimization algorithms. Some commercial LP solvers include a version of the network simplex method for this purpose. That method has the nice property that, if it is given integer flow data, it will return optimal flows that are integral [have integer values]. Integer network LPs can thus be solved efficiently without resort to complex integer programming software.

Unfortunately, many different network problems of practical interest do not have a formulation as a network LP. These include network LPs with additional linear "side constraints" (such as multicommodity flow problems) as well as problems of network routing and design that have completely different kinds of constraints. In principle, nearly all of these network problems can be modeled as integer programs. Some "easy" cases can be solved much more efficiently by specialized network algorithms, however, while other "hard" ones are so difficult that they require specialized methods that may or may not involve some integer programming. "

---

A compendium of many problems of this type and the best known (approximation) algorithms for their solution can be found at:

http://www.nada.kth.se/~viggo/problemlist/

This website provides details for a very large range of problems for which checking that a result is optimal may be relatively simple, but for which finding such a solution may be extremely difficult (typically would take an extremely long time for any large problem). These are NP-hard or NP-complete problems in the terminology of computational complexity theory (see Section 7.1.4 for more details).

### 7.2.1.1 Key problems in network analysis

The survey by Mitchell (1998, 2000) of geometrical shortest path and network optimization problems provides a further excellent source discussing such questions and solution procedures. Mitchell provides a useful summary of the range of questions that may be addressed by considering various associated parameters (Table 7-3). There are also many online sources for guidance on conducting transport network analysis, for example the US Department of Transportation planning site: http://www.plan4operations.dot.gov, the US Transportation Research Board's website: http://www.trb.org/, and the UK Transport Analysis Guidance (TAG) website: http://www.webtag.org.uk/.

*Table 7-2 Some key optimization problems in network analysis*

| Problem | Description |
|---------|-------------|
| Hamiltonian circuit (HC) | If a cycle exists from a given vertex that passes through every other vertex exactly once it is called a Hamiltonian circuit. Testing for the existence of Hamiltonian circuits in a graph is known as the Hamiltonian circuit problem (HCP). NP-complete (see further, Section 7.1.4) |
| Eulerian circuit(EC) | A circuit in a directed graph that visits every arc exactly once. A condition that a graph contains an Eulerian circuit is that the number of arcs arriving at every included vertex, $i$, must be the same as the number of arcs leaving vertex $i$ |
| Shortest path (SP) | A path between two vertices that minimizes a pre-defined metric such as the total number of steps, total distance or time, is called a shortest path. Hence this term is relative to the metric applied and even then may not be unique for any given network. Determination of shortest paths is often described as shortest path analysis (SPA). This is perhaps the central computational problem in network analysis. There are many variants of this problem, including finding the $2^{nd}$, $3^{rd}$... $n^{th}$ shortest path, finding the shortest path from a given node to all other nodes, and finding the longest path. Can be solved in linear time or better |
| Spanning tree (ST) | Given a fixed set of vertices, find a set of edges such that every vertex is connected and the network contains no cycles. Many spanning trees are possible for a given vertex set |
| Minimal spanning tree (MST) | Find a (Euclidean) spanning tree of minimum total length. Typically this will be unique, but uniqueness is not guaranteed. Solvable in near linear time |
| Steiner MST, Steiner tree | As per the MST but with additional nodes permitted that are not co-located with the original vertex set. In the (spatially) constant cost model, each additional point (known as a Steiner point) will be placed intermediate to three existing vertices and will provide a connection between these via three branches that are equally spaced (i.e. at 120 degrees) about the Steiner point. Steiner points are added to the MST, replacing MST links, if the total network length is reduced by their inclusion. NP-complete (for both Euclidean and Manhattan metrics) |
| Travelling salesman problem (TSP) | Given a set of vertices and symmetric or asymmetric distance matrix for each pair of vertices, find a Hamiltonian circuit of minimal length (cost). Typically the start location (vertex) is pre-specified and the vertices are not necessarily assumed to lie on a pre-existing network. If certain nodes must be visited before others, the task is known as a sequential ordering problem (SOP). NP-complete |
| Vehicle routing problem (VRP) | This class of problems relates to servicing customer demand (e.g. deliveries of fuel to retail garages) from a single depot, where each vehicle may have a known capacity (CVRP). If capacity is not restricted the problem in known simply as a vehicle routing problem (VRP). The number of vehicles and the number of tours of subsets of nodes are variables. The customer locations, depot location and customer demand levels are assumed to be known. The problem is to minimize the overall length of the tours, subject to the constraints. There are many variants of this problem, notably those in which there are pre-defined time windows for deliveries, problems involving pickups and deliveries, problems involving a series of depots, problems where demand is dynamically variable, problems in which link capacity constraints exist and hence may become congested, and problems where customer locations are generalized rather than fixed. Most such problems are classified as NP-hard |

| Problem | Description |
|---------|-------------|
| Transportation problem, Trans-shipment problem | The general problem of completely servicing a set of target locations with given demand levels from a set of source locations with given supply levels such that total costs are minimized is known as the transportation problem. The unit cost of shipping from each supply point to each demand point is a key input to this problem specification. This problem is an example of a Minimum Cost Flow Problem (MCFP). A generalization of the transportation problem is the trans-shipment problem. In the latter case flows from sources to targets can go via trans-shipment points, e.g. factories to warehouses to customers, rather than simply direct to customers |
| Arc routing problem (ARP) | Given a network (typically a street network or subset of a street network) find a route that completely traverses every edge, generally in both directions, that has the least cost (distance or time) subject to selected constraints (e.g. cost of turning). This problem applies to street cleaning, snow-plowing, postal deliveries, meter reading, garbage collection etc. The capacitated version of the problem is known as CARP. NP-complete |
| Facility location: p-median/p-center/ coverage | A collection of problems where the objective is to optimally locate one or more facilities within a network in order to satisfy customer requirements (demand, service level). The most commonly cited problem is minimization of total (or average) travel cost/time to or from customers (the p-median problem). Minimization of maximum distance or time is known as a p-center problem. A related set of problems seeks to ensure that all customers can be served within a fixed upper time or cost, or at least, as many as possible are served within a fixed time or cost. These are known as coverage problems. They are discussed in Daskin (1995, Ch 4) but are not explored further in this Guide, mainly because their very restrictive constraints tend to generate solutions that are too costly or ineffective to be implemented in practice. Customer demand is often assumed to be located at vertices in which case p-median solutions for p facilities serving n>p customer sites will always result in the facilities being located at network vertices (although this solution may not be unique). It is the network equivalent of the plane or free-space median location problem — a form of location-allocation task whereby facilities are located and customers are allocated to facilities. The p-median and p-center problems are NP-hard |

*Table 7-3 Sample network analysis problem parameters*

| Parameter | Questions |
|-----------|-----------|
| Objective function | How do we measure the "length" of a path? Options include the Euclidean length, $L_p$ length, link distance/time/cost etc. |
| Constraints on the path | Are we simply to get from point s to point t, or must we also visit other points or other regions along a path or cycle? |
| Input geometry | What types of obstacles or other entities are specified in the input map? |
| Dimension of the problem | Are we in 2D-space, 3D-space, or higher dimensions? Typically within GIS we only consider 2D, but transport networks may not be planar |
| Type of moving object | Are we moving a single point along the path, or is movement specified by some more complex geometry? In GIS off-road vehicular modeling is usually performed using Accumulated Cost Surface (ACS) or Distance Transform (DT) procedures applied to grid datasets rather than vector networks (see Section 4.4.2). |

| Parameter | Questions |
|---|---|
| | Constraints on routes may also be applied to vehicles of particular sizes, types or weights (e.g. height restrictions) |
| Single shot vs. repetitive mode queries | Do we want to build an effective data structure for efficient queries? Many network problems involve very similar searches — for example determining an alternative route (2nd, 3rd best) |
| Static vs. dynamic environments | Do we allow obstacles to be inserted or deleted, or do we allow obstacles to be moving along known trajectories? Flow and event dynamics may also be important considerations |
| Exact vs. approximate algorithms | Are we content with an answer that is guaranteed to be within some small margin of optimal? Larger problems in many cases cannot be solved exactly in a finite amount of time. Ideally real-world problems should be solved to within a specified level of the optimum for suitably defined subset problems |
| Known vs. unknown map | Is the complete geometry of the map known in advance, or is it discovered on-line, using some kind of sensor? Typically the geometry is known (map-able) in advance, but flows or events may not be |

*After Mitchell J S B (1998, 2000)*

## 7.2.1.2 Network analysis software

Whilst some GIS packages, such as Caliper's TransCAD and the ESRI ArcLogistics Route option, include functionality designed to solve a wide range of network analysis and associated planning and modeling tasks, problems of this type are often addressed using a range of bespoke or specialized transportation and logistics software. Some of these, such as eRouteLogistics and RouteSmart are built on/integrate with GIS packages (ESRI software in these two examples), whilst many others are purpose-built components of logistics systems, Enterprise Resource Planning (ERP) software or navigation suites. Examples include REACT, from MJC[2] (www.mjc2.com), TruckStops from MicroAnalytics (www.bestroutes.com) and Optrak (www.optrak.co.uk).

Most of the latter class of software takes into account the many practical, real world constraints that must be incorporated in operational software. Examples (from the REACT product) include: vehicle routing taking one-way streets into account; trip routing taking restricted junctions into account;

varying speeds by road type and time of day; trip routing of vehicles to avoid toll roads and toll bridges; trip routing vehicles taking account of congestion charges; delivery routing taking account of customer access constraints by time of day; night time/weekend lorry routing controls (e.g. the London 'brown' routes); weight restrictions (e.g. for truck routing); height restrictions (e.g. for truck routing); vehicle routing costs per mile/km; vehicle routing costs per hour; weight related vehicle routing costs; altitude related truck routing costs (e.g. trip routing to reduce hill climbing).

The annual review of packaged logistics software by OR/MS (the magazine of the Institute for Operations Research and Management Sciences in the USA) includes a selected list of providers for networking/routing software, with routing functionality as shown in Table 7-4. Products highlighted with a yellow background are stated to have >100 customers. Note that ILOG Dispatcher is a component of the ILOG general purpose optimization suite, which includes CPLEX, referred to later in this chapter.

*Table 7-4 Routing functionality in selected logistics software packages*

| Product | GIS support | Routing Functions | | | | |
|---------|-------------|-------------------|---|---|---|---|
| | Display/ geocode | Node Routing | Arc Routing | Real-time Routing | Daily Routing | Route Planning & Analysis |
| Descartes | Y | Y | Y | Y | Y | Y |
| Direct Route | Y | Y | Y | Y | Y | Y |
| DISC | Y | Y | Y | Y | Y | Y |
| eRouteLogistics | y | Y | Y | Y | Y | Y |
| ILOG Dispatcher | | Y | Y | Y | Y | Y |
| JOpt.SDK | | Y | | | Y | Y |
| Optrak4 | Y | Y | Y | Y | Y | Y |
| Ortec | Y | Y | Y | Y | Y | Y |
| Paragon | Y | Y | Y | | Y | Y |
| Prophesy | Y | Y | Y | Y | Y | Y |
| PTM | Y | Y | | | Y | Y |
| REACT | Y | Y | Y | Y | Y | Y |
| Roadnet | | | Y | Y | Y | Y |
| RouteSmart | Y | Y | Y | | Y | y |
| STARS | Y | Y | Y | Y | Y | y |
| StreetSync | Y | Y | Y | Y | Y | Y |
| The Logix suite | Y | Y | | Y | Y | Y |
| Toursolver | Y | | | | Y | Y |
| Truckstops | Y | Y | Y | Y | Y | Y |

Based on OR/MS Survey, 2008. *http://www.lionhrtpub.com/orms/surveys/Vehicle_Routing/vrss.html*

In addition to software that focuses on routing and logistics, there are a very large number of packages that address traffic modeling and simulation. These may deal with small-scale problems, such as the approach to intersections or traffic lights, or larger problems such as urban- and regional-scale modeling. Tools to support such modeling are sometimes grouped by scale into macro-, meso- and micro-scale classifications. At the micro-scale application-specific simulation software tends to be employed, rather than generic Cellular Automata (CA) or Agent-based Models (ABM) — see, for example, Martin Treiber's Java applet (accessible via http://www.mtreiber.de/) for a clear view of such microsimulation.

Widely used software packages exist for modeling single- or multi-mode traffic flows at a range of scales. The principal packages include: TSIS-CORSIM and SIMTraffic (extensively used for micro-simulation as well as more generic traffic modeling); Transmodeller (from Caliper, which can import data from CORSIM and SimTraffic); VISUM (produced by PTV, which they describe as a "comprehensive, flexible software system for transportation planning, travel demand modeling and network data management"); and INRO's offerings: EMME (trip forecasting) and DYNAMEQ (microsimulation, providing so-called dynamic equilibrium modeling). Figure 7-2 provides a visualization snapshot from a lane occupancy and movement simulation using DYNAMEQ. The warm colors show increased occupancy by lane where vehicles are queuing behind unprotected left-turning movements or traffic light signals. Intersection movements are colored similarly. Animated movement plots provide a more detailed breakdown of results that pinpoint the congestion. Each lane and turning movement can be color-coded according to occupancy, flow, density, speed or count.

*Figure 7-2 Visualization of lane/movement simulation (Dynameq)*

Many of these traffic and transport software packages provide a wide range of facilities, from small to large-scale modeling and forecasting, and providing sophisticated 2D and increasingly, 3D-style visualizations. Many can import from and export data to a number of standard GIS packages, most commonly supporting ESRI and MapInfo vector file formats.

### 7.2.1.3  Key problems in location analysis

Daskin (1995, Ch.1) provides a useful taxonomy of and commentary on location problems and models. We have adapted and extended his taxonomy (Table 7-5), in part using the work of Schietzelt and Densham (2003). Although Daskin's focus is on network and discrete location problems, rather than the broader sweep of network design and planar problems, this summary does offer an insight into many of the practical problems that may be encountered.

*Table 7-5 Taxonomy of location analysis problems*

| Component | Description |
|---|---|
| Planar/network/discrete | **Planar** — demand occurs anywhere in the plane (possibly represented by a deterministic or probabilistic field). Facilities may be located anywhere in the plane; **Network** — demand and facilities can only be located at network nodes or on links, and travel is restricted to the network; **Discrete** — nodes are fixed but the cost of travel between nodes is not determined by an underlying network |
| Tree/graph | Some network problems are amenable to treatment as if the graph is a tree, which can make solution far simpler |
| Distance metric | We have previously noted (Section 4.4.1) that a variety of metrics can be used in spatial analysis and this applies equally to location problems, notably planar and discrete cases |
| Facilities | The number of facilities to locate can be pre-specified (e.g. as $p$) or generated as part of the optimization process (as in the set coverage problem — see below). Problems involving the location of only one facility are often relatively straightforward to solve, and some procedures use this fact to develop heuristics that incrementally increase the number of facilities based on local optimization of the next facility added |
| Static/dynamic | Most of the problems and techniques described in this chapter are essentially static. Such methods may be applied to some dynamic problems, but in many cases these procedures require extension or alternative approaches to deal with dynamic cases. Examples include: choosing when as well as where to locate the next 1,2... facilities; incorporating dynamic demand and possibly supply into the model; modifying vehicle locations as demand varies by time of day or week (e.g. relocating emergency vehicles on standby based on time of day) |
| Private/public | The principal issue here relates to the definition of the objective function — can this be done in purely monetary (or equivalent) terms or do social, environmental and other factors require evaluation? Generally all location selection processes are part of a broader decision-making environment (as identified in the PPDAC model, Section 3.3). In public facilities location it is also often possible to dictate allocations whereas for private facilities this is almost never possible, requiring the modeling of allocation (e.g. using spatial interaction models) |
| Single/multi-objective | In most instances single-objective solutions are sought (e.g. time, distance or cost minimization). However, real-world situations are almost always multi-objective. One approach to this is to compute multiple solutions for variations in parameters that reflect the multiple objectives, and examine the nature and robustness of these solutions. This is not equivalent to true multi-objective analysis but may provide benchmarks and guidance for such problems as part of a broader analytical framework |

| Component | Description |
|---|---|
| Unique/diverse service | A unique service is one in which a single (principal) service is being modeled, such as ambulance provision. A diverse service might be a similar problem, but where different categories of ambulance service and associated vehicles and staffing were modeled — for example, full emergency call-out vehicles; individual paramedics on-call; and ambulances for non-emergency usage (e.g. transport of patients, medical supplies etc.) |
| Elastic/inelastic demand | Most models assume that demand and supply are independent. However, it must be recognized that improved supply frequently increases demand, i.e. that demand is elastic, and that supply may or may not be |
| Deterministic/adaptive/ stochastic | Many models are deterministic in terms of supply, demand and feasible solutions; others may assume demand is probabilistic and often dynamic, with solutions being sought that are optimal with respect to the inputs, but which are often adaptive reflecting changes in demand, supply and transport dynamics |
| Capacitated/uncapacitated | Basic models do not consider the capacity of facilities (e.g. warehouses, storage depots, hospitals, vehicles) or links (e.g. transport networks or pipelines) as a constraint. Tools are available that allow for the inclusion of such constraints (an example is provided in Section 7.3.5.1) |
| Nearest facility/ General demand allocation | Demand is often assumed to be allocated to the nearest facility. In capacitated models this may require that some demand is split between facilities (fractional allocation) — e.g. a retail store may need to be serviced by more than one warehouse, or patients may be sent to more distant hospitals in times of high demand or major emergencies |
| Hierarchical/single level | Some problems are intrinsically hierarchical, in that products or services are provided from larger centers (e.g. national) to smaller regional centers and on to district and local facilities (or vice versa, upwards flow rather than downwards distribution). This may apply for product or service offerings. In such problems the existence of facilities at one level (up or down) may be a pre-requisite for locating facilities at the next (e.g. large-scale regional hospitals are only provided where at least a certain number of local level medical facilities already exist). A similar example would be the design of a completely new multi-level health infrastructure for a region previously not served with these kinds of facility |
| Desirable/undesirable | Most location modeling relates to desirable facilities — the distance or cost of travel to or from facilities is to be minimized, according to some criterion. For some facilities, such as waste disposal sites, incinerators, nuclear power plants, etc. the facility location problem becomes more complex because there are often conflicting objectives. For example, the location of waste disposal sites need to be as near as possible to the waste creation points (towns say), but ideally as far away as possible from habitation |

*After Daskin (1995) and Schietzelt and Densham (2003)*

## 7.2.2 Heuristic and meta-heuristic algorithms

The term heuristic algorithm refers to the use of systematic procedures that typically trade off the quality of a solution for processing speed. Many heuristics are derived from relatively simple, commonsense ideas for finding solutions to problems, but which will not necessarily produce an optimum solution. In some instances heuristics do produce provably optimal solutions. Heuristics are defined by a set of permitted moves or *transformations* of a current solution, $Q$ say, to a new (generally improved) solution, $Q^*$. The space of all possible solutions for a given problem is known as the *search space, S,* and the space of solutions that are obtainable by a single transformation of a current solution, $Q$, is known as the *neighborhood space, N*. A comparison of a number of alternative heuristics applied to a facility location problem is provided in Section 7.4.2.3.

Heuristic algorithms will often provide a fast 'upper bound' or 'lower bound' to the value of some objective function, such as the average travel time from a set of demand locations to a set of supply locations or facilities. The 'upper bound' can provide one edge of a confidence band whose overall width can be determined if a procedure can be devised that provides a matching 'lower bound' for the problem at hand. The true upper bound *and* lower bound is the optimal solution itself — however, this value is generally unknown in advance and may be impossible to determine. An alternative approach is to solve a problem that is very similar to the problem at hand, often with fewer constraints on the permissible solutions, and for which a solution can be obtained rapidly. This is generally known as solving a 'relaxed' version of the original problem. A similar concept is to solve a set of sub-problems that collectively include all of the original dataset elements.

Once an upper and lower bound have been obtained, procedures can be devised that attempt to reduce the upper bound and raise the lower bound until they are arbitrarily close — if they meet the global optimum will have been obtained, and if not then at least the quality of the solution in terms of proximity to the optimum is known — a solution procedure that gives results that are within 5% of the optimum and can be obtained very rapidly is often preferable to a solution procedure that is optimal but which in practice may not do this using finite computer and time resources. An example of a relaxed problem might be to permit the use of Manhattan or minimax distance rather than Euclidean or network distance when assigning customers to facilities, or to entirely or partially remove one or more constraints on the problem as a temporary measure. A widely used procedure of this kind is known as Lagrangian relaxation (see further, Section 7.2.2.7).

Tests of combinatorial optimization procedures in general and heuristics in particular, often use the travelling salesman problem (TSP) as a benchmark for the quality and performance. This is because the problem is easily specified, known to be extremely difficult to solve, and may be examined using a library of available test data. In essence the TSP involves making a tour of every vertex in a given set (e.g. cities in a country, nodes on a VLSI circuit board), and returning to the starting point, such that the total tour length or cost is minimized. The distance measure used must be a metric or semi-metric, i.e. asymmetry may be permitted but distances must be positive and satisfy the triangle inequality. If there are $N$ cities there are $N!$ possible tours, so the search space is $O(N!)$, a value which rapidly becomes immensely large (this reduce slightly to $N!/2$ if the distances are symmetric and $(N-1)!/2$ if the position of the first city is pre-defined). More details on the TSP are provided in Section 7.3.5, but it is referred to frequently in other sections of this Guide. An excellent introduction to TSP problems and solutions, including Google-mapped examples, is available at:

http://www.tsp.gatech.edu/index.html

Currently the largest solved TSP cases are of the order of 86,000 'cities' and test problems for 1 million plus cities exist. Although the basic symmetric Euclidean TSP, as described above, is the most common baseline used for testing, many variants exist, including:

asymmetric edges; time windows for deliveries/collections; multiple routes (partitioned sets of cities); capacity constrained links and vehicles; and many more. Their application is also not restricted to transportation problems, but extends to many other fields of research, from printed circuit board manufacture to job scheduling to genetic sequencing.

### 7.2.2.1 Greedy heuristics and local search

So-called greedy heuristics involve a process whereby at each stage a locally optimum choice is made which may or may not lead to a globally optimum solution to some problem. As such, greedy algorithms are local search, or LS, procedures.

For example, suppose one has a set of points or vertices $\{V\}$ in the plane and you wish to create a network of edges $\{E\}$ such that every point is accessible via the network from every other point, and overall the total (Euclidean) length of the network is minimized. A greedy algorithm that solves this problem (the so-called Minimum Spanning Tree, or MST, problem) is as follows:

- Select any point $\{x\}$ from $V$ at random to start. Define the set $V^*=\{x\}$ and the set $E^*=\{ \}$

i.e. the set $V^*$ is initialized with a single point chosen at random from the source vertices, and the set $E^*$ is initialized as an empty set of edges. Then,

- Find the nearest point in the set $V$ not in $V^*$ ($v$ say) to a point in the set $V^*$ ($u$ say) and add this to the set $V^*$ together with the edge connecting $v$ and $u$ to $E^*$. If two or more points are equidistant from $V^*$ then choose one of these at random

i.e. this step ensures that at each iteration the shortest/lowest cost edge joining a point in $V^*$ to a point not yet in $V^*$ is added to the solution set and will always form a connected tree. Then,

- Repeat the preceding step until $V^*=V$. The set $E^*$ contains the MST

This is known as Prim's algorithm (Prim, 1957) and is exact in the sense that the solution it finds is globally optimal. It is also relatively fast. Kruskal's greedy algorithm for determining the MST of a weighted graph is similar in concept, but starts with the vertex set $V$ already connected such that every vertex has a direct or indirect link to every other vertex. The shortest (least weighted) link is then identified and removed, being added to the solution set. The process continues, checking that loops in the network do not occur, until the vertices in the solution set form a complete tree, which is the MST. Both of these algorithms are effectively constructive in form, gradually building the solution. Some heuristics are essentially aimed at improvement rather than construction, for example by commencing with a random or best known solution and then seeking to systematically improve upon this by a well-defined procedure (e.g. local search or iterative improvement).

Most greedy algorithms are fast but, unlike those described above, yield sub-optimal solutions and in some cases the provably worst possible solution! This *can* be the case for a similar algorithm to that described above, but where the objective is to define the shortest possible tour of the set $V$ with each vertex being visited only once, returning finally to the starting vertex (the basic Travelling Salesman Problem).

There are many variants to greedy algorithms, some of which are problem-dependent whilst others attempt to find a more systematic approach to improving the local optimum found by the procedure. For example, a greedy algorithm for a facility location problem could be to choose a set of $N$ solution locations at random and then assign all customers to the nearest facility — e.g. retail stores and customers, children and schools, medical facilities and patients. This generates a very poor solution if one is trying to minimize the average or maximum travel time by customers to facilities. An improvement to this greedy random algorithm might be a greedy add variant, whereby a single initial facility is selected at random and all customers assigned to it, and then new facilities are added one by one at random locations but subject to some additional rule, with customers re-assigned according to the 'nearest facility' rule. This *may* yield an improved solution. Repeated runs of a greedy procedure may also yield a set of results from which the best in terms of the criteria to be optimized is selected. Indeed, characteristics identified from the best solutions may assist in a progressive improvement process. So-called GRASP heuristics (greedy randomized adaptive search procedures) start with a feasible solution from a more conventional greedy algorithm and then apply a local search algorithm to try and improve on this solution. Repeated runs of the GRASP procedure give rise to an overall best solution.

### 7.2.2.2  Interchange heuristics

Heuristics that commence with one solution to a problem (typically a combinatorial optimization problem) and then systematically swap members of this initial or current solution with members that either form part of another element of this current solution or belong to the set "not a member" are called interchange heuristics. There are many examples of such heuristics. For example, the automatic zoning procedures (AZP) described in Section 4.2.11 are an example of such an interchange procedure, as is Jenk's natural breaks method for classifying univariate data (see also, Figure 4-22).

One of the best known interchange heuristics is the *n*-opt family applied to the standard form of the travelling salesman problem (TSP) with Euclidean distance metric. This is a simple improvement algorithm that applies to an existing symmetric tour of all the locations. The procedure simply takes two edges in the solution at random, say $(i,j)$ and $(k,l)$ and replaces them with $(i,k)$ and $(j,l)$ or $(i,l)$ and $(j,k)$. There are several improvements to this scheme which make a significant difference to its performance. These include checking that the revised tour contains no crossings, as this will never be the shortest configuration and only opting for interchanges to a candidate list of swaps that will yield the greatest benefit. 3-opt interchange is essentially the same as 2-

opt but taking three edges at a time. This can be more effective and is essential for asymmetric problems, but at a higher computational cost.

In the field of location modeling, a common class of problems involves identifying potential facility locations and then allocating customers to those locations. The objective is generally to minimize the cost of providing services from $p$ facilities to $m$ customers. A series of algorithms have been developed to solve such problems. One of the best known in geospatial analysis is a vertex substitution algorithm due to Teitz and Bart (1968) — see further, Section 7.4.2. The solution process systematically evaluates marginal changes to a given set of facility locations, as follows:

- An initial facility configuration is supplied to the algorithm (e.g. a random selection of $p$ locations from a candidate set of $n>p$) — this provides the first "current solution"

- The first candidate not in the current solution is substituted for each facility site in the current solution and the customers are re-allocated based on this new configuration of facilities. The substitution yielding the largest decrease in the objective function, if any, is selected for a swap

- When all of the candidates not in the current solution have been substituted for all of the sites in the current solution, an iteration is complete and the process can then be repeated

The algorithm terminates when a single iteration does not result in a swap. At termination, the interchange heuristic generates facility configurations that meet all three *necessary*, but not *sufficient*, conditions for an optimum solution to the problem: all facilities are local medians (least travel cost/distance centers) for the demand points allocated to them; all demand points are allocated to their closest facility; and finally, removing a facility from the solution and replacing it with a candidate site not in the solution always incurs a net increase or no change in the value of the objective function. Note that this solution will not in general be the global optimum, is not necessarily unique, nor is there any immediate way of identifying how good the solution found really is (i.e. how close it is to the global optimum). As with other heuristics, there are many possible variants and extensions of the core interchange procedure.

### 7.2.2.3 Metaheuristics

The term *metaheuristic* was originally coined by Glover (1986). It is now is used to refer to developments of heuristic concepts that go beyond local search (LS) procedures as a means of seeking a global optimum, typically by analogy with natural (physical or biological) processes. Examples of metaheuristics include tabu search (see Section 7.2.2.3), simulated annealing (see Section 7.2.2.6), ant systems (see Section 7.2.2.8) and genetic algorithms (see Section 8.4). A series of bi-annual international conferences on metaheuristics have been held in various locations in recent years. A number of metaheuristics can be examined and tested using the free educational program, VisualBots (www.visualbots.com), which is a basic simulation and modeling system written as a programmable ActiveX control for Excel (see, for example, the TSP project examples for implementations of simulated annealing, genetic algorithms and ant colony optimization).

The analogy of many of these procedures with biological systems is often slightly tenuous, drawing ideas rather than detail from the way ants search for food or animal genetics help to create fitter offspring. Furthermore, in many instances the techniques are applied to static problems, whereas biological systems operate in a dynamic environment, for which sub-optimal behavior that has in-built robustness and flexibility is often more important than temporary optimization — finding and eating all one's prey in the shortest possible time may exhaust their population to the point they cannot reproduce and provide you with yet more food! This observation provides not only a note of caution about such analogy-based procedures, but also one of optimism that they

may prove particularly useful in dynamical systems — indeed this has been found to be the case in fields such as dynamic telecommunications routing and real-time traffic management.

### 7.2.2.4 Tabu search

Tabu search is a metaheuristic (see Section 7.2.2.3) that aims to overcome the problem of a local search (LS) procedure (e.g. a greedy heuristic) becoming trapped at a local optimum. As such it is a general purpose extension to LS procedures that operates by permitting non-improving moves whenever a local optimum is encountered. It achieves this by recording the recent history of searches in a tabu list (a sort of short-term memory) and ensuring that future moves do not search this part of the search space, at least not for a specified number of iterations. This greatly reduces the likelihood of changing a solution configuration in a manner that will simply cycle back to the current solution. See Glover and Laguna (1997) for a full discussion of the method and variants.

Tabu search methods are thus defined by the search space, the pattern of local moves (the neighborhood structure), and the use of search memory:

- The *search space*, $S$, is simply the space (or set for purely combinatorial problems) of all possible solutions to a given problem. Note that this may be very large, or for some problems (e.g. those involving a mixture of discrete and continuous variables to be optimized) innumerably large. The search space can include infeasible as well as feasible solutions, and in some cases permitting the search to extend into infeasible regions is essential (e.g. examining possible solutions for which constraints have been relaxed)

- The *neighborhood structure* determines the set of moves, or transformations, of the current search space $S$ effected by a single iteration of the process. Hence the neighborhood, $N$, is a (typically small) subset of the search space: $N \subset S$. A simple example of such transformations is the set of interchange heuristics, where one or more elements from the current solution are interchanged with one or more elements from other parts of the current solution and/or elements that are currently outside the components of the current solution

- *Search memory*, in particular short-term search memory, is the characteristic that distinguishes tabu search from most other methods. A typical example would be the retention of a list of recent moves, whose reversal is tabu for a number of iterations (also known as the *tabu tenure*). With a network routing problem, in which customer A has just been moved from route 1 to route 2, one would prevent reversal of this interchange for a short period, in order to avoid the procedure cycling without improvement. The risk with this approach is that sometimes such moves are attractive and effective, and the process can be improved by relaxing strict tabus. The typical relaxation permitted (known as applying *aspiration criteria*) is to allow a tabu move if it results in a solution with an objective value that is an improvement on the best known value to date

Despite these protections, tabu search may still under-perform, either in terms of efficiency or quality of result. Various techniques have been devised to improve its performance, many of which are problem-specific in their design. These include: *probabilistic selection* of samples from the space *N*, in order to reduce the processing overhead and introduce randomness that again reduces the risk of encountering cycles; *intensification*, in which a number of components of the current solution (e.g. entire routes or assignments) are held fixed whilst other elements are allowed to continue being modified; and *diversification*, whereby components of the current solution that have appeared frequently or continuously since the start of the iteration process are systematically removed from the solution in order to give unused or rarely used components the chance of generating an overall improvement; *surrogate objective*

*functions* can also improve performance (though not directly quality) of a solution by reducing the overhead that is sometimes present in computing the value of the objective function. If the surrogate function is highly correlated with the objective function and is very simple to compute, it can enable many more operations to be conducted within a given time period, hence expanding the range of solutions examined; such *hybridization* is becoming an increasingly common practice, whereby techniques like tabu search are hybridized with other solution approaches such as genetic algorithms.

### 7.2.2.5 Cross-entropy (CE) methods

The CE method is an iterative procedure that can be applied to a wide range of problems, including shortest path and traveling salesman problems (TSPs). It involves two phases:

- Generation of a sample of random data (trajectories, vectors, etc.) according to a specified random mechanism (typically a Monte Carlo process), and

- Updating the parameters of the random mechanism, on the basis of the data, in order to produce a "better" sample in the next iteration

The updating mechanism makes use of the discrete version of the cross-entropy statistic. In its basic form this statistic compares two probability distributions or one probability distribution and a reference distribution. Tests by the authors of this procedure (see www.cemethod.org) on TSP problems have shown that it is capable of providing good solutions in reasonable time. However, it does not out-perform the best TSP procedures currently available (see further, Section 7.3.5), and unmodified does not take advantage of problem-specific enhancements that would improve its performance.

### 7.2.2.6 Simulated annealing

Simulated annealing is a metaheuristic devised by Kirkpatrick *et al.* (1983) and derives its name and approach from the behavior of metals and glass as they are systematically heated and re-heated and then allowed to cool steadily. The objective, as with other metaheuristics, is to obtain a close approximation to the global optimum for a given problem. The original paper by Kirkpatrick *et al.* proved that the approach would converge to the global optimum, given enough time, which encouraged considerable investigation into this, and a range of other metaheuristics for solving particularly difficult combinatorial problems. Simulated annealing can be viewed as a form of managed random walk through the solution space, $S$, in which exploration of the neighborhood space is determined by appeal to annealing behavior, which in turn relates to the temperature of the process over time. The procedure is essentially as follows:

- Define the initial configuration for the problem, e.g. a random solution set, $S_0^*$, and an initial temperature variable, $T$, and evaluate the cost, $C_0^*$, (e.g. the total distance or travel time) for this solution

- Perturb $S_0^*$ to a new neighboring state, $S_1^*$, e.g. by moving a potential facility location by some random coordinate step or by an interchange process. Compute the cost of this new state, $C_1^*$ and subtract $C_0^*$, to give the cost difference $\Delta C$

- If $\Delta C < 0$ then the new configuration has lower overall cost, so select the new configuration as the preferred current configuration. However, if the cost is higher, still retain the option of keeping the new configuration according to the so-called *Metropolis* criterion: $p = e^{-\Delta C/T}$ if $p < u$ where $u$ is a uniform random number in the range [0,1]. If the criterion applies then the temperature variable, $T$ is reduced by a factor, $\alpha$ say (e.g. $\alpha = 0.9$) and the process iterates from the previous step until some stopping criterion is reached (e.g. number of iterations, absolute or relative improvement of the objective function)

In a sense the temperate parameter controls the way in which the search space is traversed, initially in large steps and then, as the temperature reduces (the *annealing schedule*), in smaller and smaller steps until $T=0$ or another stopping criterion has been reached.

Simulated annealing is often a relatively slow technique, so modifications are often applied that are problem-specific and the result of analysis of the statistical behavior of the model, with greatly improvement performance being possible. Such changes, however, may remove the guarantee of ultimate global optimization. Significant advantages of simulated annealing include the simplicity of the basic algorithm, the low memory overhead of the procedure, and the range of optimization problems (geospatial and other) to which the approach may be applied. In the geospatial arena the procedure has been successfully applied to a variety of problems, including optimum facility location (e.g. see Muttiah *et al.*, 1996) and travelling salesman problems.

### 7.2.2.7 Lagrangian multipliers and Lagrangian relaxation

Lagrangian relaxation is a generalization of the use of *Lagrangian multipliers* in classical optimization problems, so we commence with a discussion of such problems before introducing the notion of relaxation.

The so-called "classical constrained optimization problem" applies to real-valued continuous differentiable functions (known as class $C_1$ functions), $f()$, $g()$ and is of the form:

Maximise z, where

$z = f(x_1, x_2, x_3, \ldots)$, subject to

$g_i(x_1, x_2, x_3, \ldots) = d_i$, $i = 1, 2, 3 \ldots$

or, using vector notation:

Maximise z, where

$z = f(\mathbf{x})$, subject to

$g_i(\mathbf{x}) = d_i$, $i = 1, 2, 3 \ldots$

Here the expression for z is known as the *objective function*, the expressions $g_i()$ are known as the *constraints*, the $x_i$ are variables and the $d_i$ are constants. The constraints in this case are shown as equalities — inclusion of inequalities, which is common, can be handled in a variety of ways, including the use of surrogate variables.

This class of problems can be converted into an *unconstrained optimization problem* by the use of Lagrangian multipliers. This process often simplifies the task of finding local and global maxima or minima. In the example above, all of the constraints can be moved into the objective function, and we have:

Maximise z, where

$$z = f(\mathbf{x}) + \sum_i \lambda_i \left( d_i - g_i(\mathbf{x}) \right)$$

The $\lambda_i$ components of the expression above are known as the Lagrangian multipliers. Solving the constrained problem then becomes one of maximizing or minimizing a single expression, which in turn requires determination of the introduced multipliers. These may be obtained by finding the differential of the modified objective function with respect to each $x_i$ and equating the result to zero (see Walsh, 1975, for a fuller treatment of the use of Lagrangian multipliers in such problems). Although interpretation of the Lagrangian multiplier values is not a central part of this process, in many instances they can be interpreted as a measure of the importance of the $i^{th}$ constraint.

As noted earlier, *Lagrangian relaxation* is a generalization of the above procedure. The idea is to relax the constraints by amending the objective function. The relaxed problem is then solved (if possible) and this can provide a lower (or upper) bound to the set of possible solutions to the original problem. The resultant smaller solution space can then be subjected to more systematic search or attempts can be made to narrow the upper and lower bounds until they meet.

For example, suppose that we are attempting to maximize the simple linear expression:

Maximise z, where

$$z = \sum_j a_j x_j, \text{ subject to}$$

$$g_1 : \sum_j b_{1j} x_j \leq d_1, \text{ and}$$

$$g_2 : \sum_j b_{2j} x_j \leq d_2$$

Additional conditions may be that all the $x_j$ must be greater than or equal to 0, and for problems with discrete solutions, that the solution values must be integers.

We can relax this problem whilst retaining the linear form of the objective function, by moving the constraints into the objective function whilst dropping the inequality, as follows:

$$z = \sum_j a_j x_j + \sum_i \lambda_i \left( d_i - \sum_j b_{ij} x_j \right)$$

If all $\lambda_i = 0$ the second term in the objective function disappears and thus the constraints play no part in the solution, but if any $\lambda_i > 0$ the value of the objective function we are trying to optimize is penalized (increased or decreased) when we break the constraints. By adjusting the degree to which the original problem is relaxed, varying the positive vector $\lambda$ (the Lagrangian) in a systematic manner, and/or by alternative search procedures to the reduced solution space, closer approximations to the original problem can be obtained. Lagrangian relaxation is discussed in some detail in Section 7.4.2.2, which deals with its application to optimum location problems.

The preceding discussion becomes clearer if we take a simplified example. For the purposes of this subsection we use an example provided in the excellent introductory text on combinatorial programming and spatial analysis by Scott (1971):

Maximise z, where

$z = 25x_1 + 5x_2$, subject to

$g_1 : 6x_1 + 5x_2 \leq 42$

$g_2 : -2x_1 + 10x_2 \leq 33$

$g_3 : 9x_1 - 8x_2 \leq 25$

$x_1, x_2 \geq 0$ and integer

By dealing with a problem that only involves two variables we can plot this as a graph in which each of the three constraints is shown as

a thin line (Figure 7-3A). Here the horizontal axis is $x_1$ and the vertical axis, $x_2$. The three thin colored lines correspond to the three constraints graphed as linear *equations* $g_1$ (blue), $g_2$ (green) and $g_3$ (red). The solution space is bounded by these three lines (as a result of the inequalities we have defined) and the two axes.

*Figure 7-3 LP Solution graphs*

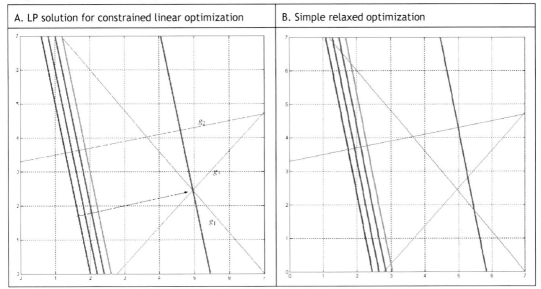

| A. LP solution for constrained linear optimization | B. Simple relaxed optimization |

The thick lines show the objective function for increasing values of z. The leftmost line is z=50, then z=55, 60 and 65. The largest possible value the objective function can take is shown by the rightmost thick line, where it just remains inside the two constraint lines illustrated and below the third constraint line.

For this problem the real-valued solution is $x_1$=4.96 and $x_2$=2.45, but integer solutions may be obtained by searching the values at the neighboring grid line intersections shown that give the highest value of the objective function, in this instance $x_1$=4 and $x_2$=3. This problem can be re-cast, but this time using

Lagrangian relaxation applied to a single constraint, as follows:

Maximise

$z = 25x_1 + 5x_2 + \lambda(25 - 9x_1 + 8x_2)$, subject to

$g_1 : 6x_1 + 5x_2 \leq 42$

$g_2 : -2x_1 + 10x_2 \leq 33$

$x_1, x_2 \geq 0$ and integer

As can be seen, the third constraint has now been incorporated into the objective function. With this change the objective function can fall outside the boundaries set by the third constraint for all values of $\lambda$>0, as shown by the rightmost line (Figure 7-3B). In this instance the same values for z as above have been used but are augmented by the relaxation element. The relaxation of the third constraint has allowed the objective function to stray beyond the limits of the fully constrained solution. In general, all the inequality constraints can be incorporated into such a relaxation process, giving the more general expression for functions $f()$ and $g()$ as apply in the classical model described earlier.

The above examples have been applied to simple linear expressions, which is not in practice necessary. However, with more complex functions and problems (e.g. constrained shortest path problems, optimum facility location problems) the use of Lagrangian relaxation has been found to be an extremely valuable tool in identifying high quality solutions within acceptable time limits.

### 7.2.2.8 Ant systems and ant colony optimization (ACO)

Ant systems draw their inspiration from the behavior of ants as they forage for food. It had been observed that ants lay trails using pheromones as they explore their environment. Successful trails (e.g. those leading to and from a food source) become reinforced as more and more ants use them (a form of learning or collective memory). This led, in the early 1990s, to research into the use of such behavioral models to solve difficult combinatorial problems such as the travelling salesman problem (TSP). The original computational model, known as Ant Systems (AS) worked reasonably well for small TSP problems but not for larger instances. This encouraged the development of more sophisticated models, particularly combining basic AS ideas with efficient local search (LS) strategies. This research area has been dominated by the work of a few key scientists, whose work is best seen via the website www.aco-metaheuristic.org, the book, "Ant Colony Optimization" by Dorigo and Stützle (2004) and Dorigo's ACO article on Scolarpedia. Their work has shown (see for example, Stützle and Dorigo, 1999) that variants of ACO can solve quite large TSP problems exactly or close to the known optimum, with acceptable levels of performance. The approach has also been found effective in vehicle routing problems with time window constraints on deliveries, and in certain dynamic routing problems. However, unlike some other meta-heuristics, its broader-scale application is less obvious although it has clear links to the field of so-called Swarm Intelligence (see further Section 8.2.3). For example, in connection with the latter, Batty, Desyllas and Duxbury (2002, 2003) successfully applied such ideas to modeling pedestrian behavior in crowded streets using pheromone surfaces rather than discrete trails. The basic ACO procedure for the TSP is as follows:

Let $m$ be the number of ants to be used, $n$ be the number of cities ($m <= n$) and $t$ be the iteration count of the process. Let $d_{ij}$ be a measure of the distance between cities, and define problem parameters: $\alpha$, $\beta$ (see below). We also define an initial pheromone value, $\tau_{ij}$ to each arc $(i,j)$ connecting cities $i$ and $j$.

- Place each of the ants on a randomly chosen city

- Construct a tour of the cities for each ant as follows: For an ant currently at city $i$ visit an unvisited city $j$ with a probability defined by the current pheromone strength for that link and on how far away the city $i$ is from $j$ (see further, below)

- Optionally improve each of the individual tours generated by the ants using a local search heuristic

- Repeat this process for each ant and when complete, update the pheromone trail values, as shown below

**Defining the probability function:** The standard probability function (i.e. should the ant now visit city $j$?) applied for ant $k$ currently at city $i$ during iteration $t$ is of the form:

$$p_{ij}^{k}(t) = \frac{\left(\tau_{ij}(t)\right)^{\alpha}\left(\eta_{ij}\right)^{\beta}}{\sum_{l \in N_i^k}\left(\tau_{il}(t)\right)^{\alpha}\left(\eta_{il}\right)^{\beta}}, \text{ where}$$

$$\eta_{ij} = 1/d_{ij}$$

In this expression the set $N$ is the currently valid neighborhood for this ant, i.e. the set of cities not yet visited. This probability function is a combination of two components: the first is the strength of the pheromone trail and the second is a distance decay factor. If $\alpha=0$ then the pheromone component has no impact and the probabilistic assignment is based on whichever city is closest, i.e. the basic greedy heuristic, whilst if $\beta=0$ assignment is simply based on pheromone trail strength, which has been found to lead to stagnation of the solutions giving sub-optimal tours. Example test values for the parameters are $\alpha=1$ and $\beta=2$

**Updating the pheromone trails**: in theory the pheromone trails could be updated continuously or after each ant has completed a tour. In practice it has been found that updating the trail values after all ants have completed an iteration is more effective. The updating involves two components: the first is to reduce all trail values by a constant factor, $\rho$ (analogous to an evaporation process); and then to add an increment based on the length of the $k^{th}$ ant's tour, $L^k(t)$, for all ants:

$$\tau_{ij}(t+1) = (1-\rho)\,\tau_{ij}(t) + \sum_{k=1}^{m} \Delta\tau_{ij}^k(t),$$

where $0 < \rho \le 1$, and

$$\Delta\tau_{ij}^k(t) = 1/L^k(t)$$

if arc $(i, j)$ is used by ant $k$, else

$$\Delta\tau_{ij}^k(t) = 0$$

This updating ensures that firstly, links do not become over-saturated with pheromones and secondly, that links visited by ants that make the shortest tours are those whose pheromone values are increased the most — a re-enforcement or learning process. Stützle and Dorigo (1999) found that the quality of solutions could be considerably improved by minor modifications to this scheme. Firstly, by restricting the maximum and minimum values the pheromone values can take, with initialized values being set to the upper limit of this range; and secondly, by only allowing updating of trail values by the best performing ant rather than all ants (this approach can also reduce the memory overhead of the algorithm considerably). With these modifications the authors were able to solve problems with 1500+ cities (e.g. TSPLIB test case fl1577) giving a range of results [22286,22358] which compares with the true optimum solution for this problem of 22249.

# 7.3 Network Construction, Optimal Routes and Optimal Tours

We now examine a number of the problems described in Table 7-2. Descriptions of each problem and examples and/or outline algorithms for their solution are provided. More detail can be found through the online and printed references provided. This is a continually developing field, an area of research in which perhaps more papers have been written and algorithms published than almost any other, so comments made here on algorithms and solvability may (will) have altered by the time of publication.

## 7.3.1 Minimum spanning tree

Given a set of vertices (points, nodes) an enormous number of possible interconnections may be made to produce a network of direct or indirect connections between vertices. The set of connections that minimizes total edge length whilst ensuring every point is reachable from every other point is known as a minimal spanning tree (MST). There is an exact solution to this problem. The algorithm involves a construction or growth process as follows: (i)

connect every point to its nearest neighbor — typically this will result in a collection of unconnected sub-networks; (ii) connect each sub-network to its nearest neighbor sub-network; (iii) iterate step (ii) until every sub-network is inter-connected. This process (which is basically Prim's algorithm described in Section 7.2.2.1), is illustrated below, with the stages of nearest neighbor linkage identified by numerical sequence values.

The MST for a set of vertices can be computed in O(nlogn) time so is in the class P. An interesting feature of the solution is that it is a subset of various other more connected forms of network including the Delaunay triangulation — see Cheriton and Tarjan (1976) and Arora (1996) for more details. Some packages (e.g. the LEDA code suite from Algorithmic Solutions) first compute the Delaunay triangulation of the point set, then generate the Delaunay diagram if necessary (a subset of the triangulation in some instances) and run the minimum spanning tree algorithm on this graph, systematically deleting edges that do not belong to the MST. Note that whilst the MST provides the shortest possible connection between all vertices, it is very susceptible to disruption since deleting any link (e.g. link failure, road accident) will result in loss of overall connectivity.

*Figure 7-4 Minimum Spanning Tree*

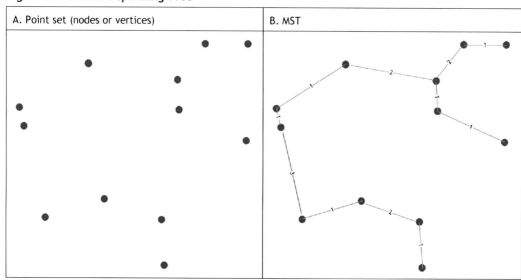

| A. Point set (nodes or vertices) | B. MST |
|---|---|

## 7.3.2   Gabriel network

A form of network that is a super-set of the MST and has a variety of uses is known as the Gabriel network, named after its principal originator, K R Gabriel (see Gabriel and Sokal (1969) for more details). The Gabriel network for a point set, such as that shown in Figure 7-4A, is created by adding edges between pairs of points in the source set *iff* there are no other points from the set contained within a circle whose diameter passes through the two points (see Figure 7-5A — black circles). In this example the green circle shown encloses another point from the set so a link between the two points used to create this circle is not included in the final solution (the straight lines). The process continues until all point pairs have been examined in this manner and linked where the condition holds (Figure 7-5B).

*Figure 7-5 Gabriel network construction*

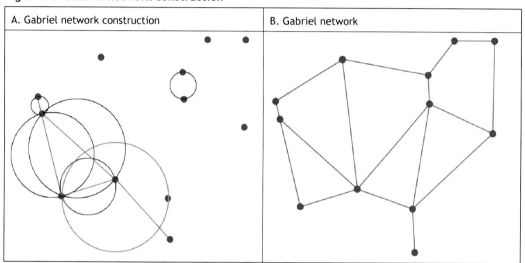

| A. Gabriel network construction | B. Gabriel network |

The Gabriel network provides a form of network that contains more links than a MST and hence provides greater connectivity especially between nearby points that are not actually nearest neighbors. It was introduced as one means of uniquely defining contiguity for a point set such that no other point could be regarded as lying 'between' connected pairs. It has been used in a variety of applications, most notably in genetic studies of populations (human and other). Examples include the research of Sokal *et al.* (1986) into the genetic makeup of the Yanomama Amerindian villages and the research by Arnaud *et al.* (1999) into land snail genetics. In each case the Gabriel network was judged to be a meaningful description of connectivity, with the option of binary or edge weighted measurement. The measure was then used to determine the spatial weights matrix in autocorrelation analyses. The MST can be produced as a subset of the Gabriel network as follows:

(i) construct an initial subset of the Gabriel network in which the additional constraint is applied that no other points may lie within the area of intersection defined by circles placed at each Gabriel network node with radius equal to the inter-node separation (see Figure 7-6B). The resulting network is called a Relative Neighborhood Network (Figure 7-6C, e.g. see implementations in Manifold GIS and PASSaGE spatial ecology software); (ii) remove the longest link in the relative network that does not break overall network connectivity; (iii) repeat step (ii) until no further reduction in overall length is achieved (see Figure 7-6D — the line identified by the arrow is the only edge requiring removal).

## Figure 7-6 Relative neighborhood network and related constructions

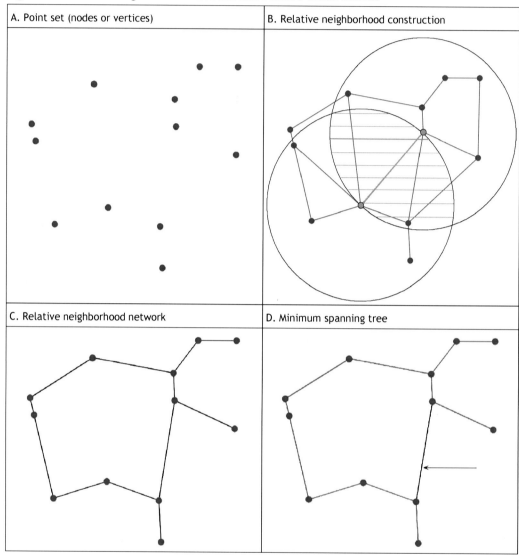

| A. Point set (nodes or vertices) | B. Relative neighborhood construction |
| C. Relative neighborhood network | D. Minimum spanning tree |

Although not specifically described in detail, this appears to be the general procedure adopted in the Manifold GIS for creating an MST. As opposed to the construction approached described earlier, this method commences with a promising solution that is a superset of the MST and reduces it until the MST is determined. A variant of the procedure is sometimes described as the $k$-MST problem, in which an MST is sought for a given subset, $k<=n$ vertices, with the remaining vertices either connected via an existing set of edges or not connected.

The various networks described so far have involved construction using Euclidean straight lines and the Euclidean metric ($L_2$). Solutions to problems such as determining the MST and many of those that are discussed in the following subsections may also be sought using other metrics. Extensive research exists into solutions that apply for the $L_1$ metric, not merely because this may provide a more meaningful measure for street patterns in many cities, but also because in unrelated areas, such as electronic circuit design and utility infrastructure planning, such metrics are often more appropriate. Examples of solutions for alternative metrics will be provided later in this chapter.

### 7.3.3 Steiner trees

A feature of the MST solutions described is that they minimize network length for a spanning tree rather than minimizing the length of a network of straight line segments connecting all vertices that permits the inclusion of intermediate points. Adding intermediate points can reduce the total network length, by a factor of up to $\sqrt{3}/2$ for the $L_2$ metric and 2/3 for the $L_1$ metric. For example, any three neighboring vertices may be connected using an intermediate (or Steiner) point that will reduce their local MST, *iff* the angle between the two legs of the local MST is less than 120 degrees (Figure 7-7A) and

the vertices are unweighted. The optimum location for an intermediate point in this case is such that each link from the chosen point to the three vertices lies at an angle of 120 degrees from the other two — i.e. they are equally spaced (Figure 7-7B).

Whilst an MST may be systematically modified in this manner, accepting solutions that reduce total network length, this will not necessarily result in a minimal length Steiner tree. Algorithms that commence with the original point set and examine a much wider range of options may yield significantly improved solutions. For example, taking 4 points at a time may identify solutions in which two additional points are warranted, with these points being themselves inter-linked. In the most general case, with $m<=n-2$ Steiner points and $n$ vertices a very large number of alternative topologies are possible — over 60,000 with just $n=7$. The Steiner MST problem is NP-hard, although efficient approximation algorithms now exist. Such facilities are not provided in current GIS software — see for example, Robins and Zelikovsky (2000) for more details.

*Figure 7-7 Steiner MST construction*

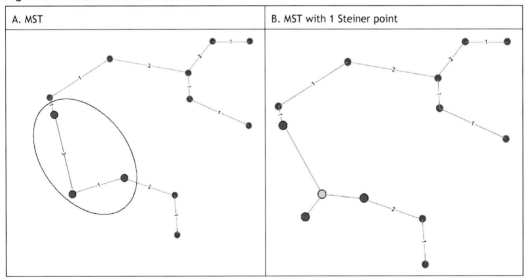

Note that these networks and solution procedures assume that network flows and directions are not relevant, and that every vertex has equal weight. If vertices have unequal weights (e.g. number of beds in a hospital, demand for certain goods, or weight of material input for some manufacturing operation) then the Steiner point solution will be altered. In fact such problems have been described briefly earlier in this Guide, in connection with locating centroids using the $L_2$ metric (Section 4.2.5.2). For $n$ vertices each of which has an associated weight, $w_i$, the least distance network in the plane from a single additional point (the point of minimum aggregate travel, MAT, or Weber point) is defined by coordinates that are determined iteratively.

The iteration equations for the MAT point, M6, are provided in Section 4.2.5.2. Typically the number of iterations required for convergence is very small (often 5 or fewer). This provides an example of a simple optimal location problem that is closely related to the Steiner network problem. If a pre-existing network is provided as part of the problem, and demand is located at the vertices, an optimal Weber point will always be found at a network vertex. An important generalization of this problem is the case where $p$ locations are sought (e.g. warehouses) to service demand at $n$ vertices (e.g. retail outlets). In this case the network-based version is known as the $p$-median problem. Such problems are discussed in more detail in Section 7.4

### 7.3.4 Shortest (network) path problems

#### 7.3.4.1 Overview of shortest path problems

Unlike some of the previous problems, the general shortest path (SP) problem requires a predefined network. The basic problem is then to determine one or more shortest (or least cost) routes between a source vertex and a target vertex where a set of edges are given. In several cases SP algorithms also provide shortest paths from a single source to all or many of the other vertices in a network as a side-effect of the procedure. Such algorithms are known as *single-source* SPAs or single-source queries. The set of shortest paths generated from a single source is known as a shortest path tree (SPT).

The determination of shortest paths can be specified as a linear programming problem, as follows. Let $s$ be the source vertex, $t$ be the target vertex and let $c_{ij}>0$ be the cost or distance associated with the link or edge $(i,j)$. Then we seek to minimize $z$, where:

$$z = \sum_i \sum_j c_{ij} x_{ij},$$

subject to

$$\sum_j x_{ji} - \sum_k x_{ik} = m, \text{ where}$$

$$m = 0 \text{ for } i \neq s,$$
$$m = 1 \text{ for } i = t$$
$$m = -1 \text{ for } i = s$$
$$x_{ij} \in \{0,1\}$$

Although this formulation enables shortest path problems to be solved by standard LP software, and is guaranteed to yield all-integer solutions, in practice it is far less efficient than utilizing specialized network aware algorithms.

Typical exact algorithms for computing shortest paths are those of Dijkstra (1959, see subsection 7.3.4.3) and Dantzig (1960, see subsection 7.3.4.2), both of which are single source SPAs. These 'greedy' algorithms applied to planar graphs with non-negative edge weights typically require $O(n^2)$ time, where $n$ is the number of vertices. However, Henzinger, Klein and Rao (1997) have shown that a near linear time algorithm is possible, i.e. $O(n)$. The complexity of Dijkstra's original algorithm can be reduced to $O(m+n\log n)$ using Fibonacci heaps, where $m$ represents the number of edges.

In some cases shortest path problems are subject to additional side constraints. For example, the shortest acceptable route in a telecommunications network may be subject to certain quality requirements — if some routes have higher quality than others, these may be preferable despite the time, cost or distance of the route being greater. Another example might be a limit on the total budget available for a given trip, where some routes have higher costs than others. Such side conditions can be incorporated into the model definition as one or more inequalities, where each network edge has not only a cost or distance value, but also one or more positive weights. Collectively these define the general Constrained Shortest Path Problem (CSPP), good solutions for which can be achieved via a number of techniques, including Lagrangian relaxation (see for example, Beasley and Christofides, 1989, and Carlyle and Wood, 2003). Unlike SPPs, which can be solved in polynomial time, CSPPs are NP-Complete.

### 7.3.4.2 Dantzig algorithm

Figure 7-8 illustrates Dantzig's step-by-step algorithm for determining the shortest path from vertex 1, 2, 3 and 4 to all other vertices in a directed planar graph (a *digraph*) with positive edge weights. The algorithm is a form of discrete dynamic programming. Figure 7-8A shows the graph and Figure 7-8B-D the steps involved in determining the shortest path from vertex 1 to 3, highlighted in red.

*Figure 7-8 Dantzig shortest path algorithm*

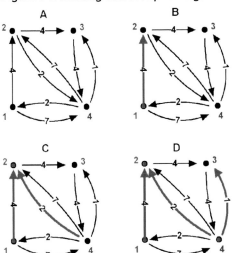

The basic steps in this procedure are as follows:

1: identify the shortest (least distance/cost/time) edge from vertex 1 – this

is to vertex 2 (*cost*=4). Add vertex 2 and the edge or link from 1 to 2 to the tagged set. If a tie occurs, arbitrarily choose one of the edges

2: identify the shortest (least cumulative cost/time) edge from vertex 1 or from vertex 2 plus edge (1,2) distance – this is to vertex 4 from 2 (*cost*=6). Add vertex 4 and edge 2 to 4 to the tagged set

3: identify the shortest (least cumulative cost/time) edge from the tagged set – this is from vertex 1 to 2 to 4 to 3 (*cost*=7)

Stop – all vertices reached; repeat from vertex 2, 3 and 4 to compute all shortest paths from every vertex

This algorithm is very similar to the standard Dijkstra procedure, which describe in subsection 7.3.4.3:

### 7.3.4.3 Dijkstra algorithm

This algorithm works by storing the cost of the shortest path found so far between the start vertex, $s$, and each target vertex, $t$. We shall denote this distance $d(t)$.

The basic steps in this classic algorithm are as follows:

1: initialize all vertices such that $d(t)=\infty$ (infinity, or in practice, a very large value) and $d(s)=0$

2: For each edge leading from $s$, add the edge length from $s$ to the current value of the path length at $s$. If this new distance is less than the current value for $d(t)$ replace this with the lower value

3: choose the lowest value in the set $d(t)$ and move the current (active) vertex to this location

4: iterate steps 2 and 3 until the target vertex is reached or all vertices have been scanned

Note that the distance to every vertex reached is contained in the vector $d(t)$. If the entry is infinity then it means the vertex is unreachable or has not been scanned. Also note that unlike the Dantzig algorithm the shortest path(s) are not generated, only their lengths. To obtain these the algorithm must be altered to retain a list of shortest path vertices, e.g. by storing both the shortest path distance and the preceding vertex address of the shortest path in the vertex label.

It should also be noted that basic Dijkstra-type algorithms provide inconsistent run-times on real-world networks, principally because such networks have very limited vertex connectivity (their adjacency matrices are very sparse). SPAs need to be either very efficient implementations of these basic algorithms or should use heuristics, such as the A* algorithm, to obtain faster solutions (e.g. for real-time/interactive applications) — see further, subsection 7.3.4.4.

### 7.3.4.4 A* algorithm

Dijkstra's algorithm is a special case of a more general algorithm known as A*. Strictly speaking A* is a goal-directed best-first algorithm. It visits nodes in an order that may be preferable (faster) than the simple sweep of all nodes that the Dijkstra algorithm adopts. To select which node to visit next it typically computes the Euclidean distance of each vertex from the target and adds to this the distance currently recorded via the network to this vertex. Vertices are visited in overall distance priority order. Typically the A* algorithm will visit fewer nodes for a specified source-target (exact) route than other algorithms and will thus on average be faster — often a lot faster.

### 7.3.4.5 GIS implementations of SPAs

Most GIS packages do not provide information on the algorithms used for this class or any similar network analysis problems, nor references to indicate the procedures used. Only the experience of using a particular implementation will confirm the nature of its behavior, both in terms of computational complexity (time and space) and quality (optimality). Systematic testing of sample networks and problems based on a range of sizes (vertices) and plotting the results will provide a good indication as to the resource requirements and practicality of using any particular software. If a preferred package (e.g. the corporate standard) does not perform in the manner desired, then solving such problems externally using tools such as Concorde, Xpress-MP or LEDA, and then re-importing the results back into the GIS, may be the best option. These latter packages, and similar software, do provide details of the algorithms used, the time complexity of their solution procedures, and in many cases optional source code and linkable library code.

Figure 7-9 illustrates the process of carrying out simple variants of SPA using ArcGIS Network Analyst and a real street network. The source dataset for the network was a shapefile of the street layout for Salt Lake City (SLC), Utah, USA. This is available as a downloadable file from the SLC authorities. Since the file is not in network-ready form it was processed using ArcCatalog to automatically create a network file that includes vertices at every intersection and end of line. Without further alteration (unrealistic in practice) this file was then used to compute the shortest path connecting four locations (Figure 7-9A). In this case the locations were selected interactively and parameters chosen for the computation. These included permitting U-turns and including two barriers (indicated by X symbols on the map).

The shortest path shown in Figure 7-9B is technically an open *tour*, or sequential ordering process, in that it is a connected series of shortest paths from 1-2, 2-3, and finally 3-4. It can also be seen as a shortest path from location 1 to location 4, with the constraint that the route must go via locations 2 and 3 — a very common requirement. A closed tour, returning to location 1, could have been generated by adding a shortest path from location 4 to 1.

*Figure 7-9 Salt Lake City — Sample networking problems and solutions*

| A. Delivery locations and road barriers | B. Shortest path solution (sequential tour from 1-4) |
| C. Shortest path solution (optimal tour from 1-4) | D. Closest facilities to an incident |

The tour described above is not optimal if the sequential condition is dropped — the tour 1-4-3-2 is shorter (Figure 7-9C). This latter tour was generated using the same dataset but this time using the Manifold package, Transform toolbar facilities. Note that there are some obvious differences in the solution map, other than the totally different routing. One of these is the lack of U-turns, an option which is not enabled in this instance. Another is the difference in default orientation of the display, which has no real significance. Manifold's solution is obtained by exhaustive search where there are 10 or fewer locations to be linked (i.e. an exact solution), and applies an heuristic algorithm (specific details are not provided) for 11+ sites. A discussion of optimal tours and associated algorithms in provided in Section 7.3.5.

Figure 7-9D shows the result of addressing a related problem — that of identifying the closest facility or facilities to a specified location such as an incident. In this example the solution has again been generated using ArcGIS, which has identified two locations within a given distance or time from an incident location at the bottom of the map, together with optimal routes to or from the incident. Note that again U-turns have been permitted and that, depending on the network characteristics (turn permissions, one-way streets, traffic speeds etc.), the route *to* an incident may well differ from the route away *from* the incident. Often, of course, the routes to and from a location will be to and from different third locations (e.g. ambulance station and hospital).

### 7.3.4.6 Further SPAs applications

Shortest path algorithms provide a key component of many problems in spatial analysis. The primary group of applications are those involving transport network routing, for example travelling from one location to another across a network with various constraints (e.g. turn restrictions, speed restrictions, directional restrictions). Extensions of this basic functionality that include other considerations such as traffic flows, second, third or $k^{th}$ shortest paths, computation of tours etc., all form standard building blocks of solutions to network and location analysis optimization problems. But there are additional application areas that are less obvious. One example is the extension of SPAs to non-network spatial environments. For example, a shopping mall, an airport or a national park, are all examples of spaces that pedestrians or maybe electronic buggies or bicycles might traverse, and computation of paths in such spaces is frequently of interest. In such cases one approach is to overlay a lattice on the available space and fully connect adjacent lattice nodes/centers or edges. This provides a high density set of links that may be used to select alternative routes — perhaps shortest routes to emergency exits

(note that this idea is not restricted to 2D spaces). An example of this idea applied to an office environment is shown in Figure 7-10, where a standard SPA algorithm has been applied with the additional constraint that a minimum distance from obstacles (e.g. desks, chairs etc.) must be maintained.

*Figure 7-10 Shortest obstacle-avoiding path*

There are many alternative approaches to solving the kind of problem illustrated in Figure 7-10. One group falls into the general area of computational geometry. In this view all elements of the problem are treated as polyhedral objects and the solution space is partitioned to identify true shortest (Euclidean) paths — in the example illustrated such methods would identify a direct path (a straight line) for the first part of the route shown, rather than the jagged route generated by the lattice-based SPA. Indeed, all lattice-based SPAs will generate biased 'shortest' routes (directionally and distance biased). One (partial) solution to such problems is to solve the lattice or raster variant of the problem first, using simple and fast algorithms, and then seek to post-optimize the resulting solution, for example by seeing if sections of the route can be straightened whilst meeting the constraints applied.

SPAs may also be applied to more abstract problems, where the network graph does not represent a spatial problem but a logical problem. Examples include searching certain types of database, or arranging a series of processes in such a way as to minimize the overall time or cost of an operation (the latter is known as a scheduling problem).

### 7.3.5 Tours, travelling salesman problems and vehicle routing

The optimal tours described in Section 7.3.4 are subsets of a more general class of problem, the travelling salesman problem (TSP). The TSP involves making a tour of every vertex in a given set, returning to the starting point, such that the tour length is minimized. Applications include: salesmen visiting customers; rubbish trucks servicing business premises; delivery trucks servicing retail outlets; security staff patrolling premises and many more. There are many non-geographic applications, ranging from VLSI design to the analysis of DNA sequences. The majority of geographic instances involve modest numbers of locations to visit (e.g. stores, cities) but variants of the problem (e.g. the need to dispatch multiple vehicles from a central depot on tours to visit their own subset of stores) can increase the problem complexity substantially. Pure TSP problems (i.e. based on a point set with no pre-defined network) are not supported within GIS packages. Where such networks are defined, very few GIS packages provide TSP functionality — one exception being TransCAD. An excellent introduction to TSP problems and solutions is provided by William Cook, one of the authors of the Concorde software package described later in this subsection) at: http://www.tsp.gatech.edu/index.html

Since every TSP tour involves visiting each location once, deleting one link from this tour will leave a spanning tree. This tree must be at least as long as the MST and will typically be longer (an upper bound for symmetric planar graphs is 1.5 times the MST length). The number, $t$, of possible tours with a symmetric (i.e. non-directed) graph consisting of $n$ vertices is $t=(n-1)!/2$. This number grows extremely rapidly with $n$ and cannot realistically be systematically evaluated for large $n$. For example, with $n=10$, $t=181,440$. Solving the problem exactly is thus an $O(n!)$ problem and has been shown to be NP-complete. An internationally collated set of test problems are provided in the dataset

known as TSPLIB. These include test datasets for symmetric and asymmetric TSPs, HCPs, SOPs and CVRPs. See www.iwr.uni-heidelberg.de/groups/comopt/software/TSPLIB95/ for more details.

A formal statement of the basic TSP is:

$$1: \min\left\{\sum_{i=1}^{n}\sum_{j=1}^{n}c_{ij}x_{ij}\right\}, \; i \neq j$$

subject to:

$$2: \sum_{\substack{i=1 \\ i \neq j}}^{n} x_{ij} = 1, \; j = 1...n$$

$$3: \sum_{\substack{j=1 \\ j \neq i}}^{n} x_{ij} = 1, \; i = 1...n$$

$$4: x_{ij} \in \{0,1\}$$

where $c_{ij}$ is the cost of travel from $i$ to $j$ (e.g. cost weighted distance), and $x_{ij}=1$ if a direct link exists from $i$ to $j$ in a tour, or 0 otherwise. Here $n$ is the number of sites in the tour, where typically $i=1$ is the tour start point (e.g. a depot) and $i=2,3,...n$ are the sites to be visited (e.g. customers).

Solutions of many TSP problems have certain attributes that may be used to assist algorithm development. These include the fact that the TSP for a point set, $S$, must lie entirely within the convex hull of the set, and any vertices located on this hull must be traversed such that their clockwise or anti-clockwise sequential arrangement is preserved. Clearly also the TSP must not be self-intersecting. Heuristic solutions, notably the Lin-Kernighan or LK-heuristic, which is a development of the $n$-opt heuristic, make use of any self-intersections that are found to generate an improved solution with the self-intersection removed by a form of symmetric resequencing or *flipping* of the order of visited nodes. The result is a very fast approximate algorithm that yields exact or near exact solutions for many problems. Exact algorithms also exist, some of which are fast. Concorde, cited earlier, uses a procedure based on linear programming and cutting plane techniques to obtain exact solutions to relatively large problems (many 1000s of vertices). This code, which is very fast with moderate-sized problems, is amongst the best available. However, users should be aware that rounding issues exist in its treatment of decimal coordinates – to avoid problems it is advisable to multiply all values by one or more powers of 10 before undertaking analyses.

There are close relationships between the generation of the Delaunay triangulations, the generation of MSTs and the solution of Euclidean (plane) TSPs. This was noted earlier on in the research into TSP heuristics, and forms the basis of some methods. To illustrate this linkage we will use a test dataset from TSPLIB consisting of $n$=130 vertices (CH130.TSP). Figure 7-11 illustrates several aspects of these relationships. Figure 7-11A shows the source point set and Figure 7-11B gives the Delaunay triangulation (DT) of this set. The total length of the edges in the triangulation is 30157 units.

Figure 7-11C and Figure 7-11D show the minimum spanning tree (MST) for the point set, produced using the Concorde software and overlain on the DT. The MST consists of 129 edges with a total length of 5166 units. Figure 7-11E and Figure 7-11F show the same pair, but in this case showing the exact TSP solution obtained using the linear programming and

cutting planes method that is implemented in Concorde. Processing on a modestly powered desktop PC was completed in a few seconds. The total number of edges in this case was 130 with a total length of 6110 units.

Finally, Figure 7-12A shows the solution provided using the LK heuristic, which was generated almost instantly for this problem. Notice that the top right corner of this solution differs slightly from that of the exact solution in Figure 7-11F. This solution also has 130 edges but a slightly greater length of 6124 units. In all cases edge weights were computed using symmetric Euclidean distances. Interestingly, with a random pattern of $n$ points with an MBR that has area A, the expected length of the Euclidean TSP has been estimated as:

$$L = k\sqrt{nA}, k \approx 3/4$$

For the example illustrated in Figure 7-11A $n$=130 and $A$=471,937 units, giving an expected tour length if the point set were random of 5874 units. The optimal result is slightly greater than this, reflecting the fact that the point set is slightly more uniform than random. With the Manhattan or $L_1$ metric the expected tour length is greater, being the same general expression but with $k \approx 19/20$.

*Figure 7-11 MST, TSP and related problems*

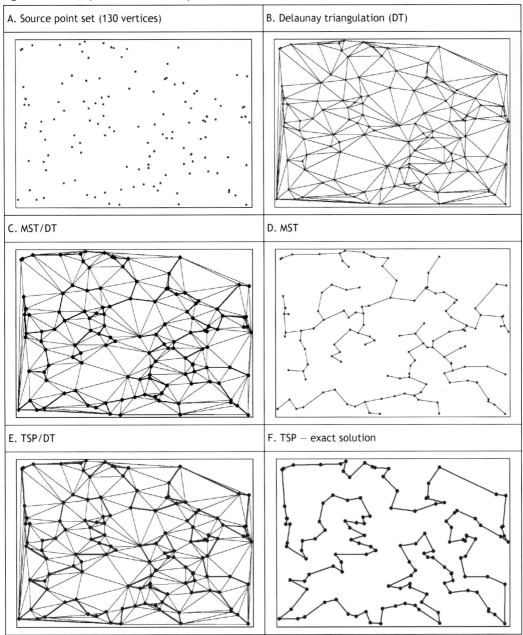

*Figure 7-12 Heuristic solution and dual circuit TSP examples*

| A. TSP — LK solution | B. Dual TSP |
|---|---|
| 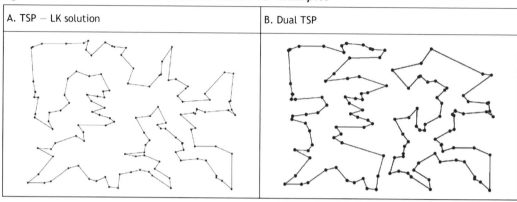 | |

### 7.3.5.1 Capacitated vehicle routing

Figure 7-12B provides one instance of a solution to a more general problem, that of determining the optimal set of $t>1$ tours for a given point set. This class of problems is known as the Vehicle Routing Problem (VRP) or Capacitated VRP (CVRP) if vehicle capacity constraints are included in the problem formulation. In this example the point set has simply been divided into left and right halves and separate optimal tours generated for each subset. The combined length of these tours is 6349 units, but it is perfectly possible for the tour length to be less than that for a single tour. Multiple tours will often utilize the same starting vertex (e.g. a single depot) but this does not substantially alter the approaches used. Separate tours can be created by breaking (dividing) the original optimal tour into discrete parts (route first-cluster second) or by separating the point sets into clusters and computing optimal or near optimal tours for each subset (cluster first-route second). There is no guarantee that the resulting multiple tours will be globally optimal, so repeated alternative subdivisions may be necessary to achieve improved solutions. Such a procedure is extremely processor intensive and hence use of algorithms such as the LK-heuristic would generally be preferred for the TSP generation step.

The two circuit TSP problem raises a number of practical issues:

- should the tours start at the same point (e.g. warehouse, bus depot...)?

- what if demand varies across the target points?

- the capacities of service vehicles may be limited and vary — what mix would be optimal?

- do tours/deliveries have to be made in certain time windows?

These questions relate to problem variants for which metaheuristics such as tabu search (see Section 7.2.2.4) have been shown to be effective, especially where time window constraints also apply (see Gendreau, Laporte and Potvin, 2002, for a fuller discussion). Problem variants such as these are addressed in several of the software packages referred to in the introduction to this chapter. Most seek optimal solutions for moderate sized problems, or provably good solutions that can be computed reasonably quickly — i.e. sub-optimal solutions, but much better than more arbitrary or user-defined plans. Individual packages vary in their approaches and often provide more than one option where complex real-world constraints and commercial criteria apply. This in turn requires careful formulation of the appropriate model, designing this using a standardized modeling structure or design tool, and then implementing the model using a high-level scripting language or code generator.

To illustrate this approach we shall use an example from the Xpress-MP optimization product with its Mosel scripting language. In this case the problem involves delivery of liquid chemicals by tanker from a refinery to 6 customer sites. The demand, *DEM*, from the sites is known (these might be regular fixed or varying amounts, delivered on a scheduled basis). Total demand in this example is 59000 liters. A symmetric shortest distance matrix is provided between all locations – map support is not provided within Xpress-MP so distance matrix creation and final display would benefit from a direct link to a GIS package or simple import/export facilities. Pairs of sites vary in separation from 12 kms to 180 kms. The capacity, *CAP*, of the delivery tanker is fixed at 36000 liters and the task is to deliver to all customers with the shortest overall distance driven. Note that a single tour would not be able to service the customers, as the tanker capacity is not sufficient, so capacity-related constraints must be added to the model formulation provided at the start of this subsection (Equations 1: to 4: in Section 7.3.5). The objective function in this instance is specified by Equation 1:, whilst the range of $i$ and $j$ in Equations 2: and 3: is from 2...$n$ as site 1 is the depot itself. We need to define additional expressions to account for customer demand and tanker capacity. Let $DEM_i$ be the demand by customer $i$, and let $q_i$ be the cumulative amount of chemical in liters delivered to all customers during a tour, up to and including customer $i$. If customer $i$ is the first in a particular tour, then $DEM_i=q_i$, which can be written as the condition:

$$5 : q_i \leq CAP + (DEM_i - CAP)x_{1i}, \; \forall i \in customers$$

If $j$ comes after $i$ in a tour then $q_i$ must be greater than the quantity delivered in the tour up to $i$ plus the quantity to be delivered to $j$. This constraint can be written as:

$$6 : q_j \geq q_i + DEM_j - CAP + CAP * x_{ij} +$$
$$(CAP - DEM_j - DEM_i)x_{ji}, \; \forall i, j \in customers, \; i \neq j$$

Although this appears rather complicated, it picks up the various cases where $i$ is not 1 and $j$ may or may not follow or precede $i$. All that remains is to add the basic quantity and capacity constraints:

$$7 : q_i \leq CAP, \; \forall i \in customers$$
$$8 : q_i \geq DEM_i, \; \forall i \in customers$$

The scripting language for Xpress-MP accepts input in almost the form shown in Equations 1: to 8:, together with the data and distance matrices described above, followed by a simple command to minimize Equation 1:. The result in this example is a solution consisting of two tours, one delivering 22000 liters to two customers, and the other delivering 37000 liters to the remaining 4 customers, with a combined tour of just under 500 kms (Figure 7-13).

*Figure 7-13 Tanker delivery tours*

Data-driven scripts that solve well-defined optimization problems may be subjected to extensive tests, and then used as the back-ends to form-based or graphical/map interfaces in order to provide solutions to a wide range of real-world problems. These higher-level interfaces can provide location, route matrix, attribute and parameter inputs (data) and submit these to the pre-built scripts for execution. Outputs (such as lists of edges comprising routes) can then be read back into the visual interface software and presented as reports, tables and maps. GIS packages such as TransCAD and ArcGIS provide a range of scripting and programming interfaces to facilitate such integration, either with the GIS package or using GIS-package facilities within another application, such as a vehicle dispatch and management system for the emergency services.

# 7.4 Location and Service Area Problems

## 7.4.1 Location problems

Optimally locating $p$ facilities to serve customer demand at $n>p$ locations is a simplified description of many locational analysis problems (many of which may be formulated as $p$-median problems – see further, Section 7.4.2). If the existence of a network is ignored, and connectivity is assumed to be by direct connection in the plane from each customer to a single, closest, facility then a simple location-allocation problem is defined – selecting locations and then allocating customers or demand to these locations according to some rule (e.g. nearest facility). Frequently, however, a network (e.g. a road network) exists together with a matrix of shortest path/least cost distances between vertices, and this provides a key input into the optimization process.

Real world problems are, of course, far more complex, since there are many other variables to be considered (e.g. availability of suitable sites, cost of sites, size of facility, access to and from sites, regulatory issues, planning controls, availability of suitable labor, timing of developments, etc.) and all of these considerations exist within a dynamic environment that affects these and core variables such as customer demand patterns, materials supply and changes in the technological, commercial and political environment. Hence optimization is only a part of a much larger decision-making process, whose importance will vary depending on the particular problem at hand (for an excellent recent discussion of some of these issues, see O'Kelly, 2008). Obtaining near (provably) optimum solutions to many problems, and understanding their robustness to variation in parameters and locational changes is often at least as important as seeking absolute optima for problems that have been very narrowly defined. Such procedures may also provide a form of benchmarking, identifying the cost associated with the "best" solution, which may then be compared with other options within a broader decision-making framework.

Research into problems such as these has a long history, with substantial progress being made from the 1960s onwards. As the range of problems tackled became broader and solution procedures required increasing use of computational power, libraries of software were developed and made available by academics, which then (directly or indirectly) were incorporated into commercial software packages. One of the first of these was the set of FORTRAN programs published (as an edited monograph and in electronic form) by Rushton, Goodchild and Ostresh in 1973. The problems addressed in this software collection included single- and multi-facility location in the plane (Euclidean metric) and on a network, together with algorithms for allocation and spatial choice modeling. At this time the single facility optimization procedures were exact, whilst multi-facility procedures utilized a variety of heuristics to obtain "good" solutions.

In the plane (i.e. with no network defined) the $p$-median problem is a form of point-set partitioning, similar to cluster analysis. Typically $p$ supply or service points are sought to service $n$ customer locations (vertices), such that each customer is allocated to a single supply point (often based on simple Euclidean proximity) and such that the total distance or cost of transport between the customers and the supply centers is minimized. If $p=1$ we have the simple computation of the Minimum Aggregate Travel (MAT) location, which may be determined using the iterative procedure described in Section 4.2.5.2. If $p>1$, however, the problem is more complicated and requires an extended solution procedure. Exact solution of the $p$-median problem in the plane is possible using branch and bound (tree-searching) algorithms. Ostresh, for example, provides such an algorithm in the FORTRAN suite referred to above (Rushton, Goodchild and Ostresh, eds., 1973). Exact solutions for larger problems and extended variants of the problem may be computationally demanding and several heuristic procedures have been devised that tests suggest will often provide optimal or near optimal solutions (with less than 3% deviation from the optimal objective function value) in many cases. Note that in planar or "free" space problems the form of the objective function can be viewed as a cost surface, whose shape may be quite complex with many small local optima. Furthermore, since sections of this surface may be relatively flat, a specific heuristic solution that is within 2% of the optimum objective function value could well be defined by a set of locations that are a considerable distance from the optimal sites. Evaluation of variation of the objective function in the neighborhood of solution points one at a time (e.g. across a grid defined within the Voronoi region of this point), can provide an insight into the form of this surface.

A simple heuristic solution for the planar $p$-median problem, most commonly attributed to Cooper (1963, 1964), is as follows:

Step 1: randomly select $p$ points in the Minimum Bounding Rectangle (MBR), or preferably within the convex hull, of the customer point set, $V$, as the initial locations for the median points

Step 2: allocate every point in $V$ to its (Euclidean) closest median point. This partitions $V$ into $p$ subsets, $V_p$

Step 3: For each of the $p$ subsets of $V$, compute the MAT point using the iterative equation referred to above (described in Section 4.2.5.2)

Step 4: iterate steps 2 and 3 until the change in the objective function falls below a preset tolerance level

Clearly the quality of the solution obtained by this heuristic is not provided. One approach to improving the solution found would be to repeat the process $k$ times with a different set of random starting points and compare the final objective value with previous runs. A better approach is to make good initial choice of the median locations, for example by some form of simple cluster analysis (e.g. the density based procedure adopted by Crimestat or a simple neighbor-based or quadrat-derived clustering). An extended version of this algorithm can be used to solve the same problem, but with capacity constraints on the supply centers. In this case allocation is more complicated and may result in some customers being served by more than one center. Experience suggests that constrained problems of this kind often yield solutions that are closer on average to the true optimum than unconstrained problems.

More recent examples of the development of collections of location modeling utilities include the public-domain C++ library known as LOLA (Library of Location Algorithms), Daskin's SITATION software, and the S-Distance project developed at the University of Thessaly in Greece (a Visual Basic V6 implementation of many discrete and network location algorithms, including a wide range of heuristics, although not yet fully completed – see further, subsection 7.4.2.3). LOLA is available for various computing platforms in both source code and in pre-compiled form with optional basic graphical user interface (GUI) and link to ESRI's ArcView GIS (using ESRI's Avenue language). LOLA utilizes a number of third party code components, including LEDA and LP-solve which we have previously referred to (LOLA's V2.0 release in December 2000 pre-dates LEDA's move to a more commercial environment). LOLA addresses both median problems (minimization of average or total travel costs) and so-called center problems (minimization of maximum travel costs, i.e. minimax problems).

As with the earlier FORTRAN-based project LOLA provides a mix of exact and heuristic solutions to problems in the plane or on networks, but in LOLA's case includes a much broader range of metrics (typically $L_p$ metrics), optional restrictions on permitted solution areas (forbidden zones, barriers), and solutions for directed and undirected networks and on trees. For network (graph) problems most solutions are designed for 1-median or 1-center problems, with solutions that may lie either at network vertices or anywhere on the network.

Figure 7-14 illustrates using LOLA to identify the best two cities in Italy from which to service demand from customer sites in a total of 39 cities. Each city included (network vertex) is taken as a customer site, with entries being of the form $(x,y,z,n)$ where $x$ and $y$ are coordinates, $z$ is the customer demand estimate and $n$ is the city name – for example:

28.00 74.00 50000 [Milano]

Coupled with this information are details on the network structure and cost. In this case data are entered as adjacency lists, in the form <from,to,weight>.

Hence as Milano is location 1 and has direct connections to Piacenza, Novara and Verona (locations 34, 17 and 13) the adjacency list is of the form:

1 34 4; 1 17 3; 1 13 22

The weights in this case might be travel or transport costs or times. The geometry of the routes in this case is unimportant. The optimum solution consists of two city locations, shown here as Opt1 and Opt2 (Piacenza and Roma). This is a very simple example but serves to illustrate the ideas involved and the basic data required. In many instances the problem LOLA addresses is where to locate a new facility given that a number of such facilities already exist. New facilities typically involve an overall construction cost (cost of site plus construction etc.).

*Figure 7-14 Optimum facility location on a network – LOLA solution*

The majority of GIS packages do not provide such capabilities directly, although many offer basic operations, such as locating a weighted mean center in the plane. TransCAD provides tools to add a number, $m$, of new facilities to an existing set (which could be empty) in a network environment, and thus has similar functionality to LOLA in this example, but here it is integrated within a GIS framework rather than linked to a separate product set. It provides tools to determine the best location to place one or more new facilities, or as many as might be required to meet a given service objective, subject to various optimization objectives (minimization of average costs, minimization of maximum costs, maximization of minimum costs). Custom-built software utilizing general purpose optimization libraries such as LEDA, CPLEX and Xpress-MP enables a wide range of problems of this type to be designed and solved in an optimal or near optimal manner. In many cases larger problems require the use of heuristic or approximation algorithms in order to obtain solutions within a reasonable time.

## 7.4.2 Larger p-median and p-center problems

### 7.4.2.1 Simple heuristics

Exact solution is possible of the network version of the $p$-median problem. In this model there are $n$ customer demand sites, each with demand weights $w_i$ and $p$ supply sites to be chosen from $m<=n$ candidates. These $p$ "median" sites will lie at vertices of the network (in fact optimal solutions may exist anywhere on the network but a theorem due to Hakimi shows that at least one optimal solution will lie entirely at network nodes, which simplifies the overall problem in many cases). In principle, for small $n$, $m$ and $p$, solutions can be found by enumerating the possible configurations, but this becomes infeasible very quickly as their values increase in size. Heuristic solutions may provide good or even optimal solutions in a reasonable time, but evaluating the quality of some of these approaches is not straightforward. Other heuristics, by their very nature, do provide bounds on the quality of their approach to

optimality.

A basic heuristic for the network-based $p$-median problem, due to Teitz and Bart (1968) and also described in Section 7.2.2.2, is known as an "interchange" method and proceeds in the following manner. Let $V$ be the set of $m$ candidate vertices, then: (i) randomly select $p$ vertices from $V$ and call this set $Q$; (ii) for each vertex $i$ in $Q$ and each $j$ not in $Q$ (i.e. in the set $V$ but not in $Q$) swap $i$ and $j$ and see if the value of the objective function is improved; if so keep this new solution as the new set $Q$; (iii) iterate step (ii) until no further improvements are found. Note that this algorithm has the potential to produce improved solutions by repeating step (i) with a different random set and/or by examining good alternative unoccupied locations (e.g. within sub-regions of the network) as preferred choices for the interchange process — see Densham and Rushton (1992) for more details.

### 7.4.2.2 Lagrangian relaxation

Because the $p$-median problem is of such importance and generality we will describe it in greater detail, together with a particularly effective solution procedure for larger problems known by the rather cumbersome name of "Lagrangian relaxation with subgradient optimization" or LR procedures. Developments of this type of approach are described by Christofides and Beasley (1982) and Beasley (1985). Essentially, this procedure is a form of "branch and bound" algorithm, whereby upper and lower bounds are determined for the problem, optionally used in conjunction with a form of tree search (branching) to produce steadily improved results.

As with many optimization problems a standard formulation of the $p$-median problem can be made as follows:

$$1 : \min \sum_{i=1}^{n} \sum_{j=1}^{m} s_{ij} x_{ij}$$

subject to:

$$2 : \sum_{j=1}^{m} x_{ij} = 1, \ i = 1, 2..n,$$

i.e.

$$2' : D=0 \ \text{where} \ D = 1 - \sum_{j=1}^{m} x_{ij}$$

$$3 : x_{jj} \ge x_{ij}, \forall i, j, i \ne j$$

$$4 : \sum_{j=1}^{m} x_{jj} = p$$

In this formulation $x_{ij}=1$ if demand location $i$ is allocated to supply location $j$, otherwise it is 0, and $x_{jj}=1$ if a facility is opened at location $j$ otherwise it is 0. These requirements can be expressed as an additional constraint equation, requiring that $x_{jj} \in \{0,1\}$

Equation 1: is the objective function, the total (or average) cost, $s_{ij}$, of servicing customer demand at locations $i=1,2..n$ from the supply sites, $j$. Here, $s_{ij}=w_i c_{ij}$ where $w_i$ is a non-zero weight value indicating the demand at customer site $i$, and $c_{ij}$ is the cost of supplying a unit of demand from supply location $j$ to customer $i$. Typically $c_{ij}$ is the shortest path distance across the network between $i$ and $j$. This information may be computed in real time or supplied as a cost/distance matrix or list. Note that in general $s_{ij}$ is not equal to $s_{ji}$. If Equation 1: is replaced with $\min\{\max\{s_{ij}x_{ij}\}\}$ then the formulation is known as the $p$-center problem (which is also known to be NP-hard). In this latter case we are trying to minimize the maximum cost of servicing demand, for example to meet pre-defined service criteria.

Equation 2: states that every customer is served by exactly one site. An alternative formulation, 2', is shown as it is used later in this subsection.

Equation 3: states that if a facility is not located at site $j$ then customer demand cannot be allocated to it.

Finally Equation 4: states that a total of $p$ facilities need to be allocated.

The $p$-median problem on a network can be

solved exactly for reasonably large problems (e.g. 1000 customer sites and 50 depots) using the LR algorithm. The solution procedure involves solving a simpler problem (a relaxation of the original problem) that does not satisfy all of the constraints (e.g. fails to satisfy Equation 2:) and then using this solution to obtain upper and lower bounds on the optimum solution. These bounds are then systematically narrowed (the subgradient optimization phase) until, ideally, the solution upper bound (which does satisfy the constraints) meets the lower bound (exactly or to within a given tolerance), providing the optimal solution.

The simpler (relaxed) problem to solve actually looks more complicated. It involves adding a set of $n$ variables (Lagrangian multipliers, $\lambda_i > 0$) into the original Equation 1:, "relaxing" the constraint in Equation 2:, as follows:

$$\max_{\lambda} \left\{ \min \left\{ \sum_i \sum_j s_{ij} x_{ij} + \sum_i \lambda_i \left( 1 - \sum_j x_{ij} \right) \right\} \right\}$$

Observe that the last term in brackets in this expression is the constraint D, which now forms part of the objective function. The problem is 'relaxed' because the constraint in Equation 2: has been removed, so it is possible for a customer to be served by/assigned to more than one site — and indeed, when one comes to solve the relaxed problem this frequently occurs. Also note that the final summation can be expanded and combined with the initial summation, as follows:

$$\max_{\lambda} \left\{ \min \left\{ \sum_i \sum_j \left( s_{ij} - \lambda_i \right) x_{ij} + \sum_i \lambda_i \right\} \right\}$$

Minimization of the main term in brackets above is thus a simple enumeration task using the first term of the expression, since the second summation is a constant. We select each of the potential sites, $j$, in turn by setting $x_{jj}=1$ and then compute the sum of the cost of servicing customer demand, $C_j$, using the selected facility minus the Lagrangian, $\lambda_i$, i.e.

$$C_j = \sum_{i=1}^{n} \left( s_{ij} - \lambda_i \right)$$

If this sum is greater than 0 it is set to 0 otherwise the value is stored and the computation proceeds for the next $j$. The $p$ smallest (largest negative) values obtained in this way are taken as the locations of the initial set of $p$-median sites. The allocation of customer sites to these selected locations is made by setting $x_{ij}=1$ if $x_{jj}=1$ and $s_{ij}-\lambda_i<0$, otherwise $x_{ij}=0$. This allocation will not generally satisfy the original constraints, but the computed total cost obtained using Equation 1: will provide a lower bound, LB, to the true optimum solution.

We now obtain an upper bound, UB, by allocating the customer sites to their nearest supply location and again computing the total cost using Equation 1:.

To obtain an optimal or near-optimal solution the values of the initial Lagrangian multipliers need to be adjusted (reduced) in such a way as to eventually satisfy the original constraints. The updated values for these multipliers are obtained using a step adjustment to their values during the previous iteration:

$$\lambda_i^{(n+1)} = \max \left\{ 0, \lambda_i^{(n)} - t^{(n)} \left( \sum x_{ij}^{(n)} - 1 \right) \right\}$$

The stepsize value at the $n^{\text{th}}$ iteration, $t^{(n)}$, is determined using an expression of the form:

$$t^{(n)} = \frac{a^{(n)} \left( UB^{(n)} - LB^{(n)} \right)}{\sum_i \left( \sum_j x_{ij}^{(n)} - 1 \right)^2}$$

Selection of suitable values for $a^{(1)}$ and the $\lambda_i^{(1)}$ is important to ensure convergence. Christofides and Beasley (1982) and Beasley (1985) suggest using $\lambda_i^{(1)}=\min(s_{ij})$ across all $j$, for all $i$ not equal to $j$, and $a^{(1)}=2$, with procedures for reducing this in subsequent iterations (e.g. progressive halving) depending

upon the convergence behavior. Note that the term in the denominator of this expression is the sum of squared 'violations' of the constraint we have relaxed, so in this case it is based on the number of customers who have been assigned to more than one supply center.

After each iteration new UB and LB value are obtained as before and the process continues until satisfactory or complete convergence has been achieved. An optional standard tree search procedure can be included at this stage if the process fails to converge. Daskin (1995, pp 225-228) provides a fuller explanation and simple numerical worked example of this procedure. For large problems the overhead of computing the initial upper bound has been found to be high, and as an alternative a simple heuristic such as the interchange method described earlier can be used. Indeed, as we have noted, the heuristic itself can sometimes produce optimal solutions directly.

Performance of the LR algorithm for a range of problems is described by Beasley (1985) and for heuristic implementations of essentially the same procedure, by Beasley (1993). A set of test data for the problems described by Beasley in these articles and a range of related problems (e.g. other problems involving depot and warehouse location, with or without capacity constraints) is available at his web site (see Appendix for details). TSPLIB can also be used as a test dataset for $p$-median software.

Problems that involve <500 vertices (customers) and modest values of $p$ (e.g. $p<50$) can be solved directly and optimally by commercial mixed integer program (MIP) solvers such as CPLEX and LINDO. Larger problems remain difficult for such software and/or may require an excessive amount of time to complete — typically an hour or more of run time. Beltran et al. (2004) use the TSPLIB dataset in their semi-Lagrangian solution approach which is built on similar ideas to those of Beasley. Their tests were implemented in MATLab in combination with the CPLEX library V8.1. They use this approach to solve large $p$-median problems (3000+ customers and up to $p=500$ supply locations) to optimality or within 1% of optimality. More recently Avella *et al.* (2006) have reported results on their earlier study of their "Branch and Cut and Price" (BCP) algorithm. BCP can be used to solve large *p*-median and related problems in conjunction with CPLEX or similar library software. They have tested their methodology against the TSPLIB and OR-Library datasets, with very encouraging results, greatly outperforming CPLEX used on its own.

### 7.4.2.3 Comparison of alternative p-median heuristics

The S-Distance software project, mentioned earlier in this subsection and described further in Sirigos and Photis (2005), provides tools to compute solutions to quite large *p*-median and *p*-center problems using a range of heuristics, together with solutions for selected coverage problems. The heuristics they implement include many of those described in Taillard (2003), Daskin (1995) and Dyer and Frieze (1985). Data may be read from various file formats, including OR-Library files and network node/link files in dbf format. These various methods may then be compared in order to obtain an estimate of their relative efficiency. For the purposes of this exercise we used an S-Distance test dataset comprising the street network in Tripolis, in the region of Arcadia, Southern Greece. The data consist of 1358 vertices and 2256 edges. Each vertex or node has an integer demand value associated with it, ranging from 1 to 137, plus 35 nodes with 0 demand. Each edge or street link has a "to-from" and/or "from-to" cost of travel assigned to it, with selected edges being designated as one-way. In this test we sought 5 locations to service the demand using several different heuristics.

Figure 7-15A to Figure 7-15C show the results of running these procedures on the test dataset. In these figures the red circles identify the solution points (median locations) and the darker lines show the network edges that each center uses to service the demand. The figure in brackets in each case shows the

objective function value, *z*, achieved, in millions of units (sum of demand times cost of travel). The basic greedy-random heuristic used by S-Distance is that defined by Dyer and Frieze (1985). This simply involves selecting the highest weighted demand point (or any at random if there are multiple locations with equal weights). The next location is then chosen by selecting the demand point that has the largest weighted distance from its nearest center. The algorithm is of complexity $O(np)$ and yields results that are within 2-3 times the optimum (and so are not very good!). By contrast, the CLS procedure often produces very good results (within 1% generally) but requires longer to run, with a complexity of at least $O(np(n+1))$. CLS is essentially a form of alternating location-allocation (ALT) procedure, like that of Cooper described earlier. Initial solutions are then perturbed according to a greedy interchange rule that attempts to swap each ALT solution point in turn with another candidate site, and examines whether the resultant solution improves the ALT local optimum.

The *greedy* heuristics shown in Figure 7-15A and B ran in almost no processor time, with the greedy-add algorithm producing a much improved *z*-value. The five locations it chose, however, are very different from those in Figure 7-15C, which was the solution found by three other algorithms: candidate list search (CLS), Lagrangian relaxation (upper bound solution, LR), and variable neighborhood search (VNS). Of these VNS was fastest to run, requiring under a second of processor time, whilst CLS took around 3 seconds and LR over 3 minutes. However, the LR procedure provides both upper and lower bounds on the solution, which in this case showed that the lower bound was 1.177, but this solution is infeasible, so it is extremely likely that the solution shown is, in fact, the true optimum. The final image, Figure 7-15D, shows the allocation of customer demand to the individual centers. The size of the colored circles reflects the demand weights assigned to the network vertices.

*Figure 7-15 Comparison of heuristic p-median solutions, Tripolis, Greece*

| A. Greedy random (z=1.526) | B. Greedy add (z=1.190) |
| C. LR, VNS and Candidate list search (z=1.180) | D. Candidate list search, Demand allocation |

*Based on data provided by S Sirigos, Dept of Planning & Regional Development, U. of Thessaly, Greece*

Similar heuristics may be applied to the *p*-center problem. The total cost of servicing demand in this case will always be greater than or equal to that for the *p*-median solution, but the maximum distance (cost of travel) for customers travelling to or from service centers will be minimized. The diagram illustrated at the start of this Guide is the *p*-center solution equivalent to that shown in Figure 7-15D. As can be seen, the selected centers are more evenly spread across the City

as the algorithm seeks to avoid any very long links between customers and service centers. Particularly noticeable are the locations of the most easterly and south-westerly service centers in this solution. It is interesting to note in this case that this *p*-center solution is very similar to the *p*-median solution illustrated in Figure 7-15B.

These network-based *p*-median and *p*-center models can be compared with the discrete location planar equivalent, where demand is located at nodes as before, but facilities may be located anywhere in the plane and the objective function is for median location. In the example shown in Figure 7-16 the facilities located are approximately optimal with respect to demand using the Euclidean metric rather than network distance. The locations are similar to those identified by the $p$-center optimization process and significantly different from the best network-based $p$-median solutions.

*Figure 7-16 Facility location in Tripolis, Greece, planar model*

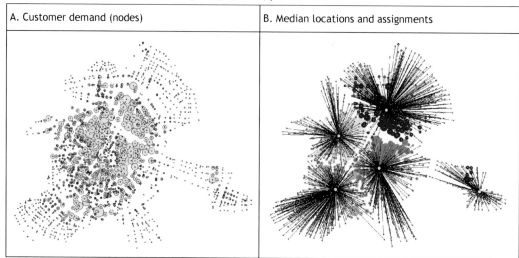

| A. Customer demand (nodes) | B. Median locations and assignments |
|---|---|

### 7.4.3 Service areas

The maps illustrating demand assignment in Figure 7-15D and Figure 7-16B provide examples of service area definition. Defining service areas or zones (often without regard to specific demand levels) is a widely supported facility within many GIS packages. These areas are typically discrete zones that are closer in distance, time or cost to specific points in the network than to any other specified point (rather like Voronoi regions in the plane — see also, Figure 4-35).

Note that the specification of service areas in this case is not the same as solving coverage problems. The latter does not assume that the locations or numbers of facility sites are known — these are outcomes of the modeling process. In the pure or set coverage problem the number of facilities must be increased until demand from all eligible customers is met within the given service parameters. This will often result in unacceptably high numbers of facilities, requiring some form of relaxation of the constraints to be of use in real-world situations. An example of such relaxation, known as the maximum coverage problem, is to pre-specify the number of facilities (or vehicles etc.) to service demand, and then seek to maximize the customer coverage within the service constraints. Relaxing the service constraints (e.g. allowing the time to reach a patient with an ambulance not to be an absolute maximum, but an average for example) leads to $p$-center and $p$-median type problem specifications.

An example of GIS-based service area functionality is provided in Figure 7-17A. This shows the locations of three ambulance stations situated in an urbanized region. In Figure 7-17B all streets closest in network distance to each station are assigned as the primary service area for each station. As noted above, this form of simple network partitioning assumes pre-defined facility locations and takes no account of variations in demand (e.g. expected accident or illness rates) or in supply (e.g. number of vehicles available). The example illustrated was generated using the TransCAD software, but similar facilities are provided in many other GIS packages, such as the v.net.alloc and v.net.iso functions in GRASS, the "service areas" facility in ArcGIS Network Analyst, AccessionGIS (a more advanced toolset, built using ArcGIS components, which incorporates multi-modal travel and timetables), the Voronoi function in SANET (see also, Figure 4-35) and the Allocation functionality provided in the TNTMips Network Analysis facility. The latter tool, for example, incorporates options to allocate service areas represented by network links based on flows to or from selected locations, with or without specifying from a range of parameters (such as demand levels, capacity constraints and travel impedance).

*Figure 7-17 Service area definition*

| A. Ambulance locations | B. Service areas (distance bands) |
| --- | --- |

### 7.4.3.1 Travel time zones

A related facility to service area definition, also provided in many GIS packages, is that of identifying travel time zones. These are typically generated as a polygon layer, overlaid on the network, indicating bands of travel times or distances. Figure 7-18 shows a set of bands that have been constructed around a point location on the Salt Lake City street network. These bands have been generated using distances in meters, with the edge of the band being the upper limit of the distance interval. Note that these zones include areas that have no roads, and the procedures for constructing such areas varies between packages, and may or may not allow zone construction procedures to be defined. Manifold implements three different options: (i) a convex hull; (ii) a buffer; and (iii) a zoning system, similar to the buffer operation, but in which off-road speeds (i.e. walking, off-road driving) are separately specified. Computation times can be very lengthy depending on the options selected and the complexity of the local network.

*Figure 7-18 Travel-time or drive-time zones*

Drive time zones — Bands: 500,1000,2000,5000 m

# 7.5 Arc Routing

The final topic in this chapter is known as Arc Routing. This is the term used to apply to a family of problems in which all links within a defined service area must be visited. It is thus a specialized routing problem.

Common variants of the problem include: those in which not all links need to be traversed; cases where some or all links are directed; cases in which links have variable traversal costs depending on direction; cases where the links and/or vehicles have capacity constraints; cases where demand varies along the links or between links; and hierarchical problems, in which one set of edges must be served before another. A thorough review and explanation of arc routing problems and their solution may be found in Moshe *et al.* (2000).

## 7.5.1 Network traversal problems

A simple example of an arc routing problem is the need to clear snow from all streets in a town in the most efficient manner. This problem and its solution are illustrated in Figure 7-19 and Figure 7-20A and B. On completion of the optimization process the operator may be issued with a route plan as a list in addition/as an alternative to a map, as shown in Figure 7-19. In this example, three depots have pre-assigned street areas to clear, as shown in Figure 7-20A. A solution plan is then shown in Figure 7-20B for one of the snow ploughs. The plan involves a systematic coverage of all streets, on both sides, with no streets being covered twice (if possible) and as few turns as possible, especially where these incur penalties. Minimizing coverage of streets that have been serviced already or have no demand for service is known as minimization of deadheading. Note that in this example U-turns are permitted, the solution involves no deadheading links (see Figure 7-19), and no explicit turn penalty has been specified. The solution illustrated was implemented using TransCAD — similar facilities are not provided in other GIS packages but are provided in a number of logistics software packages (see Table 7-4) and in add-ons to widely used GIS packages — for example, the eRouteLogistics and RouteSmart products built on the ESRI ArcGIS platform).

*Figure 7-19 Routing directions*

```
ROUTE ID 1        : depot/district 7310
Total Time        : 296.12
Deadhead Cost     : 0.00
# Deadhead Links  : 0 (out of 1090 links)
# Left Turns      : 328
# Right Turns     : 265
# U-Turns         : 215
# straight Turns  : 281
Turn Penalty Cost : 0.00
```

| No. | Movement | Street_Name | Service |
|-----|----------|-------------|---------|
| 1 | Start West on | W 3RD ST | Right |
| 2 | Left on | HUMPHREY AVE | Right |
| 3 | Left on | W 2ND ST | Right |
| 4 | U-turn on | W 2ND ST | Right |
| 5 | Right on | NEWMAN AVE | Right |
| 6 | Left on | W 4TH ST | Right |
| 7 | Left on | GARRETSON AVE | Right |
| 8 | U-turn on | GARRETSON AVE | Right |
| 9 | Left on | W 4TH ST | Right |
| 10 | U-turn on | W 4TH ST | Right |
| 11 | Left on | GARRETSON AVE | Right |
| 12 | Left on | W 5TH ST | Right |
| 13 | Left on | TRASK AVE | Right |

Another variant of this problem includes the so-called CARP or Capacitated Arc Routing Problem. This class of problems assumes that capacity constraints apply, for example the capacity of a rubbish collection or gritting vehicle, or the carrying capacity of a postman. Typically it is assumed that mean demand in constant across all routes, but clearly demand may vary depending on the type of routing service involved and neighborhood through which routes are sought (e.g. residential versus offices versus retail or a mix thereof). There may also be other considerations that are required for managing real-world arc-routing problems, such as: establishing route priorities (e.g. for clearance of main/emergency routes); multi-lane cleaning/clearing requirements; and flow issues (e.g. grit/salt spreading rate, collection/refill locations and rates). A range of exact and heuristic algorithms have been developed for the various classes of problem, often based on similar techniques to those used in solving the TSP. CARP, like the TSP, is known to be NP-complete. Yet another, closely related class of problem involves capacity constraints on the links, typically described as capacity constrained flow problems. Example applications include traffic planning, pipeline routing and some forms of telecommunications planning.

A formal statement of the uncapacitated arc routing problem is as follows: Let $E$ be a set of edges and $V$ a set of vertices for the graph $G(E,V)$ and denote by $(i,j)$ the edge from vertex $i$ to vertex $j$, with edge length $d_{ij}$. Then we have:

$$1: \min\left\{\sum_{(i,j)\in E} d_{ij}u_{ij}\right\}, \text{ subject to}$$

$$2: \sum_{(i,j)\in E} u_{ij} = \sum_{(j,i)\in E} u_{ji}$$

$$3: u_{ij} \geq 1 \ \forall(i,j)\in E$$

Here $u_{ij}$ denotes the number of times that link $(i,j)$ is used, with $u_{ij}=1$ when the problem is initialized, i.e. every edge must appear at least once in the solution. The objective function is simply minimization of overall tour length subject to constraints that ensure each edge is traversed at least once.

*Figure 7-20 Arc routing*

A. Snow plough depots and service areas

B. Arc routing plan — zone 7310

A solution to this problem can be obtained by a two-stage process:

Step 1: check to see if every vertex satisfies the necessary condition for an Eulerian circuit — i.e. do the number of inflows at every vertex equal the number of outflows. If the network is not directed this condition requires that the *degree* of every vertex is even. If the network satisfies this condition proceed to step 2. If not, then systematically add (directed) edges until the vertices do all satisfy the condition.

Step 2: Solve the ECP. This turns out to be a relatively straightforward task, although the resulting circuit is not necessarily unique. In fact there are $O(k^n)$ Eulerian circuits in any graph, where $n$ is the number of vertices and $k=K-1$, where $K$ is the minimum degree of vertices in $V$. A simple algorithm for solving the ECP is due to a little-known Frenchman called M. Fleury dating from 1885, although a perhaps better algorithm, due to Hierholzer (1873) is still widely used today. In Fleury's algorithm the term *bridge* refers to an edge that, if removed, would result in the graph becoming disconnected, i.e. forming two unconnected subgraphs. The steps are as follows (for a connected Eulerian graph):

- select any vertex as the starting point and any edge leaving that vertex, but only use a bridge if no other options are available (this requires determining whether a link is, in fact, a bridge). Add the chosen edge to the current set

- move the current vertex to the end of the chosen edge and delete this edge from the graph. If this results in the previous vertex becoming isolated (having no links) then delete the vertex also

- repeat the above steps until all edges have been deleted. The current set should now contain an Eulerian circuit

The capacitated version of this class of problems, CARP, can be solved in a similar manner. However, as it is known to be NP-hard much attention has been focused on finding good heuristics. Amongst the most effective of these is the so-called tabu search algorithm introduced by Hertz *et al.* (2000). Their procedure involves finding an initial feasible solution and seeking to improve on this by a process of systematic dropping and adding of edges. Computational tests show that this heuristic can solve medium sized problems (50 vertices, 100 edges) to within 1% of optimality in reasonable computation times, but that such times can be highly variable depending on the particular network configuration (variations of an order of magnitude in time for problems of similar size). Problems with much larger numbers of edges (e.g. detailed street networks) were also tested and solutions were obtained within 5% of the optimum on average within acceptable processing times.

# 8 Geocomputational methods and modeling[*]

This Chapter commences with an introduction to geocomputational methods and spatio-temporal model building (Section 8.1). For our purposes we consider geocomputational methods as being comprised of a family of recently devised tools that make use of computational power to address problems in spatial analysis that resist attack by alternative means. These are frequently problems in which the number of observations made or objects involved is very high, as with high resolution spatial datasets, crowd behavior and spatial data pertaining to multiple time periods.

Three principal approaches to tackling such problems are described in this Chapter, each of which owes its origins to the study of biological processes: first, in Section 8.2 we address simulation techniques that derive from models of *artificial life* and of insect and animal behavior; second, in Section 8.3 we describe a family of techniques for problem-solving that use computational models derived from the study of neurological processes; and finally, in Section 8.4 we examine problem-solving techniques based on biological reproduction and mutation processes. Sections 8.1 and 8.2 have been prepared using material researched and written by Christian Castle and Andrew Crooks of the Center for Advanced Spatial Analysis (CASA) at University College London, and subsequently updated by Andrew Crooks. Readers are also recommended to refer to the recent CASA paper by Crooks,

---

[*] The recommended citation of this chapter is: Castle C J E, Crooks A T, de Smith M J, Goodchild M F and Longley P A (2009) Geocomputational methods and modeling. Chapter 8 in de Smith M J, Goodchild M F and Longley P A (2009) Geospatial Analysis: A comprehensive guide to principles, techniques and software tools, 3rd ed., Troubador Publishing Ltd, Leicester, England

Castle and Batty (2007) which examines key challenges for Agent-based modeling.

## 8.1 Introduction to Geocomputation

### 8.1.1 Geocomputational methods

The term *geocomputation*, as defined by geocomputation.org, refers to "the art and science of solving complex spatial problems with computers". This definition captures the essence of the term geocomputation, but is too broad for the purposes of this Guide. It potentially embraces all manner of concepts, tools and techniques that form part of mainstream GIS and spatial analysis toolsets. Indeed, as individual geocomputational methods become accepted as providing effective solutions to specific spatial analysis problems, so they start to appear in more generic software with widespread usage. This is particularly apparent in some areas of remote sensing data analysis, visualization tools and in association with a number of statistical and optimization problems.

Micro-scale simulation of spatial phenomena is regarded by many as perhaps *the* archetypal geocomputational tool. Geosimulation (a term introduced by Benenson and Torrens, 2004) is discussed in Section 8.2, where cellular automata, agent-based models and the ever-expanding set of software tools to support such modeling are described. This is a very active and sometimes controversial area of geospatial modeling, which attracts much discussion amongst researchers. An important aspect of geosimulation has been the growing appreciation of its role in researching processes, particularly those involving emergent and unpredictable behaviors and outcomes, rather than always (or ever) having a strong predictive function. Section 8.2 also includes a wide-ranging discussion of the broader issues relating to spatio-temporal modeling.

Section 8.3 addresses the use of so-called *neural networks* to solve particular spatial problems, with applications ranging from image analysis to spatial interaction modeling and spatial optimization. An important area of geocomputational research relates to the problems of inferring land cover and land-use from remotely-sensed data, as well as the quest to better understand the dynamics of land-use change. A relatively recent development in this field has been the use of computational neural network (CNN) methods for both supervised and unsupervised multi-band image analysis. At one level the use of neural networks can be seen as yet another technique in the ever-expanding collection available in GIS packages such as TNTMips and Idrisi and mathematical packages such as MATLab. However, with neural network methods selection of the type of model to be used, its configuration and training, coupled with the very specific and computationally intensive procedure then adopted, separate this approach from many others available.

The final area of geocomputation we address is a class of procedures inspired by biological reproduction and 'survival of the fittest' (Section 8.4). The principal topic we cover is that of genetic algorithms (GAs) and their application to a wide range of problems in spatial analysis. Again, this is a developing field, which (for many applications) has yet to prove its superiority to alternative procedures, and is thus rarely implemented in GIS or other commercial spatial software applications. However, it does offer a novel family of methods for solving problems that have a complexity not readily addressed by other approaches. And, rather like geosimulation, the dynamics of the process can be visualized and examined, in order to obtain a clearer understanding of the underlying problem and data.

Readers of earlier chapters will have observed that many other geocomputational methods have already been described in connection with a variety of different spatial analysis problems. Examples include: the use of computationally intensive procedures to achieve desired zoning patterns (see Section 4.2.11); cluster-hunting software such as GAM/K (see Section 5.2.6); the widespread use of Monte Carlo and random permutation

techniques to generate pseudo-probability distributions and associated confidence intervals; the development of interactive data mining tools, such as the visualization techniques offered by brushing and linking (see Section 5.2); conditional choropleth mapping (see 5.2.3 and Figure 5-12); the processing of raster datasets using techniques such as distance transforms (see Section 4.4.2.2); surface analysis (see Section 6.2) and visibility analysis (see Section 6.3); and the application of heuristics and metaheuristics to combinatorial optimization problems (see Section 7.2.2). These procedures are not discussed further in this chapter and readers are referred to the individual sections of this Guide and the associated reference materials for more details in each case. The ground-breaking book "GeoComputation" edited by Openshaw and Abrahart (2000) is also a useful source discussing many of the topics covered in the subsections below.

## 8.1.2 Modeling dynamic processes within GIS

Geocomputation is a cutting edge research area within the field of GIS and geospatial analysis. For this reason it is strongly influenced by recent developments in programming, data processing and interface design. Nowhere is this more apparent than in the concern for modeling of dynamic process.

Current commercial and public domain GIS software systems all contain numerous tools for acquiring, pre-processing, and transforming data. Their use in modeling includes data management, format conversion, projection change, resampling, and raster-vector conversion. GIS also include excellent tools for visualization/mapping, rendering, querying, and analyzing model results, as well as assessing the accuracies and uncertainties associated with inputs and outputs.

Typically, all of the capabilities described above are accessible via end-user graphical and command line interfaces. However, these capabilities have recently become accessible through Application Programming Interfaces (APIs), via software libraries. The exposure of GIS APIs is a significant recent improvement, as external programmers now have access to the underlying software components or 'objects' upon which GIS software vendors base their systems. This is perhaps the most pertinent enhancement, as many of the techniques used in GIS analysis are more robust if they can be linked with an extensive toolkit of methods for simulation (see further, Section 8.1.2.2).

Recently in GIS there has also been a move to use industry-standard programming languages (e.g. Java, C++, and Visual Basic), and scripting languages (e.g. Python, VBScript, and Jscript) rather than proprietary, home grown scripting languages (e.g. ESRI's Arc Macro Language, AML, or Avenue). Interoperability standards such as the Microsoft .NET framework facilitate this process by allowing compliant packages to be called from the same script. In addition to scripts, graphical flowcharts can be used to express sequences of operations that define a model (see further, Section 3.4). One of the first graphic platforms for conceptualizing and implementing spatial models was the ERDAS software, which allows the user to build complex modeling sequences from primitive operations. ESRI's ArcGIS and Clark Labs' Idrisi are other examples of GIS products that allow models to be authored and executed in a graphical environment. In principle, graphic-model building can be used for dynamic modeling via an iterative process, where the output of one time-step becomes the input for the next. However, this method poses two problems:

- the GIS will not have been designed for an iterative process, requiring the user to re-enter the data at the beginning of each time step, and

- the time required to run a model can be considerable

The former of these problems can be overcome with scripting languages; both can potentially be overcome by integrating the GIS with a simulation/modeling (s/m) system better equipped for the task at hand. Before exploring the possibilities of linking GIS and s/m systems, the following subsection 8.1.2.1 evaluates the capability of GIS to handle space-time information, which computer simulations generate in volume.

### 8.1.2.1 Representing time and change within GIS

The subject of time within GIS has received a considerable amount of attention. Heywood *et al.* (2006) comment that, ideally, GIS would be able to represent temporal change using methods that explicitly represent spatial change, as well as different states through time. Furthermore, methods allowing direct manipulation and comparison of simulated or observational data in temporal and spatial dimensions should be catered for. In reality there are two main challenges restricting the integration of time within GIS:

1) continuous data over a period of time are rarely available for an entity or system of interest; and

2) data models and structures able to record, store, and visualize information about an object in different temporal states are still in their infancy

In the context of geocomputation the former challenge is less of a constraint since computer simulation is capable of generating an abundance of data over a continuous period of time, while much progress has been made on the latter issue. The following discussion outlines issues related to the representation of time and change, as well as approaches for incorporating space-time information within GIS. The basic objective of any temporal database is to record change over time, where change can be thought of as an event or collection of events. An event might be a change in state of one or more locations, entities, or both. Changes that might affect an event can be distinguished in terms of their temporal pattern. Peuquet (2005) has suggested four types:

- Continuous: events occurring throughout some period of time

- Majorative: events occurring most of the time

- Sporadic: events occurring some of the time, and

- Unique: events that only occur once

The distribution of events within these temporal patterns can also be very complex (e.g. chaotic, cyclic, or steady state). This is complicated further because change may occur at various rates as well (e.g. from sudden to gradual). Hence, duration and frequency are important descriptive characteristics within this taxonomy of temporal patterns.

There are three approaches for capturing space-time information within a GIS:

- location-based

- time-based, and

- entity-based

The only method of viewing a data model within existing GIS, as a space-time representation, is as a temporal series of spatially-registered 'snapshots'. Invariably this approach employs a raster data model with only a single information type stored (e.g. elevation, density, precipitation, etc.) for each cell at any one point in time. Information for the entire layer is stored for each time step, regardless of whether change has occurred since the previous step. There are several criticisms of this approach. Firstly, the data volume increases enormously, because redundant information is stored in consecutive snapshots. Secondly, the state of a spatial entity can only be retrieved by querying cells of adjacent snapshots, because information is stored implicitly between each time step. And finally, the exact point when change has occurred cannot be determined. Langran (1992) has proposed a modification of this approach. The temporal-raster (or grid) approach allows multiple values to be stored for each pixel. A new value, and the time at which change occurred for each pixel, is stored which can result in a variable number of records for each cell. Recording the time at which change has occurred allows for values to be sorted by time. The most recent value for each cell can therefore be retrieved, which represents the present state of the system.

The obvious advantage to this approach is the reduction of redundant data stored for each cell.

Peuquet and Duan (1995) have proposed a time-based approach to storing space-time information within a GIS, where change is stored as a sequence of events through time. Time is stored in increasing order from an initial point, with the temporal interval correlating to successive events. An event is recorded at the time when the amount of accumulated change is considered significant, or by another domain-specific rule. This type of representation has the advantage of facilitating time-based queries, and the addition of a new event is straightforward as it can simply be added to the end of the timeline. Furthermore, in terms of modeling an important feature of any model is its ability to represent alternative versions of the same reality. The concept of representing multiple realities over time is called *branching*. Branching allows various model simulation runs to be compared, or simulation results to be compared to observed data. The time-based approach facilitates the branching of time in order to represent alternative or parallel sequences of events resulting from specific scenarios, because it is a strictly ordinal representation.

Finally, several entity-based space-time models have been proposed. Conceptually these models extend the topological vector approach (e.g. coverage model), tracking changes in the geometry of entities incrementally through time. The amendment vector model was the first of this type, and extended frameworks have been proposed subsequently. Besides maintaining the integrity of entities and their changing topology, these approaches are able to represent asynchronous changes to entity geometries. However, the space-time topology of these vectors becomes increasingly complex as amendments accumulate through time. In addition, aspatial entity attributes can change over time. To record aspatial changes, a separate relational database is often used. However, if change occurs at a different rate between the spatial and aspatial aspects of an entity, maintaining the identity of individual entities becomes difficult, especially when entities split or merge.

Object-oriented data models have transformed the entity-based storage of space-time information within GIS and have become mainstream within commercial GIS (e.g. the geodatabase structure with ArcGIS). They have grown increasingly sophisticated, catering for a powerful modeling environment. The object-oriented data model provides a cohesive representation that allows the identity of objects, as well as complex interrelationships to be maintained through time. Specifically, temporal and location behavior can be assigned as an attribute of features rather than the space itself, which has the distinct advantage of allowing objects to be updated asynchronously.

Despite the advantages of the object-oriented data model, Reitsma and Albrecht (2006) observe that, to date, no data model or data structure allows the representation of processes (i.e. recording a process that has changed the state of an object within a model). Consequently, queries about where a process is occurring at an instant of time cannot be expressed with these current approaches. Notwithstanding, object-oriented data models are the canonical approach to the storage of space-time data generated by agent-based models and their visualization within GIS. Nevertheless, the visualization of agent-based models within GIS is still limited currently to a temporal series of snapshots.

### 8.1.2.2 Linkage/coupling versus integration/embedding

Models implemented as direct extensions of an underlying GIS, through either graphic model-building or scripts, generally make two assumptions: 1) all operations required by the model are available in the GIS (or in another system called by the model); and 2) the GIS provides sufficient performance to handle the execution of the model. In reality, a GIS will often fail to provide adequate performance, especially with very large datasets and a large number of iterations, because it has not been designed as a simulation/modeling (s/m) engine. This one-size-fits-all approach inherent in GIS is a limiting factor, and attention has therefore been focused on linking, either through coupling or integration/embedding GIS with s/m systems.

In situations where GIS and s/m systems already exist (e.g. as commercial products), or the cost of rebuilding the functionality of one system into another is too great, the systems can be coupled. Coupling can be broadly defined as the connection of two stand-alone systems by data transfer. Three types of coupling are distinguishable, although these are only a subset of the much larger fields of enterprise application integration (Linthicum, 2000) and software interoperability (Sondheim et al., 2005). The attributes of each approach from loose to tight/close are described below. Table 8-1 summarizes the competing objectives of the different coupling approaches.

**Loose Coupling**: A loose connection usually involves the asynchronous operation of functions within each system, with data exchanged between systems in the form of files. For example, the GIS might be used to prepare inputs, which are then passed to the s/m system, where after execution the results of the model are returned to the GIS for display and analysis. This approach requires the GIS and s/m system to understand the same data format; if no common format is available an additional piece of software will be required to convert formats in both directions. Occasionally, specific new programs must be developed to perform format modifications.

**Moderate Coupling**: Essentially this category encapsulates techniques between loose and tight/close coupling. For example, Westervelt (2002) advocates remote procedure calls (RPCs) and shared database access links between the GIS and s/m system, allowing indirect communication between the systems. Inevitably, this reduces the execution speed of the integrated system, and decreases the ability to simultaneously execute components belonging to the different software.

*Table 8-1 Agent-based modeling and GIS coupling*

| Objective and Explanation | Loose | Moderate | Close/Tight |
|---|---|---|---|
| **Integration Speed:** The programmer time involved in linking the programs | Fast | Medium | Slow |
| **Programmer Expertise:** Required level of software development expertise | Low | High | Medium |
| **Multiple Authorship Avoidance:** In some instances it might be necessary for the programmer to modify the original software product. Any alteration reduces the ownership responsibility. Major alterations could totally sever this link, resulting in limited or no support by the original author(s) | High | Medium | Low |
| **Execution Speed:** How rapidly does the integrated software execute? | Slow | Medium | Fast |
| **Simultaneous Execution:** Can components of the system run simultaneously and communicate with one another? Can the components operate on separate platforms? | Low | Low | High |
| **Debugging:** How difficult is it to locate execution errors in the linked system? | Easy | Moderate | Hard |

*adapted from Westervelt (2002) — grayed boxes are considered more desirable characteristics*

**Tight or Close Coupling:** This type of linkage is characterized by the simultaneous operation of systems allowing direct inter-system communication during the program execution. For example, standards such as Microsoft's COM and .NET frameworks allow a single script to invoke commands from both systems (Ungerer and Goodchild, 2002). A variant of this approach allows inter-system communication by different processes that may be run on one of more networked computers (i.e. distributed processing).

Coupling has often been the preferred approach for linking GIS and s/m systems. However, this has tended to result in very specialized and isolated solutions, which have prevented the standardization of linkage. An alternative to coupling is to embed or to integrate the required functionality of either the GIS or s/m system within the dominant system using its underlying programming language. The final system is either referred to as GIS-centric or modeling-centric depending on which system is dominant. In both instances, the GIS tools or modeling capabilities can be executed by calling functions from the dominant system, usually

through a Graphical User Interface (GUI). Compared to coupling, an embedded or integrated system is more likely to appear seamless to a user. However, in the past, integration has been based on existing closed and monolithic GIS and simulation systems, which pose a risk of designing systems which are also closed, monolithic, and therefore costly.

Interest in modeling-centric systems has increased considerably over recent years, predominately because of the development of s/m toolkits with scripting capabilities that do not require advanced computer programming skills (Gilbert and Bankes, 2002). Often the s/m toolkit can access GIS functions, such as data management and visualization capabilities, from a GIS software library. For example, the Repast toolkit exploits functions from GeoTools (a Java GIS software library) for importing and exporting data, Java Topology Suite (JTS) for data manipulation, and OpenMap for visualization. The toolkit itself maintains the agents and environment (i.e. their attributes), using identity relationships for communication between the different systems. Functions available from GIS software libraries reduce the development time of a model, and are likely to be more efficient because they have been developed over many years with attention to efficiency. Additionally, the use of standard GIS tools for spatial analysis improves functional transparency of a model, as it makes use of well known and understood algorithms. Alternatively, spatial data management and analysis functions can be developed within the modeling toolkit, although this strategy may impose substantial costs in terms of time: to program the model; to update spatial data; and to use spatial analysis functions within the model.

The GIS-centric approach is an attractive alternative, not least because the large user-base of some GIS expands the potential user-base for the final model. Analogous to the modeling-centric approach, GIS-centric integration can be carried out using software libraries of s/m functions accessed through the GIS interface. There are many examples of s/m systems integrated within commercial GIS, including: the Consequences Assessment Tool Set (CATS) system, designed for emergency response planning; the Hazard Prediction and Assessment Capability (HPAC) system, for predicting the effect of hazardous material releases into the atmosphere; and the NatureServe Vista system, for land-use and conservation planners.

Brown *et al.* (2005) have proposed an alternative approach which straddles both the GIS-centric and modeling-centric frameworks. Rather than providing functionality within one system, this middleware-based approach manages connections between systems, allowing a model to make use of the functionality available within the GIS or the s/m toolkit most appropriate for a given task. Thus, the middleware approach allows the s/m toolkit to handle the identity and relationship of, and between, agents and their environments. The GIS would then manage spatial features as well as temporal and topological relationships of the model. Essentially, the s/m toolkit handles what it is designed for (i.e. implementing the model), while the GIS can be used to run the model

and provide visualization of the output. An example of this approach is the ABM extension within ArcGIS (referred to as Agent Analyst), which allows users to create, edit, and run Repast (Python language variant, RepastPy) models from within ArcGIS.

Commenting on their experience in implementing the Agent Analyst software and dynamic modeling, ESRI scientists Johnston and Maguire (2007) found that a number of important software issues arose with this approach, confirming many of the observations we have made earlier:

- how to store and manage many outputs from simulations and scenarios

- how time is handled explicitly

- synchronizing input time series with different time intervals

- tools to analyze the simulation results

- metrics to compare and evaluate different scenarios

Current experience suggests that researchers interested in developing a geospatial model involving many interacting agents (possibly tens of thousands) with complex behaviors and interactions should consider either GIS-centric or modeling-centric integration rather than a middleware approach. A GIS is either integrated into an s/m toolkit, or vice versa; the definition of a middleware approach is essentially tight coupling (see above). At present, for many problems, commencing with a modeling-centric approach is likely to yield more effective results with fewer technical problems.

# 8.2 Geosimulation

## 8.2.1 Introduction to geosimulation

In this Section we commence with a brief description of the cell-based modeling paradigm (Section 8.2.2, below) known as cellular automata (CA), and then address the broader topic of agent-based modeling (ABM, Section 8.2.3 *et seq*) which now embraces many of the previously distinct class of CA models. Techniques of this kind have been described by some authors as *geosimulation*. As noted in Section 8.1, this is a general purpose term (introduced by Benenson and Torrens, 2004) used to describe the application of modern micro-level simulation tools to geospatial problems. Typically these problems have a well-defined (finite) spatial extent and have a dynamic context. Frequently a distinction is made between cell-based or zone-based spatial models and less formalized spatial models incorporating mobile 'agents'. In practice there are close similarities between the two types of model. Toolsets designed to support both frameworks are widely available. For example MASON (a multi-agent simulation library discussed further in Section 8.2.11) can represent continuous, discrete, or hexagonal 2D, 3D, or network data, and any combination of these.

Application-specific tools (such as those used for urban and highway traffic simulation, e.g. MATSim and TRANSIMS) are not described here, although they have been discussed briefly in Section 7.2.1.2. However, it is worth noting the planning support system UrbanSim, an open source land use modeling system written in Java which allows for the exploration of possible consequences of alternative transportation, land use and environmental policies. Various spatial datasets are used in the system such as environmental data (e.g. wetlands, slopes) and land parcel information. This information, along with employment and population data, is then used to explore future land use scenarios based on the actions and interactions of individual agents such as households and developers. For example,

households have housing preferences and value access to workplaces and shopping opportunities which influence where they want to locate. UrbanSim has been applied to several metropolitan areas in the United States including Salt Lake City, Utah. A general overview of UrbanSim can be found in Waddell *et al.* (2008) while a more technical detail can be found in Waddell *et al.* (2003).

## 8.2.2 Cellular automata (CA)

Cellular Automata (CA) are a specific type of a more general class of entities known as automata. Essentially, automata process information input to them from their surroundings, and their characteristics are altered according to rules that govern their reaction to those inputs. Typically CA are modeled as a 1-dimensional string of cells or a 2-dimensional rectangular lattice of cells. Cells are typically square, although other forms (e.g. hexagonal, irregular) are permitted.

John Conway was the first to popularize the study of 2D CA in the early 1970s, when he introduced a model called the *Game of Life*. The Game of Life has only two *states* for each cell (alive or dead, or 1 or 0) and three simple *state transition rules*: (i) **survival**: if a cell is 'alive' (i.e. its *state* is 'true' or '1', for instance) and it has two or three alive neighbors it remains alive; (ii) **reproduction**: if a cell is 'dead', but has three alive cells within its neighborhood its *state* becomes alive, and (iii) **loneliness** (less than 2 neighbors) or **overcrowding** (more than 3 neighbors): the cell dies. Despite these simple rules, the Game of Life can produce a range of complex behaviors from different initial conditions. A sample Game of Life simulation is shown in Figure 8-1, generated using NetLogo, authored by Wilensky (1998).

A more complex example, known as the 'Heatbugs' model, is illustrated in Figure 8-2. This example has also been generated using NetLogo (Wilensky, 2004; full details of the parameter settings are provided on the referenced website). In this simulation 'bugs' move around on a grid of square 'patches'.

### Figure 8-1 Game of Life Model

| A. 35% cell occupancy, randomly assigned | B. 10% cell density after simulation run; still evolving |
|---|---|

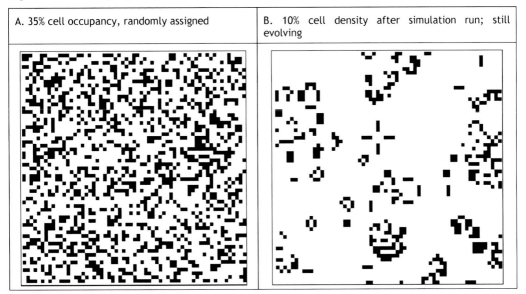

### Figure 8-2 Heatbugs Model

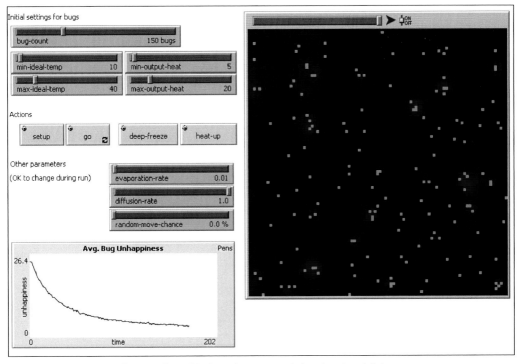

*Source (both the above figures): http://ccl.northwestern.edu/netlogo/models/*

The rules applied are: a bug may not move to a patch that already has another bug on it; each bug radiates a small amount of heat; heat gradually diffuses through the world; some heat is lost to cooling; each bug has an 'ideal' temperature it wants to be (a state of high 'happiness'); the bigger the difference between the temperature of the patch where the bug is and the bug's ideal temperature, the more 'unhappy' the bug is; when a bug is unhappy, it moves. If it is too hot, it moves to the coolest adjacent empty patch; conversely, if a bug is too cold, it moves to the warmest adjacent empty patch. Altering the model variables and parameters impacts the behavior of the 'bugs' to a greater or lesser degree, but in most instances as the simulation runs the unhappiness curve declines to a stable state. For some settings this is not the case, for example when the space is very over-crowded

Wolfram (1983) reinvigorated interest in the field when he published a paper discussing a typology of CA consisting of four classes. These classes are based on the dynamic behavior of CA and the patterns they generate, referred to as elementary cellular automata. These include, for the Game of Life example: (i) static patterns; (ii) oscillators (or periodic patterns); (iii) spaceships (patterns that repeat themselves but translated in space); and (iv) patterns that increase in population size (a range of different patterns and behaviors). A comprehensive list of patterns is included at Mark Niemiec's Game of Life web page. The unexpected complexity of the resulting behavior from the rules Wolfram identified, led him to believe that complexity in nature may be due to similar behavior.

Cellular automata, as applied in geospatial analysis, may be characterized by the following key attributes: *State variables*; *spatial framework*; *neighborhood structures*; *transition rules*; and *time*. Each is discussed briefly below.

*State variables*: these are a set of attributes for an automaton, where its 'state' describes the automaton at a particular point in time. State variables can consist of virtually any data type, but are commonly binary (e.g. 0 or 1,

blue or green, dead or alive, true or false, etc.). In many geospatial problems such limited states are too restrictive, and more complex states (including continuous variables) have been utilized. Examples might be land-use classifications, demographic taxonomies or surface attributes. Although the values of state variables typically alter as the simulation proceeds, some cell locations or attribute values may be regarded as immutable or immune to change after pre-defined transitions, and if changed to that state, remain fixed thereafter (Figure 8-1).

*Spatial framework*: CA models operate over a lattice of cells, which can be specified in any number of dimensions — typically 2D in the case of geospatial problems. A lattice can be designed using congruent cells (i.e. as a grid of cells), or any other regular shape (e.g. hexagons or triangles). However, irregular geometries such as Voronoi polygons and graphs can also be used. A lattice can be constrained to a certain size, although this size must be considered carefully as the transition rule of an automaton located adjacent to a boundary may affect the automaton's neighborhood. To resolve this issue, a lattice can be extended infinitely (within the specified dimension). However, a common alternative is to 'loop' a one-dimensional lattice back round to the initial cell, or 'wrap' a two-dimensional lattice around on both sides of the lattice so they no longer have an edge(s). Geometrically the latter option is equivalent to treating the lattice as a two-dimensional projection of a torus (a doughnut-shaped surface).

*Neighborhood structures* are localized areas around each automaton, from which inputs are obtained. Neighborhoods in CA are generally identical for each automaton. In rectangular grids these neighborhoods are commonly characterized as either 'Moore' (the cell in questions plus its eight surrounding cells), or 'von Neumann' (the cell in question and its four cardinal neighbors, or extensions of these as highlighted in Figure 8-3, adapted from Torrens, 2006) .

However, a number of variations on the CA formalism have been developed. For instance: CA combined with map algebra (Geo-Algebra; Takeyama and Couclelis, 1997); irregular or graph based cell networks (O'Sullivan, 2001 and 2002); partitions based on geographical phenomena (e.g. roads; Semboloni, 2000); or Voronoi tessellations (Shi and Pang, 2000). There is no practical reason, other than computational efficiency, to limit the shape or size of a neighborhood surrounding an automaton, although variations will obviously affect the behavior of the model. It is possible to generalize the notion of neighborhoods, to facilitate first-order, second-order (lagged) neighbors, alternative weightings, concepts of 'action at a distance' etc

*Figure 8-3 Moore and von Neumann neighborhoods*

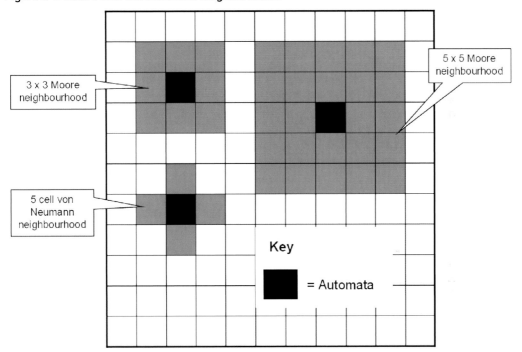

*Transition rules* determine how the state of an automaton changes over time. Automata use transition rules to determine their state, and evaluate the state of their neighbors at a particular point in time. The states of neighboring automata determine the state of each automaton in the next time step. This can remain the same or change. Traditionally, very simple deterministic transition rules were applied. More recently, models have been developed that experiment with much more complex rules, including probabilistic functions, maximization of utility, and the incorporation of complex constraints and inertia factors.

*Time* is considered as being comprised of discrete steps. Transition rules take effect at each step or increment of a discrete time interval. CA models are parallel or synchronous processors rather than serial or asynchronous processors. In parallel processing, all cells change state simultaneously at each time-step of the model clock. By contrast, in serial processing, the state of one cell has to be computed before another can begin.

In relation to modeling geographical processes, Tobler (1979) was one of the first to suggest using CA. This was followed by GIS research applying CA to a number of research questions

(Couclelis, 1985). More recently CA has been used to develop numerous models of geographical processes. A few examples include: studies of bushfires (Li and Magill, 2001); deforestation (Messina and Walsh, 2000); earthquakes (McGinnis, 2001); rainforest dynamics (Alonso and Sole, 2000); and urban systems (Candau, 2000; Torrens, 2000; Batty, 2005; Batty, 2007).

CA provides a very good medium for simulation, which has been reflected in the volume of their use. The popularity of using CA for modeling has increased considerably as the cost of computer power has decreased. Their adoption has been merited because CA provide many of the building blocks essential for modeling: *cells* serve as storage units, representing specific elements of the model system in discrete units; *lattices* serve as larger constructs of these units, where neighborhoods specify how these units network and relate to one another; *state variables* represent an infinite range of attributes for characterizing the systems conditions; and finally, *transition rules* represent processes or events that alter the system dynamically over time. Unfortunately, the inability of cells to move is a significant weakness of the CA framework. This is particularly important when trying to model mobile entities, for example pedestrians or vehicles. The inability of an automaton to move within a CA frame has catalyzed interest in Agent-Based Modeling (ABM), which is the focus of Section 8.2.3 *et seq*. While CA models can be developed with an ABM toolset, a toolset designed specifically for development of CA will have difficulty modeling the range of behaviors and dynamics necessary for ABM.

## 8.2.3 Agents and agent-based models

Although there are no fixed rules as to what constitutes an *agent*, they can usefully be defined in terms of their primary characteristics, discussed in subsection 8.2.3.2: *autonomy*; *heterogeneity*; *pro-active or reactive behavior*; *bounded rationality*; *communications capabilities*; *mobility*; and *learning capabilities*.

The term *agent-based modeling* (ABM) refers to the use of computational methods to investigate processes and problems viewed as dynamic systems of interacting *agents*. An example might be attempting to model crowd behavior in a football stadium using computational agents to represent individuals in the crowd. Agent-based models seek macro-level understanding based on micro-level processes, i.e. they involve bottom-up rather than top-down modeling. In many respects ABM and CA are very closely linked — indeed, as noted earlier, it is often possible to use ABM toolsets to model a variety of CA and in principle the reverse is possible, although this may be awkward to achieve.

The subsections that follow draw on the recent publications and research of a number of authors. Readers interested in more details should refer to these books and papers, and to the documentation associated with the toolkits that are now widely available. These publications include: Axelrod (2006); Axelrod and Tesfatsion (2006); Axtell (2000); Bonabeau (2002); Brown (2006); Casti (1997); Couclelis (2002); Crooks *et al.*(2008a); Epstein (1999); Epstein and Axtell (1996); Gilbert and Troitzsch (2005); Macal and North (2005); North and Macal (2007); O'Sullivan (2004); Parker *et al.* (2003); Parker (2005); Torrens (2004); Wooldridge and Jennings (1995); and Franklin and Graesser (1996).

### 8.2.3.1 Agent-based models

Agent-based models are comprised of multiple, interacting agents situated within a model or simulation environment (see subsection 8.2.3.2 for clarification of what may be considered as an agent). A relationship between agents is specified, linking agents to other agents and/or other entities within a system. Relationships may be specified in a variety of ways, from simply reactive (i.e. agents only perform actions when triggered to do so by some external stimulus, such as the actions of another agent), to goal-directed (i.e. seeking a particular goal). The behavior of agents can be scheduled to take place synchronously (i.e. every agent performs actions at each discrete time step), or asynchronously (i.e. agent actions are scheduled by the actions of other agents, and/or with reference to a clock).

Environments define the space in which agents operate, serving to support their interaction with the environment and other agents. Agents within an environment may be spatially explicit, meaning they have a location in geometrical space, although the agent itself may be static. For example, within a building evacuation model agents would be required to have a specific location for them to assess their exit strategy. Conversely, agents within an environment may be spatially implicit; meaning their location within the environment is irrelevant. For instance, a model of a computer network does not necessarily require each computer to know the physical location of other computers within the network.

In a modeling context, agent-based models can be used as experimental media for running and observing agent-based simulations. To this extent, they can be thought of as a miniature laboratory, where the attributes and behavior of agents, and the environment in which they are set, can be altered and the repercussions observed over the course of multiple simulation runs. Enabling the ability to simulate individual actions of many diverse agents and to measure the resulting system behavior and outcomes over time (e.g. changes in patterns of pedestrian emergency egress), means that agent-based models can be useful tools for studying processes that operate at multiple scales and organizational levels. In particular, the roots of ABM are within the simulation of social behavior and individual decision-making.

The acronym ABM will be used henceforth, but a caveat is required. There are various alternative terms (and their acronyms) applied in the literature to what, for all intent and purpose, is essentially ABM. Examples include: Agent-Based Computational Modeling, (ABCM), Agent-Based Social Simulation (ABSS), Agent Based Computation Simulation (ABCS), Agent-Based Modeling and Simulation (ABMS) and Individual-Based Modeling (IBM). Multi-Agent Systems (MAS) is another very popular term which is often, confusingly, used interchangeably to describe agent-based models. The field of MAS is a well established applied branch of Artificial Intelligence (AI), and although ABM has strong roots in the field of AI, agent-based models are not limited to the design and understanding of artificial agents. Impetus to develop MAS was spawned from problems encountered in the implementation of tasks on distributed computational units interacting with one another and with the external environment (Distributed Artificial Intelligence, DAI). The term MAS is more commonly applied outside the social sciences, for example, by computer scientists in relation to agent-oriented software development. Therefore, the MAS field can be characterized as the study of societies of artificial autonomous agents, while the ABM field can be typified as the study of artificial societies of autonomous agents. These two fields differ in more substantial ways than just their formalism (i.e. logic and AI based in the MAS domain, and mathematically based in the social science domain). However, this will not be considered here (see Conte et al., 1998 for a more detailed treatment).

More importantly, the term agent has connotations beyond ABM. For instance, agents found within agent-based models are different from mobile agent systems, which are light-weight software proxies that perform various functions for users and to some extent can behave autonomously. ABM is not the same as object-oriented simulation, although the object-oriented paradigm provides a suitable medium for the development of agent-based models. For this reason, ABM systems are invariably object-oriented.

### 8.2.3.2  Agents

There is no universal agreement on the precise definition of the term 'agent'. From a pragmatic modeling standpoint there are several features that are common to most agents:

**Autonomy:** Agents are autonomous units (i.e. operating without the influence of centralized control), capable of processing information and exchanging this information with other agents in order to make independent decisions. They are free to interact with other agents, at least over a limited range of situations, and this does not (necessarily) affect their autonomy. In this respect, agents are active rather than purely passive (see below).

**Heterogeneity:** The notion of mean-individuals is redundant; agents permit the development of autonomous individuals. Groups of agents can exist, but they are spawned from the bottom-up, as amalgamations of similar autonomous individuals.

**Active:** Agents are active because they exert independent influence in a simulation. The following active features can be identified:

> **Pro-active/goal-directed:** Agents are often deemed goal-directed, having goals to achieve (not necessarily objectives to maximize) with respect to their behaviors. For example, agents within a geographic space can be developed to find or follow a set of spatial paths to achieve a goal within a certain constraint (e.g. time), when exiting a building during an emergency.

> **Reactive/Perceptive:** Agents can be designed to have an awareness, or sense of their surroundings. Agents can also be supplied with prior knowledge, in effect a 'mental map' of their environment, thus providing them with an awareness of other entities, obstacles, or required destinations within their environment. Extending the example above, agents could therefore be provided with knowledge of building exit locations.

**Bounded Rationality:** The dominant form of modeling in the social sciences is based upon a rational-choice paradigm. Rational-choice models generally assume that agents are perfectly rational optimizers with unfettered access to information, foresight, and infinite analytical ability (Parker *et al.*, 2003). These agents are therefore capable of deductively solving complex mathematical optimization

problems in order to maximize their well-being, thereby balancing long-run and short-run payoffs in the face of uncertainty. While rational-choice models can have substantial explanatory power, some of their axiomatic foundations are contradicted by experimental evidence, leading prominent social scientists to question their empirical validity. However, agents can be configured with 'bounded' rationality (through their heterogeneity) to circumvent the potential limitations of these assumptions (e.g. agents can be provided with fettered access to information at the local level). In effect, the aforementioned 'perception' of agents can be constrained. Thus, rather than implementing a model containing agents with optimal solutions that can fully anticipate all future states of which they are part, agents make inductive, discrete, and adaptive choices that move them towards achieving goals. For instance, an agent may have knowledge of all building exit locations, but agents will be unaware if all exits are accessible (e.g. some may have become blocked through congestion).

**Interactive/Communicative:** Agents have the ability to communicate extensively. For example, agents can query other agents and/or the environment within a neighborhood, via neighborhoods of (potentially) varying size, searching for specific attributes, with the ability to disregard an input which does not match a desirable threshold.

**Mobility:** The mobility of agents is a particularly useful feature, not least for spatial simulations. Agents can roam the space in which they are situated within a model. Juxtaposed with the agent's ability to interact and their intelligence, this permits a vast range of potential uses.

**Adaptation/Learning:** Agents can also be designed to be adaptive, which can produce Complex Adaptive Systems (CAS; Holland, 1995). Agents can be designed to alter (limited to a given threshold if required) their states depending on their current states, permitting agents to adapt with a form of memory or learning, but not necessarily in the most efficient way possible. Agents can adapt at the individual level (e.g. learning alters the probability distribution of rules that compete for attention), or the population level (e.g. learning alters the frequency distribution of agents competing for reproduction).

## 8.2.4 Applications of agent-based models

Agent-based models have been developed for a diverse range of subject areas, such as: archaeological reconstruction of ancient civilizations (Axtell *et al.*, 2002; Gumerman *et al.*, 2003) ; understanding theories of political identity and stability (Lustick, 2002); understanding processes involving national identity and state formation (Cederman, 2001); biological models of infectious diseases (Eidelson and Lustick, 2004; Chen *et al.*, 2006); growth of bacterial colonies (Kreft *et al.*, 1998; Krzysztof *et al.*, 2005); single- (Emonet *et al.*, 2005) and multi-cellular level interaction and behavior (Athale and Deisboeck, 2006); alliance formation of nations during the Second World War (Axelrod and Bennett, 1993); modeling economic processes as dynamic systems of interacting agents (Agent-based Computational Economics, ACE, Tesfatsion, 2006a); company size and growth rate distributions (Axtell, 1999); size-frequency distributions for traffic jams (Nagel and Rasmussen, 1994); price variations within stock-market trading (Bak *et al.*, 1999); voting behaviors in elections (Kollman *et al.*, 1992); identifying and exploring behavior in battlefields (Ilachinski, 1997); spatial patterns of unemployment (Topa, 2001); trade networks (Epstein and Axtell, 1996); business coalitions over industry standards (Axelrod, 2006); and the analysis of social networks of terrorist groups (North *et al.*, 2004).

These examples can be construed as lying on a continuum, from minimalist academic models based upon ideal assumptions, to large scale commercial decision support systems based upon real-world data. Despite the advantages of ABM as a tool for simulation, it has not been widely adopted in geospatial research;

although there is no obvious reason why this is the case.

Thomas Schelling is credited with developing the first social agent-based model in which agents represent people, and agent interactions represent a socially relevant process. Schelling (1971, 1978, see Figure 8-4 and Figure 8-12) demonstrated that stark segregation patterns can emerge from migratory movements among two culturally distinct, but relatively tolerant, types of households. Each cell represents a household, of 'red' or 'black' type in this example. Gray indicates that the cell is unoccupied at present. The basic rule for the evolution of the grid is that households 'prefer' to live in locations where the neighbors (8-fold or 'Moore' neighborhood)  are of the same type. If a household is not 'happy' with its location, it may move elsewhere in the grid (to an unoccupied cell) or leave entirely. Even if the preference for having neighbors of the same type is quite modest (e.g. under 50%) Schelling found the process still resulted in strongly segregated groups, depending to some extent on the housing density. In the example illustrated the ratio of black to red households was set to 25% and the housing density was set to roughly 90% — with lower housing densities evolution of a stable pattern occurs very rapidly. For discussion of a more sophisticated version of this kind of model, see Batty (2007) and Crooks, Castle and Batty (2007).

ABM did not begin to feature prominently in the geographical literature until the mid-1990s, when Epstein and Axtell (1996) extended the notion of modeling people to growing entire artificial societies. The goal was to understand the emergence of patterns, trends, or other characteristics observable in society or geography. Epstein and Axtell's Sugarscape model demonstrated that agents could emerge with a variety of characteristics and behaviors suggestive of a rudimentary society (e.g. death, disease, trade, health, culture, conflict, war, etc.).

*Figure 8-4 Schelling segregation model*

| A. Initial state — random cell assignment | B. Stable evolved state |
|---|---|
|  | 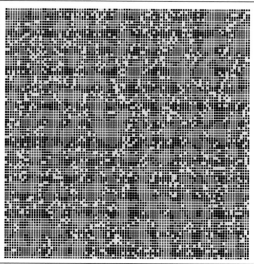 |

Epstein and Axtell describe Sugarscape as follows:

*"Sugarscape simulates the behavior of artificial people (agents) located on a landscape of a generalized resource (sugar). Agents are born onto the Sugarscape with a vision, a metabolism, a speed, and other genetic attributes. Their movement is governed by a simple local rule: 'look around as far as you can; find the spot with the most sugar; go there and eat the sugar.' Every time an agent moves, it burns sugar at an amount equal to its metabolic rate. Agents die if and when they burn up all their sugar. Agents are accumulating sugar at all times, so there is always a distribution of wealth."*

The Schelling and Sugarscape models are important early examples of ABM ideas set within a rather theoretical framework. A typical, current generation ABM model, is illustrated in Figure 8-5. This shows the a screenshot from a simulation of the movement of pedestrians (blue, red and green dots) within a subway (underground train station) hall area. This model, which may be run as a Java applet from the source site indicated or using the samples provided with the software distribution, incorporates:

- a realistic spatial framework

- multiple passengers arriving and departing

- multiple targets — ticket machines, ticket booths, platforms, shops, exits …

- free movement with obstacle avoidance

- selectable simulation speed

Models such as this provide valuable insights into spatial dynamics, in this case pedestrian behavior, which can clearly be applied in very many fields. They provide a medium where we can test ideas and hypothesis of phenomena which are not easy to do in the real world. One such example is pedestrian evacuation of a building during a fire. For example, without actually setting a building on fire we cannot easily identify people's reactions to such an event. ABM, as with simulations in general, allow for such experiments. We can recreate the building in an artificial world, populate it with artificial people, who have a set of behaviors, start a simulated fire and watch what happens. Such simulations allow the modeler to identify potential problems such as bottle necks and allows for the testing of numerous scenarios.

*Figure 8-5 Pedestrian movement simulation – Subway hall model*

This sample model is result of scientific and technical collaboration of XJ Technologies and ATN companies. The model is build on the top of AnyLogic® Pedestrian Library.

*Source: http://www.xjtek.com/anylogic/demo_models/*

Until recently the movement of agents has been dependent solely on the attributes of their immediate neighboring cells and their inhabitants, and their environments have not been based on real-world geographic features. Gimblett *et al.* (2002) were amongst the first to use real-world features. Their agent-based model was developed to evaluate the recreational use of Broken Arrow Canyon, Arizona. Specifically, current hiking, bike, and off-road trail paths were mapped in a GIS and potential alternatives simulated in order to aid management decisions of environmental protection and enhance recreational user experiences of the canyon. Dibble and Feldman (2004) have also extended the application of ABM to real-world environments by developing a three-dimensional extension to the Repast ABM toolkit. The extension has

enabled the authors to model the control of infectious disease transmission, dynamics of civil violence, and coordination of social networks within three-dimensional landscape terrains, and social and spatial networks. More recently researchers have been exploring the potential of agent-based models in virtual worlds such as in Second Life (e.g. Crooks *et al.*, 2008b) which provides opportunities for populating virtual worlds with spatial data and the creation of agent-based models which users can interact with.

The examples identified within this subsection demonstrate the vast array of subjects and disciplines that researchers have investigated through ABM. In particular, the use of ABM for experimenting and exploring with geographical phenomena is still in its infancy.

### 8.2.5 Advantages of agent-based models

Three principal advantages are claimed of agent-based over traditional top-down modeling techniques. The agent-based approach:

- captures emergent phenomena

- provides a natural environment for the study of certain systems, and

- is flexible, particularly in relation to the development of geospatial models

Emergence is a phenomenon, along with other surprising and unexpected behaviors unfamiliar to the classical sciences, such as self-organization, chaos, adaptation, etc., which are characteristic of complex systems. Neural networks (see further, Section 8.3) provide a well known example of complex structures that are capable of organized behavior as a result of the interaction of many interconnected neurons. More specifically, the study of phenomena characterized by interactions among many distinct components can be described as 'aggregate complexity'. Emergent phenomena are characterized by stable macroscopic patterns arising from local interaction of individual entities. By definition, emergent phenomena cannot be reduced to the system's parts; the whole is more than the sum of the parts. Thus, emergent phenomena can exhibit properties that are decoupled (i.e. logically independent) from the properties of the system's parts. For example, a traffic jam often forms in the opposing lane direction to a traffic accident; a consequence of 'rubber-necking'.

Studying the behavior of collections of entities focuses attention on relationships between entities. Characteristics of emergent phenomena make them difficult to understand and predict, particularly as emergent outcomes can be counterintuitive. In summary, the purpose of aggregate complexity is to arrive at understanding by reduction, and reassembly of a system of aggregate complexity, where the critical break with previous reductionist science is the attempt at reassembly. Aggregate complexity is of particular interest to spatial analysts because it implies that the local spatial configuration of interactions affects outcomes at the whole system level.

Since agent-based models describe the behavior and interactions of a system's constituent parts from the bottom up, they are the canonical approach for modeling emergent phenomena. Bonabeau (2002) has identified a (non-exhaustive) list of situations where agent-based models can be useful for capturing emergent behavior:

- **Complex interactions:** Interaction between agents is complicated, non-linear, discontinuous, or discrete (i.e. the behavior of an agent can be altered dramatically, even discontinuously, by other agents). This can be particularly useful if describing discontinuity of individual behavior is difficult, for example, using differential equations

- **Heterogeneous populations:** The ability to design a heterogeneous population of agents with an agent-based model is significant. Agents can represent any type of unit, from which intuitive collections of individual units can be formed, from the bottom up. Unlike agent-based models, aggregate differential equations tend to smooth out fluctuations. This is important because under certain conditions, fluctuations can be amplified: a system can be stable (approximately constant or exhibiting a linear trend) but susceptible to large perturbations. Heterogeneity also allows for the specification of agents with varying degrees of rationality (see above)

- **Topological complexity:** The topology of agent interactions is heterogeneous and complex. Aggregate flow equations usually assume global homogeneous mixing, but the topology of an interaction network can lead to significant deviations from predicted aggregate behavior. This is particularly poignant for social processes, because physical or social networks matter; and, when agents exhibit complex behavior, including learning and adaptation

- **Appropriate model framework**: In many cases ABM is a natural method for describing and simulating a system composed of real-world entities. The agent-based approach is more akin to reality than other modeling approaches, rendering ABM inherently suited to simulating people and objects in very realistic ways. For example, it is arguably easier to conceptualize and model how evacuees exit a building during an emergency, than to produce equations that govern the dynamics of evacuee densities. Nonetheless, because equations regarding evacuee density result from the behavior of evacuees, the agent-based approach will also enable the user to study aggregate properties. In particular, the agent-based approach can be useful when it is more natural to describe the constituent units of a system under some or all of the following conditions:

(i) The behavior of individuals cannot clearly be defined through aggregate transition rates (e.g. panic within a fleeing crowd)

(ii) Individual behavior is complex. Although hypothetically any process can be explained by an equation, the complexity of differential equations increases exponentially as the complexity of behavior increases. Describing complex individual behavior with equations can therefore become intractable

(iii) Agent behavior is stochastic. Points of randomness can be applied strategically within agent-based models, as opposed to arbitrarily within aggregate equations

- **Flexibility**: Finally, the agent-based approach to modeling is flexible, particularly in relation to geospatial modeling. Notably, spatial simulations benefit from the mobility that agent-based models offer. To reiterate, an agent-based model can be defined within any given system environment (e.g. a building, a city, a road network, a computer network,

etc.). Furthermore, agents have the ability to move within their environment, in different directions and at different velocities. Agent mobility makes ABM very flexible in terms of potential variables and parameters that can be specified. Neighborhoods can also be specified using a variety of mechanisms. The implementation of agent interactions can easily be governed by space, networks, or a combination of structures. This would be far more complex to model using mathematics, for example. Significantly, agent-based models can regulate behaviors based on interactions at a specific distance and direction. Agent-based models also provide a robust and flexible framework for tuning the complexity of agents (i.e. their behavior, degree of rationality, ability to learn and evolve, and rules of interaction). Another dimension of flexibility is the ability to adjust levels of description and aggregation. It is easy to experiment with aggregate agents, sub groups of agents, and single agents, with different levels of description coexisting within a model. Thus, the agent-based approach can be used when the appropriate level of description or complexity is unknown, and finding a suitable level requires exploration of scenarios

## 8.2.6 Limitations of agent-based models

The enthusiasm of adopting the ABM approach for geospatial modeling is curtailed by some important limitations. Although common to all modeling techniques, one issue relates to the purpose of the model; a model is only as useful as the purpose for which it was constructed. A model has to be built at the right level of description for every phenomenon, judiciously using the right amount of detail for the model to serve its purpose (Couclelis, 2002). This remains more of an art than a science (Axelrod, 2007). The nature of the system being modeled is another consideration. For example, a system based on human beings will involve agents with potentially irrational behavior, subjective choices, and complex psychology. These factors are difficult to quantify, calibrate, and sometimes justify. This complicates the implementation and development of a model, as well as the interpretation of the simulation output. However, the fundamental motivation for modeling arises from a lack of full access to data relating to a phenomenon of interest. Often, the target itself is neither well understood nor easy to access.

The development of agent-based models offers a means to increase the utility of simulation models, by closely tailoring the model and subsequent analysis to the needs of end users. In particular, the often visual communication provided by spatially explicit models (especially those coupled with GIS) can be effective at depicting formal model results to a wide range of users. Nevertheless, a model's output must be interpreted appropriately. Varying degrees of accuracy and completeness in the model inputs determine whether the output should be used purely for qualitative insight, or quantitative forecasting. Section 8.2.7 reviews the purpose of different ABM approaches in more detail.

By their very definition, agent-based models consider systems at a disaggregated level. This level of detail involves the description of potentially many agent attributes and behaviors, and their interaction with an environment. The only way to treat this type of problem in agent computing is through multiple runs, systematically varying initial conditions or parameters in order to assess the robustness of results. There is a practical upper limit to the size of the parameter space that can be checked for robustness, and this process can be extremely computationally intensive, thus time consuming. Although computing power is increasing rapidly, the high computational requirement of ABM remains a limitation when modeling large systems. Furthermore, agent-based models can be more difficult to analyze, understand and communicate than traditional analytical/ mathematical models (Grimm, 1999), as it is difficult to provide detailed descriptions of the inner workings of such models.

Finally, critics of complexity theory point out that the wide variety of surprising behavior exhibited by mathematical and computational models is rarely found in the real-world. In particular, agent-based models are very sensitive to initial conditions and to small variations in interaction rules. Consequently, modelers of complex systems are never likely to enjoy the intellectual comfort of laws. Despite this, and the other limitations that have been highlighted, ABM is a very useful tool for exploring systems that exhibit complex behavior. Complexity theory has brought awareness of the subtle, diverse, and interconnected facets common to many phenomena, and continues to contribute many powerful concepts, modeling approaches and techniques. In this vein, the following section explores the potential use of agent-based models.

### 8.2.7 Explanation or prediction?

Just as there are different types of models, each with their own characteristic features, advantages, and disadvantages, there are different ways that a model can be used. Consideration of these allows a clearer understanding of what distinguishes a good or bad model. The following discussion separates the utility of ABM into two broad categories: *explanatory* (which are often *exploratory* in nature) and *predictive* (also referred to as *prognostic* or *descriptive*). Readers are also recommended to refer back to the discussion in Section 3.3 on alternative approaches to problem-solving (the PPDAC methodology), in particular the Planning stage of the process.

The *explanatory modeling approach* strives to explore theory and generate hypotheses. The primary purpose is not to predict the future behavior of a system, but rather to provide a framework in which past observations can be understood as part of an overall process. Explanatory models generally focus on a specific aspect of a system, placing emphasis on some details of a phenomenon and ignoring others, in the hope that such laboratory explorations will lead to empirically relevant insights. These models purport to be explanatory by stating how reality should be under ideal circumstances, but they do not attempt to reproduce actual systems. The potential drawback of this approach is the lack of analytical methods to empirically evaluate ABM results (see further, Section 8.2.12). Furthermore, although explanatory models can provide considerable insights into theory, it is difficult to establish whether the final model is informative about specific real-world systems and scenarios.

The purpose of an agent-based model adopting an *explanatory approach* could be to program plausible agent behaviors and interactions that, when run as a simulation, produce similar trends and patterns to those observable through the analysis of real-world systems. A model of this nature would produce a 'candidate explanation' for the emergence of observed patterns (see Epstein, 1999 for a detailed overview of candidate explanations). The main challenge for such an application, after ensuring agent behaviors and interactions are plausible, is to develop and test alternative models to identify the range of agent representations that might produce given macro-representations.

The *predictive modeling approach* follows a fundamentally different logic to the explanatory approach. Predictive models are commonly used for extrapolation of trends, evaluation of scenarios, and the prediction of future states. More specifically, changes in initial conditions (e.g. rules governing agent behaviors and interactions, such as information available to agents, constraints upon or incentives for particular agent behavior or movement, etc.), can be used to evaluate the possible effects on the model outcome. Predictive models are designed to mimic real-world systems, and are particularly useful for scenario development and policy decisions. Parker *et al.* (2003) identify some of the key benefits of predictive modeling: in particular the authors note that by modeling at a fine scale of granularity agent-based models make very good statistical use of data at a fine resolution; in addition, because agent-based models are not constructed to meet a set of equilibrium criteria, it is possible for the model to simulate discontinuous and non-linear phenomena; and finally, by accounting

for heterogeneity and inter-dependencies, models can reflect important endogenous feedbacks between processes. However, this leads the discussion to some limitations of predictive models. Any model with positive feedback can create system behavior referred to as path dependence; where a path to a process can be very sensitive to both initial conditions and small variations in stochastic processes. For this reason, predictive modeling of a system containing positive feedbacks can be very challenging. Also, predictive models can be parameterized with too many real-world data. This can lead to an overly-fitted model (i.e. where the model's calibration is overly constrained to existing data). It may be problematic to generalize such predictive models to a large range of potential outcomes related to the system under analysis, or to analyze alternative systems.

The choice between adopting an explanatory or predictive approach to modeling is not mutually exclusive. This choice depends, in part, on the required precision of the model, which in turn is directly related to the type of information and knowledge that is required. The purpose of a model, including an agent-based model, is not necessarily to capture faithfully all aspects of a system; and this complicates this decision process further. At a fundamental level, an agent-based model can be used solely to enrich understanding of a process that is present within a system through controlled computational experimentation.

The aforementioned decision regarding the model's purpose is made harder because agent-based models do not fit easily into the classic deductive/inductive approaches to modeling. Scientists use deduction to derive theorems from assumptions, and induction to find patterns in empirical data. An agent-based modeler might use a deductive approach to develop a set of assumptions regarding the behavior and interaction of agents from a body of literature. However, in contrast to classic deduction, the simulated output of agent-based models cannot be used to prove theorems. Thus, a modeler might generate data from several different simulation runs and analyze these results with inductive methods, similar to those employed for analysis of empirical data. However, unlike the conventional process of inductive generalization, the simulated data comes from a rigorously specified set of rules rather than direct measurement of the real-world. The inability to implement ABM in either a purely deductive or inductive manner has led many authors to argue that simulation in general, and ABM in particular, presents a third way of doing science.

## 8.2.8 Developing an agent-based model

The process of building an agent-based model begins with a conceptual model, where basic questions or goals, elements of the system (e.g. agent attributes, rules of agent interaction and behavior, the model environment, etc.) and the measurable outcomes of interest are identified. It is important to 'ground' a model during the conceptualization process (i.e. establish whether simplifications made during the design process do not seriously detract from the credibility and likelihood that the model will provide important insights; Carley, 1996). It is usual for a modeler to set forth a claim as to why the proposed model is reasonable. This claim will be enhanced if the applicability of the model is not over stated, and by defining the model's limitations and scope. Grounding can be reinforced by demonstrating that other researchers have made similar or identical assumptions in their models, and by justifying how a proposed model will be of benefit in relation to pre-existing models.

Conceptualizing the fundamental aspects of an agent-based model (i.e. one or more agents interacting within an environment), juxtaposed with the distinction between explanatory versus predictive purposes of a model suggests a fourfold typology of agent and environment types (Table 8-2). Couclelis (2001) classifies agents and their environments as either being designed (i.e. explanatory) or analyzed (i.e. predictive — empirically grounded). If designed, agents are endowed with attributes and behaviors that represent (often simplified) conditions for testing specific hypotheses about general cases. Analyzed agents are intended to mimic real-world entities based on empirical data or on *ad hoc* values and assumptions that are realistic substitutes for observed processes. Similarly, the environment that agents are situated within can be designed (i.e. provided with characteristics that are simplified to focus on specific agent attributes), or analyzed (i.e. represent a real-world location).

The boundary between designed and analyzed is not always distinct, especially when *ad hoc* data are employed. Subtle but profound differences, both practical and conceptual, exist between the design or analysis approach of developing agents and their environment. A major difference in practical terms is that designing something provides direct (partial or total) control over the outcome, whereas there can only be hope that something has been analyzed 'correctly'.

Table 8-2 summaries key issues to consider when developing agents and their environment. These include: a brief description of the model; the purpose and intent of the model; verification and validation strategies used to assess the model outputs; and appropriate software for the development of a model. Once a model has been conceptualized, it must then be formalized into a specification, which can be developed into a computer program if the model is required to be run as a computer simulation. The process of formalization involves being precise about what an identified theory relating to a phenomena of interest means, and making sure that it is complete and coherent.

*Table 8-2 Agents and environments*

| | | AGENT | |
|---|---|---|---|
| | | **Designed** | **Analyzed** |
| **ENVIRONMENT** | **Designed** | **Model Description**: Abstract<br>**Purpose/Intent**: Discovery of new relationships; Existence proof<br>**Verification & Validation Strategy**: Theoretical comparison; Replication<br>**Appropriate Development Tools**: Easy to implement simulation/modeling system | **Model Description**: Experimental<br>**Purpose/Intent**: Role-playing games among stakeholders; Laboratory experiments<br>**Verification & Validation Strategy**: Repetitions; Adequacy of design<br>**Appropriate Development Tools**: Flexible simulation/modeling systems with well developed user interfaces |
| | **Analyzed** | **Model Description**: Historical<br>**Purpose/Intent**: Explanation<br>**Verification & Validation Strategy**: Qualitative: goodness of fit<br>**Appropriate Development Tools**: Advanced simulation/modeling systems linked with GIS | **Model Description**: Empirical<br>**Purpose/Intent**: Explanation; Projection; Scenario analysis<br>**Verification & Validation Strategy**: Quantitative: goodness of fit<br>**Appropriate Development Tools**: Low-level programming languages |

*adapted from Berger and Parker (2001)*

There are several reasons why computer simulation is considered more appropriate for formalizing social science theories than mathematics (which has often been used in the social sciences). First, programming languages are more expressive and less abstract than most mathematical techniques. Second, a computer simulation can deal more easily with parallel process and processes without well-defined order or actions than systems of mathematical equations. Third, a computer model can include heterogeneous agents (e.g. pedestrians with varying degrees of knowledge about a building layout), while this is usually difficult using mathematics. Finally, computer programs are (or can easily be made to be) modular, so that major changes can be made to one part of the model without requiring large changes in other parts of the program, an ability which mathematical systems often lack.

The object-oriented paradigm provides a very suitable medium for the development of agent-based models. In particular, it provides the aforementioned modularity useful for developing a computer simulation.

At the time of writing, there are many s/m systems available to assist the development stage of ABM. The majority of these s/m systems are programmed, and/or require the user to develop their model in an object-oriented language. In Section 8.2.9 we identify some of the s/m systems available for ABM, highlighting key questions that should be considered for a user to determine appropriate systems for their needs.

### 8.2.9 Types of simulation/modeling (s/m) systems for agent-based modeling

In general, two types of simulation/modeling (s/m) systems are available for the development of agent-based models: toolkits or software. Of course, an agent-based model can be programmed completely from scratch using a low-level programming language if a modeler has sufficient programming knowledge and experience (see below for disadvantages of this approach). Based on this dichotomy, toolkits are s/m systems that provide a conceptual framework for organizing and designing agent-based models. They provide appropriate libraries of software functionality that include pre-defined routines/functions specifically designed for ABM. However, the object-oriented paradigm allows the integration of additional functionality from libraries not provided by the s/m toolkit, extending the capabilities of these toolkits. Of particular interest here is the integration of functionality from GIS software libraries (e.g. OpenMap, GeoTools, ESRI's ArcGIS, etc.), which provide ABM toolkits with the greater data management and spatial analytical capabilities required for geospatial modeling.

The development of agent-based models can be greatly facilitated by the utilization of s/m toolkits. They provide reliable templates for the conceptualization, design, implementation and visualization of agent-based models, allowing modelers to focus on research (i.e. building models), rather than building the fundamental tools necessary to run a computer simulation. In particular, the use of toolkits can reduce the burden that modelers face programming parts of a simulation that are not content-specific, e.g. a Graphical User Interface (GUI), data import-export, and visualization/display of the model. It also increases the reliability and efficiency of the model, because complex parts have been created and optimized by professional developers, as standardized s/m functions.

Unsurprisingly, there are limitations of using s/m systems to develop agent-based models. For example: a substantial amount of effort is required to understand how to design and implement a model in some toolkits; the programming code of demonstration models or models produced by other researchers can be difficult to understand or apply to another purpose; a modeler will have to learn or already have an understanding of the programming language required to use the toolkit; and finally the desired/required functionality may not be present, although additional tools might be available from the user community or from other software libraries. Benenson et al. (2005) also note that toolkit use is accompanied by the fear of discovering that a particular function cannot be applied, will conflict, or is incompatible

with another part of the model late in the development process.

Probably the earliest and most prominent toolkit was SWARM, although many other toolkits now exist. At the time of writing there are more than one hundred toolkits available for ABM (see AgentLink; SwarmWiki; Multiagent Systems; and Tesfatsion for comprehensive listings). However, toolkits can vary widely with respect to: purpose, in that some toolkits have different design objectives e.g. an AI rather than social science focus, or network opposed to raster or vector model environments; level of development, in that support for models may not be ongoing and/or development may have ceased; and modeling capabilities, with respect to the number of agents that can be modeled, or the degree of interaction that is possible between them. A review of all toolkits currently available is beyond the scope of this Section. However, below (Section 8.2.11) we discuss a selection of noteworthy s/m toolkits highlighting their purpose and capabilities, together with resources providing further information.

In addition to toolkits, software is available for developing agent-based models, which can simplify the implementation process. For example, s/m software often negates the need to develop an agent-based model via a low-level programming language (e.g. Java, C++, Visual Basic, etc.). In particular, software for ABM is useful for the rapid development of basic or prototype models. However, modelers using software are restricted to the design framework advocated by the software. For instance, some ABM software will only provide limited environments (e.g. raster only) in which to model, or agent neighborhoods might be restricted in size (e.g. von Neumann or Moore). Furthermore, a modeler will be constrained to the functionality provided by the software (unlike ABM toolkits, modelers will be unable to extend or integrate additional tools) especially if the toolkit is written in its own programming language (e.g. NetLogo). Section 8.2.10 provides guidelines for choosing s/m software, whilst Section 8.2.11 identifies a selection of noteworthy software for the development of agent-based models including StarLogo, its derivative NetLogo, and AgentSheets.

## 8.2.10 Guidelines for choosing a simulation/modeling (s/m) system

Ideally, a modeler would have comprehensive practical experience in a range of modeling/simulation (s/m) systems before choosing which system to use for a specific task. Unfortunately, this is not usually feasible. For this reason several authors (Najlis et al., 2001; Serenko and Detlor, 2002; Tobias and Hofmann, 2004; Rixon et al., 2005; Roberson, 2005; Dugdale, 2006) have surveyed a number of systems, identifying key criteria that should be considered before making a decision.

General criteria include, but are not limited to:

- ease of developing the model/using the system

- size of the community using the system

- availability of help or support (most probably from the user community)

- size of the community familiar with the programming language in which the system is implemented (if a programming language is necessary to implement the model)

- is the system still maintained and/or updated?

- availability of demonstration or template models

- availability of technical details and 'how-to' documentation, etc.

Criteria relating specifically to a system's modeling functionality include:

- number of agents that can be modeled

- degree of interaction between agents

- ability to represent multiple organizational/hierarchical levels of agents

- variety of model environments available (network, raster, and vector); possible topological relationship between agents

- management of spatial relationships between agents, and agents with their environment

- mechanisms for scheduling and sequencing events, etc.

These criteria will be weighted differently depending on a modeler's personal preferences and abilities (e.g. the specification of the model to be developed, programming experience/knowledge, etc.)

Another important distinction separating s/m systems is their licensing policy: viz. whether they are open source, shareware/freeware, or proprietary. Open source s/m systems constitute toolkits or software whose source code is published and made available to the public, enabling anyone to copy, modify and redistribute the system without paying royalties or fees. A key advantage of open source s/m systems relates to the transparency of their inner workings. The user can explore the source code, permitting the modification, extension and correction of the system if necessary. This is particularly useful for verifying a model (see Section 8.2.12). The predominant open source s/m systems are toolkits (e.g. MASON, Repast, SWARM, etc.).

The distinction between an open source s/m system and a shareware/freeware system is subtle. There is no single accepted definition of the term shareware/freeware, but the expression is commonly used to describe a system that can be redistributed but not modified, primarily because the source code is unavailable. Consequently, shareware/freeware systems (e.g. StarLogo, NetLogo, OBEUS, etc.) do not have the same flexibility, extendibility or potential for verification (access to their source code), as open source systems. Similarly, shareware/freeware systems tend to be toolkits, rather than software packages.

Finally, proprietary s/m systems are available for developing agent-based models.

Proprietary systems are mainly software, developed by an organization who exercises control over its distribution and use; most require a license at a financial cost to the user. These systems have the advantage of being professionally designed and built for a specific use, and are often relatively simple to use. However, they often lack the community support found with open source or shareware/freeware systems. Moreover, since access to their source code is prohibited, a model developed with proprietary software is essentially black box. A modeler may therefore be left unsure about the inner validity of a model constructed with a proprietary system. This situation is compounded when the output of a model is emergent or unexpected.

Striking a balance between the aforementioned criteria is difficult. Unfortunately, while identifying a suitable system for the development of an agent-based model, too much time can often be expended trying to find this balance. This can be perceived as a trade off between the difficulty of developing a model (e.g. in terms of time required to program the model, understand how to develop a model with a specific system, or acquiring experience and knowledge of a programming language if required, etc.), versus the modeling power provided by the s/m system (e.g. modeling capabilities and functionality, as highlighted in Figure 8-6).

*Figure 8-6 Model development balance*

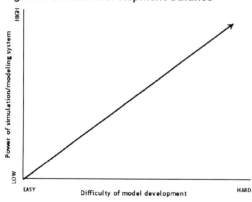

The key is striking a 'personal' balance between these criteria. For example, those more accustomed to programming may prefer the functionality and flexibility of an s/m toolkit. However, modelers who only wish to develop a basic or prototype model quickly and easily, possibly with little or no programming skills, may prefer to use packaged s/m software.

## 8.2.11 Simulation/modeling (s/m) systems for agent-based modeling

Although there are many systems available for developing agent-based models, we have selected eight for review, separated into three categories of licensing policy:

- open source (SWARM, MASON and Repast)

- shareware/freeware (StarLogo, NetLogo and OBEUS), and

- proprietary systems (AgentSheets and AnyLogic).

These systems were chosen because they largely or wholly fulfilled the criteria that they are: maintained and still being developed; widely used and supported by a strong user community; accompanied by a variety of demonstration models and in some instances the model's programming script or source code is available; and finally they are capable of developing spatially explicit models, possibly via the integration of GIS functionality.

Table 8-3, Table 8-4 and Table 8-5 summarize information relating to each system for comparison purposes, categorized by their licensing policy. These tables have been adapted from the work of Najlis *et al.* (2001) and Parker (2001). The remainder of this subsection provides further information about each system, identifying examples of geospatial models that have been developed with the system. A caveat must be noted at this point — the information provided within this subsection aims to be accurate and up-to-date. However, the systems reviewed are constantly being updated, thus modelers are advised to check each system's website to obtain the latest information.

*Table 8-3 Comparison of open source simulation/modeling toolkits*

| | SWARM | MASON | Repast |
|---|---|---|---|
| Developers | Santa Fe Institute/SWARM Development Group, USA | Center for Social Complexity, George Mason University, USA | University of Chicago, Department of Social Science Research Computing, USA |
| Date of Inception | 1996 | 2003 | 2000 |
| Website | http://www.swarm.org | http://cs.gmu.edu/~eclab/projects/mason | http://repast.sourceforge.net |
| Language | Objective-C/Java | Java | Java/Python/Microsoft.Net |
| Operating System | Windows, UNIX, Linux, Mac OSX | Windows, UNIX, Linux, Mac OSX | Windows, UNIX, Linux, Mac OSX |
| Required programming experience | Strong | Strong | Strong |
| Integrated GIS functionality | Yes (e.g. Kenge GIS library for Raster data: http://www.gis.usu.edu/swarm) | None | Yes (e.g. OpenMap, Java Topology Suite, and GeoTools). Repast simulations can also be run within ArcGIS through an extension called Agent Analyst (see below). |
| Integrated charting/graphing/ statistics | Yes (e.g. R and S-plus statistical packages) | None | Yes (e.g. Colt statistical package, and basic Repast functionality for simple network statistics). In RepastS there are automated connections to R and VisAD |
| Availability of demonstration models | Yes | Yes | Yes |
| Source code of demonstration models | Yes | Yes | Yes |
| Tutorials/'how-to' Documentation | Yes | Yes | Yes |
| Additional information | Minar *et al.* (1996)<br><br>Contributed user example models: http://www.swarm.org/index.php/Swarm:_contributed_code | Luke *et al.* (2004) | Agent Analyst Extension: www.institute.redlands.edu/agentanalyst<br>Useful weblogs: www.gisagents.blogspot.com/<br>http://crimesim.blogspot.com/ |

Table 8-3 summarizes information for three selected open source toolkits, SWARM, MASON and Repast. Each is described below:

SWARM: Designed specifically for the development of multi-agent simulations of complex adaptive systems (although agent-based models can easily be developed using SWARM as well). Inspired by research into artificial life, SWARM was designed to study biological systems, and attempts to replicate mechanisms observable in biological phenomena. In addition to modeling biological systems, SWARM has been used to develop models for anthropological, computer science, ecological, economic, geographical, and political science purposes. Examples of spatially explicit models include: the simulation of pedestrians in the urban centers (Schelhorn et al., 1999 and Haklay et al., 2001); and the examination of crowd congestion at London's Notting Hill carnival (Batty et al., 2003) highlighted in Figure 8-7. Najlis et al. (2001) identify the difficulty of learning to use SWARM as a significant factor to consider before choosing this system to develop an agent-based model, although this should be less of a problem for a modeler with strong programming skills.

*Figure 8-7 Geometric and Locational Features of the Notting Hill Carnival Swarm model*

○ entry point
□ sound system
▲ tube station (open)
△ tube station (closed)
— parade route

*Source: Batty et al. (2003)*

MASON: Multi Agent Simulation Of Neighborhood, was developed by the Evolutionary Computation Laboratory (ECLab) and the Center for Social Complexity at George Mason University. At present MASON does not provide functionality for dynamically charting model output (e.g. histograms, line graphs, pie charts, etc.) during a simulation, or allow GIS data to be imported/exported (Luke et al., 2004). However, the developers of MASON are continuing to develop further functionality, and they hope users will develop and contribute tools themselves (e.g. GIS integration). Unfortunately there is little technical documentation and a relatively small user group in comparison to some of the other systems identified within this Guide. However, 'how-to' documentation, demonstration models (e.g. simple network models; the seminal 'heatbugs' example implemented in many toolkits, see Figure 8-2), and several publications detailing the implementation and/or application of MASON are available for a prospective modeler to evaluate the system further.

Repast: Originally developed at the University of Chicago, the Recursive Porous Agent Simulation Toolkit (Repast) is currently maintained by Argonne National Laboratory and managed by the Repast Organization for Architecture and Development (ROAD: http://repast.sourceforge.net). Repast caters for the implementation of models in three programming languages: Python (RepastPy); Java (RepastJ and Repast Simphony); and Microsoft.Net (Repast.Net). RepastPy allows basic models to be developed by modelers with limited programming experience via a 'point-and-click' GUI (Collier and North, 2005). RepastPy models can subsequently be exported/ converted into Java for further development in RepastJ. Repast.Net and RepastJ allow for more advanced models to be developed, because more complex functionality can be programmed into a model. RepastPy and RepastJ are the only two open source s/m toolkits that allow the development of both raster and vector agent-based models.

Whilst still being maintained, RepastJ, Repast.NET and RepastPy have now reached maturity and are no longer being developed. They have been superseded by Repast Simphony (RepastS) which provides all the core functionality of RepastJ or Repast.NET, although limited to implementation in Java. RepastS was initially released in late 2006 and now provides the same GIS functionality of previous versions. The main improvements with RepastS over Repast 3.0 is a new optional GUI point-and-click environment for model development that generates Java classes as highlighted in Figure 8-8A; however, models can still be coded manually. Secondly an improved runtime GUI: the GUI can now be used to build displays (both in 2 and 3D); charts; output data; interrogate agents; and interface with other programs (like R for statistics or Weka for *data mining*) via a point-and-click interface at run time. This means that these tasks are done more quickly after the model has been built and compiled, and do

not feature in the underlying code at all, unlike previous Repast implementations.

The Repast development team have provided a series of articles regarding RepastS. The architecture and core functionality are introduced by North *et al.* (2005a), and the development environment is discussed by Howe *et al.* (2006). The storage, display and behavior/interaction of agents, as well as features for data analysis and presentation of models within RepastS are outlined by North *et al.* (2005b). Tatara *et al.* (2006) provide a detailed discussion outlining how to develop a "simple wolf-sheep predation" model which illustrates RepastS modeling capabilities, specifically its ability to create and display 2 and 3D agent-based models. In relation to the integration of GIS functionality the reader is referred to the tutorials by Malleson (2008) which demonstrates how to create a virtual city via the importation of shapefiles, create agents and then move the agents around a road network as shown in Figure 8-9. Furthermore, within RepastS it is possible to embed spatially explicit agent-based models directly into a 3D GIS display. For this RepastS provides methods to directly visualise agent-based models to NASA's virtual globe (Worldwind) as illustrated in Figure 8-10. This new interactive 3D GIS display allows one to visualise agents with satellite imagery, elevated terrain and other scientific datasets. Agent Analyst (Table 8-3, Repast entry) is an ABM extension that allows users to create, edit, and run RepastJ and RepastPy models from within ArcGIS (Redlands Institute, 2006). Repast has a relatively large user group and an actively supported e-mail list, as well as extensive 'how-to' documentation and demonstration models available from the system website. Useful examples of spatially explicit models created using Repast include the studying of segregation, residential and commercial location (Crooks, 2007) and the evacuation of pedestrians from within an underground station (Castle, 2007). However with the advent of 3D modeling capabilities it may be possible to model 3D problems such as air traffic, gas dispersion or more realistic pedestrian evacuation using line of sight analysis.

## Figure 8-8 RepastS point and click modeling and runtime environments

A. Visual modeling: RepastS agent editor — creation of an agent task and its linkage with behavior

B. Visual execution — the runtime displays in 2D and 3D visualization of networks

*Figure 8-9 RepastCity — importing GIS network data into Repast Simphony*

*Figure 8-10 Repast Simphony — agent-based model visualized using NASA's Worldwind*

*Table 8-4 Comparison of shareware/freeware simulation/modeling systems*

| | StarLogo | NetLogo | OBEUS |
|---|---|---|---|
| Developers | Media Laboratory, Massachusetts Institute of Technology, USA | Center for Connected Learning and Computer-Based Modeling, Northwestern University, USA | Environmental Simulation Laboratory, Tel Aviv University, Israel |
| Date of Inception | Early 1990s, Java based version 2000 | 1999 | Early 2000s |
| Website | http://education.mit.edu/starlogo | http://ccl.northwestern.edu/netlogo | http://eslab.tau.ac.il/Research/default.aspx |
| Implementation Language | Proprietary scripting | Proprietary scripting | Microsoft.Net |
| Operating System | Windows, UNIX, Linux, Mac OSX | Windows, UNIX, Linux, Mac OSX | Windows |
| Required programming experience | Basic | Basic | Moderate-Strong |
| Integrated GIS functionality | None | Yes | Yes |
| Integrated charting/graphing /statistics | Yes | Yes | Unknown |
| Availability of demonstration models | Yes | Yes | Unknown |
| Source code of demonstration models | Yes | Yes | Unknown |
| Tutorials/'how-to' Documentation | Yes | Yes | Yes |
| Additional information | OpenStarLogo website: http://education.mit.edu/openstarlogo/ | http://groups.yahoo.com/group/netlogo-users http://ccl.northwestern.edu/netlogo/docs/gis.html | User manual: http://eslab.tau.ac.il/OBEUS/OBEUSManual.pdf Geosimulation website: http://www.geosimulation.org |

Table 8-4 summarizes information for three selected shareware/freeware toolkits, StarLogo, NetLogo and OBEUS, each of which is described below.

StarLogo: is a modeling system developed at the Media Laboratory, Massachusetts Institute of Technology (MIT). Unlike the other six agent-based s/m systems discussed in this section, both StarLogo and NetLogo models are programmed procedurally, as opposed to having an object-oriented structure. Thus, models developed with StarLogo do not benefit from the similarity in abstraction shared between the agent-based and object-oriented paradigms. Furthermore, StarLogo lacks the same flexibility offered by open source systems, since modelers are constrained to the functionality provided by the system.

StarLogo has recently undergone some important changes. The original StarLogo modeling system has been released as an open source project (see OpenStarLogo) however, it is included in this section because the new version, StarLogo TNG (The New Generation) is still shareware/freeware. StarLogo TNG moves StarLogo from the 2D to the 3D realm through the use of the OpenGL graphics API and aims to lower the barrier for programming agent-based models through the use of a drag and drop programming graphical interface. Modelers can drag commands from a set of model building blocks (a block based graphical language) rather than creating models using the StarLogo syntax as highlighted in Figure 8-11 (upper image) thus allowing for rapid model development. StarLogo TNG uses OpenGL for displaying the models at run time therefore providing a 3D display termed 'SpaceLand' as show in Figure 8-11 (lower image). The terrain within such models is editable and can be manually shaped. Agents can also be programmed to move in x, y and z directions. StarLogo is very easy to use, notably for people with very little programming experience. Dynamic charting of model output during a simulation is provided. In addition, a number of demonstration models and detailed 'how-to' documentation relating to these models is supplied with StarLogo, and many more are available to download from the website. Batty *et al.* (1998) have used StarLogo to examine visitor movement within London's Tate Gallery, examining how changes in room configuration can affect visitor movement between exhibits.

NetLogo: originally named StarLogoT, is a variant of StarLogo, originally developed at the Center for Connected Learning and Computer-Based Modeling at Northwestern University. The critical distinction between the two s/m systems is that NetLogo is specifically designed for the deployment of models over the Internet. Initially both NetLogo and StarLogo only provided functionality to import image files, which can be used to define the environments within which agents are located, thus facilitating the development of spatial models. However, within NetLogo it is now possible to import both raster (in the form of .asc files) and vector data (shapefiles). This new ability opens up a range of possibilities for the easy creation of spatial agent based models, e.g. surface erosion modeling.

Using GIS data and NetLogo code it is possible to compute the slope and aspect of the terrain surface using elevation data and then simulate raindrops flowing over that surface by having agents constantly reorient themselves in the direction of the aspect while moving forward at a constant rate. Such functionality potentially lowers the barrier between coupling agent-based models and GIS to non-expert programmers. For example, the gradient example presented above could be used to model a process that relies on cost surfaces such as emergency evacuation of buildings (Crooks *et al.*, 2008a). As with StarLogo TNG, models within NetLogo can be viewed in a 3D environment however unlike StarLogo TNG it is only the agents that appear in 3D while the surface remains a 2D plane. NetLogo has been used to develop applications in disciplines varying from biology and physics to the social sciences. Extensive 'how-to' documentation, tutorials and demonstration models are available from the system website, and functionality can be extended through Application Programming Interfaces (APIs), although the source code for the system is currently unavailable.

*Figure 8-11 StarLogo TNG drag and drop programming interface and 3D view of a simulation*

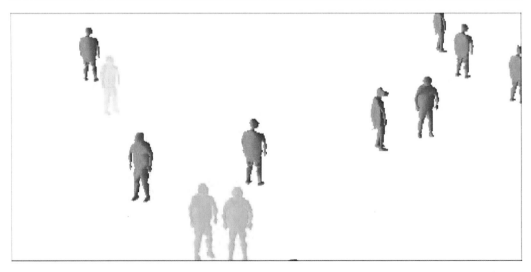

OBEUS: Object-Based Environment for Urban Simulation, was developed at Tel Aviv University, Israel. Based on the theory of Geographic Automata Systems (GAS; Benenson and Torrens, 2004 and further elaborated on with relation to OBEUS by Benenson *et al.*, 2006), it is designed for the simulation of urban phenomena; specifically in a geospatial context. GAS considers an urban system as consisting of objects that are either fixed (e.g. houses or roads) or non-fixed (e.g. people or cars). OBEUS is implemented in the Microsoft.NET framework, but relies on several third-party components (Microsoft.NET Framework, Borland C# compiler, etc.), which must be installed in order to operate the system. OBEUS provides a GUI to develop the structure of a model, although the behavior

and interaction rules of agents must be programmed using one of the Microsoft.NET languages (e.g. C#, C++, or Visual Basic, etc.). Consequently, moderate to strong programming skills are required. OBEUS has been used to develop a number of spatially explicit models, including the simulation of ethnic residential distributions within the Yaffo area of Tel Aviv between 1955 and 1995 (Benenson *et al.*, 2002, Benenson *et al.*, 2005), and street parking and urban sprawl (Benenson *et al.*, 2004). Figure 8-12 shows a Schelling-type residential dynamics model programmed in OBEUS, including an abstract grid and real-world versions demonstrating its main output windows (maps, charts and trace window).

*Figure 8-12 Outputs from OBEUS: Schelling residential dynamics model*

*Source: Benenson (2009)*

*Table 8-5 Comparison of proprietary simulation/modeling systems*

| | AgentSheets | AnyLogic |
|---|---|---|
| Developers | AgentSheets Inc., USA | XJ Technologies, Russia |
| Date of Inception | 1991 | Unknown |
| Website | http://www.agentsheets.com | http://www.xjtek.com |
| E-mail List | None | None |
| Implementation Language | Proprietary scripting | Proprietary scripting |
| Operating System | Windows, UNIX, Linux, Mac OSX | Windows, UNIX, Linux, Mac OSX |
| Required programming experience | None – Basic | Moderate |
| Integrated GIS functionality | None | None |
| Integrated charting/graphing/statistics | Yes | Yes |
| Availability of demonstration models | Yes | Yes |
| Source code of demonstration models | N /A | N /A |
| Tutorials/'how-to' Documentation | Yes | Yes |
| Additional information | Carvalho (2000), Repenning *et al.* (2000) and Repenning and Ioannidou (2004). | http://www.xjtek.com/support/forum/ Parinov (2007). |

Table 8-5 summarizes information for two proprietary toolkits, AgentSheets and AnyLogic, each of which is described in more detail below. As with many other commercial software products, both have much functionality and ongoing development that cannot be adequately described here, and readers are recommended to visit the web sites for the products to obtain more details and examples.

AgentSheets is a proprietary s/m system that allows modelers with limited programming experience to develop an agent-based model, because models are developed through a GUI (Repenning *et al.*, 2000). A number of demonstration models are available from the system website. For example, Sustainopolis is a simulation analogous to the computer game SimCity that allows investigation of pollution dispersal within a city. Furthermore, AgentSheets can be linked to real time information over the Internet (Repenning and Ioannidou, 2004).

For example, in Figure 8-13 AgentSheets is used in conjunction with real time weather feeds and used to make mountain biking recommendations in Boulder County, Colorado. Within the model, agents represent locations that are possible candidates for biking featuring real time web accessible weather sensors. This information is then used by the biker to reach a decision on where to go biking.

*Figure 8-13 AgentSheets: The Boulder Mountain Biking Advisor*

Carvalho (2000) has used AgentSheets extensively to teach undergraduate students. He comments that it is easy to use the system to develop models quickly and provides students with hands-on experience of ABM without the need to learn a programming language. However, he also found that models created with AgentSheets were limited in their sophistication (notably in terms of the complexity of representation of agent behavior and interaction). Furthermore, agents are limited to movement within a two-dimensional cell-based environment.

AnyLogic is a more sophisticated offering that incorporates a range of functionality for the development of agent-based models. For example, models can dynamically read and write data to spreadsheets or databases during a simulation run, as well as dynamically chart model output. Furthermore, external programs can be initiated from within an AnyLogic model for dynamic communication of information, and vice versa. However, AnyLogic models can only be created on Microsoft operating systems, although a

simulation can be run on any Java-enabled operating system once compiled (e.g. a Macintosh operating system). The AnyLogic website notes that models have been developed for a diverse range of applications including: the study of social, urban and ecosystem dynamics (e.g. a predator-prey system); planning of healthcare schemes (e.g. the impact of safe syringe usage on HIV diffusion); computer and telecommunication networks (e.g. the placement of cellular phone base stations); and the location of emergency services and call centers.

Further information pertaining to AnyLogic modeling applications can be found in Parinov (2007); these include imitating the functioning of a emergency department in a large hospital. However, the source code of these examples and/or documentation of these models is not available. Makarov *et al.* (2008) has used AnyLogic to study traffic jams in Moscow' and explore different scenarios for reducing such events either by road pricing or new road building.

The example illustrated in Figure 8-14 seeks to predict transport load and housing allocation (up to March 2009) within a city comprised of 5 independent zones. Each zone contains housing and business units, with various qualities of habitation and roads. Households may contain multiple members, who may work at various enterprises. Households can move in and out of the city, merge or separate, and even relocate to different zones (with an impact on travel patterns). Household members can change jobs when current ones become unsatisfactory (e.g. because of high living costs or low pay). Households whose prosperity improves may seek a better location to live within the city, which in turn may require them to purchase cars, resulting in raised $CO_2$ emissions.

*Figure 8-14 An urban and transport dynamics model developed in AnyLogic (2006)*

Source: http://www.xjtek.com/anylogic/demo_models/

## 8.2.12 Verification and calibration of agent-based models

Once developed, the ABM computer program must be verified by checking that the model behaves as expected; often referred to as *internal validation* (or *inner validity*). Whether the model itself is an accurate representation of the real-world is a different type of validity (see below). Achieving inner validity is harder than it might seem. For instance, hypotheses about the model's output can be tested under a range of input parameter settings. Perhaps the model can be examined under an extreme situation where the outcome is easily predictable. These hypotheses should yield expected results from the model because they are based on the conceptual model design. However, it is difficult for a programmer to know whether unexpected outcomes are a reflection of a mistake in the computer program (a 'bug'), logical errors of the model, or a surprising consequence of the model itself (Gilbert and Terna, 1999).

This predicament is compounded by the problem that complex systems can often produce emergent and counterintuitive results. A modeler can guard against the former of these problems by adopting 'unit tests' while programming a model. Unit testing involves the execution of the computer program after each modification of the code to check that a bug has not been introduced. Nevertheless, a modeler must still determine if unexpected results arise because of errors in the model logic, or just a feature of the system being modeled. These difficulties of verification are further compounded by the fact that most simulations rely on (pseudo-)

random numbers to generate the effects of unmeasured variables and random choices. Thus, repeated runs can be expected to produce different outcomes. Fortunately, one of the main advantages of ABMs is that they provide a natural method for describing and simulating a real-world system, which helps simplify the model logic. However, it is not uncommon to spend more time confirming that a model has been programmed correctly than programming the model itself.

The most thorough way of verifying a model is to re-implement the model using a different programming language and ideally a different ABM toolkit; a process sometimes referred to as 'docking' or 'alignment' (Axtell et al., 1996). Although this method will never attain the status of a proof, it helps the modeler become more confident as to the veracity of the model results (Hales et al., 2003). Docking is not always practical (owing to time or resource constraints) or feasible (requiring a modeler to learn a new programming language or how to develop their model in an alternative system). However, replication is one of the hallmarks of the scientific method, and is an important facet needed to confirm whether claimed results of a simulation are reliable (i.e. can be reproduced by somebody else starting from scratch). Axelrod (2006) notes that without this confirmation it is possible that specific published results could be in error as a result of programming mistakes, misrepresentation of the system being modeled, or errors analyzing the simulation results. Furthermore, replication is required to determine whether a new model can subsume a previous model. If it is not practical or feasible for a modeler to dock their model, it is critical that a thorough description of the model is provided for others to attempt replication. Unfortunately, the latter stipulation has rarely been accomplished to date; a noteworthy exception being Railsback et al. (2006). Documentation should include information regarding the source code for running the model, how to run the program, and how to understand the output. Attempts are being made to devise ontologies and protocols for model comparison, such as the ODD (overview, design concepts, details)

protocol proposed and demonstrated by Grimm et al. (2006). A worked example applied to three land use and land cover models can be seen in Polhill et al. (2008). Fortunately, the use of standardized ABM toolkits and programming languages facilitates replication. Unfortunately, it is often difficult for a modeler to provide a complete description of their model within the word limit of publications (except digital media), especially when addressing an interdisciplinary audience. Carley (1996) stresses that computer models and their output should be described and presented as separate publications.

After a modeling endeavor has been verified the final stages are to calibrate and validate the model. Calibration entails setting the model structure and parameter values in ways that accurately reflect a real-world system. Calibration typically requires data on the micro-level processes that the agent-based model is based upon. These data can be acquired through various means, such as surveys, statistical analysis of empirical data, experiments designed to obtain decision-making strategies and factors, etc. Calibration occurs in stages, usually repeated iteratively, until the outcomes of the model fit (within a reasonable tolerance) the real-world data collected. Therefore, calibration is useful for assessing the feasibility of the model to simulate the real-world system (i.e. showing that the model can generate results that match the real-world data). If the model output cannot be fitted to the real-world data, it may be necessary for the modeler to re-program aspects of the model (e.g. rules dictating agent behavior and interaction, etc.). Thus, calibration is also helpful in the verification process of the model. It should be recognized that the level of correspondence between the model and the real-world data depends in part on the purpose of the model. Hence the modeler must have confidence in the accuracy of the real-world data (e.g. ensuring that the data do not represent only extreme or improbable situations). The impulse to calibrate a model can lead to the model being overly fitted. In this situation, a model fits the real-world data but is insufficiently general to represent a diverse range of system outcomes, or be applied to other systems.

It is often argued that a model with sufficient parameters can always be adjusted until the real-world data are matched. To this extent, modelers should be wary that calibration does not guarantee the validity of a model. However, for many models this criticism is less valid. In particular, within agent-based models that represent processes with rules (e.g. the interaction and behavior of agents) rather than parameterized equations, there are often few if any parameters. Conversely, there is no guarantee that a model with a large number of rules dictating the interaction and behavior of agents can be configured to generate the observed data.

## 8.2.13 Validation and analysis of agent-based model outputs

A model is valid to the extent that it adequately represents the system being modeled. However, the validity of a model should not be thought of as binary (i.e. a model cannot simply be classified as valid or invalid); a model has a certain degree of validity (Law and Kelton, 1991). Validity can be ascertained by comparing the output of the model with comparable data collected from a real-world system. For example, to understand the output of an agent-based model it is often necessary to evaluate the details of a specific simulation 'history'. There are at least three ways in which history can be described (Axelrod, 2006):

- History can be reported as a selection of key events in chronological order. For instance, the simulation of a train station evacuation could be described at the point in time when the emergency alarm sounds, when strategic confines of the station have been evacuated (e.g. platform, escalator/stairs, ticket hall, etc.), or when the station has been fully vacated. Whilst informative, this method provides little explanatory power about the model itself

- Alternatively, the history of one agent can be documented. For example, the location of a pedestrian within the station when the emergency alarm sounds, the time taken for the pedestrian to reach strategic locations within the station thereafter (e.g. platform, escalator/stairs, ticket hall, building exit), and a summary of the route traversed by the agent. This is often the easiest type of history to understand, and can be very revealing about the way in which the model works (i.e. how the logic of the model affects agents over time)

- Finally, the history from a global viewpoint can be noted. For example, the distribution of pedestrians throughout the station may be used, to assess the usefulness of different emergency exits. Although the global viewpoint is often regarded as the best method for observing large-scale patterns, several detailed histories are often required to explain the reasons behind these observed patterns

Although the analysis of individual histories is interesting, they can be misleading; especially if the model incorporates random elements. For example, simulations often use a random number generator to imitate the decision making process of an agent (e.g. direction choices, mood preferences, etc.), to randomize the order in which agents move, or to substitute an unmeasured parameter (equivalent to the modeler making a guess in the absence of more accurate information). In order to determine whether the conclusion from a simulation run is typical, it is necessary to undertake a repeated number of simulations using identical parameters and initial conditions, but using different random number seeds. This will help distinguish whether particular patterns observed in a single illustrative history are idiosyncratic or typical. Results from these simulation runs will need to be presented as distributions, or as means with confidence intervals. Statistical analysis will be required to assess any variation in the model output, and to determine whether inferences from the simulation histories are well founded.

It is usually desirable to engage in sensitivity analysis once a model (at least for a specific set of initial conditions and parameter values) appears to be valid. The aim of sensitivity analysis is to determine the extent to which variations in the model's assumptions yield differences in the model output. The principle behind sensitivity analysis is to vary the initial conditions and parameters of the model by a small amount and observe differences in the model outcomes. For example, a model might be run several times, varying a given parameter between 10% above and below the original value. If the impact on the output is negligible, it can be assumed that the parameter is not of critical importance to the model, and its accuracy is not of major concern. However, a note of caution should be observed since complex systems can exhibit large and sudden shifts in system behavior in response to relatively small perturbations in inputs.

Sensitivity analysis is also used to investigate the robustness of the model. If the behavior of the model is very sensitive to small differences in the values of one or more parameters, the modeler might be concerned whether these particular values are correct. Unfortunately, even with a small number of variables, the required number of parameter combinations can become very large, and the resources required to perform a thorough analysis can become excessive. In practice, a modeler is likely to have a good intuition about which parameters are likely to have the largest impacts upon the output of the model, and therefore which parameters will be more critical to examine. The effect of different model versions can also be assessed by running controlled experiments with sets of simulation runs, akin to the evaluation of parameter changes. The difference in the logic of a model (e.g. changes in rules governing agent behavior and/or interaction, etc.) can be studied by systematically comparing different versions of the model. However, it is imperative that initial conditions are kept identical for any comparison to be valid.

There are a few caveats that must be considered while validating and analyzing the output of a model. Firstly, both the model and the system under analysis are likely to be stochastic. Thus, comparison between the model output and data from the real-world system are unlikely to correspond on every occasion. Whether the significance of this difference is enough to cast doubt upon the model depends partly on the expected statistical distribution of the simulation output. Unfortunately, these distributions are rarely known *a priori* and are difficult to estimate with simulations, especially if outcomes are emergent. Another problem relates to the capability of the model to make predictions, since these will almost certainly be conditional (i.e. it is unlikely that all postulated outcomes can be produced). For instance, a model may be able to produce plausible future predictions, but may not be able to recreate known past system states. Furthermore, there is a possibility that the model is correct, but the data from the real-world system are not (i.e. inappropriate assumptions or estimates could have been obtained from the data). Finally, many simulations are path dependent (i.e. the outcome of a simulation depends upon the exact initial setup chosen). Calibration and validation are arguably amongst the most challenging issues of ABM. Even though there may be correspondence between a model's output and a real-world system, this is not a sufficient condition to conclude that the model is correct (Gilbert, 2004). There are many different processes which could yield a given outcome, and just because a model generates similar outcomes does not prove that the processes included within the model account for the real-world outcome. However, a model should be regarded as a basis for reducing uncertainty about the future, from a prior state of unawareness, to one of more limited uncertainty. A model should not be considered a failure if its predictions are not perfectly accurate or if a modeler is left unsure whether processes included within the model account for the real-world outcome. It takes time and many refinements of a model, but a modeler can gradually increase their confidence in a model by testing it against real-world data in more and more ways.

# 8.3 Artificial Neural Networks (ANN)

## 8.3.1 Introduction to artificial neural networks

*Artificial neural networks* (ANNs), sometimes referred to as *computational neural networks* (CNNs), are an attempt to emulate features of biological neural networks in order to address a range of difficult information processing, analysis and modeling problems. Sections 8.3.1.3, 8.3.1.4, and 8.3.1.5 provide examples of the application of ANN to practical problems in spatial analysis, including land-use classification and spatial interaction modeling. Within the field of spatial analysis only certain types of ANNs have been found to be especially useful to date. This is not to say that other forms of ANN, developed within the computational science field, are not applicable to such problems, but rather that these areas have yet to be explored in depth. There is also considerable ongoing debate as to whether such methods simply amount to data fitting, with little or no value beyond that of description, an issue that will become clearer as we discuss the issue of generalization of such methods to unseen datasets.

Biological neurons, or nerve cells, receive multiple input stimuli, combine and modify the inputs in some way, and then transmit the result to other neurons. Most advanced animals (i.e. most life forms more complex than simple worms) have a very large number of such neurons, which in turn have vast numbers of interconnections with other neurons. This complex network structure is a biological neural network (BNN). A BNN is often divided into sub-structures that perform similar functions and the network as a whole is capable of performing very complex information processing.

The principal class of ANNs that we discuss are so-called *feedforward networks*. Of these, perhaps the most widely used is the *multi-level perceptron* (MLP) model (see Section 8.3.1.1 for more details). Other models we discuss below include *radial basis function*

*neural networks* (RBFNNs, Section 8.3.2, but also compare this with our earlier discussion of RBFs in Section 6.6.4), and *self-organizing networks* (notably SOMs, see further Section 8.3.3).

A typical feedforward ANN consists of three or more inter-connected layers of nodes — an input layer, one or more hidden intermediate layers (often just 1), and an output layer (Figure 8-15). The arrows indicate the direction of information flow, feeding information forward from input to output. Note that there may be any number of nodes at each level of the network, and not all nodes need to be connected to every node in the next layer. For example, in Figure 8-15 hidden node H2 only receives input from input nodes I1 and I3, and only provides output to node O1. This arrangement can be seen as a directed graph, or as a rather complex-looking function mapping.

*Figure 8-15 Simple 3-5-2 feedforward artificial neural network*

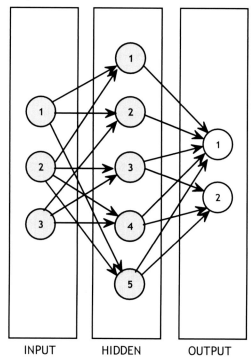

INPUT    HIDDEN    OUTPUT

The connections between the input layer and hidden layer can be described using a weight matrix, **W**, where the row/column entries $w_{ij}$ are positive or negative real-valued weights, or 0 if no connection exists. Likewise, the connections between the hidden layer and the output layer can also be viewed as a weight matrix, **Z** say, again consisting of a set of weights, $z_{jk}$. Positive weights in each case imply a reinforcement process associated with the source node or input, whilst negative weights correspond to inhibition.

### 8.3.1.1 Multi-level perceptrons (MLP)

When each node in the network is connected to every node in the next layer by a feedforward link, it is commonly referred to as a *multi-level perceptron* (MLP, Figure 8-16). The perceptron part of this description is a reference to its early development in a simpler form as a model of neuron triggering in the retina of an eye.

*Figure 8-16 MLP 3-5-2 with bias nodes*

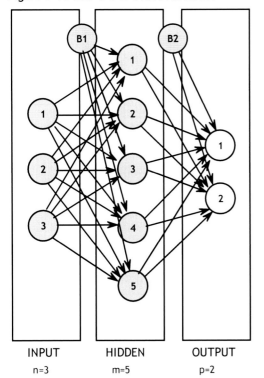

INPUT
n=3

HIDDEN
m=5

OUTPUT
p=2

By convention all nodes in the hidden layer and the output layer are also connected to a bias node. This feeds a constant input value, 1, into the set of weights, and acts in a similar manner to the constant term in a regression model. Bias node weights are treated in the same manner as per other node weights. In the MLP, with 1 bias node associated with each feedforward layer, *n* input nodes, one hidden layer with *m* hidden nodes and *p* output nodes, the **W** and **Z** weight matrices have dimensions $(n+1)\times(m)$ and $(m+1)\times(p)$. The MLP then has the architecture shown in Figure 8-16. The effective number of parameters, $\lambda$, for such a network is the sum of the number of feedforward connections (including the bias connections), so in this example $\lambda=20+12=32$.

Input data are weighted according to their $w_{ij}$ values and combined (typically summed) in the hidden layer. This weighted sum is then modified by what is known as an *activation function*. This two-step process of summation of inputs and then modification of this sum by an activation function, **g**, to create the output value can be illustrated at the node level as shown in Figure 8-17.

*Figure 8-17 ANN hidden node structure*

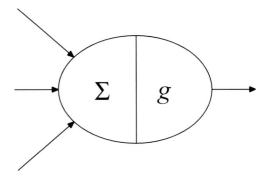

Various activation functions can be used, but the most commonly used in spatial analysis is the *logistic* or *sigmoid* function:

$$g(x) = \frac{1}{1+e^{-\beta x}}$$

where $\beta$ is a slope parameter, typically set to $\beta=1$. With this function if $x=0$ the value output is 0.5. With $x$ large and negative the output approximates 0, whilst for large positive $x$ it approaches 1 (see Figure 8-18). For large positive $\beta$ the slope of this function increases until it becomes essentially a step function from 0 to 1. The logistic function provides a model that approximates the actual response behavior of biological neurons to stimuli, but is primarily used owing to its convenient mathematical properties, as explained further below. Other commonly cited activation functions include simple step or threshold functions (of limited use in spatial analysis problems), the tanh() function (widely used)

and simple linear activation (sometimes this name is used for the identity function, which involves no change). The basic tanh() function has a range [-1,1] but may be adjusted to provide a [0,1] range if required by taking (tanh()+1)/2 (which, of course, is exactly the same as the logistic function with $\beta=2$, so the two functions can be seen to be closely related). Experience suggests that for some problems the tanh() function, which produces positive and negative values, can produce faster learning that logistic functions. Graphs of each of these functions are shown in Figure 8-18. Radial basis activation functions are described separately in Section 8.3.2.

*Figure 8-18 Sample activation functions*

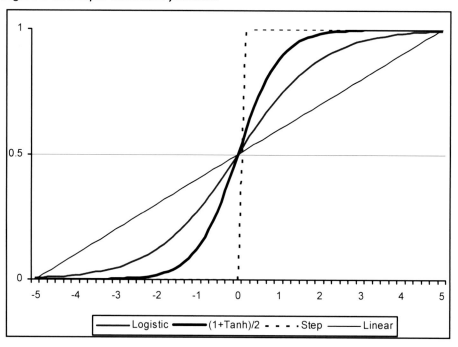

If we denote the set of inputs as a data matrix, **X**, and the set of outputs as a data matrix, **Y**, an artificial neural network is simply a mathematical operation that maps **X** to **Y**, i.e. $f : \mathbf{X} \rightarrow \mathbf{Y}$. Some authorities describe this operation as a *network function*. Typically this mapping is a form of non-linear weighted sum — indeed non-linearity is an essential feature of ANNs applied to most problems. As noted

above, the input data $\{x_i\}$ are modified twice, first by weighted summation and then by use of the activation function.

The same procedure applies to the next layer, where the hidden layer output values, $h_j$, are summed and optionally modified as per the input layer to produce the final results in the output layer, $y_k$:

$$h_j^{\cdot} = \sum_i \left( x_i w_{ij} \right), \text{ and } h_j \leftarrow g_1\left( h_j^{\cdot} \right), \text{ then}$$

$$y_k^{\cdot} = \sum_j h_j z_{jk}, \text{ and finally } y_k \leftarrow g_2\left( y_k^{\cdot} \right), \text{ hence}$$

$$y_k \leftarrow g_2\left( \sum_j g_1\left( \sum_i x_i w_{ij} \right) z_{jk} \right)$$

Although the same activation function, g(), may used for all nodes and layers, some implementations apply different activation functions at the output layer from those used for the hidden layers (e.g. linear or identity functions).

### 8.3.1.2 Learning and back-propagation for MLPs

Creating an artificial neural network, such as an MLP, does not of itself provide a direct means of solving a particular problem or class of problems. ANNs need to learn from sample datasets or subsets of a given large dataset before they can usefully be applied. Learning in the MLP case is a process of systematically adjusting the entries in the two weight matrices, $\mathbf{W}$ and $\mathbf{Z}$.

If you have one or more sets of control data, i.e. given a set of inputs, $\mathbf{i}$, and you know what the set or vector of target outputs, $\mathbf{t}$, should be, you can use this information to 'train' the network. This learning process is described as *supervised* because it implies we have prior knowledge about the nature of the solution and are supervising the training. Note that the control data may be divided into two main groups: *training data*, used to train the neural network, and *test data*, which the neural network has not previously seen, which can be used to assess the performance of the network. It is generally recommended that the control data be comprised of a substantial number of cases, in order to reasonably represent the underlying population data and to satisfactorily train and evaluate the ANN. It may be necessary to ensure that the range of values of training data variables includes the full range that may subsequently be used for validation and testing.

By contrast, *unsupervised learning* has no vector of target outputs, $\mathbf{t}$, only a vector of input data, $\mathbf{i}$. In this situation training involves identifying patterns in the input vectors that generate consistent output vectors. This process is sometimes described as *self organizing*. Both supervised and unsupervised training approaches have been applied in geospatial analysis.

Supervised learning is applied extensively in the fields of pattern recognition/classification and complex function approximation (non-linear regression). For example, suppose that the entries in the two weight matrices are initially set to random uniform [0,1] values. A set or vector of input (or training) data, $\mathbf{i}$, will be transformed as the values propagate through the network to the output, giving a set or vector of output values, $\mathbf{o}$, that will (almost certainly) not match the known correct results, $\mathbf{t}$. Individual differences or 'errors' or *error signals* at the $k^{th}$ output node are positive or negative values of the form:

$$e_k = \left( t_k - o_k \right)$$

Ideally we seek to minimize such errors by choosing an appropriate set of weights. To achieve this a convenient measure is to minimize the sum of squared errors across all output nodes, an approach which mirrors that of least squares regression. Minimization is achieved by differentiation of the sum of squared errors expression, equating this to zero, and using the result to determine the required adjustment of the initial weights. The *average* difference or error between the generated output results and the target results can be computed and tracked (e.g. graphed) using a measure that is appropriate for the problem in question. With function estimation problems it is common to compute the root mean sum of squared errors (RMSE):

$$RMSE = \sqrt{\frac{1}{N} \sum_{k=1}^{N} \left( t_k - o_k \right)^2}$$

This provides a standardized measure of the 'cost' of this solution, and the aim is to minimize this cost function, ideally reducing its value to 0 by adjusting the weights as noted above. In fact the *universal approximation theorem* states that every mapping of the form $f:X \rightarrow Y$ where X and Y are finite real-valued sets, can be approximated as closely as one wishes using a 3 layer MLP of the kind described above.

The process of learning (adjusting the entries in the weight matrices) is typically achieved through a procedure called *back propagation* with *gradient descent*. The back propagation part of this refers to the process of applying a learning rule backwards through the network, step by step — so the first step is to change the **Z** matrix entries and then to change the **W** matrix entries. The learning rule essentially adjusts the values such that at time (or *epoch*) t+1:

$$\mathbf{Z}^{t+1} = \mathbf{Z}^t + (\Delta \mathbf{Z})^t$$

and then

$$\mathbf{W}^{t+1} = \mathbf{W}^t + (\Delta \mathbf{W})^t$$

The positive or negative increments to the entries in the matrices are based on their relative contributions to the positive or negative errors in the outputs. Thus if a particular weight $z_{jk}$ is large in relation to other weights that contribute to output node k, it may need to be increased or decreased in proportion to the size and sign of the generated 'error' and the node value, $h_j$.

A simple learning rule might be of the general form:

$$z_{jk}^{t+1} = z_{jk}^t + \eta (t_k - o_k) h_j, \text{ or}$$
$$z_{jk}^{t+1} = z_{jk}^t + \eta e_k h_j$$

where $\eta$ is a small positive constant (e.g. $\eta < 0.1$) known as the *learning rate*. The initial learning rate value is often reduced during the course of iteration so that the learning rate decreases over time. This corresponds to an initial broad step learning process that makes large adjustments to the weights and later makes smaller adjustments in order to fine-tune the results (sometimes referred to as *stochastic approximation*).

In practice the learning rule provided above is not appropriate for MLPs, because it has not taken into account the use of the *activation function*. In order to incorporate this component the error signal needs to be weighted by the derivative of the activation function. A particularly nice feature of the logistic activation function:

$$g(x) = \frac{1}{1 + e^{-x}}$$

is that its derivative is simply:

$$g'(x) = g(x)[1 - g(x)]$$

and instead of using $e_k$ in the learning rule above, $g'e_k$ is used, i.e.:

$$z_{jk}^{t+1} = z_{jk}^t + \eta o_j (1 - o_j) e_k h_j$$

The $g(x) = \tanh(x)$ activation function also has a very convenient derivative:

$$g'(x) = 1 - g^2(x)$$

Essentially the same procedure is applied when computing the adjustments to the weights in the **W** matrix. However, the adjustment is slightly more complex because the error signal is now not based on the difference between output values and expected output values, but between hidden values and the back-propagated (adjusted) hidden values. These back-propagation steps correspond to a gradient descent approach to finding a local minimum of the mean squared error — see Abdi (1994) for a more detailed description and derivation of these formulas.

Having adjusted the weights for both levels, the forward propagation process takes place once more and the cost function is computed — this should now be less than or equal to the cost function for the previous time period. The process continues until reduction in the cost function ceases and/or a preset maximum number of iterations (e.g. typically more than 100) have been reached. Other variants of stopping criteria may also be provided, and separate criteria will apply to validation data (e.g. all data to be within $x\%$ of their true values). A number of additional observations should be made at this point:

(i) **local versus global minimization:** global minimization of the cost function is not guaranteed — for this reason some authors and software packages apply global minimization techniques such as simulated annealing and genetic algorithms rather than/as well as simple gradient descent in order to attempt to improve overall solutions. Faster convergence may also be achieved using more sophisticated local gradient search procedures, such as conjugate gradient methods (see Walsh, 1975, for a brief discussion of conjugate gradients).

(ii) **initialization and selection order:** initialization of weights is usually performed by random selection from a uniform distribution over a finite range. The particular initial choice of weights may affect the final outcome, depending on the nature of the problem and dataset, hence multiple initializations (e.g. 5) may be advisable in order to examine and manage this issue. Furthermore, the order in which individual weights are selected for updating can affect the process and it is common practice to select weights for updating at random until all have been updated in a given layer. Likewise, during training, it is common practice to select input vectors from the training set at random, since the selection order can affect the final trained set of weights.

(iii) **data normalization and coding:** the input dataset is generally transformed and/or pre-normalized such that all input data lie in the range [0,1]. With positive real-valued data a common procedure is to divide all input values by the maximum in the sample. Note that no distributional assumptions are made about the input data. The output dataset, if it involves distinct categories, e.g. A, B, C, D... is typically coded such that each category (output node) is assigned a binary 1 with the remainder being assigned binary 0. On completion the input and output data can be converted back to more familiar units/descriptions.

(iv) **momentum:** the number of iterations required and the quality of solutions can often be improved by amending the learning rule through the use of a *momentum factor*. This is a small multiple of the adjustment used in the preceding iteration, time $t$, effectively prolonging this adjustment, i.e. giving it *momentum* — the adjustments are thus of the form:

$$\Delta Z^{t+1} \leftarrow \Delta Z^{t+1} + \alpha \Delta Z^t \text{ and } \Delta W^{t+1} \leftarrow \Delta W^{t+1} + \alpha \Delta W^t$$

(v) **model design, over-fitting and over-training:** the number of nodes in the input and output layers are determined by the problem and how it is modeled. In most ANNs nodes are fully connected between the layers, so connection choice is not normally a requirement. The number of hidden layer units, $m$, can be specified manually (e.g. initially set to the same as the number of input nodes, $n$, or some combination of $n$ and the number of output nodes, $p$). This number, $m$, can then be systematically altered until results of the best 'quality' have been obtained. Quality is usually determined by some performance measure or multiple measures applied initially to the training data, and then examined for other datasets (see further, below). Quality is also measured in terms of model simplicity (number of parameters implied in the model structure). Some software packages attempt to compute suitable structures automatically. For example, a standard rule may be applied for selecting the number of hidden nodes, such as:

$$m = \text{int}\left(\sqrt{np}\right)$$

where int() is the integer part function. Hence with 3 inputs and 2 outputs, this rule would give $m=2$. This is the default used within Idrisi, for example. Other rules of thumb suggested by various authors include $m=(n+p)/2$, $m<2n$ and $m=2(n+p)/3$. For problems involving simple function approximation (see the worked examples in Section 8.3.1.3) the number of hidden layer units is typically set to between 3 and 10 where there is a single input and single output node.

There is a risk that neural network models perform extremely well on training data but may not perform as well on unseen data as simpler ANN models. This problem, which falls into the general category of *over-training*, often occurs when over-complex systems have been specified. There are a number of procedures for attempting to minimize over-training. One approach is to divide the control data set into three parts rather than two (a form of split-sample validation): a training set; a validation set; and a test set. With this approach the validation set is used to identify when training should be stopped, based on the leveling out of performance measures for the validation set, having first identified the neural network model which best fits the data with the minimum number of parameters — see, for example, Fischer and Gopal (1994) for a discussion of this issue in connection with spatial interaction modeling, a paper that has been republished in Fischer (2006) together with several others that address the same problem and dataset. In their model they selected an *n-m-p* model with *n*=3, *p*=1 (problem defined) and values of *m* from 5 to 50 in steps of 5, with *m*=30 being their preferred solution. This equates to a model with 151 parameters as compared with 3 parameters for the conventional spatial interaction model, suggesting that there has to be a marked improvement achieved by such models and/or other benefits (e.g. robustness, dynamic adjustment) if they are to be used in preference to conventional alternatives. An alternative approach is to apply *s*-fold cross-validation. In this case the data is divided into *s* approximately equal-sized subsets. The NN is then trained *s* times, on each occasion leaving out one of the subsets which is then used to compute the validation statistic of interest. This approach is reportedly an improvement on split-sample methods for smaller datasets, but is more computationally intensive. A third approach involves the use of a technique known as *bootstrapping*, in which random samples are taken (with replacement) rather than pre-defined or random subsets — see

Efron (1982) and Efron and Tibshirani (1997) for more details.

(vi) **forecasting**: the methods described above can be applied to time-series forecasting — indeed, this is an application area that has attracted considerable interest, notably in the financial sector. There are now a large number of software products, from Excel add-ins to multi-function integrated packages, which are specifically designed to provide 'intelligent' forecasting. For such problems it is not always necessary to have multiple inputs — for example, river flow levels can often be quite accurately predicted using existing records for daily or weekly flows over several years. However, multiple inputs, such as the inclusion of relevant correlated information (where available) such as rainfall data, catchment information, flows at related measuring points etc., may all serve to improve the model robustness and its ability to be more widely applied.

The preceding subsections have provided a description of MLPs, but their operation is not particular obvious from this information — indeed, such networks are often described as black boxes, where the inner workings are hidden from the observer, who merely provides inputs and views outputs. For this reason we now provide a small number of examples of their application.

### 8.3.1.3 MLP Example 1: Function approximation

In this example we suppose that we have a total of 21 measured values of a response (or dependent) variable, *y*, for a set of equally spaced values of an independent variable, *x* (this example is based on sample MATLAB code produced by Roger Jang, Computer Science Department, Tsing Hua University, Taiwan and also tested using the NetLab code library). The data suggest a highly non-linear relationship (Figure 8-19A). This dataset provides the training information in the form of (*x*,*y*) pairs for the model, for which there is one input node and one output node, plus a bias node for each layer. The activation function used in this case was the tanh() function, with standard gradient descent back-propagation. A learning rate of 0.02 was used with a momentum factor of 0.8 — using a higher learning rate, for example, produced far less stable RMSE behavior (Figure 8-20A and B). The stopping criteria were set to 1000 epochs (iterations) or RMSE<0.01. Weights were all initialized with a random uniform value in the range [-0.5,0.5]. Choice of the number of hidden nodes was made by varying the values between 3 and 10 and examining the fit of the model and the RMSE curve. The fitted solution shown in Figure 8-19B was based on 4 hidden nodes, this being the smallest value that provided a satisfactory fit to the sample data.

*Figure 8-19 MLP: Test data and fitted model*

A. Test response data

b. Fitted solution curve

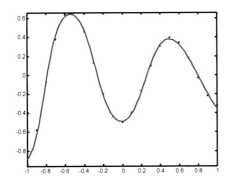

As might be expected, running the same dataset with a different MLP algorithm requires different settings to achieve the same or similar results. For example, the problem described above was also tested using software (NetLab) that uses a different (generally

faster) training procedure, known as *scaled conjugate gradients*. In this model a tanh() activation function was again used for the hidden nodes whilst a linear function was used for the output nodes. Weight matrices were initialized with scaled random values based on a Normal distribution and a learning rate of 0.02 was again used, but this program variant requires no momentum parameter. It yielded slightly improved results to those above in around 150 iterations.

*Figure 8-20 MLP: RMSE curves*

A. RMSE vs. epochs, learning rate=0.02

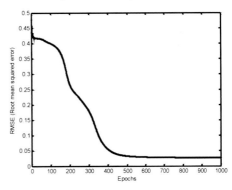

B. RMSE for learning rate=0.05

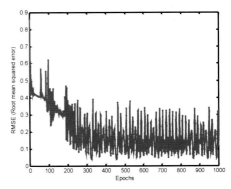

It is immediately apparent from this discussion that this ANN modeling process is effectively a form of nonlinear regression, similar to iterative least squares regression (ILSR), previously mentioned in connection with Geographically Weighted Regression in Section 5.6.3. It is also clear that the process requires a level of interaction and experimentation with the software tools, in order to determine the ideal parameter and node settings for a given function estimation problem.

### 8.3.1.4 MLP Example 2: Landcover change modeling (LCM)

In this example we use the LCM functionality included within the Idrisi GIS software (and also available for ArcGIS). This incorporates an MLP component for modeling the drivers behind landcover transitions between 1986 and 1994, as an input to specific predictions of change. The study area covers roughly 15km x 15km in part of Bolivia known as Chiquitania. It lies in the border between the Amazonian rain forest and deciduous dryland tropical forest. Existing data includes landcover in 1986 (Figure 8-21), landcover in 1994 and various vector layers (e.g. roads, rivers etc.). Fuller details of this example are provided in the Idrisi documentation.

All image/raster files used in this model are co-registered 987x927 pixels or cells, where one pixel=150mx150m. Four of the seven input rasters are generated from vector data using a simple distance transform — i.e. each pixel provides the distance to the closest object in the underlying vector set. These include urban areas, roads, streams and areas subject to anthropogenic disturbance (Figure 8-22). The underlying dataset used in this example is from the Conservation International's Center for Applied Biodiversity Science, Museo Noel Kempff Mercado, Bolivia, and supplied with the Idrisi software installation. Two of the input rasters provided the elevation and slope data for the study area, and the last of the 7 inputs is another computed raster, this time providing a measure of the likelihood of individual raster cells changing landcover based on the frequency patterns found for those cells that were subject to change in the period 1986-94.

Our principal interest is in the application of the MLP modeling and classification process (Figure 8-23) within LCM. In this instance the MLP network topology is of the form 7-7-8 (plus bias), i.e. 7 input nodes (in this instance, Bands 1, 2, 3...), all of which are real-valued raster files, 1 hidden layer with 7 nodes, and 8 output nodes. The output nodes are the 4 main land-use transitions (classes) that are taking place in the region and 4 'persistence classes' — the latter represent raster cells that might have changed between 1986 and 1994, but did not. The authors state that the inclusion of these additional output nodes assists the MLP training process. Each of the 4 main transitions observed were to the class 'anthropogenic disturbance' (class 8) and transferred from the identified classes: (i) woodland savannah; (ii) Amazonian rain forest; (iii) savannah; or (iv) deciduous forests. The MLP training site specification (Figure 8-23, center left) automatically picks a random set of cells (pixels) — i.e. training sites — to be used for training the model and a similar number of sites for testing the model. The number is chosen by examining the smallest transition in the group of four that are the principal subject of the modeling process.

As can be seen from Figure 8-23, key training parameters for the MLP modeling process are specified via this form. These include: using a dynamic learning rate, which commences with a value of 0.005 and reduces to 0.0001 — this reduction takes place over the 5000 iterations or epochs of the model, but in this example most of the training was achieved within the first 1000 epochs (see the RMSE graph in Figure 8-23); applying a momentum factor — a value of 0.5 was specified in this example; and specifying the slope parameter — the activation function used within Idrisi is the logistic or sigmoidal function, and here was applied with slope parameter (constant $a$ in Figure 8-23) of 1.

Normalization of the input raster files is not specified within the Idrisi documentation, but is assumed to be carried out by default. Three stopping criteria can be specified, although here the training stops after the maximum number of iterations has been reached. Notice that an accuracy rate of 81.5% of transitions has been obtained with this model (Figure 8-23, running statistics panel). The authors suggest that 75% is good and 80%+ is a preferable target. This figure represents the number of correctly predicted transitions for the test pixels.

*Figure 8-21 Land cover, 1986, Chiquitania*

*Figure 8-22 Distance raster (meters), anthropogenic disturbance, Chiquitania*

*Figure 8-23 MLP Classifier – Idrisi*

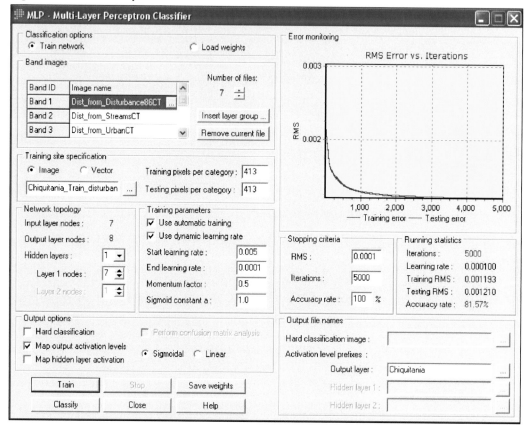

A set of four transition potential maps can then be generated using this information. One such map is shown in Figure 8-24. The next stage in the process is to use the transition potentials map, in conjunction with Markov Chain analysis (see further, CATMOG 1), to predict landcover in the year 2000, for which actual landcover information is known. This enables the quality of the MLP modeling and subsequent predictive process to be evaluated (see Idrisi documentation for more details of these steps in the modeling process).

At this point the MLP has created two weight matrices, **W** and **Z**, which may be saved for reference and optionally re-loaded for future use (see example, Table 8-6). These weights provide what the authors regard as an acceptable level of prediction of 'transition potential'. There are (7+1)x7 input weights to the 7 hidden layer nodes (**W** matrix) plus (7+1)x8 hidden layer to output nodes weights (**Z** matrix), i.e. 120 parameters for this model.

*Figure 8-24 Transition potential map*

*Table 8-6 W weights matrix, Chiquitania MLP model*

| -1.1017 | -0.5180 | -0.1645 | -3.0337 | -1.6198 | -0.1066 | -2.1134 | 0.2422 |
|---------|---------|---------|---------|---------|---------|---------|--------|
| -6.5289 | 1.4412 | -3.6655 | -3.6952 | -0.3428 | 1.7637 | -2.9166 | -0.2034 |
| 1.7461 | -0.1886 | 1.6998 | -2.0887 | 3.0947 | 0.0202 | -7.1687 | 0.1928 |
| -1.0112 | -0.4277 | 1.3041 | -0.7028 | 2.1360 | 0.4187 | 5.6591 | 0.1146 |
| 15.3872 | 0.1111 | -0.4215 | 14.3066 | 0.0078 | 0.0681 | -0.0071 | -0.1195 |
| 2.9165 | -0.3409 | 2.9754 | 5.5850 | 4.1987 | 0.0772 | -26.8881 | -0.2493 |
| 1.6520 | 0.0149 | -0.2517 | 0.2964 | -1.0419 | -0.0475 | 6.5108 | -0.1082 |

### 8.3.1.5 MLP Example 3: Spatial interaction modeling

In this example we consider a situation in which forecasts of shopping trips in region B are sought, based on data collected in region A (possibly a subset of B), or where regions A and B are the same but studied at different points in time. The data available for region A relates to attributes of source zones or origins (O), destination zones (D), a measure of the distance between each paired origin (i) and destination (j) zone, and the recorded average number of shopping trips ($T_{ij}$) per trading day. Here we assume a generalized trip model of the form:

$$T_{ij}=f(O_i,D_j,d_{ij})$$

where $f()$ is an unknown function of the attribute data and the separation measure. For example, we may have data for origin zones providing the population numbers (POPUL) and the average household incomes (HOUSINC) which are demand driver or 'push' measures;

and for destination zones we may have the retail floor space in thousands of square meters (RETAILSP) and the number of parking spaces in thousands (PARKINGSP) which are attraction or 'pull' measures. In addition, we can compute a measure of zone separation (DISTANCE), for example as Euclidean distance, network distance, estimated travel time, or some other separation measure. In total these data provide five explanatory variables (input variables) with which we seek to explain one observed variable (output), actual shopping trip levels. As mentioned previously, Fischer (2006) has studied this class of problem over many years, and has shown that ANN models can provide an excellent fit to observed data and provide good quality generalizations from such data.

A simple ANN model for the problem we have described is a 5-$m$-1 MLP, which we train using the observed data (or more generally a subset of this) and validate and/or test using the remainder of the observed data. Because the data can be seen as a set of rows, with columns corresponding to the 5 input variables and 1 output variable, they are ideally suited to simple text file, spreadsheet or database storage. Indeed, such data are similar to those found in financial and commodity trading, where a range of index, price and volume data by time of day or across days is input and closing prices, for example, are the output. ANNs have found considerable favor in this field and have resulted in the availability of a large number of desktop-based software packages and add-ins (e.g. Excel utilities) targeted specifically at this community of users. For illustrative purposes we have used one such package (from Neural Planner Software) to import a spreadsheet of simulated origin, destination and distance data (inputs) and trip levels (output) that we have generated using the specific variables described above. We have then requested the software to model the data (Figure 8-25). In this diagram thicker lines identify stronger weights, green lines are positive weights, and red lines negative weights. Bias nodes are not separately illustrated but are including in the modeling. This particular software package uses logistic activation and gradient-based

back-propagation (as described in Section 8.3.1.2) to train the network. Data are automatically normalized by the software for processing and then converted back when generating predictions. The software also estimates the preferred number of hidden layer nodes and can automatically increment these from an initial minimum value in order to obtain the best possible result. Between 1 and 3 hidden layers are catered for, but most models of this type can be accommodated with the default one hidden-layer model.

### Figure 8-25 MLP trip distribution model 1

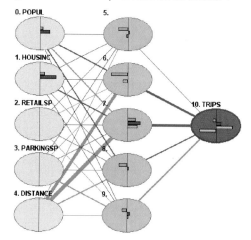

Rows from the input spreadsheet can be assigned explicitly as being for training or validation, or random samples of those provided may be used for validation. Other, non-commercial packages could equally well be used, such as NuMAP from the University of Texas at Arlington. The latter includes a range of ANN facilities and a simple user interface and data file structure. Assuming the training process yields a high quality network (i.e. excellent in terms of its fit to the validation data and any additional test data provided) its use for prediction may then be considered and compared with alternative models (e.g. gravity-based models with calibrated parameters) applied to the same datasets. However, this initial MLP modeling process did not yield good results based on fit to validation data. The process was therefore re-examined, this time log transforming the data (input and output) before commencing, adjusting the learning rate and momentum, and re-running the network modeling. The network on this occasion provided an improved fit to validation data (60% within 10% of known values – as applied to the log transformed data) using 8 hidden nodes rather than 5, as shown in Figure 8-26.

*Figure 8-26 MLP trip distribution model 2*

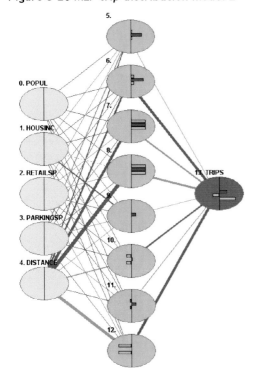

| Input Name | Importance | Relative Importance |
|---|---|---|
| DISTANCE | 24.4206 | |
| RETAILSP | 6.2171 | |
| POPUL | 5.9529 | |
| PARKINGSP | 5.6137 | |
| HOUSINC | 5.1900 | |

*The bars in the node ovals indicate the positive and negative component levels, from top to bottom: net input; activation; bias; error*

The effective number of model parameters therefore increased, which explains part of the observed improvement. In this example we have also shown the relative importance computed by the model of the input variables.

As can be seen, distance is the dominant factor, with the remaining four variables (two push and two pull factors) being of approximately equal significance.

This rather simplistic analysis highlights several issues. First, it is clear that ANN modeling is a powerful and valuable tool for modeling a wide range of data types and problems. Second, each application area presents different challenges, and application-specific modeling (e.g. selection of training, validation and test data sets; transformation and normalization of input data; network design and control parameter settings) is an important aspect of successful modeling. Finally, ANN modeling may reveal structures in the data that point the way to simpler and more general models.

### 8.3.2 Radial basis function networks

Radial basis function neural networks (RBFNNs) are essentially a combination of the ideas found in multi-level perceptrons (MLPs, Section 8.3.1.1) and those described earlier in this Guide (Section 6.6.4) under the main heading 'deterministic surface interpolation', subsection 'radial basis functions'. In addition to interpolation they can be used for function approximation, as explained further below. As before, we are attempting to find a model, or approximation, for the function mapping, $f:X \rightarrow Y$, where $X$ is the input vector or set of vectors and $Y$ is the set of matching output vectors. The standard (regression-type) RBFNN model uses the same 3 layer topology (including bias nodes) as the MLP, but the output is modeled as a linear combination of basis functions, of the form:

$$y = \sum_{j=1}^{m} w_j \varphi()$$

where the activation function, $\varphi()$, is a radial basis function. This function operates not on the input data vectors, but on the *distance* of input data vectors, $x$, from a pre-selected 'center', $c$. This center vector, $c$, has the same dimensionality as the input vector, $x$.

Figure 8-27 illustrates the architecture of the RBFNN model we describe.

The hidden layer computes the distance from the input layer data to each of the centers, and this set of distances, **D**, are then transformed before passing them to the output layer. When these center vectors are set to be the same as the input vectors the RBFNN solution will fit $f$ at the input data points, so may be used for function (or surface) interpolation and grid generation (i.e. evaluating $f$ at new data points).

*Figure 8-27 Radial basis function NN model*

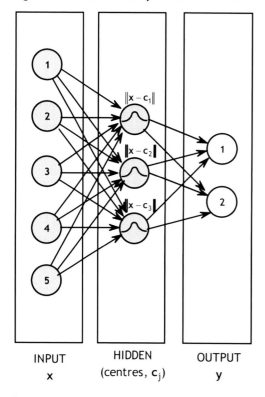

INPUT      HIDDEN      OUTPUT

x      (centres, $c_j$)      y

*Diagram based on Abdi (1994, p271)*

When the center vectors containing fewer elements than the input set the RBFNN approximates $f$. In this second case these center vectors are often initialized as random vectors within the data range of the input vectors. Making this operation explicit the equation above can be re-written as:

$$y = \sum_{j=1}^{m} w_j \varphi\left(\|\mathbf{x} - \mathbf{c}_j\|\right),$$

where $\| \ \|$ denotes the Euclidean norm.

As with other feedforward ANNs the matrix of weights, **W**, is trained using back-propagation. RBFNNs are becoming more widely used, partly because they are often faster to train and tend to suffer less than MLPs from local minima. However, their structure can make them somewhat cumbersome and brings the risk of producing models that are over-fitted. Radial basis functions, $\varphi()$, that may be used in the expressions above include the multi-quadric and simple power functions (as described in Section 6.6.4), but in most RBFNN implementations the Gaussian function is the preferred choice:

$$\varphi(\mathbf{x}) = \frac{1}{\sqrt{2\pi\sigma^2}} e^{-\left(x^2/2\sigma^2\right)}$$

The major attraction of the Gaussian is that if the centers, **c**, are distinct and the distance matrix **D** is square, the transformed matrix $\varphi(\mathbf{D})$ is non-singular and positive definite — important characteristics for standard inversion. Here the function $\varphi()$ is defined as being applied element-wise to the components of **D**. We can illustrate the RBFNN procedure with approximation of a univariate function, given a set of input data values **x** and responses, or output values, **y** (compare this description to that described in Section 6.6.4). Let the vector **c**, of centers, be the same as **x**. This means that every element of **c** will have a distance of 0 from its matching input element. Clearly if **x** is large then **c** will also be large. Effectively our dataset consists of $n$ $(x,y)$ pairs and the vector **c** is simply the set of $x$-values, $\{x\}$. The distance matrix $\mathbf{D}=\{d_{ij}\}$ is an $n$ by $n$ symmetric matrix of the separation of each $x$-value from every other $x$-value, and so has a zero principal diagonal. This distance matrix is then transformed by the activation function, $\varphi()$, where $\varphi()$ is the Gaussian function with variance parameter $\sigma^2=1$. Hence we have:

$$\varphi(\mathbf{D}) = \left[ \varphi(d_{ij}) \right] = \left[ \frac{1}{\sqrt{2\pi\sigma^2}} e^{-\left(d_{ij}^2 / 2\sigma^2\right)} \right]$$

We still require the weights matrix, **W**, in order to be able to compute the output values using the expression provided earlier. With classical RBF methods we can compute this matrix directly by inversion, as:

$$\mathbf{W} = \left[ \varphi(\mathbf{D}) \right]^{-1} \mathbf{y}$$

Using RBFNN methods the weights matrix is initialized with random vectors with values in the range of the input data, **x**, and these are used for forward propagation. The result will be differences between the expected output (y values) and those produced, i.e. errors, which are then used to adjust the set of weights by back propagation. The weight matrix is thus learnt, over a number of epochs, avoiding the need for matrix inversion. This becomes of increased value where larger problems are concerned or the structure of the problem means that the matrix **D** cannot be inverted. When this approach is applied to the dataset illustrated earlier in Figure 8-19, the results are directly comparable, but the learning process is smoother (displays a more consistent rate of improvement) than that seen with the basic MLP approach (Figure 8-20).

## 8.3.3   Self organizing networks

### 8.3.3.1   Self Organizing Maps (SOMs)

The self-organizing feature map, SOFM or SOM, is a neural network tool developed by Kohonen (1984,1995). SOMs are principally used to facilitate the visualization and interpretation of high-dimensional datasets, although they may be applied to address a number of other problems in spatial analysis. In broad terms the SOM approach attempts to find a set of attribute vectors (output vectors, effectively multi-dimensional cluster centers), which are used to represent a large set input attribute vectors. However, unlike most other clustering techniques, the set of output vectors are constrained by the SOM procedure to have a well-defined 2D (map) spatial relationship with

one another. The enforced spatial relationship is designed to ensure that similar input vectors are assigned to output vectors that are spatially near to one another in the output map. Step-by-step worked examples of the procedure are provided in Section 8.3.3.2 and Section 8.3.3.3. Software to support the SOM is available in several GIS and remote sensing packages — e.g. Idrisi, ENVI, TNTMips — in all these cases primarily as a form of unsupervised map classification. SOM facilities are also provided in some commercial neural network software packages (e.g. the Neural Network toolbox for MATLab), and the SOM Toolbox for MATLab. The latter is available free of charge under the GNU General Public License from the Helsinki University of Technology, where it was developed. In this subsection we draw on the documentation associated with the SOM toolbox for our description of the procedures involved.

The SOM map itself (the output space) is formed as a regular grid of cells or units (neurons), for example a 10x8 grid (n=80 units) or a 16x32 grid (n=512 units) — in fact the grid can be much larger if desired. The choice of grid size, form and topology may be user-definable or pre-specified, depending on the software tools being utilized. As with other forms of neural network modeling, each grid cell is connected to adjacent grid cells (neurons). However, in SOMs these connections are structured according to a spatial neighborhood relation, and this provides the key distinction between SOM and other forms of multi-dimensional analysis of this type. *Grid size* refers to the number of units or cells to be used, typically arranged as an approximately equal number of rows and columns. *Grid form* refers to the use of square or hexagonal cells (see Figure 8-28) — hexagonal cells may provide a preferable cell neighborhood arrangement. *Grid topology* refers to the way in which the grid boundary is handled. Standard topologies supported are sheet (planar grid, hence 4 edges), cylinder (grid with two opposite edges attached when computing neighborhoods — 2 edges), and toroidal (grid with both pairs of opposite edges attached when computing neighborhoods — no edges).

Each grid cell unit has an associated vector, **m**, that provides a model of the $k$-dimensional input dataset, hence the $n$ units seek to provide a model representation of the observations (e.g. multi-band source image pixels, attributes of statistical regions in a country), each of which consists of data across $k$-dimensions (e.g. feature attributes, spectral bands). These model vectors are also known as *prototype vectors* or *codebook vectors*. They can be regarded as a set of points with coordinates reflecting those of the input space or data space. In 1-, 2- or 3-dimensional space the input space and model vectors can be visualized graphically, but with higher dimensions such visualization is only possible by selecting subsets of the dimensions and plotting these individually.

*Figure 8-28 SOM grids*

Hexagonal SOM grid

Rectangular SOM grid

The SOM performs two functions: (i) the modeling of the source data with a smaller number of vectors that attempt to represent the source data as closely as possible (e.g. minimizing some measure of deviation from the observations); and (ii) the production of a topology in the SOM grid whereby similar models are close together and dissimilar models are far apart. The resulting SOM grid is not a geographic map, but a two-dimensional representation or projection of the similarity of the models applied. Typically the SOM is displayed as a gray scale or in some cases a simple colored grid (rectangular or hexagonal lattice)  with light gray or similar colors indicating clusters of similar data, whilst dark or dissimilar colors indicate divisions in the underlying models (in some implementations this representation is inverted, so that darker shades indicate similar classes). The SOM is thus a form of *data mining* tool, which may be used for this purpose alone, or as a pre-cursor to further analysis and data classification (with cells prototype vectors providing the classes). If the classification is then applied to a source spatial dataset, for example a remotely-sensed image, a map of the countries of the world, a set of point observations (e.g. medical cases and controls), or a network of streets (see Jiang, 2004) the procedure can generate a coded geographic map in addition to its functional map. Other forms of non-geographic visualization are also available, including analysis of the individual SOM unit vectors. Currently SOM procedures are provided as tools for multi-band image classification within a number of software packages, including Idrisi and TNTMips. In the following subsection (Section 8.3.3.2) we provide an example and discussion based on the TNTMips SOM implementation and we take a brief look at the Idrisi SOM facility. A second example is examined in Section 8.3.3.3, where the classic travelling salesman problem (TSP) is addressed using SOM concepts.

### 8.3.3.2 SOM unsupervised classification of hyper-spectral image data

A neural network-based unsupervised classification procedure known as a Self-Organizing Map (SOM) can be developed from an extension to the single spectrum angular mapping (SAM) analysis described in Section 4.2.12.3. In the following example the same 512x614 pixel image with 224 spectral layers provides the sample dataset. The procedure operates broadly as per the earlier discussion. The number of classes in this process is preset, in this case to 512, using a 16x32 SOM neural network. Each cell in the net, 1...k, is initially assigned a random vector, $m_k$, of values — typically these will be random numbers for each spectral band drawn from a uniform distribution over the observed range for the band in question or for all bands in the image.

The next step is to train the neural network by comparing a randomly selected pixel from the source image that has spectral vector x say, to the vectors of each neural network unit. This comparison is achieved using a *norm*:

$$d_{xk} = \|\mathbf{x} - \mathbf{m}_k\|$$

that measures the separation between the sample spectral vector, x, and the $k^{th}$ unit in the neural network, $m_k$. The measure most commonly applied is of the form:

$$d_{xk} = \sum_i (x_i - m_{ki})^2$$

where $x_i$ and $m_{ki}$ are the $i^{th}$ elements of their respective vectors. The *best matching unit* (BMU) is the SOM unit, c say, which has the smallest separation from the input vector as computed using the selected norm. The components or weights of this BMU vector are then modified using a very simple general formula:

$$m_{ci}(t+1) = m_{ci}(t) + p(t)[x(t) - m_{ci}(t)]$$

where t is the time period (iteration number or epoch) and $p(t)$ is an adjustment factor that varies with time, t. In practice $p(t)$ consists of two components:

$$p(t) = a(t)h_{cj}(t)$$

The first of these components, $a(t)$, is known as the learning rate, and is simply a fractional value that is (typically) adjusted over time. For example, if T is the total number of steps or epochs in the training period, $a(t)$ might be taken as a simple decreasing linear function of time over the interval $[0,T]$, starting at $a(0)=0.5$:

$$a(t) = a(0)(1 - t/T) \text{ or } a_t = a_0(1 - t/T)$$

The second component is the grid neighborhood time-adjusted kernel function, $h_{cj}(t)$. All vectors (j) within a specified neighborhood of the BMU, c (typically all those that relate to adjacent grid cells and/or within a specified radius, r, of c) are adjusted using a pre-selected formula, i.e. not just the central BMU, at c. In its simplest form, all map vectors (j) within grid radius r of c are adjusted equally, i.e. $h_{cj}=1$ if distance $d_{cj} \le r$ otherwise $h_{cj}=0$. Two-dimensional kernel functions of the type previously described in connection with density modeling are commonly used (see further, Table 8-7), particularly Gaussian or truncated Gaussian functions. This adjustment can be seen as migrating point c in k-space and its near neighbors towards the sample point x. This process, which is a form of sequential regression, is repeated for a substantial sample of pixels often involving thousands of iterations. If the input data are 1-, 2- or 3-dimensional the progress of the adjustment process can be visualized, for example by displaying the results every 10 epochs, providing a form of video of the progress of the procedure.

When the process has completed the individual units or grid cells will have converged to a set of vectors that provide a form of 'best representation' of the sample data. The SOM grid will contain similar vectors in close proximity to each other. These vectors can then be used to create a classified version of the source image, using the spectral angle method described earlier. The spectrum of each pixel in the source dataset is compared with the model spectra in the SOM grid and the BMU determines the classification applied. Coding nearby units in the SOM with similar or the same colors and applying these to the source dataset produces a geographic map that both identifies regions that are similar in spectral data and at the same time offers a fine level of discrimination. Figure 8-29 illustrates this classification process for the

Cuprite dataset discussed earlier in this Guide (Section 4.2.12.3).

*Figure 8-29 SOM classification of remotely-sensed hyperspectral data*

**Issues:** There are a number of important observations that should be made regarding the SOM procedure described:

- **Initialization:** the choice of the initial set of map vectors can influence both the speed of the computation and its outcome. Speed may be considerably improved by judicious choice of initial vectors in some problems, i.e. rather than random vector assignment. Multiple runs of the procedure with different initialized vectors may help to produce more consistent or robust results than a single run. For example, it is entirely possibly that two or more groups of similar vectors will be located within the SOM, but which remain isolated from each other rather than forming a single, cohesive grouping

- **Pre-processing:** with remote sensed data, factors such as atmospheric scattering, topography, surface lighting (solar effects) and data capture variables (e.g. view angle, stripes) may warrant pre-processing of the data to minimize or remove known effects

- **Normalization:** whilst it may be reasonable to expect the data values of a hyperspectral image to have a broadly similar range across the spectral bands this is not the case for general attribute data. For example, with attributes such as cases of a particular disease in sampled zones the data range might be 0-100, whilst other variables, such as the zone population or a pollutant measurement, may be in a much larger range. The latter variable might dominate the BMU computation and hence hide variations in key attributes. Pre-normalization of the data vectors, for example by ensuring each has unit variance, may be advisable in such cases. Normalizations supported within the SOM Toolbox include: variance (vectors normalized to unit variance and 0 mean); range (vector components normalized to a [0,1] range); log (simple logarithmic transformation); softmax (vector components are initially variance normalized and the results converted using the logistic function into a [0,1] range with logistic curve form); and histogram (data values are replaced by histogram bins with approximately equal numbers of observations in each bin. Bins are ordered 1, 2, 3 etc. and then finally scaled to give a [0,1] data range. Note that output data and visualizations can be produced for non-normalized, normalized or for data that has been normalized and then de-normalized prior to output

- **Missing data:** the computation of the distance metric assumes that all spectral bands or all attribute sets in the sample and final datasets are present. If one or more gaps in the data exist this can either be ignored and assumed to have little or no impact on the result, or the missing attribute data could be assumed to apply to all samples, hence effectively removing this component from the analysis

- **Masking and weighting:** it may be desirable to mask off (binary weight) or apply a variable weighting to some data in the sample or final datasets. This could be at the attribute level or the feature level

- **Learning and tuning**: it is commonly the case that different rates of adjustment are required for an initial learning period (sometimes called the ordering phase) and the subsequent fine-tuning phase of learning. In both instances similar time-dependent functions may be used, but each with different initial parameters. For example, the default parameters in the MATLab Neural Network toolbox are: 0.9 (ordering-phase learning rate, for an initial 1000 steps); max grid cell separation distance (ordering-phase neighborhood distance>1); 0.02 (tuning-phase learning rate, for subsequent steps); and 1 (tuning-phase neighborhood distance, i.e. immediate neighbors only)

- **Distance metrics**: a variety of grid or lattice distance metrics, $d_{cj}$, may be employed. Examples include: Euclidean; Manhattan (rectilinear); Box distance (directly adjacent cells in a rectangular grid 3x3 cell Moore neighborhood=1 distance unit away, or the outer cells of an expanded Moore neighborhood of 5x5 cells=2 units away etc.); and Link distance (based on connectivity steps between grid cells or nodes). Note that calculations, especially at grid edges, will vary according to the chosen grid form and topology (e.g. rectangular or hexagonal; sheet, cylinder or toroidal)

- **Neighborhood functions and Learning rate functions**: Table 8-7 provides a summary of some of the commonly used functions employed. Essentially the neighborhood functions are kernel functions of the type encountered previously

*Table 8-7 SOM neighborhood and learning rate functions*

| Functions | Name | Expressions |
|---|---|---|
| **Neighborhood functions** | Bubble | $h_{cj}(t) = \max\left\{0, 1-\left(\sigma_t - d_{cj}\right)\right\}$ |
| | Gaussian | $h_{cj}(t) = \exp(-d_{cj}^2 / 2\sigma_j^2)$ |
| | Cut Gaussian | $h_{cj}(t) = \exp(-d_{cj}^2 / 2\sigma_j^2)1\left(\sigma_t - d_{cj}\right)$ |
| | Epanechnikov | $h_{cj}(t) = \max\left\{0, 1-\left(\sigma_t - d_{cj}\right)^2\right\}$ |
| where $\sigma_t$ is the neighborhood radius at time $t$, $d_{cj}$ is the distance between map units $c$ and $j$ on the grid using the chosen grid metric, and $1(x)$ is the step function $1(x)=0$ if $x<0$ and $1(x)=1$ if $x>=0$ | | |
| **Learning rate functions** | Linear | $\alpha(t) = \alpha_0 (1 - t/T)$ |
| | Power | $\alpha(t) = \alpha_0 \left(0.005/\alpha_0\right)^{t/T}$ |
| | Inverse | $\alpha(t) = \alpha_0 (1 + 100t/T)$ |
| where $T$ is the overall training length (steps) and $\alpha_0$ is the initial learning rate | | |

Idrisi (V15 and later) includes a number of neural network modeling tools, principally provided to facilitate image analysis and classification. In Section 8.3.1.4 we showed an example of the use of Idrisi's MLP neural network facility as part of a landcover change modeling (LCM) process. In Figure 8-30 and Figure 8-31 we show the standard Idrisi SOM NN facility applied to a multi-band satellite image set. We have selected unsupervised training, but supervised training is also supported by this module. As with the MLP module, multiple input rasters are specified — here they consist of 3 SPOT images covering a region of Malawi in East Africa, with one of the bands de-striped before processing (Band 2). The input layer is thus 3 nodes, whilst the SOM output layer must be specified as an *n*-by-*n* grid. We have specified an 8x8 grid with initial clustering performed by *k*-means and a

maximum of 10 clusters. The default initial neighborhood radius was selected which reduces to 1 as training proceeds.

The process commences with the 'coarse tuning' phase, during which the network attempts to identify clusters in the input data and group similar clusters in the output layer. The second stage is to classify the map using the learnt weights, assigning a cluster ID to every pixel of the image space. In this case nine clusters were identified and then mapped as shown in Figure 8-31.

*Figure 8-30 Self Organizing Map (SOM) classification — Idrisi*

*Figure 8-31 SOM classified 3-band image*

| A. Source image — SPOT band 1 | B. SOM classified result (9 classes) |
| --- | --- |
|  | 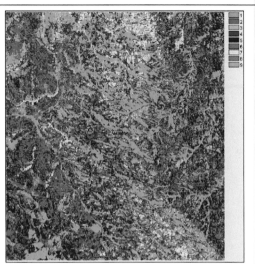 |

### 8.3.3.3  TSP optimization using SOM concepts

If the input dataset is comprised of $m$ points in 2 dimensions, the coordinates can be viewed as $m$ sets of 2-element vectors. The SOM procedure can be run with $n<m$ initial units which could be initially set to random coordinates, all set to the same coordinate (e.g. the median of the $x$- and $y$- ranges in the source data), or a simple linear spread across one or both axes. As training proceeds, the initial positions of the model vectors (i.e. the locations of the units in 2-space) will migrate towards the source data points in a manner which will minimize a separation measure of the form:

$$d_{xm} = \sum_i \left( x_i - m_i \right)^2$$

This process is essentially one of minimizing the sum of squares, so as noted earlier is a form of sequential regression. But the SOM not only adjusts the BMU but also its neighbors. This observation has led some authors to consider a variation on the SOM method that can be used as an heuristic to solve the travelling salesman problem (TSP). The

algorithm we describe is due to Angeniol *et al.* (1988), but it has since been improved by other authors and applied to well-known test problems (such as TSPLIB test ATT532). The idea with this approach is to create a tour of $M$ cities in the plane by commencing with a set of units or nodes connected together to form a 1-dimensional ring, rather like an elastic band. The objective is to progressively move the nodes that form this ring towards the $M$ cities through an iterative process, with an actual tour being obtained when each city has "captured" one node of the ring. The algorithm is as follows:

- Cities are numbered $i=1$ to $M$ and assigned coordinates:

$$\left( x_1^i, x_2^i \right)$$

- Nodes of the ring are assigned coordinates:

$$\left( c_1^j, c_2^j \right)$$

- Initially a single node ($N=1$) is generated as $(0,0)$. Nodes are added and deleted as the process proceeds. Each node on the ring has two neighbors, these being nodes $j$-1 (mod $N$) and $j$+1 (mod $N$)

- Select each city, $i$, in turn (sequentially, from 1 to $M$) in a pre-defined random order that is kept constant throughout the processing. Find the node $c$ on the ring that is closest to $i$ (minimum squared Euclidean distance). Move node $c$ and its ring neighbors closer to $i$ according to the rules described below and continue

- If the node $c$ is the closest node to more than one city, create a new node with the same coordinates. This will clearly occur frequently in the early stages of iteration, and the number of nodes will grow to at most $2M$ (from experimental evidence)

- If a node has not been selected as the closest to a city for 3 iterations it is deleted

- The movement rule applied is:

$$c_k^j \leftarrow c_k^j + f(G,n) \cdot (x_k^i - c_k^j)$$

- which can be compared with the basic SOM rule:

$$m_i^{t+1} \leftarrow m_i^t + p^t \cdot \left(x^t - m_i^t\right)$$

- In this case the function $f(G,n)$ is of Gaussian form with $n$ being the distance around the ring of each node from that chosen (where this is computed as the least distance) and $G$ is a parameter that the authors describe as the gain. The function is of the form:

$$f(G,n) = \frac{1}{\sqrt{2}} e^{-(n/G)^2}$$

- The parameter $G$ is reduced during each completed processing of the $M$ cities by a factor $(1-a)$ where $0<a<1$ (e.g. $a=0.2$). When $G$ is large all nodes move towards city $i$ with the same strength, whereas as $G$ tends to 0 only the closest node moves towards city $i$. Simulation tests on sets of up to 1000 cities showed good results (i.e. within a small percentage of the known optimum value) within modest computational time — decreasing the parameter $a$ produces better results but increases the processing time considerably. A more recent test using a slightly modified version of this algorithm applied to the ATT532 test dataset (532 US cities) produced a best result of 28,658 as compared with the known optimum solution of 27,686 (this can be verified using the Concorde software package and selecting the ATT metric — this metric is simply a Euclidean metric with an adjustment factor of the square root of 0.1)

# 8.4 Genetic Algorithms and Evolutionary Computing

Genetic algorithms, genetic programming and evolutionary computing are terms that fall within the general sphere of "Evolutionary Computation". We have previously noted that Agent-based Models can be regarded as a form of evolutionary computing, and indeed the MASON toolkit (see Section 8.2.11) has been produced by the Evolutionary Computing Laboratory at George Mason University. A useful source of information regarding many of these topics is the "Hitchhiker's Guide to Evolutionary Computing", available as an online and downloadable document set edited by Heitkötter and Beasley (2000).

## 8.4.1 Genetic algorithms — introduction

Genetic algorithms (GAs) are computationally intensive global search heuristics, or metaheuristics. They have very wide applicability, but their implementation is often highly problem specific and there is only a relatively loose understanding as to why they often work rather well. This Section provides an initial outline of GAs and how they can be applied in spatial analysis. Section 8.4.2 provides details of the main components of GAs, whilst Section 8.4.3 provides example geospatial applications and specifications for the various GA components used in these instances.

The central idea behind GAs is to mimic the Darwinian notion that selective breeding seeks optimum individuals in a given environment. In order to do this a GA requires a way of representing a solution to a (spatial) problem as if it were an individual viewed as a *chromosome* or 'genome'. Each individual (chromosome) is typically modeled as a string of codes (genes) in a particular order (see further, below). GAs then apply a *fitness function* which is used to determine which members of the population of solutions are retained and which are discarded. The fittest members are selected and a new generation is created through the genetic operations of crossover (e.g. splitting each chromosome into two parts or extracting a fixed length segment and recombining each part with the other) and mutation (e.g. simple interchange of genes within a chromosome). This gives rise to two offspring (new potential members of the solution set) whose fitness is then evaluated. The least fit member or members of the original population are then replaced with the fittest offspring and the process is iterated for a large number of generations or until some other stopping criterion is reached. A simple web-based example of a genetic algorithm in action is provided via the Netlogo models page.

Although GAs often use binary strings to represent solutions, where each bit in the string corresponds to a particular element of the solution, many representations are possible. For the travelling salesman problem (TSP) for example, with $n$ cities, a string might be used as the representation, where each element of the string contains the identity (e.g. a number, 103, 12 etc.) of each one of the cities, as shown below (note this could result in very long strings, which is not particularly efficient):

| 103 | 12 | 33 | 90 | 67 | 201 | 11 | ... | ... |
|-----|-----|-----|-----|-----|-----|-----|-----|-----|

A population of $P << n!$ randomly permutated strings can then be generated as the starting point for the population (set of prospective solutions). Each of these strings has a cost or length, $d$, and the fitness of a string can be computed as $1/d$, for example — hence the fittest strings (highest fitness values) are the shortest tours. All that remains is to run the algorithm until a stopping criterion is reached.

An outline GA procedure for solving the TSP is thus:

- Create a set of $P$ randomly permuted strings representing potential solution tours — $P$ is often very large (e.g. 100s or 1000s), in order to ensure that the solution space is well represented from the start

- Evaluate the fitness of each tour (i.e. the $1/d$ function) and sort these by fitness

- Select random pairs of solutions from all or a percentage of the population with a probability based on their fitness. For each selected pair perform a crossover combination operation. With binary strings this is simple, but with lists of cities it is more complicated since duplication of cities is not permitted, so additional checks are required (e.g. removing cities in chromosome 1 that appear in a fixed length segment of chromosome 2 and vice versa, and then appending these segments onto each other's chromosomes). Having performed this operation, mutate one or more of the genes of these offspring with a very low probability (e.g. randomly change gene 24, say, from a 1 to a 0, or randomly select two genes and swap them)

- Evaluate the fitness of the offspring

- Replace all or the least fit members of the population with the new generation (retaining the best performing individual or individuals from generation to generation is known as *elitist selection*. and often improves overall performance of the GA)

- Iterate the above steps until a specified stopping criterion has been reached

The effect of the steps described is to gradually increase the average fitness of the population, such that the fittest members (hopefully) approximate the global optimum solution. Unfortunately this may not be the case, as GAs can often converge to local optima and then stubbornly refuse to improve. Furthermore, GAs are not particularly efficient in terms of computational resources (memory, time), especially when compared with other metaheuristics such as simulated annealing. They do have the advantage of considerable flexibility, however, which combined with their overall performance can make them a very attractive option.

By systematically modifying the parameters of the algorithm (population size, mutation rate, cross-over rate and type, fitness function) significant improvements may be made. It is often also useful to combine a GA with other optimization techniques, especially local search, in order to improve the results. This is in part because GAs tend to under-perform when compared with problem-specific algorithms, but their generality often finds good initial solutions, that can then be systematically improved.

Genetic algorithms have been applied increasingly in geospatial analysis, particularly addressing demanding problems, including clustering, zone design/re-districting, model-building, map labeling, map feature simplification, constrained optimum location problems, and many more. Dijk *et al.* (2002) provide a fuller discussion, some observations from which we examine in greater detail below (Sections 8.4.2 and 8.4.3).

## 8.4.2 Genetic algorithm components

In the following subsections we provide details of the main components that make up typical genetic algorithms. For each component examples of the various optional settings for these components are provided, many of which are provided within general-purpose GA software toolsets such as GALib, from Matt Wall at MIT, and the commercial MATLab Genetic Algorithm and Direct Search Toolbox.

### 8.4.2.1 Encoding or representation

GA's require representation of possible solutions as chromosome or genome-like objects. The most widely used representations are binary strings and lists, although other representations such as trees and multi-dimensional arrays are possible. A single chromosome or genome consists of separate elements or genes., each of which contains a value (or *allele*) which may be binary, integer, real-valued or even symbolic. A typical binary coded chromosome (the gray-shaded string below) would be of the form:

| A | B | C | D | E | F | G | ... | ... |
|---|---|---|---|---|---|---|-----|-----|
| 1 | 0 | 0 | 1 | 1 | 1 | 0 | ... | ... |

where A, B, C... represent separate elements of the problem and the values '0' and '1' the presence or absence of these elements. For example, Fischer and Leung (1998) used a 68-bit string to encode a multi-layer neural network spatial interaction model, in which individual bits were assigned meanings such as: bits 1,8 and 15 = presence/absence of hidden layers 1, 2 and 3 respectively; bits 2-7 = the number of nodes in the first hidden layer (hence<64); etc.

Typical list representations might be of the form:

| 1 | 5 | 3 | 3 | 11 | 2 | 7 | ... | ... |
|---|---|---|---|----|---|---|-----|-----|

where each gene corresponds to a separate data item and the values (or alleles) 1,5,3,3... represent the assignments of individual data items to separate classes or clusters; or

| 103 | 12 | 33 | 90 | 67 | 201 | 11 | ... | ... |
|-----|----|----|----|----|-----|----|-----|-----|

where again each gene corresponds to a separate data item and 103,12,33... represent index values of these data items (e.g. identifying a set of discrete locations, such as cities or candidate facilities). Note that these last two representations require the use of very long strings as every element (gene) of the string (chromosome, genome) is a unique item from the dataset.

### 8.4.2.2 Fitness function

Specification of a suitable fitness function is a key element in the design of a successful GA. It measures how good a single individual is in terms of meeting the problem objective, e.g. minimization of total travel time. Hence for many geospatial problems the fitness function is simply based on the objective function of the problem, or some simplified or surrogate version of this that provides a suitable comparative measure and can be computed

without excessive processor overhead. The result of the fitness function is typically a real-valued number (*fitness value*), with higher values assigned to better performing individuals. These real values are generally transformed, often twice, to create a standardized score that is then used in the selection of parents for reproduction.

Fitness is typically computed for all members of the population, at each generation of the procedure, and the fitness values for all members are then ranked (first transform) such that the fittest=Rank 1 and the least fit=Rank P, where P is the population size. This ranking (*fitness rank*) is then used to guide selection of parents for reproduction, with higher ranking parents being selected preferentially. This can be achieved by randomly selecting from the top N or top x% of the ranked individuals, but more commonly some form of rank scaling is performed (second transform) and selection takes place from this modified dataset. Typically rank scaling assigns a *fitness score* to each chromosome based on its rank, r, such that better rankings (1,2,3,...) have disproportionately higher fitness scores. A standard transform is of the form:

$$s_r = \frac{c}{\sqrt{r}}, \text{ where } c = \frac{\sum_r \sqrt{r}}{N}, N \le P$$

For example, with N=P=40, c is chosen such that the sum of the transformed values = N, in this case c=3.55. A graph of the transformed ranks is shown in Figure 8-32. Other forms of scaling can be applied, such as simple inverse rank fitness scaling (e.g. of the form $s_r=k/r$, where k is a constant). These transformed values then have an effect on the subsequent selection procedures that can be used (see Section 8.4.2.4).

*Figure 8-32 Rank score transform*

### 8.4.2.3 Population initialization

Most GAs are initialized with a substantial number of chromosomes that represent alternative solutions to the problem being analyzed. The size of this population, *P*, is typically set between 100 and several 1000s, depending on the nature of the problem, the size of the solution space and the need to provide a thorough coverage of this space. Obviously, the larger this population the greater the amount of processing required. For multivariate optimization problems the population size should be significantly greater than the number of variables in the problem.

Typical initializations of population strings include simple uniform random, order-based random (random permutations), and allele-based random (i.e. randomized values). The initialization chosen will depend upon the problem and its encoding. Intelligent initialization is possible, whereby the solution space has been subjected to prior statistical analysis which is used to guide the initialization towards 'good' starting points.

### 8.4.2.4 Selection

Genetic algorithms select members of the current generation to act as parents for the next generation. Selection is biased according to the fitness of the parents, but selection of specific pairs of individuals for use in the creation of new children remains to be determined. The approach to selection depends to some extent on the way in which fitness values have been scaled. Note that the same parent may be selected multiple times, but selection of the same pair of parents may be disallowed.

There are several commonly used selection procedures:

- **Roulette:** this selection procedure treats the fitness scores as if they were parts of a pie diagram, producing under random selection a form of roulette wheel that is biased in favor of the largest segments of the wheel (i.e. the fittest individuals)

- **Tournament:** *m*>2 prospective parents are chosen at random from the population, *P*, and the fittest two are selected

- **Uniform random:** the fitness score of parents determines their probability of being selected – often achieved by an initial selection based on random selection proportionate to the fitness score for parent 1, with a fixed offset to select parent 2 (e.g. regarding all parents as laid out along a line whose segment lengths reflect their scores)

### 8.4.2.5 Reproduction

Reproduction is the process of creating a new set of children using pairs of parents selected from the current generation. In principle all parents could be candidates for selection. However, frequently only a proportion is selected for reproduction (crossover), typically 70%-80%. In addition a number of the fittest parents may be retained to the next generation, e.g. an *elite* set, say of the best 2,3 or more. It has been found, in practice, that setting a crossover percentage to 100% does not yield good solutions in most cases, and likewise reducing the percentage too much (e.g. below 20%) is also ineffective.

### 8.4.2.6 Crossover

Crossover is the process by which genetic material from one parent is combined with genetic material from the second parent to produce new offspring. The simplest form of crossover is called single-point. If the chromosome length is *n*, say, a random number between 2 and *n* is generated and the chromosome of each parent is effectively split at this point. For example, if A and B are the parents

A = [a b c d e f g h]    B = [1 2 3 4 5 6 7 8]

and the crossover point is 3, the following child is generated:

child 1 = [a b c 4 5 6 7 8]

A second child may also be generated, as follows:

child 2 = [1 2 3 d e f g h]

With two-point crossover two random numbers are generated, in a similar manner to that described above. Using the same example, with crossover points 3 and 6, we have:

child 1 = [a b c 4 5 6 g h]

A second child may also be generated, as follows:

child 2 = [1 2 3 d e f 7 8]

So-called *uniform crossover* utilizes a crossover template, a random binary vector that is the same length as the parent chromosomes. This template is used to select which genes from each parent should be crossed over. For example, if bit 1 in the template is 1, then gene 1 of parent 1 is chosen to create the first gene of the child. If bit 2 is 0 then gene 2 of parent 2 is chosen. A second child can then be generated by flipping the bit rule. With the template string: [1 1 0 0 1 0 0 0] the following children could be generated:

child 1 = [a b 3 4 e 6 7 8]

child 2 = [1 2 c d 5 f g h]

Other crossover options are possible, some of which are specific to the representation used (binary, list, tree etc.). For example, GALib supports the following crossover operators: arithmetic, blend, partial match, ordered, cycle, single point, two point, even, odd, uniform, node- and subtree-single point (see the GALib documentation for an explanation of these variants).

Heuristic (customized) crossover models may also be used, where knowledge of the problem representation and solution space can be used to ensure validly represented and hopefully fitter children are produced. For example, in many geospatial problems crossovers must be designed and checked to ensure replication of genes does not occur (e.g. a candidate location may only appear once in the list). Likewise, the spatial nature of the problem may suggest that certain types of crossover are preferable to others, for example locations that are geographically close to each other may be relevant in determining good (i.e. effective) crossover operations.

### 8.4.2.7 Mutation

Mutation is a process that randomly alters the population chromosomes in a manner that ensures greater genetic diversity and results in a broader search space than would otherwise occur. As with crossover, mutation may be achieved in many ways, some of which are representation dependent. The simplest form of mutation applies to vector representations, where a random gene is selected within each vector and with probability of, say 1%, is altered by flipping the bit (binary representations), or by swapping the allele value to a random number in the valid range for that allele. A percentage of genes may be selected for possible mutation, rather than just one. Furthermore, with some mutation models the nature and scale of mutation is governed by a statistical process (e.g. Gaussian) and has a decreasingly probability as the GA is run. With tree representations mutation may involve the swapping of tree nodes or entire sub-trees.

### 8.4.2.8 Local search

Solutions found by GAs are represented by the fittest member or members of the evolved population. Some problems may have multiple solutions with equal optimal values, whilst for others multiple solutions with comparable (not necessarily optimal) fitness may be desirable. However, GAs do not guarantee that optimal solutions will be found if they exist, nor do they provide an indication of how close they get to theoretical optimal solutions. They are generally sub-optimal, and sometimes, relatively poor or mediocre in their results. One way of improving this performance, often dramatically, is to combine the GA process with some form of local search algorithm, e.g. a greedy search or interchange search algorithm. This may be applied to all, or more typically, a subset of solutions, modifying the offspring to generate children that have significantly improved fitness, and which then replace less fit members of the population.

### 8.4.2.9 Termination

In many implementations termination of the GA occurs when a pre-specific number of iterations or *generations* have passed. Other criteria include convergence (e.g. of the fittest individual to the mean value in the population) or to a stable (non-improving) fitness value, or some combination of these options.

## 8.4.3 Example GA applications

Below we provide brief summaries of selected models that have been successfully applied to a variety of geospatial analysis problems in recent years. These examples are intended as illustrations of the range of applications and the general form of models applied. Readers are referred to the individual papers referenced for full details. As will become apparent, some implementations are clearly better than others, in terms of quality of result, computational overhead, scalability, robustness and/or flexibility.

### 8.4.3.1 GA Example 1: TSP

In the introductory section (Section 8.4.1) we provided a simple TSP sample application as a means of illustrating the basic ideas of GAs applied to a geospatial problem. The C++ library, GALib provides a coded example of such a procedure (example 26), but describes the procedure as being very poor — there are much better ways of solving the TSP, as identified elsewhere in this Guide.

### 8.4.3.2 GA Example 2: Clustering

Painho and Bação (2000) applied GAs to the problem of optimally clustering artificial and real datasets, comparing their results with those obtained by the *K*-means clustering approach and self-organizing map clustering (SOM) . On the test dataset GA outperformed *K*-means and was similar to SOM in terms of misclassifications and the standard error of cluster dispersion (SE), whilst with real data GA produced the most tightly clustered results (lowest SE). Implementation of the procedure was carried out using the C++ software library, GALib, from MIT. GA components used in this example were as follows:

*Representation*: chromosomes with $n$ genes, each gene representing an individual datapoint (hence very long chromosomes). Alleles were the cluster assignments of these genes $(1,2,...K)$. A population size of $P=100$ was used. The chromosome representation was thus of the form:

| A | B | C | D | E | F | G | ... | ... |
|---|---|---|---|---|---|---|-----|-----|
| 1 | 5 | 3 | 3 | 3 | 2 | 7 | ... | ... |

where A, B, C... represent separate data items and 1,5,3... represent the cluster assignments of these data items, i.e. the values assigned to the genes of this chromosome (the gray-shaded string). Although simple, this representation is not scalable so is of limited use for most real-world problems. A more appropriate representational model for clustering with larger datasets is one in which chromosomes have length $Kd$ where $K$ is the number of clusters and $d$ is the number of variables or dimensions of the dataset, recorded as a real variable (see for example, Demiriz *et al.*, 1999, for a fuller discussion). Each set of $d$ numbers in this arrangement represents one cluster center and cluster assignment is based on Euclidean distance rather than genome value.

*Fitness*: The fitness function chosen was based on the sum of squared error, $E$, or overall cluster dispersion statistic. Using Painho and Bação's notation:

$$E = \sum_{k=1}^{K} \sum_{x \in C_k} \|x - m_k\|^2$$

where $m_k$ is the center of cluster $C_k$. This expression is very similar to a widely used measure (for the objective function) in $K$-means clustering (see further, Section 4.2.12.2), and is generally normalized by dividing the overall sum by the number of datapoints, $N$, to give a mean squared dispersion statistic.

*Selection*: A replacement percentage of 50% was used. Other details of the selection method are not provided.

*Crossover*: A crossover probability of 90% was used. Although not specified in this article, single point crossover is the most likely to have been implemented. Clustering algorithms that use the kind of representation applied in this example often use a combination of so-called *fusion* and *fission* operators. Fusion involves taking two unique allele values and combining them into a single value, thus combining two clusters into one, whilst fission takes a single allele value and assigns it a different random value, thus breaking a cluster apart.

*Mutation*: A mutation probability of 1% was used. Again, the details are not provided but can be assumed to be single point random mutation (i.e. altering the cluster assignment of a randomly selected data item).

*Stopping criterion*: 15000 generations

### 8.4.3.3 GA Example 3: Map labeling

Dijk *et al.* (2002) analyzed the use of GAs to address the map labeling problem. This problem involves placing labels on a conventional 2D map such that (as far as possible) labels do not overlap — or more specifically, that the maximum possible number of labels on a map do not overlap. For the problem described here labels can be placed in one of four positions relative to point objects: top left, bottom left, top right, bottom right. The basic procedure was tested using a rectangular grid and 1000 points placed such that, with labels of a given fixed size, it was possible for every point to be labeled with no overlap. To remove edge effects the underlying grid was treated as a torus, i.e. wrapping both pairs of edges to give a continuous edgeless surface. Multiple runs of the GA on multiple maps of the type described were tested and the results pooled. Overall the GA performed to within 80% of the optimum, but only after some 400 million intersection tests had been computed. This result is clearly not satisfactory, but can be greatly improved as described below.

Revising the GA by the use of an heuristic crossover procedure and coupling this with a local search optimizer yielded results that were very close to the theoretical optimum with roughly 25% of the number of label intersection tests required. The results with this version of the GA were compared with the simulated annealing algorithm of Christensen *et al.* (1995) and found to be almost identical across a wide range of point set sizes. The authors conclude that the GA approach has the merit of high quality, scalability (to large numbers of points) and flexibility. The latter was exemplified by their extension of the constraints to include variable label size according to city size, special labels, preferential positioning and coastal city labeling (on the seaward side of the city in question).

*Representation*: If the possible label positions are denoted 1, 2, 3 and 4, these are the alleles of the representation, with each map point being a gene. Chromosomes are thus long strings of integers, with length equal to the number of points, *N*, to be mapped. The size of the initial population in this example was not specified. Initialization of the population involved random assignment of alleles.

*Fitness*: The fitness of a particular chromosome is simply the number of labels that do not intersect. This requires computation of label overlaps for each chromosome, which is the most processor-intensive part of the procedure.

*Selection*: Tournament, roulette and uniform selection were all tested and tournament selection proved to be the best choice. In this instance the basic tournament size chosen was 2, with the fittest parent being selected in each case. The process was repeated *n* times to select *n* parents and produce *n* children. Subsequently an *elitist* model was tested, where the two parents and two children were evaluated for fitness and the fittest two retained (i.e. this could yield a mix of parents and children).

*Reproduction*: For every pair of parents selected two children were produced, either by crossover and mutation or by cloning and mutation. Cloning simply reproduces the parent(s) in the next generation.

*Crossover*: Several alternatives were tested, with one point crossover performing best in the initial test. However, this procedure does not take into account the known spatial aspects of this problem. For this reason an alternative crossover procedure was designed that reflected the nature of the problem at hand. First, a random point on the map is selected and all neighboring points that could, in principle, contain intersecting labels were identified and marked. This set contains what may be regarded as a building block for this particular problem. The process of random selection and marking continues until 50% of all the mapped points have been marked. Then two children are generated by copying the labellings of the marked points (parent 1) as the first half of the child genome and the labellings of the unmarked points as the second half, and vice versa for the second child. The process continues for the next member of the population by selecting another random starting point. The result of this process is a pattern of crossover that disrupts the local linkage of the building blocks as little as possible. The resulting genomes can, however, be further improved by simple local optimization (see below).

*Mutation*: Mutation was ignored in this problem.

*Local search*: The initial experiment did not include a local search facility, whereas the enhanced algorithm added this operation, which substantially improved the quality of solution. Local search was conducted as follows. If the building blocks of newly produced genomes are examined it is possible to identify non-disruptive changes that will reduce the number of intersecting labels. It is also possible to apply additional positioning criteria, e.g. that coastal locations should have their labels placed in the sea. For each building block where new conflicts have arisen, the label is moved to a random available empty slot (i.e. one which no overlapping will occur as a result of the move), assuming one is available.

*Termination*: In the initial trials, this was set to 400 million intersection tests following prior experiments and consideration of available compute resources.

#### 8.4.3.4 GA Example 4: Optimum location

Correa *et al.* (2001) applied a GA to the problem of selecting 26 facilities from 43 candidate sites, each of which has capacity constraints. The search space of possible solutions is $43!/(26!*17!)$, i.e. just over $4*10^{11}$ alternative configurations. The sites to be selected needed to minimize the total travel distance to exam centers for 19,710 students. The problem is thus a classical *p*-median problem with capacity constraints. In this instance the researchers made the following choices for the GA:

*Representation*: each chromosome was assigned *p* genes (*p*=26 in this case). The value (allele) assigned to a gene was the index number of the site (hence a value from 1 to 43). A population size of *P*=100 was used

*Fitness*: Although fitness was essentially computed based on the standard total summed distance for all journeys to facilities, an additional computation was necessary to allocate students to facilities that were not their closest if facility capacity had already been reached. The procedure assigned students to their second, third... etc. nearest facility based on which student would be most disadvantaged (in terms of distance travelled) by so doing. Clearly this is an extremely processor intensive calculation.

*Selection*: Selection was based on pairs of individuals with a bias towards the fittest individuals. The individuals in the population were ranked according to fitness, 1...*P* where *P* is the population size applied to the problem (*P*=100 in this case). The selection rule used the formula:

$$s = P - floor\left(\frac{-1 + \sqrt{1 + 4rnd(P^2 + P)}}{2}\right)$$

where floor is the integer rounding down function and rnd(*x*) is a uniform random number generator over the interval [0,*x*]. With *P*=100 and selecting the first 5 pairs of results from a sample run of this selection model, the following example results (parents selected) were obtained:

(53,23) (31,7) (14,34) (88,10) (34,23)

The selection function is approximately linear with rank over the long run. Offspring were only inserted into the population if their fitness score exceeded that of the worst current member.

*Crossover*: The procedure applied was a form of one point crossover, but applied to pre-processed 'exchange vectors' rather than the source chromosome. These exchange vectors were designed to ensure that offspring do not contain duplicated locations. The exchange vector for parent 1 only contains locations that are not present in parent 2's chromosome, and vice versa. The length of each exchange vector is computed and a random number of locations less than this value in each case are swapped between the two parents.

*Mutation*: A single randomly selected location, not in the current chromosome, is selected and used to replace one gene selected at random in the individual's chromosome. The probability of mutation was set to 1%.

*Local search*: Without additional local search the test results did not perform quite as well as tabu search (see further, Section 7.2.2.4). When an interchange heuristic (that the authors describe as *hypermutation* − occurring with probability 0.5%, applied to 10% of the population, *P*) was added to the algorithm, the GA outperformed tabu search in terms of the average distance students would have to travel and the percentage being served by their geographically closest location. Processor overhead for this procedure was high, mainly due to the repeated computation of the fitness function that was required.

### 8.4.4 Evolutionary computing and genetic programming

As noted earlier, related to the field of genetic algorithms is the broader topic known as *evolutionary computing*. This field now has many strands, incorporating genetic algorithms (GAs), genetic programming (GP — see below), agent-based modeling (ABM), artificial life and cellular automata (CA), together with a range of metaheuristics applied in isolation or in conjunction with other procedures within this broad family. There have been a wide range of areas to which evolutionary computing concepts have been applied. Readers are referred to Diplock (2000) for an introduction to the subject and an application in the field of spatial interaction modeling, and to Banzhaf *et al.* (1998) for a full treatment of the subject.

Like GAs, genetic programming (GP) involves similar selection and evolutionary ideas, but instead of binary or simple numerically coded chromosomes representing members of the solution space, GP uses coded symbolic expressions or operators. The idea behind genetic programming is to evolve computer programs or models rather than solutions to optimization or similar problems. However, if one applies GA methods to GP problems two limitations are encountered: (i) finite bit strings or coded stings are unsuitable forms for developing (growing and shrinking) structures, hence tree structures are widely used for encoding rather than strings; and (ii) only certain operations produce valid programs or models, hence most GA-type reproduction and mutation mechanisms will result in invalid solutions that therefore have zero fitness. In particular, mutation operations are not normally supported within GP. Tree structures with well-defined sets of 'valid' operations (e.g. swapping entire sub-trees) can be designed to generate new solutions that have non-zero fitness, so again this architecture can assist in resolving the second of these problems.

For example, in a spatial interaction model, initial operators might include: (a) a set of basic *functions* such as +, -, /, *, ^, cos(), sin(), log(), exp() etc.; and (b) initial variables (known as *terminals*) such as origin and destination totals, inverted versions of these totals, inter-zonal distances, intervening opportunity measures etc. The aim is then to use these components, coupled with a known interaction dataset (e.g. journey-to-work data) to 'breed' or 'train' a model that fits the data as well as possible. This fit can then be compared with more conventional models in terms of sum of squared errors, for both trained datasets and untrained data. In many instances the models bred in Diplock's analysis are quite complicated, but some unexpected and quite good quality simpler models were generated, such as:

$$T_{ij} = \frac{D_j^2 e^{-d_{ij}/20}}{X_{ij}^{6/5}}$$

where $T_{ij}$ is the volume of trips from zone $i$ to zone $j$, $D_j$ is the total destination volume for zone $j$, $d_{ij}$ is the distance from zone $i$ to zone $j$, and $X_{ij}$ is a measure of intervening opportunities. Fischer and Leung (1998) tackled the same kind of problem, i.e. design of a spatial interaction model, using a combination of evolutionary methods and neural network techniques. The evolutionary component in this instance was used to select the most appropriate neural network model, which the neural network would then seek to fit to training datasets and then apply to unseen data (i.e. forecasting). Applications of GP in other fields of geospatial analysis have been limited — possibly the lack of tools to support this approach to model development has held it back, although the range of applications in related fields (e.g. ecology, land-use change forecasting, economics etc.) suggest that it remains an area open to considerable further research.

# Afterword

An important objective in developing this Guide has been to support a number of international initiatives in spatial literacy and geographic information science — of which the UK 'Spatial Literacy in Teaching' (SPLINT: www.spatial-literacy.org) programme, the TeachSpatial.org Wiki, the US National Academies 'Beyond Mapping' and Learning to think spatially initiatives, and the AAG/UCGIS Geographic Information Science and Technology "Book of Knowledge" (BoK) are currently the most prominent.

The formats in which this Guide is available make it accessible to a wide range of readers in education and the professions, and are amenable to frequent updating. We very much view the future development of the Guide as a project for the geospatial community that is never likely to be 'complete' — a more accurate title might have been 'Geospatial analysis: *towards* a comprehensive guide to principles, techniques and software tools'! To this end, we very much welcome suggestions as to topics that are missing from this current version of the Guide, as well as corrections to any errors readers may find.

These, together with any other comments, should be emailed to the authors via the web site, www.spatialanalysisonline.com

# References

Abdi H (1994) A neural network primer. J. of Biological Systems, 2(3), 247-283

Andrienko N, Andrienko G (2006) Exploratory analysis of spatial and temporal data, a systematic approach. Springer-Verlag, Heidelberg, Germany

Andrienko G, Andrienko N, Voss H (2003) GIS for everyone: the CommonGIS project and beyond. in M. Peterson (ed.) Maps and the Internet. Elsevier Science, Oxford, UK

Ahuja R K, Magnanti T L, Orlin J B (1993) Network flows: Theory, algorithms and applications. Prentice Hall, Englewood Cliffs, NJ, USA

Allan A L (2004) Maths for map makers. 2nd ed. Whittles Publishing, Dunbeath, Scotland

Alonso D, Sole R V (2000) The Divgame simulator: A stochastic cellular automata model of rainforest dynamics. Ecological Modeling, 133, 131-141

Angel S, Hyman G M (1976) Urban fields. Pion, London

Angeniol B, Vaubois G de la C, le Texier J-V (1988) Self-organizing feature maps and the travelling salesman problem. Neural Networks, 1, 289-293

Anselin L (1988) Spatial econometrics: Methods and models. Kluwer Academic Publishers, Dordrecht, NL

Anselin L (2002) Under the hood: Issues in the specification and interpretation of spatial regression models. Agricultural Economics, 17(3), 247-67

Anselin L (1995) Local indicators of spatial association — LISA. Geog. Anal., 27, 93-115

Anselin L, Bera A (1998) Spatial dependence in linear regression models with an introduction to spatial econometrics. in Ullah A, Giles D (eds.) Handbook of applied economic statistics. Marcel Dekker, New York, 237-89

Anselin L, Kim Y W, Syabri I (2003) Web-based analytical tools for the exploration of spatial data. J. of Geographical Systems 6(2), 197-218

Anselin L, Syabri I, Kho Y (2006) GeoDa: An introduction to spatial data analysis. Geog. Anal., 38, 5-22

Arnaud J-F, Madec L, Bellido A, Guiller A (1999) Microspatial genetic structure in the land snail Helix Aspersa (Gastropoda: Helicidae). Heredity, 83, 110-19

Armstrong D J (2006) The quarks of object-oriented development. Communication of the ACM, 49(2), 123-128

Arora S (1996) Polynomial time approximation scheme for Euclidean TSP and other geometric problems. Proc. 37th Ann. IEEE Symp. on Foundations of Computer Science, IEEE Computer Society, 2-11

Athale C A, Deisboeck T S (2006) The effects of EGF-receptor density on multiscale tumour growth patterns. J. of Theoretical Biology, 238, 771-779

Avella P, Sassano A, Vasil'ev I (2005) Computational study of large-scale p-median problems. Math. Program., A, 32, 215-30

Axelrod R (2006a) Agent-based modeling as a bridge between disciplines. in Tesfatsion L, Judd K L (eds.) Handbook of computational economics: Agent-based computational economics. North-Holland Publishing, Amsterdam, The Netherlands

Axelrod R (2006b) Advancing the art of simulation in the social sciences. in Rennard J-P (ed.) Handbook of research on nature inspired computing for economy and management. Idea Group, Hersey, USA

Axelrod R (2007) Simulation in the Social Sciences. in Rennard J P (ed.) Handbook of research on nature inspired computing for economy and management. Idea Group, Hershey, PA, pp. 90-100

Axelrod R, Bennett S D (1993) A landscape theory of aggregation. British J. of Political Science, 23(2), 211-233

Axelrod R, Tesfatsion L (2006) A guide for newcomers to agent-based modeling in the social sciences. in Tesfatsion L, Judd K L (eds.) Handbook of computational economics: Agent-based computational economics. North-Holland Publishing, Amsterdam, The Netherlands

Axtell R, Axelrod R, Epstein J M, Cohen D (1996) Aligning simulation models: A case study and results. Computational and Mathematical Organization Theory, 1, 123-141

Axtell R L (1999) The emergence of firms in a population of agents: Local increasing returns, unstable Nash equilibria, and power law sze distributions. Center on Social and Economic Dynamics: Working Paper No. 3, Washington, USA

Axtell R L (2000) Why agents? On the varied motivations for agent computing in the social sciences. Center on Social and Economic Dynamics (The Brookings Institute): Working Paper 17, Washington, D.C

Axtell R L, Epstein J M, Dean J S, Gumerman G J, Swedlund A C, Harburger J, Chakravarty S, Hammond R, Parker J, Parker M (2002) Population growth and collapse in a multiagent model of the Kayenta Anasazi in Long House Valley. Proceedings of the National Academy of Sciences of the United States of America (PNAS), 99(3), 7275-7279

Azis I J (1990) Analytical Hierarchy Process in the benefit-cost framework: A post-evaluation of the trans-Sumatra highway project. European J. of Operational Research, 48, 38-48

Beddeley A, Turner R (2005) Spatstat: an R package for analyzing spatial point patterns. J of Statistical Software, 12(6), 1-42. Downloadable from: (http://www.jstatsoft.org/v12/i06)

Baddeley A, Turner R, Moller J, Hazelton M (2005) Residual analysis for spatial point processes. J. of the Royal Statistical Society, Series B, 67, 617-666

Bailey K (2003) AMIS: Development and application of a GIS/Multicriteria corridor evaluation methodology. Proc. Map Asia 2003 conference, Kuala Lumpur, Malaysia

Bailey T C, Gatrell A C (1995) Interactive spatial data analysis. Longman, Harlow, UK

Bak P, Paczuski M, Shubik M (1999) Price variations in a stock market with many agents. Cowles Foundation: Discussion Paper 1132: http://cowles.econ.yale.edu

Ball G H, Hall D J (1965) A novel method of data analysis and pattern classification. Stanford Research Institute, Menlo Park, California

Banzhaf W, Nordin P, Keller R E, Francone F D (1998) Genetic Programming – an introduction. Morgan Kaufmann, San Francisco, CA, USA

Baskent E Z, Jordan G A (1995) Characterizing spatial structure of forest landscapes. Can. J. For. Res. 25, 1830-49

Batty J M, Densham P J (1996) Decision support, GIS, and urban planning. Systemma Terra, V(1), 72-76

Batty M (2001) Agent-based pedestrian modeling. Environment and Planning B, 28(3), 321-326

Batty, M (2005) Agents, Cells and Cities: New representational models for simulating multi-scale urban dynamics. Environment and Planning A, 37(8), 1373-1394

Batty M (2007) Cities and complexity. MIT Press, Cambridge, MA, USA (1st pub. 2005)

Batty M, Conroy R, Hillier B, Jiang B, Desyllas J, Mottram C, Penn A, Smith A, Turner A (1998) The virtual Tate. Working Paper 5, CASA, University College London: http://www.casa.ucl.ac.uk/publications/workingpapers.asp

Batty M, Desyllas J, Duxbury E (2002) The discrete dynamics of small-scale spatial events: Agent-based models of mobility in carnivals and street parades. Working Paper 56, CASA, University College London: http://www.casa.ucl.ac.uk/publications/workingpapers.asp

Batty M, Desyllas J, Duxbury E (2003a) Safety in numbers? Modeling crowds and designing control for the Notting Hill carnival. Urban Studies, 40(8), 1573-1590

Batty M, Desyllas J, Duxbury E (2003b) The discrete dynamics of small-scale spatial events: Agent-Based Models of mobility in carnivals and street parades. Center for Advanced Spatial Analysis (University College London): Working Paper 56: http://www.casa.ucl.ac.uk/publications/workingpapers.asp

Beasley J E (1985) A note on solving large p-median problems. European J. of Operational Research, 21, 270-73

Beasley J, Christofides N (1989) An algorithm for the resource-constrained shortest path problem. Networks, 19, 379-394

Beasley J E (1990) OR-Library: distributing test problems by electronic mail. J. of the Operational Research Society 41(11), 1069-72

Beasley J E (1993) Lagrangian heuristics for location problems. European J. of Operational Research, 65, 383-99

Beltran C, Tadonki C, Vial J-P (2004) Semi-Lagrangian relaxation. Optimization Online,: www.optimization-online.org

Benedikt M L (1979) To take hold of space: Isovists and isovist fields. Environment and Planning B, 6(1), 47-65

Benenson I (2009) Geographic Automata Systems, Geosimulation and Object Based Environment for Urban Simulation (OBEUS) Research Page: Available at http://www.tau.ac.il/~bennya/research1.html

Benenson I, Aronovich S, Noam S (2005) Let's talk objects: generic methodology for urban high-resolution simulation. Computers, Environment and Urban Systems, 29, 425-453

Benenson I, Birfur S, Kharbash V (2004) OBEUS (Object-Based Environment for Urban Simulation) Shareware Version. Association Geographic Information Laboratories Europe (AGILE), Crete

Benenson I, Birfur S, Kharbash V (2006) Geographic Automata Systems and the OBEUS software for their implementation. in Portugali, J. (ed.) Complex Artificial Environments: Simulation, Cognition and VR in the Study and Planning of Cities Springer, Berlin, Germany, pp. 137-153

Benenson I, Omer I, Hatna E (2002) Entity-based modeling of urban residential dynamics: The case of Yaffo, Tel Aviv. Environment and Planning B, Planning and Design, 29, 491-512

Benenson I, Torrens P (2004) Geosimulation: Automata-based modeling of urban phenomena. John Wiley & Sons, London

Berger T, Parker D C (2001) Examples of specific research. in Parker D C, Berger T, Manson S M (eds.), Meeting the challenge of complexity: Proceedings of a special workshop on land-use/land-cover change. Irvine, California

Berke O (2000) Modified median polish kriging and its application to the Wolfcamp-acquifer data. Discussion Paper 48/00, Univ. of Dortmund, Dept of Statistics

Berke O (2004) Exploratory disease mapping: kriging the spatial risk function from regional count data. Intl. J of Health Geographics, 3(18), 1-11 (available from Biomed Central: www.ij-healthgeographics.com)

Bernard L, Krüger T (2000) Integration of GIS and spatio-temporal simulation models: Interoperable components for different simulation strategies. Transactions in GIS, 4(3), 197-215

Bernhardsen T (2002) Geographic Information Systems − an introduction. 3rd edition, J Wiley, Hoboken, NY, USA

Berry B J L, Marble D F (1968) Spatial analysis − a reader in statistical geography. Prentice Hall, New Jersey

Berry J K (1993) Beyond Mapping: Concepts, algorithms and issues in GIS. GIS World Books, and also available online in HTML format

Besag J, Kooperberg C L (1995) On conditional and intrinsic autoregressions. Biometrika, 82, 733-46

Besag J, York J, Mollie A (1991) Bayesian image restoration, with two applications in spatial statistics. Annals of the Institute of Statistical Maths, 43, 1-59

Blastland M, Dilnot A (2008) The tiger that isn't. Profile Books, London

Bluman A G (2003) Elementary statistics: A step by step approach. 5th edition, McGraw-Hill, New York

Bonabeau E (2002) Agent-based modeling: methods and techniques for simulating human systems. Proceedings of the National Academy of Sciences of the United States of America (PNAS), 99(3), 7280-7287

Booch G (1994) Object-Oriented analysis and design with applications. Benjamin/Cummings, Redwood City, USA

Boots B N (1987?) Voronoi (Thiessen) Polygons. CATMOG 45 (op. cit.)

Borgefors G (1996) On digital distance transforms in three dimensions. Computer Vision and Image Understanding, 64(3), 368-376

Bowman A W, Azzalini A (1997) Applied smoothing techniques for data analysis: The kernel approach with S-Plus illustrations. Oxford Statistical Science Series, Oxford University Press, Oxford

Brewer C A, Pickle L (2002) Evaluation of methods for classifying epidemiological data on choropleth maps in series. Annals Assoc. Amer. Geogs., 92, 662-81

Brown D G (1998) Classification and boundary vagueness in mapping presettlement forest types. Int. J. of Geog. Information Science, 12, 105-29

Brown D G (2006) Agent-based models. pp7-13 in Geist H (ed.) The Earth's changing land: An encyclopedia of land-use and land-cover change. Greenwood Publishing Group, Westport

Brown D G, Riolo R, Robinson D T, North M, Rand W (2005) Spatial process and data models: Toward integration of agent-based models and GIS. J. of Geographical Systems, 7(1), 25-47

Brunsdon C, Fotheringham A S, Charlton M (1998) Geographically Weighted Regression − modeling spatial non-stationarity. The Statistician, 47, 431-443

Burrough P A (1986) Principles of Geographical Information Systems for land resources assessment. Monographs on Soil and Resources Survey No. 12. Clarendon Press, Oxford

Burrough P A (1989) Fuzzy mathematical methods for soil survey and land evaluation. J. of Soil Science, 40, 477-92

Burrough P A, McDonnell R A (1998) Principles of Geographical Information Systems. Oxford University Press, Oxford

Candau J (2000) Calibrating a cellular automaton model of urban growth in a timely manner. Proceedings of the 4th International Conference on Integrating GIS and Environmental Modeling:

Problems, Prospects and Research Needs, Banff, Canada

Carley K M (1996) Validating computational models. Carnegie Mellon University: Working Paper, Pittsburgh, USA

Carlson R E, Foley T A (1991) Radial Basis methods on track data. Proc. of the 13th IMACS World Congress on Computation, R. Vichnevetsky (ed.), Criterion Press, Dublin, 428- 29

Carlson R E, Foley T A (1992) Interpolation of track data with radial basis methods. Computers & Mathematics with Applications, 24, 27-34

Carlyle W M, Wood R K (2003) Lagrangian relaxation and enumeration for solving constrained shortest-path problems. Proc, 38th Annual ORSNZ Conference, Waikato, New Zealand

Carr D B, Wallin J F, Carr D A (2000) Two new templates for epidemiology applications: Linked micromap plots and conditioned choropleth maps. Statistics in Medicine, 19, John Wiley & Sons, 2521-38

Carr D B, Chen J, Bell S, Pickle L, Zhang Y (2002) Interactive linked micromaps and dynamically conditioned choropleth maps. Proceedings of the Second National Conference on Digital Government Research, Digital Government Research Center, 61-7

Carvalho J (2000) Using AgentSheets to teach simulation to undergraduate students. J. of Artificial Societies and Social Simulation, 3(3)

CATMOG, or Concepts and Techniques in Modern Geography, were published between 1975 and 1995. See CATMOG section of QMRG and listing of titles in this Guide for more details

Casti J L (1997) Would-be-worlds: How simulation is changing the frontiers of science. John Wiley & Sons, New York, USA

Castle C J E (2006) Using Repast to develop a prototype agent-based pedestrian evacuation model. Proceedings of the Agent 2006 Conference on Social Agents: Results and Prospects, Chicago, USA

Castle C J E (2007) Agent-Based Modelling of pedestrian evacuation: A study of London's King's Cross Underground Station. PhD Thesis, University College London, London, UK

Castle C E, Crooks A (2006) Principles and concepts of agent-based modeling for developing geospatial simulations. CASA Working Paper 110, University College London

Chatfield C (1975) The analysis of time series: theory and practice. Chapman and Hall, London

Cheriton D, Tarjan R E (1976) Finding minimum spanning trees. SIAM J. Comput., 5, 724-42

Clark P J, Evans F C (1954) Distance to nearest-neighbor as a measure of spatial relationships in populations. Ecology, 35, 445-53

Cederman L-E (2001) Agent-based modeling in political science. The Political Methodologist, 10(1), 16-22

Chen L-C, Carley K M, Fridsma D, Kaminsky B, Yahja A (2006) Model alignment of anthrax attack simulations. Decision Support Systems, 41, 654-668

Christensen J, Marks J, Shieber S (1995) An empirical study of algorithms for point-feature label placement. ACM Transactions on Graphics, 14(3), 203-232

Christofides N, Beasley J (1982) A tree search algorithm for the p-median problem. European J. of Operational Research, 10, 196-204

Cliff A, Ord J (1973) Spatial autocorrelation. Pion, London

Cliff A, Ord J (1981) Spatial processes: models and applications. Pion, London (an updated and extended version of their 1973 book)

Collier N, North M J (2005) Repast for Python scripting. Annual Conference of the North American Association for Computational Social and Organizational Science (NAACSOS), Notre Dame, Indiana, USA

Conte R, Gilbert N, Sichman J S (1998) MAS and social simulation: A suitable commitment. in Sichman J S, Conte R, Gilbert N (eds.), Multi-agent systems and agent-based simulation. Springer, New York

Cooper L (1963) Location-allocation problems. Operations Research, 11, 331-43

Cooper L (1964) Heuristic methods for location-allocation problems. SIAM Review, 6, 37-53

Cormen T H, Leiserson C E, Rivest R L, Stein C (2001) Introduction to algorithms. 2nd ed., MIT Press, Cambridge, Mass.

Correa E S, Steiner M T A, Freitas A A, Carnieri C (2001) A genetic algorithm for the p-median problem. Proceedings of the Genetic and Evolutionary Computation Conference (GECCO-2001), San Francisco, CA, USA

Couclelis H (1985) Cellular Worlds: A framework for modeling micro-macro dynamics. Environment and Planning A, 17, 585-596

Couclelis H (2001) Why I no longer work with agents: A challenge for ABMs of human-environment interactions. in Parker D C, Berger T, Manson S M (eds.) Meeting the challenge of complexity: Proceedings of a special workshop on land-use/land-cover change. Irvine, California

Couclelis H (2002) Modeling frameworks, paradigms, and approaches. pp. 36-50 in Clarke K C, Parks B E, Crane M P (eds.) Geographic information systems and environmental modeling. Prentice Hall, London

Cressie N A C (1991, 1993) Statistics for spatial data. John Wiley, New York (Revised edition 1993)

Cressie N A C, Chan N H (1989) Spatial modeling of regional variables. J Amer. Stat. Assoc., 84, 393-401

Cromley R G (1996) A comparison of optimal classification strategies for choroplethic displays of spatially aggregated data. Int. J. of Geog. Information Science, 10, 101-109

Cromley R G , Ye Y (2006) Ogive-based legends for choropleth mapping. CAGIS, 33(4)

Crooks A T (2006) Exploring cities using agent-based models and GIS. Proceedings of the Agent 2006 Conference on Social Agents: Results and Prospects, Chicago, USA

Crooks A T (2007), Experimenting with cities: Utilizing Agent-Based Models and GIS to explore urban dynamics. PhD Thesis, University College London, London, England

Crooks A T, Castle C, Batty M (2007) Key challenges in agent-based modeling for geo-spatial simulation. CASA Working Paper 121, University College London

Crooks A T, Castle C J E, Batty M (2008) Key challenges in Agent-Based Modelling for geo-spatial simulation. Computers, Environment and Urban Systems, 32(6), 417-430

Crooks A T, Hudson-Smith A, Dearden J (2008) Agent Street: Agent Based Modelling in Second Life: http://www.casa.ucl.ac.uk/abm/secondlife/

Dacey M (1968) A review of measures of contiguity for two and k-color maps. pp 479-95 in Berry B J L, Marble D F eds. Spatial analysis. Prentice Hall, New Jersey

Dale M R T (2000) Lacunarity analysis of spatial pattern: a comparison. Landscape Ecology, 15, 467-8

Dale P (2005) Introduction to mathematical techniques used in GIS. CRC Press, Boca Raton, USA

Dantzig G B (1960) On the shortest route through a network. Management Science, 6, 187-90

Daskin M S (1995) Network and discrete location — models, algorithms and applications. Wiley, NJ, USA

Delmelle E (2008) Sapatial sampling. Ch 10 in Fotheringham A S and Rogerson P A (eds.) op. cit.

Densham P J, Rushton G (1992) A more efficient heuristic for solving large p-median problems by heuristic methods. Papers in Regional Science, 71, 307-329

de Smith M J (2004) Distance transforms as a new tool in spatial analysis, urban planning and GIS. Environment & Planning B, 31, 85-104

de Smith M J (2006) Maths for the mystified. Troubador Publishing Ltd, Leicester, UK

de Smith M J (2006a) Determination of gradient and curvature constrained optimal paths. Computer-aided Civil and Infrastructure Engineering, 21, 17-31

Deutsch C V, Journel A G (1992, 1998) GSLIB geostatistical software library and user's guide. Oxford University Press, New York

Dibble C, Feldman P G (2004) The GeoGraph 3D computational laboratory: Network and terrain landscapes for Repast. J. of Artificial Societies and Social Simulation, 7(1): http://jasss.soc.surrey.ac.uk/7/1/7.html

Dijk S F van, Thierens D, Berg M T de (2002) Using genetic algorithms for solving hard problems in GIS. GeoInformatica, 6(4), 381-413

Diggle P J (1983) Statistical analysis of spatial point patterns. Academic Press, London

Diggle P J (1990) A point process modeling approach to raised incidence of a rare phenomenon in the vicinity of a prespecified point. J. Royal Stat. Soc., A, 153, 349-62

Dijkstra E W (1959) A note on two problems in connexion with graphs. Numerische Mathematik, 1, 269-71

Diplock G (2000) Genetic programming: a new approach to spatial model building. Ch 9 in Openshaw S, Abrahart R J, eds. (2000) GeoComputation. Taylor and Francis, London

Dixon C, Leach B (1977) Sampling methods for geographical research. CATMOG 17

Dodge M, Kitchin R (2001) Atlas of Cyberspace. available as a free PDF file from: http://www.kitchin.org/atlas/index.html (originally published by Adison-Wesley).

Dodge M, McDerby M, Turner M (eds.) (2008) Geographic visualization: Concepts, tools and applications. J Wiley

Dorling D (1996) Area cartograms: Their use and creation. Concepts and Techniques in Modern

Geography (CATMOG), 59, Geo Abstrcts Ltd, Norwich, UK (Copy available as PDF from http://www.qmrg.org.uk/?page_id=141 )

Dougenik J A, Chrisman N R, Niemeyer D R (1985) An algorithm to construct continous area cartograms, Professional Geographer, 37 (1), 75-81

Douglas D H (1994) Least cost path in GIS using an accumulated cost surface and slope lines. Cartographica, 31, 37-51

Douglas D H, Peucker T K (1973) Algorithms for the reduction of the number of points required to represent a digitised line or its caricature. The Canadian Cartographer, 10, 112-22

Draper G, Vincent T, Kroll M E, Swanson J (2005) Childhood cancer in relation to distance from high voltage power lines in England and Wales: a case-control study. British Medical J., 330, 4 June 2005, 1-5

Dubin R (2008) Spatial weights. Ch 8 in Fotheringham A S, Rogerson P A, eds. op.cit.

Dubois G, Saisana M (2002) Optimal spatial declustering weights – comparison of methods. Proc. Annual Conf. International Assoc. for Math. Geology, Berlin, 479-84

Dugdale J (2006) An evaluation of seven software simulation tools for use in the social sciences: http://www.irit.fr/COSI/training/evaluationoftools /Evaluation-Of-Simulation-Tools.htm

Dunn J C (1973) A fuzzy relative of the ISODATA process and its use in detecting compact well-separated clusters. J. of Cybernetics, 3, 32-57

Dyer M E, Frieze A M (1985) A simple heuristic for the p-center problem. Operations Research Letters, 3, 285-8

Eastman J R (1989) Pushbroom algorithms for calculating distances in raster grids. Proceedings, Autocarto 9, 288-97. Available as a downloadable pdf from: http://mapcontext.com/autocarto/proceedings/aut o-carto-9

Ebisch K (2002) A correction to the Douglas-Peuker line generalization algorithm. Computers & Geosciences, 28, 995-7

Efron B (1982) The Jackknife, the Bootstrap and other resampling plans. Philadelphia: SIAM

Efron B, Tibshirani R J (1997) Improvements on cross-validation: The .632+ bootstrap method. J. American Stat. Assoc., 92, 548-560

Eidelson B M, Lustick I (2004) VIR-POX: An agent-based analysis of smallpox preparedness and response policy. J. of Artificial Societies and Social Simulation, 7(3). Available at: http://jasss.soc.surrey.ac.uk/7/3/6.html

Emonet T, Macal C M, North M J, Wickersham C E, Cluzel P (2005) AgentCell: A digital single-cell assay for bacterial chemotaxis. Bioinformatics, 21(11), 2714-2721

Epanechnikov V A (1969) Nonparametric estimation of a multidimensional probability density. Theor. Probab. Appl., 14, 153-8

Epstein J M (1999) Agent-based computational models and generative social science. Complexity, 4(5), 41-60

Epstein J M, Axtell R (1996) Growing artificial societies: Social science from the bottom up. MIT Press, Cambridge, USA

ESRI (1996) Automation of map generalization – the cutting edge technology. ESRI, Redlands, CA, USA: http://downloads.esri.com/support/whitepapers/a o_/mapgen.pdf

Fedra K (1996) Distributed models and embedded GIS: Integration strategies and case studies. in Goodchild M F, Steyaert L T, Parks B O (eds.) GIS and environmental modeling: Progress and research issues. GIS World Books, Fort Collins, 413-8

Fischer M M (2006) Spatial analysis and geocomputation: Select essays. Springer, Berlin

Fischer M M, Lung Y (1998) A genetic-algorithms based evolutionary neural network for modeling spatial interaction data. The Annals of Regional Science, 32(3) 437-458. reprinted as Ch 8 in Fischer M M (2006)

Fisher N I (1993) Statistical analysis of circular data. Cambridge University Press, Cambridge

Fisher W D (1958) On grouping for maximal homogeneity. J. of the American Statistical Association, 53, 789-98

Foresman T W ed. (1998) The history of geographic information systems: Perspectives from the pioneers. Prentice Hall, Upper Saddle River, NJ, USA

Fortin M-J, Dale M R T (2008) Spatial autocorrelation. Ch 6 in Fotheringham A S and Rogerson P A (eds.) op. cit.

Fotheringham A S, Rogerson P A, eds. (2008) The SAGE handbook of spatial analysis. Sage Publications Ltd.

Fotheringham A S, Brunsdon C, Charlton M (2002) Geographically Weighted Regression: The analysis of spatially varying relationships. Wiley, New York

Fotheringham A S, Charlton M, Chris Brunsdon, Nakaya T (2005) Model selection issues in Geographically Weighted Regression. Proc., Geocomputation 2005 Conference, Ann Arbor, Mi. USA

Franklin S, Graesser A (1996) Is it an agent, or just a program? A taxonomy for autonomous agents. Proceedings of the Third International Workshop on Agent Theories, Architectures, and Languages, Springer-Verlag

Freeman M F, Tukey J (1950) Transformations related to the angular and the square root. Annals of Mathematical Statistics, 21, 607-11

Gabriel K R, Sokal R R (1969) A new statistical approach to geographic variation analysis. Systematic Zoology, 18, 259-78

Gaile G L, Burt J E (1980) Directional statistics, CATMOG 25 (op. cit.)

Galea E R, Gwynne S (2006) Principles and practice of evacuation modeling (7th Edition). Fire Safety Engineering Group — University of Greenwich, London

Gardner R H, O'Neill R V (1991) Pattern, process, and predictability: the use of neural models for landscape analysis. pp 289-307 in Turner M G, Gardner R H, eds. (1991) Quantitative Methods in Landscape Ecology. Springer-Verlag, New York

Gastner M T, Newman M E J (2004) Diffusion-based method for producing density-equlizing maps, Proc. National Academy of Science, 101, 20, 7499-7504

Gendreau M, Laporte G, Potvin J-Y (2002) Metaheuristics for the capacitated VRP. pp 129-154 in Toth P, Vigo D eds. (2002) SIAM Monographs on Discrete Mathematics and Applications

Getis A D, Griffith D A (2002) Comparative spatial filtering in regression analysis. Geog. Anal., 34, 130-40

Getis A D, Ord J K (1992) The analysis of spatial association using distance statistics. Geog. Anal., 24, 189-206

Getis A D, Ord J K (1995) Local spatial autocorrelation statistics: Distributional issues and an application. Geog. Anal., 27, 287-306

Gilbert N (2004) Agent-based social simulation: Dealing with complexity. University of Surrey, Guildford, UK

Gilbert N, Bankes S (2002) Platforms and methods for agent-based modeling. Proceedings of the National Academy of Sciences of the USA, 99(3), 7197-7198

Gilbert N, Terna P (1999) How to build and use agent-base models in social science. Mind & Society, 1, 57-72

Gilbert N, Troitzsch K G (2005) Simulation for the social scientist. Open University Press, UK

Gimblett H R, Richards M T, Itami R M (2002) Simulating wildland recreation use and conflicting spatial interactions using rule-driven intelligent agents. pp 211-243 in Gimblett H R (ed.) Integrating geographic information systems and agent-based modeling techniques for simulating social and ecological processes. Oxford University Press, Oxford

Glover F (1977) Heuristics for integer programming using surrogate constraints. Decision sciences, 8, 156-166

Glover F (1986) Future paths for integer programming and links to artificial intelligence. Computers and operations research, 13, 533-549

Glover F, Laguna M (1997) Tabu search. Kluwer Academic Publishers, Univ of Colorado

Gold C M, Thibault D (2001) Map generalization by skeleton retraction. Proceedings, International Cartographic Association, Beijing, China, 2072-81

Golledge R G, Rushton G (1972) Multidimensional scaling: Review and geographical applications. Commission on college geography, Tech. Paper 10, Washington DC, Assoc. of Amer. Geogs.

Goodchild M F (1986) Spatial autocorrelation. CATMOG 47 (op. cit.)

Goodchild M F (2005) GIS, spatial analysis, and modeling overview. in Maguire D J, Batty M, Goodchild M F (eds.) GIS, spatial analysis and modeling. ESRI Press, Redlands, California

Goodchild M F, Mark D M (1987) The fractal nature of geographic phenomena. Annals of Association of American Geographers, 77, 265-78

Goodchild M F, Kemp K K eds. (1990) NCGIA Core Curriculum in GIS. National Center for Geographic Information and Analysis, University of California, Santa Barbara, CA, USA

Goodchild M F, Longley P A (1999) The future of GIS and spatial analysis. In Longley et al. (1999, op cit), 567-80

Goodchild M F, Parks B O, Steyaert L T, eds. (1993) Environmental modeling with GIS. Oxford University Press, New York

Goodchild M F, Proctor J (1997) Scale in a digital geographic world. Geographical and Environmental Modeling, 1, 5-23

Goodchild M F, Steyaert L T, Parks B O, Johnston C, Maidment D, Crane M, Glendenning S eds. (1996) Environmental modeling: Progress and research issues. GIS World Books, Fort Collins, CO, USA

Goovaerts P (1997) Geostatistics for natural resources evaluation. Oxford University Press, New York

Goovaerts P (1999) Geostatistics in soil science: state-of-the-art and perspectives. Geoderma, 89, 1-45

Griffith D A (2005) A comparison of six analytical disease mapping techniques as applied to West Nile Virus in the coterminous United States, Intl. J of Health Geographics, 4:18. Available from: http://www.ij-healthgeographics.com/content/4/1/18/

Grimm V (1999) Ten years of individual-based modelling in ecology: What have we learned, and what could we learn in the future? Ecological Modelling, 115(2-3): 129 − 148

Grimm V et al. (2006) A standard protocol for describing individual-based and agent-based models. Ecological Modelling, 198(1-2): 115-126

Gumerman G J, Swedlund A C, Dean J S, Epstein J M (2003) The evolution of social behavior in the prehistoric American southwest. Artificial Life, 9(4), 435-444

Gustafson E J (1998) Quantifying landscape spatial pattern: What is the state of the art. Ecosystems, 143-56

Gustafson E J, Parker G R (1992) Relationships between landcover proportion and indices of landscape spatial pattern. Landscape Ecology 7, 101-10

Haggett P, Chorley R J (1969) Network analysis in geography. E Arnold, London

Haining R (2003) Spatial data analysis − theory and practice. Cambridge University Press, Cambridge, UK

Haining R (2008) The special nature of spatial data. Ch2 in Fotheringham A S and Rogerson P A (eds.) op. cit.

Haklay M (2004) Map calculus in GIS: a proposal and demonstration. Int. J. Geog. Information Science, 18, 107-25

Haklay M (2006) Comparing map calculus and map algebra in dynamic GIS. Ch 5 in Drummond J, Billen R, Forrest D and Jo E. eds. (2006) Dynamic & mobile GIS: Investigating change in space and time, Taylor & Francis/CRC

Haklay M, O'Sullivan D, Thurstain-Goodwin M, Schelhorn T (2001) '"So go downtown": Simulating pedestrian movement in town centers. Environment and Planning B: Planning and Design, 28(3), 343-359

Hales D, Rouchier J, Edmounds B (2003) Model-to-model analysis. J. of Artificial Societies and Social Simulation, 6(4): http://jasss.soc.surrey.ac.uk/6/4/5.html

Hanrahan P, Ebert D S, Musgrave F K, Peachey D, Perlin K, Worley S, eds. (2003) Texturing and modeling: A procedural approach. 3rd ed., Morgan and Kaufmann, San Francisco

Harris R, Sleight P, Webber R (2005) Geodemographics, GIS and neighborhood targeting. J Wiley & Sons

Harvey D (1969) Explanation in geography. E Arnold, London

Harvey M J, Barbour R W (1965) Polygon fitting of Microtus Ochrogaster as determined by a modified minimum area method. J of Mammology, 46, 398-402

Hawley K, Moellering H (2005) A comparative analysis of areal interpolation methods: A preliminary report. Proc. Auto-Carto 2005, CaGIS

Heitkötter J, Beasley D, eds. (2000) The Hitch-Hiker's Guide to Evolutionary Computation: A list of Frequently Asked Questions (FAQ). USENET: comp.ai.genetic

Henzinger M R, Klein P, Rao S (1997) Faster shortest-path algorithms for planar graphs. J. Comput. Syst. Sci., 55, 3-23

Hertz A, Laporte G, Mittaz M (2000) A tabu search heuristic for the capacited arc routing problem. Operations Research, 48, 129-35

Herzog A (2003) Developing cartographic applets for the Internet. in Peterson M P (ed.): Maps and the Internet, Vol. 1 115-128, Pergammon/Elsevier

Heywood I, Cornelius, S, Carver S (2006) An introduction to geographical information systems (3rd Edition). Pearson Education, UK

Hillier B et al. (1993) Natural movement: or, configuration and attraction in urban pedestrian movement. Environment & Planning B, 20, 29-66

Holland J H (1995) Hidden order: How adaptation builds complexity. Addison-Wesley, Reading

Horne B K P (1981) Hill shading and the reflectance map. Proc. IEEE 69, 14-47

Howe T R, Collier N T, North M J, Parker M T, Vos J R (2006) Containing agents: Contexts, projections, and agents. Proceedings of Agent 2006 Conference on Social Agents: Results and Prospects, Chicago, USA. See:

http://agent2007.anl.gov/2006procpdf/Agent_2006.pdf

Hubert L J, Golledge R G (1982) Comparing rectangular data matrices. Environment and Planning A, 14(8), 1087-1095

Hudson-Smith A (2008) Digital Geography: Geographic visualization for urban environments., CASA Publications, UCL, London

Huff D (1993) How to lie with statistics. W W Norton & Co, New York

Hutchinson M F (1988) Calculation of hydrologically sound digital elevation models. Proceedings, Third International Symposium on Spatial Data Handling, Sydney, Columbus, International Geographical Union, 117-33

Hutchinson M F (1989) A new procedure for gridding elevation and stream line data with automatic removal of spurious pits. J. of Hydrology 106, 211-32

Hutchinson M F (1996) A locally adaptive approach to the interpolation of digital elevation models. In Proceedings, Third International Conference/Workshop on Integrating GIS and Environmental Modeling, Santa Fe, NM. Available online from NCGIA

Ikonen L, Toivanen P (2005) Shortest routes on varying height surfaces using gray-level distance transforms. Image and Vision Computing, 23, 133-141

Iliffe J, Lott R (2008) Datums and map projections for remote sensing, GIS and surveying. 2$^{nd}$ Edition. Whittles Publishing, Dunbeath, Scotland

Ilachinski A (1997) Irreducible semi-autonomous adaptive combat (ISAAC): An artificial-life approach to land combat. Center for Naval Analyses, Virginia, USA

Isaaks E H, Srivastava R M (1989) An introduction to applied geostatistics. Oxford University Press, New York

Jacquez G M (1996) A $k$ nearest neighbour test for space-time interaction. Statistics in Medicine, 15, 1935-1949

Jaeger J A G (2000) Landscape division, splitting index, and effective mesh size: new measures of landscape fragmentation. Landscape Ecology 15, 115-130

Jain A K (1989) Fundamentals of digital image processing. Prentice-Hall, Englewood Cliffs, NJ

Jacquez G M, Meliker J R (2008) Case-control clustering for mobile populations. Ch19 in Fotheringham A S and Rogerson P A (eds.) op.cit.

Jenks G F, Caspall F C (1971) Error on choroplethic maps: Definition, measurement, reduction. Annals of American Geographers, 61, 217-44

Jenson S, Domingue J (1988) Extracting topographic structure from digital elevation data for geographic information system analysis. Photogrammetric Engineering and Remote Sensing, 54, 1593-600

Jiang B (2004) Selection of streets from a network using self-organizing maps. Trans. in GIS, 8, 335-350

Jiang B, Claramunt C (2002) Integration of Space Syntax into GIS: New perspectives for urban morphology. Trans. in GIS, 6(3), 295-309

Johnston K M, Maguire D (2007) Agent-based modeling: Position statement. UCSB/UCL Workshop on Agent-Based Modeling of Complex Spatial Systems, April 14-16, 2007, Santa Barbara, CA, USA

Jones K H (1998) A comparison of algorithms used to compute hill slope as a property of the DEM. Computers & Geosciences, 24, 315-23

Kabos S, Csillag F (2002) The analysis of spatial association on a regular lattice by join-count statistics without the assumption of first-order homogeneity. Computers & Geosciences, 28, 901-910

Keitt T H, Urban D L, Milne B T (1997) Detecting critical scales in fragmented landscapes. Conservation Ecology, 1, 4

Kempf-Leonard K ed. (2005) Encyclopaedia of social measurement. Elsevier, San Diego, CA, USA, 921-6

Kikpatrick S, Gelatt C D, Vecchi M P (1983) Optimization by simulated annealing. Science, 220 (4598), 671-680

King G, Rosen O, Tanner M A (2004) Ecological inference: New methodological strategies. Cambridge University Press, Cambridge UK

Kohonen T (1984) Self-organization and associative memory. Springer-Verlag, Berlin

Kohonen T (1995) Self Organizing Maps. Springer-Verlag, Berlin

Kollman K, Miller J H, Page S E (1992) Adaptive parties in spatial elections. The American Political Science Review, 86(4), 929-937

Kreft J-U, Booth G, Wimpenny W T (1998) BacSim, a simulator for individual based modeling of bacterial colony growth. Microbiology, 144, 3275-3287

Kristinsson H, Jonsson M T, Jonsdottir F (2005) Pipe route design using variable topography distance transforms. Proc. IDETC/CIE ASME 2005 International Design Engineering Technical Conference

Krzysztof K, Dzwinel W, Yuen D A (2005) Nonlinear development of bacterial colony modeled with cellular automata and agent objects. International J. of Modern Physics C, 14(10), 1385-1404

Kulldorf M (1997) A spatial scan statistic. Communications in Statistics: Theory and Methods, 26, 1481-1496

Kulldorf M, Hjalmars U (1999) The Knox method and other tests for space-time interaction. Biometrics, 55, 544-552

LaGro J Jr (1991) Assessing patch shape in landscape mosaics. Photogrammetric Eng. Remote Sens. 57, 285-93

Langran G (1992) Time in geographic information systems. Taylor and Francis, London

Law A M, Kelton D (1991) Simulation modeling and analysis. (2nd Edition), McGraw-Hill, New York, USA

Levine N (2007) CrimeStat: A spatial statistics program for the analysis of crime incident locations (v3.1). N Levine & Associates, Houston, TX, and the National Inst. of Justice, Washington, DC. See: http://www.icpsr.umich.edu/CRIMESTAT

Levy S (1993) Artificial Life: The quest for a new creation. Penguin Books, London

Li H, Reynolds J F (1993) A new contagion index to quantify spatial patterns of landscapes. Landscape Ecology, 8,155-62

Li L, Zhu L, Sui D Z (2007) A GIS-based Bayesian approach for analyzing spatio-temporal patterns of intra-city motor vehicle crashs. J of Transport Geog., 15, 274-285

Li X, Magill W (2001) Modeling fire spread under environmental influence using a cellular automaton approach. Complexity International, 8, 1-14

Lichstein J W, Simons T R, Shriner S A, Franzreb K E (2002) Spatial autocorrelation and autoregressive models in Ecology. Ecological Monographs, 72, 445-63

Lindsay J B (2005) The Terrain Analysis System: A tool for hydro-geomorphic applications. Hydrological Processes, 19, 1123-30

Linthicum D S (2000) Enterprise application integration. Addison-Wesley, Boston

Longley P A (2004) Geographical Information Systems: On modeling and representation. Progress in Human Geography, 28(1), 108-116

Longley P A, Batty M, eds. (1997) Spatial analysis: Modeling in a GIS environment. J Wiley & Sons, New York

Longley P A, Batty M, eds. (2001) Advanced spatial analysis – the CASA book of GIS. ESRI Press, Redlands, CA, USA

Longley P A, Goodchild M F, Maguire D J, Rhind D W (1999) Geographic information systems: Principles, techniques, management and applications. 2nd ed., J Wiley, New York

Longley P A, Goodchild M F, Maguire D J, Rhind D W (2005) Geographic information systems: Principles, techniques, management and applications. Abridged edition, J Wiley, Hoboken.

Longley P A, Goodchild M F, Maguire D J, Rhind D W (2005) Geographic information systems and science. 2nd ed., J Wiley, Chichester, UK; and 3$^{rd}$ edition (forthcoming)

Longley P A, Harris R (1999) Towards a new digital data infrastructure for urban analysis and modeling. Environment and Planning B, 26, 855-78

Love R F, Morris J G (1972) Modeling intercity road distances by mathematical functions. Oper. Res. Quart., 23, 61-72

Love R F, Morris J G, Wesolowsky G O (1988) Facilities location, models and methods. North-Holland, New York

Luke S, Cioffi-Revilla C, Panait L and Sullivan K (2004) MASON: A New Multi-Agent Simulation Toolkit. SwarmFest 2004, Eighth Annual Swarm Users/Researchers Conference, University of Michigan, Ann Arbor, Michigan USA

Lustick I (2002) PS-I: A user-friendly agent-based modeling platform for testing theories of political identity and political stability. J. of Artificial Societies and Social Simulation, 5(3): http://jasss.soc.surrey.ac.uk/5/3/7.html

Macal C M, North M J (2005) Tutorial on agent-based modeling and simulation. in Euhl M E, Steiger N M, Armstrong F B, Joines J A (eds.), Proceedings of the 2005 Winter Simulation Conference. Proceedings of the 2005 Introductory Tutorials section at: http://www.wintersim.org/pastprog.htm

Mackaness W A, Ruas A, Sarjakoski T L (eds.) (2007) Generalization of geographic information; Cartographic modeling and applications. Elsevier, Netherlands

Mackay R J, Oldford R W (2000) Scientific method, statistical method, and the speed of light. Working Paper 2000-02, Department of Statistics and Actuarial Science, University of Waterloo, Ontario, Canada

Maguire D J (1995) Implementing spatial analysis and GIS applications for business and service planning. in Longley P A, Batty M (eds.) GIS for business and service planning. GeoInformation International, Cambridge, UK

Maguire D J (2005) Towards a GIS platform for spatial analysis and modeling. in Maguire D J, Batty M, Goodchild M F (eds.) GIS, spatial analysis and modeling. ESRI Press, Redlands, California, USA

Maguire D, Batty M, Goodchild M F eds. (2005) GIS, spatial analysis and modeling. ESRI Press, Redlands, CA, USA

Mandelbrot B B (1982) The fractal geometry of nature. W. H. Freeman and Co., New York

Mannan B, Roy J (1998) Fuzzy ARTMAP: supervised classification of multi-spectral remotely-sensed images. International Journal of Remote Sensing, 19, 767-774

Manson S M (2001) Simplifying complexity: A review of complexity theory. Geoforum, 32(3), 405-414.

Manson S M (2003) Epistemological possibilities and imperatives of complexity research: A reply to Reitsma. Geoforum, 34(1), 17-20

Manson S M (2007) Challenges to evaluating models of geographic complexity'. Environment and Planning B: Planning and Design, 34, 245-260

Mantel N (1967) The detection of disease clustering and a generalized regression approach. Cancer Research, 27, 209-220

Makarov V L, Bakhtizin A R, Zhitkov V A (2008) Agent-Based Model for traffic jams in Moscow. ABS[2] Agent Based Spatial Simulation International Workshop, 24-25 November 2008, Paris, France, Available at http://s4.csregistry.org/ABS2

Malleson N (2008) RepastCity — A demo virtual city. Available at http://portal.ncess.ac.uk/access/wiki/site/mass/repastcity.html

Mardia K V, Jupp P E (1999) Directional statistics. 2nd ed., John Wiley, Chichester

Martin D J (1996) Geographic information systems: Socio-economic applications. Routledge, London

Martin D (2000) Census 2001: making the best of zonal geographies. Paper presented at the Census of population: 2000 and beyond, conference, University of Manchester, 22-23rd June 2000

Masser I, Campbell H, Craglia M eds. (1996) GIS diffusion: The adoption and use of geographical information systems in local government in Europe. Taylor & Francis, Bristol, PA, USA

Matheron G (1973) The intrinsic random functions and their application. Advances in Applied Prob., 5, 439-68

McGarigal K, Marks B J (1995) FRAGSTATS: spatial pattern analysis program for quantifying landscape structure. Gen. Tech. Report PNW-GTR-351, USDA Forest Service, Pacific Northwest Research Station, Portland, OR, USA

McGinnis S A (2001) On the effects of geometry in discrete element numerical earthquake simulations. Ph.D. Thesis, University of Colorado

McHarg I L (1969) Design with nature. Natural History Press, Garden City, New York

McMaster R B, Shea K S (1992) Generalization in digital cartography. Washington DC, Association of American Geographers

Mennis J, Leong J, Khanna R (2005a) Multidimensional map algebra. Presented at the 8th International Conference on Geocomputation, Ann Arbor, MI, USA

Mennis J, Viger R, Tomlin C D (2005b) Cubic map algebra functions for spatio-temporal analysis. Cartography and Geographic Information Science, 32, 17-32

Mennis J, Hultgren T (2006) Intelligent dasymetric mapping and its application to areal interpolation. Cartography and Geographic Information Science, 33, 179-194

Messina J P and Walsh S J (2000) The application of a cellular automaton model for predicting deforestation. Proceedings of the 4th International Conference on Integrating GIS and Environmental Modeling: Problems, Prospects and Research Needs, Banff, Canada

Miller H J, Shaw S-L (2001) Geographic information systems for transportation. Oxford University Press, Oxford

Milne BT (1991) Lessons from applying fractal models to landscape patterns. pp. 199-235 in Turner M G, Gardner R H (eds.) Quantitative methods in landscape ecology. Springer-Verlag, New York

Minar N, Burkhart R, Langton C, Askenazi M (1996) The Swarm simulation system: A toolkit for building multi-agent simulations: http://www.santafe.edu/

Mitasova H, Mitas L (1993) Interpolation by regularised spline with tension. Math. Geol., 25, 641-55

Mitchell A (1999) The ESRI guide to GIS analysis, Volume 1: Geographic patterns and relationships. ESRI Press, Redlands, CA, USA

Mitchell A (2005) The ESRI guide to GIS analysis, Volume 2: Spatial measurements and statistics. ESRI Press, Redlands, CA, USA

Mitchell B R (2006) Comparison of programs for fixed kernel homerange analysis. June 2006 newsletter, The Wildlife Society, GIS Working Group.

Mitchell J S B (1998) Geometric shortest paths and network optimization. Handbook of Computational Geometry, Elsevier Science, Sack J-R, Urrutia J, eds. (2000) Chapter 15, 633-701. Draft available as a PDF from http://www.ams.stonybrook.edu/~jsbm/publications.html

Mitchell T (2005) Web mapping illustrated: using open source GIS toolkits. O'Reilly Media. http://www.oreilly.com/catalog/webmapping/

Moore I D, Grayson R B, Landson A R (1991) Digital terrain modeling: A review of hydrological, geomorphological and biological applications. Hydrological processes, 5, 3-30

Moore I D, Lewis A, Gallant J C (1995) Terrain attributes: Estimation methods and scale effects, in Jakeman A J, Beck M B, McAleer M J (1995) Modeling change in environmental systems. John Wiley, New York

Moran P A P (1948) The interpretation of statistical maps. J. of the Royal Statistical Society B, 10, 243-51

Moran P A P (1950) Notes on continuous stochastic phenomena. Biometrika, 37, 17-23

Moshe D ed. (2000) Arc routing: Theory, solutions and applications. Kluwer Academic Publishers, Amsterdam

Muttiah R S, Engel B A, Jones D D (1996) Waste disposal site selection using GIS-based simulated annealing. Computers and Geosciences, 22(9), 1013-1017

Najlis R, Janssen M A, Parker D C (2001) Software Tools and Communication Issues. in Parker D C, Berger T, Manson S M (eds.), Meeting the challenge of complexity: Proceedings of a Special Workshop on Land-Use/Land-Cover Change, Irvine, California

Nakaya T, Fotheringham A S, Brunsdon C, Charlton M (2005) Geographically weighted Poisson regression for disease association mapping. Statist. in Med., 24, 2695-717

National Research Council of the National Academies (2006) Beyond Mapping: meeting national needs through enhanced geographic information science. The National Academies Press, Washington DC

Neteler M, Mitasova H (2008) Open Source GIS: A GRASS GIS approach. 3rd Ed., Springer, New York. http://www.grassbook.org

North M, Macal C M, Vos J R (2004) Terrorist organization modeling. North American Association for Computational Social and Organizational Science Conference 2004, Pittsburgh, USA

North M J, Howe T R, Collier N T, Vos J R (2005a) The Repast Simphony development environment. Proceedings of the Agent 2005 Conference on Generative Social Processes, Models, and Mechanisms, Chicago, USA. Available at http://agent2007.anl.gov/Agent_2005.pdf

North M J, Howe T R, Collier N T, Vos J R (2005b) The Repast Simphony runtime system. Proceedings of the Agent 2005 Conference on Generative Social Processes, Models, and Mechanisms, Chicago, USA. Available at http://agent2007.anl.gov/Agent_2005.pdf

North M J, Macal C M (2007) Managing business complexity: Discovering strategic solutions with Agent-Based Modelling and simulation. Oxford University Press, New York, NY

O'Brien L G (?) The statistical analysis of contingency table designs. CATMOG 51

Oden N (1995) Adjusting Moran's I for population density. Statistics in Medicine 14, 17-26

Okabe A, Boots B, Sugihara K, Chiu S N (2000) Spatial tessellations: Concepts and applications of Voronoi diagrams. 2nd ed., J Wiley, New Jersey

Okabe A, Okukuki K-I, Shiode S (2006a) The SANET Toolbox: New methods for network spatial analysis. Trans in GIS, 10(4), 535-550

Okabe A, Okukuki K-I, Shiode S (2006b) SANET: A toolbox for spatial analysis on a network. Geog. Anal., 38, 57-66

Okabe A, Satoh T (2008) Spatial analysis on a network. Ch23 in Fotheringham A S, Rogerson P A (eds.) op.cit.

Okabe A, Satoh T, Sugihara K (2009) A kernel density estimation method for networks, its computational method and a GIS-based tool. Int. J. of Geographical Information Science, 23(1), 7-32

O'Kelly M E (2008) Applied retail location models using spatial interaction tools. Ch22 in Fotheringham A S, Rogerson P A (eds.) *op.cit.*

Openshaw S (1977) A geographical solution to scale and aggregation problems in region-building, partitioning and spatial modeling. Transactions of the Institute of British Geographers NS 2, 459-72

Open Geospatial Consortium Inc (2006) OpenGIS implementation specification for Geographic Information. Simple feature access, Part 1: Common architecture. Ref: OGC 06-103r3, 2006-10-05

Openshaw S (1984) The modifiable areal unit problem (Concepts and Techniques in Modern Geography, (CATMOG), 38. Geo Abstracts Ltd, Norwich, England. Copy available as PDF from http://www.qmrg.org.uk/?page_id=141 )

Openshaw S, Abrahart R J, eds. (2000) GeoComputation. Taylor and Francis, London

O'Sullivan D (2001) Exploring spatial process dynamics using irregular cellular automaton models. Geog. Anal., 33(1), 1-18

O'Sullivan D (2002) Understanding the difference that space can make: Towards a geographical agent modeling environment. Proceedings of the Agent 2002 Conference on Social Agents: Ecology, Exchange, and Evolution, University of Chicago and Argonne National Laboratory

O'Sullivan D (2004) Complexity science and human geography. Transactions of the Institute of British Geographers, 29(3), 282-295

O'Sullivan D, Unwin D J (2003) Geographic information analysis. J Wiley, New Jersey

O'Sullivan F (2005) Factors affecting Radon levels in houses: A GIS study around Castleisland, County Kerry, South-West Ireland. Unpub. MSc Thesis, Dept of Geomatic Engineering, University College London

Painho M, Bação F (2000) Using genetic algorithms in clustering problems. Proc. GeoComputation 2000 available via http://www.geocomputation.org/

Parinov S I (2007) New possibilities for simulations of socio-economic systems. Artificial Societies, 2(3-4): 23-53. Available at http://www.artsoc.ru/html_e/journal.htm

Parker D C (2001) Object-Oriented packages for agent-based modeling: http://mason.gmu.edu/~dparker3/

Parker D C (2005) Integration of geographic information systems and Agent-Based Models of land use: Challenges and prospects. Pp. 403-422 in Maguire D J, Batty M, Goodchild M F (eds.), GIS, Spatial Analysis and Modeling, ESRI Press, Redlands, CA

Parker D C, Manson S M, Janssen M A, Hoffmann M J, Deadman P (2003) Multi-Agent systems for the simulation of land-use and land-cover change: A review. Annals of the Association of American Geographers, 93(2), 314-337

Perry J N, Liebhold A M, Rosenberg M S, Dungan J, Meriti M, Jakomulska A, Citron-Pousty S (2002) Illustrations and guidelines for selecting statistical methods for quantifying pattern in ecological data. Ecography 25, 578-600. Obtainable from: http://www.rothamsted.bbsrc.ac.uk/pie/sadie/rep rints/subgroup1_ecography.pdf

Peuquet D J (2005) Time in GIS and geographical databases. in Longley P A, Maguire D J, Goodchild M F, Rhind D (eds.) Geographical information systems: Principles, techniques, applications, and management (Abridged Edition). John Wiley & Sons, New York

Peuquet D J, Duan N (1995) An event-based spatio-temporal data model (ESTDM) for temporal analysis of geographic data. International J. of Geographical Information Systems, 9(1), 2-24

Piantanakulchai M (2005) Analytical Network Process model for highway corridor planning. Proc. ISAHP 2005, Honolulu, Hawaii

Pickover C A (1990) Computers, pattern, chaos and beauty: graphics from an unseen world. New York, St. Martin's

Plotnick R E, Gardner R H, O'Neill R V (1993) Lacunarity indices as measures of landscape texture. Landscape Ecology, 8, 201-11

Plotnick R E, Gardner R H, Hargrove W W, Pretegaard K, Perlmutter M (1996) Lacunarity analysis: a general technique for the analysis of spatial patterns. Phys. Rev. E53, 5461-8

Polhill J G, Parker D, Brown D, Grimm V (2008) Using the ODD protocol for describing three Agent-Based social simulation models of land-use change. J. Artificial Societies and Social Simulation, 11(2) 3. Available at http://jasss.soc.surrey.ac.uk/11/2/3.html

Pratt W K (1991) Digital Image Processing. 2nd ed. J Wiley, New York

Prim R C (1957) Shortest connection networks and some generalizations. Bell System Technical J., 36, 1389-1401

Railsback S F, Lytinen S L, Jackson S K (2006) Agent-based simulation platforms: Review and development recommendations. Simulation, 82(9), 609-623

Rana S ed. (2004a) Topological data structures for surfaces: An introduction to geographical information science. J Wiley & Sons

Rana S (2004b) Two approximate solutions to the Art Gallery problem. International Conference on Computer Graphics and Interactive techniques, Los Angeles (available from http://eprints.ucl.ac.uk/

Rana, S (2006) Isovist Analyst - An ArcView extension for planning visual surveillance. in: Proceedings ESRI User Conference 2006, San Diego, CA, USA

Rana S, Wood J (2000) Weighted and metric surface networks — new insights and an interactive application for their generalization in TCL/TK. Working Paper 25, Center for Advanced Spatial Analysis, University College London

Rangel T F L V B, Diniz-Filho J A F, Bini L M (2006) Towards an integrated computational tool for spatial analysis in macroecology and Biogeography. Global Ecology and Biogeography, 15, 321-327

Ratti C (2001) Urban analysis for environmental prediction. Unpub PhD thesis, Univ. of Cambridge, UK

Ratti C, Baker N, Steemers K (2004) Energy consumption and urban texture. Energy and Buildings, 37, 762-6

Ratti C, Richens S (2004) Raster analysis of urban texture. Environment and Planning B, Planning and Design, 31, 297-309

Reitsma F (2003) A Response to simplifying complexity. Geoforum, 34(1), 13-16

Reitsma F, Albrecht J (2006) A process-oriented data model. in Drummond J, Billen R, Forrest D, João E (eds.) Dynamic & mobile GIS: Investigating change in space and time. Taylor & Francis, London

Repenning A, Ioannidou A (2004) Agent-based end-user development. Communications of the Association of Computing Machinery, 47(9): 43-46

Repenning A, Ioannidou A, Zola J (2000) AgentSheets: End-user programmable simulations. J. of Artificial Societies and Social Simulation, 3(3)

Rey S J, Janikas M V (2006) STARS: Space-time analysis of regional systems. Geog. Anal., 38, 67-86

Richards J A (1986) Remote sensing digital image analysis. Springer-Verlag, Berlin

Rixon A, Moglia M, Burn S (2005) Bottom-up approaches to building agent-based models: Discussing the need for a platform. Proceedings of the Joint Conference on Multi-Agent Modeling for Environmental Management, Bourg-St-Maurice, France

Robins G, Zelikovsky A (2000) Improved Steiner tree approximation in graphs. Proc. 10th Ann. ACM-SIAM Symp. on Discrete Algorithms, ACM-SIAM, 770-9

Rodrigue J-P, Comtois C, Slack B (2006) The geography of transport systems. Routledge

Rojas R (1996) Neural Networks - A systematic introduction. Springer-Verlag, Berlin, New-York

Roy J R (2004) Spatial interaction modeling: A regional science context. Springer

Rushton G, Goodchild M F, Ostresh L M eds. (1973) Computer programs for location-allocation problems. Monograph No. 6, Dept. of Geography, Univ. of Iowa, Iowa, USA

Russell S, Norvig P (2003) Artificial intelligence: A modern approach. Prentice Hall, USA

Saaty T L (1980) The Analytical Hierarchy Process. McGraw-Hill, New York

Saaty T L (1999) Fundamentals of the Analytical Network Process. Proc. Of ISAHP 1999, Kobe

Sandwell D T (1987) Biharmonic spline interpolation of GEOS-3 and SEASAT altimeter data. Geophysical Research Letters, 2, 139-142

Sawada M (1999) ROOKCASE: An Excel 97/2000 Visual Basic (VB) Add-in for exploring global and local spatial autocorrelation. Bull. Ecological Soc. America, 80, 231-4

Scott A J (1971) Combinatorial programming, spatial analysis and planning. Methuen, London

Semboloni F (2000) The growth of an urban cluster into a dynamic, self-modifying spatial pattern. Environment and Planning B: Planning and Design, 27, 549-564

Schelhorn T, O'Sullivan D, Haklay M, Thurstain-Goodwin M (1999) STREETS: An agent-based pedestrian model. Center for Advanced Spatial Analysis (University College London): Working Paper 9, London

Schelling T C (1971) Dynamic models of segregation. J. of Mathematical Sociology, 1, 143-186

Schelling T C (1971) Micromotives and macrobehavior. W W Norton & Co

Schietzelt T, Densham P (2003) Location-allocation in GIS. In Longley & Batty (2003) op cit, 345-65

Serenko A, Detlor B (2002) Agent toolkits: A general overview of the market and an assessment of instructor satisfaction with utilizing toolkits in the classroom. McMaster University (School of Business), Ontario, USA

Shannon C, Weaver W (1949) The mathematical theory of communication. Univ. Illinois Press, Urbana, IL, USA

Shaw M, Thomas B, Davey Smith G, Dorling D (2008) The Grim Reaper's road map: An atlas of mortality in Britain, Policy Press, Bristol, UK

Sherman G (2008) Desktop GIS: Mapping the planet with Open Source. Pragmatic Bookshelf. http://www.pragprog.com/titles/gsdgis/desktop-gis

Shi W, Pang M Y C (2000) Development of Voronoi-based cellular automata: An integrated dynamic model for geographical information systems. International J. of Geographical Information Science, 14(5), 455-474

Silverman B W (1986) Density estimation for statistics and data analysis. Chapman and Hall, New York

Simpson E H (1949) Measurement of diversity. Nature, 163, 688

Sirigos S A, Photis Y N (2005) A prototype planning support system for scenario location analysis. Proceedings of Xth International Symposium on Locational Decisions, 2-8 June, Seville

Slocum T A, McMaster R B, Kessler F C, Howard H H (2008) Thematic Cartography and Geographic Visualization. 3rd Edition, Prentice-Hall, NJ, USA

Smith W H F, Wessel P (1990) Gridding with continuous curvature splines in tension. Geophysics, 55, 293-305

Sokal R R, Smouse P E, Neel J V (1986) The genetic structure of a tribal population, the Yanomama indians. XV. Patterns inferred by autocorrelation analysis. Genetics, 114, 259-87

Sondheim M, Gardels K, Buehler K (2005) GIS interoperability. in Longley P A, Maguire D J, Goodchild M F, Rhind D (eds.) Geographical information systems: Principles, techniques, applications, and management (Abridged Edition), John Wiley & Sons, New York

Steinitz C (1983) Geographical information systems: a personal historical perspective, thee framework for a recent project, and some questions for the future. The European Conference on Geographic Information Systems, Genoa, 1993. Available from: http://www.gsd.harvard.edu/studios/brc/framework/steinitz.txt

Stouffler S A (1940) Intervening opportunities: A theory relating mobility and distance. Amer. Soc. Rev., 5, No. 6

Stratton R D (2004) Assessing the effectiveness of landscape fuel treatments on fire growth and behavior. J. of Forestry, 102(7), 32-40

Stratton R D (2006) Guidance on spatial wildfire analysis: Models, tools and techniques. USDA Forest Research, Gen Tech Report RMRS-GTR-183. Available from: http://www.firemodels.org/downloads/farsite/publications/stratton_rmrs_gtr_183_v16.pdf

Taillard E D (2003) Heuristic methods for large centroid clustering problems. J. of Heuristics, 9, 51-74

Takeyama M, Couclelis H (1997) Map dynamics: Integrating cellular automata and GIS through geo-algebra. International J. of Geographical Information Science, 11(1), 73-91

Tarboton D G, Bras R L, Rodriguez-Iturbe I (1991) On the extraction of channel networks from digital elevation data. Hydrological Processes, 5, 81-100

Tarboton D G (1997) A new method for the determination of flow directions and upslope areas in grid digital elevation models. Water Resources Research, 33, 309-19

Tatara E, North M J, Howe T R, Collier N T, Vos J R (2006) An introduction to Repast Simphony modeling using a simple predator-prey example. Proceedings of the Agent 2006 Conference on Social Agents: Results and Prospects, Chicago, USA. Available at http://agent2007.anl.gov/2006procpdf/Agent_2006.pdf

Teitz M B, Bart P (1968) Heuristic methods for estimating the generalized vertex median of a weighted graph. Operations Research, 16, 955-61

Tesfatsion L (2006) Agent-based computational economics: A constructive approach to economic theory. in Tesfatsion L, Kenneth L (eds.), Handbook of computational economics. North-Holland Publishing, Amsterdam, the Netherlands

Thomas R W (1977) An introduction to quadrat analysis. CATMOG 12

Tjøstheim D (1978) A measure of association for spatial variables. Biometrika, 65, 109-114

Tobias R, Hofmann C (2004) Evaluation of free Java-libraries for social-scientific agent-based simulation. J. of Artificial Societies and Social Simulation, 7(1). Available from http://jasss.soc.surrey.ac.uk/7/1/6.html

Tobler W (1963) Geographic area and map projections, Geographical Review, 53, 59-78

Tobler W (1973) Choropleth maps without class intervals?." Geographical Analysis, 3, 262-265

Tobler W, Wineberg S (1971) A Cappadocian speculation. Nature, 231(5297), 39-42

Tomlin C Dana (1990) Geographic Information systems and cartographic modeling. Prentice-Hall, New Jersey

Tomlinson R F (1967) An introduction to the geo-information system of the Canada Land Inventory. ARDA, Canada Land Inventory, Department of Forestry and Rural Development, Ottawa

Tomlinson R F (1970) Computer based geographical data handling methods. In New Possibilities and Techniques for Land Use and Related Surveys, ed. I. H. Cox. World Land Use Occasional Papers No. 8, Geographical Publications Ltd., Berkhamsted, Herts, England

Topa G (2001) Social interactions, local spillovers and unemployment. Review of Economic Studies, 68, 261-295

Torrens P M (2000) How land-use-transportation models work. Center for Advanced Spatial Analysis (University College London): Working Paper 20, London

Torrens P M (2004) Simulating sprawl: A dynamic entity-based approach to modeling North American suburban sprawl using cellular automata and multi-agent systems. Ph.D. Thesis, University College London, London

Torrens P M (2006) Geosimulation and its application to urban growth modelling. pp. 119-136 in Portugali J (ed.) Complex Artificial Environments: Simulation, cognition and VR in the study and planning of cities. Springer, Berlin, Germany

Torrens P M, Benenson I (2005) Geographic automata systems. International J. of Geographical Information Science, 19(4), 385-412

Tou J T, Gonzales R C (1974) Pattern classification by distance functions. Addison-Wesley, Reading, MA

Tukey J W (1977) Explanatory data analysis. Addison-Wesley, Reading, MA

Turner A (2004) Depthmap 4, a researcher's handbook. UCL Bartlett School of Architecture, London. Available from: http://www.vr.ucl.ac.uk/depthmap/

Turner M G, Gardner R H, eds. (1991) Quantitative methods in landscape ecology. Springer-Verlag, New York

Ungerer M J, Goodchild M F (2002) Integrating spatial data analysis and GIS: A new implementation using Component Object Model (COM). International J. of Geographic Information Science, 16(1), 41-53

Urban D L (2003) Spatial analysis in ecology: Mantel's test. National Center for Ecological Analysis and Synthesis, Univ of California, Santa Barbara. Available from the NCEAS: http://www.nceas.ucsb.edu/scicomp/SciCompDocuments.html

Vaughan R (1987) Urban spatial traffic patterns. Pion, London

Vincenty T (1975) Direct and inverse solutions of geodesics on the ellipsoid with application of nested equations. Survey Review XXII, 176, 88-93. A spreadsheet implementation of this algorithm can be found at: www.ga.gov.au/geodesy/datums/calcs.jsp

Visvalingam M, Whyatt J D (1991) The Douglas-Peucker algorithm for line simplification: re-evaluation through visualization. Computer Graphics Forum 9, 213-28

Vos J R (2005) Repast .NET: The Repast framework implemented in the .NET. Annual Conference of the North American Association for Computational Social and Organizational Science (NAACSOS), Notre Dame, Indiana, USA

Waddell P, Borning A, Noth M, Freier N, Becke M, Ulfarsson G (2003) Microsimulation of urban development and location choices: Design and implementation of UrbanSim. Networks and Spatial Economics, 3(1): 43-67

Waddell P, Wang L, Liu X (2008) UrbanSim: An evolving planning support system for evolving communities. pp. 103-138 in Brail R K (ed.) Planning support systems for cities and regions. Lincoln Institute of Land Policy, Cambridge, MA

Wall M M (2004) A close look at the spatial structure implied by the CAR and SAR models. J of Statistical Planning and Inference, 121, 311-24

Walsh G R (1975) Methods of optimization. John Wiley & Sons, London

Wegener M (2000) Spatial Models and GIS. in Fotheringham A S, Wegener M (eds.) Spatial models and GIS: New potential and new methods. Taylor and Francis, London

Westervelt J D (2002) Geographic information systems and agent-based modeling. pp 83-104 in Gimblett H R (ed.) Integrating geographic information systems and agent-based modeling techniques for simulating social and ecological processes. Oxford University Press, Oxford

Whyatt J D, Wade P R (1988) The Douglas-Peucker line simplification algorithm. Society of University Cartographers Bulletin, 22, 17-25

Whitcomb R F, Lynch J F, Klimkiewwicz M K, Robbins C S, Whitcomb B L, Bystrak D (1981) Effects of forest fragmentation on avifauna of the eastern deciduous forest. pp 125-205 in R L Burgess and D M Sharpe, editors. Forest island dynamics in man-dominated landscapes. Springer-Verlag, New York

White G C, Garrott R A (1990) Analysis of wildlife radio-tracking data. Academic Press, San Diego

Wilensky U (1998) NetLogo Life model. http://ccl.northwestern.edu/netlogo/models/Life. Center for Connected Learning and Computer-Based Modeling, Northwestern University, Evanston, IL

Wilensky U (2004) NetLogo Heatbugs model. http://ccl.northwestern.edu/netlogo/models/Heat bugs. Center for Connected Learning and Computer-Based Modeling, Northwestern University, Evanston, IL.

Wilson A G (1967) A statistical theory of spatial distribution models. Transportation Research, 1, 253-69

Wise S (2002) GIS basics. Taylor & Francis, London

Wolfram S (1983) Statistical mechanics of cellular automata. Review of Modern Physics, 55, 601-643

Wolfram S (2002) A new kind of science. Wolfram Media, USA

Womble W H (1951) Differential systematics. Science, 114, 315-22

Wong D (2008) The modifiable areal unit problem (MAUP). Ch 7 in Fotheringham A S and Rogerson P A op .cit.

Wooldridge M, Jennings N R (1995) Intelligent agents: Theory and practice. Knowledge Engineering Review, 10(2), 115-152

Worboys M, Duckham M (2004) GIS — A computing perspective. 2nd ed., CRC Press, Boca Raton, Florida

Yasui Y, Liu H, Beach J, Winget M (2000) An empirical evaluation of various priors in the empirical Bayes estimation of small area disease risks. Statistics in Medicine, 19, 2409-20

Zadeh L (1965) Fuzzy sets. Information and Control, 8, 338-22

Zambon M, Lawrence R, Bunn A, Powell S (2006) Effect of alternative splitting rules on image processing using classification tree analysis. Photogrammetric Engineering and Remote Sensing, 72(1), 25-30

Zeiler M (1999) Modeling our world: The ESRI guide to geodatabase design. ESRI Press, Redlands, California

Zeverbergen L W, Thorne C R (1987) Quantitative analysis of land surface topography. Earth Surface Processes and Landforms, 12, 47-56

Zhang J, Goodchild M F (2002) Uncertainty in geographic information. Taylor and Francis, London

Zhang C, Franklin S E, Wulder M A (2004) Geostatistical and texture analysis of airborne-acquired images used in forest classification. Int. J. Remote Sensing, 25, 4, 859-865

Zhou Q, Liu X (2004) Analysis of errors of derived slope and aspect related to DEM data properties. Computers & Geosciences 30, 369-78

# CATMOG Guides

The following is a complete listing of the series known as CATMOG, or Concepts and Techniques in Modern Geography, which were published between 1975 and 1995. All these brief guides are out of print but most are available from www.qmrg.org.uk as free PDF downloads.

1   Collins, Introduction to Markov chain analysis

2   Taylor, Distance decay in spatial interactions

3   Clark, Understanding canonical correlation analysis

4   Openshaw, Some theoretical and applied aspects of spatial interaction shopping models

5   Unwin, An introduction to trend surface analysis

6   Johnston, Classification in Geography

7   Goddard & Kirby, An introduction to factor analysis

8   Daultrey, Principle Components Analysis

9   Davidson, Causal inferences from dichotomous variables

10  Wrigley, Introduction to the use of logit models in geography

11  Hay, Linear programming: elementary geographical applications of the transportation problem

12  Thomas, An introduction to quadrat analysis (2nd ed.)

13  Thrift, An introduction to time geography

14  Tinkler, An introduction to graph theoretical methods in geography

15  Ferguson, Linear regression in geography

16  Wrigley, Probability surface mapping. An introduction with examples and FORTRAN programs

17  Dixon & Leach, Sampling methods for geographical research

18  Dixon & Leach, Questionnaires and interviews in geographical research

19  Gardiner & Gardiner, Analysis of frequency distribution

20  Silk, Analysis of covariance and comparison of regression lines

21  Todd, An introduction to the use of simultaneous-equation regression analysis in geography

22  Pong-wai Lai, Transfer function modeling: relationship between time series variables

23  Richards, Stochastic processes in one dimensional series: an introduction

24  Killen, Linear programming: the Simplex method with geographical applications

25  Gaile & Burt, Directional statistics

26  Rich, Potential models in human geography

27  Pringle, Causal modeling: the Simon-Blalock approach

28  Bennett, Statistical forecasting

29  Dewdney, The British census

30  Silk, The analysis of variance

31  Thomas, Information statistics in geography

32  Kellerman, Centrographic measures in geography

# R-Project spatial statistics software packages

See: http://www.r-project.org/. R is a system for statistical computation and graphics. It consists of a language plus a run-time environment with graphics, a debugger, access to certain system functions, and the ability to run programs stored in script files. Selected spatial analysis packages are listed in the Table below. Descriptions are those provided by the package authors. Many of the Spatial functions are described at: http://cran.r-project.org/web/views/Spatial.html

An R-Spatial page with news and comments is provided by Arizona State University:

http://geodacenter.asu.edu/r-spatial-projects/

A full set of course notes for analyzing spatial point patterns using R is available from CSIRO at: http://www.csiro.au/resources/Spatial-Point-Patterns-in-R.html

| Package (links) | Description | Features |
|---|---|---|
| ads | Spatial point patterns analysis | Perform first- and second-order multi-scale analyses derived from Ripley's K-function, for univariate, multivariate and marked mapped data in rectangular, circular or irregular shaped sampling windows, with test of statistical significance based on Monte Carlo simulations. |
| aspace | A collection of functions for estimating centrographic statistics and computational geometries from spatial point patterns | A collection of functions for computing centrographic statistics (e.g., standard distance, standard deviation ellipse), and minimum convex polygons (MCP) for observations taken at point locations. A tool is also provided for converting geometric objects associated with the centrographic statistics, and MCPs into ESRI Shapefiles |
| DCluster | Functions for the detection of spatial clusters of diseases | A set of functions for the detection of spatial clusters of disease using count data. Bootstrap is used to estimate sampling distributions of statistics |
| fields | Tools for spatial data | Fields is for curve, surface and function fitting with an emphasis on splines, spatial data and spatial statistics. The major methods include cubic, robust, and thin plate splines, multivariate Kriging and Kriging for large data sets. One main feature is any covariance function implemented in R can be used for spatial prediction. There are also useful functions for plotting and working with spatial data as images |
| GeoXp | http://cran.r-project.org/web/packages/GeoXp/index.html<br><br>Interactive exploratory spatial data analysis (manual is in French) | GeoXp is a tool for researchers in spatial statistics, spatial econometrics, geography, ecology etc allowing to link dynamically statistical plots with elementary maps. This coupling consists in the fact that the selection of a zone on the map results in the automatic highlighting of the corresponding points on the statistical graph or reversely the selection of a portion of the graph results in the automatic highlighting of the corresponding points |

| Package (links) | Description | Features |
| --- | --- | --- |
| | | on the map. GeoXp includes tools from different areas of spatial statistics including geostatistics as well as spatial econometrics and point processes. Besides elementary plots like box plots, histograms or simple scatterplots, GeoXp also couples with maps Moran scatterplots, variogram cloud, Lorentz Curves,...In order to make the most of the multidimensionality of the data, GeoXp includes some dimension reduction techniques such as PCA |
| geoRglm | Package for generalized linear spatial models | Functions for inference in generalized linear spatial models. The posterior and predictive inference is based on Markov chain Monte Carlo methods. Package geoRglm is an extension to the package geoR, which must be installed first. |
| grasp/grasper | Generalized Regression Analysis and Spatial Prediction for R | GRASP is a general method for making spatial predictions of response variables (RV) using point surveys of the RV and spatial coverages of Predictor variables (PV) |
| maptools | Tools for reading and handling spatial objects | Set of tools for manipulating and reading geographic data, in particular ESRI shapefiles. Includes facilities for Google Earth grid and KML creation, ASCII grid reading, output to Mondrian, WinBUGS etc. |
| spatial | Functions for Kriging and Point Pattern Analysis | |
| sp | A package that provides classes and methods for spatial data. Note that sp has its own Sourceforge page. see: http://r-spatial.sourceforge.net/ | The classes document where the spatial location information resides, for 2D or 3D data. Utility functions are provided, e.g. for plotting data as maps, spatial selection, as well as methods for retrieving coordinates, for subsetting, print, summary, etc. |
| spBayes | Univariate and Multivariate Spatial Modeling | spBayes fits Gaussian univariate and multivariate models with Markov chain Monte Carlo (MCMC) |
| spatclus | Arbitrarily Shaped Multiple Spatial Cluster Detection for Case Event Data | Multiple cluster location and detection for 2D and 3D spatial point patterns (case event data). The methodology of this package is based on an original method that allows the detection of multiple clusters of any shape. A selection order and the distance from its nearest neighbor once pre-selected points have been taken into account are attributed at each point. This distance is weighted by the expected distance under the uniform distribution hypothesis. Potential clusters are located by modeling the multiple structural change of the distances on the selection order. Their presence is tested using the double maximum test and a Monte Carlo procedure |
| spatgraphs | Graphs for spatial point patterns | Graphs, graph visualization and graph component calculations, meant to be used as a tool in spatial |

| Package (links) | Description | Features |
|---|---|---|
| | | point pattern analysis |
| spatstat | http://cran.r-project.org/web/packages/spatstat/index.html<br><br>Spatial Point Pattern analysis, model-fitting, simulation, tests. See further<br><br>http://www.spatstat.org/ | A package for analyzing spatial data, mainly Spatial Point Patterns, including multitype/marked points and spatial covariates, in any two-dimensional spatial region. Contains functions for plotting spatial data, exploratory data analysis, model-fitting, simulation, spatial sampling, model diagnostics, and formal inference. Data types include point patterns, line segment patterns, spatial windows, and pixel images. Point process models can be fitted to point pattern data. Cluster type models are fitted by the method of minimum contrast. Very general Gibbs point process models can be fitted to point pattern data using a function ppm similar to lm or glm. Models may include dependence on covariates, interpoint interaction and dependence on marks. Fitted models can be simulated automatically. Also provides facilities for formal inference (such as chi-squared tests) and model diagnostics (including simulation envelopes, residuals, residual plots and Q-Q plots) |
| spdep | Spatial dependence: weighting schemes, statistics and models. See documentation for details:<br><br>http://cran.r-project.org/web/packages/spdep/spdep.pdf | A collection of functions to create spatial weights matrix objects from polygon contiguities, from point patterns by distance and tessellations, for summarizing these objects, and for permitting their use in spatial data analysis, including regional aggregation by minimum spanning tree; a collection of tests for spatial autocorrelation, including global Moran's I, APLE, Geary's C, Hubert/Mantel general cross product statistic, Empirical Bayes estimates and Assunção/Reis Index, Getis/Ord G and multicolored join count statistics, local Moran's I and Getis/Ord G, saddlepoint approximations and exact tests for global and local Moran's I; and functions for estimating spatial simultaneous autoregressive (SAR) lag and error models, weighted and unweighted SAR and CAR spatial regression models, semi-parametric and Moran eigenvector spatial filtering, GM SAR error models, and generalized spatial two stage least squares models |
| spgwr | Geographically weighted regression<br>http://cran.r-project.org/web/packages/spgwr/ | The function implements generalised geographically weighted regression approach to exploring spatial non-stationarity for given global bandwidth and chosen weighting scheme. |
| splancs | Spatial and Space-Time Point Pattern Analysis in R and S | Point pattern analysis, including kernel density, Ripley K, Ghat and Fhat functions |
| trip | Trip pattern analysis | Analysis of spatial trip data, notably animal tracking information |

# Fragstats landscape metrics

The table below provides details of the 100+ metrics supported by Fragstats. Many of these measures are very similar, and can be considered as highly correlated. Full details of the computations associated with each metric can be found in the Fragstats documentation. Functions of this type can also be found in other packages such as the Pattern functions of SAGA, PASSaGE and the TEXTURE set of image transform operators in Idrisi.

| Landscape metrics | | Shape Index |
|---|---|---|
| **Area/density/edge metrics** | | Fractal Dimension Index |
| Patch Area | | Linearity Index |
| Patch Perimeter | | Related Circumscribing Circle |
| Radius of Gyration | | Contiguity Index |
| Total (Class) Area | | Perimeter-Area Fractal |
| Percentage of Landscape | | Perimeter-Area Ratio Distribution |
| Number of Patches | | Shape Index Distribution |
| Patch Density | | Fractal Index Distribution |
| Total Edge | | Linearity Index Distribution |
| Edge Density | | Related Circumscribing Circle Distribution |
| Landscape Shape Index | | Contiguity Index Distribution |
| Normalized Landscape Shape Index | | Perimeter-Area Fractal Dimension |
| Largest Patch Index | | Perimeter-Area Ratio Distribution |
| Patch Area Distribution | | Shape Index Distribution |
| Radius of Gyration Distribution | | Fractal Index Distribution |
| Total Area | | Linearity Index Distribution |
| Number of Patches | | Related Circumscribing Circle Distribution |
| Patch Density | | Contiguity Index Distribution |
| Total Edge | | **Core area metrics** |
| Edge Density | | Core Area |
| Landscape Shape Index | | Number of Core Areas |
| Largest Patch Index | | Core Area Index |
| Patch Area Distribution | | Average Depth Index |
| Radius of Gyration Distribution | | Maximum Depth Index |
| **Shape metrics** | | Total Core Area |
| Perimeter-Area Ratio | | Core Area Percentage of Landscape |

| | |
|---|---|
| Number of Disjunct Core Areas | Clumpiness Index |
| Disjunct Core Area Density | Aggregation Index |
| Core Area Distribution | Interspersion & Juxtaposition Index |
| Disjunct Core Area Distribution | Mass Fractal Dimension |
| Core Area Index Distribution | Landscape Division Index |
| Total Core Area | Splitting Index |
| Number of Disjunct Core Areas | Effective Mesh Size |
| Disjunct Core Area Density | Percentage of Like Adjacencies |
| Core Area Distribution | Contagion |
| Disjunct Core Area Distribution | Aggregation Index |
| Core Area Index Distribution | Interspersion & Juxtaposition Index |
| **Isolation/proximity metrics** | Landscape Division Index |
| Proximity Index | Splitting Index |
| Similarity Index | Effective Mesh Size |
| Euclidean Nearest-neighbor Distance | **Connectivity metrics** |
| Functional Nearest-neighbor Distance | Patch Cohesion Index |
| Proximity Index Distribution | Connectance Index |
| Similarity Index Distribution | Traversability Index |
| Euclidean Nearest-neighbor Distance Distribution | Patch Cohesion Index |
| Functional Nearest-neighbor Distance Distribution | Connectance Index |
| Proximity Index Distribution | Traversability Index |
| Similarity Index Distribution | **Diversity metrics** |
| Euclidean Nearest-neighbor Distance Distribution | Patch Richness |
| Functional Nearest-neighbor Distance Distribution | Patch Richness Density |
| **Contrast metrics** | Relative Patch Richness |
| Edge Contrast Index | Shannon's Diversity Index |
| Contrast-Weighted Edge Density | Simpson's Diversity Index |
| Total Edge Contrast Index | Modified Simpson's Diversity Index |
| Edge Contrast Index Distribution | Shannon's Evenness Index |
| Contrast-Weighted Edge Density | Simpson's Evenness Index |
| Total Edge Contrast Index | Modified Simpson's Evenness Index |
| Edge Contrast Index Distribution | |
| **Contagion/interspersion metrics** | |
| Percentage of Like Adjacencies | |

# Web links

## Associations and academic bodies

Association of American Geographers (AAG): http://www.aag.org/

Association of American Geographers , Spatial Analysis SIG: http://www.fsu.edu/~geog/sam/

Association of American Geographers (AAG), Geographic Information Systems and Science SIG: http://geography.sdsu.edu/aaggis/

Association for Geographic Information (AGI): http://www.agi.org.uk/

Birkbeck College, University of London: http://www.bbk.ac.uk/gisconline/

Center for Advanced Spatial Analysis (CASA): http://www.casa.ucl.ac.uk

Center for Spatially Integrated Social Science (CSISS): http://www.csiss.org/

Center for Computational Geography: http://www.ccg.leeds.ac.uk/

Center for Computational Geostatistics http://www.uofaweb.ualberta.ca/ccg/

European Commission Joint Research Center (CEC/JRC) - a web forum for Geostatistics and Spatial Statistics supported by the European Commission: http://www.ai-geostats.org

EURO Working Group on Locational Analysis: http://www.vub.ac.be/EWGLA/homepage.htm

Free GIS Organization - portal and mailing list: http://www.freegis.org/

Geoscience Australia: http://www.ga.gov.au/

Geospatial Information and Technology Association (GITA): http://www.gita.org/

GIS.COM - geospatial portal sponsored by ESRI: http://www.gis.com

INFORMS OR/MS: http://www2.informs.org/Resources/Computer_Programs/

International Association of Crime Analysts (software list): http://www.iaca.net/Software.asp

International Association for Mathematical Geology (IAMG): http://www.iamg.org/

Market Research Society, Geodemographics Knowledgebase: http://geodemographics.org.uk

National Cancer Institute, GIS: http://gis.cancer.gov/

NCGIA Core curriculum: http://www.geog.ubc.ca/courses/klink/gis.notes/ncgia/toc.html

Open Geospatial Consortium (OGC): http://www.opengeospatial.org

Open Source Geospatial Foundation (OSGeo): http://www.osgeo.org/

Open Source Technology Group (OSTG),

   Sourceforge: http://sourceforge.net

   LP-solve website managed at Sourceforge: http://lpsolve.sourceforge.net/5.5/

Optimization compendium and best known solutions: http://www.nada.kth.se/~viggo/problemlist/

Optimization Online: www.optimization-online.org

Royal Geographical Society/Institute of British Geographers: http://www.rgs.org/

Royal Geographical Society/Institute of British Geographers: Quantitative Methods Research Group: http://www.qmrg.org.uk/

Spatial analysis laboratory, (SAL), University of Illinois: http://geodacenter.asu.edu/

Spatial Analysis Laboratory, University of Thessaly, Greece:
http://www.prd.uth.gr/res_labs/spatial_analysis/index_en.htm

SPLINT: Spatial Literacy in Teaching: http://www.spatial-literacy.org

UK Census Dissemination Unit (CDU): http://census.ac.uk/cdu/

UK 2001 Census Output area construction: http://www2.geog.soton.ac.uk/research/oa2001/

GB Ordnance Survey: http://www.ordnancesurvey.co.uk/

UNIGIS: http://www.unigis.net/

University Consortium for Geographic Information Science (UCGIS): http://www.ucgis.org

US National Institute of Justice (crime analysis software): http://www.ojp.usdoj.gov/nij/maps/software.htm

USGS: http://www.usgs.gov/

USGS Spatial Data Transfer Standard: http://mcmcweb.er.usgs.gov/sdts/

USGS Spectral Lab: http://speclab.cr.usgs.gov

US National Research Council of the National Academies: http://www.nationalacademies.org/

US National Research Council of the National Academies: Geographical Sciences Committee:
http://dels.nas.edu/besr/gsc.shtml

US National Research Council of the National Academies: Mapping Science Committee:
http://dels.nas.edu/besr/msc.shtml

# Online technical dictionaries/definitions

ESRI GIS Dictionary: http://support.esri.com/index.cfm?fa=knowledgebase.gisDictionary.gateway

Mathworld: http://mathworld.wolfram.com/

NIST Dictionary of algorithms and data structures: http://www.nist.gov/dads/

University of California GIS Abbreviations Dictionary:
http://www.lib.berkeley.edu/EART/abbrev2.html#index

# Spatial data, test data and spatial information sources

## Selected national and international data and information sources

Collins Bartholomew - commercial map datasets for UK, Europe and World, in MapInfo or ESRI SHP formats:
http://www.bartholomewmaps.com/

GB Ordnance Survey: http://www.ordnancesurvey.co.uk/

EDINA — Repository of UK Digital Mapping data and related resources (academic access):
http://www.edina.ac.uk/maps/ and http://www.gogeo.ac.uk/ (the EDINA Geoportal)

ESRI Managed Geography Network: http://www.geographynetwork.com/

Eurostat - European statistics data library and mapping service: http://ec.europa.eu/eurostat

Geo-community portal: http://www.geocomm.com/

King's College London Geodata portal:
http://www.kcl.ac.uk/schools/sspp/geography/research/emm/geodata

MAGIC — Repository of UK Environmental and related data: http://www.magic.gov.uk/

NAVTEQ - Road navigation datasets for over 70 countries: http://www.navteq.com/about/data.html

UK Geospatial information Gateway (Data and Standards documents): http://www.gigateway.org.uk/

United Nations data library (datasets by country on many variables and multiple time periods): http://data.un.org/

US Census Bureau: http://www.census.gov/geo/www/index.html

US Geological Survey: http://www.usgs.gov/

US National Spatial Data Infrastructure: http://www.fgdc.gov/nsdi/nsdi.html

US one-stop geoportal: http://gos2.geodata.gov/wps/portal/gos

World Bank: http://www.worldbank.org/data

### Transport planning and analysis

US Department of Transportation planning site: http://www.plan4operations.dot.gov

US Transportation Research Board: http://www.trb.org/

UK Transport Analysis Guidance (TAG): http://www.webtag.org.uk/

### Network analysis test datasets

TSPLIB: http://www.iwr.uni-heidelberg.de/groups/comopt/software/TSPLIB95/ and via http://www.tsp.gatech.edu/index.html

OR-LIBRARY: http://people.brunel.ac.uk/~mastjjb/jeb/info.html

# Statistics and Spatial Statistics links

Online statistical methods and definitions e-Handbook, the "NIST/SEMATECH e-Handbook of Statistical Methods": http://www.itl.nist.gov/div898/handbook

The R Project for statistical computing: http://www.r-project.org/

Spatial analysis laboratory, (SAL), University of Illinois: http://www.sal.uiuc.edu/ (see R-Geo menu item)

Spatial statistics and environmental sciences (SSES) Program, Ohio State: http://www.stat.ohio-state.edu/~sses/

Kelly Pace's spatial statistics page (MATLab toolkit and general spatial statistics site): http://www.spatial-statistics.com/

# Other GIS web sites

Geo-Community (Portal): http://www.geocomm.com/

Geo:connexion magazine (monthly): http://www.geoconnexion.com/

GeoPlace: http://www.geoplace.com/

GEOInformatics: http://www.geoinformatics.com/

GeoSpatial Solutions: http://www.geospatial-solutions.com/

GIS Professional/Geomatics World: http://www.pvpubs.com/index.php

GIS User: http://www.gisuser.com/

GISWiki: http://en.giswiki.net/

Directions Magazine: http://www.directionsmag.com/ and its sister publication

Location Intelligence: http://www.locationintelligence.net

GIS@development: http://www.gisdevelopment.net/

GIS Lounge: http://gislounge.com/

GIS Café: http://www.giscafe.com/

Spatial News at Geocomm: http://spatialnews.geocomm.com/ and for a list of GIS Viewers: http://spatialnews.geocomm.com/features/viewers2002/

Vector1: http://vector1media.com/

# Index

Drift · 376, 383, 387
Drive-Time Zones · 205, 397
DTM (definition) · 37

# E

Earthquake Modelling · 456
Ecological Fallacy · 89, 298
Ecological Regression · 298
EDA · 37, 236, 239
Edge · 544
Edge Effects · 62, 69, 112, 171, 176, 255, 256, 263, 277, 310, 316, 326, 352, 515
    Filtering · 223
Edge Labelling · 394
EDM (definition) · 37
Effective Number of Parameters · 302
Eigenvalue · 295
Eigenvalue (definition) · 55
Eigenvector (definition) · 55
Electronic Distance Measurement · 37
Elitist Selection · 510
Ellipsoid · 109, 114, 185, 187
Ellipsoid (definition) · 37
Emergency Planning · 31, 103, 404, 405, 424, 429, 451, 457, 458, 463, 481, 484
Entropy · 146, 155, 160, 243, 410
Entropy (definition) · 50
Erosion · 224
Error Signal · 489, 490
ESDA · 37, 236, 238, 239, 243, 244, 292, 299, 308
ESTDA · 236
Eulerian Circuit · 399
Evolutionary Computing · 518
Excess risk · 170, 310
Exponential Integral Function · 364
Exponential Integral Function (definition) · 54

# F

Factor Analysis · 139, 141
Factorial Kriging · 387
Feature · 107, 108, 152, 153, 163, 185, 203, 268, 319, 331
    Amalgamation · 116
    Central · 119
    Central · 121
    Extraction · 158
    Generalization · 116
Feature (definition) · 38
Feature Extraction · 234, 318, 330
Feature, Central · 91
Field · 314
Fill · 186, 336, 345
Filtering · 26, 39, 105, 220, 312, 320, 333, 334

Blurring · 222
Edge · 222
Embossing · 222
Frequency Domain · 223
Gaussian · 222
High-pass · 221
Low-pass · 220
Non-linear · 223
Roberts Method · 222
Sharpening · 222
Smoothing · 222
Symmetric · 222
Fire Spread · 200, 258, 456
First-order Process · 73
Flow · 217, 258, 345, 346, 347, 348, 401
Flow Accumulation · 347
Flow Analysis · 210
Focal · 164, 219, 220, 222, 223, 247, 256, 257, 356
Focal Functions · 219
Fourier Analysis · 369, 382
Fractal · 51, 124, 149, 211, 252, 255, 256, 257, 306, 320, 321, 350, 369, 376, 381, 543, 544
Fractal Dimension · 149
Fractal Terrains · 321
Fragstats · 149, 253, 279, 543
Freeman-Tukey · 310
    Angular Transform (definition) · 53
    Square Root Transform (definition) · 52
Friction · 193, 200, 217
    Angle · 196
Fuzzy Boundaries · 153

# G

Gabriel Network · 417
GAM · 176, 244
Gamma Function (definition) · 54
Gaussian · 207, 304, 335, 379
Gaussian Sequential Simulation · 388
Gaussian Smoothing · 356
Gaussian Surface · 341, 350
Geary C · 282, 290, 293
Generalised Least Squares · 296
Generalization · 66, 116
Genetic Algorithms · 397, 509
    Chromosome · 509
    Crossover · 513
    Encoding · 510
        Alleles · 510
        Genes · 510
    Fitness Function · 509, 511
    Fitness Score · 511
    Initialization · 512
    Local Search · 514
    Mutation · 514
    Optimum Location · 517

# H

# I

# J

## K

Kappa Index · 249
Kernel · 149, 173, 176, 179, 221, 351, 381
  Gaussian · 220
Kernel (definition) · 39
Kernel Density · 149, 171-81, 269, 301
  Adaptive Selection · 176
  Networks · 178
Kernel Density Function
  Exponential · 176
  Gaussian · 176, 179
  Quartic · 176
  Triangular · 176
Kernel Smoothing · 334
KML · 24, 217
KMZ · 24
Knox Test · 271
Kolmogorov-Smirnov Test · 251, 263, 373
Kriging · 73, 351, 354, 363, 372, 376, 382, 384, 385, 386, 387, 388
Kurtosis · 45
Kurtosis (definition) · 50

## L

Lacunarity · 257
Lagrangian · 306, 363, 383, 435
Lagrangian Multipliers · 411, 434
Lagrangian Relaxation · 411, 433
Landscape Metrics · 124, 252, 253
Laplacian · 222
Lattice · 41, 71, 158, 232, 237, 281, 282, 298, 310, 424
  Analysis · 226
  Cellular Automata · 452
  Hexagonal · 182
  Metrics · 505
  Rectangular · 196
  SOM · 502
ldd network · 345, 347
Learning Rate · 490, 493, 494, 499, 503, 505
Least Cost Paths · 190, 191, 193
Least Squares · 294, 317, 319, 351, 368
  Iteratively Reweighted · 304
  Weighted · 296, 302, 368
Level Sets · 81, 337, 356
Line Frequency · 179
Line of Sight · 337, 339, 340
Line Smoothing · 114
Linear Programming · 398
LineString · 40
Linking · 27, 81, 213, 236, 244, 318, 522
LISA · 238, 290, 291
Local Drainage Direction · 217, 335, 345
Local Functions · 219

Local Outliers · 239, 244
Local Polynomial · 352, 355, 363, 365, 366, 367
Locational Analysis · 27, 189, 430
Logistic · 487
Logistic Function · 297, 490, 494, 504
Logistic Function (definition) · 52
Logistics · 31, 391, 401, 402, 441
Logit · 296
Logit (definition) · 52
Lower Quartile · 286
Lower Quartile (definition) · 47
Lp-Metric · 188

## M

Madograms · 289, 381
Majority · 219, 223
Majority (definition) · 45
Mantel Test · 271
  Proximity Analysis · 273
Map Algebra · 26, 164, 179, 193, 219, 224, 350, 356
  Calculus · 220
  Multidimensional · 220
Map Calculus · 220, 320
Map Transformation (definition) · 41
Markov Chain Monte Carlo (MCMC) · 309
Masking · 92, 156, 230, 247, 377
Matrix
  Determinant · 54, 111, 365
  Inverse (definition) · 54
  Positive Definite · 54
  Positive Semi-definite · 54
  Singular · 54
  Symmetric (definition) · 54
  Trace · 302
  Trace (definition) · 55
  Transpose (definition) · 54
MAUP · 132
Maximum (definition) · 46
MBR · 39, 117, 120, 121, 124, 152, 235, 243, 245, 261, 262, 264, 359, 361, 364, 426, 431
MCFP · 398, 400
Mean
  Arithmetic (definition) · 46
  Directional · 212
  Geometric · 121, 259
  Geometric (definition) · 46
  Harmonic · 121
  Harmonic (definition) · 46
  Olympic (definition) · 47
  Power (definition) · 46
  Trim (definition) · 47
  Weighted · 120, 123, 178, 222, 241, 247
  Weighted (definition) · 46
Mean Absolute Deviation · 49
Mean Deviation (definition) · 49

Parsimony Objective · 93, 295, 297
Path · 194, 334, 392
pCentre · 433
pCentre · 400
PCP · 264
Percentile · 136, 169
Periodograms · 369, 381
Piecewise Function · 319
PIP · 121
Pits · 194, 318, 330, 334, 335, 345, 347, 368
Pixel · 165, 166, 220, 224, 314, 346, 363
Pixel (definition) · 39
Plan Convexity · 329
Planar · 43, 111, 125, 159, 188, 226, 330, 333, 365
  Enforcement (definition) · 39
Planar (definition) · 39
Planimetric Area · 111
pMedian · 433
pMedian Problem · 400
Point Density · 171
Point in Polygon · 122
Point Kriging · 382
Point Pattern
  Clustering · 261
  CSR · 261
  Density · 260, 261
  Edge Correction · 262, 264
  Standard Distance · 261
Point Patterns · 259
  Contagion · 260
  Covariates · 259
  Marked · 259
  Nearest Neighbor · 260
Point Sampling · 230
Point Weeding · 114, 115, 151
Poisson Distribution · 50, 250
Poisson Distribution (definition) · 52
Polygon · 26, 36, 38, 45, 105, 107, 109, 111, 114, 116, 119, 121, 122, 124, 127, 128, 149, 150, 153, 154, 159, 161, 163, 164, 166, 203, 204, 232, 262, 264, 282, 289, 290, 336, 351, 361, 366, 372
Polygon (definition) · 39, 40
Polygon Decomposition · 123
Polygon Fitting · 150
Polyline · 36, 107, 108, 115, 121, 125, 185, 211, 328, 356
Polyline (definition) · 40
Polynomial Regression · 352, 366, 367
Power (statistical) · 91
Power Transforms · 53
PPDAC · 86, 87, 91, 95, 308
PPGIS · 95, 102
Precision Farming · 230
Predictor Variables · 294, 298, 302
Principal Components Analysis · 141, 295
Probability Density · 75
Probability Kriging · 386

Product Moment Correlation · 45, 301
Profile Curvature · 317
Profiles · 185, 328, 333, 340, 351, 377
Profiling · 328, 352, 366
Proximity · 68, 85, 127, 159, 234, 256, 276, 300, 338, 544
  Bands · 276
Proximity Matrix Analysis · 272
PTAS · 395
Pushbroom Algorithm · 194
Pycnophylactic · 129

# Q

Quadrat · 171, 226, 232, 247, 250
Quantile · 137, 169, 382
Quintic functions · 320

# R

Radial Basis · 209, 351, 354, 355, 363, 364, 372, 382
Radial Basis Function
  Completely Regularised Spline · 364
  Inverse Multiquadric · 364
  Multilog · 364
  Multiquadric · 363, 364
  Spline
    Cubic · 364
    Tension · 364
  Thin Plate Spline · 363, 364
Radio Transmission Analysis · 339
Random Walk · 216, 388
Range (definition) · 47
Raster Data Model · 40, 315
Rate Smoothing · 170
Raw Rates · 169
Re-districting · 128, 130
Reflexive · 263
Regression · 71, 115, 178, 225, 227, 234, 244, 247, 292, 294, 296, 298, 299, 300, 301, 302, 303, 311, 315, 352, 366, 367, 383, 386
  CAR · 298
  Conditional Autoregressive · 298
  Ecological · 298
  Hedonic · 294, 298
  Linear · 215, 298, 305, 306
  Logistic · 298, 304
  Multiple · 298
  Multivariate · 298
  Poisson · 298, 304
  SAR · 298, 305
  Simultaneous Autoregressive · 298
RELATE · 163
Relative Neighbourhood Network · 417

# Digital globe visualizations of Mars - Hill-shaded and colored DEMs

© NASA, 2008. Google Earth KML files